Yankee Leviathan

Yankee Leviathan

The Origins of Central State Authority
in America, 1859–1877

RICHARD FRANKLIN BENSEL

New School for Social Research

CAMBRIDGE
UNIVERSITY PRESS

Published by the Press Syndicate of the University of Cambridge
The Pitt Building, Trumpington Street, Cambridge CB2 1RP
40 West 20th Street, New York, NY 10011-4211, USA
10 Stamford Road, Oakleigh, Melbourne 3166, Australia

© Cambridge University Press 1990

First published 1990
Reprinted 1994, 1995

Library of Congress Cataloging-in-Publication Data is available

A catalogue record for this book is available from the British Library

ISBN 0-521-39136-9 hardback
ISBN 0-521-39817-7 paperback

Transferred to digital printing 2003

TO MY MOTHER AND FATHER

Contents

Preface

I have pursued several goals in writing this book. The first was to somehow anchor an analytical description of American political development "at the beginning" of national state formation. As will become clear, I think, in the course of the book, the American state emerged from the wreckage of the Civil War. The state that early American nationalists had previously attempted to establish at the Constitutional Convention in 1787 had become a mere shell by 1860 – a government with only a token administrative presence in most of the nation and whose sovereignty was interpreted by the central administration as contingent on the consent of the individual states. This antebellum government was not so much overthrown by the Civil War as rendered anachronistic. In the process, prewar constitutional doctrine and administrative tradition became the ineffective weapons of the regime's opponents as they attempted to prevent the Republican party from consolidating the power and authority of the new Union state. Other than these pleas for a return to "the Constitution as it was," the modern state's inheritance from the antebellum period was nil. In that sense, then, an account of American state formation can begin with the Civil War with little lost in historical continuity or theoretical generality.

A second goal has been to put forward, in contrast to both the "class conflict" and "consensus" interpretations of American political development, a more encompassing and alternative analysis of the impact of southern separatism on the formation of the American state. The search for potential comparisons within the European state system has led many scholars to focus on things that did not happen in the United States, such as the absence of strong social democratic movements in the late nineteenth and early twentieth centuries. While such nonevents serve as useful foils to what actually occurred, they tend to reinforce a continuing preoccupation with European experience. In contrast, recognition of the primacy of southern separatism in American state formation – the large something that did happen – emphasizes the membership of the United States in that class of nations that have had as one of their most prominent developmental influences the ebb and flow of separatist threats to national cohesion. Some European regimes, such as Great Britain and Spain, have also experienced significant separatist pressure. But many of the most comparable cases, such as the Soviet Union, India, and Canada, are located outside of Europe.

Another characteristic of American state formation during the Civil War was the almost complete fusion of party and state in the northern Union. During the decade in which the Union first suppressed the Confederacy through war and subsequently attempted a partial reorganization of the southern political economy, the Republican party exercised without significant challenge central state authority in the name of northern-led nationalism. Again European experience can provide a few parallels, but the most comparable cases of nationalist party-states have arisen outside Europe altogether: the PRI in Mexico, the Congress Party in India, the Bolsheviks in the early years of the Soviet Union, and so on.

The final aspect of comparative state development that has influenced the writing of this book can be traced to the Civil War itself. During the conflict America held not one, but two central states and these states were locked in mortal combat. The material requirements of the battlefield compelled the southern Confederacy to pursue a relatively statist war mobilization. In contrast, the northern war effort mobilized materiel and men by relying on voluntary contracts within a comparatively robust capitalist market. Since the formal structures of the northern and southern regimes were almost identical at the beginning of the Civil War, differences in the way in which they developed during the conflict can be attributed to both their contrasting social bases and the capacity of their respective societies to supply armies at the front. Thus, general questions concerning the impact of war and economy on state formation can be addressed by comparing the experiences of the Union and Confederate nations.

In one form or another over the last five years, I have taken up all of these issues with my colleagues in the Proseminar on State Formation and Collective Action held at the New School for Social Research. To all of them – especially Charles Tilly, Ira Katznelson, Andrew Beveridge, Jytte Klausen, Fred Murphy, and Dan Kryder – I owe a special debt for their advice and criticism. I am also grateful to those students in the Committee on Historical Studies who helped me gather and organize the materials that went into this book, particularly Chris Mele, Kenneth Trippel, David Turner, and Perry Chang. With a sharp eye and ready pen, Kim Geiger edited a rough draft of the book during the spring of 1989. After my revisions introduced more errors and nonsequiturs, Elizabeth Sanders again scoured the manuscript during the summer and fall.

Much of the credit for whatever virtues this book possesses must go to my often-failing attempts to avoid her marginal notations. Richard Valelly and Eric Foner read the manuscript for Cambridge University Press and contributed much appreciated advice. Another large debt is owed to my editor, Emily Loose, who, with seemingly limitless patience, recommended a vast number of improvements in organization and argument. Other scholars who read and commented on portions of the manuscript, often very early drafts, were Stephen Skowronek, Karen Orren, Elaine Swift, Kim Voss, Thomas Alexander, Allan Lichtman, Toyo Nagata, and H. Douglas Price. I must also thank the National Endowment for the Humanities and the Institute for Humane Studies for their research support. As is the tradition in our family, I offered my son, Seth, responsibility for all the remaining errors in this book. However, he refused and carefully explained that no one would read his own books if he gave away his reputation like that.

I

Modernization, southern separatism, and state formation in American political development

The American state both survived and was transformed by the Civil War. The national state survived in the sense that its territorial integrity and political institutions remained intact.[1] In the middle of the nineteenth century, these minimal conditions of state existence were threatened by southern separatism and could only be met through a successfully prosecuted civil war.[2] If the war's outcome had been different, alternative historical trajectories would have replaced the United States with at least two nations, ultimately perhaps more, and in the process profoundly disrupted the established traditions and institutions of the American state inherited by the northern remainder of the nation. Union victory in the Civil War minimized these disruptions but, even so, the impact of the conflict destroyed political traditions and continuity in at least one-third of the reconstituted nation.

A new American state emerged from the Civil War in the sense that the conflict settled long-standing questions of whether the national government was to possess the fundamental attributes of territorial and governmental sovereignty or was to serve only to coordinate the foreign relations of the constituent, federated states. Such questions only have contingent historical answers. In the American case, the answer depended on whether the northern Union possessed the will and strength to impose its formulation upon the South. If the Union had lost the Civil War,

1. Theda Skocpol gave these minimal expectations a slightly different emphasis in her "Bringing the State Back In: Strategies of Analysis in Current Research," in Peter B. Evans, Dietrich Rueschemeyer, and Theda Skocpol, eds., *Bringing the State Back In* (Cambridge: Cambridge University Press, 1985), p. 16.
2. As used in this book, the term *separatism* refers to the secessionist demands of a geographically concentrated subsection of a nation and the general, broad-based resistance to national political integration if and when secessionist demands are clearly unrealistic and/or forcibly repressed.

southern independence would have answered this question by affirming the right of federated states to secede. Union victory thus created the American state by conferring upon it the fundamental attributes of territorial and governmental sovereignty. In fact, the very process of secession, war, and reunification both strengthened the American state in every dimension of institutional design and substantive policy and committed the entire apparatus to the promotion of northern industrial development and western settlement.

The major institutions of what had been an extremely weak antebellum state thus survived the war and emerged as the unchallenged sovereign power within the American republic. In the process, the state experimented with policies as statist and far-reaching as any in American history. Many of these lapsed in the postwar period with the abandonment of efforts to reconstruct the southern political economy, but a few, including the commitment of the American state to modernizing policies associated with the industrial and financial sectors of the North, persisted and laid the basis of subsequent political development.

The Civil War and the American state

The Civil War and Reconstruction periods encompassed three stages by which a starkly defined and exclusive political coalition captured the nascent American state, infused that state with vast powers to remake the national political economy, and, finally, was compelled by internal contradictions within the alliance to compromise its own control of the state apparatus. The first of these stages entailed *capture:* the ascent to power of a cohesive political-economic alliance (the Republican party) combined with the exit of its major opponent (the southern plantation elite). Up to the point of capture, the American state had been little more than an arena in which contending forces and coalitions in the national political economy competed over decisions related to continental settlement and foreign policy. The secession of the South and the decision of the North to attempt military reunification produced an *explosive expansion* of central state authority within the framework of the Republican alliance. Part of this explosive expansion can be attributed to the enactment and implementation of the political economic agenda of the groups allied within the Republican party. The secession of the South in effect broke the logjam behind which this agenda had languished in the years just prior to the Civil War and a major portion of state expansion was composed of policies that had been proposed and debated in the prewar period.[3] The mobilization of the northern political economy for war, however, both provided the major impetus for state expansion and re-shaped the antebellum agenda. The war had an even greater impact on the structure and substantive policies of the emergent southern Confederacy.

Prosecution of the war, implementation of the major elements on the northern agenda, and the reentry of the South into the political system all combined to *compromise control* of the central state by the Republican party and allow the development of internal contradictions within the alliance to halt expansion. As an increasing divergence of interest within the alliance spawned factional conflict within the Republican party, support for reconstruction of the southern political economy withered away. With the return of former Confederate nationalists to Congress, the Democrats became a competitive alternative to the Republicans in national politics. All of these factors – Republican factionalism, the return of former Confederates, and Democratic competition – brought the Civil War party-state to an end. The Civil War and Reconstruction period thus encapsulated several stages in which a starkly defined and exclusive party coalition captured the nascent American state, infused the central government with vast powers to remake the national political economy, and, finally, was compelled by internal contradictions within its alliance to compromise its own control of the state apparatus. The process delineated by these three stages produced the context for the Compromise of 1877 – the resolution of the Hayes–Tilden presidential election in the Republican's favor and the associated withdrawal of Union troops from the South. This, in turn, slowed the pace of post-Reconstruction state development. Once it became possible for the "rebel" South to participate in a winning presidential coalition, the state bureaucracy became a potential balance-wheel between rival political-economic coalitions. With that possibility of a balance-of-power position in national politics and the emergence of civil service protection from partisan influence, the state could at last begin to develop a "statist" sensibility, an identity and interest apart from any class or partisan interest.[4]

From 1861 to 1877, the American state and the Republican party were

3. See, for example, David M. Potter, *The Impending Crisis: 1848–1861* (New York: Harper Torchbooks, 1976), pp. 390–1.
4. With appropriate caveats, the developments of this period correspond to one of Michael Mann's conditions for the emergence of state autonomy: the creation of "a certain 'space'... in which a state elite could manoeuvre, play off classes against war factions and other states, and so stake out an area and degree of power autonomy for itself." See Michael Mann, "The Autonomous Power of the State: Its Origins, Mechanisms and Results," *Archives Europeennes de Sociologie* 25 (1984), pp. 186–7.

essentially the same thing; the federal government was simply the vehicle of common interests in economic development associated with northern finance, industry, and free soil agriculture.[5] By 1877, party and state had become dissociated to such an extent that the individual factions of the Republican party, particularly finance capital and western agrarians, could entertain alliances with the Democratic party and the general interests of state sovereignty and expansion were no longer the exclusive province of northern Republicans. From a statist perspective, this dissociation might be viewed as the silver lining that accompanied Reconstruction's failure. While we can easily exaggerate this transition from unmediated party rule to state-centered pluralistic nationalism (which, in any case, occurred slowly), the transition from a revolutionary party-state to state-centered pluralism is still significant, and possibly generalizable as an historical process.[6] This process can be profitably contrasted with more conventional theories of modernization.

Modernization and American state development

Samuel Huntington and others have argued that political modernization has involved three elements. The first of these has been the rationalization of authority throughout the nation – which is accomplished by the destruction of decentralized institutions which might resist the extension of that authority. The second has been the differentiation of new political functions and the development of specialized institutions to perform those functions. The last factor in modernization has been the broadening of political participation, primarily through the emergence of mass-based political parties. In most European societies, modernization occurred in

5.   As C. Vann Woodward put it, "the Republican party had ... become the conservative party, spokesman of vested interests and big business, defender of an elaborate system of tariffs, subsidies, currency laws, privileged banks, railroads, and corporations. ... The old Whig element of the North that had combined with the Free-Soil Democrats and Abolitionists in the fifties to form the Republican party was on top in 1876 and had written its antebellum economic program into law." *Reunion and Reaction: The Compromise of 1877 and the End of Reconstruction* (Boston: Little, Brown, 1966), p. 35.
6.   Within the scope of this book, "unmediated party rule" and "state-centered pluralistic nationalism" can be viewed as polar opposites. Unmediated party rule describes a regime that meets three criteria: (1) a political system in which a single party dominates all other contenders for power; (2) the dominant party coalition excludes important groups and classes in the national political economy from almost all participation in government decision making; and (3) membership in the dominant party is the most important single qualification for office holding within the state bureaucracy. In contrast, state-centered pluralism describes a political system in which two or more parties are serious contenders for power, the social bases of competing political parties contain at least a fraction of all important groups and classes in the national political economy, and party membership is not a qualification for bureaucratic service.

that order: first, the extension and consolidation of central state power; second, bureaucratic specialization; and, last, popular political participation. In America the order was reversed, and it is said that the early emergence of broad political participation in the form of manhood suffrage was premature because it aborted the development of the specialized and politically insulated bureaucracies necessary to a strong central government.[7] The nineteenth-century patronage-based party system was characterized by issueless competition and retarded the growth of a strong state because it allowed constantly shifting public opinion to sweep unhindered through the structure of government, preventing the erection of stable, insulated, and self-conscious bureaucratic forms. From this perspective, the late nineteenth century was a period in which the nascent institutions of a modern state groped blindly through a whirlwind of patronage, corruption, and sloganeering in an attempt to "recast" (Stephen Skowronek's word) the basis of American government.

Modernization itself "involves such basic changes in the structure of a society as rapid economic development, urbanization, industrialization, the creation of an integrated national economic and political structure, and generally, the spread of market-oriented capitalist economic relations and of mental attitudes viewing continuous social change as natural and desirable." From this perspective, the American Civil War was a part of the process by which the "modernizing" North integrated the "premodern" South into the national political and economic system. Painted in even broader strokes, the American Civil War appears as but one of many conflicts in the nineteenth-century world economy by which industrializing regions and nations successfully penetrated and reorganized the socioeconomic bases of less-developed, usually agrarian societies.[8]

7. Samuel P. Huntington, *Political Order in Changing Societies* (New Haven, Conn.: Yale University Press, 1968), pp. 93–139. Huntington also accepts Cyril Black's argument that Union victory in the American Civil War marked the "consolidation of modernizing leadership" in the United States (p. 46). Also see Stephen Skowronek, *Building a New American State: The Expansion of National Administrative Capacities, 1877–1920* (Cambridge: Cambridge University Press, 1982), pp. 6–8, 39–40; Gianfranco Poggi, *The Development of the Modern State* (Stanford, Calif.: Stanford University Press, 1978), p. 93; Charles C. Bright, "The State in the United States during the Nineteenth Century," in Charles Bright and Susan Harding, eds., *Statemaking and Social Movements: Essays in History and Theory* (Ann Arbor: University of Michigan Press, 1984), pp. 123–4.
8. The quotation is from Eric Foner, *Politics and Ideology in the Age of the Civil War* (New York: Oxford University Press, 1980), p. 20; also see S. N. Eisenstadt, *Modernization: Protest and Change* (Englewood Cliffs, N.J.: Prentice-Hall, 1966); and George Fredrickson, ed., *A Nation Divided: Problems and Issues of the Civil War and Reconstruction* (Minneapolis: Burgess, 1978); Raimondo Luraghi, "The Civil War and the Modernization of American Society: Social Structure and Industrial Revolution in the Old South before and during the War," *Civil War History* 18 (September 1972): 230–50; Barrington Moore, Jr., *Social Origins of Dictatorship and Democracy: Lord*

While generally sympathetic to the modernization school, the theoretical perspective of this book parts company with some of the assumptions and conclusions of that approach. First, the connection
between modernization and state development is more complicated than
many of these scholars suggest. In one formulation of the thesis, state
expansion in the late nineteenth century was the indicated response to
two developmental imperatives: the emergence of inter- and intraclass
conflict that accompanied rapid growth in the capitalist economy and a
general, equally rapid increase in social complexity. These imperatives
provided the context, even the necessity, for the emergence of a "modern"
American state in the sense that quasi-autonomous administrative structures would have made the management of class conflict and the coordination of complex social functions possible.[9] Recognition of these
objective requirements by influential elements of the national elite, it is
argued, will (and did) move the state forward on a modernizing trajectory
even in cases, such as the American one, where the statist response was
painfully slow and often inadequate.

Without exception, scholars associated with the developmental school
have viewed the industrializing, urban North as the bearer of American
modernization and the Civil War as presenting one of the most important
administrative challenges of the nineteenth century. On the basis of these
two facts, it could be argued that the response of the modernizing North
to the requirements of the American Civil War should have been much
more state-centered and administratively advanced than that of the comparatively underdeveloped South. In fact, however, many features of the
Confederate war mobilization were far more statist and modern than
their counterparts in the Union (see Chapter 3). This appraisal does not
in itself vitiate a connection between modernization and state development. For example, the theoretical framework could be amended by
interpreting war mobilizations as statist responses driven more by the
battlefield challenge presented by the enemy than by the domestic consequences of economic development, thus excepting war from the normal
course of state development. Even so, proper recognition and correct
implementation of the statist response to such challenges requires a modern sensibility not often attributed to the southern plantation elite. On
these grounds alone, we might conclude that the (already contingent)

    and Peasant in the Making of the Modern World (Boston: Beacon Press, 1967), ch.
    3; Richard D. Brown, *Modernization: The Transformation of American Life, 1600–
    1865* (New York: Hill and Wang, 1976), ch. 7; and C. E. Black, *The Dynamics of
    Modernization: A Study in Comparative History* (New York: Harper & Row, 1966),
    p. 111.
9. Skowronek, *Building a New American State*, p. 11. Also see Bright, "The State in the
    United States during the Nineteenth Century," pp. 121–58.

connection between modernization and state development in the nineteenth century was somewhat looser than has been suggested.

A second problem with the thesis as applied to the American case arises out of the tendency to assume a "unitary" society in the sense that modernization policies advance the development of the entire society or are a response to external challenges arising out of increased participation in the world system.[10] On both counts, the reality was very different in the United States in the nineteenth century. In the United States, central state policies promoted modernization primarily in the North and, to a lesser extent, the West. Economic development took place in those regions at the expense of the southern periphery, which fell further and further behind the remainder of the nation throughout the late nineteenth century (see Chapter 7).[11] State-sponsored modernization in the South (such as the replacement of slavery with more market-oriented versions of peonage) was carried out only incidentally, if at all, for national developmental

10. This preoccupation with national destiny led Barrington Moore to pose, as a counterfactual possibility, "what would have happened had the Southern plantation system been able to establish itself in the West by the middle of the nineteenth century and surrounded the Northeast. Then the United States would have been in the position of some modernizing countries today, with a latifundia economy, a dominant antidemocratic aristocracy, and a weak and dependent commercial and industrial class, unable and unwilling to push forward toward political democracy." *Social Origins of Dictatorship and Democracy*, p. 153. Given the climatic constraints on the territorial expansion of the southern plantation economy and the fact that antebellum southern political systems were, with few exceptions, as fully democratic as any in the North and more democratic than any contemporary European system, the historical possibility of this counterfactual faces major theoretical and empirical difficulties. The point, however, is not to criticize Moore's vision but, instead, to suggest a reason why he chose to project a southern-dominated United States rather than the much more plausible separation of the South into a new nation. Moore's "unitary" counterfactual was chosen over southern independence, I would argue, because he wanted to compare the American experience with the unitary histories of Britain, France, and Japan. In the process, however, he implicitly confused a hypothetical contest over control of the national political economy with a struggle for separate national existence. An exception to the mainstream emphasis on *national* modernization is David F. Good, "Uneven Development in the Nineteenth Century: A Comparison of the Habsburg Empire and the United States," *Journal of Economic History* 46 (March 1986): 137–51.
11. See, for example, Richard A. Easterlin, "Regional Income Trends, 1840–1950," in S. E. Harris, ed., *American Economic History* (New York: McGraw-Hill, 1961); and Easterlin, "Interregional Differences in Per Capita Income, Population, and Total Income, 1840–1950," in *Trends in the American Economy in the Nineteenth Century* (Princeton, N.J.: Princeton University Press, 1960), pp. 85–9. Though this book will take the position that the Civil War on the whole contributed to the modernization of the American nation, that contention is subject to a number of important qualifications and is even susceptible to repudiation in terms of national economic growth. See, for example, Thomas C. Cochran, "Did the Civil War Retard Industrialization?" and Stanley L. Engerman, "The Economic Impact of the Civil War," in Ralph Andreano, ed., *The Economic Impact of the American Civil War* (Cambridge, Mass.: Schenkman, 1967), pp. 167–79, 188–209.

reasons.[12] The primary purpose and impact of such policies was a weakening of the political economic base of the southern plantation elite, not the promotion of social efficiencies arising out of free market allocation of the southern labor supply.

Nor can the modernization of the American state be ascribed to external challenges arising out of increased participation in the world system. America's relative isolation in the western hemisphere presented the emergent world power with opportunities for territorial and market expansion, not challenges to national survival. Unlike many states within the intensely competitive European system, the United States could more or less ignore foreign challenges for months at a time, if not years, without endangering national independence. This relative isolation focused American state development much more intensely and exclusively on questions of internal cohesion and political integration than was the case for major European states. As part of this global perspective, modernization theories commonly interpret the American Civil War as part of a worldwide expansion of market capitalism. The conflict thus becomes a product of exogenous forces in the world economy that compelled hitherto isolated and relatively backward regions to link up with and participate in production for global markets. This interpretation is problematic in that such forces were not evident at all in the antebellum secession crisis (which unfolded in an international vacuum) and in that southern plantations already constituted the most internationally integrated sector of the

12.   The most general form of the modernization thesis maintains that the replacement of slavery with some form of labor market and the removal of plantation-elite opposition in national politics were necessary steps for the economic development of the United States and says little or nothing about their impact upon the South. In fact, the combination of these two alterations in the national political economy produced an environment in which representatives of southern plantation and subsistence agriculture could not resist the massive redistribution of wealth and resources to the northern economy that enabled American industrialization to proceed. For that reason alone, the Civil War can be interpreted as a modernizing event for the northern industrial system and, plausibly, for the nation. Just as certainly, however, the policies of the federal government during the Civil War and Reconstruction retarded southern economic development by systematically redistributing wealth to the North. Secondary consequences of this redistribution of wealth include strong southern opposition to central state expansion and progressive disfranchisement of blacks and poor whites in the last decades of the nineteenth century. A complete account of the demodernizing influence of the Civil War upon the American South would include references to all three impacts: retardation of economic development, resistance to central state expansion, and a retreat from mass-based political participation. See, for example, J. Morgan Kousser, *The Shaping of Southern Politics: Suffrage Restriction and the Establishment of the One-Party South, 1880–1910* (New Haven, Conn.: Yale University Press, 1974) for an account of disfranchisement; and Richard Bensel, *Sectionalism and American Political Development, 1880–1980* (Madison: University of Wisconsin Press, 1984), ch. 3, for a description of southern opposition to expansion of the central state in the late nineteenth century.

American economy. During the war itself, foreign powers continued to stand aside, though the war disrupted the British textile industry and shifted the loci of world cotton cultivation to areas securely within the British sphere of influence. In fact, when foreign pressure did appear, European states threatened to intervene on the side of the less-developed Confederacy and thus could be said to have hindered northern efforts to modernize the southern economy.

In the American context, modernization theory seriously understates the influence of purely state-centered concerns as proximate causes of the Civil War. Two of these concerns were the managed development of the western frontier and the suppression of separatism as a fundamental threat to national unity. These concerns may be associated with modern states such as the Soviet Union but are hardly unique to them. Since the end of the French Revolution, all central states that were not monarchies have resisted the secession of contiguous territory with some degree of violence.[13] Similarly, it is not clear what the "modernizing" choice was during Reconstruction. There were two broad alternatives. One was expensive, state-centered reorganization of the southern political economy with consequent constraints on national economic growth (caused by, for example, higher levels of taxation), deleterious impact on the position of the United States in the world economy (for example, because of disorganization in cotton production), and potential intensification of class conflict in the industrial economy.[14] The other alternative was an accommodation with the southern plantation elite that would enable efficient northern exploitation of the southern export economy during the industrialization period of American development (through the redistribution of wealth under the operation of the tariff and military pensions).[15] These choices posed a trade-off between central state expansion and economic development that, in effect, distinguished political from economic modernization.

All of these caveats aside, the modernization model does invite, even compel, cross-national comparison and attention to the global context within which the Civil War was fought. In addition, the model allows

13. In fact American policies aimed at pacification of the separatist South had interesting parallels in the less successful efforts to integrate Ireland and Algeria into the parent states of Britain and France (to take but two examples). In all three cases, the central state relied on settlers or other sponsored groups to represent state interests and neglected or suppressed indigenous groups.

14. On apprehension that land distribution to freedmen would have inhibited cash crop production, see, for example, Foner, *Politics and Ideology*, p. 111. For a broad suggestion of one way that Reconstruction could have intensified class conflict throughout the national political economy, see Chapter 5 of this book.

15. For the regional redistributive impact of military pensions and the tariff, see Bensel, *Sectionalism and American Political Development*, pp. 62–73.

the consideration of alternative developmental trajectories as historical possibilities and places the conflict within a set of fairly well-defined economic and political processes.

Overview

This book examines one case of revolutionary state formation: the United States between 1859 and 1877. Capture of the antebellum state by the Republican party brought on the American Civil War, which, in turn, permitted the development of a party-state resting on a broad economic coalition capable of fighting and winning the world's first modern, industrial war. The conditions of Civil War allowed the party to secure its hold on the state by disfranchising disloyal citizens, expanding the suffrage to dependent freedmen, and imposing martial law and other security measures throughout most of the nation (see Chapter 3).[16] Yet the character that state formation assumed during the war limited this party-state's capacity for further expansion. The party-state's leaders created a clientele, finance capitalists, that then limited the development of the national state, despite the fact that Union victory and Reconstruction presented an opportunity for a second phase of state-building. As a result of these limits, the party-state eventually reached a stalemate in the late nineteenth century – a state similar to the one that existed in the antebellum period in that the political economic coalitions supporting and opposing state expansion had many parallels. Consequently, a new state-building problem (inadequate administrative capacity) gradually replaced the old (southern separatism), but the resolution of this new problem occurred within the structures imprinted upon the American state by the revolutionary Republican party. For these reasons, the Civil War, even more than the end of British colonial rule, represents the true foundational moment in American political development.

The American state that emerged from the late nineteenth century was primarily the result of successful repression of southern separatism and the pursuit of economic advantage over the South by the industrializing regions of the Northeast and the Great Lakes. The Republican party coalition that enacted these policies constructed the American state upon two principles. The first was a robust nationalism that made loyalty to

16. For other national experiences in which one-party regimes, economic development, and political modernization have been connected, see Joseph LaPalombara and Myron Weiner, "Origin and Development of Political Parties," in their *Political Parties and Political Development* (Princeton, N.J.: Princeton University Press, 1966), pp. 17, 37–8.

the Union a prerequisite for representation in state institutions. This nationalism found its purest expression in military reconstruction of the South following the Civil War but also can be ascribed to martial law rule in the border regions during the war itself and to sporadic attempts to nationalize suffrage rights after the period known as Reconstruction ended. The second principle proposed a political economy in which central state power could sweep aside regional and local barriers to the development of a national capitalist market and directly assist in the construction of the physical and financial infrastructure necessary for that market.

During the years just prior to the Civil War, the uncompromising hostility of southern Democrats to state expansion and their growing nationalism – embracing the broader ideology supporting secession and the formation of an independent state – were based on a realistic appraisal of the current direction of the national political economy and the rise of the Republican party (see Chapter 2). They were a reaction to several trends: increasing penetration of the South by institutions and processes associated with the northern political economy, and the imminent exclusion of most of the South from participation in those political coalitions that were to control the central state. By contrast, northern Republicans became a "nationalist" force only as their class coalition occupied the national seats of power and were able to impose their developmental program upon the remainder of the nation.[17] In the southern Confederacy, nationalism was a response to the external threat represented by northern Republicans; the relative unity of the South during the Civil War can be attributed to this defensive position. In the northern Union, the war against southern separatism was driven by the need to maintain the newly dominant position of the Republican coalition in the domestic political economy. Both the offensive character of Republican

17. The basis of Republican nationalism was clearly different from that underlying nineteenth-century European state formation, where the two criteria guiding state development were "the principle of 'nationality,' by which a state would claim that populations currently subject to a neighboring state were 'nationally' the same as the claimant's own population and hence should join the latter in a single system of rule ... [and] 'natural borders,' physical boundaries that would provide the state with military defensibility and a sense of integrity and completeness." Neither of these justifications for nationalist claims fits the American case (a nation made up of immigrants can hardly lay claim to ethnicity, and "natural borders" are a much less relevant consideration in the context of an extremely weak central state and little international competition). The nationalists who suppressed southern separatism neither maintained that Southerners were ethnically "American" nor that the natural, defensible borders of the United States included the Gulf of Mexico and the western boundary of Texas. Poggi, *Development of the Modern State*, p. 90.

nationalism and the exclusive nature of the ruling coalition help explain
the comparative dissension within the northern Union during the war
(see Chapter 3).[18]

An immediate consequence of secession is a change in the scope and
content of the political economy of the parent nation. This change alters
the strategic considerations that supported the position of formerly dominant classes and thus can undermine the cohesion of a ruling class coalition. For example, the Republican coalition of yeoman agriculture and
industrialists would probably have rapidly fractured in a political system
that did not include the southern plantation economy. Without the South,
the national political economy would have lacked the major reservoir of
wealth that the coalition could potentially redistribute to its own members
and the base of the party would have narrowed as each sector sought to
impose redistributive claims upon the other. Thus the viability of a dominant class coalition changes with the scope of the political economy
potentially subject to central state rule. If an independent southern nation
had been successfully established, the two wings of the Republican alliance might themselves have become separatist in the new northern
political economy. In sum, then, southern secession posed serious risks
for the continued viability of the Republican coalition in the North and,
if successful, could have begun a process of centrifugal distintegration of
the entire Union.

The Confederate and Union states started the American Civil War with
almost identical governmental structures, and their close similarity per-
mits a study of comparative central state evolution that is unique in world
history (see Chapter 3). The Confederacy absorbed the physical plant
and personnel of the federal government throughout the South, adopted
a constitutional framework that was almost a verbatim copy of the federal
model, and passed legislation that adopted without change almost all
antebellum federal statutes. When the war began, the two national governments were more similar in formal structure and established bureaucratic routine than any other two states in history. This meant that their
expansion and development during the war was almost *solely* the product
of the nature of the challenge presented by the war itself and the differences in their internal political economies (slave-plantation versus
industrial–free soil systems). The combination of both factors served

18. In this context, Seward's proposal to begin a war with Spain and France over Santo
     Domingo and Mexico revealed the new secretary of state's profound awareness of
     the narrow basis of northern nationalism during the early months of the Lincoln
     administration. Seward evidently believed that such a foreign crisis might reunite the
     nation (by creating an external threat) and thus avoid civil war. Lincoln rejected the
     suggestion. James M. McPherson, *Battle Cry of Freedom: The Civil War Era* (New
     York: Oxford University Press, 1988), p. 270.

to produce central states of roughly equivalent overall strengths but with significant and surprising internal differences.

The strong Confederate state that emerged out of the southern war mobilization was remarkable in a number of respects. From a modernizing perspective, the premodern plantation elite that staffed and led the Confederate mobilization should have been hostile to the formation of an advanced state apparatus. The South did, in fact, oppose expansion of the central state both before and after the Civil War when the region belonged to a larger American political system that included an increasingly powerful northern economy. Furthermore, this southern opposition was reinforced by a states' rights political ideology and a conservative posture on constitutional interpretation that suggested a pervasive decentralizing world view on the proper role of a national government in economy and society. The claim has often been made that this ideological world view carried over into the construction and operation of the Confederacy.

The problem with this interpretation of southern state formation is that it never compared the administrative structure and policies of the central governments of the Union and the Confederacy. If, as I will maintain here, the South created in the Confederacy a central state at least as strong as the one that guided Union war mobilization, we can begin to distinguish between states' rights ideology, on the one hand, as a determinative world view and, on the other, as a pragmatic political program. From the latter perspective, both decentralist opposition to a strong federal government (when the South was in the Union) and support for a strong Confederate state can be viewed as defensive strategies directed against the hegemonic influence of the northern industrial economy in the middle and late nineteenth century. Thus, explanations of the antithetical positions of plantation and industrial elites in American development should assign the primary part to highly divergent regional political economies and only a tactical role to ideological principles. In the Union, the South needed states' rights in order to organize a consistent and broad institutional opposition to central state growth. Out of the Union, the South jettisoned states' rights and built a central state much stronger than either the antebellum or post-Reconstruction federal governments, a government to mobilize resistance to the military forces of the Union. That it did this in the space of one year from secession underscores the limiting, tactical context of states' rights philosophical concerns.[19] In fact, one of the great ironies of American political development

19. This subordination of ideological "worldview" to the strategic position of the economic base does not deny the partially independent existence of ideological concerns as policy systems in which class coalitions can identify and project their "rights" into

is that a central state as well organized and powerful as the Confederacy did not emerge until the New Deal and subsequent mobilization for World War II. Only then, some seven decades later, did the American state begin to approximate the bureaucratic controls on property and labor that had enabled the South to resist the Union during the Civil War.

The Union government chose to finance the northern war mobilization by expanding the power of the central state in three directions: abandoning the gold standard in the domestic economy and conferring legal tender status on paper currency (greenbacks); creating a national bank system that abolished locally chartered banks of issue and effectively nationalized the currency; and permanently placing (through the national bank system) a large part of the national debt with finance capitalists (see Chapters 4 and 5). The net effect of all these choices was the creation of a dependent financial class tied to the success of central state extraction and fiscal policy generally. Within the new financial system designed by the Union, however, the interests of finance capitalists became antithetical to radical Republican efforts to reconstruct the South and the new financial elite ultimately forced retrenchment and helped to bring an end to Reconstruction. In effect, by taking the form it did, Union financial policy mortgaged a radical Reconstruction of the South even before the war ended. The failure of Reconstruction, in turn, effectively ended further significant central state expansion for the remainder of the nineteenth century.

Chapters 4 and 5 thus recount one example of postwar "conservative reaction" and specify a process with some cross-national and historical applicability. The thesis they present may also reconcile some of the apparent divergence of interpretation between southern Reconstruction and postwar monetary policies that now characterizes much of American historiography. In addition, they posit a political-economic explanation for at least one of the ways in which the process of state expansion in any specific period can be self-limiting (by creating new groups and interests in the national political economy that retard further expansion). The way in which the North chose to finance the Civil War *created*, through its own structure, crucial, unforeseen limitations on the growth of the state in the late nineteenth century.

Once we recognize that both the Union and Confederate states were comparatively strong and that the federal government's Reconstruction policies were the most ambitious effort to remake society in American

the future. For an excellent example of this kind of interpretation, see Eric Foner, *Free Soil, Free Labor, Free Men: The Ideology of the Republican Party before the Civil War* (New York: Oxford University Press, 1970).

history, the major question associated with American state formation in the nineteenth century is not to explain its weakness but to explain why those Civil War and Reconstruction governments were dismantled. Since those governments coexisted with robust democratic systems, it cannot be the case, as most modernization theorists would have it, that wide popular access to the ballot necessarily debilitated state-building efforts. Nor can the political party competition in which antebellum, Civil War, and Reconstruction voters participated be described as a charade. The major parties, in fact, presented much more concrete and substantial political economic programs between 1859 and 1877 than ever before or since in American history.

An explanation for the disappearance of the Civil War/Reconstruction state and its replacement by the laissez-faire model of the Gilded Age is proposed at the end of Chapter 6 and distinguishes the respective interests of plantation owners and industrialists with regard to the exercise of central state authority. Plantation owners in a slave economy and for some time after the Civil War were separatist (by which is meant that they denied the legitimacy of state authority). After Reconstruction, this position was modified but, even then, resistance to central authority had a strong separatist theme. By contrast, northern industrialists were fervent nationalists and consistently favored the expansion of central state authority in two primary areas: the suppression of southern separatism and the imposition of a unified market economy throughout the entire nation. One of the main themes of Reconstruction, in fact, combined these areas by supporting the development of a free labor market in the South which would, it was hoped, encourage the emergence of indigenous, self-sustaining loyalist elements in the former states of the Confederacy.

Union victory determined the shape of the national political economy by forcefully including the plantation South within its boundaries. This victory both identified the Republican party with the survival of the state and opened up possibilities for interregional redistribution of wealth that would not have otherwise been possible. Furthermore, the central state's identification with northern economic development following the Civil War associated state power with modernization of private economic and institutional organizations. This alignment of state, region, and party only required a spare institutional apparatus dedicated to the suppression of local regulatory barriers to interstate trade and investment.[20] The

20. The agency of the central state most responsible for the emergence of national markets in the post-Reconstruction era was the judiciary, the very model of lean administrative organization. For example, Charles W. McCurdy has argued that "The Supreme Court's commerce clause decisions of the 1875–1890 period were of immediate importance to large-scale manufacturers and had an enduring influence on American

southern plantation elite, on the other hand, preferred a central state either too weak to overcome the centrifugal thrust of local governments or, failing that, a state just strong enough to thwart the designs of northern industrialists by imposing federal regulation on interstate commerce and investment. This interpretation, for example, can explain why John Reagan of Texas could be both the postmaster general of the Confederacy and, twenty years later, the major political proponent of the Interstate Commerce Commission, the precedent-setting extension of central state authority over the nation's railroads. As Confederate postmaster, Reagan followed his first and his deepest desire for a separate political existence for the South. His support for the ICC was an act of desperation, of self-defense against the rampaging forces let loose by industrialization. The impetus for that Commission, the Sherman Antitrust Act, and subsequent efforts to regulate the giant corporations that sprang up in the postwar decades came from western and southern agrarian efforts to restrain the economic nationalism of eastern industrialists, thus creating the first of the administrative agencies and insulated bureaucracies that have come to typify the modern state.[21] That these early efforts failed to accomplish their purpose and, instead, were turned to very different ends by the agents of northern industrialists and financiers should not obscure either their origins in the political economy or the fundamental alignment of central state authority with northern economic development.

Within this interpretation, it is possible to suggest that the economic nationalism of the industrial North was the original impetus behind American state expansion in the late nineteenth century. It was this drive to unify the national marketplace that eventually broke the back of southern separatism. Social and political reconstruction failed because the

economic growth for they firmly established the Supreme Court's role as the umpire of the nation's [internal] free-trade network." He observes that the cases leading to these decisions were generated by the legal counsel of the giant corporations whose growth was further encouraged by these Supreme Court rulings. In other words, the cases in some instances followed the initial expansion of corporate enterprise and then accelerated a further concentration of economic power. "American Law and the Marketing Structure of the Large Corporation, 1875–1890," *Journal of Economic History* 38 (September 1978): 631–49.

21. For example, on the decision to substitute the Reagan bill for the much weaker Senate version of the proposed Interstate Commerce Act, every one of the 52 Confederate veterans who voted supported the strengthening substitute. In sharp contrast, Union veterans broke almost two to one (43 to 22) against aggressive central-state regulation of railroad rates. For further discussion of the significance of this particular vote and the Interstate Commerce Act, see Elizabeth Sanders, "Industrial Concentration, Sectional Competition and Antitrust Politics in America, 1880–1980," Karen Orren and Stephen Skowronek, eds., *Studies in American Political Development* 1 (1986), pp. 154–6. On southern agrarian influence on state expansion generally, see Elizabeth Sanders, *Farmers, Workers and the State, 1880–1916* (Chicago: University of Chicago Press, forthcoming).

installation of federally sponsored loyalist groups in the South implied broader policies of wealth distribution that threatened private property rights and had no natural northern constituency. Economic nationalism, on the other hand, had a vigorous, powerful clientele in northern industrialism. Thus, the defensive reaction to economic nationalism – southern support for an infant administrative state – was, in fact, intended to restrain the rampaging forces of northern development. In the last decades of the nineteenth century, northern idealists and reformers who desired a more conventional, European-style state were frustrated, first, because they were only marginally relevant to the major problem facing the nation (southern separatism) and, second, because those elements in the political system most opposed to state expansion (aside from regulation of northern capitalist expansion) ultimately became their most likely allies.[22]

I propose an alternative explanation for the comparative weakness of the American state in the late nineteenth century that has these elements: (1) The Republican class coalition that captured the federal government just prior to the Civil War subsequently produced the central state's confrontation with southern separatism. (2) The major problem facing state-builders was thus not associated with a robust democracy, but southern separatism. (3) In confronting separatism, the central state moved from violent repression to a state-centered solution (involving Reconstruction), and, finally, to a (loosely effected) market integration. (4) In sum, American state formation assumed the form of a northern, industrial program in which incomplete political integration coincided with the creation of national markets and corporate consolidation.

There were, then, at least five different American states in the late-nineteenth century: the self-effacing antebellum state; the two national governments of the Civil War; the highly centralized Reconstruction state; and the market-oriented state that followed the withdrawal of military troops from the South. None of them bears much resemblance to classic European models, but they don't resemble one another very much, either. They are linked together by their focus on one central problem, the persistent demands of southern separatism.

22. For example, see Sanders, "Industrial Concentration, Sectional Competition and Antitrust," pp. 142–214.

2

The political economy of secession and civil war

The American man-of-war is a noble spectacle. I have seen it enter
an ancient port in the Mediterranean. All the world wondered at it,
and talked of it. Salvos of artillery, from forts and shipping in the
harbor, saluted its flag. Princes and princesses and merchants paid
it homage, and all the people blessed it as a harbinger of hope for
their own ultimate freedom. I imagine now the same noble vessel
again entering the same haven. The flag of thirty-three stars and
thirteen stripes has been hauled down, and in its place a signal is
run up, which flaunts the device of a lone star or a palmetto tree.
Men ask, "Who is the stranger that thus steals into our waters?"
The answer contemptuously given is, "she comes from one of the
obscure republics of North America. Let her pass on."
                    – Senator William H. Seward in the United States Senate,
                                                    January 12, 1861

Any study of the origins of the American state must address two questions
posed by the Civil War: Why did the South secede from the Union? and
why did the North resist secession?[1] Both questions, from a political-
economy perspective, involve the relationship of the two regions to the
American state. For the South, the American nation in 1860 was a confederation of sovereign states. Its continued existence threatened the plantation economy and promised little, if any, advantage to the region's
immediate or long-term interests. For the North, the American state was
a military and customs union that, properly exploited, could encourage
the territorial expansion of the capitalist northern economy and ensure
American preeminence in the world system. By 1861, the Republican
party was well on the way to converting the political-economic program
of the North into a nationalist ideology that promised a much wider and

---

1. In a slightly different form, Eric Foner asked the same two questions in his *Free Soil,
    Free Labor, Free Men: The Ideology of the Republican Party before the Civil War*
    (New York: Oxford University Press, 1970), p. 316.

18

more vital role for the central government.[2] This vision held nothing for the South; while Seward of New York was dreaming of American men-of-war in the Mediterranean, Southerners envisioned conquering abolitionist armies in Georgia. These predictions of the future shape and direction of the national political economy were in no way inconsistent.

Thus the plantation South both controlled the American state and became its most serious opponent in the years just before the Civil War. This period ended with the ascension to national power of the northern Republican party and the subsequent secession of the South from the Union. In the ensuing Civil War, a northern Union and a southern Confederacy fought over whether the plantation South would be reincorporated into a northern-dominated nation. In this chapter, the origins of southern secession and the Civil War are examined from several perspectives. An examination of the political and economic topography of antebellum America introduces a larger overview of the root sources of sectional tension in the national political economy. A following analytical description of the 1859–60 contest for the speakership of the House of Representatives illustrates both the broad terms of potential compromise between the sections and their rejection by southern political leaders. The chapter concludes with a comparison of the patterns of legislative support for prewar central state expansion and for a repressive response to southern secession. This comparison demonstrates the close linkages between the antebellum program for northern economic development, expansion of central state authority, and military suppression of southern separatism. The changing position of the sections in the national political economy made secession and civil war highly likely but not unavoidable. What made these events unavoidable were several political elements: the absence of constraints on the progressive radicalization of the Republican party, the self-defeating nature of the compromise measures proposed to the South, and the potential disintegration of the northern Union if the South were allowed to secede.

The future of slavery

Secession drew upon at least three interrelated interpretations of the future of the southern political economy. First, Southerners viewed the growing strength of the Republican party as a threat to the interests of

2. In contrast to long-standing arguments in support of individual state sovereignty and a constitutional right of secession, a nationalist ideology emerged comparatively late in the antebellum period. See, for example, Kenneth M. Stampp, *The Imperiled Union: Essays on the Background of the Civil War* (New York: Oxford University Press, 1980), pp. 3–36.

both slavery and the plantation system generally. Second, secessionists thought that disentanglement of the South from the antebellum state would be comparatively easy and would not invite foreign intervention in the region. Finally, southern political leaders recognized that the continuing rapid expansion of the North made successful separation increasingly problematic. In strictly economic terms, secession should be sooner rather than later. However, projections of the future shape of the national political economy and the viability of secession carried, by their very nature, substantial uncertainty. They were thus open to debate and potentially debilitating disagreement. Ultimately, the timing of secession was determined by two factors: (1) a triggering event that appeared to verify the fears of the least favorable projections of the South's future under Republican rule and (2) calculations of the ability and intention of the North to resist secession.

No one expected that Republican control of the presidency would mean the immediate abolition of slavery. Yet every Southerner realized that many Republicans considered destruction of the "slave power" to be the primary reason for the new party's existence. In an address in Boston, for example, Senator Henry Wilson of Massachusetts had promised that the Republicans "shall arrest the extension of slavery, and rescue the Government from the grasp of the slave power. We shall blot out slavery in the national capital. We shall surround the slave States with a cordon of free States and, in a few years, not withstanding the immense interests combined in the cause of oppression, we shall give liberty to the millions in bondage."[3] Speaking in the Senate, William Seward had previously argued that struggle between the free and slave states was unavoidable.

> The question of slavery in the federal territories...involves a dynastical struggle of two antagonistical systems, the labor of slaves and the labor of freemen, for mastery in the Federal Union. One of these systems partakes of an aristocratic character; the other is purely democratic. Each one of the existing states has staked, or it will ultimately stake, not only its internal welfare, but also its influence in the federal councils, on the decision of that contest. Such a struggle

3. The speech was reprinted in the *Appendix to the Congressional Globe* 36:1:249, April 23, 1860. Charles Sumner, Wilson's Massachusetts colleague, followed this address with one of the most vitriolic condemnations of slavery ever heard in the United States Congress. In it, Sumner likened slavery to "a bloody touch-me-not, and everywhere in sight now blooms the bloody flower. It is on the wayside as we approach the national Capitol; it is on the marble steps which we mount; it flaunts on this floor. I stand now in the house of its friends. About me, while I speak, are its most sensitive guardians." For the full text, see *Congressional Globe* 36:1:2590–603, June 4, 1860. On June 15, a *New York Times* editorial noted that Sumner's address had been formally endorsed by the Massachusetts legislature and favorably received throughout the North.

is not to be arrested, quelled or reconciled, by temporary expedients or compromises.⁴

In his famous speech, "The Irrepressible Conflict," delivered in Rochester, New York, on October 25, 1858, Seward held that a "slave power" held sway in the land. Using their influence in the seat of government, slavery's advocates intended to carry out a master plan for maintaining the institution's position in the nation:

> By continued appliances of patronage and threats of disunion, they will keep a majority favorable to these designs in the senate, where each state has an equal representation. Through that majority they will defeat, as they best can, the admission of free states and secure the admission of slave states. Under the protection of the judiciary, they will, on the principle of the Dred Scott case, carry slavery into all the territories of the United States now existing and hereafter to be organized. By the action of the president and the senate, using the treaty-making power, they will annex foreign slaveholding states. In a favorable conjuncture they will induce congress to repeal the act of 1808, which prohibits the foreign slave trade.... Thus relatively increasing the number of slave states, they will allow no amendment to the constitution prejudicial to their interest; and so, having permanently established their power, they expect the federal judiciary to nullify all state laws which shall interfere with internal or foreign commerce in slaves.⁵

Only the success of such a plan, Seward contended, could prevent the victory of free labor over slavery and its ultimate extinction. Republicans such as Wilson and Seward promised active intervention and were not to be dismissed lightly. Seward, for example, was the leading candidate for his party's presidential nomination. Most Republicans, however, were content to simply cite "irrepressible conflict" between the free labor and slavery economies and to predict the latter's ultimate, inevitable extinction.⁶

4. George E. Baker, ed., *The Works of William H. Seward* (New York: AMS Press, 1972; reprint of an 1884 edition), p. 575.
5. Ibid., p. 294. Seward urged that this struggle was "an irrepressible conflict between opposing and enduring forces, and it means that the United States must and will, sooner or later, become either entirely a slaveholding nation, or entirely a free-labor nation.... It is the failure to apprehend this great truth that induces so many unsuccessful attempts at final compromise between the slave and free states, and it is the existence of this great fact that renders all such pretended compromises, when made, vain and ephemeral." Ibid., p. 292.
6. See, for example, Representative Henry Waldron of Michigan in the *Congressional Globe* 36:1:1873, April 26, 1860. Stated in an ambiguous, neutral way, the "irrepressible conflict" theme drew some unusual support in the South. For example, John C. Calhoun, the states' rights leader, had also predicted systemic conflict between

By openly embracing industrial protection and neutralizing immigrant opposition by rebuffing nativism, the Republican party consolidated its preeminent position throughout the free states.[7] Between 1856 and 1860, the party's explosive growth in the border regions of the North, California, and the industrial regions of the East more than counterbalanced the slight erosion of Republican strength in the original areas of Free Soil party sentiment (upstate Illinois, southern Wisconsin, Michigan, the Western Reserve of Ohio, central New York state, and New England).

By 1860, the Republicans had also elaborated an integrated, internally coherent critique of slavery and the southern plantation economy that allowed both radicals and moderates to coexist within the party. Radicals could justify federal intervention on the grounds that the extinction of slavery was inevitable anyway. Moderates could urge restraint for the same reason.[8] In this critique, there was nothing to prevent moderates from moving to the radical position and, as Eric Foner notes, a "commitment to the reconstruction of southern society ... was actually quite common throughout the party."[9]

In fact, neutral observers had good reasons to doubt that so-called moderates within the party would resist, even passively, the abolitionist

northern and southern societies. Clement Eaton, *The Growth of Southern Civilization: 1790–1860* (New York: Harper & Row, 1963), pp. 309–11. Threats of active intervention only strengthened secessionist sentiment. Allan Nevins, *The Emergence of Lincoln*, vol. 2 (New York: Charles Scribner's Sons, 1950), pp. 279–80.

7. The Republicans also defused racist resistance to their opposition to slavery. On this and racism in the North generally, see Stampp, *Imperiled Union*, pp. 109–22; Leon F. Litwack, *North of Slavery: The Negro in the Free States, 1790–1860* (Chicago: University of Chicago Press, 1971); Foner, *Free Soil, Free Labor, Free Men*, pp. 261–300; John M. Rozett, "Racism and Republican Emergence in Illinois, 1848–1860: Reevaluation of Republican Negrophobia," *Civil War History* 22 (June 1976): 101–15. Rozett maintains that there was a closer connection between "free soil" and "Republican" sentiment, on the one hand, and black equality than is often believed to be the case – consequently, southern apprehension that territorial exclusion would be followed by an attack on slavery was, in fact, justified. However, Republican attitudes were by no means reflected in northern law. The abstract of the *Revised Code of Indiana*, for example, summarized the dismal position of northern blacks before the war: "1. Negroes and mulattoes not allowed to come into the State. 2. All contracts with such negroes and mulattoes declared to be void. 3. Any person encouraging them to come, or giving them employment, to be fined from $10 to $500. 4. Negroes and mulattoes not to be allowed to vote. 5. No negro, or mulatto having even one-eighth part of negro blood, shall marry a white person; and punishes a violation of the law with from one to ten year's imprisonment, and fine of from $1,000 to $5,000. 6. Any person counseling or assisting such marriage shall be fined from $100 to $1,000, and the marriage to be void. 7. Negroes and mulattoes are not allowed to testify against white persons, or send their children to the free schools with white children, or hold any office." *Congressional Globe* 36:1:1903, May 2, 1860.

8. For a summary of the Republican ideological critique of the southern plantation economy, see Foner, *Free Soil, Free Labor, Free Men*, pp. 40–72.

9. Ibid., p. 52.

plans of their more radical colleagues. In many respects, the Republican party was both a zealous abolitionist crusade and an organization led by professional, rather conventional politicians.[10] Once the party succeeded in prohibiting slavery in the territories, these leaders would have had to find new campaign issues to justify the party's continued existence. Given the abolitionist base, the achievement of the party's initial goals would almost certainly have been followed by an escalating attack on slavery. The continuing search for votes would have moved the party from prohibition in the territories to abolition in the District of Columbia, to a ban on the interstate movement of slaves, and, finally, to an assault on the institution within the slave states themselves. To argue that such a dynamic would not have moved professional politicians in this direction, one would have to assume that the leadership could have found and would have wanted to impose some other issue as the basis of the party's identity. Alternatively, it might be suggested that the party would have refused to exploit the slavery issue beyond the territorial question and, instead, have risked possible stagnation and collapse. Even neutral observers should have viewed these expectations with serious skepticism. Most Southerners would have dismissed them out of hand.

They could, for example, point to the capitulation of the moderates when Representative Harrison Blake of Ohio proposed a wholesale assault on slavery by the federal government. The preamble to Blake's resolution read: "The chattelizing of humanity and the holding of persons as property is contrary to natural justice and the fundamental principles of our political system, and is notoriously a reproach to our country throughout the civilized world, and a serious hindrance to the progress of republican liberty among the nations of the earth." The resolution itself instructed the Judiciary Committee "to inquire into the expediency of reporting a bill giving freedom to every human being and interdicting slavery wherever Congress has the constitutional power to legislate on the subject." Anticipating that the proposal would embarrass the opposition, gleeful Southerners overrode objections by moderate Republicans to legislative consideration of the resolution and, as the voting continued, even tentatively moved (then withdrew) a resolution of censure against those Republicans who refused to vote. Although a few Republican moderates attempted to explain that their position on slavery lay somewhere between abolition and indifference, most toed the radical line. When the dust settled, almost two-thirds (60 of 95) of all northern congressmen voted for the resolution, including even greater majorities

---

10.   The best account of the party's formative years is William E. Gienapp, *The Origins of the Republican Party, 1852–1856* (New York: Oxford University Press, 1987).

among delegations from New England, upstate New York, the Great Lakes region, and newly settled Minnesota and Iowa (see Map 2.1).[11]

Though the resolution, once southern votes were tallied, lost by a sizable margin, Blake had forced moderates to concede: (1) that slavery violated "the fundamental principles" of the American "political system"; (2) that slavery therefore violated the Constitution (otherwise the Constitution would itself violate these principles); and (3) that legislation to abolish slavery, even in the South, should be enacted by Congress. While no one believed that such action was politically feasible in the spring of 1860, Southerners would have been equally rash to believe that Republican moderates would have found the will to resist radical proposals once the party occupied the White House. And, while Republican moderates were yielding to Blake's initiative, the high abstention rate among Anti-Lecompton Democrats and Americans offered little solace to the South (see Table 2.1). A significant minority of even these tiny party fragments could not, it seemed, withstand Republican radicalism.

Even without attempting to abolish slavery outright, the advent of a Republican administration promised potentially lethal changes in the political economy within which the institution operated. As both friend and foe recognized, Republican control of the federal government would allow the party:

1. to create numerous free states out of the western territories (thereby ensuring free state dominance in the Senate and Electoral College);
2. to encourage the flight of slaves into neighboring free states by, among other things, repealing the fugitive slave law (thus forcing slaveholders to emigrate into more secure regions of the deep South, thereby eroding support for slavery in the border states);
3. to abolish slavery in the western territories, federal forts, navy yards, and the District of Columbia;
4. to dismantle constitutional protections for slavery, including reversal of the Dred Scott decision, by either formally amending the Constitution or appointing antislavery judges to the Supreme Court;
5. to prohibit all interstate trade in slaves;
6. to eliminate southern censorship of the mails and thus allow antislavery literature and newspapers to flood the region;
7. to insinuate an antislavery party into the very heart of the South through the dispensation of federal patronage.[12]

11. *Congressional Globe* 36:1:1359–62, March 26, 1860.
12. On February 10, 1860, Senator Robert Toombs of Georgia wrote, in a letter to Alexander Stephens (the future vice-president of the Confederacy), that the dispensation of federal patronage by a Republican president "would abolitionize Maryland in a year, raise a powerful abolition party in Va., Kentucky and Missouri in two

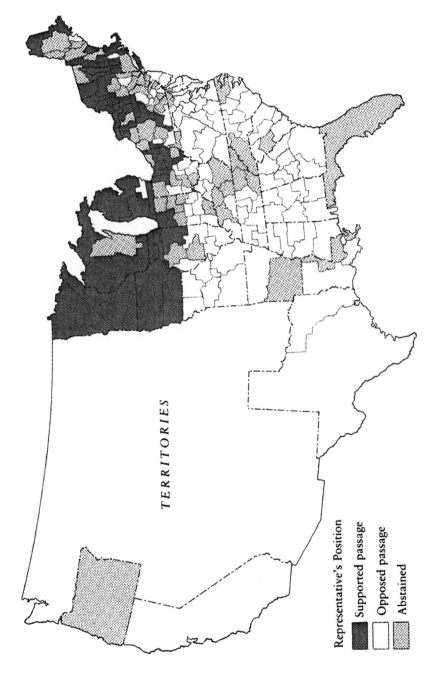

Map 2.1 Passage of a resolution proposing legislation "interdicting slavery," March 26, 1860. *Source:* Analysis of roll call data by author.

TERRITORIES

Representative's Position

Supported passage

Opposed passage

Abstained

Table 2.1. *Party breakdown on Blake Resolution interdicting slavery*

| | Percentage of party members voting | | |
Party	Yea	Nay	Abstaining
Republicans	54.1 (60)	10.8 (12)	35.1 (39)
Anti-Lecompton Democrats	0	61.5 (8)	38.5 (5)
Americans	0	61.5 (16)	38.5 (10)
Administration Democrats	0	83.9 (73)	16.1 (14)
All congressmen	25.3 (60)	46.0 (109)	28.7 (68)

Note: These four parties were the organizations into which the membership eventually divided. Though allegiances shifted over the life of the Thirty-sixth Congress, the memberships of each of these four parties were routinely referred to as formal organizations during legislative debate and caucused together for mutual consultation. For membership composition at the beginning of the Thirty-sixth Congress, see *Congressional Globe,* 36:1:1–2, December 7, 1859.
Source: Calculations from roll call in the *Congressional Globe,* 36:1:1359–62, March 26, 1860.

The implementation of such a program, both Republicans and slaveholders believed, would cause the institution to atrophy and finally disappear.[13]

For a number of reasons, including the maintenance of a balance in the Senate between free states and slave states and a widespread belief that slavery needed virgin land in order to survive and prosper, the abolition of slavery in the western territories became the focal point of sectional competition. Though slavery could not expand into the West because of the hostility of the climate to cotton cultivation, many southern

> years, and foster and rear up a free labour party in [the] whole South in four years."
> Ulrich B. Phillips, ed., *The Correspondence of Robert Toombs, Alexander H. Stephens, and Howell Cobb,* in the *1911 Annual Report of the American Historical Association,* vol. 2 (Washington, D.C., 1913), p. 461.

13. This list is a composite of similar predictions made by Representative Albert Jenkins of Virginia in the *Appendix to the Congressional Globe* 36:1:260–3, April 26, 1860; *The Kentucky Statesman,* January 6, 1860, cited in Dwight Lowell Dumond, *Antislavery Origins of the Civil War in the United States* (Ann Arbor: University of Michigan Press, 1964; reprint of the 1939 edition), pp. 116–17; Foner, *Free Labor, Free Soil, Free Men,* pp. 119, 122–3; and Gilbert Graffenreid Glover, *Immediate Pre-Civil War Compromise Efforts* (Nashville, Tenn.: George Peabody College for Teachers, 1934), pp. 10, 18. As Senator Alfred Iverson of Georgia put it, "the power of this Federal Government could be so exercised against the institution of slavery in the southern States, as that, without an overt act, the institution would not last ten years. We know that ... and seeing the storm which is approaching, although it may be seemingly in the distance, we are determined to seek our own safety and security before it shall ... overwhelm us with its fury." *Congressional Globe* 36:2:102, December 17, 1860.

congressmen insisted upon a (largely symbolic and purposeless) "slave code" for the territories. Such a code would commit the federal government to slavery's protection in the West, perhaps slow settlement of the territories and thus postpone their admission into the Union, and, most important, promote the breakup of the Democratic party and thus hasten southern secession.[14] On the other hand, many Republicans, including Lincoln, viewed the containment of slavery within its present bounds as the one development that would doom the institution without outright abolition.[15]

Many leaders on both sides of the slavery issue subscribed to some version of the soil exhaustion thesis. This thesis held that cultivation of cash crops by means of slave labor rapidly exhausted the productive capacity of the land. Lower crop yields decreased land values and stimulated a westward migration of slaves (either with their masters or through sale).

Without territorial expansion, the value of slaves would decline with their decreasing marginal productivity, slaves would increase as a proportion of the total population, and owners would resort to heavier discipline and commit fewer resources to the support of slaves. As William Barney observed, "Very few planters would have agreed to a political economy where the value of their slave property steadily depreciated or their monopolization of the South's sources of wealth and status aspirations was eroded by competing centers of power. . . . Southerners were certain that the most vital function of their society – its ability to assimilate and control slaves – would be destroyed by the confinement of slavery."[16] Under this thesis, the expansionary imperatives of slavery and

14. By pressing for a slave code for the territories, southern states' rights advocates threatened to impose a policy on the Democratic party that the northern wing, led by Stephen Douglas, could and would not tolerate. At best, these southerners were indifferent to their party's survival in the North; at worst, their strategy was intended to destroy the last cross-sectional party and thus further polarize the nation as another step leading to separation. See David M. Potter, *The Impending Crisis, 1848–1861* (New York: Harper & Row, 1976; completed and edited by Don E. Fehrenbacher), pp. 401–4; Nevins, *The Emergence of Lincoln,* vol. 2, pp. 175–81.

15. Nevins, *The Emergence of Lincoln,* vol. 2, pp. 178, 403; Foner, *Free Soil, Free Labor, Free Men,* pp. 115–6.

16. William L. Barney, *The Secessionist Impulse: Alabama and Mississippi in 1860* (Princeton, N.J.: Princeton University Press, 1974), pp. 15–18, 313. The fullest expression of the thesis is in Eugene D. Genovese, *The Political Economy of Slavery: Studies in the Economy and Society of the Slave South* (New York: Vintage, 1967), especially ch. 4. Also see W. H. Yarbrough, *Economic Aspects of Slavery in Relation to Southern and Southwestern Migration* (Nashville, Tenn.: George Peabody College for Teachers, 1932), pp. 3, 26–55, and William Chandler Bagley, Jr., *Soil Exhaustion and the Civil War* (Washington, D.C.: American Council on Public Affairs, 1942), pp. 78, 85–90. Contemporary Southerners, such as Representative Zebulon Vance of North Carolina, agreed: "By surrounding the slave States with free territory, and

the westward drive of free labor came into direct and irresolvable conflict in the western territories and made the Civil War or something very like it inevitable.

The soil exhaustion thesis has come under attack from several directions. One objection notes that slavery would not have been strangled by Republican containment for at least three decades or more. It would have taken that long to occupy the vast stretches of vacant land within the South in 1860.[17] In addition, the southern plantation economy was so robust and the price of slaves so high that an argument for imminent collapse cannot reconcile southern economic and political expectations. As the *New York Times* editorialized on October 1, 1860, "The South was never so rich, powerful, and prosperous, as at the present moment, when its politicians look upon it as on the brink of ruin, by the overthrow of a favorite political dogma." Seemingly oblivious to political crisis, the soaring price of slaves was evidence both of economic prosperity and the rapid expansion of cotton cultivation.[18] These objections can be lodged most effectively against a broad regional analysis of the slave economy. They do not hold up when individual states are considered. If, for example, a prohibition on the interstate movement of slaves were enacted, the institution would have rapidly developed the pathological traits predicted by the soil exhaustion thesis in most eastern slave states.

The most powerful objection to the soil exhaustion thesis, however, is that the territories themselves were so physically inhospitable to slavery

building us in with an impassable wall, you would eventually *force* the abolition of slavery. Our population would become so dense, and our slaves so numerous, that we could not live; their value would depreciate to nothing; and we would not be able to keep them." *Congressional Globe* 36:1:1162, March 14, 1860.

17. Gavin Wright, *The Political Economy of the Cotton South: Households, Markets, and Wealth in the Nineteenth Century* (New York: W. W. Norton, 1978), pp. 132–3. Also see Roger L. Ransom, *Conflict and Compromise: The Political Economy of Slavery, Emancipation, and the American Civil War* (New York: Cambridge University Press, 1989), pp. 53–60.

18. On the incongruity of historically high slave prices and political crisis, see Wright, *Political Economy of the Cotton South*, pp. 144–50. Mark Schmitz and Donald Schaefer have provided new support for the traditional argument "that the net effect [of territorial expansion] upon slave owners – in particular those on the slave-exporting eastern seaboard – was positive. The thesis is that the marginal product of slave labor increased with new land supplies and was capitalized into higher slave values. This gain more than offset the losses due to the concurrent decline in the price of cotton due to an outward shift in cotton supply." "Paradox Lost: Westward Expansion and Slave Prices before the Civil War," *Journal of Economic History* 41 (June 1981): 402–7. One strong implication of the argument in this article is that it was economically advantageous and, therefore, rational for eastern slave states to support the territorial expansion of slavery. The analysis, however, omits the strictly "political" factors in the calculation: Eastern slaveholders would have supported expansion regardless of the marginal economic costs because the settlement of new slave states was the only way of defending the institution within the American state.

that even southern politicians who argued for a slave code did not believe the institution could be planted there. The most likely territory to evolve into a slave state was New Mexico but, even there, seven years of "propagandism, positive legislation, and executive compliance," all intended to encourage slavery, had produced only twenty-two slaves.[19] Even so, Republicans in the House of Representatives attempted in the spring of 1860 to abolish slavery in the territory.[20]

During the secession crisis, the party reversed ground and offered to admit New Mexico into the Union as a slave state. This apparent concession to the South was widely viewed as insignificant because both free- and slave-state congressmen predicted that New Mexico, of its own accord, would abolish slavery in the near future.[21] If even Southerners believed the territories to be inhospitable, the soil exhaustion thesis predicts not the inevitability of the Civil War but the unavoidable, long-term extinction of slavery. In the short term, however, the South could still seek to retard settlement of the western territories by imposing a slave code (in order to delay their admission as free states) and the North could, equally reasonably, encourage settlement by prohibiting the institution. Both strategies had, as their primary object, not the definition of the limits of slavery, but the determination of the speed with which the North would reap political advantage from the admission of the western territories as states.

Closed to the West, the southern domain of slavery seemed to be contracting as well. Perhaps the single best indication of the institution's retreat was the growth of an indigenous free black population. By 1860, free blacks composed large fractions of the population along the northern border of the slave South, in the Appalachian highlands and old eastern piedmont, in the Catholic portion of Louisiana and Gulf Coast to the east of New Orleans, and along the Rio Grande (see Map 2.2). In Delaware, slavery had been almost completely abolished by gradual, voluntary emancipation (91.7 percent of all blacks were free). In Maryland, free blacks (49.1 percent) almost outnumbered slaves and in Virginia they composed over 10 percent of the black population. North Carolina

19. James Ford Rhodes, *History of the United States, 1854–1860*, vol. 2 (New York: Macmillan, 1919), p. 313. In testimony before the House Committee of Thirty-three, the federal district judge of New Mexico gave the population of the territory as 750 whites, 2,000 Mexicans who were U.S. citizens, 3,000 Mexican aliens, 44,000 "peons," 44,000 "half-civilized" Indians, and 50 slaves "mostly servants of army and Federal officers," *New York Times*, December 27, 1860.

20. *Congressional Globe* 36:1:2045, May 10, 1860. Similar prohibitions of slavery were subsequently passed for the remainder of the western territories, pp. 2066–77, May 11, 1860.

21. *New York Times*, December 27, 1860; Rhodes, *History of the United States*, vol. 2, p. 314; Nevins, *Emergence of Lincoln*, vol. 2, p. 408.

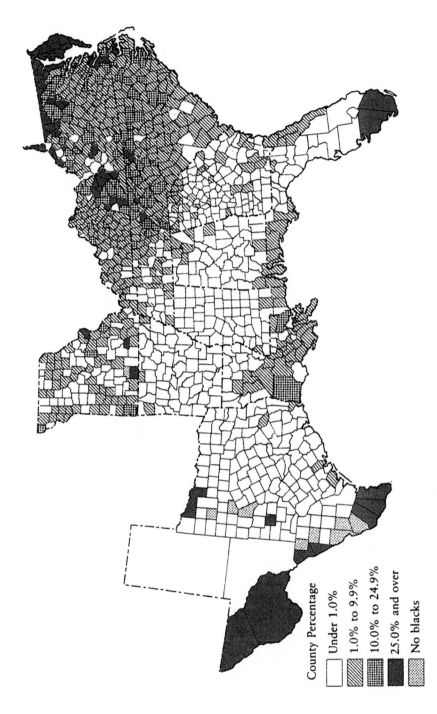

Map 2.2 Free blacks as a percentage of the total black population, 1860. *Source:* Calculations by the author from the *1860 Census.*

County Percentage

Under 1.0%

1.0% to 9.9%

10.0% to 24.9%

25.0% and over

No blacks

(8.4 percent) and Louisiana (5.3 percent) also held substantial numbers of free blacks.

Free blacks tended to reside in the oldest regions of the South, especially those where intensive cultivation over several centuries had depleted the soil or in highland, marginally productive areas. They were also numerous along the border with the North, where proximity to free territory increased the risk to slaveholders that their chattels might escape. As the *Texas Almanac* explained, the decreasing number of slaves in counties along the Rio Grande "arises from their proximity to Mexico, making this kind of property a very uncertain one."[22] The relatively high percentage of free blacks in border regions was the product of both greater rates of manumission (possibly because of lower slave values) and the exodus of slaves and slaveowners to more secure territories. Older regions of the South, as well, inherited the free population that represented the cumulation of prior acts of manumission over the centuries.

In almost every state, slaves composed a smaller proportion of the total black population in cities than in the surrounding countryside. The apparent incompatibility of slavery with the industrial and commercial economies of urban communities has been attributed to a number of factors. Eugene Genovese, for example, cites the absence of a prosperous yeoman farmer class in the South and, thus, the lack of a broad regional market for manufactured goods. He also describes plantation society as a "pre-capitalist economy" that discouraged capital investment in areas other than land or slaves.[23] Fred Bateman and Thomas Weiss have concluded that the lack of industrialization reflected "the decisions of planters, acting individually and without legal constraints to shun manufacturing opportunities" but that the southern slaveholding elite would have, eventually, exploited the higher returns offered by industry.[24]

Neither argument implies a retreat by slavery in the face of continuing urbanization. In the first case, cities would fail to develop in the South altogether. In the second, expanding industrial communities would come to include a large percentage of slaves in the work force. In fact, however, the South's largest cities were hostile environments for slavery because of their large free-black populations, social diversity (including relatively large immigrant communities), robust market dynamics, and, often, close proximity to free states.[25] In the larger cities, slavery was a dying insti-

22. *Texas Almanac for 1857* (Galveston: Richardson, 1856), pp. 70–1.
23. *The Political Economy of Slavery*, pp. 157–240; also see Yarbrough, *Economic Aspects of Slavery*, ch. 5.
24. *A Deplorable Scarcity: The Failure of Industrialization in the Slave Economy* (Chapel Hill: University of North Carolina Press, 1981), pp. 160–3.
25. Dumond, *Antislavery Origins*, p. 13; Richard C. Wade, *Slavery in the Cities* (New York: Oxford University Press, 1964), pp. 3, 246. For contrary views that emphasize

tution and the capital investment and industrial workers that spurred urban growth came disproportionately from the North. The long-term projection from these trends had to include the probable loss of border-state support for slavery in the national House of Representatives and, less immediately, in the Senate. In fact, many Confederate nationalists would have been reluctant to include the border states in the new southern republic, even if they had seceded, because the latter were destined to become manufacturing areas.[26]

The tension between the institution and the market economy of competitive capitalism was nowhere more evident than in the southern legal system. As Mark Tushnet has argued, there were two partial, though ultimately unsatisfactory, solutions to the incompatibility between slavery and a robust capitalist economy. The first, the insulation of the law of slavery into a separate code apart from commercial and labor market law, had already been tried in the South, and was slowly but surely failing. The second solution was the breaking of political ties with the North. While the erection of a separate political economy in the South would have retarded the disruptive invasion of capitalist legal and economic relations from the North, slavery would still have been under siege because of the extensive integration of plantation production into the rhythms and commercial routines of the world economy.[27]

the comparative productivity of slave labor in agricultural areas, see Claudia Dale Goldin, *Urban Slavery in the American South, 1820–1860: A Quantitative History* (Chicago: University of Chicago Press, 1976), pp. 123–8, and Heywood Fleisig, "Slavery, the Supply of Agricultural Labor, and the Industrialization of the South," *Journal of Economic History* 36 (September 1976): 572–97.

26. Letter from William Gilmore Simms to William Porcher Miles, February 26, 1861, quoted in Nevins, *Emergence of Lincoln*, vol. 2, p. 430. For a statistical description of industrial development in the South and the plantation economy generally see J. D. B. DeBow, *The Industrial Resources, Statistics, etc. of the United States*, vols. 1–3, 3rd ed. (New York: D. Appleton, 1854). For secessionist fears that slavery was a vulnerable institution in the border states, see Eric Foner, *Politics and Ideology in the Age of the Civil War* (New York: Oxford University Press, 1980), p. 51; William W. Freehling, "The Editorial Revolution, Virginia, and the Coming of the Civil War: A Review Essay," *Civil War History* 16 (March 1970): 68–71.

27. Mark V. Tushnet, *The American Law of Slavery: 1810–1860* (Princeton, N.J.: Princeton University Press, 1981), pp. 6–10. As Tushnet puts it, "the dilemma of Southern slave law [was] that slave relations generated a totalistic concern for both humanity and interest at the same time that Southern society was inserted into a bourgeois world economy whose well-developed bourgeois world-view pervaded the consciousness of all who took part in trade in the world markets." For the legal definitions of a slave under southern law, see *Congressional Globe* 36:1:2591, 2596, June 4, 1860. For the texts of laws prohibiting the mistreatment of slaves, see *Appendix to the Congressional Globe* 36:1:337, May 19, 1860. The paternalistic aspect of slavery led southern congressmen to unreservedly condemn the "irresponsible" form of labor–capital relations in the North. These condemnations ranged from John Reagan of Texas ("There is oppression wherever power and wealth are brought to bear upon labor, and exists in every civilized community on earth.") to Muscoe Garnett of

While slavery was a viable, even robust economic institution in the South as a whole, the system was under serious and sustained political attack. In fact, from the perspective of the South, the assault on slavery by northern abolitionists was the most important economic cause of the Civil War.[28] Other factors, such as the tariff and incremental nationalization of the economy, were less salient except in that they increased the political resources available to abolitionist radicals.[29]

Virginia ("in the northern portion of this Republic, under the influence of universal suffrage, which so generally prevails, the whole power of the Government is rapidly being concentrated into the hands of the corporations, lords of the loom which control the opinions of men, and use their power to grind down the operatives to the lowest depths of degradation, and which control your politics, by aid of corruption and moneyed influence. Your laboring millions groan beneath their oppression. They strike for better wages; but your capitalists combine to crush them down.") to William Porcher Miles of South Carolina ("Do we, in times of want and pressure, when your mobs are glaring with hungry eyes at the luxuries of the rich, while a scanty crust, perhaps, is all that they have to eke out a wretched existence; when, during your bitter winters, thousands, thrown out of employment by the fluctuations of trade and commerce acting upon your manufactories, moody and reckless, stand ready, at the bidding of any demagogue, to commit acts of open violence, do we, or any of our people, ever attempt to spur them on?"). *Congressional Globe* 36:1:1876, April 27, 1860; 2024, May 9, 1860; and *Appendix to the Congressional Globe* 36:1:69, January 6, 1860. For general reviews of the literature in which Southerners condemned the workings of the free labor system in the North, see Peter Kolchin, "In Defense of Servitude: American Proslavery and Russian Proserfdom Arguments, 1760–1860" *American Historical Review* 85 (October 1980): 813–14, and Wilfred Carsel, "The Slaveholders' Indictment of Northern Wage Slavery," *Journal of Southern History* 6 (November 1940): 504–20.

28. For a review of the recent literature on the economic causes of the Civil War, see Susan Previant Lee and Peter Passell, *A New Economic View of American History* (New York: W. W. Norton, 1979), ch. 10; Wright, *The Political Economy of the Cotton South*, pp. 128–57; Foner, *Free Soil, Free Labor, Free Men*, pp. 2–10, 314–15. For a contemporary southern interpretation of the vitality of slavery as a producer of wealth, the salience of cotton in the northern and British economies, and the future prospects for a successful economic and political union between the sections, see Thomas Prentice Kettell, *Southern Wealth and Northern Profits* (New York: George W. and John A. Wood, 1860). For the contention that the incipient shift of economic and political power to the North caused secession and the Civil War, see Nevins, *Emergence of Lincoln*, vol. 2, pp. 466–8.

29. As Representative Reuben Davis of Mississippi noted in a letter to a constituent, the internal development policies of the North could not be contained but would spill over into an attempt to reconstruct the basis of southern society: "The interest of the New England States is in direct and positive antagonism with that of our own, and will ever continue so to be, and will every year of the duration of the Republic, become more and more aggressive. The original object of the leaders of the New England States was the acquisition of the balance of power to be exerted in favor of their peculiar interest, and to give them the ascendancy in the Government. But, having raised the storm, it is now directing itself against our labor system, and they are no longer able to control it to their interest. Many of their wise men see and feel that it is now likely to involve both North and South in one common ruin; *yet the fatal step cannot be retracted.* Having arrived at its present point, we of the South must not only look to, but prepare for the only result that can spring out of the

The nonslaveowning South

This analysis of secession has so far omitted a discussion of the interests of nonslaveowning Southerners. One common explanation for the wide support by poor whites for southern separatism has focused on the overt manipulation of public opinion and political competition by a unified slaveowning elite occupying an overwhelmingly dominant economic position in southern society.[30] This interpretation views the interests of the white nonslaveholding class as hostile to slavery and explains their acquiescence in secession as, in part, a product of elite censorship and coercive enforcement of a proslavery consensus.[31] Others have contended that the abolition of slavery presented poor southern whites with the prospect of increased economic competition, social disorder, and the creation of an unassimilable group fundamentally hostile to southern interests in the American political economy.[32]

A more balanced view holds that slavery had no discernible impact on the economic interests of most nonslaveholding southerners because their subsistence existence was almost entirely detached from the national and world economies. For other poor whites, the dependence of slave plantations on cash crops provided a vast market for the production of foodstuffs that otherwise might not have existed. For another group, perhaps the smallest in number, the hostility of the plantation economy to industrialization retarded the development of comparatively attractive wage-labor opportunities.[33] This view interprets the censorship of political debate in the South as both an expression of a regional consensus on slavery and the requirements of labor discipline within the institution. Periods of political tension, for example, usually heightened fear of slave revolt and brought renewed calls for white unity.[34] This interpretation

present state of things." Italics in the original. First printed in the Grenada, Mississippi, *Locomotive* and dated January 14; reprinted in the *New York Times*, February 14, 1860.

30. For a concise summary of the literature on elite manipulation, see Barney, *The Secessionist Impulse*, pp. 38–49. On the concentration of wealth in the slaveholding elite, see Gavin Wright, " 'Economic Democracy' and the Concentration of Agricultural Wealth in the Cotton South, 1850–1860," *Agricultural History* 44 (January 1970); 63–93.

31. For a contemporary interpretation of the interests of poor whites and the most outstanding example of southern censorship of antislavery material, see Hinton Rowan Helper, *The Impending Crisis of the South* (New York: Burdick Brothers, 1857).

32. Nevins, *Emergence of Lincoln*, vol. 2, p. 148.

33. Robert R. Russel, "The Effects of Slavery upon Nonslaveholders in the Ante Bellum South," *Agricultural History* 15 (April 1941): 54–71.

34. See, for example, accounts of slave plots, "alarms," and "excitement" in the South during the presidential election carried in the *New York Times*, October 19, 1860. Such reports, of course, can also be interpreted as elite manipulation of public opinion

can also point to the relatively open process of political competition within the South itself (aside from censorship on the question of slavery). Ralph Wooster, for instance, observes that the increasing number of property holders and slaveowners among political officials during the 1850s coincided with significant strides toward democratization of the political process.[35] In addition, the prolonged, intense debate over disunion and southern independence in the three decades between 1830 and 1860 seems to have ensured that all aspects of slavery were publicly considered. Finally, aside from the relatively small group of southern whites who lost potential employment opportunities in industry, the northern political-economic program of tariffs, internal development, and national economic integration had very little appeal, particularly when measured against the social and economic insecurity that appeared to accompany emancipation.

Comparative advantages of a southern nation

In several respects, the southern decision to secede was a relatively easy choice to make. One reason Southerners could contemplate regional independence with such equanimity was the complete absence of major competing states in the western hemisphere.[36] In the decade preceding the Civil War, the American drama was acted out in a vacuum and, while secession would create a hostile and major power to the north of a southern confederacy, this development promised to be no more com-

but, as Eric Foner has argued, "the experience [in the Caribbean islands] and similar events in the 1880s in Brazil, should remind us again of the dangers of subversive ideas among the slave population, and the reality of southern fears that the very existence of a hostile central government was a threat to the stability of their peculiar institution." *Politics and Ideology*, p. 30; also see Robert William Fogel and Stanley L. Engerman, *Time on the Cross: The Economics of American Negro Slavery* (Boston: Little, Brown, 1974), pp. 39–40, and Robert Brent Toplin, "The Spectre of Crisis: Slaveholder Reactions to Abolitionism in the United States and Brazil," *Civil War History* 18 (June 1973): 129–38.

35. By 1860, for example, the only state in the region that retained a property requirement for serving as governor was North Carolina. Ralph Wooster, *Politicians, Planters and Plain Folk: Courthouse and Statehouse in the Upper South, 1850–1860* (Knoxville: University of Tennessee Press, 1975), pp. 118–29; also see Chilton Williamson, *American Suffrage from Property to Democracy, 1760–1860* (Princeton, N.J.: Princeton University Press, 1968), pp. 223–80; Edward Pessen, "How Different from Each Other Were the Antebellum North and South?" *American Historical Review* 85 (December 1980): 1136–8.

36. For the growth and political expression of southern nationalism, see John McCardell, *The Idea of a Southern Nation: Southern Nationalists and Southern Nationalism, 1830–1860* (New York: W. W. Norton, 1979), pp. 277–335.

plicated than continued coexistence within the federal union.[37] In fact, secession would free the South to pursue expansionary policies in Mexico, Cuba, and Central America against countries that were clearly unable to resist the new Confederacy. Everything considered, independence expanded international opportunities for the South without increasing insecurity.

Division of the antebellum state apparatus was also relatively uncomplicated for a number of reasons. First, the federal structure of the American state meant that a good portion of state activity would carry over into the new nation without the slightest interruption or difficulty. The laws and government of South Carolina governing property or the economy, for example, would not be affected in any way by withdrawal from the Union. The small size of the central state and its restriction to a narrow range of activities meant that secessionists could risk the total collapse of federal functions with indifference. The atrophied military establishment, itself a product of American isolation in the western hemisphere, made secession even more attractive. A second reason southern nationalists expected to easily dismantle the state apparatus can be traced to their anticipation of high cohesion within southern society. High social cohesion carried with it expectations for an absence of political disorder during secession and the wholesale defection of federal officeholders. In the actual event, these expectations were fulfilled; secession was accompanied by almost no rioting, public demonstrations by opponents, or other breaches of the peace that might have distracted the consolidation of power by the new regime, and the Confederacy absorbed southern extensions of the central state almost completely intact (see Chapter 3).

Perhaps the most important factor operating against secession was the economic ties that had grown up between the North and South. The failure of the South to break commercial relations with the North, in retaliation for abolitionist demonstrations, indicates the durability of market-driven trade networks. Boycotts of "black Republican" New York commercial houses and attempts to reorganize the cotton trade so that southern cities would become major export and import centers all foundered.[38] The overall failure of economic boycotts of northern goods

37. Just how impoverished were American foreign relations during this period is illustrated by David Potter's *The Impending Crisis: 1848–1861*. Aside from a few references to European nationalism as a foil for his examination of the American experience, Potter comments on foreign nations only as opportunities for national expansion (i.e., Cuba, Mexico, and the countries of Central America) or as potential obstacles to expansion (e.g., Spain in the case of Cuba).

38. On the failure of southern boycotts to affect New York commercial traffic, see the *New York Times*, March 14, 1860. The one area where voluntary boycotts seemed effective was newspaper circulation. The fervently antislavery and Republican *New*

and firms was frustrating to secessionists and, to cite but one example, led the state of Georgia to impose a fine of $2,000 on citizens selling goods to residents of the free states.[39] This step, taken as the state moved toward secession, could not be enforced as long as Georgia remained in the Union because of its manifest interference with interstate commerce. Once independence was attained, however, the South was able to forcefully impose the economic boycott that voluntaristic cooperation never achieved.

In fact, wherever secession seemed likely to erect a new international boundary, expectations of a serious disruption of economic ties and trade networks strongly affected political sentiment on disunion. Northern Alabama, for example, was reluctant to secede as long as Tennessee remained in the Union because the region's natural trade outlet was the Tennessee River (which would be blocked if Tennessee failed to join the Confederacy).[40] For similar reasons, Representative H. Winter Davis predicted that, because "Western Virginia belongs to the Valley of the Mississippi ... Virginia can never withdraw from the existing Confederacy undivided; her western boundary will be the Blue Ridge."[41] Five months later, when Virginia voted on a secession ordinance, counties beyond the Blue Ridge gave large majorities against secession and subsequently, as Davis had predicted, formed a separate state within the federal union.[42] Davis reserved his most cogent analysis, however, for his own state of Maryland and native city of Baltimore. He began by noting that, if Maryland joined the Confederacy, "slaveholders lose their only guarantee for the return of their slaves" and continued:

> Every commercial line of communication is severed. Custom house barriers arrest her merchants at every frontier. Her commerce on the ocean is the prey of every pirate, or the sport of every maritime power. Her great railroad loses every connection which makes it valuable. If two republics divide the territory of the United States, Maryland is ruined.

York Tribune, for example, experienced a circulation loss in the deep South of 14 percent between 1859 and 1860 even as national distribution increased by over 33 percent. In those states that were to compose the Confederacy readers consumed less than 0.5 percent of the weekly printing (circulation data from the *New York Times,* April 11, 1860, p. 6).
39. *New York Times,* December 20, 1860.
40. Roy Franklin Nichols, *The Disruption of American Democracy* (New York: Macmillan, 1948), p. 417.
41. Davis made this prediction on January 2, 1861. Bernard C. Steiner, *Life of Henry Winter Davis* (Baltimore: John Murphy, 1916), p. 175.
42. For the county results and analysis, see Richard Orr Curry, *A House Divided: Statehood Politics and the Copperhead Movement in West Virginia* (Pittsburgh: University of Pittsburgh Press, 1964), pp. 23–6, 141–9.

Davis contended that free trade, a likely southern policy, would retard Baltimore's mushrooming industry and, because of its location on the anticipated perimeter of the Confederacy, the city could never be the commercial "emporium" of the South. Secession would give New York control of Baltimore's western trade without appreciably increasing southern traffic. He went on to predict that the state's tax burden would increase because of the necessary maintenance of a standing army to guard Maryland's northern boundary and that Maryland itself would always be the most militarily vulnerable part of a new southern nation.[43] Similar arguments could be made for every region and major city along a possible Confederate frontier.[44]

Away from the frontier, both New Orleans and New York City saw their commercial interests seriously threatened. New Orleans' commitment to secession was potentially compromised by its position as the port of entry for Mississippi River traffic.[45] By 1860, however, most commodities moving through the port originated in the South (such as cotton, sugar, tobacco, and molasses) because the Erie Canal and the developing northern rail network had already diverted midwestern grain to the East. Similar developments, including the completion of the Illinois and Michigan Canal (1848), help explain the rise of the city of Chicago and a reorientation of Cincinnati's commercial interests away from the South (and the Ohio River steamboat) to the East (and the trans-Appalachian railroad).[46] By 1860, the *New York Times* was crowing,

43. Quoted in Steiner, *Henry Winter Davis*, pp. 173–4. For an analysis of Baltimore's position in the national political economy and impact on secession sentiment, see William C. Wright, *The Secession Movement in the Middle Atlantic States* (Rutherford, N.J.: Fairleigh Dickinson University Press, 1973), p. 22; and James Weston Livingood, *The Philadelphia–Baltimore Trade Rivalry, 1780–1860* (New York: Arno Press and New York Times, 1970), ch. 6. Later, however, all ten of Baltimore's representatives in the state legislature backed secession. Gary Browne, *Baltimore in the Nation, 1789–1861* (Chapel Hill: University of North Carolina Press, 1980), pp. 214–15.

44. For disunion sentiment in Delaware, New Jersey, and Pennsylvania, see Wright, *Secession Movement*, pp. 78–85, 113, 134–7, 147–54, and 162. On the interdependence of the antebellum urban system, see Allan Pred, *Urban Growth and City Systems in the United States, 1840–1860* (Cambridge, Mass.: Harvard University Press, 1980), ch. 4.

45. The *New York Times* (October 17, 1860), for example, argued that Louisiana "can never be counted in any scheme of disunion, for New Orleans must still continue to be the great emporium of the Mississippi Valley." The city, however, supported Louisiana's withdrawal from the Union. Perry H. Howard, *Political Tendencies in Louisiana*, rev. ed. (Baton Rouge: Louisiana State University Press, 1971), p. 98.

46. Eliot Alfred Rosen, The Growth of the American City, 1830 to 1860: Economic Foundations of Urban Growth in the Pre–Civil War Period, unpublished Ph.D. thesis, New York University, 1953, pp. 176–8, 196, and 227. On the growth of commercial ties between the Great Lakes and Upper Mississippi Valley, on the one hand, and northeastern ports, see T. W. Van Metre, *An Outline of the Development of the*

"Already have we taken nineteen-twentieths [of the trade] of the Upper Mississippi from its natural outlet" in New Orleans.[47] While the development of northeastern commercial ties bound the Midwest to the North, New York City retained a vast and thriving interest in the transatlantic cotton trade that committed the city to a policy of appeasement even after the outbreak of war.[48]

By and large, the division of the national political economy into two separate spheres threatened havoc only in the Missouri, Ohio, and Potomac river basins. The remainder of the southern plantation economy, including both subsistence and cash crop agriculture and urban commercial interests, could contemplate secession with indifference or enthusiasm. In the border regions, however, the economic consequences of trade disruption accentuated the preexisting ambivalence toward slavery and secession caused by the area's growing manufacturing and commercial commitments. In sum, wherever the international boundary was drawn, the new frontier region would find its trade network and commercial ties seriously disrupted. As it turned out, the new frontier carved a line along the southern boundary of the very regions with the weakest economic commitment to slavery.

Both the fundamental unity of the deep South and the ambivalence of the border states was reflected in the political negotiations between the great slave and free sections in the late antebellum period. We now turn to a brief analytical description of the speaker's contest in the House of Representatives during the winter of 1859–60. That contest will serve

Internal Commerce of the United States, 1789–1900 (Baltimore: Williams and Wilkins, 1913), pp. 11–14; George Rogers Taylor, *The Transportation Revolution, 1815–1860* (New York: Harper Torchbooks, 1968), pp. 74–103; and A. L. Kohlmeier, *The Old Northwest as the Keystone of the Arch of American Federal Union* (Bloomington, Ind.: Principia Press, 1938), pp. 167–225.

47. December 24, 1860 (the paper also reported tonnage shipped over the Erie Canal, 1836–60, and the New York Central and New York and Erie Railroad, 1852–60). For the impact of western trade on property values within the city, see April 7, 1860. For the railroad's impact on the development of financial markets in New York City during the antebellum period, see Alfred D. Chandler, Jr., *The Visible Hand: The Managerial Revolution in American Business* (Cambridge, Mass.: Harvard University Press, 1977), pp. 91–3.

48. On the cotton trade, see Robert Greenhalgh Albion, *The Rise of New York Port: 1815–1860* (New York: Charles Scribner's Sons, 1939), pp. 95–121, 390–421. Outside of Congress, the most eloquent expression of sympathy for the South was Stephen Colwell's *The Five Cotton States and New York; or, Remarks upon the Social and Economic Aspects of the Southern Political Crisis* (New York: no publisher information, January 1861), especially pp. 6, 9–12, 22–34, and 55–64. Such appeals led Wendell Phillips to observe, "The saddest thing in the Union meetings of last year was the constant presence, in all of them, of the clink of coin – the whistle of spindles, the dust of trade. You would have imagined it was an insurrection of peddlers against honest men." *New York Times*, November 9, 1860. Phillips was delivering an address in Boston.

as a vehicle for the exploration of the antebellum party system, for the connection between the structure of the national political economy and possible compromises that might have delayed or prevented secession, and for the deep cleavages, in addition to slavery, that rent the American nation prior to the Civil War. This contest also highlights the strategic context in which southerners chose to forgo further compromise with the North – in this case, over tariff protection for industry – in favor of secession.

Issues dividing the Thirty-sixth Congress

The most important issue dividing the membership of the House of Representatives in the last antebellum Congress was, of course, slavery. Although almost every public decision was evaluated at least partially in terms of its consequences for slavery, the central focus of the struggle was over the institution's extension into the territories. The forces for and against slavery represented, as Seward described them, two systems "so incompatible . . . that every new state which is organized within our ever extending domain makes its first political act a choice of the one and the exclusion of the other, even at the cost of civil war, if necessary."[49] While other decisions, such as annexation and the disposal of the public lands under the homestead bill, were also important, the slavery issue was usually decided at two stages in the life of a territory: its initial organization and later admission into the Union as a state.

Following the Dred Scott decision in 1857, slavery could not be prohibited – either by Congress or the territorial legislature – in any territory. The decision shifted congressional attention to statehood as the most important legislative action affecting the institution's expansion. It was in this context that the Buchanan administration proposed the admission of Kansas under the proslavery "Lecompton constitution." The admission of Kansas as a slave state consumed almost the entire attention of Congress and the Buchanan administration in 1858 and the subsequent general election was largely conducted as a referendum on that issue. Congressmen could, and did, assume many different and sometimes contradictory positions on the different ramifications of slavery in the national political economy; however, the single most important test of pro- or antislavery sentiment, a test that opened wide and unbridgeable chasms within the established parties, was the stand of the membership of the Thirty-sixth Congress on the Lecompton constitution.[50]

49. "The Irrepressible Conflict" in Baker, ed., *Works of William Seward*, p. 291.
50. For a discussion of the various party positions on the Kansas question, see Robert R. Russel, "Constitutional Doctrines with Regard to Slavery in Territories," *Journal*

By the winter of 1859–60 the admission of Kansas as a slave state had become politically impossible. The population of the state was overwhelmingly opposed to the institution and becoming more so. But the issue would not and could not die for two reasons. First, something had to be done about the territory. Under Buchanan's leadership the representatives of the slave states had conceded that Kansas was eligible for statehood (even while losing on the status of slavery). While admission could be delayed, it could not be denied. Second, the prospective entry of Kansas into the Union underscored the rapidly growing political and economic strength of the free states. Even though the political forces supporting slavery seemed to be more adept than those hostile to its extension, demographic trends and the inhospitality of the remaining territories to plantation culture strongly indicated the future subordination of the "slave power" in national policies.

Although only one battle in the struggle over slavery – and a battle irretrievably lost at that – the vote on admission of Kansas under the Lecompton constitution marked congressmen not only on the issue at hand but also on the entire panoply of issues associated with the interests of the institution. Positions on the Lecompton constitution thus served to divide the membership of the House and provided the single most important criterion by which candidates for the speakership were measured.

Slavery, however, was not the only issue dividing the House, nor can that struggle be isolated from economic competition between the free- and slave-state societies. The slave economy produced cotton, a product that either earned foreign exchange for the United States in world markets or was sent north to be manufactured in New England mills. The resulting interdependence between the slave and free economies cut both ways. On the one hand, southerners emphasized the reliance of northern manufacturing on cotton culture as a reason why acquiescence in southern demands was unavoidable.[51] On the other hand, that same interdependence seemed, to northerners, to make southern threats of disunion increasingly unrealistic. Seward, for example, contended that, "Commercial interests bind the slave states and the free states together in links of gold that are riveted with iron, and they cannot be broken by passion or by ambition. Either party

---

of *Southern History* 32 (November 1966): 466–86. Also see Ransom, *Conflict and Compromise*, pp. 149–55.

51. See, for example, a speech delivered by James Stewart of Maryland in *Congressional Globe*, 36:1:109, December 12, 1859. For the sensitivity of northern business to the connection between slavery and industrial prosperity, see Stampp, *Imperiled Union*, p. 198; Thomas H. O'Connor, *Lords of the Loom: The Cotton Whigs and the Coming of the Civil War* (New York: Charles Scribner's Sons, 1968).

will submit to the ascendancy of the other, rather than yield to the commercial advantages of this Union."[52]

Economic interdependence, however, did not imply economic equality. The growing economic supremacy of the Northeast was obvious to all concerned and greatly influenced the calculations of both sides of the slavery issue. To northern Republicans, the failure of the South to keep pace with the rest of the country was "due to the inherent error of the system [of slave labor] itself."[53] They maintained that "the slave states not only build no great cities, but they build no great states" while the natural destiny of New York City was to be "the metropolis of the continent."[54] In contrast to the "sluggish, turbid and desolating stream of slave labor issuing from fifteen slave states," there was "an ever increasing volume of free labor issuing from sixteen free states.... These two variant floods cannot be mingled, but one necessarily repels and excludes the other" because a slave economy, in all its aspects, was inimical to manufacturing and industry.[55] Measures taken by the national government to encourage western settlement, to provide protection to domestic industry by raising the tariff on imports, and to develop a continental transportation network were advocated by northerners as policies that unleashed the energies of free labor and thus hastened the eminent destiny of the nation.

Southerners saw these same manipulations of the national political economy as the root cause of northern industrial might and southern economic underdevelopment. William Boyce of South Carolina made the argument best when he listed the economic grievances of his region as

> the tariff...the disbursements of the Government [which favored the North]...the law by which the coastwise trade is confined exclusively to American ships, the practical advantage of which law is confined almost exclusively to the northern states...the law which gives American ship-builders...a monopoly of building ships which sail under the American flag...the law which gives codfish bounties to the people of Massachusetts...the law which, under the form of

---

52. "Nebraska and Kansas: Second Speech," delivered in the Senate on May 25, 1854, in Baker, ed., *Works of William Seward*, p. 476.
53. Seward, "Freedom in Kansas," ibid., p. 601.
54. Seward, "The Republican Party and Secession," a speech delivered in New York on November 2, 1860, ibid., p. 418.
55. Seward, "The Political Parties of the Day," a speech delivered in Auburn, New York, on October 21, 1856, ibid., p. 282. In an address to the "laboring men" of Auburn on November 5, 1860, Seward claimed "slavery will not tolerate one of you upon its soil" because "slavery wants as little of the industry of the white man in the nation as possible." "The Night before the Election," ibid., pp. 426–7.

the reciprocity treaty, exempts the people of the North along the Canadian frontier from paying duties... all of these great industrial laws are so favorable to northern interests that they cannot be improved upon... [they have] given the North everything and reserved nothing for [the South], except the poor privilege of paying tribute to the victorious industry of the imperial North.[56]

These measures, and not the institution of slavery, Boyce argued, prevented the South from keeping pace.

As northern Republicans saw it, the political power of the slave economy retarded national development not only by spreading the institution into the West (for this advance could be stopped), but also by thwarting northern industrial expansion. The developmental problem facing industrial Republicans in the antebellum era was the forging of a durable alliance between the manufacturing East and the agricultural Midwest. The task confronting the South was to play the two great free-state regions against each other. In fact, serious strains existed within the emerging northern alliance, strains that were exposed when disunion seemed imminent. During the speakership contest, for example, Charles Larrabee of Wisconsin predicted that southern secession would be followed by further division of the nation:

> Provisional governments would be formed, one South, one West –
> and by the West I mean all the country watered by the Mississippi – and one Northeast. I tell you, gentlemen from the New England States, very frankly, for I think it is true, that there is very little in common between the Northwest and yourselves, and in such a contingency as a disruption of the Union, we can hardly look for any unity of sentiment between us. I think we would not act together.[57]

56. *Congressional Globe*, 36:1:308, January 3, 1860. See also the speeches by Martin Crawford of Georgia, ibid., p. 163, December 15, 1859, and James Pugh of Alabama, ibid, p. 407, January 11, 1860. For a discussion of the economic factors, in addition to slavery, that led to disunion, Henry H. Simms, *A Decade of Sectional Controversy, 1851–1861* (Chapel Hill: University of North Carolina Press, 1942), ch. 8, "Sectional Divergence over Economic Factors." For more on these policy conflicts, see, in order: William W. Bates, *American Navigation, the Political History of Its Rise and Ruin* (New York: Houghton Mifflin, 1902); Samuel E. Morison, *The Maritime History of Massachusetts, 1783–1860* (New York: Houghton Mifflin, 1921); John B. Sanborn, *Congressional Grants of Land in Aid of Railways* (New York: Arno Press, 1981); George M. Stephenson, *The Political History of the Public Lands from 1840 to 1862* (New York: Russell and Russell, 1967); and, on all policy conflicts as viewed from the South, Herbert Wender, "Southern Commercial Conventions, 1837–1859," in *Johns Hopkins University Studies in Historical and Political Science*, Series 48 (Baltimore: 1930), chs. 5–10.

57. *Congressional Globe*, 36:1:174, December 17, 1859.

The existence of these strains between the Northeast and Old Northwest clearly entered into the calculations of secessionists in Congress.[58]

Against the charge that industry had made their party into a vehicle for northeastern interests, New England Republicans promoted "free soil" as a policy that outweighed all the real and imagined liabilities cited by southerners and northwestern Democrats. With reference to the speakership contest, their western allies itemized the many other benefits they expected to derive from a Republican victory. While a Republican Speaker would ensure "the protection of American commerce," a Democrat in the chair would make certain "that the committees shall be so stocked and constituted that the rivers and harbors of the West shall have no protection whatever." Republican support for a homestead bill was cited as an additional reason for backing a Republican candidate.[59] In the end, the cohesive appeal of free soil and economic development proved far stronger than the antithetical implications of tariff protection and northeastern "exploitation." The northern alliance held.

Other than slavery, the tariff was the most important single issue dividing the membership of the Thirty-sixth Congress. The alignment on the tariff did not closely follow the fault lines imposed by slavery and New England economic prowess. Many members in the North, primarily antislavery Democrats, opposed protection, while a sizable minority of southerners, usually American party members of Whiggish lineage, supported a high tariff. In fact, the tariff was the most important issue dividing an otherwise united South, and Democrats from the region often bitterly attacked their American party opponents on this issue.[60] Throughout the South, but particularly in the slave states

58. In support of his argument that disunion would ultimately proceed peaceably, one South Carolina congressman first postulated the unacceptably high costs of civil war, and then continued, "We would hold out inducements, too, to the Northwest, for the Mississippi is a natural peacemaker." After southern control of the export trade of the Old Northwest had effectively neutralized the latter region, William Boyce predicted that New England would become increasingly vulnerable to the designs of foreign powers, particularly Great Britain. This vulnerability, he speculated, would ultimately lead to a thorough constitutional revision in which the New England states would be compelled to accept a smaller apportionment of members within the U.S. Senate. *Congressional Globe* 36:1:311–12, January 3, 1860.

59. Representative John Farnsworth of Chicago, *Congressional Globe*, 36:1:230, December 23, 1859.

60. In berating an American colleague from his state, for example, Democrat John Wright charged that a Republican tariff would "tax the people of Tennessee, in order to put money into the hands of northern capitalists. . . . [It would] raise the taxes on the poor farmers, who cultivate the hillsides and valleys of the mountain country . . . twenty or thirty per cent., to make them pay the additional price for the iron hoes and plows

bordering the North, the American party members won seats in districts in more industrialized areas that could benefit from tariff protection.[61]

The cleavage that cut most obliquely across the alignment on slavery was nativism. Anti-Catholic and anti-immigrant in orientation, nativism found its strongest adherents in the American party, North and South, and in those Republicans of recent American party antecedents.[62] The elections had devastated the ranks of the Know-Nothings in the House of Representatives. Within the remnants of the American party — now almost irrelevant to the course of the nation — concern with foreign immigration and Catholicism could merge almost imperceptibly into paranoid fixation. The "ultra-Protestant" Thomas Nelson of Tennessee, for example, claimed that "A foreign emigration society was organized in Europe, more than twenty years ago, which had three objects in view. One of these was to furnish a market in this country, through emigrants,

by which they earn a livelihood, in order that the rich ironmongers of the North may be made richer, and the poor people of Tennessee made poorer, and this under the pretense of protecting American industry." *Congressional Globe*, 36:1:397, January 10, 1860.

61. In the states that later became the Confederacy, the districts represented by Democrats had an average value-added in manufacturing (per capita) of $7.43, slightly below the American party average of $8.48. The difference was greater in border state districts where the Democratic constituencies averaged $12.97 and the Americans $22.51. Calculated from data in the Secretary of the Interior, *1860 Census of Manufacturing* (Washington, D.C.: Governmental Printing Office, 1865).

62. For an exploration of the social factors and economic context that underlie nativism in the antebellum period, see Michael F. Holt, "The Politics of Impatience: The Origins of Know Nothingism" *Journal of American History* 60 (September 1973): 309–31. On the importance of nativism in the late antebellum period, see Potter, *The Impending Crisis*, pp. 241–61; and W. Darrell Overdyke, *The Know-Nothing Party in the South* (Gloucester, Mass.: Peter Smith, 1968). During the struggle over the admission of Kansas, William Seward decried the influence of nativism on American politics because it drew attention away from the fight against slavery. Seward argued, "The question of the day is not about natives and foreigners, nor about protestants and Roman Catholics, but about freemen and slaves. . . . If the American people divide and one portion, being a minority, declare for freedom; while another portion, being also a minority, declare against foreigners and catholics; and a third, larger than either, declare for slavery, nothing is obtained against foreigners and catholics, nothing against slavery. . . . Thus it is apparent that the issue raised by the Know-nothings, whatever may be its merit, is an immaterial, irrelevant, and false issue. . . . It will, I think, be hereafter regarded as one of the caprices of politics that a system of combination so puerile was ever attempted in the United States." Baker, ed., *Works of William Seward*, pp. 283–4. Thus it was that Seward and much of the Republican party could be both antinativist and protectionist. Nativism had to be opposed because it divided free-state political forces and, therefore, allowed slavery to persist and even extend its range. For these reasons, nativism and protectionism were not only theoretically unrelated, but they were also, in the practical political world, openly contradictory and mutually defeating programs.

for British manufacturers; the second was, to furnish a home to the emigrant; and the third and last was, to make Romanism the predominant religion of the country."[63]

Most congressional districts sympathetic to immigrants were represented by northern Democrats. While northern Democrats were opposed to slavery (and thus found it difficult to support southern nominees for the chair), they also had grave misgivings about the varnished-over nativists that composed much of the Republican party membership.[64] While the most important factor in the strategic calculations of the major party leaders was the great chasm separating the free- and slave-state members, nativism and the tariff, more than any other issues, shaped the day-to-day tactics in the speaker's contest. As we shall see, the election of a compromise candidate to the House speakership depended upon southern acquiesence in a protective tariff for northern iron and steel manufacturers. Southern congressmen were repeatedly presented with such compromise opportunities and consistently rejected proslavery candidates who also supported tariff protection. These refusals illustrate both the

63. *Congressional Globe*, 36:1:52, December 7, 1859. The "ultra-Protestant" label is taken from Overdyke, *Know-Nothing Party in the South*, p. 33. In his recent book, *The Origins of the Republican Party*, William Gienapp has stressed the significance of the nativist, Know-Nothing vote as a serious complicating factor in the rise of the Republican party. His point is well taken, but it doesn't appear that nativism as an issue could ever have constituted a fundamental alignment in the party system. Slavery/ free soil factionalism, for example, easily and completely dissolved the national base of the American party. Even in the period before the rise of the Republicans, irresolvable disputes over slavery were involved in the large majority of convention schisms that led to bolting rump caucuses and separate electoral tickets. More to the point, parties in the late antebellum period were organizations that drew their importance and viability from patronage and other spoils of office (including the enactment of policy outcomes such as the admission of Kansas), not as cultural totems to which voters owed their allegiance much as they would a church. Gienapp describes a Republican party that gathered a wide range of potential interests and politicians together under one tent (holding open conventions in which anyone could participate, for example). Such a party could develop because voter allegiances were so weak, ever shifting between competing factions and parties, as Gienapp demonstrates. The emergence of the "Republican" party was not destined to succeed (any more than another gathering, under another tent such as the "People's" party in Indiana and Pennsylvania was destined to fail); what was instead almost inevitable was that a northern-based, antislavery party would arise. In making his case, then, Gienapp places too much emphasis on parties instead of issues as the fundamental factors in antebellum politics.

64. Noting the recent conversion of William Moorhead of Pittsburgh to the Republican party, William Montgomery of Pennsylvania charged that Moorhead had previously seen "hopes for office in the American organization; and he crawled into the caves, garrets, and cellars where 'Sam' [an allegorical figure representing the spirit of Know-nothing rituals and beliefs] congregated; took all the horrid oaths and learned the secret grips of that order.... The gentleman has forgotten his oaths and pledges now; his holy horror of foreigners and Catholics." *Congressional Globe*, 36:1:515, January 18, 1860.

narrow limits within which the southern leadership would entertain compromise with the North and the self-defeating nature of the concessions offered the South. Compromise programs that accelerated northern industrial development would only have postponed secession and, in the meantime, strengthened the comparative position of the North in the national political economy.

Sectional conflict and the speaker's contest of 1859

The 1858 elections awarded a majority to none of the parties in the House of Representatives and the first crisis facing the Thirty-sixth Congress thus arose over the selection of a speaker, a post that was unusually important in 1859 for reasons that went beyond the institutional politics of the chamber.[65] As the contest began in an atmosphere reeking of sectional hostility, a Maryland congressman urged the 237 "members from various States of the Confederacy – not delegates from a consolidated people, but ambassadors from great sovereignties" to take into consideration "all the great questions connected with the present state of the Union" before selecting the new Speaker.[66] On January 30, 1860, just before the end of the struggle, "almost the entire population of the District, including thousands of strangers, flocked to the capitol... to witness... the election of a Speaker. The crowd in and around the Capitol was estimated at from twenty to thirty thousand, not one-fourth of whom could gain admittance. Every passage, stairway, and retiring room was packed with the excited throng, which remained undiminished up to the hour of adjournment."[67]

It would be difficult to exaggerate the sense of impending violence that

65. For one thing, the speaker appointed, with the consent of the House, members to the standing and select committees that drafted legislation and conducted congressional investigations. This appointment power was unusually important in 1859 because the Buchanan administration, it was commonly thought, was guilty of a wide variety of dubious and corrupt practices related to the distribution of patronage and government contracts. A speaker opposed to the administration could appoint select committees to investigate and expose these practices. A friendly speaker could prevent congressional inquiry (since the Senate was safely Democratic). In addition, the newly elected speaker would appoint the membership of the standing Committee on Elections that would determine the contested election cases then before the House. The decisions in these cases might change the partisan balance in a few strategically important state delegations. Since it was already anticipated that at least four major presidential candidacies would be launched in 1860 and since the House of Representatives would decide who won the presidency if the Electoral College produced no decision, the composition of the Committee on Elections might influence, even determine, the outcome of the presidential election.
66. *Congressional Globe*, 36:1:108, December 12, 1859.
67. *New York Times*, January 31, 1860. The population of the District of Columbia in 1860 was 61,122.

hung over the House during this period.[68] Southern members repeatedly
threatened disunion if a member of the "treasonable, incendiary and
revolutionary Black" Republican party were elected president.[69] Many
agreed with a South Carolina member who defined sectional loyalty in
terms that already set up the South as an independent nation: "There is
a treason now known to the South greater than the treason of disunion,
and that is treason to the South itself, and her constitutional rights."[70]
Many, if not most, members came to the House floor carrying weapons.
Southern representatives, "following the custom, then so prevalent in
that section of the country," brought weapons almost as a matter of
course. Northern colleagues "felt themselves forced to adopt the custom
by the threats hurled at them from across the chamber."[71] Only two days
into the contest, the Democrats were described as "armed to the teeth"
and, if a blow had been struck, it would not have been "the ordinary
combat of former years, but war to the knife."[72] Two events, John
Brown's raid on Harper's Ferry and the publication of Hinton Helper's
antislavery book, *The Impending Crisis of the South,* shaped the course
of the speakership struggle. Less than two months before the House of
Representatives opened the session, Brown and his men attacked the
armory at Harper's Ferry, immeasurably heightening southern fear of
northern-inspired and -organized slave insurrections. Three days before
the House met, Brown was hanged by the state of Virginia while church
bells tolled in grief throughout the North. Less than two weeks later, his
men followed him to the gallows. Both the raid and northern reaction

68. Much of the following account is drawn from Richard Bensel, "The Antebellum
     Political Economy and the Speaker's Contest of 1859," delivered to the 1985 Annual
     Meeting of the American Political Science Association, the New Orleans Hilton,
     August 29–September 1, 1985. The most complete published account, though dated,
     is Ollinger Crenshaw, "The Speakership Contest of 1859–1860: John Sherman's
     Election: A Cause of Disruption," *Mississippi Valley Historical Review* 29 (December
     1942): 323–38. Brief accounts can be found in Nichols, *Disruption of American
     Democracy,* pp. 270–6; Potter, *Impending Crisis,* pp. 386–91; Rhodes, *History of
     the United States,* vol. 2, pp. 418–28; and Nevins, *Emergence of Lincoln,* vol. 2,
     pp. 116–24. Also see, Victor Hicken, "John A. McClernand and the House Speak-
     ership Struggle of 1859," *Illinois State Historical Society Journal* 53 (Summer 1960):
     163–78.
69. Albert Rust of Arkansas, *Congressional Globe* 36:1:270, December 28, 1959. One
     month into the contest, the *Washington Era* could count eleven members who, in its
     opinion, had "threatened or justified disunion," January 5, 1860. A subsequent enu-
     meration quoted thirteen southern House members who had supported secession
     upon election of a "Black" Republican president. *Congressional Globe* 36:1:840–1,
     February, 20, 1860. Many more members stopped just short of advocating secession.
70. Milledge Bonham, *Congressional Globe,* 36:1:167, December 16, 1859.
71. Hubert Fuller, *The Speakers of the House* (New York: Arno Press, 1947; reprint of
     1909 edition), p. 136; Willard H. Smith, *Schuyler Colfax: The Changing Fortunes
     of a Political Idol* (Indianapolis: Indiana Historical Bureau, 1952), p. 125.
72. *New York Times,* December 8, 1859.

to the executions made the emergence of a successful bisectional candidate for the speakership extremely difficult.[73]

Helper had intended his book to rouse the nonslaveowning southern white from his unthinking acquiesence in the political program and goals of the slaveholding elite. The book was seized upon by Republican leaders as a possible campaign tract and a shorter "compendium" was planned. In advance of the compendium's preparation, the signatures of prominent congressional Republicans were solicited as endorsements of the work. The resulting circular was a request for funds to offset the costs of preparing and printing the compendium and was sent out to potential Republican subscribers.[74] Forty-three Republican members of the Thirty-sixth Congress – among them the leading party candidates for the speakership, John Sherman and Galusha Grow – had signed the circular. Helper's uncondensed, original text was filled with highly incendiary prose and contained many thinly veiled threats of violence against southern slaveowners. Against the background of John Brown's raid, these threats made southern support for any candidate who signed the circular impossible.

The Republicans, the largest party organization, were 110 members strong. They were fervently and unanimously opposed to the admission of Kansas under the Lecompton constitution, widely but more weakly associated with nativism, and supported a protective tariff. The 88 Administration Democrats were identified with President Buchanan, particularly with the administration's support for the Lecompton admission of Kansas, and opposed the Republicans on all three major issues confronting the Thirty-sixth Congress. For the most part, the Administration Democrats shared the Republican preoccupation with slavery, placed lower but still high significance on the tariff issue, and were largely indifferent toward nativism.

The Americans and the Anti-Lecompton Democrats held the balance of power in the House. By 1859, all but three of the 26 House members of the American party represented slaveholding districts and all of these members supported the institution. However, some Know-Nothing congressmen opposed the Lecompton constitution for partisan reasons and, thus, for these members alone, that issue was not an accurate test of their sentiments on slavery generally. Most Americans were, of course, obsessed with the nativist issue and also strongly advocated government-

73. A brief account of the effect of John Brown's raid on sectional relations can be found in ch. 14 of Potter, *Impending Crisis.*
74. A copy of the circular with the list of signatures was printed in the *Congressional Globe,* 36:1:16–17, December 6, 1859. See, also, Nichols, *Disruption of American Democracy,* p. 272.

sponsored national development and a protective tariff. Their rank-ordering of the importance of the three issues was the inverse of the one held by Republicans and Administration Democrats. The 13 Anti-Lecompton Democrats, as the name suggests, fervently opposed the admission of Kansas as a slave state and had each bolted their party over that issue. Since, to a man, they represented northern districts with fairly sizable immigrant populations, these members strongly opposed the nativist measures advocated by the Americans. Though latent divisions over the tariff probably existed within this small group of congressmen, none surfaced during the speakership contest because the issue did not rank high in their order of priorities.

In sum, Republicans and Anti-Lecompton Democrats opposed the Administration Democrats on Buchanan's policy toward Kansas and on slavery generally. The Americans split over Lecompton, favored slavery, but were more concerned with other issues. On the tariff, the Republicans and Americans backed protection, a stand opposed by the administration's supporters. Anti-Lecompton Democrats split on the tariff but were largely distracted by other issues. Nativism brought the Americans and Anti-Lecomptonites to loggerheads but, for the most part, was irrelevant to the larger party organizations. Overlaying all of these cleavages were partisan rivalries which, in the North, pit Anti-Lecompton Democrats against Republicans and, in the South, drew apart Americans and Administration Democrats. This intraregional competition made cooperation among these pairs of parties very difficult.

Given these intense cleavages within the membership and given the fact that no party drew the allegiance of a majority, the election of a speaker on the basis of policy positions alone was widely recognized as all but impossible. Because they played but a small role in the voting decisions of members outside their respective parties, the personal characteristics and leadership qualities of the nominees could not compensate for the policy contradictions within every potential coalition.[75]

This, then, was the situation facing the House of Representatives at the beginning the Thirty-sixth Congress: a membership deeply riven by differences over slavery, economic policy (most notably the tariff), and

75. In fact, the member finally chosen as speaker, William Pennington of New Jersey, subsequently gained a reputation as "one of the worst-equipped and most incompetent" presiding officers of the House and was defeated for reelection only nine months after his elevation to the chair. Nevins, *Emergence of Lincoln*, vol. 2, p. 124. More charitably, Mary Parker Follett described Pennington's qualifications for office as "some legal attainments, dignity of manner, equanimity of temper, and an undoubted integrity and impartiality." She concludes that he "made a respectable presiding officer" although he was "notably ignorant of the practice of the House." *The Speaker of the House of Representatives* (New York: Burt Franklin, 1974; reprint of a 1902 edition), p. 95.

nativism, and further divided into four party factions. Given the distribution of issue preferences and the intensity with which they were held, the most appealing candidate would be Anti-Lecompton, protariff, and nativist (with weakly held positions on each), for the membership contained a nominal majority on all three issues. In addition, given the intense rivalry existing between the parties, the successful candidate would be a recent convert from the now defunct, and thus nonthreatening Whigs. Finally, he would probably be a Northerner and a Republican, for such members formed the largest part – though not a majority – of the House. Freshman Representative William Pennington of New Jersey had all of these characteristics, but, before he was elected, after fifty-nine days and forty-four ballots, the membership voted on ninety other candidates (see Table 2.2). Including Pennington, members receiving at least some votes at some time during the contest comprised 38 percent of the 237 members of the House.

At several different points in the struggle southern Democrats could have elected a southern American to the speakership if they had been willing to compromise on the tariff. Both John Gilmer and William N. H. Smith of North Carolina could have drawn enough support from the Pennsylvania and New Jersey delegations, including some Republicans, to be elected if the southern Democrats had swung behind their candidacies. The crucial tests came on the seventh ballot (December 16, 1859), the eighteenth (December 22), and the thirty-ninth (January 27, 1860). On each of these occasions intense bargaining between congressmen interested in tariff protection for iron, the southern Americans, and Administration Democrats placed the decision squarely in the hands of the latter. Each time southern Democrats refused to barter the tariff in return for the protection of slavery's interests that control over the organization of the House would have given them.

The success of both the Gilmer and Smith candidacies depended upon a combination of Administration Democrats, the southern wing of the American party, and Pennsylvania Republicans. The key to a viable coalition between the three factions was to allow an American candidate to offer a protective tariff to attract Republicans and a proslavery position to pull in Administration Democrats. This combination lay behind John Gilmer's candidacy. Since Gilmer was the largest slaveholder in the House of Representatives, his slavery credentials were beyond southern Democratic criticism. However, Gilmer opposed a slave code for the territories and, thus, was sufficiently moderate to draw northern votes.[76]

Gilmer came closest to the speaker's chair on the seventh and the

76. *Congressional Globe* 36:1:218–19, December 22, 1859; 36: 1:514, 516, January 18, 1860.

Table 2.2. *Chronology of the speakership contest in the Thirty-sixth Congress*

Date	Event
October 16–18, 1859	John Brown and his men raid Harper's Ferry.
December 2, 1859	John Brown is executed at Charlestown, Virginia, less than 100 miles from the capital.
December 5, 1859	The House of Representatives meets for the first time. John Sherman of Ohio defeats Galusha Grow of Pennsylvania for the Republican nomination. Thomas Bocock of Virginia is put forward by the Administration Democrats. (During the war, Bocock later serves as the speaker of the House of Representatives in the First and Second Confederate Congresses.) Thirty-five votes are scattered among other candidates.
December 7–9, 1859	Bocock's candidacy peaks with 38.1 percent of the vote on the second and third ballots.
December 16, 1859	Pennsylvania Republicans temporarily defect to John Gilmer of North Carolina on the seventh ballot, pushing his total to 36 votes. The Americans invite Administration Democrats to join the coalition. Sherman's vote falls to 42.3 percent, his poorest showing as the Republican candidate.
December 19, 1859	On the twelfth ballot, Bocock withdraws as the Administration Democrat nominee. On this and the next four ballots no candidate opposing Sherman draws more than 19 percent of the vote.
December 20, 1859	Sherman draws 48.9 percent of all votes cast on the sixteenth ballot – three short of victory. He was to come this close to election on two other ballots: the twenty-eighth (January 6) and the thirty-third (January 11).
December 21, 1859	The Administration Democrats concentrate their votes on John Millson of Virginia. Millson draws 96 votes on this, the seventeenth, ballot, and is only 18 short of election. This is the closest any Democrat, Administration or Anti-Lecompton, would come to victory.
December 22, 1859	Pennsylvania Republicans again temporarily defect to Gilmer on the eighteenth ballot. The Americans again invite Administration Democrats into the coalition. His total climbs to 36 votes as both Sherman and Millson slip.
December 23–27, 1859	On the twentieth and subsequent two ballots, none of Sherman's challengers draws more than 12 percent of the vote.
December 28, 1859	Horace Maynard of Tennessee, the American party candidate, draws 31 percent of the vote on the twenty-third ballot.
December 29, 1859	On the twenty-fourth ballot the Administration Democrats nominate Charles Scott of California, who polls 39 percent of the vote. Scott was one of the few western, free-state Democrats to support Administration policy on Kansas, and

Table 2.2 *(cont.)*

Date	Event
	his nomination was an attempt to bridge Democratic divisions over slavery in the territories.
January 5, 1860	As the Administration Democratic nominee, Clement Vallandigham draws 69 votes, 32 percent of the total. On the next ballot (the twenty-seventh), the regular Democrats shift back to Bocock, who only polls 56.
January 7, 1860	At the urging of Stephen Douglas, the Democrats nominate Andrew Hamilton of Texas. On the twenty-ninth ballot, he pulls 89 votes, 42 percent of the total. This was to be the second best showing by any Democrat but Hamilton never gains the backing of all the Anti-Lecompton wing of the party.
January 8, 1860	A committee composed of representatives of the three parties opposing Sherman and the Republicans meets to consider possible compromise candidates but cannot reach agreement.
January 12, 1860	Hamilton's support has gradually fallen to 75 votes by this, the thirty-fourth ballot. The House did not vote again for 13 days.
January 25, 1860	The Administration Democrats return to Bocock on the thirty-fifth ballot but he only polls 51 votes – less than half of Sherman's total. The regular Democrats stay with Bocock through the thirty-eighth ballot.
January 27, 1860	On the thirty-ninth ballot, the Administration Democrats and Americans combine on William N. H. Smith, a North Carolina American, and push Sherman into second place for the first time since he became the Republican nominee. The balloting, accompanied by an unprecedented number of vote changes, explanations in the form of speeches, and intense bargaining, takes hours to complete. At one point, Smith actually has an unofficial majority of the votes. His showing forces the Republicans to abandon Sherman.
January 30, 1860	On the fortieth ballot, the Republicans nominate William Pennington of New Jersey, who recaptures the lead but falls three votes short of a majority. Only six votes are cast for candidates other than Smith and Pennington. On the forty-first ballot, Pennington falls only two votes short as four votes are given to outside candidates.
January 31, 1860	The American–Administration Democrat alliance breaks up and the Democrats attempt to unite on John McClernand of Illinois, an Anti-Lecompton Democrat allied with Stephen Douglas. McClernand's nomination is a last-ditch attempt to prevent renegade Anti-Lecompton Democrats from joining the Republicans. On this, the forty-third ballot, McClernand runs 25 votes behind Pennington, who is but one vote shy of election.

Table 2.2 (*cont.*)

Date	Event
February 1, 1860	On the forty-fourth ballot, Pennington wins the speakership with 117 of 233 votes cast. He receives only one vote from the slave states – H. Winter Davis, an American from Baltimore, Maryland. Pennington's leading opponent, McClernand, polls only 85 votes. Pennington is escorted to the chair by Thomas Bocock of Virginia and John Sherman of Ohio.

eighteenth ballots. The first of these closely followed the opening of formal negotiations between the American party and Administration Democrats. The former had caucused on the evening of December 10 and agreed to nominate Gilmer. A committee of three Democrats had waited on the Americans and proposed an alliance on the following terms: if Bocock, their candidate, polled 93 votes or more, then the Americans would support his election; in return, the Democrats would pledge to support Gilmer if he drew more than 28 votes. At this time the Americans rejected the proposal. On December 13 the Americans extended a nearly identical offer to the Democrats, but the two parties failed to reach agreement.[77]

With the accession of a dozen Republicans and one Anti-Lecomptonite, Gilmer's support surged to 36 votes on the following day. It remains unclear whether their decision violated any agreement between the parties, but in any event the Democrats did not shift their votes to Gilmer. On December 21 the Americans again broached the possibility of a coalition with the Administration Democrats, but the negotiations were inconclusive. On the next day, Gilmer's vote was again augmented by Republican defections from Sherman, but the Administration Democrats once more remained aloof.[78] Seventeen free-state members supported Gilmer on either the seventh or eighteenth ballots: 13 Republicans, one Anti-Lecompton Democrat, and three Americans. Twelve of the Repub-

77. *New York Times*, December 12 and 16, 1859; *Congressional Globe* 36:1:138–9, December 13, 1859; *Washington Evening Star*, December 12, 1859.
78. *Washington Era*, December 22, 1859; *New York Times*, December 17, 1859; Overdyke, *The Know-Nothing Party in the South*, p. 168; James Vaulx Drake, *Life of General Robert Hatton* (Nashville, Tenn.: Marshall and Bruce, 1867), pp. 181, 184; *Congressional Globe* 36:1:205–6, 210–11, December 21, 1859.

licans came from Pennsylvania.[79] As he rejected Gilmer's candidacy, one southern Democrat described the proposed bargain as one in which the Pennsylvania Republicans offered "a compromise that they will not say anything more than they have said on the slavery question if you will give them a protective tariff... [but] every Democrat at the South is opposed to the doctrine of protection for the sake of protection."[80]

Smith's candidacy came much later in the contest and tentatively brought together a solid coalition of Administration Democrats and Americans plus a scattering of Anti-Lecompton Democrats and a small band of protectionist Republicans. The one New Jersey and four Pennsylvania Republicans who originally voted for Smith grew more disenchanted with him as the long thirty-ninth ballot progressed. They were initially attracted because he seemed to be, as they were, a nativist who supported a protective tariff and would be a moderate on the slavery issue. As the voting continued, however, Smith first disavowed nativism (in order to hold the Anti-Lecompton Democrats) and, subsequently, when his position on a territorial slave code was called into question, he refused to commit himself. Even then these members might have stayed with Smith if he had made an explicit commitment on the tariff. This commitment was, in fact, sought by one Pennsylvania Republican who later explained:

> After having cast the vote, as I did, for Mr. Smith... and after having heard, from the other side of the House, statements that seemed to put Mr. Smith in an equivocal position in reference to the American party... I thought it absolutely necessary for me to make myself sure beyond a doubt of that gentleman's position upon the subject of industrial protection. I accordingly called upon that gentleman at his seat in the House and asked him... "Will you organize the Committee of Ways and Means in such a manner as to protect the interests of Pennsylvania?"... That gentleman could give me no firm and positive and satisfactory declaration upon the subject... [This response was disappointing] in the estimation of the Pennsylvania delegation, charged, as they are with the guardianship of practical questions of vital moment to capital and labor. After having received from Mr. Smith the assurance that he could give no positive infor-

79. On Gilmer's attractiveness to Pennsylvania Republicans, see *Congressional Globe* 36:1:218–19, December 22, 1859; 36:1:403, 405, 413, January 11, 1860.
80. *Congressional Globe* 36:1:464, January 16, 1860. For the reasons given by Administration Democrats for their failure to back Gilmer, see *Congressional Globe* 36:1:367, January 7, 1860; *Washington Evening Star*, January 4, 1860. On the refusal of southern Democrats to "pledge a protective tariff as the price of Pennsylvania support," see Nichols, *Disruption of American Democracy*, p. 274.

mation upon the subject, I said to my colleague, Mr. Wood, in the first instance, and afterwards to others, that it was time to sound the bugle of retreat, because we were misled.[81]

Though Smith almost certainly favored tariff protection in theory, it is just as certain that he "had promised to give the principal committees to the Democrats" as the price of their support.[82] Once given, that promise prevented the candidate from giving contradictory assurances to his Republican supporters. Once again, the intransigence of Administration Democrats on the tariff issue prevented the election of a southern Speaker. When the Republican leadership indicated that Sherman would step down in favor of either Corwin or Pennington, all the defectors but one backed away from Smith and, five ballots later, Pennington was elected to the chair.[83]

The struggle over the speakership of the House of Representatives in 1859 was the most serious, sustained effort to resolve those disputes that threatened to dissolve the Union.[84] Every section and every party partic-

81. *Congressional Globe* 36:1:636, January 30, 1860; *New York Times*, January 31, 1860.

82. Gerald S. Henig, *Henry Winter Davis: Antebellum and Civil War Congressman from Maryland* (New York: Twayne Publishers, 1973), p. 124.

83. On the three ballots following Sherman's retirement from the contest, the House of Representatives was presented with a choice between very similar candidates. Both Smith and Pennington, the new Republican nominee, were freshman congressmen with no previous service, thinly varnished and recently converted Whigs, moderates on the slavery issue, mildly protariff (though Smith's hands were tied on this issue) and nativist, and personally unknown to a majority of the membership. Their anonymity, moderation, and ambiguous party antecedents allowed them each to hold the more extreme members within their respective coalitions and to maximize their appeal to marginal members caught in the middle of the great sectional dispute. When these marginal members finally fell in line, they, almost without exception, went with their section.

84. The conclaves that nominated Lincoln, Douglas, Breckinridge, and Bell only represented their respective party organizations. In addition, the conventions sought to blur the issues dividing the nation, not to craft specific guarantees between the sections. James McPherson, *Battle Cry of Freedom: The Civil War Era* (New York: Oxford University Press, 1988), pp. 213–22; Nichols, *Disruption of American Democracy*, pp. 288–322; Nevins, *Emergence of Lincoln*, vol. 2, pp. 203–28, 266–72; Dwight L. Dumond, *The Secession Movement, 1860–1861* (New York: Macmillan, 1931), pp. 92–112. After Lincoln's election, the House and the Senate both created committees to search for possible solutions to the secession crisis. While the "Committee of Thirty-three" and the "Committee of Thirteen," respectively, were entrusted with the task of crafting an acceptable and wide-ranging adjustment of sectional differences, the deep South began to leave the Union just as these committees started deliberations. Once the southern states began to secede, realistic bargaining stopped because further negotiation undercut the viability of secession and most southern leaders had already chosen that course. Albert D. Kirwan, *John J. Crittenden: The Struggle for the Union* (Lexington: University of Kentucky Press, 1962), pp. 374–

ipated in the deliberations. Furthermore, because the office could influence almost every dimension of federal policy, the negotiations over the speakership took into consideration the multidimensionality of the cleavages that produced secession. Finally, the congressmen who participated in the contest were highly skilled and articulate spokesmen for their respective positions; if there had been a chance, at that late date, of crafting an acceptable and durable compromise between the sections, these men should have found it. In the end, the only course open to the South, aside from defeat and disunion, was to trade government-sponsored economic development for temporary protection for the interests of slavery. Since tariff-sponsored industrial expansion would further accentuate the South's isolation and impending minority status in the national political economy, southern Democrats refused the bargain.[85]

Summary of the political-economic causes of secession

In refusing to bargain, southern Democrats were choosing secession.[86] By 1860, Republican radicals were a more or less immediate threat to slavery, the party's program promised little good and much harm for the plantation economy, disentanglement of the state apparatus appeared to be easy, and the deep South, at least, could anticipate division of the national political economy with equanimity. Secession came not just because the cultural and partisan bonds of the American nation had, one by one, snapped. Secession also came because the political economic foundation for unity was extremely weak and any attempt to strengthen that foundation by increasing economic integration threatened the long-term interests of the plantation economy.

421; David M. Potter, *Lincoln and His Party in the Secession Crisis* (New Haven, Conn.: Yale University Press, 1942), pp. 204–8.

85. On March 16, 1860, for example, Robert Toombs wrote, in a letter to Alexander Stephens, that "Penn. wants a tariff man and of course expects the Dem. party now to swallow its past history to secure her support, doubtful at least." Phillips, ed., *Correspondence of Robert Toombs, Alexander H. Stephens, and Howell Cobb*, p. 465. For a recent analysis that supports southern unwillingness to compromise, see Lee and Passell, *A New Economic View of American History*, p. 215. On the negative economic impact of the tariff on the southern plantation economy, see Thomas F. Huertas, "Damnifying Growth in the Antebellum South," *Journal of Economic History* 39 (March 1979): 98–9.

86. That a cohesive group of committed secessionists served as congressmen and senators during the Thirty-sixth Congress (1859–61) and played key roles in promoting southern secession has long been acknowledged. See, for example, Alabama Representative David Clopton's letter quoted in Nevins, *Emergence of Lincoln*, vol. 2, pp. 386–7; also, Potter, *Lincoln and His Party*, p. 4.

All contemporary projections of the future evolution of the national political economy involved a degree of uncertainty. That uncertainty plus the ambivalence of subsistence farmers and border regions operated against proponents of southern independence. The timing of secession was determined by events largely outside the control of southern nationalists and, although disunion sentiment was growing rapidly between 1858 and 1860, John Brown's raid on Harper's Ferry was probably a necessary catalyst.[87] While cutting the ground out from under southern unionists, that event, and the North's reaction to it, confirmed the most pessimistic projections of slavery's future in the American nation. The only policy concessions the South could make to block a consolidation of northern interests behind the Republican party were those that, self-defeatingly, would further accelerate expansion of the northern capitalist economy. As one Cooper River planter contended, "We must do it now or never."[88]

The 1860 census and subsequent reapportionment of the House of Representatives and Electoral College confirmed the growing political and economic influence of the North. This shift, in turn, threatened to break the national deadlock over slavery by delivering control of the central state to the Republican party. From slavery's perspective such trends provided a dismal backdrop to the dissolution of the national Democratic party and Lincoln's election (achieved without the benefit of the 1860 reapportionment). While John Brown's raid strengthened pessimistic projections of slavery's future, Lincoln's victory determined the precise timing of secession: the period after the election but before inauguration.[89] In this interim, President Buchanan's southern sympathies promised to paralyze the federal government and preclude any effective northern resistance.

In the months preceding the presidential election, however, even well-informed observers who expected a Republican victory did not view disunion as unavoidable.[90] On October 22 the *New York Times* assumed

87. Avery Craven, *The Coming of the Civil War* (Chicago: University of Chicago Press, 1942), pp. 400–12.
88. Printed in the *New York Weekly Tribune*, November 17, 1860, quoted in Nevins, *Emergence of Lincoln*, vol. 2, p. 334.
89. Lincoln's election "caused almost as great an outburst of joy in Charleston and New Orleans as it did in Boston." Frederic Bancroft, *The Life of William H. Seward*, vol. 2 (New York: Harper and Brothers, 1900), p. 1. In a pamphlet written during the middle of the war, the speaker of the North Carolina House of Commons agreed: "The election of Mr. Lincoln was perhaps hailed with greater joy at Charleston [by secessionist Democrats] than at New York." R. S. Donnell, *A Voice from North Carolina* (New York: Anson D. F. Randolph, 1863), p. 9.
90. See, for example, the frequent, almost daily shifts between optimism and pessimism

that Lincoln's election would lead South Carolina and the Gulf Coast states to secede but predicted that North Carolina, Tennessee, and Arkansas "will firmly adhere to the Union." On the day before the election the paper was more optimistic and judged that there was "no great risk" that the South would secede. On the day after the balloting, the *Times* interpreted Constitutional Union party victories in the upper South as having "substantially dispelled all the danger of disunion which the election of Lincoln was supposed to involve."

Postelection attempts to compromise sectional divisions centered around two initiatives. Outside the government the Washington Peace Conference brought together well-meaning elder statesmen from both sections but was never seriously considered as an alternative to congressional negotiations.[91] A separate congressional initiative spawned both a Committee of Thirteen in the Senate and a Committee of Thirty-three in the House. While more substantial than the Washington Peace Conference, deliberations within these committees discovered no common ground between Republican radicals and southern secessionists. Plagued by Republican intransigence and southern preoccupation with the progress of the secession movement, these panels were recognized as futile almost as soon as they were established.[92] From the very beginning, southern congressmen refused to serve on these committees or regarded their deliberations with hostility.[93]

Even as these committees deliberated, caucuses of southern representatives and senators were declaring that sectional differences were hopelessly irreconcilable and urging the immediate secession of the South.[94]

in the *New York Times*, July 26; August 20, 24; September 10, 28, 29; October 12, 20, 29, 31; November 2, 6, 7.
91. The *New York Herald* described the convention as a gathering of "political fossils who would not have been disinterred but for the shock given the country by the crisis." Quoted in Nevins, *Emergence of Lincoln*, vol. 2, p. 411.
92. On December 13, nine days after its creation, the Committee of Thirty-three was described as a "coffin" by Isaac Morris, an otherwise sympathetic Douglas Democrat. *Congressional Globe* 36:2:87.
93. Both George Hawkins of Florida and William Boyce of South Carolina asked to be excused from service on the House committee. Though he consented to serve, Reuben Davis of Mississippi viewed the purpose of the committee to "arrest the present noble and manly movements of the southern States to provide... for their security and safety out of the union." On December 30, Miles Taylor of Louisiana, Warren Winslow of North Carolina, and George Houston of Alabama withdrew without resigning. *Congressional Globe* 36:2:22–3, 37, 59–61 (December 6, 10–11, 1860); *New York Times*, December 31, 1860. On the futility of House deliberations, see Nevins, *Emergence of Lincoln*, vol. 2, pp. 385, 388, 405; Potter, *Lincoln and His Party*, pp. 89–101; and Foner, *Free Soil, Free Labor, Free Men*, p. 144.
94. *New York Times*, December 10 and 14, 1860; Nevins, *Emergence of Lincoln*, vol. 2, p. 398; Glover, *Pre–Civil War Compromise Efforts*, pp. 110–26, 151. A telegram

The last hope of compromise lay with the incoming administration. Lincoln wrote Seward indicating he was willing to guarantee that slavery in the District of Columbia, the interstate slave trade, and federal fugitive slave laws would remain safe under his administration and that he would permit New Mexico to come in as a slave state.[95] By this point, however, such guarantees did not even give pause to secessionists. With these presentiments, rejection of the Crittenden compromise, the most serious compromise proposal, was but a formality.[96] Once Jefferson Davis and Lincoln assumed leadership of their respective governments, both had strong political reasons for viewing compromise initiatives as dangerous distractions that retarded the nationalist mobilization of public opinion.[97]

The northern decision to suppress the South

In one sense, the reasons why the North suppressed southern separatism are much simpler than the causes of secession. While the incongruous place of the plantation economy in a political system dominated by expansionist industrial capitalism was responsible for secession, the imperatives of survival (for the slave economy) are difficult to specify in the absence of a well-established theory of state-centered political economy. On the other hand, all modern states aside from monarchies have repressed the secession of contiguous territory and, in the absence of foreign intervention, they have done so successfully in most cases. From this perspective, it would have been surprising, indeed, had the North chosen to let the South go without a fight. But the observation that all states repress separatism is an observation without a theoretical explanation; several reasons for the strong tendency toward repression can be offered for the American case.

In the first instance, separatism threatens the viability of the state in the international system. Such a development, by weakening the capacity of both the parent and newly created states to defend national territory, provides opportunities for intervention, domination, and even absorption

from Washington reporting a caucus of secessionist Senators on January 5, 1861, appeared in the Charleston, South Carolina, press on January 7. The caucus adopted resolutions urging immediate secession and took other measures for the purpose of orchestrating the movement in Congress. *1861 American Annual Cyclopaedia* (New York: D. Appleton, 1862), p. 125.

95. Nevins, *Emergence of Lincoln*, vol. 2, p. 447.
96. The proposal was named for its author, Senator John Crittenden of Kentucky. For the text of the compromise, see Glover, *Pre–Civil War Compromise Efforts*, pp. 153–6. For the parliamentary maneuvers through which Sherrard Clemens of Virginia became the sponsor of the Crittenden compromise in the House, see Nichols, *Disruption of American Democracy*, pp. 454–5, 484–5.
97. Stampp, *Imperiled Union*, pp. 177–87.

by foreign powers. However, such consequences are much more likely to be realized in a regional system of relatively strong states than in one where the dissolving nation clearly dominates all proximate countries. It would be difficult, if not impossible, to explain northern repression of the South as the result of a fear of subsequent foreign domination. The North was much more concerned with a lost opportunity for imperial greatness than with foreign subjugation.[98]

A second reason for the strong tendency toward repression is the impact a successful separatist movement would have on the political institutions and constitutional processes of the parent state. The legitimation of secession as a possible political option seriously weakens centralizing tendencies that would otherwise compel political and administrative integration and immeasurably strengthens the political position of the remaining regions in their own quarrels with the central state. Thus, one experience with unopposed secession threatens to begin an irreversible process of national disintegration with unpredictable consequences for the economy and international security. In the case of the United States, southern secession spawned a public reconsideration of the terms of union within almost every section. Only New England exhibited an unreservedly nationalist response to southern withdrawal in the months prior to the attack on Fort Sumter.

Other regions of the North were much more ambivalent. New York's political leaders, including Representative Daniel Sickles and Mayor Fernando Wood, even proposed that the city secede and form a free port of entry similar to Bremen or Hamburg.[99] As early as April 1860, Senator Milton Latham was contending that his state of California would be viable as a separate, independent republic.[100] In the Middle Atlantic

98. See, for example, this passage from a Senate address Seward delivered in 1854, "Political ties bind the Union together – a common necessity, and not merely a common necessity, but the common interests of empire – of such empire as the world has never before seen. The control of the national power is the control of the great western continent; and the control of this continent is to be in a very few years the controlling influence in the world." "Nebraska and Kansas: Second Speech," in Baker, ed., *The Works of William Seward*, p. 476. This interpretation found an echo in New Orleans when a southern sympathizer, the French consul, declared, "The war of conquest undertaken by the North is meant much less to maintain the union than to defend its threatened and greatly imperiled financial and commercial interests." – Letter from Count E. de Mejan to the French government (June 22, 1861) cited in Gordon Wright, "Economic Conditions in the Confederacy as Seen by the French Consuls," *Journal of Southern History* 7 (May 1941): 196–7.

99. Nichols, *Disruption of American Democracy*, p. 402; George Fort Milton, *Eve of Conflict: Stephen A. Douglas and the Needless War* (New York: Houghton Mifflin, 1934), p. 520; Wright, *Secession Movement*, pp. 14, 176–80, 189–91, 198–202; *New York Times*, December 11, 1860.

100. *Congressional Globe* 36:1:1728–9, April 16, 1860. Latham later demurred when

states, a few major political leaders and many less important figures debated the possible advantages of a "central confederacy" which could extend from New York to Norfolk, Virginia. When Governor John Letcher spoke to the Virginia Assembly in December 1860, he predicted that this central confederation would dominate the four new nations that would inherit the territory of the United States.[101] Midwestern sectionalists, who feared the triumph of industrialism and the predominance of New England, foresaw that a civil war could transform them into "slaves and serfs of New England." They recognized that the closing of the competitive Mississippi River system would put them at the mercy of the Great Lakes shipping interests and the east–west railway trunk lines, owned mainly by New York and Boston capital. Some astute Midwesterners feared that New England industry and northeastern capital would exploit their section through the Republican party.[102] In Missouri, the *New York Times* reported, "leading gentlemen . . . are privately discussing the question of the separate independence of that State."[103] Two weeks later, the paper repeated another rumor – this one attributed to "Frontier State" senators and representatives (in particular, Samuel Woodson of Missouri). The speculation claimed that the three northern regions (New England, Pacific states, and Middle Atlantic/Midwest) were discussing with the South the possibility of "forming a league or confederacy uniting the different sections in all the essential powers and purposes of national defense and international commerce."[104]

As these rumors indicate, the choice for the North posed by southern secession was never between one nation and two but between one nation and many. Though there was little doubt that the new Republican administration would commit the central government to a policy of repression, there also can be little doubt that failure to do so would have fatally strengthened the centrifugal forces already operating within the federal union. The major problem facing northern leaders was finding a popular basis for unifying the free states behind a policy of coercion.[105] A moral

Representative Charles Scott wrote a letter to the *Washington Constitution* advocating a policy of independence and neutrality for California. See the *New York Times*, December 10 and 24, 1860.

101. Wright, *Secession Movement*, pp. 13–14, 85–8, 103–6, 113–21, 213–21.
102. Frank L. Klement, *Clement L. Vallandigham and the Civil War* (Lexington: University Press of Kentucky, 1970), p. 59. As the Midwest considered the problem of interrupted commerce on the Mississippi River, this secessionist speculation was replaced by support for coercive reintegration of the South into the Union. *New York Times*, December 12 and 19, 1860; Milton, *Eve of Conflict*, pp. 520–1, 532; Robert W. Johannsen, ed., *The Letters of Stephen A. Douglas* (Urbana: University of Illinois Press, 1961), pp. 504–5. On the possible economic consequences of midwestern secession, see Kohlmeier, *Old Northwest*, pp. 226–31, 243–4.
103. December 17, 1860.
104. December 31, 1860.
105. In an editorial titled "Why Not Let South Carolina Secede?," the *New York Times*

appeal for the abolition of slavery during this period would have driven the border states into the southern confederacy and made a policy of repression materially impossible.[106] The only other popular basis was an imperialistic nationalism.

Nationalism has two major components. One is the legitimation of the national community's resistance to penetration by the world economy or domination by foreign states. As a result, nationalist ideologies are often more salient features of countries subject to intense international political and economic pressure than of those comparatively removed from the competition of major foreign powers. For that reason, the relative isolation of the United States on the North American continent contributed to the comparative unimportance of nationalism in American life prior to secession.[107]

The second is an ideologically justified insistence that the resources of the central state be mobilized in support of the interests of the dominant groups in a society. In fact, the ambivalent relationship between the state and major groups in the national political economy was an equally important factor behind the antebellum weakness of American nationalism. For decades prior to the Civil War, the national government had been dominated by the political agents of plantation slavery. As the dominant group, these representatives of the slave South had been able to fend off the development schemes of the industrializing Northeast and agrarian West but had been unable to impose their own program upon the rest

attempted to assign responsibility for a coercive policy to the "Constitution": "The whole country would feel relieved if South Carolina could be translated out of this Federal vale of tears into some region of solitary sovereignty, where she would have none to molest or make her afraid. But the trouble in the case is, it can't be done. We can no more let her go out of the union than she can go out of her own accord. The Constitution imposes upon the Federal Government duties towards the States as well as upon the States duties towards the Federal Government." This fatalistic appeal to an abstract concept detached from political reality illustrates the difficulty northern leaders encountered in discovering a moral basis for coercion. The *New York Weekly Tribune* even admitted that the South had a right to secede: "Whenever a considerable section of our Union shall deliberately resolve to go out, we shall resist all coercive measures designed to keep it in. We hope never to live in a republic whereof one section is pinned to the residue by bayonets." November 17, 1860, quoted in Nevins, *Emergence of Lincoln*, vol. 2, p. 338.

106. In the years immediately preceding the Civil War, the abolitionists Wendell Phillips and William Lloyd Garrison repeatedly advocated that the North separate from the South. See, for example, Phillips' speech in the Athenaeum (printed in the *New York Times*, March 21, 1860) and the text of a disunion resolution adopted by Garrison's followers in Albany, New York on February 2, 1859, printed in Horace Greeley and John F. Cleveland, eds., *A Political Textbook for 1860* (New York: Negro Universities Press, 1969; reprint), p. 173; also, Glover, *Pre-Civil War Compromise Efforts*, pp. 38–42.

107. See, for example, James H. Kettner, *The Development of American Citizenship, 1608–1870* (Chapel Hill: University of North Carolina Press, 1984), pp. 248–86, and McCardell, *Idea of a Southern Nation*, pp. 227–76.

of the nation. Their lack of success and the impending loss of national power made these Southerners separatists, not nationalists. On the other hand, Lincoln's election heralded the ascension to power of a broad alliance of northern industrial capital, labor, and land-owning farmers. As the alliance emerged as a contender for the dominant position in the national political economy, the Republican party became the vehicle for its political program. Enshrined in the party platform, the program of the northern alliance now loomed as the master plan for the political economy as a result of the 1860 election. Along with America's isolation in the world system, the recent ascent of the alliance to dominance accounts for the hesitancy with which the North embraced a nationalist response to secession; a more reflexive nationalism would only develop after expectations of continued preeminence were supported by unfolding events.[108] Anticipating that the alliance would subsequently dominate the political economy, the social base of the Republican party became the social base for a sweeping program of central state repression.

The Republican plan for the national political economy

Four major candidates ran for president in 1860. Two of them, Stephen Douglas of Illinois and John Breckinridge of Kentucky, inherited the northern and southern wings of the Democratic party. Douglas represented the Anti-Lecompton opponents of slavery and Buchanan's policy in Kansas. Breckinridge was the nominee of Administration Democrats and was supported by presidential patronage. A third candidate, John Bell, was nominated by the Constitutional Union party, a new organization created out of the Whiggish remnants of the American party just months before the election. The fourth candidate was Abraham Lincoln. The conventions nominating these candidates drafted very different platforms. Bell's Constitutional Union party, for example, contended:

108. A successful separatist movement rearranges the position of all groups remaining in the parent nation and thus changes the position of the previously dominant group in the national political economy. The alteration of positions narrows the breadth of the dominant group because secession removes a major class of subordinate interests ("losers") and a redistribution of wealth within the remaining portion of the political economy would take place primarily among former beneficiaries ("winners"). For that reason, groups opposed to southern secession might have, after the nation had divided, themselves become separatist in the *new* national political economy. The most separatist groups in the South, on the other hand, should become the most fervent supporters of their new state. The definition of a dominant group is thus heavily dependent on the territorial scope of the national political economy and the social and economic groups that the boundaries of the state enclose.

> Experience has demonstrated that Platforms adopted by the partisan
> Conventions of the country have had the effect to mislead and deceive
> the people, and at the same time to widen the political divisions of
> the country, by the creation and encouragement of geographical and
> sectional parties.[109]

Having said this, the party recognized "no political principle other than The Constitution of the Country, The Union of the States and The Enforcement of the Laws." This platform might be characterized as a nationalist rebuff to separatism, except that the party did not say what should happen if constitutional principles could not be preserved. For many Southerners, federal protection of slavery in the territories was a constitutional obligation. To them, any violation by the Republican party of this constitutional "principle" would justify disunion. On this argument and on all of the other major issues in the election, Bell's party expressed no opinion. As a program for the national political economy, the platform of the Constitutional Union convention promised nothing more than political stalemate. While ostensibly neutral, such a program would ultimately yield advantage to the North because of that section's much more robust expansion.

A little less ambiguous was the National Democratic (Douglas) party platform. The party took no position on secession or on the disposition of the public lands. A plank tacitly supporting the Dred Scott decision was rejected by the convention, but nothing was adopted in its place. Blanket endorsement of the 1856 "Cincinnati" platform provided the only indication of party positions on the admission of Kansas, the tariff, and federal aid to internal development projects.

The Breckinridge wing of the party also endorsed the "Cincinnati" platform (except the tacit endorsement of the free state admission of Kansas).[110] In other respects, the Breckinridge convention drafted a positive, albeit southern program for the political economy – a policy of federal protection for slavery in the territories and annexation of foreign lands where slavery might reasonably be expected to take root (i.e., Cuba). No encouragement would be given to industrial growth or homestead agriculture. This program promised to retard free-state expansion into the western territories, to decelerate capitalist expansion in the North, and to create new slave states in conquered lands bordering the Caribbean. A political economy shaped by such principles gave the best

109. Greeley and Cleveland, eds., *Political Textbook for 1860*, p. 29.
110. For a summary of objections to the admission of Kansas posed by southern Democrats loyal to the administration, see the *New York Times*, April 2, 1860, and *Congressional Globe* 36:1:1662, April 11, 1860.

(but hardly sanguine) chance of maintaining a balance of power between free and slave states.

The major difference between the Douglas and Breckinridge platforms was over slavery in the territories. The northern wing of the Democratic party would commit the federal government to a policy of neutrality under which the citizens residing in the territories would decide slavery's status. In practice, "popular sovereignty" would have effectively banned slavery in all the western territories, including, ultimately, New Mexico. In all other respects, the Douglas and Breckinridge platforms were virtually identical. Even though Douglas himself held slaves, the two candidates diverged much more sharply than did their respective platforms. When war broke out, Douglas gave strong support to the Lincoln administration, including a mission to southern Illinois to gain that region's backing for the Union.[111] Breckinridge, on the other hand, left the Senate for a generalship in the southern army and ended the conflict as the Confederate secretary of war. The Bell, Breckinridge, and Douglas platforms all promised near term stalemate between free- and slave-state interests in the national political economy. None could have prevented such a stalemate from ultimately evolving into northern hegemony, but each committed the central state to active retardation of or neutrality toward northern expansion.

The Republican program for the national political economy, on the other hand, threw the entire weight of the federal government behind the expansion of northern industry and homestead agriculture. Beginning with a declaration that secession was treason, the party not only promised to prohibit slavery in the western territories but also favored homestead legislation that would actively promote free state settlement. Republican support for a protective tariff for industry and central state aid for internal development united eastern capitalism with western yeoman agriculture. As a program for northern economic expansion, the weakest link in the Republican platform concerned immigrants. Here the party promised opposition to new restrictions on immigration or citizenship by either the federal or state governments. Though the Douglas and Breckinridge planks were comparatively more generous, the Republican position satisfied a large portion of the immigrant population.[112]

The central state's role in the Republican program was primarily as

---

111. Douglas owned slaves in his capacity as executor of his first wife's estate and trustee for his sons' inheritance. Craven, *Coming of the Civil War*, pp. 333–4; Johannsen, ed., *The Letters of Stephen A. Douglas*, pp. 509–11.
112. George M. Stephenson, *A History of American Immigration, 1820–1924* (New York: Russell and Russell, 1964), pp. 125–33; Foner, *Free Labor, Free Soil, Free Men*, pp. 226–60.

an umbrella for market-centered internal development and only second-
arily as an active agent for capitalist expansion. The platform did not
reveal any inclination to regulate investment or direct economic activity
beyond the mild manipulations of land distribution, development of rivers
and harbors, and a tariff on imports. Aside from prohibiting slavery in
the territories (which merely hastened and ratified the inevitable), southern interests were not discriminated against except and insofar as those
interests stood in the way of northern development. The platform broke
the stalemate in the political economy in the North's favor and projected
a durable reign of northern hegemony, a hegemony within which Southerners feared that Republican radicals would mobilize the central state
behind the abolition of slavery as well.

In terms of central state authority, the Republican program was only
marginally more statist than the Breckinridge platform. Both would commit the federal government on slavery in the territories: the Republicans
behind a prohibition and Breckinridge in back of a federal slave code
for the institution's protection. If anything, the Breckinridge position
promised a larger role for the central state because a slave code would
have to be enforced against the wishes of a majority of the territorial
population while the Republican prohibition was, for the most part, self-
executing. For similar reasons, rigorous enforcement of the fugitive slave
law (the Breckinridge position) was more statist than a vague promise
to execute the laws (the Republican stance). Similarly, the disposition of
the public domain, either to homestead settlers or through revenue-
oriented public sale, was a weak policy in statist terms. Both alternatives
withdrew public lands from federal control and entered them into the
market economy where further development would largely be determined
by private interests. It could be argued that the Republican program was
marginally more statist in that the terms under which land transfer occurred encouraged the formation of a particular type of society (free-
state yeoman agriculture).

That policy, however, sacrificed another statist goal (the generation of
revenue) that could have been maximized by the Breckinridge program.[113]
In any case, Breckinridge's party was more concerned with slowing the
rate of western settlement, which general land sale, compared to free
homestead grants, would have done. The acquisition of Cuba, a Breckinridge proposal, would also have implied a larger central state than the
Republican's apparent endorsement of the status quo. Republican policies
on internal development and the tariff, on the other hand, were inter-

113. Land sales, however, constituted only a small fraction of total federal revenue, 10
      percent of total customs receipts between 1824 and 1855. *Appendix to the Congres-
      sional Globe* 36:1:346, May 4, 1860.

ventionist in nature. A protectionist tariff, in particular, was a state-enhancing policy peculiarly adapted to import-sensitive sectors of the economy. Because the South could not benefit from any tariff position other than unrestricted trade and because most internal development projects appeared to strengthen the position of northeastern commercial and manufacturing centers in the economy, the Breckinridge convention did not present a positive, state-centered alternative to these Republican planks.

Even conceding the relatively similar statist content of the two programs, however, the Republican platform promised to create a stronger central state in that only its program could break the stalemate in the national political economy and repress the centrifugal force of southern separatism. By comparison, the Breckinridge program committed the federal government to a promotion of slavery that could only delay, not prevent, the rise of northern economic and political dominance. The Breckinridge program could not have strengthened the central state because it did not rest on a compelling political-economic base and because its implementation would have forced the most vital, dynamic elements of the national political economy to assume a hostile orientation toward the central state.[114]

Legislative evidence for the emergence
of northern hegemony

Much of the preceding interpretation of the political and economic context of the secession crisis has drawn upon secondary materials and has moved rapidly over events upon which entire books could and have been written. There is, however, one crucial element that the secondary literature does not provide: empirical evidence of the close linkage of, on the one hand, support for the free labor–industrial capital program for the national political economy and, on the other, backing for a state-

---

114. Foner, *Free Soil, Free Labor, Free Men,* pp. 134–5. The most dynamic sectors of the national political economy were those associated with industrial expansion, the growing autonomy of the nation's financial system from European influence, and rapid settlement of the western frontier. Each sector provided increasing support for a more powerful position for the United States both in the world economy and in the international system of independent states. Even though the plantation system was also expanding at a brisk pace, the interests of the cotton South were antithetical to these larger, northern sectors. Thus, while plantation production might have been the most dynamic element in an independent southern Confederacy, northern development required at least indifference toward, if not exploitation of, the cotton economy. And the future of the American state was tied to the development of the North if only because that section already encompassed a large majority of the nation's wealth and population.

centered repression of southern separatism. The legislative voting patterns described in this section document, first, that the northern program for national development drew consistent support from almost all Republicans and large fractions of the much smaller minor parties of the North and, second, that this developmental coalition was also the major source of resistance to southern secession.

These voting patterns also demonstrate that impending passage of the northern program was, along with the Republican party's hostility to slavery, a major factor in the South's decision to secede – thus completing the connections between state-sponsored northern development, the antislavery position of northern political leaders, and northern suppression of secession. As the evidence suggests, the struggles over slavery, state sponsorship of northern economic expansion, and the subsequent mobilization of the North for war were all deeply embedded in the same contest for sectional supremacy in the national political economy. It would, therefore, be incorrect to distinguish, as many scholars have done, Republican antislavery proposals (as derived from moralistic ideological principles) and the suppression of secession (as nationalist support "for the Union") from the impending passage of the northern developmental program. Each element was but a different facet in a much broader and more fundamental shift in the locus of power within the national political economy.

Every Republican proposal for the development of the northern economy was deliberated in the House of Representatives during 1860. Several, such as the homestead bill and tariff legislation, actually passed the chamber before the Republican national convention met in Chicago on May 16. Taken together, the voting patterns on these proposals illustrate the close, interlocking interests of the northern alliance and the deep penetration the Republican program made into the demoralized ranks of the other organized parties (Tables 2.3–2.5). The first of these votes occurred on Representative Justin Morrill's bill to use revenue from the sale of public lands to establish agricultural ("land-grant") colleges in each of the states. Similar legislation had passed the House and Senate during the Thirty-fifth Congress only to be vetoed by Buchanan. This time Morrill's bill survived a tabling motion (see Table 2.3) but, after a postponement, was not reconsidered, presumably because another veto could not be overridden. After the South left the Union, agricultural college legislation easily moved through Congress and became law in 1862.[115] Though the proposal was not formally a part of the Republican

115. Paul W. Gates, *Agriculture and the Civil War* (New York: Knopf, 1965), pp. 261–4. Gates attributed southern opposition to Morrill's bill to a regional reluctance to educate "at public expense the people who actually farmed." His interpretation is

Table 2.3. *Congressional support for internal development in the Thirty-sixth Congress*

	Legislative proposal					
Membership category	Agricultural colleges (March 7, 1860)	Homestead (March 12, 1860)	Tariff (May 11, 1860)	Steamboat passenger bill (May 18, 1860)	Rivers and harbors (June 20, 1860)	Pacific railroad (Dec. 20, 1860)
Party						
Republicans	94.1% (85)	100.0% (85)	96.6% (89)	73.3% (75)	96.7% (91)	77.8% (81)
Anti-Lecompton Democrats	66.7 (9)	100.0 (10)	62.5 (8)	77.8 (9)	33.3 (3)	14.3 (7)
Americans	90.5 (21)	10.0 (20)	76.9 (13)	38.1 (21)	73.7 (19)	45.0 (20)
Administration Democrats	1.6 (63)	27.3 (66)	5.2 (58)	32.7 (55)	3.8 (53)	35.6 (59)
Manufacturing						
Over $80.00	70.0% (20)	100.0% (24)	90.9% (22)	72.7% (22)	91.3% (23)	91.3% (23)
$20 to 79.99	91.1 (45)	88.1 (42)	94.1 (51)	69.8 (43)	87.5 (48)	67.5 (40)
$10 to 19.99	56.2 (48)	79.6 (49)	63.2 (38)	60.5 (38)	70.3 (37)	61.0 (41)
$ 0 to 9.99	36.9 (65)	22.7 (66)	21.1 (57)	33.3 (57)	27.6 (58)	33.3 (63)
Immigrants						
Over 20%	71.8% (39)	90.0% (40)	89.2% (37)	75.0% (36)	92.9% (42)	76.9% (37)
5.0 to 19.9%	70.5 (78)	87.0 (77)	72.7 (77)	64.7 (68)	75.8 (66)	68.9 (74)
Under 5.0%	37.7 (61)	18.8 (64)	27.8 (54)	30.4 (56)	27.6 (58)	24.1 (54)
Status of slavery						
Free state	80.7% (109)	99.1% (115)	86.5% (111)	72.0% (100)	87.7% (106)	74.5% (106)
Slave state	26.1 (69)	1.5 (66)	14.0 (57)	26.7 (60)	20.0 (60)	24.6 (61)
Sectional stress	65.3	80.3	78.1	56.9	68.9	53.4

Source: Analysis of roll call data. Manufacturing categories are based on value-added per capita data for congressional districts calculated from the *1860 Census*. Immigrant categories are calculated from data on the percentage of the congressional district white population classified as foreign born in the *1860 Census*. Sectional stress scores measure the regional polarization of voting alignments on the roll call (see Richard F. Bensel, *Sectionalism and American Political Development, 1880–1980*, pp. 443–9).

70

Table 2.4. *Slave-state support for internal development in the Thirty-sixth Congress*

Membership category	Legislative proposal					
	Agricultural colleges	Homestead	Tariff	Steamboat passenger bill	Rivers and harbors	Pacific railroad
Party						
Americans	89.5% (19)	0.0% (18)	70.0% (10)	42.1% (19)	70.6% (17)	38.9% (18)
Administration Democrats	2.0 (50)	2.1 (48)	2.1 (47)	19.5 (41)	0.0 (43)	18.6 (43)
Manufacturing						
$20 to $79.99	60.0% (5)	0.0% (5)	50.0% (4)	66.7% (6)	66.7% (6)	50.0% (6)
$10 to $19.99	16.7 (12)	0.0 (9)	25.0 (8)	50.0 (10)	28.6 (7)	14.3 (7)
$ 0 to $ 9.99	25.0 (52)	1.9 (52)	8.9 (45)	15.9 (44)	12.8 (47)	22.9 (48)
Immigrants						
Over 20%	50.0% (6)	0.0% (4)	33.3% (3)	60.0% (5)	80.0% (5)	50.0% (4)
5.0% to 19.9%	7.7 (13)	9.1 (11)	18.2 (11)	55.6 (9)	12.5 (8)	46.2 (13)
Under 5.0%	28.0 (50)	0.0 (51)	11.6 (43)	17.4 (46)	14.9 (47)	15.9 (44)
Slavery						
50.0% and over	0.0% (16)	0.0% (14)	0.0% (12)	27.3% (11)	0.0% (12)	0.0% (10)
25.0% to 49.9%	27.3 (22)	0.0 (25)	8.7 (23)	20.8 (24)	13.0 (23)	21.7 (23)
0% to 24.9%	38.7 (31)	3.7 (27)	27.3 (22)	32.0 (25)	36.0 (25)	35.7 (28)

Source: Analysis of roll call data. Manufacturing categories are based on value-added per capita data for congressional districts calculated from the *1860 Census.* Immigrant categories are calculated from data on the percentage of the congressional district white population classified as foreign born in the *1860 Census.*

Table 2.5. *Free-state support for internal development in the Thirty-sixth Congress*

Membership category	Legislative proposal					
	Agricultural colleges	Homestead	Tariff	Steamboat passenger bill	Rivers and harbors	Pacific railroad
Party						
Republicans	94.1% (85)	100.0% (85)	96.6% (89)	73.3% (75)	96.7% (91)	77.8% (81)
Anti-Lecompton Democrats	66.7 (9)	100.0 (10)	62.5 (8)	77.8 (9)	33.3 (3)	14.3 (7)
Americans	100.0 (2)	100.0 (2)	100.0 (3)	0.0 (2)	100.0 (2)	100.0 (2)
Administration Democrats	0.0 (13)	94.4 (18)	22.2 (11)	71.4 (14)	20.0 (10)	81.2 (16)
Manufacturing						
Over $80	70.0% (20)	100.0% (24)	90.9% (22)	72.7% (22)	91.3% (23)	91.3% (23)
$20 to $79.99	95.0 (40)	100.0 (37)	97.9 (47)	70.3 (37)	90.5 (42)	70.6 (34)
$10 to $19.99	69.4 (36)	97.5 (40)	73.3 (30)	64.3 (28)	80.0 (30)	70.6 (34)
$ 0 to $ 9.99	84.6 (13)	100.0 (14)	66.7 (12)	92.3 (13)	90.9 (11)	66.7 (15)
Immigrants						
20.0% and over	75.8% (33)	100.0% (36)	94.1% (34)	77.4% (31)	94.6% (37)	80.0% (35)
5.0% to 19.9%	83.1 (65)	100.0 (66)	81.8 (66)	66.1 (59)	84.5 (58)	73.8 (61)
0% to 4.9%	81.8 (11)	92.3 (13)	90.9 (11)	90.0 (10)	81.8 (11)	60.0 (10)

Source: Analysis of roll call data. Manufacturing categories are based on value-added per capita data for congressional districts calculated from the *1860 Census*. Immigrant categories are calculated from data on the percentage of the congressional district white population classified as foreign born in the *1860 Census*.

platform, the Morrill bill was an integral part of the party's developmental policy.

Five days after the chamber turned back the tabling motion on agricultural college legislation, the House of Representatives passed the homestead bill (see Table 2.3). This proposal, more sweeping than the version finally sent to the White House, would have granted free homesteads of 160 acres to any man over twenty-one.[116] In the upper chamber, Senator James Mason accused the North of intending to use the homestead bill to assure itself "command and control of the destinies of the continent.... It is part of this 'measure of empire' to connect, as belonging indissolubly to it, the whole slavery question with the homestead policy ... a political engine and a potent one" for an attack on the very existence of the South.[117] Here too, enactment finally came only after the South had seceded and Lincoln assumed the presidency.

Along with the homestead bill, the tariff was the centerpiece of the Republican program and an upward revision of duties, particularly on iron, passed the House of Representatives on May 11, 1860 (see Table 2.3). The *New York Times* termed Section 7, the iron schedule, "devoted to the peculiar interests of Pennsylvania iron and coal ... its conception required the continuous sitting for days of several leading gentlemen of Pennsylvania, in and out of Congress. Of course it suits them. Would it be fair to say that this portion of the bill is drawn as a special appeal to the people of that State in behalf of the nominee of the Chicago Convention? It is certainly true."[118] One of these Pennsylvania "iron" men outlined to the House chamber the developmental theory that lay behind the tariff:

> Every enlightened nation, whatever homage it may have paid in documents to the theory of free trade has pursued a widely different policy, and relaxed the protective system only when domestic manufacturers have been firmly rooted.... Free trade may ... be considered as the object to which society is tending; but protection must

probably too narrow; the South, at this point, opposed every measure that promised to strengthen the federal government except those favoring slavery.
116. For the text of the final version of the homestead bill vetoed by Buchanan, see Greeley and Cleveland, eds., *Political Textbook for 1860*, pp. 188–93. For a history of the South's opposition to homestead legislation, see Roy M. Robbins, *Our Landed Heritage: The Public Domain, 1776–1936* (Lincoln: University of Nebraska Press, 1962), pp. 169–82; Benjamin Horace Hibbard, *A History of the Public Land Policies* (Madison: University of Wisconsin Press, 1965), pp. 371–85.
117. Quoted in James T. DuBois and Gertrude S. Mathews, *Galusha A. Grow: Father of the Homestead Law* (Boston: Houghton Mifflin, 1917), pp. 212–13. Mason's fear, of course, was that rapid settlement of the West by free homesteaders would so strengthen abolitionist sentiment as to doom slavery.
118. March 28, 1860.

be the means of arriving at it. Suppose free trade is established in a
new and poor country: what will that country produce? I do not
deny but that it can develop some favored industry by a natural
privileged situation; but foreign competition would stifle in their bud
all those things which it requires in order to prosper – capital, skillful
workmen, experienced overseers, easy communication, and a good
market; in fact, all the conditions which time alone can give. A
transition, consequently, is indispensable; and to preach free trade
to a country which does not enjoy all these advantages, is nearly as
equitable as to propose that a child contend with a grown man."[119]

Sent on to the Senate, the Democratic majority in that chamber blocked
passage until southern secession produced a bare protectionist majority.
Buchanan, himself a Pennsylvanian, signed the bill.

Of all the major developmental measures facing the Thirty-sixth Congress, the most anomalous was the steamboat passenger bill. Introduced
by Republican Elihu Washburne of Chicago, the legislation strengthened
regulatory standards and punitive levies on steamboat masters and owners to ensure proper operation and maintanence of the vessels.[120] Though
the measure enjoyed the backing of the Buchanan administration and
only expanded an ongoing federal policy, Southerners contended that the
bill was an "unconstitutional" infringement upon the rights of the
states.[121] The steamboat passenger bill was unique among antebellum
measures in that it contemplated the regulation of economic activity
without intending either to prohibit that activity altogether (as by banning
slavery in the territories) or encourage economic expansion (as by tariff
protection).

During the First Session of the Thirty-sixth Congress, members of the
House of Representatives introduced forty different bills proposing river
and harbor improvements. Three-quarters of these proposed federal development of waterways in the Northeast and Midwest. Five were introduced by members from border slave states, and only five more
suggested projects in the deep South (these were to be located in four
western states: Arkansas, Louisiana, Tennessee, and Texas). Many were

119. Representative James Campbell, *Congressional Globe* 36:1:1845, 1847, April 24,
     1860. For data on trade patterns and customs receipts, see 36:1:1834–6, 1946–50,
     April 23 and May 7, 1860. For Seward's views on the tariff, see Bancroft, *Life of
     William H. Seward*, pp. 46–51.
120. *New York Times*, April 7 and May 3, 1860. The *Times* endorsed the bill. For a
     brief description of antebellum regulation of steamboat operation, see D. S. Han-
     chett, "Government Aid and Commercial Policy," in Emory R. Johnson, T. W. Van
     Metre, G. G. Huebner, and D. S. Hanchett, *History of Domestic and Foreign
     Commerce of the United States*, vol. 2 (Washington, D.C.: Carnegie Institute, 1915),
     pp. 261–2.
121. *Congressional Globe* 36:1:2126, May 16, 1860. For the text of the bill, see
     36:1:2177–9.

contained in an omnibus bill reported out of the Commerce Committee, brought to the floor, and defeated under a motion to suspend the rules (requiring a two-thirds majority) on June 20, 1860.[122] Like the Morrill agricultural college bill, this rivers and harbors proposal faced a certain veto from the White House and Republicans did not pursue the measure beyond the creation of a public record.[123]

The Douglas, Breckinridge, and Republican conventions all endorsed federal aid for the construction of a railroad connecting the Pacific coast with the eastern railroad network. Few opposed a Pacific railroad in theory – in part because California and Oregon made this project their highest political priority and these states often determined the balance of power between free- and slave-state forces. When specific route proposals were suggested, however, rotating majorities frustrated the development of a compromise agreement. In Robert Russel's words:

> The greatest obstacle in the way of Pacific railway legislation lay in the inability to agree upon a route or routes. If a bill were framed for a central route the advocates of northern and southern routes would unite with the small, compact minority altogether opposed to government aid and defeat it. If the bill provided for two roads, or for three roads, or for one main trunk with several branches to take care of the chief contenders of the terminus, the votes gained by such log-rolling processes were always offset by votes lost on the ground that the project was too costly for the country to bear.

Nothing changed the shape of this struggle until the secession of the South left the choice of a route up to the North alone.[124]

The Speaker appointed a select committee on the Pacific railroad on March 9, 1860, and that panel considered the route problem for the next eight months. From the very beginning, a "central route" from the western border of Iowa or Missouri to San Francisco drew the most attention and, as the committee deliberated, advocates developed a wide range of arguments for its support. These supporting arguments included a claim that construction of a railroad through the Salt Lake region would help discourage polygamy among the Mormon settlers (by exposing the community to national values), would provide an overland route to the East for the gold mining center at Pike's Peak and the silver lodes in Nevada, would follow the "time-tested" trails of western emigrants, and would

122. *Congressional Globe*, 36:1:3195–6.
123. Nevins, *Emergence of Lincoln*, vol. 2, pp. 194–5.
124. "The Pacific Railway Issue in Politics prior to the Civil War," *Mississippi Valley Historical Review* 12 (September 1925): 198. See also Robert R. Russel, *Critical Studies in Antebellum Sectionalism: Essays in American Political and Economic History* (Westport, Conn.: Greenwood, 1972), pp. 127–44.

be the most militarily secure of all alternatives.[125] Just before the bill reached the floor, the committee added a southern route because, as the *New York Times* noted, "Texas, Louisiana and Arkansas are now wavering in their allegiance to the Union. They are calculating its value; their people will not fail to perceive that their only hope of a connection with the Pacific is dependent on the preservation of the Union."[126] Earlier in the session, Andrew Hamilton of Texas had openly threatened disunion if the Pacific railroad bill only provided a central route.[127] After addition of a southern route, southern congressmen supported the bill and the legislation passed the House on December 20, 1860 – the same day South Carolina seceded from the Union.

Five of these six developmental measures received more support from Republican members than from any other party in the House (see Table 2.3). The one exception, the steamboat passenger bill, involved federal regulation of private economic activity, but even here legislation would not have passed the House without strong Republican backing. The relatively weak Republican support for the Pacific railroad was the result of disenchantment among members favoring a northern route to Puget Sound and others opposed to southern concessions. Whiggish American party members supported agricultural colleges, the tariff, and rivers and harbors appropriations. The small band of Anti-Lecompton Democrats opposed only rivers and harbors and railroad legislation. Democrats loyal to the Buchanan administration, on the other hand, opposed every developmental measure by a large margin.

Reflecting the strong manufacturing base in the Northeast and the prodevelopment orientation of industrial capitalism, the voting patterns revealed a strong relationship between per capita value-added in manufacturing and support for development. This relationship was most evident in voting on the twin pillars of the Republican program for the national political economy: the homestead and tariff bills. The connection between districts with large foreign-born populations and development followed a very similar pattern, largely because immigrants chose to settle in the North in overwhelming numbers. In most cases, the dichotomy between free states and slave states produced more stark divisions over development than either manufacturing or immigrant classifications. Sectional stress scores calculated from the behavior of trade area delegations

125. For the membership of the committee, see *Congressional Globe* 36:1:1086. The
      New York Times closely followed the committee's deliberations: April 4, 6, 7, 9,
      17, 26; June 5, 12; November 16; December 3, 7, 1860.
126. December 21, 1860.
127. *Congressional Globe* 36:1:2446–7, May 29, 1860. For other debate, see 36:1:2330–
      3, 2440, 2442, May 24 and 29, 1860.

– some of which transcended boundaries between free states and slave states, closely tracked free- versus slave-state patterns but also reflected internal divisions within delegations that spanned the North–South line.[128]

When slave-state members are considered alone, the relationship between support for internal development proposals and manufacturing or foreign born population is weaker but persists (see Table 2.4). The division over internal development between American party members and Administration Democrats, on the other hand, widens when Southerners are considered alone. Only on the homestead bill, where one Administration Democrat from St. Joseph, Missouri, strayed from the southern fold, did Buchanan Democrats give more support to internal development than American party members. Many of the prodevelopment Americans represented relatively industrialized districts containing comparatively large immigrant populations, primarily in the states of Kentucky and Maryland. As would be expected, a positive relationship between support for internal development and these characteristics of capitalist market expansion (manufacturing and foreign born population) also produced a significant negative connection between slaveholding and the Republican program for the national political economy. No congressman representing a district in which more than half of the population was composed of slaves voted for anything other than the steamboat passenger bill. Southerners from districts less than a quarter slave, on the other hand, cast over a fourth of their votes for every measure except the homestead bill. The evident Republican seduction of American party members from more industrial, less plantation-oriented districts underlined the dismal prospects for slavery's future in the border states and the contracting political base of the plantation economy in the nation as a whole.

In the North, the Republican program drew such wide support as to overwhelm any relationship between manufacturing or immigrant populations and support for internal development (see Table 2.5). For example, two-thirds of the members representing districts with a per

128. Sectional stress scores were derived from the voting behavior of "trade area" delegations in the House of Representatives. Trade areas are the terriorial units containing the nation's leading urban centers and their respective tributary hinterlands. In 1860 the leading urban centers were defined as those with 8,000 population or more. To qualify, the city also had to have been seventy-five or more miles by rail from any larger center. The application of these criteria yielded a total of forty-seven trade areas. For a more complete methodological description, comparable trade area boundaries in 1880 and 1890, and an explanation of the sectional stress index, see Richard Franklin Bensel, *Sectionalism and American Political Development, 1880–1980* (Madison: University of Wisconsin Press, 1984), pp. 415–50.

capita value-added in manufacturing under ten dollars voted for the tariff while all members from districts over eighty dollars voted for the homestead bill. The closely interlocking interests of the yeoman agriculture–industrial capital alliance within the Republican party persuaded sizable fractions – even majorities – of the other party fragments on every measure. Even as support for the Republican program was spilling over into the northern border regions of the slave economy, Republican initiatives drew significant backing from nonmanufacturing regions on the southern border of the free states (often represented by Douglas or Administration Democrats) and in New York City with its large immigrant population and close economic ties to the South. Nineteen of 147 northern congressmen, all Republicans, voted for all six development measures.

Internal development and repression
of southern separatism

Between the secession of South Carolina and the inauguration of Lincoln, Congress considered many responses to the withdrawal of southern states from the union. Most of these proposals were either concerned with the military capacity of the federal government or the direct exercise of federal authority in the South and contemplated coercive reintegration of the South into the Union. While Republicans and Southerners used these resolutions and bills to indicate their respective positions, neither proponents nor opponents of coercion made a sustained effort to enact legislation.[129] Still, the voting patterns represent congressional sentiment on a possible coercive response to secession and reveal important differences between party and regional groupings that can be connected to support for the Republican program for internal development. The first resolution was proposed by Roger Pryor of Virginia on December 31, 1860, and stated that "any attempt to preserve the Union between the States of this Confederacy by force would be impracticable, and destructive of republican liberty."[130] After a brief and one-sided discussion in which southern members attempted, unsuccessfully, to engage Republicans in a debate over federal coercion, Pryor's resolution was tabled (98 to 55).

In order to better guarantee the security of Washington, the Republicans subsequently brought legislation to the floor of the House that would have imposed a loyalty oath on the militia of the District of Columbia. One Virginia Democrat, Daniel de Jarnett, contended the bill

---

129. Potter, *Lincoln and His Party*, pp. 273–4.
130. *Congressional Globe* 36:2:220.

"foists into the service of the United States an army of six thousand men to constitute a Praetorian guard to overawe the South" while another, Muscoe Garnett, viewed it as a step toward "military dictatorship." This measure passed by a comfortable margin (120 to 42).[131]

On February 14, 1861, the issue of troops in the District of Columbia came up again when Lawrence Branch of North Carolina offered a resolution claiming "that the quartering of troops of the regular Army in this District and around the Capitol, when not necessary for their protection from a hostile enemy, and during the session of Congress, is impolite and offensive, and, if permitted, may be destructive of civil liberty; and in the opinion of this House, the regular troops now in this city ought to be forthwith removed therefrom."[132] Once more Southerners argued that stationing loyal troops in the capital strongly implied that Northerners contemplated coercion of the seceding states. By now, however, the Confederate Congress had convened in Montgomery, Alabama, and the withdrawal of southern congressmen from Washington had decimated antirepression ranks. Only thirty-five members voted against a Republican motion to table Branch's resolution.

On the same day that Jefferson Davis took the oath of office as president of the Confederate States of America, Benjamin Stanton of Ohio brought legislation to the floor that extended federal authority to call up the militia in "case of insurrections against the authority of the United States." Arguing that the extension was "the most harmless thing in the world," Stanton claimed that the bill "merely supplies an accidental omission" in the original enabling act of 1795.[133] This proposal obviously contemplated active coercion of the South and drew more opposition, 68 votes, than the more-or-less defensive measures involving the capital.

Just days before Lincoln assumed office, the House of Representatives took up two additional coercive measures. Considered almost consecutively, the first provided emergency authority for the erection of alternative sites for collecting duties in the southern states and proposed that federal authority be enforced even if it meant offshore collection from naval vessels. Considered under suspension of the rules – a parliamentary motion which required a two-thirds vote for passage, the bill lost when only a simple majority of the members backed the proposal (103 to 62). A subsequent measure, brought before the House by Henry Dawes of

131. *Congressional Globe* 36:2:606, January 29, 1861.
132. *Congressional Globe* 36:2:917.
133. *Congressional Globe* 36:2:1001, February 18, 1861. Also see Potter, *Lincoln and His Party*, pp. 274–7; Nichols, *Disruption of American Democracy*, pp. 478–9; Anonymous, *Mr. Buchanan's Administration on the Eve of the Rebellion* (New York: D. Appleton, 1866), pp. 153–61.

Massachusetts, sought to censure the secretary of the navy for "accepting without delay or inquiry the resignations of officers of the Navy who were in arms against the Government when tendering the same."[134] Condemning the secretary's actions as "highly prejudicial to the discipline of the service and injurious to the honor and efficiency of the Navy," the resolution survived a tabling motion (57 to 96) and moved the government slightly closer to a punitive definition of disloyal acts by federal officers.

Of those voting on these proposals, only one northern congressman, Democrat William English of southern Indiana, consistently opposed coercion. English, who was Buchanan's legislative spokesman during the struggle over Kansas in the Thirty-fifth Congress, voted against three measures and supported none. Only two Southerners, Green Adams of eastern Kentucky and Henry Winter Davis of Baltimore, consistently backed coercion. Davis, who was the only slave-state congressman to vote for Speaker Pennington, voted for four coercive measures while opposing none. Adams supported three proposals and abstained on the other three. Overall support for coercion was concentrated in the northern portions of the free states (see Map 2.3). Southern Ohio and Illinois produced the greatest number of northern votes against coercion. In the South, members from Tennessee and Kentucky cast most of the slave-state votes for an aggressive federal response to secession. The deep South left the Union before members from those states could create a record on coercion. Only one member from the deep South, Joshua Hill of Georgia, ever cast a vote for federal repression.

For slave-state members, support for internal development legislation early in the Thirty-sixth Congress was closely related to backing for an aggressive federal policy toward secession during the months preceeding Lincoln's inauguration (see Table 2.6 – the homestead bill is not included because only one Southerner voted for it). Support for the tariff and rivers and harbors appropriations, closely followed by agricultural college legislation, were the best predictors of union sentiment later in the term. Aside from the February 14 resolution on the quartering of troops in Washington, no slave-state member who voted against the tariff ever voted for federal coercion of the South. Though a close connection obtained between allegiance to the American party, the tariff, and federal coercion of the South, support for the tariff was a better predictor of union sentiment among southern congressmen than membership in the American party.

---

134. *Congressional Globe* 36:2:1422–3, March 2, 1861. For a description of the customs duties bill, see *Appendix to the Congressional Globe* 36:2:70, January 18, 1861.

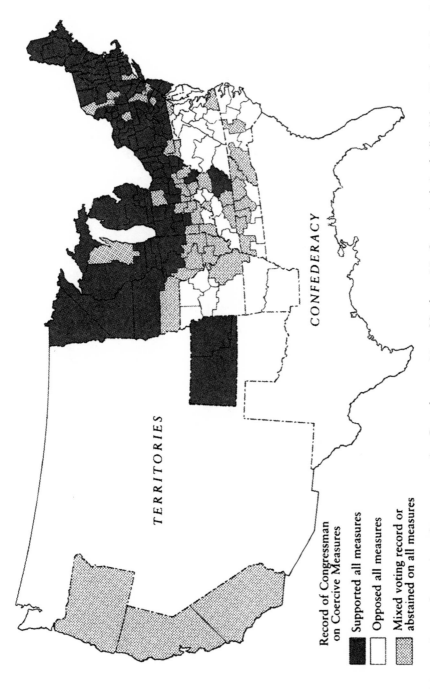

Map 2.3 Support for coercive resistance to secession, December 20, 1860 to March 4, 1861. *Source:* Analysis of roll call data. For description of the six bills and resolutions, see Table 2.5 and text.

Table 2.6. *Relationship between slave-state support for internal development and opposition to secession*

Representatives voting for internal development proposals	Response to secession*					
	Coercive resistance (Dec. 31, 1860)	Militia oath (Jan. 28, 1861)	Troops in D.C. (Feb. 14, 1861)	Call up militia (Feb. 18, 1861)	Collection of duties (March 2, 1861)	Censure secretary (March 2, 1861)
Tariff						
For:	80.0% (5)	87.5% (8)	87.5% (8)	16.7% (6)	0.0% (6)	33.3% (3)
Against:	0.0 (29)	0.0 (20)	5.9 (17)	0.0 (23)	0.0 (19)	0.0 (20)
Agricultural colleges						
For:	81.8% (11)	66.7% (18)	80.0% (15)	5.9% (17)	0.0% (16)	11.1% (9)
Against:	9.7 (31)	0.0 (20)	5.3 (19)	0.0 (23)	0.0 (20)	0.0 (22)
Steamboat passenger bill						
For:	50.0% (10)	45.5% (11)	50.0% (10)	11.1% (9)	0.0% (7)	16.7% (6)
Against:	18.5 (27)	23.8 (21)	22.7 (22)	0.0 (27)	0.0 (22)	0.0 (20)
Rivers and harbors						
For:	83.3% (6)	90.9% (11)	90.0% (10)	9.1% (11)	0.0% (9)	33.3% (3)
Against:	14.3 (28)	5.0 (20)	10.5 (19)	0.0 (22)	0.0 (21)	0.0 (21)
Pacific railroad						
For:	36.4% (11)	50.0% (12)	45.5% (11)	0.0% (13)	0.0% (11)	0.0% (9)
Against:	19.4 (31)	16.0 (25)	22.7 (22)	0.0 (24)	0.0 (24)	0.0 (21)

*Percentage of representatives voting for or against specific development measures who also supported a coercive response to secession on indicated measures.

Source: Analysis of roll call data.

In the North, congressional support for an aggressive response to secession was very broad and deep, but even here the relationship between internal development and union sentiment was strong (see Table 2.7). Again positions on the tariff, rivers and harbors, and the Pacific railroad are the best predictors of subsequent attitudes on coercion. More than 90 percent of congressmen supporting these internal development bills backed each proposal for repression; the one exception arose when only 89.9 percent of those who had previously supported agricultural colleges later voted to table the December 31 resolution opposing coercion. Opponents of internal development never matched the enthusiasm with which supporters embraced repression and, in fact, cast more than half their votes against coercion on the last three unionist initiatives.

These patterns outline the close connection between the Republican program for the national political economy and nationalist resistance to secession in the House of Representatives. Though mediated to some extent by party organizations, congressional support for both internal development and an aggressive federal response to secession tied advantage in the national political economy (the ability to impose favorable policies) to nationalist unionism. The flip side of that connection, of course, is that the bitterest opponents of the Republican program were secessionists; they had become nationalists within an alternative political system.

Northern nationalism was built on the tariff–homestead axis within the Republican party. The party's firm commitment to the tariff was evident in the intense bargaining for the speakership of the House and in the broad consensus within party ranks on passage. Though Republicans had their eye on Pennsylvania and New Jersey votes in the 1860 presidential election when constructing the tariff plank in the Chicago platform, the commitment of the party cannot be called "tentative."[135] The process by which homestead yeoman agriculture, abolition of slavery, and industrial protection came together within the Republican program for the national political economy was paralleled by the development of an ideology that reconciled these demands in one coherent vision. The southern plantation economy was the major target of these trends. Nothing in the Republican program suggested any internal (to the party or, more broadly speaking, to the North) restraint on the expanding demands

135. Eric Foner's term, *Free Soil, Free Labor, Free Men*, pp. 175–6. Foner, however, later returns to a stronger theme, pp. 191–2. Also see Rhodes, *History of the United States*, vol. 2, pp. 478–80; James L. Huston, "A Political Response to Industrialism: The Republican Embrace of Protectionist Labor Doctrines," *Journal of American History* 70 (June 1983): 35–57.

Table 2.7. *Relationship between free-state support for internal development and opposition to secession*

Representatives voting for internal development proposals	Response to secession*					
	Coercive resistance	Militia oath	Troops in D.C.	Call up militia	Collection of duties	Censure secretary
Tariff						
For:	92.3% (65)	97.7% (88)	98.7% (78)	97.7% (88)	96.5% (85)	92.6% (81)
Against:	60.0 (15)	80.0 (10)	88.9 (9)	30.8 (13)	35.7 (14)	23.1 (13)
Agricultural colleges						
For:	89.8% (59)	98.7% (78)	100.0% (75)	97.5% (80)	96.1% (77)	91.7% (72)
Against:	58.8 (17)	76.5 (17)	61.5 (13)	38.9 (18)	42.9 (14)	37.5 (16)
Steamboat passenger bill						
For:	88.1% (59)	90.0% (60)	95.2% (63)	81.8% (66)	84.5% (58)	78.3% (60)
Against:	61.5 (13)	91.3 (23)	91.7 (24)	80.8 (26)	79.2 (24)	77.8 (18)
Rivers and harbors						
For:	91.2% (68)	97.4% (78)	97.5% (80)	96.4% (84)	94.0% (84)	92.5% (80)
Against:	66.7 (6)	87.5 (8)	70.0 (10)	41.7 (12)	25.0 (8)	22.2 (9)
Pacific railroad						
For:	86.4% (59)	95.0% (60)	94.0% (67)	84.1% (69)	84.4% (64)	78.3% (60)
Against:	73.7 (19)	91.3 (23)	95.2 (21)	75.0 (24)	81.8 (22)	79.2 (24)

*Percentage of representatives voting for or against specific development measures who also supported a coercive response to secession on indicated measures.

Source: Analysis of roll call data by author.

of settlers, abolitionists, or industrialists.[136] Even if the South had entered the bidding for the support of one of these groups (which it refused to do), leaders of the slave-state forces could not have outbid northern competitors within the Republican umbrella organization.

The American state in the secession crisis

In 1860 the weak American state did not have the will or capacity to play a mediating role between the great free- and slave-state sections. Restricted to a very few functions such as the collection of customs duties and delivery of the mail, the federal government contained no statist-bureaucratic element that could prepare for the secession crisis. The best approximation to such a bureaucratic statism, able to rise above sectional particularism and to respond soley to the imperatives of state preservation, should have been the American military. Here the most important unit was the United States Army, led for the last nineteen years by General-in-Chief Winfield Scott. But Scott, instead of taking steps that would have minimized the debilitating effects of southern resignations on the officer corps and seeking to maintain the neutrality of the military, urged that Buchanan's secretary of war accept the separation of the South as an accomplished fact because, compared to "the laceration and despotism of the sword," a lesser evil would be to allow the fragments of "the great Republic to form themselves into new Confederacies." This letter was written just before Lincoln's election. On the day before Lincoln's inaugural, Scott wrote William Seward, the new secretary of state, that the best attitude for the administration to take toward secession should be to say "wayward sisters, depart in peace."[137]

Even so, Scott's attitude toward secession was more statist than the near treasonable stances of cabinet officers within the Buchanan administration. The secretary of war, John Floyd of Virginia, was viewed as so sympathetic to the South that the state of South Carolina asked him to deliver a shipment of "rifle muskets with sword bayonets" only eight days before the state was to secede from the Union. (The secretary replied that he had no authority to comply with the request.[138]) On the day South Carolina seceded, Floyd ordered the delivery of 124 ten-inch Columbiad

---

136. The best account of the growth of the Republican coalition is Foner's *Free Soil, Free Labor, Free Men,* especially pp. 13, 28–9, 36–7, 133.

137. Anonymous, *Mr. Buchanan's Administration,* pp. 99–101; Glover, *Pre–Civil War Compromise Efforts,* p. 30.

138. William Porcher Miles, the congressman through whom South Carolina made the request, subsequently left for the state secession convention. *New York Times,* December 13, 1860. For southern attempts to repeal the law blocking the transfer of arms, see December 20, 1860.

cannons to forts in Mississippi and Texas from the Alleghany Arsenal in Pittsburgh, Pennsylvania. Only after public protests, threats of mob interdiction of the shipment, and congressional intervention did Buchanan countermand Floyd's order.[139] On December 29, the *Troy Arena* reported that the secretary had ordered the Watervliet Arsenal to ship ten thousand muskets to Georgia and these guns had headed South on December 14.[140] The activities of the secretary of war were only part of what the *New York Times* termed "uncontradicted" reports of a disunion plot within the cabinet.[141] Centered around the secretary of the treasury, Howell Cobb of Georgia, the reports led many – Stephen Douglas among them – to fear a southern conspiracy to take over the capital and occupy the government with the open connivance of the outgoing administration.[142]

Even the highest levels of the military bureaucracy were compromised by disloyalty. On the day before Lincoln's inauguration, General-in-Chief Winfield Scott held a conference in which he and his staff discussed security arrangements including the disposition of troops. That night, after drafting a record of the meeting and orders for the positioning of troops, Scott's secretary resigned his commission and departed for the South carrying this sensitive information with him.[143] President Buchanan himself believed both, on the one hand, that no state could secede and, on the other hand, that the federal government did not have the authority to use force to prevent disunion. Presiding over a squabbling cabinet of traitorous Southerners and bellicose Northerners, the president attempted only to prevent an outbreak of hostilities before the Lincoln administration relieved him of further responsibility.[144] While his attitude toward the central government was not disloyal, his leadership was nonetheless ambivalent and ineffective.

Responsibility for the interests of the central government during this period fell primarily on Seward, Lincoln's designated secretary of state, and the Republican leadership of the House of Representatives. Pitts-

---

139. *New York Times*, December 25, 26, 27, 28, 1860; Wright, *Secession Movement*, p. 160; Nevins, *Emergence of Lincoln*, vol. 2, p. 375. Later that year, after he had returned to the South, Floyd was publicly praised as a Confederate patriot. *1861 American Cyclopaedia*, p. 124.
140. Cited in the *New York Times*, December 29, 1860. For more on the distribution of arms to the South during 1860, see *1861 American Cyclopaedia*, p. 123.
141. October 26, 30; November 6, 1860.
142. Nevins, *Emergence of Lincoln*, vol. 2, p. 293; Seward, *Seward at Washington*, vol. 2, pp. 487, 490–1, 497, 513–14; Bancroft, *Life of William H. Seward*, vol. 2, p. 20; Henry Adams, *The Great Secession Winter of 1860–1861 and Other Essays* (New York: A. S. Barnes, 1963), pp. 1–32.
143. Seward, *Seward at Washington*, vol. 2, pp. 514–15.
144. Anonymous, *Mr. Buchanan's Administration*, pp. 125–8; Nevins, *Emergence of Lincoln*, vol. 2, pp. 341–2, 361.

burgh's congressman turned to the chairman of the House Committee on Military Affairs, for example, during the uproar over cannon shipments from the Alleghany Arsenal. But, even though the Republicans controlled the House and steadily gained influence in the Senate as southern senators resigned, neither chamber was capable of directing a bureaucratic counteroffensive to the secessionist campaign.[145] Given the disarray within the highest political councils of the government, centralized direction and coordination of federal installations throughout the nation rapidly deteriorated. Operations in these installations often, particularly in the South, began to take on a surreal character.[146]

During this period, Seward was a central figure around whom federal loyalists could rally. Though his apparently sincere efforts to reach a compromise were hamstrung by Lincoln's refusal to yield on territorial questions, the New York senator presented a conciliatory attitude even as he gave expression to a comprehensive "statism."[147] Dwelling on a vision of America's potential greatness, preeminent influence in the world community of nations, and problems of national security, Seward could neither prevent the absorption of post offices and district courts into the

145. On Republican gains in the Senate, see Rhodes, *History of the United States,* vol. 2, p. 312, and the reorganization of committees reported in *Congressional Globe* 36:2:536, January 24, 1861. Those Southerners who remained were often openly hostile to any effort to preserve the Union. During debate on a naval appropriations bill, for example, Roger Pryor of Virginia swore he would "sink" the navy "in the abyss of the ocean before I would grant it a farthing." *Congressional Globe* 36:2:346, January 12, 1861.
146. In the Gosport, Virginia navy yard, for example, the "disturbed condition of the country during the early months of 1861 did not put a stop to the work of improvement and repairs at the yards. Everything went on, under the current appropriations, as if no interruption was anticipated; though at the same time those of the inhabitants who favored the secession movement were actively preparing for civil war. Men were organized into companies and drilled on every hand. Officers of the Navy resigned their commissions – some as the States in which they resided passed the so-called ordinances of secession, others on their arrival in the United States from abroad, and many of those who remained in the service to the last moment talked rebellion in greater or less degree; and for a time it was difficult for commanding officers or for the Department to know exactly upon whom to rely. It was, therefore, not at all strange that the veteran officer in command at Gosport yard should not only have been very ill-advised but that the dangers surrounding his position should have been greatly exaggerated; and particularly was he cautioned by his counselors against committing any act which being regarded as hostile, should 'inaugurate civil war!' " Edward P. Lull, *History of the United States Navy-Yard at Gosport, Virginia* (Washington: Government Printing Office, 1874), p. 45. Federal officers later deserted when Confederate forces captured the yard. Ibid., pp. 50–9.
147. *Congressional Globe* 36:2:341–4, January 12, 1861. For other examples of Republican nationalist sentiment, see John Sherman's speech during debate on the army appropriation bill, 36:2:450–6, January 18, 1861, and Senator Ben Wade's address, 36:2:99–104, December 17, 1860.

new Confederacy nor forge an effective response to this challenge to federal sovereignty.

From the sidelines, president-elect Lincoln made his own views known in a letter to the editor of the *New York Courier and Examiner*: "I think we should hold the forts, or retake them, as the case may be, and collect the revenue. We shall have to forgo the use of the federal courts, and they that of the mails, for a while. We cannot fight them into holding courts, or receiving the mails. This is an outline of my view; and perhaps suggests sufficiently, the whole of it."[148] While apparently restrained, Lincoln's recommendations would have meant the opening of civil war. By this time, federal officials could neither retake southern forts nor collect customs duties in South Carolina without the use of military force. In fact, even Republican nationalists did not want the outgoing administration to undertake such aggressive ventures. Lincoln and his advisors sought only to stiffen the Buchanan administration's response to secession so that central state authority didn't dissolve altogether before inauguration day, to ensure an orderly transfer of power to the new administration (at least in the capital and in the North), and to assure the border states of Republican solicitude for their interests during the crisis.[149] When March 4 finally arrived, control of the central state was transferred from South to North, from slave state to free, and the federal government was infused with northern nationalism.

Statism and breaking the deadlock in the national political economy

If the statist program for the national political economy is defined solely as the maximization of central state authority (and not necessarily the promotion of dominant group interests), then the statist program for resolving conflict over slavery included: (1) regulation of slave importation into the United States; (2) federal intervention in the territories; (3) striking down efforts by the individual states in the North to frustrate operation of the fugitive slave law; and (4) opposition to any compromise measure that limited central state authority (such as an unrepealable constitutional clause protecting slavery). The first two points in this program were neutral toward slavery; the central government could regulate slave importation by either prohibiting or encouraging the traffic and could intervene in the territories by banning, regulating, or protecting slavery. The third point would advantage slavery by ensuring unham-

---

148. Dated December 29, 1860, and quoted in Stampp, *Imperiled Union*, pp. 169–70.
149. Potter, *Lincoln and His Party*, p. 251.

pered federal execution of the fugitive slave law, while the last would operate against slavery by denying the institution any federal guarantee that came at the expense of central state authority.[150] These four points described a general program that moved toward a comprehensive, state-centered regulation of slavery throughout the national political economy. Such a program would be unambiguously statist in that it would expand central state authority and create a state-centered position from which sectional competition might be managed.

No major group in antebellum American society was interested in the entire program. The Republican party approached the statist ideal by proposing to prohibit slave importation (as was already done), to prohibit slavery in the territories, and to oppose most compromise measures that limited central state discretion. The Republican position on personal liberty laws was ambiguous but a majority of the party at least gave lip service to their repeal. Likewise, slave-state members could support regulation of slave importation, a territorial slave code, and a prohibition of personal liberty laws. In view of their increasing isolation in American society, however, slave-state congressmen could not forgo constitutional guarantees. Douglas Democrats were comparatively hostile to the federal government, advocating "popular sovereignty" in the territories and passage of almost every compromise measure proposed in either chamber. This conception of the central state's role in internal development left the fate of the nation up to the fortunes of electoral politics in extremely small and isolated frontier communities. No theory of state development could easily accommodate such an abdication.

Confronted with the existence of Mormon polygamy in the Territory of Utah, for example, Douglas Democrats were forced by their popular sovereignty position to assert that Congress had no right to override the territorial legislature (which had expressed the popular will by legitimating polygamy). Because this interpretation apparently committed

150. On the operation of federal policy, see Stanley W. Campbell, *The Slave Catchers: Enforcement of the Fugitive Slave Law, 1850–1860* (Chapel Hill: University of North Carolina Press, 1970). The Virginia legislature reported that every New England state, Pennsylvania, New York, New Jersey, Michigan, and Wisconsin prohibited public officials or citizens from aiding execution of the federal fugitive slave law. Five of these also denied the use of public buildings to any master seeking to return a slave, seven provided legal defence to the fugitive, three declared the slave free if brought into the state by the master, and New Hampshire declared any slave free unconditionally. *Congressional Globe* 36:1:1828, April 23, 1860. On December 17, 1860, the House of Representatives approved a resolution condemning personal liberty laws and recommending their repeal (153 to 14). For the most extreme proposed restriction of central government authority over slavery, see the constitutional amendment proposed by Emerson Etheridge of Tennessee. *Congressional Globe* 36:2:279, January 7, 1861. Also see a resolution passed February 11, 1861, 36:2:857.

them to a defense of polygamy (a suicidal political position), the Douglas Democrats suggested that the territory be divided in half and that the two pieces be separately attached to Nevada and what later became Colorado. Settlers in the two territories could then change the popular will of the Mormon community (by outvoting Brigham Young's follow- ers) and thus prohibit polygamy where the federal government could not.[151]

Slave-state congressmen also wanted to prohibit multiple wives, but their theory of the state was only slightly less convoluted. Some argued that Congress could not act at all because the federal government had no authority to enact and enforce criminal law in the territories. They noted that nothing in the Constitution provided such power.[152] For them, the territories constituted a loophole unanticipated by that document. A few argued that their interpretation still allowed congressional protection for slavery in the territories because slavery was, in some sense, recognized by the Constitution (see below).

Many more slave-state members contended that Congress had the power to prohibit polygamy because all the states in the Union did so and the federal government could act as the collective agent of the states.[153] Conversely, they maintained that Congress could not prohibit slavery because fifteen states supported the institution. In fact, Congress could enact a slave code because slaves-as-property were recognized by the Constitution and because all states must honor "contracts" executed

151. *Congressional Globe* 36:1:1515, April 3, 1860.
152. *Congressional Globe* 36:1:1410, March 28, 1860; *Appendix to the Congressional Globe* 36:1:195–8, April 4, 1860.
153. Roger Pryor's rendition of this slave state position is worth examining: "In the interest of slavery, I repudiate the suggestion that its rights in the Territories may be impaired by any legitimate act of Federal legislation. The authority of Congress over the Territories is exclusive, but not absolute, being restricted by the nature of its trust and the principles of the Constitution. The Territories are the common property of the States, and the power of Congress over them cannot be perverted to the partial advantage of any section . . . its exclusion by Congress from the Federal territory would be in flagrant derogation of the rights of the South and the equitable spirit of the Constitution. . . . But polygamy enjoys no such recognition and no such protection. It is not only unknown to the Constitution but is repugnant to every principle of republican government. It does not exist in any State; but, on the contrary, is prohibited by penal enactment, in every State of the Union. Hence I affirm that its suppression in the Territories by the direct agency of Congress would promote the established policy of the States. . . . There is, then, no association, no alliance, no analogy between polygamy and slavery; and the prohibition of the one system by an exertion of Federal power in no way impairs the security of the other." *Congressional Globe* 36:1:1496, April 2, 1860. Emerson Etheridge called Pryor's position "the late edition of the Democratic catechism, to wit: that every citizen who goes into the Territories carries with him the laws of his domicile – in other words, that every southern man who carries a slave into the Territories carries also with him the slave laws of the State whence he emigrates." Ibid. 36:1:1498.

within any of the states, a position that found succor in the Dred Scott decision.[154] Though this position reconciled hostility to polygamy with the promotion of slavery without conceding to Congress a right to prohibit the latter (no mean accomplishment), the slave-state theory was fraught with difficulties. The existing states, for example, regulated economic and social activity in many more and diverse ways than slavery and marriage. Nothing in this theory specified how coherent territorial regulation could be developed, say on the establishment of banks, out of this diversity.

The Gordian knot tied by the Douglas and slave-state Democrats was left to the nationalist Republicans. As early as 1856, the party platform had asserted "That the Constitution confers upon Congress sovereign power over the Territories of the United States for their government, and that in the exercise of the power it is both the right and duty of Congress to prohibit in the territories those twin relics of barbarism – polygamy and slavery." The Republican solution to the territorial knot, unqualified national sovereignty, was integrated, in turn, with a program intended to reinforce northern hegemony.[155]

Because northern nationalists and southern separatists so completely divided the terrain of the antebellum political system, no purely statist program could develop the anemic apparatus of the federal government. The central government had no identity apart from that imparted by the sectional forces that occupied the seat of power. While a more developed state might have been able to turn a brokering position between hostile sectional alliances into an opportunity for bureaucratic expansion and insulation from electoral influence, in the actual case the first priority for those who wished to strengthen the central state had to be to break the deadlock between free labor and slavery interests by conferring hegemony upon one or the other. The rapid demographic and economic expansion of the North, as well as the party's relatively statist program, heavily tilted the decision toward the Republicans. Compromise with the South could only have weakened, perhaps irretrievably, the authority and le-

---

154. *Appendix to the Congressional Globe* 36:1:249, April 23, 1860. Over half of the pages in Greeley and Cleveland's *Political Textbook for 1860* were devoted to summaries of the debate over extension of slavery into the territories (particularly Kansas).

155. Douglas believed that the Republicans so aggressively pursued the territorial question because they actively desired southern secession in order to secure "a permanent Republican ascendancy in the Northern States." Johannsen, ed., *Letters of Stephen Douglas,* pp. 504–5. All 108 voting Republicans supported a federal prohibition of polygamy; 18 of 21 American party members from the South and 6 of 7 Anti-Lecompton Democrats did so as well. Only 22 of 78 Administration Democrats supported the bill and almost all of these were Northerners. *Congressional Globe* 36:1:1853, April 24, 1860.

gitimacy of the central government and retarded northern economic development. Without guarantees for slavery and even with them, Republican control of the central state doomed slavery to an early end.[156]

The most important barrier to expansion of the central state in the last antebellum years was southern separatism, not because the South was philosophically hostile to central state power (as the Confederate experience was to demonstrate), but because a successful defense of the interests of plantation slavery ensured continued stalemate over control of the national political economy. In an odd way, then, secession itself was an enormously facilitating event in American state formation because disunion ensured the identification of the Republican party with the central state and brought on a massive enlargement of governmental authority in the North. When the South seceded, the central state, the Republican party, and the imperatives of northern political economy became inextricably intertwined. From this point until the end of Reconstruction, the interests of state expansion and the Republican party were almost synonymous.

Returning to the two questions with which this chapter began, we can now answer that the South seceded because the impending shift in control of the central state portended permanent subordination of the interests of the cotton South within the national political economy, as well as

156. This chapter has proposed an interpretation of secession and the Civil War that is, in many respects, similar to Barrington Moore's evaluation of the conflict as "The Last Capitalist Revolution." *Social Origins of Dictatorship and Democracy: Lord and Peasant in the Making of the Modern World* (Boston: Beacon Press, 1967), ch. 3. Moore, however, tends to slight state-centered factors such as the very real threat Republican control of the American state posed to the social and economic underpinnings of slavery. The Republican program for the national political economy not only promised to accelerate northern expansion but would have also further encouraged the already rapid penetration of market capitalist relations into the South. In addition, while abolitionists were a minority within the party, achievement of even a limited antislavery program almost certainly would have led the Republicans to escalate their attacks on the institution. Such an escalation would have both justified the party's continued existence and provided a broad rationale for the agrarian–industrial coalition whenever economic issues needed support. Under these conditions, the question is not Moore's "Why did the South secede?" but, rather, "Why should the South have remained in the Union?" On the other hand, Moore readily concedes the economic argument for the Republican program and East–West coalition. What he neglects to consider is the state-centered, national-unity reasons why the North chose to repress southern separatism. As Moore saw it, once secession occurred, war was inevitable; the northern decision to conquer the South did not require an explanation. In place of the more political and state-centered interpretations offered here, he proposes a more sociological emphasis on differences between the "bourgeois" North and "aristocratic" South that does not, strictly speaking, seem necessary and may very well be misleading. As will be discussed in the next chapter, for example, the Confederate state contained very little that could be described as "aristocratic" and, in fact, began existence as a near carbon copy of the one in the North.

increasingly hostile policies toward the institution of slavery. Tactical compromise within the framework of the Union promised only a postponement of subordination and attacks on slavery while accelerating northern economic expansion. On the other side of the ledger, few reasons for continued allegiance to a northern-dominated Union existed. The antebellum central state was so small that disengagement from the federal apparatus was a simple matter. No powerful competing nation would threaten either a northern or southern state on the North American continent. And the interests of the South and North in the future direction of the national political economy were so antithetical as to be irreconcilable over the long term.

The North suppressed secession because the separation of the South would have weakened, perhaps irremediably, bonds between the remaining states of the Union. In addition, loss of the South would have created a new political economy in which the basis of the Republican-led alliance of eastern industry and western yeoman agriculture would have rapidly dissolved as the two wings of the party struggled over the competing interests of industrial expansion and agricultural settlement. Thus, both national and party cohesion required suppression. The combination of southern secession and northern suppression led to the establishment of two strong central states within the territory previously occupied by the antebellum federal government. In the following chapter, we turn to a comparison of these Union and Confederate states and again link their characteristics and policies to their respective political economies.

3

War mobilization
and state formation
in the northern Union
and southern Confederacy

Part I: Introduction and overview

Prior to 1861, no nation had attempted a full mobilization of a society's material and human resources. The American Civil War brought forth two such mobilizations and, by twentieth-century standards, was thus the first modern war.[1] Comparison of these two mobilizations – one directed in the North by the Union, the other in the South by the Confederacy – provides the basis for understanding the connection between northern economic development and the rapid construction of the American party-state both during and after the Civil War. Study of the Union war effort demonstrates its dependence upon unregulated capitalist markets and industrial production. The northern war effort left the industrial and agricultural sectors almost untouched by central state controls and only skimmed the surface of northern labor pools with the draft (although

1. See, for example, Marvin A. Kreidberg and Merton G. Henry, *History of Military Mobilization in the United States Army, 1775–1945* (Washington, D.C.: U.S. Department of the Army, 1955), p. 83; Jay Luvaas, *The Military Legacy of the Civil War: The European Inheritance* (Lawrence: University of Kansas Press, 1988; reprint of 1959 edition), pp. 203–33. The American Civil War is commonly conceded to have been the largest military conflict in the world between 1815 and 1914. Cyril Black, *The Dynamics of Modernization* (New York: Harper & Row, 1966), p. 111. Although the Napoleonic Wars rivaled the American Civil War in magnitude (as measured by numbers of troops), European mobilization efforts did not attempt full-scale logistical support of field armies and, thus, did not involve a full subordination of the national economy to central state control. See, for example, Samuel E. Finer, "State- and Nation-Building in Europe: The Role of the Military," in Charles Tilly, ed., *The Formation of National States in Western Europe* (Princeton, N.J.: Princeton University Press, 1975), pp. 144–55. The major difference between the two conflicts that enabled a much more comprehensive economic mobilization in the American Civil War was the development and utilization of the railroad in military supply. Edward Hagerman, *The American Civil War and the Origins of Modern Warfare: Ideas, Organization, and Field Command* (Bloomington: Indiana University Press, 1988), pp. xi–xii.

military recruitment of volunteers through bounties and other incentives mobilized huge numbers of men). The only sector to feel the full force of central state authority was the financial system. There the war effort stimulated the emergence of an American class of finance capitalists free from European dominance and restructured capital markets by replacing gold bullion with Union greenbacks as the basic unit of monetary exchange. Both of these changes brought the United States Treasury into a much more intimate and influential relationship with the nation's capital markets and the financial system generally. The Union state was strongest, however, not on its home territory in the North but in the construction and execution of policies intended to subjugate and pacify the rebellious South. These policies – abolition of slavery, reconstruction of the southern political economy, and direct military rule – were the most state-enhancing measures for the North during the war.

In terms of the mobilization of national material and manpower resources, however, it was the Confederate state, not the market-oriented state of the Union, that was by many measures the modern response to the political economic challenge of war. Thrown up in a matter of months by the agrarian, economically underdeveloped South, the all-encompassing economic and social controls of the Confederacy were in fact so extensive that they call into question standard interpretations of southern opposition to the expansion of federal power in both the antebellum and post-Reconstruction periods.[2] Southern reluctance to expand federal power in those periods has been attributed variously to regional sympathy for laissez-faire principles, the "precapitalist" cultural origins of the plantation elite, and a general philosophical orientation hostile to state development.[3] When the impressive ambitions and

---

2. Some of the material in this chapter originally appeared in "Southern Leviathan: The Development of Central State Authority in the Confederate States of America," Karen Orren and Stephen Skowronek, eds., *Studies in American Political Development*, vol. 2 (New Haven, Conn.: Yale University Press, 1987), pp. 68–136. Among those who have also stressed the strength of the Confederate state are Curtis Arthur Amlund, *Federalism in the Southern Confederacy* (Washington, D.C.: Public Affairs Press, 1966); Louise B. Hill, *State Socialism in the Confederate States of America*, (Charlottesville, Va.: Historical Publishing, 1936); and Raimondo Luraghi, "The Civil War and the Modernization of American Society," *Civil War History* 18 (September 1972): 230–50. See also Richard E. Beringer, Herman Hattaway, Archer Jones, and William N. Still, Jr., *Why the South Lost the Civil War* (Athens: University of Georgia Press, 1986), ch. 1.

3. On the ideological "world view" of the southern plantation elite, see, for example, Eugene Genovese, who contends that "the Southern world" was characterized by a "premodern quality...imparted to it by its dominant slaveholding class" and that the "planters" who composed this class "were not mere capitalists; they were pre-capitalist, quasi-aristocratic landowners who had to adjust their economy and ways of thinking to a capitalist world market" in order to sell their produce. *The Political Economy of Slavery: Studies in the Economy and Society of the Slave South* (New York: Vintage,

achievements of the Confederate state are recognized, however, such explanations of southern hostility to the expansion of federal power seem, at best, incomplete. It would appear that the South's opposition to the North's industrial and commercial policies provided the impetus for both the region's opposition to a strong American state in the Union and support for a centralized Confederate regime after secession. Southern support for a strong Confederate and a weak American state (before and after the Civil War until the end of Reconstruction) can thus be viewed as a consistent strategy intended to minimize the anticipated deleterious impact of the northern industrial program on the plantation South.[4]

Questions of state strength aside, a second lesson to be learned from the American Civil War involves the relationship between the economic base and the form of state organization. War mobilizations compel states to extract a much larger share of a society's resources than are usually collected through peacetime taxation. The resulting efforts to channel resources and manpower into war force states to exploit many more sources of revenue more completely than they would during peacetime. As a consequence, the search for new and more productive revenue sources during war encourages central states to reshape their taxation policies ever more closely to the form of societal production. While a state at peace may leave many sectors and activities untouched and con- centrate levies on luxuries such as liquor and tobacco, a state at war is often compelled to extract revenue from almost all areas of societal

1967), pp. 3, 23. Barrington Moore describes the antebellum South as a "capitalist civilization... but hardly a bourgeois one" characterized by a "defense of hereditary privilege." *Social Origins of Dictatorship and Democracy: Lord and Peasant in the Making of the Modern World* (Boston: Beacon Press, 1966), p. 121. Eric Foner labels the South as one of the two "great pre-modern cultures within American society" (along with Irish immigrants), *Politics and Ideology in the Age of the Civil War* (New York: Oxford University Press, 1980), p. 26. For a dissent from these interpretations of the South as "precapitalist" or "premodern," see Edward Pessen, "How Different from Each Other Were the Antebellum North and South?" *American Historical Review* 85 (December 1980): 1145–7.

4. After the end of Reconstruction southern resistance to northern economic penetration increasingly assumed the form of support for central state regulation of national cor- porations (railroad rates and antitrust legislation). This backing for a stronger central state role in the economy was, of course, very different from the Republican program for the nationalization of markets and subsidization of northern economic expansion. For evidence of the continuity of southern opposition to northern economic policy, see Richard Franklin Bensel, *Sectionalism and American Political Development, 1880– 1980* (Madison: University of Wisconsin Press, 1984) chs. 3–6. Also see Robert Royal Russel, *Economic Aspects of Southern Sectionalism 1840–1861* (New York: Russell and Russell, 1960), p. 166, and Elizabeth Sanders, "Industrial Concentration, Sectional Competition, and Antitrust Politics in America, 1880–1980," in Orren and Skowronek, eds., *Studies in American Political Development*, vol. 1 (1986): 142–214.

production, thus molding the state apparatus in a way that complements and exploits the strengths and organizing structures of economic activity. When the necessary requirements of a war effort lie well within the material capacity of a society, capitalist states can rely upon voluntary, open-market contracts for military supplies and manpower. A reliance on voluntary transactions for men and materiel molds the war mobilization to available societal resources by drawing first upon the marginal productive capacity of an economy and labor pools. Since these transactions are voluntary, the war effort both guarantees a rate of return high enough to encourage new investment in war production and leaves relatively untouched other sectors with higher rates of return.

On the revenue side, the fit between a capitalist state at war and the organizing structures of the economic system may be even closer. When war requirements fall well within the material capacity of a society, a capitalist state can extract revenue from the self-renewing stream of transactions and commerce through which economic activity is carried out. The state molds the revenue system to the organizing structures of the economy by adjusting the rate of extraction to the carrying capacity of the various sectors and locating state extraction at the most visible, easily monitored points in the stream of commerce. In a wealthy state at war, the government has several related objectives: to raise the maximum amount of revenue possible, to preserve the flow of commerce subject to taxation (for example, by avoiding tax rates so high as to destroy production or markets), and to maintain the visibility of markets and production (for example, by avoiding rates so high as to drive robust markets into underground, unmonitored black markets). In these ways, then, wealthy capitalist states at war are brought into a much closer relationship with the societal forms of production and markets.

Only when efforts to harness existing productive potential are not sufficient to meet the challenge presented by the enemy do states attempt to innovate or go beyond the prewar forms of societal production. In terms of material capacity and manpower potential, the Union did not face such a challenge in the Civil War and the war effort became a more-or-less capitalist, market-oriented response to the requirements of mobilization, well within the potential of northern society and well molded into its forms and structures.[5] By contrast, the Confederate war effort far outstripped the productive capabilities of the prewar economy and compelled a much more innovative, almost futuristic mobilization of

5. For a parallel, somewhat broader logic undergirding European state formation, see Charles Tilly, "States, Coercion, and Capital," *Center for Studies of Social Change Working Paper Series*, no. 75, July 1988, pp. 15–21.

resources. As a consequence, the southern mobilization was far more state-centered and coordinated than its northern counterpart.[6]

Yet another lesson can be drawn from the relationships of both wartime states to their social bases. In an explosive burst of governmental creativity and activism, both states expanded their administrative bureaucracies and associated powers. Because their respective social bases were so different (the industrial, free-labor organization of northern society stood in stark contrast to the agrarian, slave-labor plantation system of the South), comparison of the state-building experience in the two nations provides an important opportunity to study the influence of social development on state formation. What makes this opportunity unique is the fact that the two nations created their respective states almost from scratch and were thus compelled, within a short span of time, to decide questions of organizational structure and authority across the full breadth of potential state activity. As if this were not enough, these two American states began their wartime expansion with almost identical formal constitutional structures in which a president, a congress, local governments of limited sovereignty, elections, and other aspects were assigned almost identical roles. No two independent states in the history of the world have ever possessed more similar formal political systems. The similarity is particularly striking during the crucial early months of the war; later both the Union and Confederacy would move to shape the form and quality of societal influence in ways that reflected increasingly divergent state-building trajectories.

The core of the evidence presented in this chapter is an analysis of the most important state-building decisions in the Confederate and Union congresses. A majority of these decisions presented almost identical questions of state organization and authority to Civil War legislators, the delegated representatives of their respective social bases. Other decisions represent areas in which one of the respective states moved further along a statist dimension than did the other. In both policy areas, the organization and performance of the two states are compared.

The strength and effectiveness of the two states were determined by

6. The interpretation put forward here assumes little preexisting state-centered orientation on the part of the participants in Union or Confederate public life. As Stephen Skowronek has observed, state building in America has been, at best, a haphazard process in which most of the participants have not comprehended the statist implications of what they were doing. *Building a New American State: The Expansion of National Administrative Capacities, 1877–1920* (Cambridge: Cambridge University Press, 1982). During the American Civil War and particularly in the Confederacy, this process was even more haphazard than it would become in the late-nineteenth-century United States. The South did not have a natural reform elite such as the one that emerged from the cultural and financial centers of the Northeast, nor did the region have the leisure to contemplate state-building proposals as an integrated program.

their wartime needs. These needs differed; for example, the Union experienced more serious internal social division but could afford to fight a "guns and butter" war, while a more united Confederacy was forced to mount a full mobilization of its society. The comparative strength of the two central state structures is best measured, however, against an ideal "executive/bureaucratic" conception of state enhancement in which contextual factors are downplayed (see the discussion of the theoretical framework below).[7]

Early Union and Confederate state development

In creating the administrative apparatus necessary to orchestrate the southern war effort, the Confederate state started from scratch. The Union, while only a little better organized, possessed at least an administrative shell. Moving rapidly, the Confederacy had, by the beginning of hostilities, provisionally adopted all then-existing U.S. laws until "altered or repealed," as well as a Confederate Constitution which was almost identical to the U.S. framework. In addition, the southern branches of the federal bureaucracy had been absorbed intact and the administrative departments of the Confederacy unabashedly mimicked their northern counterparts. These choices made the new Confederate state almost a carbon copy of the Union government left behind in Washington.[8] Where the South deviated from the

7. This interpretation of Union and Confederate experience tacitly assumes that a government designed in accord with commonly held statist principles is the most effective way to mobilize resources in a war. See, for example, Alan S. Milward, *War, Economy and Society: 1939–1945* (Berkeley: University of California Press, 1979), especially chs. 1–3. Obviously, this axiom should be most stringently applied to the inherently weaker of the parties involved in military conflict; the stronger side may pursue both guns and butter and still win a war (as did the Union). In fact, the economic inferiority of the Confederacy was so great as to, in and of itself, impose limits on central state development. For a general comparison of the Union and Confederate war mobilizations that emphasizes the respective material capacities of the two societies, see Roger L. Ransom, *Conflict and Compromise: The Political Economy of Slavery, Emancipation, and the American Civil War* (New York: Cambridge University Press, 1989), pp. 172–215.

8. A comparison of the texts of the two constitutions is provided in Jefferson Davis, *The Rise and Fall of the Confederate Government*, vol. 1 (New York: Thomas Yoseloff; reprint 1958), appendix K. On Confederate adoption of U.S. laws, see Wilfred Buck Yearns, *The Confederate Congress* (Athens: University of Georgia Press, 1960), pp. 32, 36. The rules and organization of the Confederate Congress were also largely taken from procedures used in the North (pp. 34–5). On similarities between Confederate and Union administrative design, see Paul P. Van Riper and Harry N. Scheiber, "The Confederate Civil Service," *Journal of Southern History* 25 (November 1959): 448–70. Robert C. Black described the Confederate quartermaster bureau as a "photographical reproduction of the old United States organization," in *The Railroads of the Confederacy* (Chapel Hill: University of North Carolina Press, 1952), p. 50. On the

organizational model set by the United States, its innovations often strengthened administrative capacity.⁹

In the spring of 1861, Montgomery, Alabama, was filled with devoted proponents of states' rights and individual liberty, armed with a philosophical rhetoric sharpened and polished by long years passed in political combat in the halls of the federal Congress.¹⁰ Among other things, the Constitution drafted there prohibited government-subsidized internal improvements, barred a protective tariff, and allowed the legislature of an individual state, under certain circumstances, to impeach an officer of the national government. However, these and other weakening provisions turned out to be little more than cosmetic adornments. By the middle of 1862, for example, the Confederate government had practically vitiated the first two prohibitions on grounds of military necessity and no Confederate official was ever impeached.¹¹

In other areas, such as the term of office and authority of the chief executive, Confederate practice and the Constitution were more centralized than those of the Union. Although isolated phrases could be attributed to the states' rights ideology and doctrine of minimal central state power with which Southerners left the Union, other passages proved more than an adequate base for an expansion of Confederate authority into all aspects of southern life. Among the most important were a necessary and proper clause, an injunction concerning faithful execution of the laws, a modified supremacy clause, and an oath of allegiance to the Confederacy imposed upon the officers of the individual states. Much of this, as was the case for most of the document, was taken verbatim from the antebellum Constitution. Thus, although it is true that the framers of the fundamental law of the Confederacy had been opposed to "the expansive interpretation given the federal Constitution" by northern nationalists and wished to constrain similar

adoption of Union judicial practice and precedents by the Confederacy and a general account of Confederate administration, see Amlund, *Federalism in the Southern Confederacy*, pp. 65, 83, as well as ch. 6, and William M. Robinson, Jr., *Justice in Grey* (Cambridge, Mass.: Harvard University Press, 1941).

9. Noting that the Confederate Department of Justice was the first bureau of its kind in America, William Robinson also observed that it was "the first such subdivision of government in an Anglo-Saxon country.... In 1861 no department of justice existed in the United States and the attorney general simply presided over a small office consisting of one assistant and three clerks." *Justice in Grey*, p. 27.

10. About one-third (85 of 267) of all Confederate congressmen and senators had previously served in the U.S. Congress. The percentage was higher in the Senate (55 to 48 percent in the First and Second Confederate congresses) than in the House (39, 32, and 21 percent in the Provisional, First, and Second congresses, respectively). Thomas B. Alexander and Richard E. Beringer, *The Anatomy of the Confederate Congress* (Nashville, Tenn.: Vanderbilt University Press, 1972), pp. 24–5.

11. Amlund, *Federalism in the Southern Confederacy*, p. 22.

constitutional developments in the new southern nation, the most striking feature of the new framework was that it "prescribed for the Confederacy much the same kind of union which the Southerners had dissolved," a document that under the pressure of civil war proved fully as expansive as that in the North.[12]

The process by which the South absorbed and adapted federal administrative systems allowed the Confederate state to rapidly extend at least a token presence into the most remote reaches of its domain. The establishment of the Post Office Department of the Confederacy, for example, entailed tacit cooperation with the Union in the transfer of control to the southern nation, a vigorous campaign to bring federal employees into the new department, the use of federal equipment and supplies (including stamps), and the adoption, with minor changes, of the previous administrative organization of mail delivery. By 1862, the Confederate government was maintaining 8,300 local post offices, of which number 8,228 had been previously established by the U.S. government. By 1863, postal service was provided throughout the Confederacy with regular delivery to all territory under southern control (see Map 3.1).[13]

This general pattern of withdrawal from federal authority and reestablishment under the Confederacy was repeated throughout the South.[14] Federal courts, customshouses, arsenals, and lighthouses became extensions of the new Confederate state without changes in personnel or interruption of activity. Confederate courts, for example,

---

12. Amlund, *Federalism in the Southern Confederacy*, pp. 17–18 (and, generally, 17–27); Emory M. Thomas, *The Confederate Nation: 1861–1865* (New York: Harper & Row, 1979), p. 64; Charles R. Lee, Jr., *The Confederate Constitutions* (Chapel Hill: University of North Carolina Press, 1963), pp. 82–140.

13. "The Postmaster-General's Report," in *Confederate States Almanac for 1863* (Augusta, Ga.: H. C. Clarke, 1863), pp. 51–2. The Confederate Post Office Department absorbed the existing Union administration in the South without change. See Walter F. McCaleb, "The Organization of the Post Office Department of the Confederacy," *American Historical Review* 12 (October 1906): 66–74; E. Merton Coulter, *The Confederate States of America: 1861–1865* (Baton Rouge: Louisiana State University Press, 1950), pp. 125–6. For the postal routes charted in Map 3.1, see Post Office Department of the Confederacy: *Instructions to Post Masters* (Richmond, Va.: Ritchie and Dunnavant, 1861); *A List of Establishments, Discontinuances, and Changes in Name of the Post Offices in the Confederate States since 1861; Report of the Postmaster-General, April 29, 1861* (Montgomery, Ala., 1861); *Report of the Postmaster-General, November 27, 1861* (Richmond, 1861); *Advertisement of December 31, 1862, Inviting Proposals for Carrying the Mails...from July 1, 1863 to June 30, 1867* (Richmond, Va., February 28, 1862); *Report from the General Post Office Department to the Postmaster General* (Richmond, Va., November 22, 1861).

14. For a good discussion of the rapid consolidation of power in the Confederate central government, see the *1861 American Annual Cyclopaedia* (New York: D. Appleton and Company, 1873), pp. 126–37; for an itemized description of federal forts, arsenals, and lighthouses absorbed by the Confederacy, see pp. 315–23.

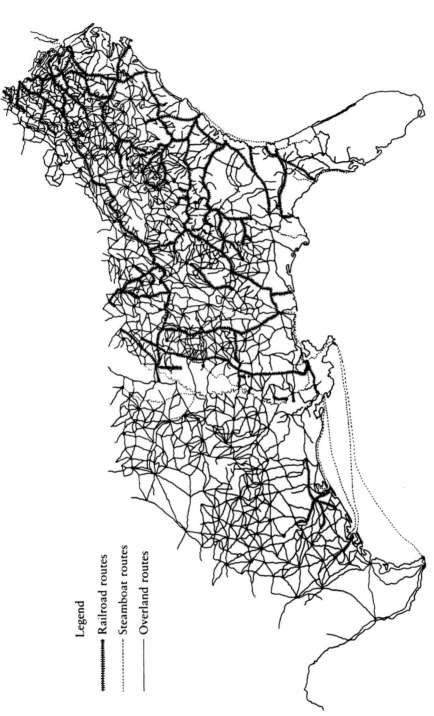

Legend

✙✙✙ Railroad routes

········ Steamboat routes

——— Overland routes

Map 3.1 The postal system of the Confederacy: Contract routes and terminals, ca. 1862–3. *Sources: Advertisement of December 31, 1862, Inviting Proposals for Carrying the Mails of the Confederate States (Florida, Georgia, South Carolina, North Carolina, and Virginia) from July 1, 1863 to June 30, 1867; Report to the Postmaster-General of the General Post Office Department (November 22, 1861); A List of Establishments, Discontinuances, and Changes in Names of the Post Offices in the Confederate States since 1861; Report of the Postmaster General to the President (February 28, 1862).*

continued to process cases that were inherited from federal dockets while the new Patent Office encouraged southern citizens to register federal patents "for the term...yet unexpired" under federal regulations.[15] The net result of all these defections and the transfer of federal installations to southern control was to replicate the administrative design of the antebellum Union throughout the Confederacy. In one of the finishing touches to this first period of rapid state formation, Confederate revenue stations were established in March 1861 at major railroad junctions and river landings where northern goods commonly entered the South.[16]

Ultimately, however, most of the bureaucratic expansion of the Confederate state was built upon new foundations that had little or no precedent in antebellum experience. Much of this expansion was attributable to the central state mobilization of men and materiel for war. At its peak, for example, the civil service of the Confederacy totaled some 70,000 employees, over 80 percent of whom were in the War Department. The Post Office Department employed another 9,000 (13 percent) and the Treasury about 2,800 (4 percent). Most of the remaining civil employees worked for the navy and only a handful were housed in the Justice and State departments. The dominance of military activity in state operations was also expressed in the War Department's share of overall expenditures – over 90 percent in 1864, outside expenses related to debt service.[17] As was also true of the Union, most Confederate bureaus employed far more civil servants in the field than they did in the capital. Employees working for the War Department in the city of Richmond, for example, composed less than one-half of one percent of all civilian employment in the department.[18]

At the time the Union divided, the federal government had a much larger presence in the North than it did in the South (see Map 3.2). In the free states, the larger volume of mail generated by the more com-

---

15. *Rules and Directions for Proceedings in the Confederate States Patent Office* (Richmond, Va.: Enquirer Book and Job Press, 1861), p. 4; see, also, *Report of the Commissioner of Patents for 1862*, Confederate States Patent Office (Richmond, Va., 1863).

16. *1861 American Cyclopaedia*, p. 131; *New York Times*, March 29, 1861.

17. Van Riper and Scheiber, "The Confederate Civil Service," p. 450. For a description of the creation, structure, and operation of the Treasury Department, see Richard Cecil Todd, *Confederate Finance* (Athens: University of Georgia Press, 1954), pp. 1–24; Confederate States of America, Treasury Department, *Report of the Secretary of the Treasury* (Richmond, Va., n.d.), p. 2. The reporting period was April 1 to October 1, 1864.

18. Confederate States of America, War Department, *Report of the Secretary of War* (Richmond, Va., November 3, 1864), p. 23; Richard Goff, *Confederate Supply* (Durham, N.C.: Duke University Press, 1969), p. 127.

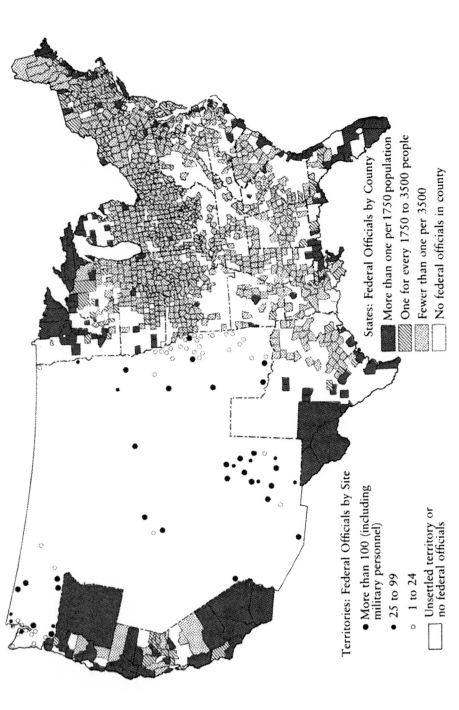

Territories: Federal Officials by Site

- ● More than 100 (including military personnel)
- ● 25 to 99
- ○ 1 to 24
- ☐ Unsettled territory or no federal officials

States: Federal Officials by County

■ More than one per 1750 population
▨ One for every 1750 to 3500 people
▨ Fewer than one per 3500
☐ No federal officials in county

Map 3.2 Regional distribution of federal officials, 1859. This includes all federal officials receiving a cash income of $200 or more and those who were paid fees in the performance of their duties. *Source: 1859 Official Register of the United States and 1859 Annual Report of the Secretary of War.*

mercialized economy tended to raise the incomes of postmasters above $200 a year and the greater import trade of cities along the northeastern coast and Canada led to the establishment of comparatively large customshouses for collection of the tariff.[19] Almost the entire strength of the United States Army was concentrated along the Pacific Coast and adjacent interior or the western frontier (particularly Minnesota, Texas, and the New Mexico and Kansas territories). Reflecting the lack of threat British Canada presented to American security, there were only two detachments with garrisons greater than twenty-five men stationed along the border from the eastern edge of the Washington Territory to Maine.[20] Much of the interior of the slave states had been almost devoid of federal officials. An inhabitant of the South could travel through great swaths of the southern and central Appalachian upland, the Ozark region of Missouri and Arkansas, and the piney wood sections of Alabama, Georgia, Louisiana, and Texas without encountering another citizen who owed a significant portion of his livelihood to federal employment. The southern coast, on the other hand, was comparatively thickly populated with official representatives of the federal government. Within what became the Confederacy, the largest federal establishments – often buttressed by navy yards, forts, and customshouses – were in the port cities of Pensacola (381 employees), New Orleans (242), Charleston (190), Norfolk (131), and Mobile (69).[21] While the federal presence could be locally impressive in some cases (particularly on the western frontier), the most remarkable feature of this distribution of agents is how little in the way of state apparatus the Confederate and Union states inherited from the antebellum federal government.

19. Two hundred dollars was probably about a quarter to a fifth of what an unskilled laborer in a federal shipyard received as an annual wage. Though necessarily somewhat arbitrary, the income threshhold adopted in this analysis was intended to separate those officials who had some material stake in their continued federal employment from those who, at best, received little more than a symbolic honorarium. Because their income was tied to the amount of postal revenue their office generated and because many of their offices were little more than counter space in a small country store, some of the nation's postmasters, for example, received less than a dollar a year from the federal government. To take just one case, the $200 threshhold excluded some 95 percent of Alabama postmasters in 1859.

20. The garrisons were Fort Mackinac, Michigan, and Plattsburgh Barracks, New York, with 57 and 59 men, respectively. The troops stationed in the Washington Territory were protecting settlers and officials surveying the United States border with Canada from Indian attack.

21. In Charleston, South Carolina, where the war began, the customshouse employed 44 officials, the post office contributed 13 workers and the local arsenal an additional 10. Fort Moultrie in Charleston harbor held a garrison of 113 men. The remaining handful of federal employees were scattered between the assistant treasurer's office, steamboat inspectors, a pension agent, and the federal district court.

Theoretical framework for an analysis of Civil War state formation

Once created, the Union and Confederate states adopted increasingly different policies that were to propel them along divergent developmental trajectories. However, before examining those policies and their implications for northern and southern state formation, we must sketch a framework within which these policies can be systematically compared. Discussions of comparative state expansion commonly conflate three different aspects of the state: (1) structure, including organization and activity; (2) relations between the state and its citizens and subjects, including public popularity and loyalty; and (3) relations between a state and other states in the international system, including diplomatic position and military power. When these three aspects are not distinguished from one another, the relationships between policy and popularity, authority and power, and organizational structure and legitimacy are impossible to analyze. For this reason the conceptualization of state strength put forward in this chapter emphasizes only the characteristics that fall under the first, structural aspect of the state. Under the criteria advanced here, whether or not a policy choice encourages public obedience (by enacting popular measures, for instance) or enhances the legitimacy with which the citizenry views state sovereignty does not influence our evaluation of whether or not the measure represents a positive step in state development.

Similarly, we are less interested in whether a particular state is strong vis-à-vis other states in terms of raw military power but are, instead, much more concerned with whether or not that state is comparatively well organized according to statist principles. Even though the existing literature on the state almost always fails to apply theoretical principles to specific aspects of central state organization, most work displays an apparent consensus on broad principles of state development.[22] The taxonomy of central state authority developed in this section is anchored within that consensus and addresses both the structural design of the state and the substantive content of its policies. This taxonomy divides

22. Peter B. Evans, Dietrich Rueschemeyer, and Theda Skocpol, "On the Road toward a More Adequate Understanding of the State," in *Bringing the State Back In* (Cambridge: Cambridge University Press, 1985), pp. 347–66. On the theoretical principles underlying state-centered approaches to political development, see Skowronek, *Building a New American State*, pp. vii–x, 3–46; Theda Skocpol and Kenneth Finegold, "State Capacity and Economic Intervention in the Early New Deal," *Political Science Quarterly* 97 (Summer 1982):255–78; Theda Skocpol, "Political Response to Capitalist Crisis: Neo-Marxist Theories of the State and the Case of the New Deal," *Politics and Society* 10 (1980): 155–201; and Stephen D. Krasner, *Defending the National Interest: Raw Materials Investments and U.S. Foreign Policy* (Princeton, N.J.: Princeton University Press, 1978), pp. 5–34.

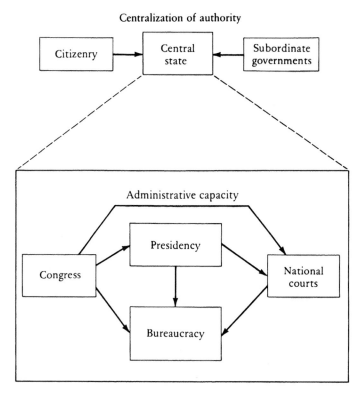

Figure 3.1
Structural dimensions of central state power.

central state structure and authority into seven distinct dimensions and will guide our subsequent comparative evaluation of the Union and Confederate states.

Structural design. The structural design of a strong state can be conveniently divided into two dimensions: centralization of authority and administrative capacity. The first dimension contains all measures that concentrate decision-making authority within one of the institutions of the central state (see Figure 3.1). The administrative capacity dimension covers the interior design of the central state itself. Thus, a proposal to give the Confederate Supreme Court jurisdiction over cases that arise within the court systems of the individual states falls under the first, centralization of authority, dimension because it entails the subordination of individual state courts to the national tribunal. Similarly, measures that confer the power of appointment of military officers upon the president instead of lodging that authority with the individual states or with enlisted men fall under the centralization heading.

While the centralization dimension, in this formulation, subsumes all measures that concentrate authority in the central state, the administrative capacity dimension encompasses all proposals that allocate authority between the various branches of the state itself. Since generally accepted administrative principles favor the executive bureaucracy over the legislative and judicial branches, statist alternatives are those that further the autonomy and discretionary authority of the central state bureaucracy. From the perspective of strong-state advocates, the least attractive of the major central state institutions is the Congress. In fact, the permeability of Congress to the influence of private interests has consistently persuaded analysts to regard the national legislature as incapable of long-term planning in the public interest and to consider statutory specification (the flip side of legislative delegation) as inconsistent with technologically effective and efficient administration. At one extreme many scholars implicitly assume that Congress is so penetrated by outside influence that it is not statist at all, but is basically just a popular assembly through which central state authority is wrested from society.

In practice, because of its own direct responsibilities and position at the top of the administrative hierarchy, the office of the presidency is often indistinguishable from the remainder of the state bureaucracy. For this reason, the interior design of a strong state would favor presidential appointment of military officers over congressional specification in statutory law. Presidential authority would be favored, also, in questions involving the breadth of legislative delegation: the statist alternative always confers greater administrative discretion. The comparatively few instances where a distinction must be drawn between the president and the bureaucracy include civil service provisions and the structural location of discretionary authority. Because all presidents are elected officials, the office of the presidency is an avenue of societal influence that, from a statist perspective, is less insulated than a career civil service. Measures that further insulate the state bureaucracy, even from presidential influence and control, thus represent enhancements of structural strength. Examples of such state-enhancing measures include civil service rules governing recruitment and advancement and the formal designation of career bureaucrats (instead of the president or political appointees) as the recipients of discretionary authority. The assignment of discretionary power to a career bureaucracy has an insulating impact on the exercise of state authority even though the executive may still influence any final administrative decision.

For parallel reasons, the national courts should, under this strong-state paradigm, give way to the central state bureaucracy. Like the bureaucracy, the national court system is normally composed of career state officials who, aside from initial appointment, are insulated from political influence. Although the national courts share many of the characteristics of long-term planning, coordination, and administrative hierarchy that describe an ideal statist bureaucracy, judicial authority is, at best, redundant in a perfectly designed state and, at worst, in direct competition with the task-oriented design of the bureaucracy.[23] When, however, the judiciary is in direct competition with the president or Congress, the statist model favors the courts because of the latter's superior statist characteristics. Thus, the structural design of a strong state systematically favors the expansion of bureaucratic authority over that of the other three branches, the courts over the president and Congress, and the president when in competition with the legislative branch.

Neither of the structural dimensions says anything, at this point, about the substantive content of central state policy. They are concerned only with the skeletal form of the state. In that respect, they are consistent with the commonly understood institutional conditions for state centralization and the emergence of administrative capacity: (1) clear lines of bureaucratic authority; (2) insulation from purely political or partisan influence; (3) the development of a bureaucratic culture that encourages state agents to identify themselves with the broadest interests of the state; and (4) the specialization of task assignment and performance within the career bureaucracy.[24] As a set of criteria by which policy choices can be evaluated according to their statist implications, the centralization of authority dimension presents few difficulties. Policy measures falling within the dimension either strengthen or weaken the design of the central state in its decision-making arrangements with the citizenry or local governmental units.

23.   This interpretation does not deny that national judiciaries have often and particularly in the United States played a central role in state expansion. Nor does it deny that the courts have often carried out many classically statist responsibilities (such as regulation and enforcement of private contracts). Instead, the text only recognizes that, from a statist perspective, there appears to be no role for the judiciary that could not be better performed by a unit of an integrated central bureaucracy.

24.   See, for example, Skowronek, *Building a New American State*, pp. viii, 15, 20, 47. The separation of centralization of state authority and administrative capacity into distinct dimensions parallels to some extent Michael Mann's *infrastructural* and *despotic* forms of state power. "The Autonomous Power of the State: Its Origins, Mechanisms and Results," *Archives Europeenes de Sociologie* 25 (1984): 186–7. For a theoretical exploration emphasizing the role of a formally organized bureaucracy in a legal system of political domination and the connection between (1) bureaucracy; (2) capitalist market development; (3) political modernization; and (4) central state expansion, see Max Weber, *On Law in Economy and Society* (New York: Touchstone, 1954), pp. xxxi–xxxv, 40.

This conceptualization of administrative capacity distinguishes between the social functions or purposes of state activity and the conditions under which central states develop the ability to operate independently of the social base from which they emerged.[25] Under this conception of administrative capacity, policy alternatives are evaluated as to their effectiveness in generating and sustaining the institutional conditions that are expected to support the ability of state agents to: (1) expand state direction and coordination of societal activity; (2) rationalize state policy by eliminating administrative contradictions and lacunae; and (3) deepen the social base of the state (for example, through the creation of dependency relations with subordinate social groups). This conceptualization directly relates the structure and policies of the state to the dynamics of the political system (such as party competition and suffrage qualifications) upon which the process of state expansion and the state apparatus itself ultimately rest. In short, when the structural principles associated with bureaucratic autonomy are satisfied, state bureaucracies are said to possess "administrative capacity." State agents within such bureaus are theoretically able to effectively exploit political opportunities for further societal penetration by, for example, creating and leading political coalitions that support further enhancement of central state authority. These state agents are defined as career officials in the central state bureaucracy, a definition that excludes party appointees, advisors to elected officials, and individuals in the intelligentsia not formally connected to the state. Though the latter groups also create and lead political coalitions through which central state authority is expanded (as did the Republican party during the Civil War), they are all deeply embedded in the larger political economy and society. Without the emergence of administrative capacity within the bureaucracy, the influence of these social groups both promotes societal penetration of the state apparatus and commits state policy to specific interests in the larger political economy. Such penetration and commitments also expand central state authority, but central state strength is always compromised by these close ties to an underlying social base.

These two structural dimensions of central state authority relate only

---

25. Under the social functions of state activity, for example, we might ascribe a set of societal "challenges" or "needs" (say, those associated with the process of industrialization). Administrative capacity would then be defined as the institutional conditions under which the central state successfully responds to these societal needs. For a general description of the most widely acknowledged state functions, see Skowronek, *Building a New American State*, pp. 10–11, and, more narrowly, Skocpol and Finegold, "State Capacity," pp. 275–6.

to the design of the state, particularly the process of decision making and its location within the state apparatus.

Substantive content. A completely formulated conception of a strong state must move beyond structural design and encompass the substantive content of central state policy. Here, these substantive policies have been categorized into five dimensions: citizenship, property rights, client-group formation, extraction, and involvement in the world system. The citizenship dimension takes in all the non–property-related rights and duties of individual citizens in their relations with the central state. Any narrowing in these rights, including central state proscription of religious practices or political beliefs and discrimination between ethnic groups, implies an expansion of central state power. Similarly, policies that dictate the use of labor in service to the state or reduce the ability of individuals to resist such policies enhance central state power.

The control-of-property dimension includes all policy measures that increase the authority of the state over the use and ownership of property. Many internal revenue measures fall into this category, as do all forms of state regulation of private economic activity and marketplace relations. Labor contracts between private parties are also included when and if central state intervention does not carry an obligation on the part of labor to service the needs of the state. This distinction rests upon the direct impact of labor regulation upon private property rights (for example, the profitability of production). While manpower drafts involve obligations at least tangentially related to private property, these obligations are much more deeply embedded in the central state's definition of citizen duties and societal membership.

The client-group dimension contains measures that create a dependency relation between individuals and the central state. Such measures can be divided into at least three subcategories. Those involving pensions, welfare payments, salaries from government employment, and income substitutes (such as price controls on commodities sold to targeted groups in the population) generally insulate individuals from the marketplace. This insulation is the result of a reduction of their exposure to market forces by way of dependence on government-derived income. A different type of dependency is involved in the issuance and distribution of long-term debt securities by the central state. Acceptance of these securities involves individuals in the future viability and strength of the central state but does not, in itself, reduce exposure to market forces. Debt relationships are involved, again, in the currency policy of the central state. Manipulation of the definition of legal tender (as for the repayment of public and private debt) and government discretion over the inherent value of the currency enhance the authority of the central state. Reliance on a gold standard and enforcement of a gold clause in contractual debt relations, by contrast, substantively reduce the dependence of private individuals on the discretionary exercise of central state authority.

The sixth dimension, extraction, focuses directly on measures that sustain state operations within society. This category includes most measures that forcibly reallocate societal resources and production from the private economy into the state treasury. The resources that are drawn into the state through extraction take the form of fungible assets that may be used in the marketplace to fund government operations. These fungible assets (usually money) are collected through processes (usually taxation) that have as their primary purpose the extraction of wealth from the private economy. Where extraction activities are heavily influenced by alternative policy goals (as in the effect of a protective tariff upon the domestic economy) or where the claims of the state on private production assume the same form as state consumption (as in the confiscation of crops in order to feed armies in a military campaign), they fall within other dimensions of state activity (world system and property, respectively, in the two examples).

The seventh and last dimension concerns those measures that describe the relationship of the central state with the remainder of the world system, including other central states. These policies include trade relations between national and world economies (for example, tariffs, import quotas, export subsidies, state-to-state economic aid and trading arrangements), diplomatic relations with foreign nations (treaty negotiations, military conflict, formal international alliances), and broadly conceived policies of internal development. Most measures in the last category involve the settlement of unoccupied territory, territorial expansion, or the administration of territorial possessions. Some, like the institution or manipulation of restrictions on immigration, involve the future composition of the citizenry and domestic labor force. Others promise to shape internal settlement patterns and to integrate disparate regional economies. In the late nineteenth century, the transcontinental railway and the Homestead Act were the two most prominent measures falling under this heading.

Like much of the literature on state formation, all seven dimensions of comparative state strength put forward here are grounded in an ideal "executive/bureaucratic" conception of state development.[26] These cat-

---

26. The adoption of this "ideal" conception of state organization and activity does not entail a normative assertion that statist principles somehow indicate the "proper" policies states should adopt. Instead, these principles have been accepted and expanded upon as a means of establishing a common yardstick against which the

egories are intended to be exhaustive in the sense that all policy choices can be classified within one of the dimensions.[27] The dimensions themselves play several roles in the following analysis. In the first place, the taxonomy should facilitate comparison of legislative support for state expansion through an examination of congressional voting patterns. Such a comparison, in turn, would help locate support for the expansion of state authority by specific groups and interests within the larger northern and southern societies. Without some prior classification, such comparisons would be frustrated by the wide variety and apparent individuality of the hundreds, sometimes thousands of legislative measures considered annually. In this sense, the taxonomy serves as a frame within which comparisons between northern and southern state development can be made and, in addition, guides the selection of a representative sample of the most important developmental policies for intensive study. This taxonomy is not an a priori classification. Each element can be derived from theoretical concerns that find repeated expression in the literature on state formation (for example, administrative capacity), in the philosophical discussion of natural and constitutional rights (citizenship), or in conventional distinctions between the role of the state in different policy areas (for example, the distinction between domestic and foreign policy). Several dimensions reflect a concern with more than one of these separate areas of theoretical discussion (see Table 3.1).

Part II: A comparison of Union and Confederate state formation

This analysis of state-building efforts during the Civil War focuses on a comparison of legislative support for selected, crucial decisions that either

---

structural and substantive strength of states might be measured. Among the most interesting aspects of the policies and structures to be studied is their implications for encouraging further state expansion (for example, by creating "client groups" dependent on the continued exercise of central state authority). Also of interest are the ways in which internal state organization and policies reflect their constitutive social bases and the external challenges each state faces. However, these concerns do not imply that policies dictated by statist principles are or were necessarily the "best" or "most efficient" responses to these challenges or the needs of their constitutive societies.

27.   For the most part, the dimensions are also mutually exclusive. However, this property is not completely developed because clear dimensional boundaries can only be based upon a fully articulated theory of the emergence and exercise of central state authority. In the absence of such a complete theory, exclusive policy boundaries can be constructed only by cataloging a vast number of policies involving the exercise of state power.

Table 3.1. *Dimensions of central state authority*

Centralization of authority: Measures involving the transfer of decision-making authority from subordinate governments and the citizenry to the central state; in the case of individual citizens, such measures do not involve a substantive expansion of central state activity but, only, the allocation of influence and control over that activity; in the case of subordinate governments, such measures include the review of subordinate government decisions by central state institutions and the form of subordinate government participation in central state decision making.

Administrative capacity: Measures involving a broadening or narrowing of bureaucratic discretion and long-term planning capacity within the central state; these measures affect only institutions within the central state itself; in analyzing policy, reference is made to a hierarchy based on relative insulation from societal or outside political influence (the state bureaucracy, national courts, presidency, and, last, the legislature).

Citizenship: Measures involving the religious practices, political beliefs, ethnic identity, and rights and duties of citizens in their relations with the state; this category excludes measures affecting property but includes all measures concerning the physical movement and labor of citizens (such as conscription).

Control of property: Measures involving the control or use of property by individuals or institutions other than the central state itself, including expropriation, regulation of the marketplace, and labor contracts between private parties.

Creation of client groups: Measures that increase the dependence of groups within society upon the continued existence and viability of the central state; includes only measures that provide income or income substitutes to individuals (pensions, employment by central state institutions, welfare, and price-control programs for specific groups in society), that establish future-oriented obligations that depend on state viability (the issuance of long-term debt), and that control the value of the currency (the gold standard and redemption of paper money).

Extraction: The coercive diversion of material resources from society into the central state apparatus; extraction measures skim wealth and resources from the flow of commerce and marketplace transactions without significantly redirecting or influencing the volume of these transactions (unlike otherwise similar measures falling under the property, client-group, or world-system dimensions); primarily forms of light taxation or manipulations of the financial system such as gradual inflation of the currency.

The central state in the world system: Measures concerning the relationship of the central state and nation with other states and the world economy; these include access to foreign markets (licensing, import quotas, export subsidies, and tariffs), diplomatic relations (membership in international organizations, treaties, and military conflict), immigration restrictions, and broadly conceived policies of internal development (the construction of a railroad to the Pacific Ocean, the Homestead Act, and administration of territorial possessions).

significantly expanded or retarded the growth of central state power.[28] While a verbatim record of the legislative proceedings of the Union Congress has survived in the *Congressional Globe* and can be supplemented with a large number of personal and journalistic accounts of decision making, the Confederate Congress provides a much poorer record of southern state-building efforts. This paucity of information concerning the operation and internal politics of the Confederate Congress arose for a number of reasons. First, many, if not most, of its most important deliberations were conducted in secret session. The injunction of secrecy largely prevented contemporary coverage of legislative debates and may have discouraged members from setting down a more complete record of their participation in diaries or memoirs. The lack of official records constitutes a second and equally serious limitation on historical knowledge of the southern legislature. Stringencies imposed by the war effort led the Congress to forgo a verbatim record of its proceedings. During the war, the Congress, along with many other Confederate institutions, delayed publication of many of its reports and even journals (which were later published by the U.S. Congress).[29] Despite these deficiencies in the historical record, however, the information essential to an understanding of the structure and administration of the Confederate state, as well as the voting behavior of congressmen on specific issues, can be retrieved from official documents.

This comparison first describes those tests of legislative support for state expansion that involved closely similar policy choices in both the Union and Confederate Congresses. These *symmetrical* policy choices represent a wide sampling of the most important war measures considered in the Union and Confederacy. The significance of some of these, such as conscription and suspension of the writ of habeas corpus, rests upon a consensus in the scholarly community. Others, such as the initial decision to publicly fund construction of a private railroad branch line, are less commonly discussed.[30] A broad sampling of *nonsymmetrical* but

28. This study focuses on the House of Representatives in both the Union Congress and the Confederate Congress because the lower chamber contained many more members than the respective Senates. The greater number of members allows the analysis of voting patterns to reflect the support of the social base for state expansion in some detail (constituency sentiment in units smaller than an entire state). In contrast, senators not only represented much larger constituencies but were also indirectly selected (through their respective state legislatures) by those constituencies.

29. *Journal of the Congress of the Confederate States of America, 1861–1865*, 7 vols. (Washington, D.C.: Government Printing Office, 1904–5). This record is subsequently referred to by chamber (for example, *Journal of the Confederate House of Representatives*) and congressional session. These volumes also contain the *Journal of the Confederate Constitutional Convention*.

30. One of the best general reviews of precedent-setting legislative decisions for the Union

equally important decisions has also been included. Each of these legislative contests lacked a close parallel in the other nation's legislative
chamber but are necessary to a full-bodied comparison of the two state-
building efforts.

The comparisons of Union and Confederate state performance and
legislative support for state formation are made in forty-two policy
areas.[31] Each evaluation of state performance begins with the relatively
narrow policy issue raised by deliberations in the legislature and expands
into a broad discussion of related government structures and operations.
A few of the most important comparisons, such as that concerning conscription policy, necessitate lengthier treatment. Though each comparison
is but a sample of the contour and content of the respective governmental
systems, taken together they permit a quite detailed and complete interpretation of Confederate and Union state-building achievements. A full
analysis of the voting patterns that underlay each of the legislative decisions concludes the chapter.

The detailed comparisons that follow thus serve several purposes. On
the one hand, they provide the necessary background for an investigation
into the contrasting social bases of Union and Confederate state expansion. On the other, these comparisons of state development in individual
policy areas support broadly textured characterizations of state—society
relations under the two regimes. These characterizations are drawn in
the concluding section of this chapter. Finally, this review requires a
practical application of abstract "statist" principles through which the
comparative performance of the two states might be evaluated. Through
these comparisons the implications of a structural conceptualization of
state strength are explored in a way that gives empirical meaning to
abstract statist principles. The following discussion begins with an examination of policy decisions within the two structural dimensions, centralization of authority and administrative capacity.

1.   Centralization of authority

The Union and Confederate congresses debated and subsequently voted
on three representative policies that centralized authority within their

Congress is Leonard P. Curry's *Blueprint for Modern America: Nonmilitary Legislation of the First Civil War Congress* (Nashville, Tenn.: Vanderbilt University Press,
1968). Also see Allan G. Bogue, *The Congressman's Civil War* (Cambridge: Cambridge University Press, 1989), pp. xiv–xv, 140. For the South, see Amlund, *Federalism in the Southern Confederacy*, specifically pp. 44–63.

31.   In twenty of these policy areas decisions made by the Union and by the Confederacy
were similar. The other twenty-four were concerned with questions unique to either
Union or Confederate experience.

respective states: adoption of procedural rules ensuring that at least some legislative deliberations would be conducted in secret session; legislation that gave the president authority to commission military officers (taking that power away from the governors of the individual states); and resolutions expelling legislators who had been duly elected by their constituencies. In addition to these parallel developments, four nonsymmetrical decisions have been included. Most of these involved Union policies: the service of border-state militia outside their own states, the creation of a Freedmen's Bureau, nationalization of the currency, and the enactment of a general Reconstruction policy intended to reform the southern political economy after the war was over. Only one important nonsymmetrical policy, concerning the scope of the proposed supreme court's jurisdiction, emerged in the Confederate Congress.

Secret sessions. As has been noted, Congress is commonly considered to be the least statist of the major branches of American government, owing primarily to the permeability of the national legislature to public influence through elections. Any measure that insulates individual members of Congress from public pressure and electoral competition increases the autonomy of the institution and furthers the integration of the legislature with the other, more statist-oriented branches. The most important such measure adopted by the Union and Confederate states was the institution, through congressional resolution, of secret sessions from which the public and members of the press were excluded and concerning which congressmen were enjoined from discussion outside the chamber.

The northern House of Representatives began the war with a rule requiring secret sessions when "confidential communications" were received from the president, but the rule did not provide for the punishment of members who violated the integrity of the proceedings. On January 29, 1862, the House rectified this oversight by ordering the expulsion of any member who publicly revealed any information or action taken within a secret session. Throughout the life of the Thirty-seventh and Thirty-eighth congresses, however, the House rarely conducted its deliberations in secret and the rule was seldom, if ever, used.[32] In sharp

---

32. The previously existing 137th rule of the House (without sanctions) was reprinted in the *Congressional Globe* 37:2:554, January 29, 1862. The text of the slightly different, proposed joint rule appears on the same page. The House tabled a motion to reconsider the main question on this new rule by a recorded vote of 79 to 54 and the new resolution subsequently passed by voice vote. The recorded vote basically frustrated the delaying tactics of the new rule's opponents and, thus, a "yea" vote for tabling tended to strengthen the statist orientation of the House. For a brief parliamentary history of the secrecy rule in U.S. House of Representatives, see Asher C. Hinds, *Hinds' Precedents of the House of Representatives of the United States*, vol. 5 (Wash-

contrast, most major Confederate policies were discussed and adopted
in secrecy, and secret sessions were convened throughout the life of the
Confederate Congress.[33] From a statist perspective, this Confederate policy was superior to the much more open deliberations of the Union
Congress.[34]

Appointment of military officers by state governors. The early mobilization of manpower into the Union and Confederate armies shared
roughly similar characteristics. Both began their mobilizations with a
presidential proclamation calling for the enlistment of troops from the
(largely nonexistent) militia controlled by the individual states. Both nations also placed the first stages of mobilization under the administrative
direction of state governors who issued their own facilitating proclamations. Above and below the Mason Dixon line, local notables (plantation owners in the South, wealthy individuals in the North, and
politicians in both sections) called for the organization of volunteer regiments at designated mustering points. When these regiments came up
to strength, these notables were elected as commanding officers by the
men they had attracted into their units and, as officers, were subsequently
commissioned by their respective governors. The troops then took an
oath of allegiance to the nation and authority over them was assumed
by the central government.[35] The two armies mobilized in this way were
almost entirely composed of men who had never before served in the
military. On January 1, 1861, the regular army of the federal government
contained just over 16,000 officers and enlisted men scattered over 100
posts throughout the West, a few installations on the Atlantic coast, and
a handful of arsenals. Of the 1,098 officers serving in the regular army,
some 29 percent resigned or abandoned their commissions and joined

ington, D.C.: Government Printing Office 1907), entry numbers 7247–8, pp. 1094–
5. Also see Bogue, *The Congressman's Civil War*, p. 102.

33. Many members of the Confederate House complained that secret sessions made a
mockery of the "representation" role of elected representatives. On several occasions,
these members offered resolutions that would have made it more difficult for the
House to invoke secrecy. The roll call on one of these resolutions – requiring that
one-fifth of the members in attendance approve a motion to go into secret session –
was the vote that best parallels the Union decision (*Journal of the Confederate House
of Representatives*, 1:1:52, March 4, 1862).

34. Once again, this comparison is restricted to conformity with statist principles of central
organization and does not imply, for example, that secrecy in legislative deliberations
was a more effective means of maintaining civilian morale.

35. Kreidberg and Henry, *History of Military Mobilization*, pp. 116–9; Fred Albert Shan-
non, *The Organization and Administration of the Union Army, 1861–1865*, vol. 1
(Gloucester, Mass.: Peter Smith, 1965), pp. 159–70, 186–92; Coulter, *Confederate
States*, p. 329–31.

Table 3.2. *Loyalty of regular army officers to the Union*

	Joined the	
Category	Union	Confederacy
Southern officers trained at West Point	162	168
Southern officers previously appointed from civilian life	1	129
Northern officers	622	16
Totals	785	313

the Confederate military (see Table 3.2).[36] Defections included the last four secretaries of war to serve the antebellum Union (George Crawford of Georgia, Charles Conrad of Louisiana, Jefferson Davis of Mississippi, and John Floyd of Virginia), the adjutant general (Samuel Cooper), and the quartermaster general of the United States (Joseph E. Johnston).[37]

This reservoir of experienced officers was employed in very different ways in the Union and the Confederacy. The northern government, in what can only be viewed as a mistake, kept intact what remained of the regular army and thus prevented the distribution of experienced commanding officers throughout the new and vastly larger volunteer army. As a result, officers of the regular army were seriously underutilized while northern volunteers were usually led, at least early in the war, by inexperienced, powerful politicians or other notables.[38] The Confederacy, on the other hand, rapidly absorbed defecting officers into the volunteer forces and thus held an early advantage over the North in the exploitation of available command experience. This early advantage was, in part, due to the fact that most antebellum regular army units contained personnel

36. The sixteen northern officers who went South had, in most cases, married southern women. Marcus Cunliffe, *Soldiers and Civilians: The Martial Spirit in America, 1775–1865* (New York: Free Press, 1973), pp. 340–1, 373–4; E. B. Long, *The Civil War Day by Day* (New York: Da Capo, 1985), p. 709; Kreidberg and Henry, *History of Military Mobilization*, pp. 90, 115–7. The wide difference in defection rates between West Point–trained southern officers and those appointed from civilian life (as political patronage) suggests that formal training in the academy was at least partially successful in promoting loyalty to the federal government. See, for example, James L. Morrison, "The Struggle between Sectionalism and Nationalism at Ante-Bellum West Point, 1830–1861," *Civil War History* 19 (June 1973): 138–48.
37. Kreidberg and Henry, *History of Military Mobilization*, pp. 86, 89, 115–7; on the disruptive impact of southern defections on the federal military, see A. Howard Meneely, *The War Department, 1861: A Study in Mobilization and Administration* (New York: Columbia University Press, 1928), pp. 106–7. For a list of Confederate officers who previously served in the U.S. Army, see the *1863 American Cyclopaedia*, pp. 19–20.
38. Kreidberg and Henry, *History of Military Mobilization*, p. 97; Shannon, *Organization and Administration*, p. 164.

drawn from all parts of the United States and thus did not defect to the
Confederacy as units.[39] Because defecting officers came into the Confederacy as individuals, distribution throughout the volunteer forces was
almost automatic.

Aside from conscription, the most difficult issue frustrating professionalization of the Union and Confederate military forces concerned the
appointment of officers to command in the volunteer army. In practice,
the statist position was presidential appointment (which faced competition primarily from the commissioning authority of governors). Both
states moved to transfer appointment power from governors to the president in roughly the same way and at the same rate.[40]

Expulsion of members of Congress. Other than instituting secret sessions,
one of the most significant ways in which a central state can reduce or
shape the influence of the citizenry on governmental decisions is by regulating the process through which officials are selected and imposing
qualifying conditions on office holding. Such screens allow the state to
regulate personnel recruitment and, in effect, negate or limit popular
influence on the selection of central state agents. This can be done, for
example, through restrictions on suffrage eligibility which control access

39. Because the regular army was the only branch of the antebellum state that combined
     men from both free and slave states in the same units, military garrisons were the
     only surviving representatives of federal authority in the South after secession. Other
     branches appointed personnel from the surrounding regions in which they stationed
     officials and went over to the Confederacy en bloc. Thus Fort Sumter's symbolic role
     as the sole remaining federal presence in Charleston, South Carolina, was, in part,
     preordained by the distinctive administrative design of the army.
40. Coulter, *Confederate States*, pp. 329–31; Shannon, *Organization and Administration*,
     p. 170; W. H. H. Terrell, *Indiana in the War of the Rebellion: Report of the Adjutant
     General* (Indiana Historical Bureau, 1960; reprint of a 1869 edition), pp. 106, 108.
     In an important test of legislative support for this statist development in the North,
     the Union House of Representatives rejected an amendment to the bill establishing
     federal conscription authority on February 25, 1863 (55 members favored the amend-
     ment while 104 opposed). The amendment would have given governors (instead of
     the president) authority to appoint officers for army units organized under the draft
     (*Congressional Globe* 37:3:1292). The clearest test of Confederate congressional
     sentiment occurred on the adoption of an amendment to the 1862 conscription bill.
     As approved by the House, the amendment gave to governors the authority to com-
     mission officers who had been elected by enlisted men. The original provision, to be
     struck out by the amendment, had given commissioning authority to the president.
     Both alternatives contemplated a system that relied primarily on election by enlisted
     men. The chief difference between them lay in the location of the formal commis-
     sioning authority and, thus, in the relative centralization of the military hierarchy.
     See the *Journal of the Confederate House of Representatives* 1:1:224, April 14, 1862;
     though the amendment was adopted by the Confederate House, the conscription act
     was returned to the original, state-enhancing text before enactment. *Official Records
     of the Union and Confederate Armies*, ser. IV, vol. 1, p. 1095 (for the appointment
     provisions in earlier enrolling legislation, see pp. 302, 826, 925).

to the ballot and thus prevent some portions of the citizenry from influencing the selection of elected officials. Office-holding requirements (such as age, residence, and citizenship) and loyalty oaths similarly restrict the pool of eligible candidates for elected office or bureaucratic service. The most rigorous method used by the Union and Confederate Congress was the expulsion of duly elected members. Three members were expelled by the Union House of Representatives during the four years of war. All represented border-state districts and were charged, accurately, with disloyalty to the Union government. Two were similarly expelled from the Confederate House, one from north Alabama and the other from Tennessee. All five expulsions might be expected under conditions of civil war. The Union members were expelled because they failed to resign before joining the Confederacy. One of the expelled Confederates defected to the Union under similar circumstances. Only the expulsion of Henry Foote of Tennessee by the Confederate House set a slightly more important precedent as a potential control on the views and activities of legislators. One of the most vocal members of the House, Foote was a leading critic of administration policy and the foremost advocate of a war effort that would rely exclusively upon the uncoerced nationalism of the citizenry.[41]

Service of militia outside the state. This is the first of the five nonsymmetrical decisions involving centralization of authority within either the Union or Confederate states. The decision involved the service of border-state troops beyond the boundaries of their states. The issue arose after

41. For expulsions from the Union House of Representatives, see the *Biographical Directory of the American Congress, 1774–1971* (Washington, D.C.: Government Printing Office, 1971), notes to pp. 175–83; and U.S. Congress, Joint Committee on Congressional Operations, *House of Representatives Exclusion, Censure and Expulsion Cases from 1789 to 1973* (Washington, D.C.: Government Printing Office, 1973), pp. 143–4. For the recorded vote and accompanying debate on the expulsion of John B. Clark of Missouri from the Union House, see *Congressional Globe* 37:1:116–7, July 13, 1861 (the vote was 94 yea, 45 nay – almost exactly the two-thirds majority required under the Constitution). At the time of his expulsion, Clark was an officer in the prosecessionist Missouri State Guard and later became a Confederate congressman. An attempt to expel Foote for attempting to cross over into Union lines failed in the Confederate House on a recorded vote on January 24, 1865 (51 members favored expulsion, 25 opposed – the Confederate Constitution required an affirmative vote by two-thirds of the entire membership and abstentions killed this first expulsion effort). See *Proceedings of the Confederate Congress*, vol. 52, p. 215–16, November 15, 1864 (published as vols. 44–52 of the *Southern Historical Society Papers* [Richmond, Va., 1923–59]). These volumes, which contain abstracts and summaries of the deliberations of the Confederate Congress printed originally in the Richmond *Examiner,* are hereafter cited as *Proceedings.* Foote subsequently passed through the lines on the way to Washington and the Confederate House of Representatives expelled him.

President Lincoln had negotiated agreements for the enrollment of state militia into the federal army with the governors of Maryland and Missouri and backed passage of a similar arrangement for the enrollment of Kentucky troops. In all three cases, these agreements exchanged a relatively strong, but qualified guarantee that the militia would not have to serve beyond state lines in return for their incorporation into the Union army. Even though this concession facilitated the organization of border-state troops for local garrison duty along the Confederate frontier, Republican nationalists strongly opposed this pragmatic adjustment of Union sovereignty.[42] Though the nationalization of militia forces in the South faced a different set of problems, Confederate experience in this policy area was roughly similar.[43]

Establishment of the Freedmen's Bureau. The American Civil War emancipated approximately four million slaves and these new "freedmen" presented the Union with an opportunity to remake the southern political economy even as the war raged on. During 1863 and 1864 Congress considered several proposals for the establishment of a separate agency to administer Union policy toward the freedmen. In the new bureau finally established in March 1865, Congress consolidated refugee relief efforts, freedmen's affairs, and land redistribution.[44] Though land redistribution was soon stopped by Andrew Johnson's pardon policy (which exempted

42. The recorded vote on this issue arose over the adoption of a Senate amendment providing that "no volunteers or militia from any State shall be mustered into the service of the United States on any terms or conditions confining their service to the limits of said State or vicinity; and if any such volunteer militia are in service contrary to the provisions of this act the same shall be discharged." *Congressional Globe* 37:2:614, February 3, 1862; for general debate, see pp. 610–13. The House of Representatives rejected this central state–enhancing amendment (65 to 85). In his final report on Union conscription, Provost Marshal James B. Fry noted that casualties were much lower for border-state forces than for northern free-state troops because the former were used primarily in local garrison duty far away from the front line. See the *Final Report of the Provost Marshal General*, part 1, p. 74, in *Report of the Secretary of War, 1865–1866*, part 3 (Washington, D.C.: Government Printing Office, 1866). Militia service is a nonsymmetrical policy area because the issue never came to a vote in the Confederate Congress.

43. Frank Owsley's representation of Confederate performance as fatally hampered by limitations on national mobilization (in *State Rights in the Confederacy* [Chicago: University of Chicago Press, 1925]) has recently been effectively challenged by Beringer et al., *Why the South Lost the Civil War*, appendix 1, pp. 443–57.

44. For contemporary discussion of the condition of refugees and freedmen throughout the South, see the *1865 American Cyclopaedia*, pp. 370–8, 394–5, 515–16, 787–8, 793–4. The test of congressional sentiment included here arose on March 1, 1864, when the Union House of Representatives narrowly passed legislation similar to the final act (*Congressional Globe* 38:1:566, 69 members supported passage, 67 opposed). Disagreement between the House and Senate postponed final passage until the following year.

most former Confederates from confiscation) and government relief programs for refugees rapidly wound down with the close of the war, the bureau's activities also included more persistent efforts to promote the transition of the southern political economy from slavery to contractual, market-oriented forms of labor relations. Organized as a military bureaucracy, the agency sought to impose order on sometimes anarchic communities, imposed labor contracts on both plantation owners and freedmen as the Union attempted to reorganize and reestablish commodity production, and sometimes preempted local courts if the latter failed to protect black interests. These and other activities carried out by the bureau represented a broad expansion of central government authority in areas previously exclusively controlled by the individual states.[45] The Confederacy, of course, possessed no counterpart to the Freedman's Bureau.

Reconstruction (the Wade–Davis Bill). Even more sweeping was the process created by the Union for the political reconstruction of the South. Though Lincoln's initial efforts in Arkansas and Louisiana suggested a passive policy, Congress subsequently moved to enact a much more active general program that would have dramatically reapportioned political influence among the major groups within the southern political economy. Named for a senator from Ohio and a congressman from Maryland, the Wade–Davis Bill proposed to appoint interim military governors to administer captured Confederate territory, to restrict suffrage eligibility and office holding to whites who had remained loyal to the Union (a tiny fraction of the southern population), and to repudiate all government contractual obligations created by the Confederacy or southern state governments.[46] These and other provisions of the bill effectively transferred many aspects of individual state sovereignty to the national government and, thus, vastly centralized political authority. Though Lincoln

45. Eric Foner, *Reconstruction: America's Unfinished Revolution, 1863–1877* (New York: Harper & Row, 1988), pp. 68–70; Robert H. Bremner, *The Public Good: Philanthropy and Welfare in the Civil War Era* (New York: Alfred A. Knopf, 1980), pp. 115–19, 126–8; William S. McFeely, *Yankee Stepfather: General O. O. Howard and the Freedmen* (New York: W. W. Norton, 1968); James Smallwood, "Charles E. Culver, A Reconstruction Agent in Texas: The Work of Local Freedmen's Bureau Agents and the Black Community," *Civil War History* 27 (December 1981): 350–61.

46. Foner, *Reconstruction*, pp. 61–2; Michael Les Benedict, *A Compromise of Principle: Congressional Republicans and Reconstruction, 1863–1869* (New York: W. W. Norton, 1974), pp. 70–83. The Wade–Davis bill passed the House on May 4, 1864. *Congressional Globe* 38:1:2108; for debate, see pp. 2105–8. Seventy-three members supported passage, 59 opposed.

vetoed this bill, Congress ultimately enacted very similar policies during Andrew Johnson's administration.

Nationalization of the currency. As part of the northern effort to fund the war, the Union created a new national banking system (discussed separately in the review of extraction policies). Banks that joined the new system were allowed to issue "national bank notes" that were, in effect, a national currency (along with legal tender greenbacks). In the beginning these notes circulated alongside currency issued by the hundreds of state-chartered banks that already existed. In order to eliminate the notes issued by these latter institutions and thus centralize authority over the currency in the national government, a prohibitively high tax, 10 percent, was imposed on the circulation of state-chartered bank notes. While collecting almost no revenue, the tax effectively drove these notes out of the money supply and strongly encouraged the absorption of state-chartered banks into the national bank system. Both results strengthened the Union government's authority over the national financial system at the expense of the individual states.[47] Because the Confederacy failed to establish an equivalent to the Union national bank system, southern currency continued to be composed of a mixture of Confederate treasury notes, money issued by the individual state governments, and currency issued by banks chartered by the state governments.

Jurisdiction of the Confederate Supreme Court. One of the most important centralization questions facing the Confederacy concerned the possible jurisdiction of the Confederate Supreme Court over cases originating in the separate judicial systems of the individual states. The question arose not in the Confederate Congress but during the Constitutional Convention, when the framers included appeals from the highest tribunals of the individual states in the Supreme Court's jurisdiction.[48] An attempt to delete this authority was defeated when the delegations tied in the voting. If the Confederacy had subsequently enacted the legislation nec-

47. The tax was narrowly adopted by the U.S. House of Representatives on February 18, 1865. *Congressional Globe* 38:2:906; 69 members supported the amendment imposing the tax, 66 opposed. Albert S. Bolles, *The Financial History of the United States, 1861 to 1885*, vol. 3 (New York: Augustus M. Kelley, 1969), p. 194.
48. An amendment to exempt these cases from the jurisdiction of the Supreme Court was offered from the floor of the convention on March 7, 1861. Louisiana, South Carolina, and Texas supported this restriction on central state authority; Alabama, Georgia, and Mississippi voted for an expansive jurisdiction; and Florida's delegation split evenly. *Journal of the Confederate Constitutional Convention*, pp. 880–1; also see Lee, *Confederate Constitutions*, p. 108.

essary to establish the Supreme Court (discussed later in the text), the extension of jurisdiction to include decisions of the higher courts of the individual states would have formally written into fundamental law the power necessary for national supremacy and thus immeasurably concentrated authority within the central state. The Union Constitution already provided for federal review of cases arising within the courts of the individual states and the question did not come up in the North.

A total of eight policies have been described under the dimension of centralization of authority. In four of these areas of potential expansion, the Union and Confederate states traveled essentially parallel trajectories (with a possible slight statist advantage to the Confederacy in one or two instances). The expulsion of disloyal members, the erosion of the appointment authority of state governors over military officers, the nationalization of militia service, and the jurisdictional breadth of the respective supreme courts all assumed the form of comparatively equivalent arrangements in the two central governments. After the nationalization of the northern currency, the Union held a clear advantage in national financial policy. And, while the Confederacy was never presented with an opportunity to consider parallel measures, both Union Reconstruction and freedmen policies represented extraordinarily important preemptions of individual state sovereignty by the central government. The Confederacy was clearly more statist in only one area: the insulation of the legislature from societal influence by the institution of secret sessions. On the whole, therefore, Union measures to centralize authority were considerably more in keeping with statist design principles than those of the southern Confederacy. Both central states represented significant advances over the antebellum Union government.

2.   *Administrative capacity*

Administrative capacity is improved by any expansion of discretionary authority lodged within central state bureaucracy and by any arrangement that insulates the bureaucracy from purely political or partisan influence. Among the four branches, the bureaucracy is the most statist, followed by the national courts, the presidency, and Congress, respectively. Thus, two kinds of legislative choice fall under the rubric of administrative capacity: those that transfer authority for decisions on specific policies among the branches of the central state and those that promise to increase the general autonomy of any branch and its independence from the influence of a less statist branch (for example, civil service rules that help insulate the bureaucracy from executive influence).

Military academy appointments. The largest and most important bureaucracy in both the Union and Confederate states was, of course, the army, and one of the most pressing tasks associated with constructing a more efficient and insulated state apparatus was the depoliticization of military appointments. In the Union, the issue arose in connection with the appointment of cadets to the military academy at West Point. When the South seceded, the defection of southern cadets left behind many vacancies in the academy. To fill these vacancies and also to expand presidential influence over the selection of cadets, legislation was introduced in the Union Congress that gave the president authority to appoint cadets to those vacancies caused by secession. The number of such appointments was to equal the number of (former) representatives and senators from the eleven states of the Confederacy but, unlike prior appointments, the president might select these cadets from anywhere in the Union without soliciting the recommendation of congressmen or senators.[49]

In the Confederacy, the clearest and perhaps most hotly contested struggle between executive and legislative appointment arose over the appointment of midshipmen to the naval academy. When the Confederate Congress passed a bill reallocating authority over appointments to each individual representative and senator, President Davis vetoed the measure. In his veto message, he cited the formal allocation of powers under the Confederate Constitution, which he interpreted as assigning all appointments of officers to the executive. After vigorous debate, the House of Representatives sustained the veto and thus preserved presidential appointment authority.[50] The Union and Confederate states thus experienced similar struggles over the depoliticization of appointments. Although both Lincoln and Davis attempted to restrict the influence of congressmen and senators (who made recommendations largely motivated by electoral and patronage considerations), the Confederate pres-

49. The bill, which also prescribed a loyalty oath and execution for "desertion" to the enemy, survived a tabling motion on July 30, 1861, by a vote of 72 to 51. *Congressional Globe* 37:1:348–9; for debate, see pp. 347–9. A similar, though more narrowly framed issue arose over the appointment of midshipmen to the Union naval academy. *Congressional Globe*, 37:3:748–9, February 5, 1863; 37:3:888–94, February 11, 1863. On antebellum involvement of congressmen in cadet selection, see James L. Morrison, Jr., *"The Best School in the World": West Point, the Pre–Civil War Years, 1833–1866* (Kent, Ohio: Kent State University Press, 1986), pp. 62–4; Stephen E. Ambrose, *Duty, Honor, Country: A History of West Point* (Baltimore: Johns Hopkins Press, 1966), pp. 128–9.

50. *Journal of the Confederate House of Representatives*, 2:2:500–2, January 26, 1865; *Proceedings*, 52: 232, January 26, 1865. A majority (40 to 36) of the House of Representatives voted to override the veto but fell short of the two-thirds required by the Confederate Constitution.

ident more effectively and resolutely resisted congressional pressure. In practice, then, the Confederate state possessed an advantage over the more political practice of the Union in this policy area.

Presidential removal of military officers. The Union and Confederate mobilizations brought many incompetent or otherwise undesirable individuals to command in both armies (although the wide distribution of defecting federal officers throughout the volunteers partially alleviated the problem in the South). The removal of these incompetent officers became a goal of both governments, but strong resistance to reform developed among those who viewed their removal as an affront to states' rights or the democratic rights of enlisted men. In the North, the Union moved, in the Army Act of July 22, 1861, to establish military commissions to review all officers in volunteer regiments.[51] Those judged incompetent were to be removed upon the president's approval of the commissions' recommendations. Within weeks, Congress considered additional legislation to expand this removal power to include professional officers in the regular army. In the House of Representatives the question was posed in such a way as to make inclusion of the professional officers one of the major issues. This question presented an interesting problem from a statist perspective because the inclusion of professional officers diminished the independence of the military bureaucracy from presidential influence.[52]

In October 1862, the Confederacy confronted this issue in roughly the same way by enacting legislation creating military boards to inquire into the competence of officers and recommend dismissal where necessary. Although the Confederacy acted later than the Union, the southern government purged the officer corps more aggressively than did the North.[53]

51. See *Official Records*, ser. III, vol. 1, pp. 380–3 (General Orders No. 49) for the text of the act; also, p. 349 (General Orders No. 47).
52. The House of Representatives decisively rejected the amendment to review professional officers, 99 to 17. *Congressional Globe* 37:1:429, August 3, 1861.
53. The issue of insulation of the military bureaucracy from presidential influence arose most clearly on the adoption of an amendment to a bill for "the organization of the Navy." An amendment was offered that provided that "No officers appointed under the provisions of this act shall be finally dismissed from the service except upon the finding of a court-martial or court of inquiry after charges duly preferred." The amendment would have restricted presidential authority to dismiss naval officers by providing for review by professional officers, thus partially insulating the naval bureaucracy from executive influence. The statist position failed when the amendment was defeated 13 to 17. *Journal of the Provisional Confederate Congress*, p. 125, March 11, 1861. For the text of the October 1862 act, see *Official Records* ser. IV, vol. 2, pp. 205–6; examinations of officers elected after enrollment in the national army were conducted as early as May 1862. See *Official Records*, ser. IV, vol. 1, pp. 1122–3, General Orders No. 36; Coulter, *Confederate States*, pp. 330–1. At least

On the whole, however, there was little difference between the organization or performance of the two Civil War states with respect to the nationalization and bureaucratic insulation of their respective officer corps.

Court of claims. Six nonsymmetrical decisions, two for the Union and four for the Confederacy, are included under the heading, administrative capacity. The first of these involved a proposed strengthening of the jurisdictional power of the federal court of claims. This body was originally established under the antebellum federal government in 1855 and reviewed claims arising from contracts made with the national government. As originally structured, the court of claims could not render a final decision but could only report back to Congress the facts of the case and the court's recommendation. In order to satisfy claims, Congress was thus compelled to pass appropriate legislation. As a development that shifted a portion of state activity from the legislature to a judicial body, the establishment of the court represented a statist enhancement of administrative capacity.

In 1862 the Union Congress considered a bill that would have made all verdicts of the court final except certain cases involving large sums which might be appealed to the Supreme Court.[54] Had it become law (it died in the Senate), this legislation would have represented a statist development in further insulating the judicial process from congressional influence. Although the Confederacy never established a court of claims, much of the same kind of activity was carried out within the central bureaucracy and the district courts where Congress had little or no influence over the decisions.[55] In practice, the Confederate arrangement was probably marginally more compatible with statist principles than the more legislative, political process in the Union.

Board of admiralty. The vast expansion of the northern navy during the Civil War concentrated great power in the hands of the politically appointed secretary of the navy and his closest subordinates. As Representative H. Winter Davis of Maryland described the arrangement produced by the war,

---

1,700 Confederate officers were dismissed or led to resign; outright dismissals in the Union army amounted to only a "few hundred" with a correspondingly less important influence on decisions to resign from the service. Shannon, *Organization and Administration*, pp. 186–7.

54. *Congressional Globe* 37:2:1671–7, April 15, 1862. The decision included in the voting analysis involved the defeat of a motion to table (kill) the bill (83 to 40, p. 1677).

55. Coulter, *Confederate States*, p. 123.

> The organization of the Navy Department... leaves the whole re-
> sponsibility of the construction of all naval vessels, their forms, struc-
> ture, armament, machinery, and materials, limited ˙only by the
> amount of money appropriated for their construction, at the irre-
> sponsible discretion of... three persons... for, the organization of
> the Navy Department is a Secretary who administers it, an Assistant
> Secretary who administers him, and the chiefs of bureaus who are
> the ministerial fingers and hands of the gentleman at the head of the
> Navy Department. Such an organization of a Navy Department exists
> nowhere else in the civilized world among naval Powers.

In order to involve professional naval officers in making decisions for
the department, Davis and other critics proposed the establishment of a
board of admiralty modeled on the admiralty offices of the British navy.
Such a body would have strengthened the statist design of the Navy
Department by routinely and formally soliciting the advice and official
recommendations of professional officers before the secretary could act.
The Union Congress, however, defeated the proposed reform.[56] Since the
Confederacy also did not create a board of this kind, the two national
experiences were roughly equivalent in this area of potential state
enhancement.[57]

General staff. During the early stages of mobilization, both the Union
and the Confederacy created highly personalized military structures in
which aides to the commanding officer were often tied to him through
family or friendship relations. When the commanding officer changed
postings or stepped down, his aides and immediate subordinates would
be replaced by those similarly tied to the new commanding officer. In an
attempt to professionalize the command structure, an amendment was
offered in the Confederate House that would have added the following
language to previously passed legislation organizing the general staff of
the army:

> Adjutants appointed by the President shall be deemed officers of the
> general staff, shall be regarded as part of the commands to which
> they are attached and not as belonging to the personal staff of the
> officer [under] whose orders they may be serving for the time being,

56. For the text of the proposed legislation, see the *Appendix to the Congressional Globe*
    38:2:41, February 3, 1865; for debate on the floor of the House of Representatives,
    see 38:2:35, 41–6, February 3, 1865; 38:2:46–9, February 4, 1865; the proposal
    drew the support of 60 members of the House, but the opposition of 70 more
    congressmen. *Congressional Globe* 38:2:628, February 7, 1865.
57. For a description of the administrative structure of the Confederate Department of
    the Navy, see Joseph T. Durkin, *Stephen R. Mallory: Confederate Navy Chief* (Chapel
    Hill: University of North Carolina Press, 1954), pp. 136–45.

and shall, where competent, be promoted in their several army corps as assistant adjutant and inspector generals to fill vacancies according to seniority.[58]

Although there were other attempts to professionalize the officer corps, few were so focused on the problem of transforming a military structure that originated largely in the personal recruitment efforts of individual members of the landed aristocracy into a permanent bureaucracy in which the separate organization of units, not their leaders, provided administrative continuity. Although the Union Congress never addressed this issue as directly as did the Confederacy, the northern state probably had a more professionalized staff organization than did the South.[59]

Exemptions from conscription. The Confederate draft was a much more complete manpower policy than the conscription policy of the Union. One of the features of the Confederate program that gave southern conscription its strong statist character was the extensive categorization of occupational exemptions, which gave the Confederacy almost total control over manpower allocation in the economy. Their one drawback was that they were written into statutory law and therefore more rigid and subject to legislative influence than a purely statist design would prescribe.

58. Offered by John Baldwin of Virginia, the amendment passed the House by a wide margin (37 to 22). *Journal of the Confederate House of Representatives*, 1:2:533–4, October 11, 1862. The amendment apparently followed previous administrative attempts to professionalize staff organization (see General Orders No. 53, July 31, 1862, *Official Records*, ser. IV, vol. 2, p. 26). President Davis had previously strengthened the office of the Confederate Adjutant General as an alternative to the creation of a general-in-chief of the southern armies. The thrust of the legislative amendment and existing practice was, apparently, to insulate the adjutant general's field officers from the influence of field generals. See Herman Hattaway and Archer Jones, *How the North Won: A Military History of the Civil War* (Urbana: University of Illinois Press, 1983), pp. 107–8.

59. For other examples of legislation relating to the organization of a general staff of the army, see R. C. Gilchrist, *General Orders of the Confederate States Army* (Columbia, S.C.: Evans and Cogswell, 1864), pp. 86–7, 92–7. A related but separate issue involved the appointment of a "commanding general" to administer the Confederate military and serve just below President Davis. Because of the president's strong opposition, a commanding general was not created until the war was almost over. Yearns, *Confederate Congress*, p. 108; Coulter, *Confederate States*, p. 332. Unlike the Confederacy, the Union separated centralized direction of the northern army from the executive office of the president from the very beginning of the war and, in 1862, attached most corps staff officers to their units as opposed to their commanders (see the "Act to Amend the Act Calling Forth the Militia . . . July 17, 1862" and General Orders No. 212, December 23, 1862 in *Official Records* ser. III, vol. 2, pp. 281, 953–4). For comparisons of Union and Confederate command structures that gives a slight edge to the North, see Hattaway and Jones, *How the North Won*, pp. 101–10, 117–24; Hagerman, *The American Civil War and the Origins of Modern Warfare*, p. xvi.

In an early contest over the determination of exempted occupations, the Confederate Congress rejected legislation that would have lodged all authority over exemptions with the secretary of war.[60] In their deliberations, congressmen expressed opposition to the sheer power over the southern economy that would be placed in the hands of the War Department. Not only would the legislation have transferred authority from Congress to the president; implicit in the debate was the recognition that discretionary power in the hands of the central state carried much more coercive potential than categorical statutory exemptions. Discretion, for example, allowed the state to grant exemptions as an inducement for compliance in other governmental policies, thus furthering the complete mobilization of resources behind the southern war effort.[61]

Approximately one year after this bill was defeated, however, the Confederate Congress granted "the Secretary of War, under the direction of the President" the power to "exempt or detail such other persons [in addition to those already exempt] as he may be satisfied ought to be exempted on account of public necessity."[62] Because the South carried out a state-directed allocation of manpower administered by a largely autonomous bureaucracy, Confederate conscription embodied a classic expression of statist principles never approached by the much more market-oriented policies of the Union.

Civil service test. Although necessary to bureaucratic professionalization, the depersonalization of recruitment and promotion, taken alone, is not a sufficient guarantee of competent administrative performance. As bureaucratic functions specialize, personnel can no longer transfer freely between units, and demonstrated expertise becomes a critical factor in appointment to office. The Confederate Congress confronted this aspect of administrative capacity on March 11, 1863, when Muscoe Garnett of Virginia offered an amendment to a bill "to provide and organize engineer troops to serve during the war." The amendment would have specified that "no officer shall be appointed or promoted under authority of this law until his qualifications have been tested by examination under rules

60. The bill was very short and the most important clause read, "the Secretary of War shall...with the approval of the President, exempt from all military service, or detail for specified purposes, such person or persons as...he may deem essential for the good of the service or the general interests of the country." *Journal of the Confederate House of Representatives*, 1:3:36–7, 40–1, January 21–22, 1863. This statist proposal was narrowly defeated (35 to 39).
61. For a general sampling of debate on this exemption bill, see *Proceedings*, 47:173, 181, 183, 205, 211–12 (January 21–27, 1863).
62. See "An Act to Organize Forces to Serve during the War," approved February 17, 1864, in *Official Records*, ser. IV, vol. 3, pp. 178–81 (General Orders No. 26).

to be prescribed by the War Department, and appointment shall be made from those passing such examination in the order of merit."[63] The impetus for the amendment came from the reputed poor training of officers in the engineering corps.[64] A civil service test or other examination of competency strengthens administrative capacity because it transfers influence over recruitment and promotion from the president (and, indirectly, the Senate) to the bureaucracy. Though this southern decision focused narrowly on the examination of military engineers (an area in which Union state performance was probably superior to the South), the Confederacy generally relied upon much more objective, competency-based criteria in making appointments in both the civil and military services than did the more politicized and patronage-oriented Union.[65]

A Confederate Supreme Court. Throughout the life of the Confederacy, the judicial branch was hampered by the failure of Congress to organize the Supreme Court provided for in the Confederate Constitution. Although that failure also carried important implications for states' rights, over the lifetime of the Confederate state the decision prevented the judiciary from successfully competing with the executive and legislative branches for influence. While the absence of a supreme court probably liberated, on occasion, the more statist bureaucracy, its absence had a negative effect on overall administrative capacity.[66]

63. *Journal of the Confederate House of Representatives,* 1:3:172. The amendment was rejected on a roll call vote (24 to 45). For the text of the law ultimately passed by Congress (without a competency test), see *Public Laws of the Confederate States of America, Third Session, First Congress* (Richmond, Va.: R. M. Smith, 1863), pp. 98–9. For the military regulations that implemented the statute, see General Orders No. 66 (May 22, 1863) in *General Orders of the Confederate States Army, 1863,* pp. 70–1.
64. See, for example, James L. Nichols, *Confederate Engineers,* Confederate Centennial Studies, no. 5 (Tuscaloosa, Ala.: Confederate Publishing, 1957), p. 32.
65. Van Riper and Scheiber, "The Confederate Civil Service," p. 470.
66. The provisional constitution stipulated that judges of the district courts would, sitting together, compose the Confederate Supreme Court. Congress passed the necessary implementing legislation on March 16, 1861, but, before the court could convene, it passed a second statute providing that the court would not meet until organized under the permanent Constitution by the First Confederate Congress. The only serious subsequent attempt to establish the court came in the spring of 1863. At this time, however, the House of Representatives voted (39 to 30) to suspend consideration of the bill until the next session of Congress. With this postponement, serious efforts to organize the court ceased. Sidney D. Brummer, "The Judicial Interpretation of the Confederate Constitution," in *Studies in Southern History and Politics* (New York: Columbia University Press, 1914), p. 107; for the text of the act postponing organization of the court, see *Acts and Resolutions of the Third Session of the Provisional Congress,* pp. 6–7; Robinson, *Justice in Grey,* pp. 420–34, 474–91. For background on the decision not to organize the court, see John Christopher Schwab, *Confederate States of America: 1861–1865* (New York: Burt Franklin, 1968), pp. 219–20. On

Despite the failure of the Confederate Congress to establish a supreme court, the absence of this relatively statist institution was not, for a number of reasons, a serious impediment to the administrative performance of the Confederate state. In the first place, both the national district courts and the courts of the individual states were largely staffed by judges who had renounced their allegiance to the Union, resigned their federal posts, and been reappointed to the Confederate judiciary. Both these judges and those newly appointed were aware of and followed precedents established by the antebellum Supreme Court of the United States. Despite the absence of a supreme tribunal in the Confederacy, this practice unified constitutional interpretation throughout the South (incidentally minimizing differences between the constitutional law of the two nations), and generally strengthened the claims of the central government. Second, on his own initiative, the attorney general of the Confederacy reviewed laws enacted by the individual states for conformity with the Constitution, advised the government not to respect those that he considered unconstitutional, and generally consolidated some of the functions of a supreme court in the executive branch.[67] Although the attorney general became less assertive in the last years of the Confederacy, his decisions consistently favored central state power.

A pervasive tendency by the highest courts of the individual states to sustain the exercise of national authority also minimized any difficulties that otherwise might have arisen from the failure to establish a Confederate Supreme Court. Most of the cases implicating national sovereignty related in one way or another to conscription, and here the record of the individual state courts almost universally favored Richmond.[68] In fact, the courts were so compliant that some scholars have cited their record as one reason the Confederate Congress failed to establish a national tribunal. For all these reasons, the absence of a Confederate Supreme Court probably was not a serious menace to Confederate interests.[69]

the structure and operation of the Confederate courts generally, see Robinson, *Justice in Grey*, pp. 39–69.

67. Amlund, *Federalism in the Southern Confederacy*, p. 83; Brummer, "Judicial Interpretation of the Confederate Constitution," p. 132; Rembert W. Patrick, ed., *The Opinions of the Confederate Attorneys General* (Buffalo: Dennis, 1950), p. xx.

68. Brummer, "Judicial Interpretation of the Confederate Constitution," p. 133; Robinson, *Justice in Grey*, p. 436; J. G. de R. Hamilton, "The State Courts and the Confederate Constitution," *Journal of Southern History* 4 (November 1938): 425–48; Amlund, *Federalism in the Southern Confederacy*, pp. 88–92; Albert Burton Moore, *Conscription and Conflict in the Confederacy* (New York: Hillary House, 1963), pp. 162–90; John K. Bettersworth, *Confederate Mississippi: The People and Policies of a Cotton State in Wartime* (Philadelphia: Porcupine Press, 1978; reprint of a 1943 edition), pp. 72–4, 80.

69. Robinson, *Justice in Grey*, pp. 435–6; Amlund, *Federalism in the Southern Confederacy*, pp. 84, 93.

Regardless of these apparently mitigating factors, the northern Union was much stronger than the Confederacy in this area of administrative capacity.

This brief review of the administrative capacity of the Union and Confederate states has focused on eight important areas in which major tests of legislative sentiment occurred. In the policy areas involving presidential removal of officers and the board of admiralty, neither the Union nor the Confederacy exhibited greater conformity to statist principles of internal administrative organization. The Union probably had a slight advantage in the professionalization of military staff personnel, while the southern state was slightly superior in making appointments to the military academies, determining claims made against the government, and relying on demonstrations of competence in civil and military appointments. The Union had a clear advantage with respect to establishment of a supreme court while, in the most striking comparison, the Confederate state developed a discretionary, comprehensive manpower policy within the apparatus of the Bureau of Conscription and the Department of War that went far beyond anything the Union ever envisioned as a possibility. Though this record is mixed, the administrative design of the Confederate state appears to have been more consistent with statist principles than the Union. The southern statist orientation was most pronounced in questions allocating relative influence between the executive and Congress and between Congress and the central bureaucracy.[70] Seen another way, a major comparative source of state strength in the Confederacy was the structural weakness of the Confederate Congress in the southern central government.

In several instances, the policy areas that gave rise to the administrative decisions discussed in this section also involved important substantive issues of citizenship duties to the state. In the case of manpower conscription, Confederate policy was both administratively and substantively more statist than the Union because Confederate controls on the allocation of labor were both implemented by a more insulated bureaucracy, and more encompassing. In the case of the judiciary, administrative organization and citizenship policies are more complexly related. On the one hand, Union administrative organization was more statist because the North maintained a complete judicial hierarchy while the Confederate system lacked a supreme court. On the other hand, Union policy was also more statist because the North more thoroughly *limited* the power of the courts to review decisions made by the chief executive and the

70. See, for example, the three policy areas involving legislative authority: decisions of the Court of Claims, academy appointments, and discretionary authority over draft exemptions.

state bureaucracy. This apparent inconsistency is raised and resolved in the discussion of comparative Union and Confederate policies toward the suspension of the writ of habeas corpus in the following section.

3. Citizenship

Of all dimensions of central state authority, the American Civil War most profoundly shaped future state–society development in the relations of individual citizens to the state. Under the pressure of material and political mobilization, both the Union and Confederate states restructured the rights and duties of citizens in ways that reflected both roughly parallel developmental trajectories and major differences in the nature of the challenge each faced. In the Confederacy, the expansion focused on the duty of citizens to provide labor to the state and explored the potentially broad implications of a full, categorical mobilization of the manpower of the South. The Union enacted a much less comprehensive conscription policy. However, the northern state was comparatively aggressive in the repression of dissident political organizations and vocal opposition in the press. Within both nations, but particularly in the Union, the war transformed slaves into freedmen, thus moving them from one dimension (property) to another (citizenship).

Conscription. The decisions to conscript men into the military and to grant to the president the authority to suspend the writ of habeas corpus were the most significant state power-enhancing measures ever adopted by the Confederate state. The only measure that might compete in importance was embodied in legislation that regulated the already existing practice of impressment.[71] (During the Civil War, "impressment" referred to the forcible appropriation of property by the state in return for at least token compensation, the amount to be decided by government agents). The first conscription act was passed by the Confederate House of Representatives on April 14, 1862, and enacted into law two days later. This act declared all able-bodied, white males between the ages of eighteen and thirty-five subject to service in the Confederate military and retained those already enrolled in the army for an additional three years. Conscription dramatically centralized control over the organization of the military forces of the Confederacy by eliminating or severely reducing most aspects of participation by individual state governments. Conscrip-

---

71. For a general history of conscription in the Confederacy, see Moore, *Conscription and Conflict;* Schwab, *Confederate States of America,* pp. 193–202.

tion also enmeshed the individual citizen in a direct and subordinate relationship to central state authority.[72]

The original Confederate conscription act predated a much weaker Union policy by over a year and was the first military draft in American history. It was extensively enforced.[73] Even so, the unrelenting requirements of the war effort demanded an even harsher manpower policy. In November of 1864, the secretary of war advocated an end to all exemptions except those "officers actually essential to the conduct of the Confederate and State Governments" and that all other able-bodied men "without distinction, be at once devoted to the sacred duty [of] defending their country in the field."[74] Conscription, particularly discretionary authority over the granting of exemptions, gave the Confederate government almost complete command over the labor force throughout the southern economy. In turn, the Confederate government's control over the supply of labor gave the central state indirect control over industrial and agricultural production, including profit margins on government contracts and price ceilings on agricultural produce.[75]

72. The combination of conscription with suspension of the writ of habeas corpus vastly increased the vulnerability of the individual citizen to central state controls. Suspension in effect made conscription decisions involving individual men unappealable and thus gave conscription agents complete discretion over the determination of exemptions and eligibility. For the South, see Moore, *Conscription and Conflict*, pp. 86–7; for the North, James Ford Rhodes, *History of the United States*, vol. 4 (New York: Macmillan, 1920), p. 417.

73. In 1864 the chief of the Confederate Bureau of War noted, "The conscription is now being pressed mercilessly. It is agonizing to see and hear the cases daily brought into the War Office, appeal after appeal and *all* disallowed. Women come there and weep, wring their hands, scold, entreat, beg, and almost drive me mad. The iron is gone deep into the heart of society." Robert Kean, *Inside Confederate Government*, edited by Edward Younger (New York: Oxford University Press, 1957), p. 174.

74. Confederate States of America, War Department, *Report of the Secretary of War* (Richmond, Va., 1864), p. 7. In describing the improvements embodied in the 1864 revision, Richard Goff has observed that from "an administrative viewpoint the act left little to be desired, except for the exemption of officialdom and professionals." Charles Ramsdell praised the same act because it abolished previously protected exemptions and "authorized the Secretary of War to detail men for certain necessary civil services" which left "factory owners . . . entirely at the mercy of some government bureau." Goff, *Confederate Supply*, pp. 95, 163; Charles W. Ramsdell, *Behind the Lines in the Southern Confederacy* (Baton Rouge: Louisiana State University Press, 1944), p. 102.

75. Amlund, *Federalism in the Southern Confederacy*, pp. 63–71, and Charles W. Ramsdell, "The Control of Manufacturing by the Confederate Government," *Mississippi Valley Historical Review* 8 (December 1921): 235. As an example of agricultural price controls, see Goff, *Confederate Supply*, p. 162. Goff adds that the "broad exemption-and-detail provisions" of the third conscription act (February 17, 1864) "put the government in a general position to control farm and factory labor, and in the face of mounting subsistence shortages, the act, together with subsequent War Department rulings, spelled out government controls over agriculture with even greater precision."

The Confederate government seems to have most actively exercised this command over the supply of labor in relation to central state direction of private wool, cotton, leather, shoe, and general ordnance production.[76] The most extensive use of exemption authority was, however, in relation to Confederate direction of railroad operations.[77] Control of railroad traffic, in turn, complemented the state's influence over industrial production because, given the shortfall in railway capacity, control of railroad operations was roughly equivalent to control over the allocation of raw materials. Compliant factories were systematically favored by Confederate quartermasters. Outside the conscription-centered system of industrial and agricultural controls, the provisions of an "Act to Lay Taxes for the Common Defence and Carry on the Government of the Confederate States," amended February 17, 1864, effectively conferred upon the central government potential licensing authority over all major trades, businesses, and occupations.[78] Together, Confederate direction of railway operations, taxation, and conscription conferred upon the central government almost absolute control over the southern economy. At all times, however, the manpower authority embodied in the conscription and exemption acts was far and away the most important source of central state influence.[79] The final report of the Bureau of Conscription, issued

76. Ramsdell, "The Control of Manufacturing," pp. 234–40, 245–6. For an example of military enforcement of labor in detailed or exempted occupations, see R. H. P. Robinson, *General Orders of the Confederate States Army, 1863* (Richmond, Va.: A. Morris, 1864), no. 30 (March 18, 1863), p. 28: "conscripts or detailed men leaving their employment without written permission shall be reported to the nearest enrolling officer, to be tried and punished as deserters."

77. Goff, *Confederate Supply*; Amlund, *Federalism in the Southern Confederacy*, pp. 47–8; Francis B. C. Bradlee, *Blockade Running during the Civil War: And the Effect of Land and Water Transportation on the Confederacy* (Salem, Mass.: Essex Institute, 1925), p. 255; and Charles W. Turner, "The Virginia Central Railroad at War, 1861–1865," *Journal of Southern History* 12 (November 1946): 513.

78. Dozens of different occupations and businesses were assigned specific taxes that could have easily become prohibitive. *Laws of Congress in Regard to Taxes, Currency, and Conscription* (Richmond, Va.: James E. Goode, 1864), pp. 3–20.

79. The enforcement of conscription also threatened to turn the Bureau of Conscription into a central manpower agency for employment within the Confederate government itself. For General Orders No. 7 (January 19, 1863) which recognized the exempted status of Post Office Department employees, see *General Orders of the Confederate States Army, 1863*, p. 8. On the implications of conscription enforcement on Ordnance Bureau operations, see Frank E. Vandiver, "Makeshifts of Confederate Ordnance," *Journal of Southern History* 17 (May 1951): 190. On a conscription-induced shortage of clerks in the Treasury Department, see Todd, *Confederate Finance*, pp. 10–11. On John Whitner's difficulties in preparing a record of the Confederate Constitutional Convention (because conscription officers repeatedly drafted his assistants), see Ulrich B. Phillips, ed., *The Correspondence of Robert Toombs, Alexander H. Stephens, and Howell Cobb* in the *Annual Report of the American Historical Association, 1911*, vol. 2 (Washington, D.C.: 1913), pp. 602–3. On the relationship

in 1865, estimated that 177,000 men had been enrolled from areas east of the Mississippi. In his *Conscription and Conflict*, Albert Moore concluded that the bureau's estimate should be raised to at least 300,000 (effectively accounting for between 30 and 50 percent of all enlistments).[80]

For many reasons, the Union implemented a much weaker manpower policy than did the South. In the first place, the North instituted a federal draft almost a year after the Confederacy.[81] By this time the war was, as it turned out, almost half over and many of the possible connections between conscription and control of industrial production would not have had time to develop even if northern policy had been as comprehensive at that in the South. In fact, however, Union conscription was structured so that a comprehensive manpower policy was completely beyond the reach of the northern government. The Union draft allowed exemptions for physical or mental disability, for specified family relationships involving dependents, and for high federal or state officials but, unlike Confederate policy, did not offer occupational deferments. In some respects, Union conscription resembled a system of taxation by offering (until summer 1864) exemptions to anyone willing to pay the government $300 and, throughout the war, allowed draftees to hire a substitute to serve in their place. (Early in the war, the Confederacy also allowed substitution, but the practice was abolished in December 1863.) Both nations offered bounties to volunteers, but only the Union devoted both a comparatively and absolutely large portion of the government's resources to cash incentives.[82] Finally, the quotas assigned to the individual states of the North could be filled by sending agents into occupied regions of the South to enlist freed slaves.[83] Because of these "free-market" as-

between departmental operations and conscription enforcement generally, see Goff, *Confederate Supply.*
80. Pp. 355–8. Many "voluntary" enlistments were, in fact, the result of the imminence of conscription. Also see Thomas, *The Confederate Nation*, p. 155.
81. The Union House of Representatives passed the conscription bill on February 25, 1863 (115 members supported passage, 48 opposed; *Congressional Globe* 37:3:1293). For the text of the conscription law, see Frank Moore, ed., *Rebellion Record*, vol. 1 (New York: G. P. Putnam, Henry Holt, 1864), pp. 270–4.
82. For accounts and descriptions of the Union draft, see the *1863 American Cyclopaedia*, pp. 361–71; *1864 American Cyclopaedia*, pp. 32–5; *1865 American Cyclopaedia*, pp. 30–2; Shannon, *Organization and Administration*, pp. 259–323; and Eugene C. Murdock, *One Million Men: The Civil War Draft in the North* (Madison: State Historical Society of Wisconsin, 1971). Bounties paid out by the Union (including those offered by state and local governments) are estimated to have totaled $750 million – more than all quartermaster expenditures for the entire war, about as much as all regular salaries paid to the troops after enlistment, and five times as much as all ordnance expenditures. Kreidberg and Henry, *History of Military Mobilization*, pp. 108–10.
83. *1863 American Cyclopaedia*, pp. 25–6; for a sample of legislative debate on this

pects of northern conscription policy, the Union drafted only a fraction of all men who finally served in the war and those who did serve were not chosen as part of a larger, comprehensive manpower program.[84] In contrast, Confederate conscription allocated labor throughout the mobilized southern economy.[85] The implications of this more statist policy reached beyond the direct supply of manpower to the front and deep into the very fabric of industrial and agricultural production.[86]

Suspension of the writ of habeas corpus. The power of the judiciary to demand that the executive (or monarch) justify the detention or imprisonment of citizens can be traced back to the Magna Charta. In brief, the writ of habeas corpus compels agents of the executive to produce the

policy, see *Congressional Globe* 38:1:845, February 26, 1864; Terrell, *Indiana in the War*, pp. 72–3.

84. Only 6 percent of all men who served in the federal army can be directly attributed to the draft although some doubtless volunteered because conscription presented them with a harsher alternative. Kreidberg and Henry, *History of Military Mobilization*, p. 108. As Coulter summarized the comparative Civil War experience, "No wheel of fortune was necessary [in the South], as was the case in the North, for all were in the army, and it was merely a matter of reaching them and either exempting them or sending them on to camps of instruction, from which they would later be sent to the army.... In some [southern] communities the country had been swept clean of men." *Confederate States of America*, pp. 323–5.

85. Some scholars have argued that Confederate conscription policy was counterproductive in that, according to these critics, the southern government lost more in civilian morale than it gained in manpower. See, for instance, Coulter, *Confederate States*, pp. 327–8. These critics operate within a logic that can claim that the Confederate state would have been "stronger" if it had abolished conscription and relied upon volunteers in military recruitment. Such a definition of a strong state allows them to identify and connect political "mistakes" to the effectiveness of the Confederate war effort. While the attractiveness of that logic should be clear, the problematic conflation of state authority and societal impact should be equally obvious. In addition, the inclusion of considerations of political efficacy in a conception of state strength inevitably involves contextual factors of the political environment that would ultimately reduce every instance of state development to idiosyncratic exceptionalism. For example, the calculation of advantage in a trade-off between morale and manpower, if such a trade-off indeed existed, is inextricably grounded in a specific historical context. For my limited purposes, the text assumes that a state designed according to statist principles maximizes the effectiveness of war mobilization. This assumption allows a full analysis of the Union and Confederate performance but excludes contextual factors that may have influenced the efficacy of individual war measures.

86. Kreidberg and Henry, *History of Military Mobilization*, p. 136 and, generally, 136–7, 139. Published by the U.S. Army in 1955, this work listed a number of lessons to be learned from the experience of the Civil War. As the accompanying discussion made clear, the Confederate mobilization was considered more applicable to modern warfare in almost every respect other than the utilization of black soldiers. Other scholarly evaluations have also favored the South. See, for example, Shannon, *Organization and Administration*, p. 269; Murdock, *One Million Men*, pp. 24–5; Coulter, *Confederate States of America*, p. 145.

"body" of the prisoner named in the writ and explain his detention under the law. The United States Constitution recognized this English and colonial right in Article I, Section 9 and further provided that the writ could only be suspended "when in cases of rebellion or invasion the public safety may require it." From one perspective, the writ is not a right of citizenship but, instead, represents an allocation of authority between the judiciary and the executive bureaucracy. The writ of habeas corpus, in effect, assigns authority to the judiciary to review and overturn actions taken by the executive and his agents. How much the rights of individual citizens are protected by the writ depends on how the courts use that authority and the nature of the laws under which the executive may justify the detention of citizens. Suspension of the writ thus transfers authority from the courts to the executive; on its face then, suspension may be a negative development in terms of administrative capacity (because the judiciary has a more statist role than that played by an elected chief executive).[87] However, since the courts can only use this power to limit state authority over the citizenry, the writ also has even more important substantive implications on the breadth of central state authority that outweigh its potential impact on administrative capacity. Everything considered, these substantive considerations support an interpretation of suspension as an expansion of central state authority.

During the American Civil War, both the Union and Confederate states suspended the writ. In the North, Lincoln first suspended the power of the courts to review detentions along the rail corridor between Philadelphia and Washington, D.C., on April 27, 1861. His action was in response to civilian attacks on Union troop movements in the city of Baltimore. Because Congress was not in session, Lincoln's proclamation was an aggressive assertion of executive power, in that congressional concurrence, commonly considered to be required by the Constitution, was not evidenced by supporting legislation. Lincoln's unilateral action led the Chief Justice of the Supreme Court, Roger B. Taney, to rule that the proclamation was unconstitutional and therefore void. However, citing Lincoln's proclamation, the military commander to whom the rul-

---

87. In terms of administrative organization, evaluation of the statist implications of suspension turns on whether the central bureaucracy systematically exercises power over the citizenry (as in conscription) or whether the chief executive implements more discretionary controls (represses dissent by jailing political opponents, for example). In most cases, suspension of the writ would probably enhance statist organization in the first instance (by removing an impediment to bureaucratic policy). In the latter instance, suspension might weaken state organization by failing to provide for systematic review of decisions by a lesser branch of the government (lesser in terms of statist principles). These considerations again underscore the complex and often ambiguous role of the judiciary in statist theory.

ing was addressed simply refused to comply with Taney's order.[88] Subsequent proclamations extended the suspension to the rail corridor between Philadelphia and Maine, the entire states of Kentucky and Maryland, the city of St. Louis, and, ultimately, the entire nation. The power conferred upon federal authorities was almost absolute. When speaking with the British ambassador, William Seward, the secretary of state, only slightly overstated his power when he said, "I can touch a bell on my right hand and order the imprisonment of a citizen of New York; and no power on earth except the President can release them."[89] For all practical purposes, federal detention under suspension of the writ and arrests of citizens under martial law were one and the same thing.[90] Execution of central state policy in both cases was carried out by the military under executive direction and the sweeping repression of dissent and public resistance to Union policy tended to blur any distinction between civilian and military rule.

Both suspension of the writ and martial law were used by the Union to detain thousands of individuals who represented real and imagined threats to the security of the government, and to close down dissident newspapers or influence their editorial policy.[91] In most elections held in

88. James G. Randall, *Constitutional Problems under Lincoln* (Urbana: University of Illinois Press, 1964), pp. 120–4, 161–3. On December 8, 1862, the U.S. House of Representatives passed legislation retrospectively endorsing all presidential suspensions between April 1861 and December 1862, voiding all litigation that had already or might arise under those proclamations, and conferring upon the president full, discretionary authority over suspension in the future. This bill passed by a 2 to 1 margin (90 yea votes to 45 nay – this is the legislative test of statist sentiment in the North). *Congressional Globe* 37:3:22; for a public protest against passage of this bill, signed by 37 members of the House, see pp. 165–6, December 22, 1862; for subsequent deliberations, see pp. 1102–7, February 19, 1863; p. 1479, March 2, 1863; for the text of the final act, see *1863 American Cyclopaedia*, pp. 255–6.
89. Quoted in Meneely, *War Department*, p. 224n.
90. *1861 American Cyclopaedia*, pp. 438–42. In the Confederacy, also, most civil and military officers considered suspension of the writ and martial law inextricably connected. Even before the presidential authority was used to suspend the writ, for example, "numerous arrests were made in the Confederate States by the civil and military authorities, both State and federal, on charges of treason and on suspicion of aiding and abetting the enemy. Many of the arrests made by military commanders were, to say the least, extraconstitutional. Some were in the broad twilight zone between war crimes and treason. The Army usually refused to yield a prisoner on a writ of habeas corpus on the ground that no civil court had power to inquire into the detention of prisoners of war . . . on the theory that upon dissolution of the Old Union every citizen had the right to determine whether he would remain a citizen of the United States or go with his State to the new Confederacy." The interpretation of citizenship related in the last portion of this passage was supported by a U.S. Supreme Court decision handed down in 1830 in a case arising out of the American Revolution. Robinson, *Justice in Grey*, p. 385.
91. For both specific and general descriptions of detentions under suspension, see *1861 American Cyclopaedia*, pp. 354–62; *1862 American Cyclopaedia*, pp. 508–16; *1863*

the border states during the war the military relied on martial law to screen eligible voters and influence results in favor of candidates who supported the Union war effort. In Maryland, the federal government seized secessionist members of the state legislature and, in Baltimore, a federal commander even stopped the sale of pictures of Confederate military officers and political leaders.[92] Viewed in its entirety, federal suspension of the writ was notable both for a broad realization of its repressive potential and for the fact that the executive claimed unilateral authority for its exercise.

In the South, Jefferson Davis was comparatively less assertive than Lincoln in several respects. For one thing, the Confederate president never suspended the writ without first requesting and receiving congressional approval for this authority. For another, even when granted this power, Davis never used suspension as sweepingly or with as much overt political purpose.[93] As in the North, suspension of the writ reinforced the discre-

American Cyclopaedia, pp. 469–91, 518–25; *1864 American Cyclopaedia*, pp. 421–5; for the entire war, the Provost Marshal's office in Washington reported some 38,000 arrests, including detentions of draft violators and prisoners of war as well as "offenders against the State." *1865 American Cyclopaedia*, pp. 414–21. For accounts and lists of newspapers closed by military authorities or destroyed by mobs (often with the tacit approval of local representatives of the Union government), see *1861 American Cyclopaedia*, pp. 328–30; *1863 American Cyclopaedia*, pp. 423–5; *1864 American Cyclopaedia*, pp. 389–94; *Frank Leslie's Illustrated Newspaper*, October 5, 1861; Long, *Civil War*, pp. 108–11, 119–20, 158, 316, 319, 321, 326, 362, 504. While the number of newspapers that were closed was quite large, James Rhodes concluded that the "public prints were substantially untrammelled" because many papers violently critical of the Union war effort continued to publish. *History of the United States*, vol. 3, p. 440.

92. Rhodes, *History of the United States*, vol. 3, pp. 440–1; *1863 American Cyclopaedia*, pp. 530–1, 606–16; *1864 American Cyclopaedia*, pp. 451–3; *1865 American Cyclopaedia*, pp. 568–76; Long, *Civil War*, pp. 66, 79, 90, 108, 127, 151–2, 186, 261, 270–1, 325, 409, 534, 696. Commenting on the use of martial law in Maryland, the British ambassador to the United States, Lord Lyons, wrote Earl Russell on September 16, 1861: "A war has been made at Baltimore upon particular articles of dress, particular colors, portraits of Southern leaders and other supposed symptoms of supposed disaffection. The violent measures that have been resorted to have gone far to establish the fact that Maryland is retained in the Union only by military force." Quoted in Bradley T. Johnson, *Maryland*, vol. II of *Confederate Military History* (Atlanta: Confederate Publishing Co., 1899), p. 95.

93. The Confederate Congress passed legislation authorizing suspension on four separate occasions. The first law was approved February 27, 1862, which, after a second act passed April 19, was set to expire on October 13, 1862 (thirty days after the next meeting of Congress). On that date, Congress approved a third suspension act, which, again, was set to expire thirty days after the next meeting of Congress. On February 13, 1863, the authority expired, only to be renewed one year later, on February 15, 1864, under a fourth and final law. The renewal expired ninety days after the next meeting of Congress, August 1, 1864. Under the first and subsequent laws, authority to suspend the writ was given for all arrests made by the central government for offenses against the Confederacy. The fourth statute detailed these offenses, including treason, desertion, sabotage, and unlawful intercourse with the enemy, but, in prac-

tionary power of the executive at the expense of the national judiciary and the rights of the citizenry. In the South, however, suspension was also a measure that concentrated authority in the central government at the expense of the individual states. Because the Confederacy never established a supreme court and because the district courts tended to be the pliant tools of executive policy, most writs were issued by the courts of the individual states. In the absence of a fully integrated national judiciary, the suspension acts thus allowed Confederate officials to ignore the otherwise definitive rulings of local and individual state courts. In Georgia and North Carolina, in particular, suspension of the writ was thus viewed as a direct assault on states' rights.[94]

In response to invasion by the Union army, Davis used his powers of suspension for the first time to declare martial law in Norfolk and Portsmouth, Virginia, on February 27, 1862. Three days later martial law was extended to include Richmond and all areas within ten miles of the city. His proclamation suspended the writ of habeas corpus, replaced all civil authority (the mayor excepted) with military rule, and closed all distilleries and liquor stores. Similar proclamations under the first suspension act later included other areas of Virginia, the city of Memphis, the Department of East Tennessee, and much of the territory surrounding Charleston, South Carolina. Proclamations issued by either the president or individual military commanders extended suspension to the cities of Mobile, New Orleans, Atlanta, and Salisbury, North Carolina; the entire states of Arkansas and Texas; and portions of Louisiana and Mississippi.[95] Even so, most arrests under martial law were probably related to the sale of liquor by civilians to enlisted men, usually in camps.[96] In

tice, it was almost as broad a grant of authority as the original. Schwab, *Confederate States of America: 1861–1865*, p. 186–92; Amlund, *Federalism in the Southern Confederacy*, p. 106. Texts of the various acts can be found in *A Digest of the Military and Naval Laws of the Confederate States, Provisional and First Congresses* (Columbia, S.C.: Evans and Cogswell, 1864), pp. 132ff; the text of the February 15, 1864, act can be found in *Public Laws of the Confederate States of America, Fourth Session, First Congress*, pp. 187–8. Considering their profound implications for individual liberty and for the relative influence of the judicial systems of the individual states, suspension acts passed the Confederate Congress with relative ease. For a general history, see Robinson, *Justice in Grey*, pp. 389–415; Yearns, *Confederate Congress*, pp. 150–60; Alexander and Beringer, *Anatomy of the Confederate Congress*, pp. 166–73; Thomas, *Confederate Nation*, pp. 150–2.

94. See, for example, the text of "Resolutions on the Suspension of Habeas Corpus" (March 19, 1864) in *Acts of the General Assembly of the State of Georgia*, pp. 152–4.

95. Long, *Civil War*, p. 176; Schwab, *Confederate States of America*, pp. 186–7; Owsley, *State Rights in the Confederacy*, pp. 151–2, 157–60; Coulter, *Confederate States of America*, p. 337; Bettersworth, *Confederate Mississippi*, p. 78.

96. See, for example, the summary of "Sentences by Court-Martial" carried in the Richmond *Dispatch*, December 5, 1862.

1862 the Confederate secretary of war expressed the hope that "this revolution may be successfully closed without suppression of one single newspaper in the Confederate States" and, indeed, only one paper (in Knoxville, Tennessee) seems to have been closed by national authorities; only one other (in Raleigh, North Carolina) was destroyed by mob action.[97]

The writ of habeas corpus was formally suspended by congressional action for only eighteen months and President Davis was unwilling to suspend the writ by executive proclamation.[98] In other periods, however, Confederate military officers often acted as if the writ were formally suspended, by resorting to martial law. The military thus partially filled the breach in periods when the Confederate Congress failed to pass enabling legislation. Even allowing for these supporting, extrastatutory efforts, however, the Confederate experience with suspension of the writ and martial law was considerably less statist than the administrative structure and implementation in the North.[99]

Emancipation amendment. The destruction of slavery also introduced important changes in the citizenship dimension. Before the Civil War, most national and individual state government policies considered slaves solely as property and regulated the institution of slavery largely as a matter of property rights. Since property rights were almost entirely controlled by local governments, most aspects of slavery in the antebellum period did not involve either questions of citizenship (because slaves were not considered citizens) or central state authority. The Emancipation Proclamation of September 1862 was the first major step toward extending national authority over the institution of slavery and placed many former slaves under the citizenship dimension of central state authority for the first time. Even more important was passage of the emancipation amendment to the Constitution of the United States, which abolished

97. Coulter, *Confederate States of America*, p. 503; Long, *Civil War*, pp. 131, 408; *1861 American Cyclopaedia*, pp. 438–42. Bettersworth similarly concluded that "there was almost no restriction upon the freedom of the press in Mississippi during the war." *Confederate Mississippi*, p. 337.

98. The roll call chosen as a test of legislative sentiment on suspension was recorded on passage of the bill that renewed executive authority originally granted on February 27, 1862 (*Journal of the Confederate House of Representatives*, 1:2:518, October 9, 1862). Thirty-eight members supported passage, 29 opposed.

99. Suspension of the writ in the northern Union tightened the hold of Republicans on the local as well as national state apparatus. For example, under martial law and suspension powers, Governor Morton exercised virtual dictatorial authority over the state of Indiana from 1863 to 1865 after the state legislature, controlled by the Democratic party, refused to enact war measures. See Allan Nevins, *The War for the Union: War Becomes Revolution, 1862–1863* (New York: Charles Scribner's Sons, 1960), pp. 390–2.

slavery throughout the Union. From a statist perspective, the Thirteenth Amendment should be interpreted as a major expansion of central state authority not so much because slavery was abolished but because the central state in effect nationalized governmental regulation of American black labor in the process of emancipating slaves.[100] Though the Confederacy nationalized some aspects of slaves as property (for example, by making slaves susceptible to confiscation and impressment), no southern measure extended central state authority over slavery as much as did Union-sponsored emancipation.

All three citizenship policies examined in this section suggest that northern and southern state performance matched the comparative requirements of the war effort in both the Union and the Confederacy. Manpower shortages forced the South to adopt a fully developed conscription program and, through it, a comprehensive, centrally controlled allocation of labor throughout the southern economy. In contrast, the relative absence of disloyalty in the South allowed the Confederacy to adopt less rigorous measures to suppress dissent and suspend civil judicial process. The Union also moved more aggressively with respect to slavery and emancipation. Northern state expansion in the latter case arose out of the political economic structure of the war itself – most slaves resided beyond Union lines, and thus the interests of slaveowners were largely unrepresented in the northern political system at the very same time that emancipation promised to aid the Union war effort. While southern conscription conformed more closely to statist principles than did the Union draft, the northern state held an advantage in the other two policy areas and, probably, in the citizenship dimension of central state authority overall.

Of all the other dimensions of central state authority, citizenship was probably the dimension most closely related to the control of property. One major reason for this linkage was the dual nature of central state intervention in the organization and allocation of labor in the private

100. Because Lincoln drew his authority from his constitutional powers as commander in chief of the nation's armed forces, the Emancipation Proclamation only freed slaves in areas controlled by the Confederacy. In only those areas were slaves able to contribute to southern resistance and thus vulnerable to presidential decisions intended to reduce the material resources available to the rebellion. In those areas already controlled by the Union, Lincoln was unable to abolish slavery by presidential fiat, because slaves could not contribute to the Confederate war effort. See, for example, *1863 American Cyclopaedia*, pp. 594–6. The Thirteenth Amendment passed the House of Representatives on January 31, 1865 (119 yea votes, 56 nay; *Congressional Globe* 38:2:531). The Thirteenth Amendment did not confer citizenship upon former slaves; that was done by the subsequent, Fourteenth Amendment. Until the latter's ratification, freedmen were in a position vis-à-vis the central government similar to that occupied by unnaturalized immigrants.

economy. Emancipation transformed property into citizens, while conscription obligated other citizens to labor for the state. Another reason these dimensions were so closely linked was that state policies in both areas tended to complement each other in practice, particularly in the Confederacy.

4. *Control of property*

In the area of property relations, the Confederacy was considerably more statist than the Union. As a result of policies that sometimes contravened rather clear provisions of the Confederate Constitution and moved southern society into novel arrangements between state agents and private property owners, the Confederate state gained control over the use and disposition of private property in many sectors of the southern economy. Most of these sectors bore an immediate, direct relation to the requirements of military supply. Other government policies, such as the production of salt and the impressment of gold coin and plate, were less directly connected to the war effort.[101] Almost all central state activities had parallels administered by the governments of the individual states. In most cases these parallel activities complemented, rather than competed with, the central government's mobilization effort.[102] Confederate control of the southern economy was most complete in quartermaster stores (other than food) and munitions.[103] Perhaps the best example of such control was the operation of the Confederate Nitre and Mining Bureau. Faced with severe shortages of ordnance, the Confederate state, through the bureau, granted advances of 50 percent toward the capital cost of private production of nitre (potassium nitrate used in the manufacture of gunpowder) and the mining of coal and iron, in addition to claiming authority over the production and operations "of any mine or manufactory" necessary "to secure an adequate supply." As a consequence of these activities, Confederate bureaus came to underpin the southern economy. Throughout the South, "country and city teemed with

101. Because of a shortage of natural deposits in the South, salt production became an unusually important government activity in the Confederacy. See, for example, Goff, *Confederate Supply*, pp. 78–128; William Watson Davis, *Civil War and Reconstruction in Florida* (New York: Columbia University Press, 1913), pp. 205–10. The best overall treatment is Ella Lonn, *Salt as a Factor in the Confederacy* (New York: Columbia University Press, 1933).
102. For general accounts of individual state activity, see May Spencer Ringold, *The Role of the State Legislatures in the Confederacy* (Athens: University of Georgia Press, 1966), pp. 39–56, and Amlund, *Federalism in the Southern Confederacy*, ch. 9.
103. Amlund, *Federalism in the Southern Confederacy*, pp. 68–74; and Ramsdell, "Control of Manufacturing," pp. 231–49.

officious agents of the new bureaucracy who sometimes impressed into service what they could not buy."[104]

Because the material resources of the North were so much greater than those in the South, Union efforts to control private firms or create state-owned productive capacity were much less extensive. The most impressive northern accomplishments from a statist perspective were the early use of slaves as soldiers and confiscation of the property of citizens who cooperated with the Confederacy. In both cases northern policy acted upon that portion of the citizenry defined by the war as the enemy while Confederate expansion in the area of property relations reorganized and partially socialized the economic base of the "loyal" society of the South. If the South had won the Civil War, the statist precedents and experience of the conflict might have endured in the Confederate state because they were originally applied to the social base of the nation itself. Under the same conditions, Union precedents would probably have been irrelevant to the postwar state because they would have applied to an "alien" people beyond the reach of a defeated Union government. Even with northern victory, Union policy precedents that applied exclusively or almost exclusively to the South were significantly less enduring than those which applied to indigenous northern society.

In the following section Union and Confederate policies are compared in eight general areas of potential central state control of property relations. Although they are generally representative, these policy areas do not include a few of the most significant aggrandizing actions of the Confederate state (such as the entry of the government into large-scale manufacturing activity), because central state expansion in these exceptional areas was so consensual that congressmen did not record their votes on these issues. For those policy areas where either Union or Confederate congressmen did have an opportunity to express their opinions, most entailed substantially parallel or symmetrical expansions of state activity, although several more represented idiosyncratic developments. This review begins with comparison of government policy toward the construction and operating control of the largest and most complex industrial systems in both the Union and the Confederacy – railroads.

104. Lester J. Cappon, "Government and Private Industry in the Southern Confederacy," in *Humanistic Studies in Honor of John Calvin Metcalf* (Charlottesville: University of Virginia, 1941), p. 187. For a description of the manufacture of munitions and other war material by Confederate arsenals, see pp. 163–8, 172–4, and 177–8. On the extent of Confederate control of economic production, see Goff, *Confederate Supply*, pp. 32, 103; General Orders No. 85 (June 16, 1863), *General Orders of the Confederate States Army, 1863*, pp. 96–7; Ramsdell, *Behind the Lines in the Southern Confederacy*, pp. 73–4.

Railroad construction subsidies. Perhaps no decision more clearly revealed the precipitate renunciation of southern political tradition than
the passage of a bill to extend Confederate aid to the Richmond and
Danville Railroad. In the federal Congress, most Southerners had consistently opposed government assistance in the construction of internal
improvements, because they viewed such activity as unconstitutional and
interpreted aid as an enhancement of the power of the central government
at the expense of the states.[105] This opposition carried over into the
formative months of the Confederacy, and as a consequence, the Provisional Congress as Constitutional Convention adopted a provision prohibiting almost all types of government assistance.[106]

Despite this constitutional prohibition, Jefferson Davis advocated Confederate aid in the construction of a rail connection between Danville,
Virginia, and Greensboro, North Carolina, as early as the fall of 1861.
Arguing that government assistance would be premised on military necessity rather than commercial advantage, the administration gained
congressional approval on February 7, 1862, with almost two-thirds of
those voting supporting government aid. Once the precedent had been
set, the Confederacy engaged in numerous construction projects. While
the government stated that assistance was available only for rail lines of
military value, the nature of military operations during the Civil War
and of Confederate strategy (with its emphasis on perimeter defense)
conferred some military relevance upon almost all projects. The real
limitation on Confederate-sponsored rail expansion was not ideological
opposition but a chronic shortage of iron.[107]

The Union built or subsidized many more miles of track than the
Confederacy during the war. Some of this trackage was laid down as the
result of land grants to private railroad corporations. Other track was
built as part of the tactical operations of various military campaigns and
did not require specific congressional approval. The best comparable
northern example of government-sponsored railroad construction arose
as a result of legislation authorizing the completion of a line between the
Ohio Valley and East Tennessee. Endorsed by Union generals commanding forces in this theater, the proposed railroad had clear military

105. The individual states of the South, however, were actively involved in railroad
      construction and operation in the antebellum period. See, for example, Peter Wal-
      lenstein, *From Slave South to New South: Public Policy in Nineteenth-Century
      Georgia* (Chapel Hill: University of North Carolina Press, 1987), pp. 33–9.
106. Lee, *Confederate Constitutions*, p. 95.
107. Black, *The Railroads of the Confederacy*, pp. 148–9, 162, 200; *Journal of the
      Provisional Confederate Congress*, 781–2, 819, 821 (February 10 and 14, 1862);
      Journal of the Confederate House of Representatives 1:1:260, 1:2:480 (April 17
      and October 2, 1862); Coulter, *Confederate States of America*, pp. 270–2.

value and the same kind of commercial potential as the Virginia–North Carolina line built by the Confederacy.[108] Comparison of Confederate and Union state performance in this policy area is made difficult by the fact that the South did not possess the material resources to carry out any but a few construction projects. The Union, however, was aggressive only in using railroad construction as a means for structuring the broad outline of frontier development (considered separately later in this chapter).[109] Allowing for the constraining impact of iron scarcity on Confederate policy and the fact that much of Union activity took place in the western territories (considered separately as a "world-system" policy), the two central states delivered roughly similar performances with respect to railroad subsidization and construction in previously settled regions of their respective nations.

Control of railroads. Like government construction assistance, Union and Confederate control of railroad operations significantly expanded central state authority. The Confederate House of Representatives passed legislation that would have established "consultations" between railroad officials and the secretary of war as early as April 17, 1862. As reported by the House Committee on Military Affairs, the bill would have invested all railroad officials with military rank and subjected them to military discipline, thus centralizing control over all operations within the Confederate military.[110] Floor amendments, however, systematically stripped the measure of its strongest provisions and left the bill only a pale shadow of the form in which it was introduced. When the Senate failed to consider the bill, the legislation died. On May 1, 1863, the Confederate Congress subsequently enacted a law giving the executive branch wide discretionary authority over operations, schedules, and the impressment of railroad property either as a penalty for noncooperation or wherever necessary to maintain more essential lines.

By February 1864 the Confederate Army could directly control all private rail operations if it wished to do so.[111] Using this authority and

108. The U.S. House of Representatives passed the joint resolution authorizing construction on May 31, 1864 (64 yea, 56 nay; *Congressional Globe* 38:1:2611).
109. Where construction subsidies to railroads were part of a national policy of territorial expansion and political integration of remote frontier regions, government aid falls under the world-system dimension where, for example, land grants to what became the Union Pacific Railroad are discussed. In contrast, construction subsidies considered under the property-control dimension mandated a state role in the rail network established within the already settled and integrated regions of the nation.
110. Black, *The Railroads of the Confederacy*, pp. 97–8.
111. The authority for military direction of rail operations was contained in General Orders No. 15 (February 15, 1864): "As the various railroads of the Confederacy for the transportation of troops, supplies, and munitions of war are under the control

the power to impress into government service both railroad employees and rolling stock, the War Department gradually assumed direction of southern rail traffic without overtly socializing the railroad system. Even so, on November 3, 1864, the secretary of war requested stronger measures to further centralize rail operations, and on February 28, 1865, Congress enacted legislation confirming the secretary's unqualified control over all rail operations and subjecting employees to military discipline.[112] Although these two acts (of May 1, 1863, and February 28, 1865) were more powerful measures than the bill that failed in 1862, the earlier measure had established the original precedent concerning central state control over the operations and property of private industrial corporations.[113]

The Union government claimed authority "to take possession of any or all the railroad lines in the United States, their rolling stock, their offices, shops, buildings, and all their appurtenances" in legislation passing the northern House of Representatives on January 29, 1862.[114] The bill empowered the Union state to prescribe operating rules and regulations and, in cases of outright confiscation, to force employees into "the military force of the United States, subject to all restrictions imposed by the rules and articles of war." On February 11, 1862, this authority was transferred to Brevet Brigadier General D. C. McCallum by Secretary of War Stanton. Despite this potentially broad power to directly control railroad operations, however, the Union almost exclusively relied on open-market contracts for the supply of railroad services in the northern free states. A general rate agreement between the railroads and the Union government governed all market transactions between the two parties during the war and was sufficiently lucrative to prevent actual administration of line operations by the government. With minor exceptions

of the Quartermaster's department, the orders of commanding generals, and other officers, relating to such transportation by railroad, will be immediately furnished to the Quartermaster-General, in order that arrangements may be made in time to harmonize the various routes so as to prevent accidents and delays." *Official Records*, ser. IV, vol. 3, p. 77.

112. Black, *The Railroads of the Confederacy*, pp. 121–2, 164–75, 280–1. The 1863 act gave administrative control to the quartermaster general. *General Orders of the Confederate States Army, 1864*, p. 17. Also see General Orders No. 2 (January 3, 1863) and No. 26 (March 7, 1863) issued before the May 1, 1863, law. *General Orders of the Confederate States Army, 1863*, pp. 4–5, 24–5; and Goff, *Confederate Supply*, p. 105, 110–11; Ramsdell, *Behind the Lines in the Southern Confederacy*, p. 97; *Report of the Secretary of War*, p. 14; Coulter, *Confederate States of America*, pp. 280–1; Bettersworth, *Confederate Mississippi*, pp. 136–40.

113. The 1862 bill passed the House with 39 yea and 33 nay votes. For the roll call and text of the bill, see *Journal of the Confederate House of Representatives* 1:1:251–4, April 17, 1862; also, *Proceedings*, 45:148–9.

114. *Congressional Globe* 37:2:547–8.

(such as short stretches of line in Maryland and Pennsylvania during the Gettysburg campaign), all railroads actually operated by the Union lay entirely in the Confederate states. These operations were quite substantial, employing at the peak some 25,000 men, 2,000 miles of track, 400 locomotives, and over 6,000 cars.[115]

Of the two experiments in governmental control, the Confederacy turned in a stronger performance from a statist perspective. While the southern state is often criticized for administrative disorganization and slow recognition of the importance of an efficient rail system to military operations, the Confederate state did attempt direct control of the entire rail network of the South.[116] By contrast, the Union limited government control and operation to the military railroads that directly supplied the front in hostile territory. While the Union experience was impressive as a demonstration and exploitation of the material, industrial advantage of the northern economy, the performance did relatively little to expand potential state control of private enterprise.

Regulation of financial markets. Both the Union and Confederate states attempted to regulate financial markets during the Civil War, but the configuration of their respective economies led them down different developmental paths. In the South, the most important attempt to control financial markets first arose when the Confederate House of Representatives passed legislation prohibiting acceptance of U.S. greenbacks on April 30, 1863. As approved by the House, the prohibition was considerably broader than a simple prohibition on Union currency, as it included a ban on the securities of northern state governments and private corporations chartered under northern law. This measure later failed in the Confederate Senate. A second bill, narrower in scope, moved through the House on December 24, 1863, and became law on February 6, 1864. This legislation prohibited the circulation of U.S. currency but exempted postage stamps and the activity of authorized Confederate officials. While this law may have driven some currency transactions underground, the

115. Union administration of railroads is described in *Report of Brevet Brigadier General D. C. McCallum*, Exec. Doc. No. 1: House of Representatives: 39th Congress, 1st Session, (Washington, D.C.: Government Printing Office, 1866), Ser. Rec. 1251, especially pp. 1–39. Also see, Meneely, *The War Department*, pp. 126, 199, 235, 238–46; Philip Shaw Paludan, *"A People's Contest": The Union and Civil War, 1861–1865* (New York: Harper & Row, 1988), pp. 139–43.
116. On the inadequacy of Confederate administrative performance, see Black, *The Railroads of the Confederacy*, pp. 294–5; George Edgar Turner, *Victory Rode the Rails: The Strategic Place of the Railroads in the Civil War* (Indianapolis: Bobbs-Merrill, 1953), pp. 233–4. For a contemporary description of the condition of Confederate railroads, see *1863 American Cyclopaedia*, pp. 208–9; *1864 American Cyclopaedia*, pp. 193–203.

greenback price of Confederate notes was widely known and quoted in most major southern cities.[117]

In the North, the most significant attempt to regulate financial markets was one result of the suspension of the gold standard in the winter of 1861–2. After suspension, the price of Union currency began to float against gold and, as the northern state emitted more and more greenbacks, these began to rapidly depreciate. Many Northerners believed that the depreciation of greenbacks was caused in some way by speculation on the New York gold exchange, and, in fact, short-term fluctuations in the gold value of greenbacks were often connected to how well Union armies were doing in the field. From these beliefs and connections, many Union congressmen concluded that gold trading on the exchange was, at best, unpatriotic or, at worst, traitorous. These congressmen combined to pass legislation prohibiting almost all organized trading in gold. Since much of the developed world was on a gold standard, this attempt to prohibit open trading in gold amounted to an attempt to control the rate of foreign exchange between greenbacks and other national currencies.[118]

This prohibition had an immediate, disastrous impact on the value of Union currency as many traders, representing otherwise legitimate import/export firms and financial houses, were forced into black market transactions. The greenback plummetted against gold and foreign trade was seriously disrupted during the two weeks the prohibition was in effect. Reversing direction, Congress repealed the ban on July 1, 1864.[119] As conceived and implemented, the prohibition was a primitive attempt to regulate foreign exchange transactions by removing them from organized trading in an open market and, by thus prohibiting certain types of transactions, to influence the gold value of greenbacks. This attempt failed because, as many congressmen and financial journals noted, speculation on the exchange could not by itself cause a shortage of gold.[120]

117.   The only roll call vote on either of these measures occurred on April 30, 1863 when the first bill survived a tabling motion (16 to 52). *Journal of the Confederate House of Representatives* 1:3:466–7. For congressional debate on the second bill, see *Proceedings* 50:102, 105 (December 22, 1863), and 147–8 (December 29, 1863). The text of the later bill appears on pp. 125–6 (December 24, 1863).
118.   This legislation passed the U.S. House of Representatives on June 14, 1864 by a vote of 76 to 62. *Congressional Globe* 38:1:2936–7.
119.   *Congressional Globe* 38:1:3468; Bolles, *Financial History of the United States*, pp. 142–7.
120.   As Representative John Broomall of Pennsylvania put it, gold's "fluency is like that of water; and the attempt to buy up the gold market would be like that to drain the Potomac by dipping or pumping. . . . Suppose such an attempt should be made by the entire horde of New York brokers combined. The whole commercial world and the whole mining interests would conspire to thwart them. If gold should thereby become more valuable in New York than in Boston, Philadelphia, Liverpool, a constant stream of it would flow in from all quarters to restore the disturbed balance

Currency controls seldom work effectively for very long even in more advanced states than the Civil War Union and Confederacy. They didn't work at all in either of these cases. In spite of this failure, the Union experience with financial markets was significantly more statist than that of the Confederacy. While outright regulation failed, the Union successfully developed other methods of intervening in the open market (largely in connection with the placement of government debt instruments and the payment of gold interest) that greatly enhanced the central state's role in national and international capital markets (see Chapter 4). The history of Confederate finance contains no parallel to the growth of Union intervention in open money markets.

Slaves as soldiers. Of all the legislation passed by the Confederate Congress, the one law that most perfectly demonstrated the depth of southern nationalism and its new life independent of the slave culture that had originally given birth to the Confederacy was the bill providing for the arming and freeing of the slaves. Prior actions involving the use of blacks in the southern war effort included the organization of a regiment of free blacks by the state of Louisiana in April 1861 and the enlistment of Creoles for the defense of Mobile by the state of Alabama in November 1862. The Confederate Congress first authorized the impressment of slaves as laborers in military operations in 1863 and significantly expanded that authority the following year.[121]

Serious congressional debate on the possible arming of slaves appears

---

...all the efforts of all the brokers' boards and gamblers in christendom cannot vary its price from that exchangeable value, except to a small extent and for a limited period." *Appendix to the Congressional Globe* 38:2:50, February 7, 1865. It should be noted, however, that this analysis does not preclude the possibility of short-term "corners" on the gold exchange.

121. The two general accounts of the background of this legislation are N. W. Stephenson, "The Question of Arming the Slaves," *American Historical Review* 18 (January 1913): 295–308, and Thomas R. Hay, "The South and the Arming of the Slaves," *Mississippi Valley Historical Review* 6 (June 1919): 34–73. Also see Moore, *Conscription and Conflict in the Confederacy*, pp. 343–9; *1864 American Cyclopaedia*, pp. 193–203. The state of Alabama impressed slaves as laborers as early as 1862, and the legislature authorized the enlistment of Creoles in "An Act: To Authorize the enrollment of the Creoles of Mobile" (November 20, 1862). *Acts of the Called Session, 1862 and of the Second Regular Session of the General Assembly*, pp. 37–40, 162. The Confederate army impressed slaves as laborers in Mississippi as early as February 1862. Bettersworth, *Confederate Mississippi*, pp. 169–70. For military regulations relating to slave impressment, see *General Orders of the Confederate States Army, 1863*, pp. 190–2; also, Ira Berlin et al., *Freedom: A Documentary History of Emancipation, 1861–1867*, ser. 1, vol. 1 (*The Destruction of Slavery*) (Cambridge: Cambridge University Press, 1985), pp. 665–73. For the text of the second impressment act (February 17, 1864), see Robert F. Durden, *The Gray and the Black* (Baton Rouge: Louisiana State University Press, 1972), pp. 51–3.

to have begun with the *1864 Report of the Secretary of War.* In his message, the secretary observed that conscription or impressment of slaves as soldiers "would of course require the concurring legislation of each State . . . because to the States belong exclusively the determination of the relations which their colored population, or any part of them, shall hold." This position conceded to the central state the power to impress slaves into the army and to arm them, but gave to the individual states exclusive authority to emancipate slaves from bondage. Because emancipation was believed, evidently by all who considered the matter, to be an essential feature of the proposal to arm slaves, the cooperation of the individual states would be required. But, the secretary added, "while it is encouraging to know this resource for further and future efforts is at our command, my own judgment does not yet either perceive the necessity or approve the policy of employing slaves in the higher duties of soldiers." In his annual message to Congress on November 7, President Davis stopped short of advocating the impressment of slaves as soldiers, but added "should the alternative ever be present of subjugation or of the employment of slaves as soldiers, there seems no reason to doubt what should be our decision."[122]

For the next four months, Congress and the southern nation argued the case for and against arming slaves. During this period most congressmen made the transition from "the Confederate States of America *and* slavery" to "the Confederate States of America *without* slavery." On February 11, 1865, the Confederate House of Representatives appointed a special committee of thirteen members (one from each state) to consider legislation enabling slaves to serve as soldiers. That committee brought back to the House a bill providing for the conscription of "300,000 troops . . . to be raised from such classes of the population, irrespective of color, in each state, as the proper authorities thereof may determine." Nothing in the bill mandated emancipation "except by consent of the owners and of the states," although all expected emancipation to follow. With the strong backing of President Davis, Governor Smith of Virginia, and General Robert E. Lee, this bill cleared the House on February 20, 1865. The best test of congressional sentiment, however, occurred on an amendment adopted just prior to passage. Offered by Charles Conrad of Louisiana, the amendment inserted presidential authority to call for troops under the terms discussed above and isolated the issue of arming the slaves from the remainder of the bill. Approved by a wide margin (46 to 29), the amendment demonstrated the depth of nationalist sentiment in the House – and its detachment from the pres-

122. Hay, "The South and the Arming of the Slaves," p. 52.

ervation of slavery. As such, the bill presented the Confederate House with the chamber's stiffest challenge: whether or not the "rights" of private property in slaves should be violated, both individually and as a system, as part of the military effort directed by the central state of the Confederacy.

The Confederate Congress finally forwarded the slaves-as-soldiers legislation to Davis on March 13, 1865, and the Confederate president immediately signed it into law. General Orders No. 14, the implementing bureaucratic directive, specified first that "No slave will be accepted as a recruit unless with his own consent and with the approbation of his master by a written instrument conferring, as far as he may, the rights of a freedman." The directive stated further that "All officers... are enjoined to a provident, considerate, and humane attention to whatever concerns the health, comfort, instruction, and discipline of these troops, and to the uniform observance of kindness, forbearance, and indulgence in their treatment of them, and especially that they will protect them from injustice and oppression." As Emory Thomas notes, this paternalistic injunction apparently set a standard of "equal treatment" for black soldiers in the ranks.[123]

Under legislation passed on July 12, 1862, the Union Army began to accept blacks for labor or other service. Subsequent legislation, passed by the U.S. House of Representatives in February 1863, authorized the enrollment of blacks as soldiers, and a third act of February 24, 1864, subjected blacks to the draft. Although the northern Congress empowered the army to enlist blacks only after prolonged and bitter discussion, the Union ultimately made much wider use of them in the military than did the Confederacy. In theory, northern enrollment of freedmen and slaves was restricted until 1864 to those who had been free before the war or legally emancipated by the Union war effort (by the Emancipation Proclamation). In practice, federal recruitment often failed to distinguish between those who had been formally emancipated and those who had

---

123. *Proceedings* 52:337; *Journal of the Confederate House of Representatives* 2:2:611–12, February 20, 1865. For the complete text of the bill as enacted, see Durden, *The Gray and the Black*, pp. 202–3. Passage came too late for implementation. On April 28, 1865, for example, "the major-general commanding in Florida directed ten prominent citizens of Florida each 'to proceed at once to raise a company of negroes to be mustered into the service of the Confederate States for the War' but Lee had already surrendered at Appomattox on the ninth, nearly three weeks previously." Davis, *Civil War and Reconstruction in Florida*, pp. 227–8. Durden, *The Gray and the Black*, pp. 249–50, 268–9; Thomas, *The Confederate Nation*, pp. 296–7; Clarence L. Mohr contends that arming of the slaves might have provided willing troops for the Confederacy if the war had continued. *On the Threshold of Freedom: Masters and Slaves in Civil War Georgia* (Athens: University of Georgia Press, 1986), p. 291.

escaped from their legal owners.[124] By 1865 all slaves who enlisted in the Union army, and their families, were emancipated under federal law. Because of the clear parallel with Confederate action, Union recruitment of blacks as soldiers is considered a policy falling under the property dimension of central state authority. Though the Confederate decision to enlist slaves probably was of more symbolic importance, the overall experience and material use of blacks as Union military auxiliaries and troops conformed much more closely to statist principles.

Confiscation. The programmatic confiscation of private property is one of the most effective ways of reshaping a national political economy and promoting strong central state penetration of societal structures. As part of their mobilizations, both the Union and Confederate states confiscated the property of those who failed to support their war efforts. These policies both punished treason and strongly encouraged citizens to affirm loyalty to their respective governments. On both sides, confiscation targeted elite, property-rich segments of the population.

Under martial law, the Union began to confiscate property in contested areas of the border states and occupied regions of the Confederacy very early in the war. Some of these uncoordinated, disjointed efforts were legitimated under an August 1861 statute that freed all slaves who were used in direct supporting roles in the Confederate war effort. This act was a somewhat narrower version of a bill that originally advocated a broader definition of treasonous use and a wider range of confiscatable property.[125] Even under this law, however, Union confiscation was not limited to slaves. In November 1861, for example, northern authorities seized ships in New York harbor that were wholly and partially owned by Southerners. In January 1862 the military began to seize the property of secessionists in St. Louis if they did not pay assessments for the support of Union refugees.[126]

124. Kreidberg and Henry, *History of Military Mobilization*, p. 113; *1864 American Cyclopaedia*, p. 36; Curry, *Blueprint for Modern America*, p. 66; Paludan, "A People's Contest", pp. 208–214; Foner, *Reconstruction*, pp. 7–8. The roll call included in the voting analysis was taken on a motion to table (kill) the bill that became the 1863 act. *Congressional Globe* 37:3:282, January 12, 1863. The motion was turned back by a large margin (54 to 83). For subsequent deliberations on the 1863 bill, see 37:3:557, January 27, 1863; 570–83, January 28; 598, January 29; 633–5, January 30; 688–90, February 2. For the indifference of federal officers to the formal status of slave enlistees, see Berlin et al., *The Destruction of Slavery*, pp. 34–5, 110–11.

125. For the text of the August 6, 1861, act, see *Hunt's Merchants' Magazine and Commercial Review*, November 1861, pp. 525–6; for a brief description of the act, see *Congressional Globe* 37:1:409, August 2, 1861.

126. *Hunt's*, November 1861, p. 526; Long, *Civil War*, p. 163.

In an attempt to both broaden the scope of confiscation and make wartime seizures permanent, the House of Representatives created a select Committee on the Confiscation of Rebels on April 28, 1862. After considering a wide variety of possible policies, the committee reported back a bill that confiscated the property of Confederate leaders immediately and all others who supported the rebellion after a grace period. Though the bill provided for limited judicial review of seizures, the Union government could have freely confiscated most southern property under this legislation.[127] After further deliberations in the Senate, a somewhat weaker bill was sent to the president on July 12, 1862.[128] Though some potentially important steps were taken to implement this legislation, Union confiscation policy remained haphazard and tentative until Andrew Johnson's postwar pardons effectively scuttled the whole program.[129]

Compared to the northern Union, the Confederacy moved more rapidly and established a more systematic and comprehensive confiscation policy. Under a May 1861 law the Confederate state sequestered all debts owed by Southerners to northern individuals and firms. Under a subsequent act, passed by the Confederate House of Representatives on August 24, 1861, all the property of alien enemies of the southern nation was made liable to seizure and most easily traceable property was readily confiscated. These early seizures included northern investments in southern corporations (such as the stocks and bonds of railroads and banks), bank deposits, and state and local debt. Government inspection of public and corporate records facilitated execution of the law.[130]

As in the North, confiscation did not amount to very much in the end. Beyond an initial wave of feverish expropriation, the Confederacy showed

127. For the creation and appointment of the select committee, see *Congressional Globe* 37:2:1846, April 28, 1862; for general debate on the wide variety of confiscation proposals, see 37:2:1766–72, 1788–90, April 22–3, 1862; for the text of the House bill, see 37:2:2360–1, May 26, 1862. The measure passed the House (82 to 68 – this is the roll call included in the voting analysis).

128. The original House bill had been, by this time, merged into a larger measure that included both emancipation and colonization abroad of slaves. This omnibus bill is discussed later in this chapter as a world system policy. For a legislative history, see Curry, *Blueprint for Modern America*, pp. 88–95.

129. For a contemporary discussion of federal confiscation, see *1863 American Cyclopaedia*, pp. 219–25; *1865 American Cyclopaedia*, pp. 202–3. Also see Foner, *Reconstruction*, pp. 51, 158–9; Curry, *Blueprint for Modern America*, pp. 99–100.

130. For the text of the bill, see *Rebellion Record*, vol. 1, pp. 19–23. Before passage in the House, the bill survived a tabling motion 51 to 9. *Journal of the Provisional Congress*, pp. 402–3. This is the roll call included in the voting analysis. For enforcement and implementation, see *1861 American Cyclopaedia*, pp. 148–9, 433; *1864 American Cyclopaedia*, pp. 203–4; *Rebellion Record*, pp. 213–14.

little enthusiasm for property seizures.[131] However, the nature of the problem facing the two regimes differed in ways that ultimately led the Confederacy to develop a more statist position. The Union targeted the property of southern citizens, which was primarily in the form of landed estates, slaves, livestock, and fixed assets generally. As a result, northern confiscation policy both treated southern citizens as individuals (potentially loyal or disloyal) and struck at forms of property in which formal ownership was often difficult to determine (because it was not clearly documented). Both of these policy aspects as well as the fact that the Union ultimately provided for rather strict judicial review made most seizures legally suspect and, over the long term, unenforceable. Southern policy, on the other hand, struck for the most part at the investments of foreign enemies of the Confederate state (not, as the Union did, at traitorous citizens of the state) and confiscated without discrimination all the property of these enemies. Although the southern courts could review seizures, the entire program was much more sweeping and unambiguous than the northern counterpart. The potential impact of these two programs on their respective political economies also differed. For the North, confiscation promised at least a much larger role for the central state in the adjudication of southern property rights and, possibly, wholesale redistribution of wealth between loyal and disloyal elements of the southern population. For the South, seizure liquidated northern capitalist investments and thus portended an end to Union commercial influence in the Confederate economy.[132]

Bankruptcy. Though a national bankruptcy law was not enacted until after the Civil War, the U.S. House of Representatives passed a bankruptcy bill December 12, 1864.[133] Recognizing the impact of Confederate sequestration and confiscation on northern creditors, the measure excluded from its benefits "all those who in any way have given aid or comfort to unlawful disputation of the authority of the Government" but otherwise promised to nationalize the adjudication of creditor rights with reference to the assets of insolvent firms and individuals.[134] If the bill had been enacted, the Union would have taken an important step toward the creation of a nationalized market for commercial investment and trade. Because the measure failed, the structure and operation of the

131. Coulter, *Confederate States of America*, pp. 123–4.
132. Neither policy set a precedent in American political development; for a listing of confiscation laws passed by the colonies during the Revolutionary War which seized the property of Tories, see *Congressional Globe* 37:2:2194–5, May 19, 1862.
133. *Congressional Globe* 38:2:24. The roll call included in the voting analysis recorded 76 members yea, 56 nay.
134. *Congressional Globe* 37:3:223–4, January 7, 1863.

Union state held no advantage in this area over the Confederacy, which did not consider the subject at all.

Impressment. From a state-building perspective, a much more significant development was the systematic impressment of private property as the primary means of supplying the Confederate military. Simply defined, impressment involved involuntary transactions in which the state compelled citizens to exchange supplies for currency, bonds, or promises to pay at some future date. What distinguished impressment from confiscation were these exchanges of government obligations for property and the fact that impressment, unlike confiscation, fell for the most part on loyal citizens. Again unlike confiscation, impressment activity was not intended to remake the national political economy by weakening the position of targeted social groups but was, instead, meant to supplement other means of supplying armies in the field. Large-scale impressment began in the autumn of 1861 when inflation and shortages in the marketplace drove prices to prohibitively high levels. By the fall of 1862, the Confederate government had vastly expanded the scope of impressment activity, and state agents were routinely seizing military supplies from blockade runners, speculators, plantations, farms, railroads, factories, distilleries, and mines. Although the Confederacy attempted to make this activity "as palatable as possible" by paying the prices that prevailed in the open market, impressment remained a practice outside the law, and irregularities in implementation caused wide public resentment.[135] In response, Congress placed authority for impressment in the statutory code in the spring of 1863.[136]

This legislation established price-setting boards of assessment to regulate impressment activity. Appointed by President Davis and governors of the individual states, the boards published official price schedules to be followed by officers who impressed supplies. These schedules invariably set prices below marketplace levels and, as the war continued, evolved into a national system of price controls.[137] Later, the Confederate

135.   Goff, *Confederate Supply*, pp. 41–2, 97; *1863 American Cyclopaedia*, pp. 206–8, 447; Schwab, *Confederate States of America*, pp. 202–9. For examples of implementing directives and application in specific sectors of the economy, see General Orders No. 31 (March 19, 1863). *General Orders of the Confederate States Army, 1863*, pp. 29–30 and General Orders No. 49 (April 23, 1863) *Official Records*, ser. IV, vol. 2, p. 511.

136.   On February 13, 1863, the Confederate House of Representatives overwhelmingly passed this impressment measure (52 to 7). *Journal of the Confederate House of Representatives* 1:3:107. The accompanying roll call is included in the voting analysis.

137.   For the text of the March 26, 1863, act and an April 27, 1863, amendment, see *Public Laws of the Confederate States of America, Third Session, First Congress,*

Congress enacted a tax "in kind" on farmers that required payment of "one tenth of the wheat, corn, oats, rye, buckwheat or rice" produced.[138] In practice, this tax further routinized impressment activities as it also reduced the internal revenue system to barter. As a result of these actions, the Confederate state established almost complete control over the price and availability of military supplies and slave labor throughout the southern economy. In contrast, the Union relied almost as exclusively on market forces and open competition for military contracts for the provision and pricing of goods and services.

Destruction of property. One of the most extreme measures that a central state can undertake with reference to the private economy is the uncompensated seizure and destruction of property. An amendment providing such authority was offered to a bill ordering the burning of cotton, tobacco, and other property likely to fall into Union hands. William Miles, the chairman of the Committee on Military Affairs of the Confederate House of Representatives, contended that the "destruction of the cotton was the first consideration, and the compensation a matter of detail." After adopting the amendment (45 to 39), the House of Representatives subsequently backtracked a bit and passed a Senate bill providing for both the destruction of property and compensation.[139] The

pp. 102–4, 127–8. In addition to regulating the impressment of supplies, this act also provided for the impressment of slaves for labor. Implementing orders can be found in General Orders No. 161 (December 10, 1863) which set out regulations concerning procedures for the appeal of the decisions of impressing officers. *General Orders of the Confederate Army, 1863,* pp. 223–4. For examples of price schedules used by impressment officers, see *General Orders of the Confederate States Army, 1863,* pp. 65–70, 114–18, 139–44, 154–64, 203–4, 217–22; *General Orders of the Confederate States Army, 1864,* pp. 8–13, 75–80, 92–7. For evidence that price schedules and impressment practices evolved into a fairly centralized form of price control, see Goff, *Confederate Supply,* p. 98; General Orders No. 34 (April 1, 1863), *General Orders of the Confederate States Army, 1863,* pp. 32–3 (setting prices for beef hides to be paid by the army); and General Orders No. 10 (January 30, 1864), *General Orders of the Confederate States Army, 1864,* p. 13 (which extended impressment authority to "all materials essential to the production and manufacture of iron").

138. *Laws of Congress in Regard to Taxes, Currency, and Conscription,* p. 14.
139. The amendment struck the language "and the owners thereof shall receive just compensation therefore from the Confederate Government under such laws and regulations as may hereafter be established by Congress." *Journal of the Confederate House of Representatives* 1:1:60, March 5, 1862; *Proceedings,* 44:99–104, 117, March 5 and 7, 1862; *1862 American Cyclopaedia,* pp. 259–62. The roll call on the amendment was included in the voting analysis. On the burning of cotton by Confederate authorities generally, see Stanley Lebergott, "Through the Blockade: The Profitability and Extent of Cotton Smuggling, 1861–1865," *Journal of Economic History* 41 (December 1981): 882–3; in Mississippi, see Bettersworth, *Confederate Mississippi,* p. 85.

Union never established a formal policy for the destruction of property owned by loyal citizens.

Of the eight policy areas concerning property relations reviewed in this section, the Confederate state had a marginal to substantial advantage in three areas: control of railroads, confiscation, and the destruction of property. In addition, the southern state was decisively more statist in the most comprehensive and regime-shaping policy area: the impressment of private property under centrally controlled pricing and potential expropriation authority. In some respects, impressment and other Confederate controls on property emerged as central state responses to the absence of well-developed commodity markets and a chronic shortage of materiel generally.[140] Under these conditions, the South in a sense leapfrogged the more market-oriented (and thus less state-centered) Union war effort and produced a war mobilization very similar in some ways to the American experience in World War II. Comparatively statist policies for the Union were limited to the use of slaves as soldiers (a practice roughly equivalent in many instances to their uncompensated emancipation) and Treasury participation in financial markets. Both were important developments in central state authority and the latter held, under a paper currency system, the potential for sophisticated central state direction of investment and economic growth. Massive Treasury-led reorganization of the nation's financial system also transformed finance capitalists into one of the most influential "clients" of the Union state.

5. Creation of client groups

Client groups are those segments of the general population that are dependent upon the central state for a major fraction of their total income. Government policies that create client groups include those that provide income or income substitutes to individuals (for example, pensions, employment by central state institutions, welfare benefits, and price-control policies that apply to targeted groups in society), that establish future-oriented obligations that depend on state viability (for example, long-term debt or land warrants for frontier settlement), and that control the value of the currency (for example, the gold standard and redemption of paper money). For reasons that will become apparent in the following

---

140. The southern state's reliance upon impressment as a procurement practice has sometimes been attributed to the weakness of the Confederate currency. That weakness, in turn, has been attributed to the failure of the Confederate state to pass sufficiently comprehensive tax legislation and to enact legal tender legislation. See, for example, Alexander and Beringer, *Anatomy of the Confederate Congress*, p. 140. Both of these policy decisions are discussed later in this chapter.

discussion of individual policy areas, client-group creation is often intimately related to both the control-of-property and extraction dimensions of central state authority.

Legal tender notes. When the Union government went off the gold standard in the winter of 1861–2, the Treasury Department immediately began to experience difficulty in persuading the public to accept its notes. In response and as part of a comprehensive funding policy, the Union adopted legislation that made irredeemable paper currency (greenbacks) a legal tender for all debts public and private except the payment of interest on the national debt and customs duties.[141] By making greenbacks a legal tender, the Union in effect modified every money-denominated contract in the North by substituting the irredeemable paper currency for the formerly obligatory payment in gold. This substitution, in turn, effectively nationalized the payment clauses of private and public contracts in the northern economy and tied these agreements to the future financial policy of the central state. (For example, an inflationary expansion of the money supply would diminish the value of the principal owed by all debtors.) Greenbacks were later joined by a new national banking system that vastly expanded the central state's role in operation of financial markets. As Representative Samuel Cox of Ohio noted, through these policies "the party in power ... have established a paper-money banking system, under the control of the General Government, which concentrates power in the Administration ... and gives it control over the property and pecuniary interests of the people."[142] Even though the Confederate state issued vast quantities of paper currency, the national government never made this currency legal tender in public and private contracts.[143]

141. By making the greenback a "legal tender" for public and private debts, the Union in effect made the acceptance of paper currency mandatory in all contracts and transactions in which money changed hands if those obligations were to be enforceable in court. Before this legislation was adopted, creditors could have refused greenback payments and required, for example, gold – a contractual requirement that before 1862 was legally binding.

142. *Congressional Globe* 38:1:2683, June 2, 1864. For a legislative history of the legal tender clause and greenbacks generally, see Curry, *Blueprint for Modern America*, pp. 188–96. The roll call included in the voting analysis occurred on passage of the legal tender legislation. *Congressional Globe* 37:2:699, February 5, 1862. The bill was approved with 93 members voting yea, 59 nay.

143. Although both the Confederate secretary of the treasury and Jefferson Davis opposed legal tender legislation, enactment enjoyed broad support outside the government. Both the Richmond *Dispatch* and Charleston *Courier* backed legislation "as an accommodation to the loyal and a check to the disloyal" and interpreted refusal to accept Confederate notes as evidence of a "latent infidelity to the Southern cause." Schwab, *Confederate States of America*, pp. 86–101, 161. For a sample of congres-

Treasury debt. Another method of creating a client group is the issuance of government bonds, a strategy pursued by both the Union and Confederate states out of necessity. Bonds drawn on the credit of the government create an interest in the general viability and extractive (revenue) capacity of the state. Those who buy and hold these bonds, usually the more property-rich classes of society, are thus brought into a clientele relationship with the state. Compared to the Union, southern financial policy heavily relied on the voluntary acceptance of paper currency and only late in the war moved to fund government activity through major placements of debt.[144] In the North, however, both taxation and debt funded a much larger portion of the war.[145] One common difficulty with bonds, from a statist perspective, is that they can be marketed, and, once they are sold, the seller no longer has an enduring interest in the welfare of the state. In the North (but not in the South), this deficiency was alleviated by the erection of a national banking system that strongly encouraged banks to invest the major part of their capitalization in Union debt (described below and in the following chapter). Thus Union policy was considerably more statist in two respects: debt issues comprised a larger portion of the entire effort to fund the war and were, at least in part, permanently placed with finance capitalists, an important element in the national political economy.

sional sentiment on Confederate legal tender proposals, see *Proceedings,* 47:45 (October 3, 1862), and 49:27–8 (March 25, 1863); Eugene M. Lerner, "Money, Prices, and Wages in the Confederacy, 1861–1865," in Ralph Andreano, ed., *The Economic Impact of the American Civil War* (Cambridge, Mass.: Schenkman Publishing, 1967), pp. 31–60. The roll call included in the voting analysis occurred on an amendment that would have made Confederate notes "a legal tender in the payment of all private debts," offered on January 14, 1864. *Journal of the Confederate House of Representatives,* 1:4:632. The amendment was defeated (36 to 28).

144. The roll call selected for voting analysis was recorded on passage of "An Act to Reduce the Currency and to Authorize a New Issue of Notes and Bonds" (*Journal of the Confederate House of Representatives,* 1:4:644, January 16, 1864). This act attempted to compel the holders of Confederate currency to purchase government bonds and thus absorb the "excess" currency that was then producing a runaway inflation throughout the economy. Though the implementation of this complicated act ultimately failed to halt the falling value of the southern dollar, the choice presented to Confederate congressmen clearly indicated the statist alternative in this policy area. For a description of the act, see Todd, *Confederate Finance,* pp. 74–7 (and, on debt policy generally, 25–84).

145. The roll call included in the voting anlysis was taken on adoption of the conference report for the first major debt act of the Thirty-seventh Congress (*Congressional Globe* 37:1:383, August 1, 1861). The report was adopted (83 to 35). This measure gave the secretary of the treasury authority to issue $150 million in government bonds. As described in Chapter 4, the placement of these bonds both tied the solvency of major banks in New York, Philadelphia, and Boston to the future success of Union financial policy and, within a matter of months, brought on the suspension of gold payments by both these banks and the national treasury.

Homesteads in the Confederacy. As part of its confiscation policy, the Union ordered that land in the southern states be seized if the owner supported the Confederate war effort or failed to pay taxes imposed by the northern government. On May 12, 1864, the House of Representatives passed legislation that would have opened up this land to settlement by Union veterans, both white and black, under provisions similar to the national homestead act.[146] If this bill had become law, these settlers would have been tied to the Union state both during the probationary period when these veterans would have established their statutory qualifications to the land and afterward when title would have been protected by federal authorities against prospective challenge under southern state and local governments. Thus the legislation would have created a client group loyal to the Union state throughout the former states of the Confederacy. Although this proposal was never enacted, the Union did establish a broad homestead policy for the western frontier that not only created an important clientele in the national political economy but also and more importantly shaped the developmental trajectory of the United States.[147] The southern state never considered adoption of a parallel program and, thus, never established a comparable state-enhancing precedent in this policy area.

Military pensions. Very early in the life of the southern nation, the Provisional Congress of the Confederacy adopted a motion to postpone indefinitely consideration of an invalid pension bill and, thus, refused to support southerners who had been on the pension rolls of the United States.[148] While the Union never faced a parallel choice that would have as strikingly determined the fate of the federal pension system, the North did continue the antebellum program and even expanded eligibility and benefits. Although only some 10,700 veterans received pensions before

146. *Congressional Globe* 38:1:2253. The roll call included in the voting analysis approved the bill (75 to 64).
147. The vote on the Homestead Act was not included in this review of central state policy decisions because legislative support was overwhelming (106 to 16 on passage in the House of Representatives) and because the alignment (aside from absent Southerners) was very similar to the antebellum roll call studied in Chapter 2. If this vote had been included, homestead land grants would have been treated under the world-system dimension of central state authority. For a general history of legislative deliberations on the Homestead Act during the Thirty-seventh Congress, see Curry, *Blueprint for Modern America*, pp. 100–8.
148. The roll call included in the voting analysis was taken on this motion to postpone (which carried, 26 to 10). *Journal of the Confederate Provisional Congress*, p. 216, May 13, 1861. In 1858 the Department of the Interior reported 907 invalid pensioners from the eleven states that became the Confederacy. "Names of Invalid Pensioners, &c.," Exec. Doc. 119: House of Representatives: 35th Cong., 1st Sess., Ser. Rec. 959 (Washington, D.C.: James P. Steedman, 1858).

the war began, the system was rapidly expanded into a vast veteran-centered welfare system involving, by 1880, hundreds of thousands of recipients.[149]

Redistribution of income. Individual state and local governments in both the Union and the Confederacy readily initiated programs of assistance to soldiers' families once their war mobilizations began to draw upon men whose incomes constituted the primary means of support for their dependents.[150] In support of local efforts to provide indigent relief, the Confederate government instituted a tax on slave overseers who were exempted by law from conscription. The proceeds of this levy were then turned over to the relief agencies of the individual states – in effect, a redistribution of income from the owners of plantations to the large yeoman-farmer class of the South. On October 1, 1862, Representative Robert Trippe of Georgia proposed to include within the scope of this tax all exempted men – not just overseers – except those employed in a civilian or military capacity by the individual states and those physically or mentally incapacitated. Each man so exempted would be asked to pay "five dollars on every hundred dollars" worth of real and personal property and "five dollars on each hundred dollars of salary or fees or pay for personal services he may have received during the present year." Although Trippe's amendment failed and Confederate redistribution efforts at the national level remained focused on overseers, even this token southern effort to redistribute income between the classes set a statist precedent in a policy area that the Union entirely neglected.[151]

149. On the development of the Civil War pension system, see William H. Glasson, *Federal Military Pensions in the United States* (New York: Oxford University Press, 1918), pp. 123–280.

150. These programs spread rapidly throughout the South and by the end of the war comprised a large fraction of all individual income. In Alabama, for example, 10,263 families were on relief during 1862 (10.6 percent of all families). This total rose to 31,915 (33.3 percent) in 1863 and to 37,521 (37 percent) in 1864. In one rural hill county, 59 percent of all families were on indigent relief in 1863. Bessie Martin, *Desertion of Alabama Troops from the Confederate Army* (New York: Columbia University Press, 1932), pp. 128–34, 174–87. On the general response of state governments, see Ringold, *Role of the State Legislature in the Confederacy*, pp. 77–80; Davis, *Civil War and Reconstruction*, pp. 188–9; *1863 American Cyclopaedia*, pp. 423–5, 447; Wallenstein, *From Slave South to New South*, pp. 99–120. For public assistance to soldiers' families in the cities and towns of Massachusetts, see William Schouler, *A History of Massachusetts in the Civil War*, vol. 2 (Boston: William Schouler, 1871). For a brief comparison of northern and southern efforts at the individual state and local level, see Bremner, *The Public Good*, pp. 72–7. Bremner notes that northern assistance was rather meager compared to the much more substantial bounties offered at the time of enlistment, while nominally impressive southern policies were rapidly vitiated by soaring currency inflation.

151. Trippe's sweeping proposal drew the support of more than a third of all House

Price control. A different kind of redistribution was involved in the price-control policy of the Confederacy. There, plantations run by exempted overseers were compelled to sell surplus agricultural production to the government or soldiers' families at prices set by the impressment boards. Adopted as an amendment to the "Act to Organize Forces to Serve during the War" on February 3, 1864, the price-control provision effectively covered all plantations employing twenty or more slaves and many with less than that number.[152] Since the price schedules regulating impressment were set far below market levels and since food was the major form of civilian expenditure during the war, this provision was, in all probability, an even more effective means of redistributing income from the owners of plantations to indigent families than the 1862 tax discussed previously. Confederate performance in this policy area was more statist than that of the Union, which never established a program of civilian price controls.

Veteran soldiers' home. It was for budgetary reasons that President Jefferson Davis not only opposed the creation of a national pension system but even vetoed legislation to establish a veteran soldiers' home. When the president's veto message was received in the Confederate House of Representatives, backers emphasized that wounded veterans from areas overrun by Union armies had nowhere to go. Although the soldiers' home bill first passed the House by a margin of over 8 to 1 (the vote was 59 to 7), supporters mustered fewer than 40 percent of the ballots on a motion to override the veto.[153] As a result, the Confederacy never established a national home for disabled soldiers. In contrast, the Union inherited from the antebellum period a home founded in 1851 in Washington, D.C., and continued its operation during the war.

Of all the dimensions of central state authority, client-group creation was probably the policy area in which the Civil War states were both the least developed and experienced the least growth. From a statist perspective, the Union turned in a generally superior performance. The

members voting (22 to 42). *Journal of the Confederate House of Representatives* 1:2:476. For executive and administrative actions undertaken by the Confederacy in support of local relief efforts, see Paul D. Escott, " 'The Cry of the Sufferers': The Problem of Welfare in the Confederacy," *Civil War History* 23 (September 1977): 228–40.

152. The amendment was adopted in the House by a vote of 42 to 25. *Journal of the Confederate House of Representatives*, 1:4:742–3, February 3, 1864. For the final statute, see General Orders No. 26 (March 1, 1864), *General Orders of the Confederate States Army, 1864*, p. 35. On the relationship between conscription and price control in Florida, see Davis, *Civil War and Reconstruction*, pp. 214–15.

153. *Proceedings*, 50:242–3, 256 (January 15, 18, 1864). For the text of the president's veto, see *Journal of the Confederate Congress* 1:4:808–10, and for the override vote, pp. 848–9 (February 17, 1864).

northern advantage was particularly marked in central state finance, where the Union effectively combined extraction policy and client-group creation in a way that insinuated Treasury operations into the very marrow of the national financial system. The northern state was also more successful in the establishment of programs that tied veterans to the government – another policy area comparatively neglected by the South. The Confederacy was not, however, entirely inactive. The structural design of policies that combined conscription, price control, and income redistribution to soldiers' families suggests a sophistication and statist ambition that might ultimately have taken the southern government into a more class-sensitive, welfare-state direction.[154]

6. Extraction of resources

The boundaries between extraction and the other dimensions of central state authority are often indistinct. To some extent, the vagueness of these boundaries is a reflection of differences in the relation of individual policies to the structure and operation of state power. Extraction policies draw resources from society into the state irrespective (or largely so) of planned or conscious intervention in societal relations within the larger political economy. On the other hand, closely related policies under the other dimensions have a direct and larger impact on the position of social groups in the political economy and their ties to the state. Client-group policies, for example, have as one major consequence of their implementation the establishment of direct dependency between a societal group and central state viability. As was discussed in the previous section, the development of client-group ties and the extraction of resources need not be mutually exclusive activities, and under perhaps the best statist designs they are not. Similar interpretations can be attached to most "control-of-property" and some "world-system" policy areas (examples are impressment and the tariff, respectively). Most policies with derivative extraction implications are considered under other headings in order to bring out their other, broader political economic characteristics. This section includes policies that meet two related conditions. First, these policies are not generally intended to restructure the larger political economy, although the possibility that they might have that outcome is never entirely absent. Second, these methods of extracting resources from society tend to skim revenue from the flow of economic activity in the larger society without substantially altering the pattern or volume of that ac-

154. The redistributive impact of these policies was reinforced by the progressive structure of Confederate income tax rates (see Table 3.4). By comparison, the Union schedule was almost flat.

tivity. In some sense, then, extraction is the primary, purposeful goal of these programs.

Direct taxes/internal duties. The first major extraction policy enacted by both the Union and the Confederacy involved direct taxes. As set down by both the northern and southern constitutions, these levies were assigned to the several states within each nation according to their respective populations. The Union passed legislation authorizing $20 million in direct taxes on individuals according to their real estate and slave holdings. The individual states were given the opportunity to assume these tax obligations and thus, in practice, to substitute their own taxation systems for the collection of these federal revenue obligations. All states in the North except Delaware ultimately substituted their own collections for the direct tax alternative.[155] The Confederacy imposed similar direct taxes through legislation enacted August 19, 1861, and collected about as much revenue under this law as did the Union under the August 5, 1861, statute.[156] As contributions to their respective financial programs, these two schemes ultimately turned out to be unimportant (well under 10 percent of all receipts during the war in each case). Their significance arises from their role as precedents for later expansions of central state revenue capacity. As such, the Union and the Confederate states turned in relatively similar performances in this area of extraction policy.

Internal revenue. By and large, direct taxes fell almost exclusively on tangible forms of wealth such as land and slaves that were characteristic of a rural, agrarian economy.[157] They were also gathered by the individual

155. Bolles, *Financial History*, pp. 16–18; Harry Edwin Smith, *The United States Federal Internal Tax History from 1861 to 1871* (n.p.: Hart, Schaffner, and Marx, 1914), pp. 15–23. The roll call included in the voting analysis occurred upon initial passage of the bill in the House of Representatives. *Congressional Globe* 37:1:331, July 29, 1861. Seventy-seven members supported the tax, 60 opposed. For tables displaying the apportionment of direct taxes, population, and the amount of real and personal property by states, see ibid., p. 280, July 26, 1861. Other provisions in the bill levied unimportant internal duties on carriages, gold and silver watches, and liquor. A tax on incomes of 3 percent over $600 was also included in this version of the bill.
156. Todd, *Confederate Finance*, pp. 130–4. Votes on this August 19 act were unanimous. The roll call selected for inclusion in the voting analysis arose on a motion to table "a bill to raise revenue." *Journal of the Confederate House of Representatives* 1:2:497, October 6, 1862. The bill was tabled (36 to 28).
157. The agrarian emphasis of direct taxes was not lost on rural congressmen. As Representative Sidney Edgerton of Ohio, a Republican, complained, "the farmers of the country are to have their lands pledged as security for the payment of [the national] debt, while the great stockholders, the money lenders, and the merchant princes of Wall Street, and all the great capitalists, are to go free, and bear none of these burdens." *Congressional Globe* 37:1:282, July 26, 1861; also see pp. 306–8, July 27, 1861.

states, not by the central government, and collections thus depended on the cooperation of the individual states. Internal revenue taxes, on the other hand, targeted liquid capital and monetary transactions, which were much more heavily concentrated in large cities and were collected by a thoroughly nationalized bureaucracy within the central state. Acting first, the Union established an internal revenue system on July 1, 1862, that placed license fees on almost every occupation or service function in the northern economy; reached almost all monetary transactions through excise, ad valorem, and stamp duties; raised the maximum rate on incomes from 3 to 5 percent; and imposed levies on inheritance.[158] As one European writer noted, "The citizen of the Union paid a tax every hour of the day, either directly or indirectly, for each act of his life; for his movable and immovable property; for his income as well as his expenditure; for his business as well as his pleasure."[159] Reaching into almost every hamlet and town through a network of 185 collection districts, the new Bureau of Internal Revenue rapidly became the most coercive civilian agency of the national government. Aside from the military itself, no other bureaucratic expansion in the nineteenth century brought so many citizens into direct contact with central state authority.

One year after the Union, the Confederacy established a very similar revenue system. The southern law imposed a one-time-only ad valorem tax of 8 percent on all farm and forest products; reached most professional services and retail trade through occupational licenses and levies on gross sales; burdened "speculative" commodity transactions with a tax of 10 percent on profits; created a "tax-in-kind" of 10 percent on all agricultural produce grown in 1863; and imposed an income tax.[160] Though the two systems were not precisely comparable, southern levies

158. For a description of the taxes imposed by this law and the operation of the system during the Civil War, see Amasa A. Redfield, *A Hand-book of the U.S. Tax Law* (New York: John S. Voorhies, 1863); George S. Boutwell, *A Manual of the Direct and Excise Tax System of the United States* (Boston: Little, Brown, 1863); George S. Boutwell, *The Tax-payer's Manual* (Boston: Little, Brown, 1866); Smith, *Federal Internal Tax History*, p. 52, 313–18. For a legislative history of the act, see Curry, *Blueprint for Modern America*, pp. 170–80. The roll call included in the voting analysis occurred upon passage of the act in the House of Representatives. *Congressional Globe* 37:2:1577, April 8, 1862. The vote was lopsided (125 to 14).

159. Carl Von Hock, an Austrian, quoted in Frederic C. Howe, *Taxation and Taxes in the U.S. under the Internal Revenue System, 1791–1895* (New York: Thomas Y. Crowell, 1896), p. 65.

160. Todd, *Confederate Finance*, pp. 136–45; Coulter, *Confederate States of America*, pp. 178–81; *1863 American Cyclopaedia*, pp. 227–8. The roll call included in the voting analysis was recorded on passage of the bill in the House. *Journal of the Confederate House of Representatives* 1:3:234–5, March 23, 1863. The bill passed by a wide margin (50 to 30). For the text of the original House version of the act, see ibid., pp. 219–28. For the text of the law as enacted, see "The Tax Act Approved April 24, 1863" (n.p.: pamphlet published by the Confederacy).

Table 3.3. *Selected license fees imposed by the Union and the Confederacy*[a]

Occupation/Facility	Confederacy	Union
Apothecaries	$50	$10
Auctioneers	50	20
Bankers	500	100
Billiard rooms	40[b]	5[b]
Butchers and bakers	50	0
Confectioners	50	10
Distillers	200	50
Doctors	50	10
Lawyers	50	10
Peddlers	50	5–50
Photographers	50	10–25
Retail liquor dealers	100	20
Theaters	500	100
Tobacconists	50	10
Wholesale liquor dealers	200	100

[a]Under the April 24, 1863, and July 1, 1862, acts, respectively. See sources cited in the text.
[b]Per billiard table.

appear to be at least as high as (if not higher than) those imposed by the North (see Tables 3.3 and 3.4). This conclusion depends, in part, on the rough equivalency between the stamp duties upon which the Union relied and the southern taxes on gross sales (which ranged up to 20 percent on the gross revenue of distillers). Within a year after passage, the Confederacy had collected $82 million under the internal revenue act from 338 collection districts in ten states. This total does not include proceeds from the tax-in-kind, which were estimated at $40 million by March 1, 1864, and had no parallel in the Union.[161] Even allowing for a currency inflation that worked to the North's advantage, Confederate collections compare very favorably with the $39 million returned to the Union during the federal system's first year.[162]

Measured by statutory rates, coverage, and revenues collected the Con-

161. In comparing Union and Confederate extraction policies, we should also note that systematic impressment of supplies in the South increased the comparative rates at which the Confederacy extracted resources from the economy. Impressment had no counterpart in the North.
162. Todd, *Confederate Finance*, p. 145; *1864 National Almanac and Annual Record* (Philadelphia: George W. Childs, 1864), p. 192. The rapidly changing values of both the Confederate dollar and the Union greenback and a general lack of information concerning when these revenues were received make any comparison of collections in gold equivalents extremely difficult. See, for example, Eugene M. Lerner, "Money, Prices, and Wages in the Confederacy, 1861–65," and Wesley C.

Table 3.4. *Income taxes levied in the Confederacy and the Union*

Income Bracket or Exemption	Confederate	Union
Exemption	First $500	First $600
$ 500 to 1,500	5%	3%
1,500 to 5,000	10	3
5,000 to 10,000	12.5	3
over 10,000	15	5

Note: These are marginal tax rates under the April 24, 1863, and July 1, 1862, acts, respectively. See sources cited in the text. On salary income the Confederacy exempted the first $1,000, imposed taxes of 1 percent on the next $1,500, and 2 percent on income above $2,500.

federate internal revenue system extracted more wealth from that erected by the Union. This does not, however, imply that southern financial policy was a success – far from it. The South established a system after a crucial one-year delay that seriously undermined the value of Confederate currency and made many civilian monetary transactions with the government unwelcome. In addition, the Confederate advantage in internal revenue could not begin to replace the advantage the Union enjoyed in collections from customs duties. Measured in gold, the tariff alone extracted more resources from the northern economy than the remainder of the revenue system. In contrast, no manipulation of customs duties could possibly deliver substantial revenue to the Confederacy after the Union naval blockade of southern ports became effective. This deficiency could not be made up by raising the rates already imposed by the southern internal revenue system, because those rates were already so high that administration was difficult and evasion rampant. Technically, major portions of the Confederate revenue system were not perceptibly different from partial confiscation, and they destroyed the forms of commerce from the flow of which, theoretically, they were intended to skim wealth.[163]

While the Confederacy erred in not establishing a system in the first year of the war, the revenue problem the South faced was probably unsolvable. The Union, however, extracted wealth from a much larger, more commercially developed economy in which more modest tax rates

Mitchell, "The Greenbacks and the Cost of the Civil War," in Adreano, ed., *The Economic Impact of the American Civil War*, pp. 31–60, 85–97. Even so, Confederate collections were made from a much smaller stream of commerce than those in the North and, everything considered, probably constituted a significantly greater burden on the population.

163. The Confederate system verged on partial confiscation because those compelled to remit internal revenue duties were unable to pass on these taxes to the consumers they served and, thus, at least part of these taxes assumed the form of central state consumption of private capital.

could deliver revenue from renewable flows of capital and goods. In addition, full participation in the world economy produced, for the Union, even greater revenue from another source, customs duties. Limiting comparison to the respective internal revenue systems, discounting the southern experience for tardy response, but giving the Confederacy an overall superiority in comprehensiveness and design, a general evaluation of comparative central state performance in this policy area must view Union and Confederate efforts as approximately equivalent.

National banks. The initial establishment of the national bank system has been classified as an extraction policy for several reasons. Most important, during the Civil War membership in the federal system was voluntary. As a consequence, the exercise of central state authority in this policy area did relatively little to reshape property relations. For similar reasons, while the formation of national banks during this early period created a client group dependent in potentially significant ways on the viability of the central state, these banks could fairly easily turn in their national charters, exit from the system, and thus end the clientele relationship with the government. In fact, the strongest role of the national bank system established in 1863 appears to have been as a consumer and marketer of federal debt.[164] These institutions purchased Union debt on their own account as legally required security for the issuance of national bank notes. The banks also worked closely with the Treasury and appointed agents to market government bonds throughout northern society. While these extraction-related characteristics were the most prominent features of the system before 1865, the postwar system possessed much more powerful implications for clientele-group formation and for property relations (discussed in Chapter 4). In creating the national bank system, the Union took a major step in central state development that had no parallel in the southern Confederacy.

As has been stressed, this review of extraction policy is not a full comparison of the respective financial policies of the Union and Confederate states. A full comparison would take the analysis into policy areas in which extraction is a secondary feature (an example is the "legal tender" quality attached to Union greenbacks) or may not even be quan-

---

164.   The roll call included in the voting analysis was recorded on passage of the national bank bill in the House of Representatives. *Congressional Globe* 37:3:1148, February 20, 1863. Seventy-eight members supported the bill, 64 opposed. For the final text of the national bank law, see *1863 American Cyclopaedia*, pp. 295–304; for a brief history of legislative consideration, see Curry, *Blueprint for Modern America*, pp. 204–6; also, Paludan, *"A People's Contest,"* pp. 122–6; Albert S. Bolles, *The Financial History of the United States*, vol. 3 (New York: D. Appleton, 1894), pp. 127–8.

tifiable in monetary terms (an example is conscription of manpower). As defined here, extraction policies do not substantially restructure the political economies in which they operate. Instead, they are programs framed so as to allow the central state to draw wealth from production and commercial transactions without altering the terms of internal trade or the distribution of activity among economic sectors; the rate and point at which the state appropriates resources are, in fact, often chosen so as to minimize impact on the political economy. In a narrow sense, the Union outperformed the Confederacy in the extraction of resources because the former established a national bank system without parallel in the South. In a larger sense, however, the comparative wealth of the North allowed the Union to create a classic market-centered revenue system molded to the shape and potential of the northern economy while the material disadvantages under which the Confederacy operated compelled the South to push taxation policies beyond mere extraction into outright confiscation (as in impressment and internal revenue policies). More than any other aspect of central state development, the emergence of relatively statist policies within the extraction dimension usually depends on the existence of the kind of well-developed and commercialized economy that the North possessed. In less favorably endowed societies, such as the Confederacy, aggressive taxation consumes the very marrow of production and destroys open markets.

7. The world system

From a statist perspective, the relationship of the nation to the remainder of the world system would be largely determined by a professional career bureaucracy insulated from the parochial concerns of internal domestic politics. In such a government, the bureaucracy would base the broad internal development and foreign policies of the country on the national interest, free from the short-term political interests that otherwise divide the polity, restrict bureaucratic freedom of action, and debilitate long-term planning capacity. Under the world-system dimension we consider the broad policies that a state might enact as part of such a statist design.

Tariff. Customs duties both extract resources from the economy and protect domestic producers from foreign competition, to an extent varying with the size of the duty. A tariff that minimized protection and maximized revenue might conceivably fall under the extraction dimension of central state authority. The most important feature of the Union tariff, however, was the openly protectionist schedules that encouraged the domestic expansion of almost every manufacturing sector in the northern economy. These schedules were particularly effective in directing capital investment into iron and steel production, so much so that iron and steel producers can be numbered among the most important clients of the Union government from the close of the Civil War until the end of the century.

Even before Lincoln was inaugurated, the last antebellum Congress enacted the Morrill tariff of March 2, 1861, which has been called "the first triumph of Northern industrial over Southern agricultural economy." This act was followed by an August 1861 revision that again raised duties in many schedules. The subsequent tariff act of June 30, 1864, again increased duties, this time to levels that became prohibitive for many goods and commodities.[165] As a statist program for reshaping the pattern of investment and development of the national political economy, the 1864 tariff had few, if any, equals in the nineteenth century.

In one of its few deviations from the antebellum federal framework, the Confederate Constitution prohibited the establishment of a tariff intended "to promote or foster any branch of industry." This provision, with its limitations on the discretionary authority of the central state to shape internal development through manipulation of the terms of foreign trade, weakened the formal structure and power of the Confederate government. Prior to its adoption on February 9, 1861, the Provisional Congress had continued in force the existing U.S. tariff enacted in 1857. Although the early decision to continue existing schedules was motivated by the desire of representatives from border states (for example, North Carolina, Tennessee, and Virginia) to protect their home industries from foreign competition, later reductions and modifications, adopted May 21 and August 3, 1861, removed most duties in excess of those required for revenue.[166] Included among the changes the South made in the 1857 schedules was the addition of a section providing for the duty-free ad-

165. Herbert Ronald Ferleger, *David A. Wells and the American Revenue System, 1865–1870* (New York: Private printing, 1942), p. 119. For a discussion of the 1864 act and excerpts from congressional debate, see Edward Young, *Customs-Tariff Legislation of the United States* (Washington, D.C.: Government Printing Office, 1877), pp. cxxxii–ix; for a comparison of individual schedules under the 1857, March 1861, and August 1861, and 1864 tariffs, see pp. 40–97. The roll call included in the voting analysis was taken upon passage of the 1864 act in the House of Representatives. *Congressional Globe* 38:1:2751, June 4, 1864. Eighty-one members voted for the revision, 26 opposed.

166. In order to entice imports of war materiel and encourage those willing to run the blockade, the Confederacy also reduced duties in other schedules. Richmond *Daily Examiner*, May 25, 1861; Yearns, *Confederate Congress*, pp. 162–7. For Confederate tariff schedules, see the Richmond *Daily Examiner*, April 12 and June 18, 1861.

mission of "breadstuffs" from the Northwest, special treatment that was intended to reduce opposition to southern independence in the western half of the Union.[167]

In spite of the constitutional ban on import duties, protectionist sentiment was strong in some quarters of the Confederacy, and attempts were made to expand the tariff into the gray area between revenue collection and import protection.[168] Such efforts, however, proved counterproductive, because they provoked an even larger movement to repeal the tariff entirely and open the South to unrestricted free trade in the world economy. During debate on one such free-trade proposal, Representative John Perkins of Louisiana noted that the measure had been "recommended by the Legislatures of Georgia, Texas, and South Carolina ... by a very large number of the merchants of New Orleans, and by the Chamber of Commerce of Charleston... [and] by the Commercial and Planters convention that met in Georgia," adding that the secretary of the treasury's "statement showed that the revenue collected from imports [since July 1861] was just about equal to the expense of collection... we surrender nothing whatever of the revenue in point of fact." The House of Representatives subsequently adopted the bill, which would have entailed an unqualified commitment to free trade by the Confederate state; however, the Senate failed to consider the proposal, and Confed-

167. Other changes provided for free navigation of the Mississippi from the river's mouth to the northern border of the Confederacy, repealed U.S. navigation laws, with their hated monopoly on the coastal trade for American vessels, and imposed an export tax on cotton of one-eighth of a cent per pound. (An export tax was then and still is prohibited by the United States Constitution.) Russel, *Economic Aspects of Southern Sectionalism*, pp. 259–60, 273–4. Although important as a precedent, the export duty produced almost no revenue for the government (about $6,000 total in specie during the war). Schwab, *Confederate States of America*, pp. 240–2; Todd, *Confederate Finance*, pp. 123–4. As one of the last acts of the first session, the Provisional Congress prohibited the exportation of cotton to the North. Since, as the Richmond *Daily Examiner* noted, the naval blockade prevented exports to Europe, the sale of cotton to the Union would have damaged southern interests by stimulating the northern economy (May 27 and June 5, 1861). For examples of Union regulation of northern trade with the Confederacy, see *1862 American Cyclopaedia*, pp. 227–34; *1864 American Cyclopaedia*, pp. 189–93; *1865 American Cyclopaedia*, pp. 184–6.

168. On March 8, 1862, for example, Representative Augustus Wright of Georgia presented to the Confederate House of Representatives a letter from Colonel Wade S. Cottran, President of the Bank of the Empire State in which the latter argued that investment in iron production should be encouraged by a protective tariff. *Proceedings*, 44:123. See, more generally, Todd, *Confederate Finance*, p. 128. While southern industry was insulated from the world economy as long as the Union blockaded southern ports, private manufacturers were often reluctant to expand their facilities because they feared that the end of the war would again expose them to foreign competition.

erate tariff policy remained focused on revenue – though, as Perkins observed, most customs offices probably operated at a loss.[169]

The free-trade bill was a potential blow to the foreign-policy powers of the Confederate state because it neither yielded revenue to the government nor created dependent economic sectors protected by a state-maintained tariff wall. In creating these dependent sectors, it should be noted, the state would also have provided central direction and encouragement to internal economic development. Between the twin goals of revenue enhancement and economic development, a theory of central state authority cannot choose; each contributes to the authority and influence of the state in a different way. A theoretically consistent endorsement of free-trade principles, however, entails the renunciation of both statist alternatives. Adoption of such principles not only weakens the revenue capacity of the government and forgoes one of the most powerful means of directing the shape of internal development, but also leaves the home market vulnerable to exploitation by other central states through their own trade policies.

In the end, the Confederate state both repudiated pure free-trade principles by rejecting abandonment of the tariff as a revenue policy and vitiated most of the significance of the constitutional ban on protectionism through control of blockade-running shippers (see below). The southern export duty on cotton was also a novel expansion of central state authority over foreign commerce. On the whole, however, the Union exploited both the revenue potential and the protectionist possibilities of the tariff with much more confidence and statist sensibility than did the Confederacy.

Negotiated peace. Both the Union and Confederate states conferred upon their respective presidents wide discretion over the articulation of war goals and foreign policy generally. This discretionary authority, however, was a heavily contested prerogative in both political systems. In the South, presidential control of foreign relations was most commonly challenged by congressmen who wished to prod the executive into talks with the Union government in Washington. These congressmen emerged as a political force as the prospects for an outright Confederate military victory diminished. Always a distinct minority, the group had an essentially conservative goal: a negotiated peace in which the South would gain the

169.	*Proceedings,* 45:59–61, April 2, 1862. The roll call included in the voting analysis arose upon passage of this free trade proposal (67 to 16 – a "nay" vote conforms to the statist position). *Journal of the Confederate House of Representatives,* 1:1:170–1. Also see Todd, *Confederate Finance,* p. 128.

practical equivalence or substance of independence. As many scholars and contemporary observers have noted, it was never clear – particularly after Lincoln's victory over McClellan in the 1864 presidential election – why the Union would consider negotiating such a peace.

The most serious attempt to propose negotiations was contained in a joint resolution offered by James T. Leach of North Carolina, a member, as Alexander and Beringer put it, of the "lunatic fringe." Leach proposed that delegations from the individual states request that President Davis offer a ninety-day armistice to the U.S. government as a precondition to negotiations concerning a peace in which individual state sovereignty and independence would be secured. Although not explicitly binding on Davis, the measure was aptly perceived as an infringement upon the president's foreign policy prerogatives. After brief debate, the joint resolution was tabled by a large majority.[170]

In the North, President Lincoln was challenged by a similar peace movement that sought to open up congressionally sponsored negotiations with southern representatives. While a few of these members openly advocated Confederate independence, most viewed formal negotiations as a way of developing and proposing guarantees for the protection of southern interests in a reunited nation. These guarantees would then be ratified as new amendments to the Constitution. This movement was most powerful early in the war when subjection of the Confederacy seemed unlikely.[171] These proposals for peace negotiations carried negative statist implications for several reasons. In the first place, they threatened to replace presidential control of foreign relations with some form of congressional direction of foreign policy. Such a transfer of influence would lodge governmental authority in a less statist branch (which would, nothing else considered, place the decision within the "administrative-capacity" dimension). Even more important, however, than the structural implications of peace proposals were their potential substantive impact. "Peace," in both instances, would have been accompanied by serious qualifications of national sovereignty, a consideration that properly

---

170. *Anatomy of the Confederate Congress*, p. 295; Yearns, *Confederate Congress*, 171–83; *Journal of the Confederate House of Representatives* 2:1:84–5, May 23, 1864. Sixty-two members supported the statist position (to table the motion for peace negotiations), 21 members opposed the motion.

171. The roll call included in the voting analysis was taken on a "peace resolution" offered only a week after the first battle of Bull Run, a disastrous defeat for Union forces only a day's march outside Washington. At that time almost a third of all congressmen supported congressionally sponsored negotiations with commissioners appointed by the "so-called Confederate States." The measure, however, was defeated (41 to 85). *Congressional Globe* 37:1:331, July 29, 1861.

places these decisions under the world-system dimension. Since both political systems rejected these peace initiatives, the Union and the Confederacy turned in similar performances in this policy area.[172]

Union Pacific Railroad. Construction of a transcontinental railroad connecting California with western extensions of the major eastern trunk lines carried several important implications for the position of the United States in the world system. As a broad policy on internal development, the railroad proposed to channel settlement along a route chosen by the government and to share state-sponsored sales of land (theoretically in the form of homesteads) with a private, albeit relatively heavily regulated corporation. The link also promised to promote national security by facilitating the movement of troops and military supplies between the west coast and the more populated east. Because California harbored substantial secessionist sentiment in its own right and viewed proposed construction of the railroad as a serious governmental commitment to the Pacific community, the project also promised to promote national unity. Passage of the Pacific Railroad Act of July 1, 1862, was, for these reasons, an active assertion of central state authority by the northern Union.[173]

Colonization/emancipation/confiscation. The confiscation of southern property and emancipation of slaves presented the Union with developmental questions even more profound than the settlement of the western frontier. As far as that response was articulated during the Civil War years, Union policy combined several related programs, concerning emancipation, confiscation, and colonization. In terms of future national de-

172. If this comparison were broadened to include congressional pressure and influence over the conduct of the war itself, the Union political process would have to be evaluated as distinctly less statist than that of the Confederacy. See, for example, the interventionist activities of congressional "radicals" who directed the secret hearings and investigations of the Joint Committee on the Conduct of the War. T. Harry Williams, *Lincoln and the Radicals* (Madison: University of Wisconsin Press, 1965).

173. For a discussion of the politics of the act, see Chapter 2. Also see Curry, *Blueprint for Modern America*, pp. 120–36; Nelson Trottman, *History of the Union Pacific: A Financial and Economic Survey* (New York: Augustus M. Kelley, 1966), pp. 3–22; Paludan, "*A People's Contest*," pp. 135–9. For a discussion of the importance of the Pacific railroad in countering California separatist sentiment and promoting economic integration with the remainder of the nation, see Joseph Ellison, *California and the Nation, 1850–1869* (Berkeley: University of California Press, 1927), pp. 170–88; Kerry A. Odell, "The Integration of Regional and Interregional Capital Markets: Evidence from the Pacific Coast, 1883–1913," *Journal of Economic History* 49 (June 1989): 306. The roll call included in the voting analysis was recorded upon passage of the act in the House of Representatives. *Congressional Globe* 37:2:1971, May 6, 1862. The bill passed easily (79 to 49).

velopment, the emancipation of southern blacks was interpreted as giving freedmen a choice of residence and nationality. Land and other property confiscated from disloyal Southerners would be used to subsidize the colonization abroad of those freedmen who chose to settle under another flag. (That most, if not all, blacks would choose to emigrate was never doubted.) Finally, in order to complete this program, the president would negotiate the location and terms of colonization with other countries. In theory, approximately four million blacks were to be removed from the United States and permanently relocated abroad. In broad terms, authority for these policies had already been enacted when the House of Representatives considered funding for the program.[174] The section of the appropriations bill in which the funding was provided specified that the spending authority was intended "to enable the President to carry out the act of Congress for the emancipation of the slaves in the District of Columbia, and to colonize those to be made free by the probable passage of a confiscation bill, $500,000, to be repaid to the Treasury out of confiscated property, to be used at the discretion of the president in securing the right of colonization of said persons made free, and in payment of the necessary expenses of their removal." Although a motion to strike this section was defeated (41 to 70), the United States never carried out this program of confiscation-subsidized colonization.[175] Still, however, the northern government's half-hearted efforts to impose this state-centered "solution" to the problem of the freedmen surpassed, from a statist perspective, any policy ever developed in the Confederacy.

Blockade cargo. Some of the first "world-system" policies that turned the Confederate state in an interventionist direction were those that prohibited cotton exports to the Union except where sales were conducted by authorized Confederate officials. This prohibition was later expanded to include all staple crops, but it was almost impossible to enforce. Trade with nations other than the Union primarily took the form of evading the blockade imposed by the Union navy and was much easier to monitor and control.[176] In 1863 the Confederacy sought to compel vessels running

174. Bogue, *Congressman's Civil War*, pp. 47–8.
175. *Congressional Globe* 37:2:3331, July 14, 1862. For a history of this legislation, see Curry, *Blueprint for Modern America*, pp. 36–56; for a chronology of Lincoln's efforts to negotiate a site for colonization, see Long, *Civil War*, pp. 55, 179, 241, 251, 292, 303, 459. For a discussion of possible emancipation/colonization schemes, see Senator Doolittle of Wisconsin's comments in the *Appendix to the Congressional Globe* 37:2:94–101, April 11, 1862.
176. Yearns, *Confederate Congress*, pp. 135–8. On the importance of blockade running to the Confederate war effort and its scale in general, see Bradlee, *Blockade Running during the Civil War;* Gordon Wright, "Economic Conditions in the Confederacy as seen by the French Consuls," *Journal of Southern History* 7, no. 2 (May 1941):

the blockade to dedicate one-third to one-half of all cargo space to government imports. This statute, however, exempted vessels chartered or owned by the individual states, an exception that frustrated Confederate efforts to centralize import controls.

In February 1864 the Confederate government assumed control of 50 percent of the export/import trade upon adoption of a law prohibiting the importation of luxuries and another giving the president wide discretionary power over exports. Under the latter, enacted February 6, 1864, the president was given control over the "exportation of cotton, tobacco, military and naval stores, sugar, molasses, and rice" and authorized to use the army and navy to enforce Confederate trade regulations. President Davis aggressively used this authority, and an effective centralization of much of the foreign trade of the Confederacy was achieved. In fact, executive control was viewed with so much alarm that the Confederate Congress subsequently passed two measures intended to weaken presidential authority. Davis stopped each of these measures with vetoes.[177] This unprecedented imposition of central state controls on the flow of foreign trade was never contemplated in any form by the Union.

The Union and Confederate states occupied very different positions within the world system during the Civil War. The Union enjoyed unrestricted access to the remainder of the world economy even while imposing a naval blockade on trade between the southern state and other nations. The Confederate economy was comparatively isolated by the blockade and, beyond a handful of oceanic raiders, was unable to threaten the flow of foreign goods into the North. The Union, in addition, inherited the vast western frontier from the antebellum federal government while, aside from west Texas, the Confederacy was a relatively settled country. Finally, the emancipation policies of the North held significant implications for possible state-centered direction of national development. Any program that promised to eliminate private rights to over half the wealth of a society (such as the emancipation of slaves in the South did) must create an immense opportunity, from a statist perspective, for government determination of the disposition of that property. In the case of slavery, the Union first timidly moved toward relocation abroad and, only sub-

200–2; Hill, *State Socialism in the Confederate States of America*, pp. 8–9; Lebergott, "Through the Blockade," pp. 867–8; and in Florida, Davis, *Civil War and Reconstruction*, pp. 198–203.

177. General Orders No. 43 (April 16, 1864), *General Orders of the Confederate States Army, 1864*, pp. 84–6 (includes implementing regulations). For the text of the statute, see *Public Laws of the Confederate States of America, Fourth Session, First Congress*, pp. 181–3. The House originally approved the law on January 28, 1864 (61 to 11; *Journal of the Confederate House of Representatives* 1:4:703). Also see, Hill, *State Socialism in the Confederate States of America*, pp. 14–23.

sequently, toward an expanding notion of black citizenship accompanied by federal guarantees of fundamental civil and voting rights. The Confederacy could not, of course, contemplate similar programs without destroying its social base and was never presented with the opportunity to impose a parallel form of expropriation upon northern wealth.

These differences between northern and southern experience offer a tempting explanation for comparative Union and Confederate state performance within the world-system dimension. The relatively minor advantage of the Union in the tariff and colonization policy areas and the major superiority that must be attached to the transcontinental railroad appear to represent the exploitation of policy alternatives that were more or less closed to the South. Similarly, the Confederate imposition of export/import controls, a major initiative not duplicated in the North, could be considered a response to a challenge (the naval blockade) not faced by the Union. In these ways, the two states were unquestionably shaped by the challenges and the opportunities each faced during the war. On the other hand, the two regimes also reflected the nature and limitations of their respective social bases, including the organizational forms their respective nationalist movements assumed. In the next, concluding section of this chapter, we will consider the ways in which these elements – battlefield challenge, social base, and organizational form – contributed to Union and Confederate state formation.

Part III: Summary comparison of Union and Confederate state organization and performance

While there will always be disagreement over the evaluation of Union and Confederate performance in some of the forty-two policy areas analyzed here, the evidence clearly indicates superiority, from a statist perspective, for one of the two states in most comparisons of individual policies. Each of the comparisons, listed in Table 3.5, samples a portion of the respective contours and content of the two states. Some policy areas, such as the establishment of a home for veterans or authority for military academy appointments, are relatively unimportant even as they help to fill out this broad survey of comparative state development. Others represent much more significant areas of potential state expansion. In this select group would fall, for example, conscription, suspension of the writ of habeas corpus, government impressment of property, the internal revenue system, and the tariff. Further comparison can isolate thematically related sets of policies in which one of the two regimes held significant advantages over the other. This analytical strategy, in fact, leads us to view the two regimes from radically different perspectives.

Table 3.5. *Summary comparison of structural and operational strength of the Union and Confederate states*

Dimension		Policy area	Stronger state
1. Centralization of authority	a)	Secret sessions	Confederacy
	b)	States appoint officers	Neither
	c)	Expulsion of members	Neither
	*d)	Militia outside state	Neither
	*e)	Freedmen's Bureau	Union
	*f)	Reconstruction	Union
	*g)	Nationalization of currency	Union
	*h)	Supreme court jurisdiction	Neither
2. Administrative capacity	a)	Academy appointments	Confederacy
	b)	Removal of officers	Neither
	*c)	Court of claims	Confederacy
	*d)	Board of admiralty	Neither
	*e)	General staff	Union
	*f)	Exemptions	Confederacy
	*g)	Civil service test	Confederacy
	*h)	A supreme court	Union
3. Citizenship	a)	Conscription	Confederacy
	b)	Habeas corpus	Union
	*c)	Emancipation	Union
4. Control of property	a)	Railroad subsidy	Neither
	b)	Control of railroads	Confederacy
	c)	Financial markets	Union
	d)	Slaves as soldiers	Union
	e)	Confiscation	Confederacy
	*f)	Bankruptcy	Neither
	*g)	Impressment	Confederacy
	*h)	Destruction of property	Confederacy
5. Creation of client groups	a)	Legal tender notes	Union
	b)	Treasury debt	Union
	*c)	Homesteads in Confederacy	Union
	*d)	Military pensions	Union
	*e)	Redistribution of income	Confederacy
	*f)	Price controls	Confederacy
	*g)	Veteran soldiers' home	Union
6. Extraction of resources	a)	Direct taxes/internal duties	Neither
	b)	Internal revenue	Neither
	*c)	National banks	Union
7. World system	a)	Tariff	Union
	b)	Negotiated peace	Neither
	*c)	Pacific railroad	Union
	*d)	Colonization/confiscation	Union
	*e)	Blockade cargo	Confederacy

Note: All policy areas are discussed in the text under their appropriate headings. Asterisked entries are policy areas in which either the Union or Confederate House of Representatives (but not both) recorded votes. In all other areas, both the Union and Confederate chambers recorded votes.

Confederate advantages over the Union were most prominent in both the administrative design of the southern state and in policy areas relating to government control of property and labor. Much of the South's superiority in administrative design was due to the relative weakness of the Confederate Congress vis-à-vis the executive and central state bureaucracy. That legislature, in turn, was comparatively insulated from societal influence because most deliberations were conducted in secret and many members represented districts behind Union lines, which gave them unusual freedom from direct constituency pressure. These related developments placed the Confederate Congress in a distinctly secondary but supportive role in southern state formation.

The most impressive accomplishment of the Confederate state was the extensive apparatus the South established in order to mobilize manpower and materiel. Considered as a whole, the Confederate state attempted to direct a mobilization of men and materiel as complete and as centrally directed as any in American history. Detailed comparison of individual policy areas cannot fully convey the comprehensive nature of southern state controls, the interlocking application of these programs in the field, or their aggressive exercise by implementing Confederate officers and agents. In this section, we can consider the synergistic impact of some of the most salient features of this system. Based primarily on conscription and impressment policies, Confederate controls brought the southern factory, railroad, and plantation into the war effort even where formal legal authority was lacking. Conscription, for example, not only sent men to the front but also, through military details and categorical exemptions, allocated labor throughout the southern economy, thus providing the foundation for further expansion of central state authority over other portions of the political economy and social relations.[178] The exemption of overseers on plantations with twenty or more slaves, for example, was both a necessary measure for maintaining agricultural production and a major irritant in class relations in that poor, non–slave-owning whites were sent to the front while much of the plantation elite enjoyed exemption from military service. In partial redress of this grievance, the Confederate state taxed exempted overseers and returned that revenue to soldiers' families while making surplus plantation production available to the government and soldiers' families under regulated schedules that

178. As Emory Thomas put it, "There were approximately 1,000,000 white men between eighteen and forty-five in the Confederacy. At one time or another about 750,000 of these men were Confederate soldiers. If the number of men exempted from service or detailed from service to perform some vital civilian task is added to that, the total involved in the war would very nearly approximate the South's military population." *Confederate Nation*, p. 155.

set prices below market levels. Seen in combination, these policies committed the Confederate state to an active role in the amelioration of class
conflict as the state moved beyond mere exploitation of the material
potential of the plantation economy. From this position, the Confederacy,
had it survived, could have undertaken an even more interventionist
reorganization of the southern political economy (along the lines suggested by the enlistment of slaves as soldiers and their simultaneous
emancipation – a policy adopted during the last month of southern
independence).

During the first year of conscription, suspension of the writ of habeas
corpus helped overcome resistance to the draft in areas that came under
presidential proclamations. Later, after upholding conscription's constitutionality, the judiciaries of the individual states enforced compliance.
Under conscription, categorical exemptions and the allocation of enlisted
men to factory production brought most industrial and railroad operations within the ambit of Confederate controls. Simply put, firms could
not operate without labor and the Confederacy controlled the supply of
able-bodied workers. Any factory or rail line considered nonessential or
uncooperative could find its labor force confiscated by the Confederate
state and reallocated to another use.[179] Direct central state investment in
industrial firms also subjected them to Confederate controls on production, prices, and profits. (Much of the total industrial capacity of the
South was in fact owned and operated by the Confederacy.)

Impressment of materiel reached units of production through the compensated confiscation of property and was used to compel civilian property holders to turn over supplies to the government. The authority was
applied to both slaves and other forms of property, including factories
and agricultural harvests, and dated from the very beginning of the war.
Though impressment originally emerged as a martial law power exercised
by armies in the field, the practice was later bureaucratized through an
explicit statutory grant of authority to the military and the establishment
of price-control boards. Even more detailed provisions affecting railroads,
slave labor, and factory production followed. Because of the close as-

---

179. See, for example, James Michael Russell, *Atlanta, 1847–1890: City Building in the
     Old South and the New* (Baton Rouge: Louisiana State University Press, 1988),
     pp. 100–6. Russell also discusses Confederate-directed industrial war production in
     Atlanta, including the operations of the nationalized arsenal and the use of con-
     scription authority to break strikes. For a general description of the number and
     occupation of military details during the war, see a tabular report prepared by the
     Bureau of Conscription in *Official Records*, ser. IV, vol. III, pp. 1101–10. On strikes
     and conscription generally, see Coulter, *Confederate States of America*, pp. 236–8;
     for the North, see David Montgomery, *Beyond Equality: Labor and the Radical
     Republicans, 1862–1872* (New York: Alfred A. Knopf, 1967), pp. 100–1.

sociation between impressment and martial law, the practice was almost always unappealable (though civilians might appeal price decisions to the impressment boards). When used in conjunction with other authority to control railroad operations, impressment centralized the transport and, therefore, the supply of industrial raw materials in the hands of Confederate agents. Without raw materials, industrial operations would grind to a halt and impressment authority was sometimes used to assign war production priorities and render some productive capacity redundant. By the time the twin policies of conscription and impressment and their derivative applications met in the city or countryside, the susceptibility of manufacturers and the great plantations to Confederate command was complete.[180]

Although other features of the Confederate state similarly demonstrate the comprehensive mobilization of the southern nation, the synergistic combination of conscription and impressment policies constituted the foundation of the Confederate war effort.[181] Although some aspects of these and other policies were spelled out in law, most authority conferred upon the central state allowed executive or bureaucratic discretion. And, although this discretion could theoretically have been used to enhance the planning capacity and centralizing tendencies of the state, in practice both technological deficiency (primarily in telegraphic communication

180. At the beginning of the war, the South was almost entirely deficient in war-making capital plant and skilled labor. Josiah Gorgas, "Contributions to the History of the Confederate Ordnance Department," *Southern Historical Society Papers* 12 (January and February 1884): 69. For the impact of Confederate war mobilization and manufacturing operations upon various cities and states, see Frederick F. Siegel, *The Roots of Southern Distinctiveness: Tobacco and Society in Danville, Virginia, 1780–1865* (Chapel Hill: University of North Carolina Press, 1987), pp. 153–8; Kenneth Coleman, *Confederate Athens* (Athens: University of Georgia Press, 1967), pp. 95–100; Emory M. Thomas, *The Confederate State of Richmond: A Biography of the Capital* (Austin: University of Texas Press, 1971), pp. 23–4; Florence Fleming Corley, *Confederate City: Augusta, Georgia, 1860–1865* (Columbia: University of South Carolina Press, 1960), pp. 46–61; in Georgia, see Mohr, *On the Threshold of Freedom*, pp. 120–89, and T. Conn Bryan, *Confederate Georgia* (Athens: University of Georgia Press, 1953), pp. 101–17; for a general overview of Confederate control of the southern economy, see Thomas, *Confederate Nation*, pp. 134–5, 152–5, 206–16; Beringer et al., *Why the South Lost the Civil War*, pp. 215–18; Cappon, "Government and Private Industry in the Southern Confederacy," pp. 151–89; Frank E. Vandiver, *Ploughshares into Swords: Josiah Gorgas and Confederate Ordnance* (Austin: University of Texas Press, 1952), pp. 55–127, 136–271; Victor S. Clark, *History of Manufacturers in the United States*, vol. 2 (New York: Peter Smith, 1949), pp. 41–53.

181. For an example of how conscription and impressment authority were coordinated in nitre production, see General Orders No. 41 (May 31, 1862) and No. 66 (September 12, 1862), Adjutant and Inspector General's Office, *General Orders of the Confederate States Army from January 1862 to December 1863* (Columbia, S.C.: Evans and Cogswell, 1864), pp. 55, 78.

but later extending to transportation) and chronic shortages in materiel and manpower forced a much more decentralized control apparatus upon the Confederacy.[182] These same factors meant that similar administrative structures in the Union and the Confederacy would have burdened the southern political economy with much greater logistical demands (in terms of the allocation of manpower to bureaucratic service, government traffic over transportation and communication networks, and other matters) than would have been required in the North. Even if the two war mobilizations had been equally state-centered, the much higher proportional demands of the Confederate war effort on the southern political economy would have produced a much more complete transformation of that agrarian society than the comparatively unobtrusive requirements of the Union on the northern industrial system.

As shortages of materiel became more acute, individual bureaus assumed control over resources essential to their operations and allocated commodities to other departments within the government. The Nitre and Mining Bureau, for example, socialized mineral extraction and iron production by taking over mines and foundries or by so dominating their operations that outright confiscation was unnecessary.[183] The Subsistence and Quartermaster's departments obtained exclusive purchasing rights in the domestic market through the power of impressment and thus became the sole agent in the allocation of cotton textile production. As the war continued, all agencies became increasingly dependent on running the naval blockade as the domestic economy, sundered by invasion and cavalry raids, failed.[184] The individual citizen was almost entirely helpless before these policies. Armed with immense and largely unappealable discretionary power, Confederate civilian and military agents improvised temporary solutions to the problem of supplying and arming a military force capable of holding at bay an army backed by one of the world's leading industrial powers.[185]

182. Gorgas, "History of the Confederate Ordnance Department," pp. 74, 79; Vandiver, *Ploughshares into Swords*, pp. 179, 214. For a general account of administrative decentralization in the western Confederacy, see James L. Nichols, *The Confederate Quartermaster in the Trans-Mississippi* (Austin: University of Texas, 1964).
183. Vandiver, *Ploughshares into Swords*, pp. 115, 161–3; Marion O. Smith, "The Sauta Cave Confederate Niter Works," *Civil War History* 29 (December 1983): 293–315.
184. Goff, *Confederate Supply*, pp. 157–8. The Confederate bureaucracy rapidly became a disciplined institution that could, even after the evacuation of Richmond just days before Appomattox, send instructions to an impressment officer in Louisiana informing him that "the duty intrusted to you is a delicate one, and care will be taken not to interfere with any planter so as to curtail the provision crop which he may be cultivating." Trexler, "The Opposition of Planters to the Employment of Slaves," p. 218.
185. In terms of "modern" industrial capacity, the northern Union may have ranked as high as third in the world, after the United Kingdom and France. Paul Bairoch,

The Union, in fact, enjoyed manpower reserves and potential economic capacity that vastly surpassed southern resources in almost every respect. Ranging from a 2 to 1 advantage in railroad mileage to a 10 to 1 advantage in the value of annual manufacturing production, the Union drew on a vast reservoir of industrial and financial potential. With a 4 to 1 preponderance in incorporated bank capital, a multiple of two or more in manpower, and real and personal property that exceeded southern wealth (including slaves) by a margin of 3 to 1, the enormous size of the northern political economy allowed the Union to develop a capitalist version of the southern, quasisocialist war mobilization.[186] Neither price controls, central state allocation of raw materials, nor expropriation of private production units can be found in the northern mobilization. Instead, lucrative contracts and excess productive capacity allowed the Union to rely on open-market agreements in order to mobilize materiel. What passed for conscription in the Union was also, in effect, a heavily market-oriented policy that neither comprehended the varying relevance of occupations to the war effort nor mobilized a significant fraction of northern manpower. In these respects, the Union state apparatus appears relatively anemic when compared to the Confederacy and, in fact, the southern state was a much more pervasive and encompassing presence in the daily life of southern society than the Union government was in the North.[187] The northern mobilization was, however, distinguished by several developments that were forever beyond the reach of the Confederacy. For one thing, a relatively prosperous economy allowed the Union to create and expand client-group policies that had no parallel in the South. The Homestead Act, veterans' pensions, and an array of financial measures all tied the welfare of important groups in the political economy to the success or failure of the central government. Because of this relative material abundance, the Union was able to devise policies that brought in enough revenue to fund the war effort and yet did not destroy the

"International Industrialization Levels from 1750 to 1980," *Journal of European Economic History* 11 (Fall 1982): 269–334.
186. On the superiority of northern economic and manpower capacity, see Richard N. Current, "God and the Strongest Battalions," in David Donald, ed., *Why the North Won the Civil War* (Baton Rouge: Louisiana State University Press, 1960), pp. 3–22; Beringer et al., *Why the South Lost the Civil War*, pp. 8–13; James M. McPherson, *Battle Cry of Freedom: The Civil War Era* (New York: Oxford University Press, 1988), p. 318–20; Long, *Civil War Day by Day*, 721–8.
187. As one North Carolina congressman lamented toward the end of the war (in debate summarized by the Richmond *Examiner*): "There was too much of brass button and bayonet rule in the country. The land was alive with them [Confederate officials]. They were as thick as locusts in Egypt. Richmond was full of them. Even in his little town they were so thick that he could not walk without being elbowed off the streets by them." *Proceedings*, 52:242 (January 27, 1865).

flow of commerce from which they skimmed wealth. The core financial policy of the Union ultimately evolved into a symbiotic program through which the northern state traded the organization of a national financial market in return for an (albeit not entirely willing) accommodation of finance capitalists to the needs of the Treasury. In all these respects, the policies of the Union state melded into the processes of the northern capitalist economy.[188] The most striking feature of Union state formation was the reliance on unregulated capitalist markets through which the central state drew upon northern economic and manpower resource potential. In contrast, almost every revenue arrangement in the South sooner or later turned into outright expropriation and, thus, drove goods out of the visible stream of commerce as citizens and firms attempted to hide their activities from the unbearable demands of the Confederate war effort. While more statist in design and operation, the Confederacy imposed comparatively cannibalistic demands on the southern political economy while the voluntarist structures of the Union reinforced the renewable vitality of northern commerce and productive capacity. While the quasisocialist response of the Confederacy to the challenge presented by Union invasion should be viewed as a remarkable leap beyond the premodern social base upon which the southern state rested, the Union mobilization carried little revolutionary potential and can be interpreted as an incrementalist, though accelerated adaptation of central state capacity and design to advancing industrial and commercial interests.[189]

So far, the Union and Confederate states have been compared with respect to domestic policies that organized their national political economies and citizenries. From a statist perspective, the Confederate experience compares favorably and can be considered superior to that of the Union in these areas. Both states, however, also implemented policies that targeted the property, citizens, and social relations of the other, alien political economy. For the Confederacy, these policies were largely limited to the confiscation of northern property holdings in the South, restrictions on trading with the North, and negotiations with the Union over the exchange of prisoners of war.[190]

188. For a theoretical discussion of possible extraction strategies that is compatible with Confederate and Union policies and their outcomes, see Margaret Levi, *Of Rule and Revenue* (Berkeley: University of California Press, 1988), ch. 2.

189. On the adaption of the mode of central state extraction to the emergence of an exchange economy, see Charles Tilly, "Reflections on the History of European State-making," p. 54; Gabriel Ardant, "Financial Policy and Economic Infrastructure of Modern States and Nations", pp. 166, 176, 220, both articles appear in Tilly, ed., *The Formation of National States in Western Europe.*

190. For a brief review of Confederate policy toward the exchange of prisoners and prisoners of war generally, see Bensel, "Southern Leviathan," pp. 119–21.

Both Union and Confederate armies operated under similar interpretations of martial law but, because they occupied extensive areas of the South, northern commanders had many more opportunities to exercise this authority. In this policy area, the Union did not shy away from an aggressive exploitation of opportunities for central state enhancement. As Sherman moved through Georgia, for example, he ordered that:

> If any farmer or peaceable inhabitant is molested by the enemy, viz., the Confederate army or guerrillas, because of his friendship to the National Government, the perpetrator, if caught, will be summarily punished, or his family made to suffer for the outrage; but if the crime cannot be traced to the actual party, then retaliation will be made on the adherents to the cause of the rebellion; should a Union man be murdered, then a rebel selected by lot will be shot – or if a Union family be persecuted on account of the cause, a rebel family will be banished to a foreign land. In aggravated cases, retaliation will extend as high as five for one. All commanding officers will act promptly in such cases, and report their action after the retaliation is done.[191]

While the sweeping and arbitrary repression of subject civilian populations which this order advocated appears to be exceptional, the command was based on a general principle that the authority of the Union state over the rebellious South was unlimited – a principle that provided the foundation for much of Union state development during the Civil War and subsequent Reconstruction era.

As northern troops moved South, the Union was presented with three major problems of varying urgency. The earliest appearing and most urgent of these problems concerned the immediate security of Union forces operating in hostile territory. Though impressive as an example of the potentially great power with which martial law can cloak a commander, Sherman's order also illustrates the transient nature of such authority. Once such orders are revoked they leave little evidence in the political economy of their past operation or influence. More significant are those actions intended to undermine or destroy the resource base of the enemy. In this category might fall the burning of Jackson, Mississippi, Atlanta, Georgia, Columbia, South Carolina, and the plantations and farms along Sherman's march to the sea. Even more important, however, were the confiscation of property owned by Confederate citizens, the emancipation of slaves, and the enrollment of southern blacks in the Union army. Grounded in martial law and the extraordinary war powers of the executive, these policies reshaped property and social relations in

191. The order was issued January 14, 1865. *1865 American Cyclopaedia*, p. 391.

190 *Yankee Leviathan*

Table 3.6. *Pacification of the secessionist South and central state development in the Union*

Policy category	Measures adopted or proposed
Union efforts to restructure southern property relations	*Emancipation and slaves as soldiers: Elimination of property rights in black slaves.
	*Confiscation: Expropriation of property owned by citizens who aided the Confederate war effort.
Union control over political and economic institutions	*Reconstruction: Participation by loyal southerners in a controlled process in which: (1) governmental institutions would be thoroughly reorganized; and (2) the political dominance of loyal elements in the South would become self-sustaining.
	*Freedmen's Bureau: Central state redefinition of southern plantation labor relations and adjudication of black–white contractual agreements. Possible land redistribution.
	*Homesteads in the Confederacy: Land redistribution to Union veterans, both white and black.
Role of freedmen in long-term national development	*Colonization/confiscation: Central state directed resettlement of blacks abroad.
	Self-sustaining loyal southern elite: Property redistribution, blacks become yeoman farmers.
	Client group of the central state: No property redistribution, but political and civil rights/dominance secured by direct central state intervention.
	Central state withdraws from active intervention in the southern political economy: Disloyal whites return to political–economic dominance.

Note: Asterisked programs are described in the text as actual or potential Union policy choices. While those programs not asterisked were not formally entertained by the Union Congress during the Civil War, all were seriously considered during the Reconstruction era that immediately followed.

the South and effected far-reaching and permanent changes in the southern political economy (see Table 3.6).

The least urgent problem facing Union commanders, but the one that carried the widest potential for central state expansion, was the permanent pacification of southern communities and the establishment of loyal governments in conquered territory. Here, secession and war had destroyed the antebellum governing authorities that might have mediated central state policy toward the South. The creation of new governmental structures in the South, combined with emancipation and more active confiscation policies, could have remade the entire political economy by revamping the distribution of property between major societal groups and by making wartime loyalty to the Union a permanent condition for access to political power.   The Wade–Davis Bill, the establishment of the Freedmen's Bureau, and the contemplated but never enacted southern homestead policy represent the kind of statist initiatives either considered or experimentally attempted as part of a larger pacification program. Though reconstruction of the southern political economy ultimately failed to create a new and dominant loyalist class, the experience nonetheless represented an extremely important expansion of central state capacity.

Among the long-term pacification choices open to the Union, four alternatives stand out, all involving different roles for blacks and the central state in the southern political economy. The only one formally considered in the Union Congress as a comprehensive program would have resettled freedmen abroad and thus eliminated any significant black participation in subsequent national development. This alternative was first tentatively adopted and then rejected when property confiscation was abandoned and receptive colonies could not be found. The abandonment of property confiscation also undermined the practicality of policies intended to establish freedmen as economically independent yeoman farmers. Without the emergence of land ownership by freedmen, loyal Southerners would be dependent clients of the Union government and their political influence would rest ultimately on continued central state intervention in southern political processes. In the years immediately following the war, this alternative was, by default, Union policy (see Chapter 6). With the withdrawal of Union troops from the South, disloyal whites returned to political dominance throughout former Confederate territory. This brief review of possible alternative trajectories indicates the potential scope and influence of Union occupation and pacification policies on national development; as the postwar period unfolded, the Union chose the least statist of these possibilities.

Thus, in conclusion, we can say that the Confederacy was much stronger than the Union with respect to central state direction and control of the domestic political economy. This comparative advantage was particularly marked in the policy dimensions associated with administrative design and governmental control of property and manpower. On the other hand, the Union established highly statist policies for directing the pacification of the conquered South and for determining the broad contours of national development and the position of the nation in the world system. In most of these areas, the Confederacy never had an opportunity to attempt comparable expansions of state authority. Given the very

different evaluations of central state strength that could be supported by
evidence drawn from either broad perspective, a single, summary statement of comparative state strength is impossible. Each was strong in
different ways.

We now turn to an examination of the social bases of the Union and
Confederate states. The following sections identify those social groups
and economic classes that elected congressmen who subsequently provided legislative support for central state expansion during the American
Civil War. Looking at the legislative patterns of support and opposition
to the state-expanding policies previously identified in this chapter reveals
those groups and classes that consistently gave political backing to statist
policies across the wide range of substantive and organizational issues
raised during Union and Confederate state formation. These groups and
classes were the social bases of their respective states. With reference to
their respective antebellum citizenries, the Union was apparently founded
upon a much narrower social base than the Confederacy; in fact, the
social base of the latter was so broad as to encompass almost the entire
southern nation. In addition, societal support for state expansion was
funneled through two very different political arrangements. In the North,
a very strong political party thoroughly controlled the central state and
directed its activities. In the South, the party system disappeared and a
fluid, executive-led congressional coalition granted ever-increasing discretionary power to a more autonomous central bureaucracy. In some
respects, these developments were surprising. In other respects, they might
have been predicted.

Social bases of the Union and Confederate states

The South's decision to secede and the North's decision to resist secession
by force of arms were both directly related to the emergence of diametrically antithetical interests concerning the future course of the national political economy (see Chapter 2). What little growth in central
state activity that occurred in the late antebellum period was driven by
the industrial expansion of northern free-labor society and was characterized by a strong predisposition to impose a broad, capitalist market
design on the nation through an activist developmental program. The
slave-based, plantation economy of the South could only retard, not
prevent implementation of that program. The American Civil War was
an extension of that antebellum conflict; therefore, we might expect a
high level of agreement between antebellum alignments over policies
associated with the northern, Republican program for the national political economy and wartime expansion of the Union and Confederate

states. This expectation would view the respective states as agents of the political-economic interests to which they owed their emergence. As such, we would then expect the emergence of a strong central state to be supported by free-labor, frontier, and industrial sectors in the northern Union and slavery-dependent, plantation sectors in the southern Confederacy.

Still, central state expansion on the vast scale of the northern war mobilization radically diverged from the antebellum Republican design for the national political economy. The war mobilization not only imposed a much stronger role for the central state in the national political economy; it also created at least one new major economic class (finance capitalists) and destroyed another (slaveholders). In the process, more than a few antebellum developmental advocates may have lost their way between state-aided economic expansion and violent suppression of southern separatism. For the South, the link between opposition to the formation of a stronger antebellum state and support for a stronger Confederate apparatus was even more tenuous. While both positions could be traced to opposition to the developmental program of the North, the reversal snapped most ties to antebellum principles concerning the proper role and scale of central state activity. While residual hostility to northern hegemony and the emergence of a robust southern nationalism may have helped replace these broken links to decentralized federalism, more than a few secessionists may have lost the trail between southern separatism and Confederate leviathan.

As noted in the opening of this chapter, the American Civil War presents a unique opportunity to compare the dynamics of central state expansion in two very different political economies. What makes the opportunity unique is the almost identical initial designs of the Confederate and Union states. In the middle portion of this chapter, the resulting policy choices and operational arrangements of the Union and Confederate states were described and traced to the challenges each faced in their respective mobilizations. This section moves to analysis of the social bases of northern and southern state formation by comparing the legislative coalitions that supported Union and Confederate state expansion. First the two Congresses are compared on issues involving similar portions of the state apparatus and parallel developmental trajectories. These decisions allow a close comparison of the social bases of the two regimes on almost identical policy choices involving central state expansion. In order to round out this analysis, legislative behavior in the two lower chambers is also compared on a number of nonsymmetrical decisions involving either idiosyncratic state expansion initiatives or choices in which only one of the chambers recorded their votes. In brief, Union and

Confederate legislative support for state expansion are compared on almost identical congressional decisions in which differences in policy characteristics are minimized. Other, nonsymmetrical decisions reveal legislative support for expansion with respect to those policies unique to each state. Together, the voting patterns on both symmetrical and non-symmetrical issues allow characterization of the social bases of Union and Confederate state expansion.[192]

In order to carry out these comparisons, analytical categories have been chosen that distinguished between the major characteristics of the northern and southern political economies during the antebellum and Civil War periods. In both the Union and Confederate House of Representatives, for example, congressmen have been categorized according to the characteristics of their districts with respect to manufacturing activity, the presence of foreign-born populations, and slave holding. Slave holding has frequently been considered the most significant ecological correlate of secession sentiment and, later, southern nationalism, and the categorical distinction drawn here touches on many previous interpretations of antebellum and Confederate politics.[193] For the Union, a simple distinction between "free" and "slave" congressional districts is sufficient because of the small number of the latter after secession. For the Confederacy, all congressmen represented slave-holding constituencies; therefore, these are further divided into three subcategories according to the proportion of slaves in their respective populations: High, 50 percent and more; Medium, 25 to 49 percent; and Low, under 25 percent.

The classification of districts according to per capita value added in manufacturing is based upon the widely accepted argument that the industrialization process generates social and economic demands for the expansion of central state authority and administrative capacity. Here

192. With one major exception in each case, both the Union and Confederacy were open, competitive democracies during the Civil War in which we might expect elected representatives to the national government to reflect the interests and wishes of their electorates. This connection between delegate and voter allows us to interpret these representatives as the agents of their respective portions of the nation's society. The major exception is the border-state regions from Maryland to Missouri, in which the political process was either subjected to state repression (in the case of the Union) or fell outside the control of the state and normal elections could not be conducted (in the case of the Confederacy). The analysis in this chapter relies on a relatively uncomplicated methodology in order to allow possible cross-national and historical comparison and to make the text accessible to readers from a range of academic disciplines. For more on the advantages and drawbacks of roll call evidence as a means of understanding political development, see Bensel, *Sectionalism and American Political Development*, pp. 25–31.

193. In their exhaustive analysis, Alexander and Beringer considered only the slave-holding characteristics of the members themselves. *Anatomy of the Confederate Congress*, pp. 59–65.

all Union and Confederate congressional districts were divided into three categories on the basis of manufacturing activity: High, constituencies in which per capita value-added exceeded $60.00 in 1860; Medium, between $10.00 and $59.99; and Low, under $10.00. The Union House of Representatives contained districts in all three categories. The Confederate House held no districts in the highest category and so, in practice, was divided into only two groups: Medium and Low.[194]

Because of the significance of nativist–immigrant cleavages in antebellum party coalitions and competition, Union and Confederate House districts have also been classified according to the proportion of foreign-born residents in the white population. The three categories are: High, constituencies in which the foreign-born proportion equaled or exceeded 20 percent; Medium, between 5 and 19 percent; and, Low, under 5 percent. The Union House held numerous districts in all three categories (with the smallest number classified as Low). In the Confederacy, only six districts fell in the highest category, so the High and Medium categories were combined.

In addition to these ecological characteristics, congressional constituencies were also analyzed from several more or less political perspectives. For example, a distinction was made between "contested" (Kentucky, Missouri, and West Virginia) and "secure" districts, a fundamental cleavage widely recognized in the literature on the Union and Confederate Congresses.[195] With a handful of exceptions, politically contested districts were those located in states represented in both the Union and Confed-

194. Districts with modest levels of manufacturing (over ten dollars value-added per capita) included many of the leading cities of the South: Mobile, Alabama; Columbus and Savannah, Georgia; Louisville, Kentucky; New Orleans, Louisiana; St. Louis, Missouri; Wilmington, North Carolina; Charleston, South Carolina; Chattanooga, Nashville, and Memphis, Tennessee; and Arlington, Lynchburg, Petersburg, Richmond, and Wheeling, Virginia. In all, twenty-eight districts in the Confederate House of Representatives produced a total value-added in manufacturing greater than ten dollars per capita according to the 1860 census. Maps of counties included in Confederate districts can be found in John Brawner Robbins, Confederate Nationalism: Politics and Government in the Confederate South, 1861–1865, unpublished doctoral dissertation, Rice University, 1964. With the exception of a few cities such as Atlanta and Augusta, Georgia, and Norfolk, Virginia, the value-added in manufacturing category divides the South along both an urban–rural and an industrial–agrarian axis. Southern manufacturing everywhere, however, was only a pale shadow of northern industrialization.

195. The dichotomy can be found in Alexander and Beringer, *Anatomy of the Confederate Congress*, though they use a different terminology ("exterior" and "interior") and mean something different (all districts occupied by Union forces are "exterior" – a category that increases in size throughout the war; see p. 135). They find that the exterior–interior division is the single most important cleavage in the Confederate Congress. Yearns also emphasizes its significance in *Confederate Congress*, pp. 225–6. For the North, see Joel H. Silbey, *A Respectable Minority: The Democratic Party in the Civil War Era, 1860–1868* (New York: W. W. Norton, 1977), pp. 67–8, 99.

eracy. The Union, for example, never recognized the secession of Missouri or Kentucky, while the Confederacy admitted both. All districts from these two states belonged in the contested category of both the Union Congress and Confederate Congress. Similarly, West Virginia is included because the Confederacy continued to admit congressmen from the region even after the North brought the new state into the Union. All of these districts were in some sense contested in that peace negotiations might have determined their final disposition between the two nations. The North also allowed a scattering of districts in Louisiana, Tennessee, and Virginia into the House of Representatives without (re)admitting their respective states into the Union. These constituencies were certainly contested in the sense that military stalemate or southern victory would have eliminated all northern claims to their territory. For the same reason, they were, however, securely held by the Confederacy. In these isolated cases, districts were identified as contested in the Union Congress and secure in the Confederacy.

From almost the beginning of the war, most thoughtful Confederates conceded Kentucky and Missouri (and, later, West Virginia) to the Union as a necessary outcome, barring miracles, of any negotiations attending independence. But despite these reservations, twenty-three congressmen (seven from Missouri, twelve from Kentucky, and four from western Virginia) continued to serve in the First and Second Confederate Congresses.[196] Contact with their constituencies was impossible: As John Crockett of Kentucky noted in debate, "In Kentucky every Southern man is marked."[197] Congressmen from secure regions viewed these delegates

196. These members composed just over one-fifth of the Confederate House of Representatives. The failure of officially sponsored conventions to ratify a secession ordinance prevented most objective observers from considering Kentucky and Missouri as integral parts of the Confederacy. Doubt concerning resolve over the retention of "West Virginia" led the Virginia General Assembly to request that the Confederate Congress formally support inclusion of the territory in the new southern nation. The resolution subsequently passed by Congress stated, "That in no event will this government consent to a division or dismemberment of the state of Virginia, but will assert and maintain her jurisdiction and sovereignty to the uttermost limits of her ancient boundaries, at any and every cost" (approved June 4, 1864), but probably did little to allay the General Assembly's fears. *A Digest of the Military and Naval Laws of the Confederate States, Provisional and First Congresses*, pp. 315–16.

197. *Proceedings*, 44: 117. By 1863 major portions of the Confederacy had fallen under the control of Union armies and the normal conduct of elections became impossible in these areas. In the states of Arkansas, Kentucky, Louisiana, Missouri, and Tennessee the Confederate Congress ordered "general ticket" elections by which means refugees and residents of unoccupied territory could cast a vote for a candidate in each of the individual districts of the state. The candidate receiving the greatest number of votes was then declared eligible to serve in the Confederate Congress as the representative from the district in which he was a candidate. Yearns, *Confederate Congress*, p. 43; Bensel, "Southern Leviathan," n. 11. Under these circumstances,

as representing rotten boroughs that diluted the influence of the remaining, legitimate areas of the Confederacy. In 1864, for example, Josiah Turner of North Carolina wrote to his wife that he "would rather plough and feed hogs than legislate ... with Missouri and Kentucky to help me."[198] Later, near the end of the war, the Confederate House of Representatives formally debated resolutions questioning the legitimacy of representation in the Confederate Congress of areas overrun by Union armies.[199]

Though these areas were securely occupied by northern armies, they also presented serious political problems to the Union. Open civilian disloyalty, partial secession (and subsequent disintegration) of portions of the local government, and guerrilla warfare destroyed most semblance of administrative order in these districts. In response, the Union army assumed an active role in the administration of elections, imposed loyalty oaths as a condition of suffrage, shut down opposition newspapers, banned public assemblies called by the Democratic party, and, thus, enforced formal Union sovereignty in the border states. By the end of the war, the Union government ruled these regions either directly through martial law or indirectly through governments more or less propped up by military power.[200]

electoral participation was predictably low; between 1,000 and 1,200 voters, for example, elected Kentucky's Confederate congressmen in 1864. *1864 American Cyclopaedia*, p. 454.

198. Quoted in Yearns, *Confederate Congress*, p. 225.
199. Alexander and Beringer, *Anatomy of the Confederate Congress*, pp. 66–7; and *Proceedings*, 52:266–9, January 31, 1865.
200. Philip J. Avillo, Jr., "Ballots for the Faithful: The Oath and the Emergence of Slave State Republican Congressmen, 1861–1867," *Civil War History* 22 (June 1976): 164–74; Richard H. Abbott, *The Republican Party and the South, 1855–1877: The First Southern Strategy* (Chapel Hill: University of North Carolina Press, 1986), p. 21. For election law, loyalty oaths, implementing military orders, and election results in Kentucky, see *1863 American Cyclopaedia*, pp. 567–9, and *Congressional Globe* 37:3:1160–1, February 21, 1863; for an account of military influence in the 1865 elections, see *1865 American Cyclopaedia*, pp. 463–6; for the formation of a provisional court and government and military rule in Louisiana, see *1863 American Cyclopaedia*, pp. 586–94, 770–6; for the expulsion of "disloyal persons" from Missouri by the Union army, see *1863 American Cyclopaedia*, p. 653; for a long and detailed condemnation of military interference in border-state elections, see *Appendix to the Congressional Globe* 38:1:55–71, March 3–4, 1864; for a defense of military interference, see *Appendix to the Congressional Globe* 38:1:85–98, March 23–4, 1864; for test oaths, politics, and military conduct of elections in Maryland, see *1863 American Cyclopaedia*, pp. 616–24, *1864 American Cyclopaedia*, pp. 496–506, and *1865 American Cyclopaedia*, pp. 526–7. As will be evident in the voting analysis, this rather heavy-handed activity by the Union army apparently had only a moderate impact on the expression of loyalist and statist sympathies by border-state congressmen. In the Union Congress, border-state representatives elected under these extensive political controls gave much less support

Legislative behavior was also analyzed in terms of formally organized party structures (for the Union), loyalty to the presidential administration of Jefferson Davis (for the Confederacy), and sectional stress (compared for both states). Party organizations can be studied in the North because the Union inherited and consolidated the antebellum party system. In the South, the party system dissolved and no clear substitute emerged. Thus, a strictly comparable analysis of the influence of party organizations on the two state-building experiences is not possible.[201] Analysis of sectional stress within the two political systems allows us to compare the significance of latent separatist forces in the Union and the Confederacy.[202]

Political alignments on state-building issues

Constituency slave holdings were not an important factor in the voting alignments of the Confederate Congress on major state-building issues (see Tables 3.7 and 3.12). If anything, congressmen from districts with relatively few slaves tended to support central state expansion slightly more strongly than members from districts in which slaves were more numerous, but the results are so generally ambiguous that no conclusion is possible. Within individual policy areas, those districts with few slaves provided more support for market-centered state policies (such as those regarding legal tender notes, internal revenue, and the tariff) than did congressmen representing plantation constituencies. Before too much is made of that finding, however, note that nonplantation districts generally supported expansions of state extraction capacity and property controls (impressment, destruction of property, and price controls) more often

to northern state expansion than their counterparts in the Confederate Congress gave to the southern state.

201. The potential impact of antebellum party allegiance upon southern congressmen as a source of ideological and programmatic predispositions is not studied here because Alexander and Beringer have previously analyzed its influence in their *Anatomy of the Confederate Congress,* with generally inconclusive findings.

202. Before connecting the voting patterns in the Confederate Congress to the political economic characteristics of individual districts, we should remember that many of these votes were cast in secret sessions that prevented public announcement of members' positions. These secret sessions created an environment in which we cannot automatically assume that electorates could influence their representatives. However, these members were originally elected by their constituencies and, as much of the debate in both public and secret sessions indicates, remained intensely sympathetic to the interests of their districts when deliberating on Confederate policy. Furthermore, the records of these secret sessions were to become public at some point in the future and extreme discrepancies between public and secret legislative behavior would have damaged the credibility of these politicians in either future office holding or private life. We can probably assume that secrecy freed members from some measure of constituency pressure in the short term, but that the broader patterns of Confederate state formation reflected district sentiment.

Table 3.7. *Symmetrical state-building measures: The relationship of congressional support to slavery in constituency populations*

State dimension		Policy decision	Congressional support for symmetrical state-building decisions				
			Union		Confederacy		
			Free-state congressmen	Slave-state congressmen	Percent of slaves in district		
					Low	Medium	High
Centralization of authority	a)	Secret sessions	61.4% (114)	47.4% (19)	69.0% (29)	65.7% (35)	50.0% (24)
	b)	States appoint officers	71.2% (132)	37.0% (27)	55.6% (27)	44.1% (34)	45.0% (20)
	c)	Expulsion of member	67.2% (125)	71.4% (14)	67.9% (28)	56.7% (30)	83.3% (18)
Administrative capacity	a)	Academy appointments	59.5% (111)	50.0% (12)	52.0% (25)	33.3% (33)	66.7% (18)
	b)	Removal of officers	84.5% (97)	89.5% (19)	0.0% (2)	78.6% (14)	14.3% (14)
Citizenship	a)	Conscription	75.6% (135)	44.8% (29)	76.0% (25)	60.6% (33)	66.7% (21)
	b)	Habeas corpus	72.0% (118)	29.4% (17)	80.0% (15)	41.9% (31)	61.9% (21)
Property	a)	Railroad subsidy	47.1% (104)	93.7% (16)	94.4% (18)	54.8% (31)	50.0% (18)
	b)	Control railroads	84.2% (120)	57.1% (21)	62.5% (24)	43.7% (32)	62.5% (16)
	c)	Securities trading	53.7% (121)	64.7% (17)	77.3% (22)	64.0% (25)	90.5% (21)
	d)	Slaves as soldiers	72.2% (115)	0.0% (22)	70.0% (30)	51.6% (31)	69.2% (13)
	e)	Confiscation	63.4% (123)	14.8% (27)	81.8% (11)	87.5% (32)	82.4% (17)

Table 3.7 (continued)

| State dimension | Policy decision | Union | | Confederacy | | |
| | | Free-state congressmen | Slave-state congressmen | Percent of slaves in district | | |
				Low	Medium	High
Client groups	a) Legal tender notes	64.1% (131)	57.1% (21)	68.4% (19)	29.6% (27)	38.9% (18)
	b) Treasury debt	77.7% (103)	20.0% (15)	50.0% (24)	50.0% (26)	65.0% (20)
Extraction	a) Internal revenue	89.7% (117)	90.9% (22)	70.4% (27)	62.1% (29)	54.2% (24)
	b) Direct taxes/internal duties	63.6% (118)	10.5% (19)	40.0% (15)	36.7% (30)	57.9% (19)
World system	a) Tariff	77.3% (97)	60.0% (10)	28.0% (25)	21.1% (38)	5.0% (20)
	b) Negotiated peace	77.6% (107)	10.5% (19)	80.0% (25)	58.8% (34)	91.7% (24)
Average state-building support (all eighteen policy decisions)		70.1%	47.2%	62.4%	52.3%	58.6%

Note: Confederate congressmen are divided into three categories as follows: Low includes all congressmen from districts in which slaves composed less than 25 percent of the total population, Medium includes districts from 25 to 49 percent, and High includes those 50 percent and above. Population data was taken from the 1860 Census. Maps of counties included in Confederate districts can be found in John Brawner Robbins, Confederate Nationalism: Politics and Government in the Confederate South, 1861–1865, unpublished doctoral dissertation, Rice University, 1964.

Table 3.8. *Symmetrical state-building measures: Congressional support from contested and politically secure areas*

State dimension		Policy decision	Congressional support for symmetrical state-building decisions			
			Union		Confederacy	
			Secure	Contested	Secure	Contested
Centralization of authority	a)	Secret sessions	60.0% (120)	53.8% (13)	59.7% (72)	75.0% (16)
	b)	States appoint officers	70.3% (138)	33.3% (21)	40.6% (64)	76.5% (17)
	c)	Expulsion of member	66.9% (127)	75.0% (12)	61.4% (57)	84.2% (19)
Administrative capacity	a)	Academy appointments	59.3% (113)	50.0% (10)	41.7% (60)	68.7% (16)
	b)	Removal of officers	87.1% (101)	86.7% (15)	43.3% (30)	No districts
Citizenship	a)	Conscription	76.1% (142)	31.8% (22)	61.5% (65)	92.9% (14)
	b)	Habeas corpus	71.4% (119)	31.2% (16)	53.3% (60)	85.7% (7)
Property	a)	Railroad subsidy	47.2% (106)	100.0% (14)	57.1% (56)	100.0% (11)
	b)	Control railroads	82.4% (125)	62.5% (16)	51.7% (60)	66.7% (12)
	c)	Securities trading	54.4% (125)	61.5% (13)	75.9% (54)	78.6% (14)
	d)	Slaves as soldiers	69.7% (119)	0.0% (18)	57.1% (56)	73.7% (19)
	e)	Confiscation	60.5% (129)	19.0% (21)	84.5% (58)	100.0% (2)

Table 3.8 (continued)

| | | Congressional support for symmetrical state-building decisions | | | |
| | | Union | | Confederacy | |
State dimension	Policy decision	Secure	Contested	Secure	Contested
Client groups	a) Legal tender notes	62.8% (137)	46.7% (15)	38.9% (54)	70.0% (10)
	b) Treasury debt	75.7% (107)	18.2% (11)	52.5% (59)	63.6% (11)
Extraction	a) Internal revenue	90.2% (122)	88.2% (17)	56.1% (66)	92.9% (14)
	b) Direct taxes/internal duties	61.8% (123)	7.1% (14)	44.8% (58)	33.3% (6)
World system	a) Tariff	77.8% (99)	50.0% (8)	14.7% (68)	40.0% (15)
	b) Negotiated peace	74.1% (112)	14.3% (14)	73.2% (71)	83.3% (12)
Average state-building support (all 18 decisions for the Union/ 17 decisions for the Confederacy)		69.3%	46.1%	51.4%	75.6%

Note: For the Union, congressmen from contested areas include those representing districts in Kentucky, Louisiana, Missouri, Tennessee, and Virginia. For the Confederacy, congressmen from contested areas include those representing districts in Kentucky, Missouri, and what is now West Virginia. No congressmen from contested districts had been admitted when the Confederate Congress voted on presidential authority to remove military officers from command. For the Confederacy, therefore, the summary percentages at the bottom of the table exclude this decision.

Table 3.9. *Symmetrical state-building measures: The relationship of congressional support to manufacturing activity*

State dimension	Policy decision	Union			Confederacy	
		Manufacturing activity			Manufacturing activity	
		High	Medium	Low	Medium	Low
Centralization of authority	a) Secret sessions	51.9% (27)	63.0% (81)	56.0% (25)	62.5% (24)	62.5% (64)
	b) States appoint officers	72.7% (33)	69.1% (97)	44.8% (29)	56.5% (23)	44.8% (58)
	c) Expulsion of member	45.8% (24)	71.7% (92)	73.9% (23)	60.0% (20)	69.6% (56)
Administrative capacity	a) Academy appointments	87.0% (23)	55.0% (80)	40.0% (20)	55.6% (18)	44.8% (58)
	b) Removal of officers	76.5% (17)	87.8% (74)	84.0% (25)	66.7% (6)	37.5% (24)
Citizenship	a) Conscription	70.6% (34)	77.1% (96)	50.0% (34)	81.8% (22)	61.4% (57)
	b) Habeas corpus	78.3% (23)	69.0% (87)	48.0% (25)	60.0% (15)	55.8% (52)
Property	a) Railroad subsidy	60.0% (20)	54.3% (70)	46.7% (30)	68.7% (16)	62.7% (51)
	b) Control railroads	89.7% (29)	82.1% (84)	64.3% (28)	61.1% (18)	51.9% (54)
	c) Securities trading	72.0% (25)	53.7% (82)	45.2% (31)	68.7% (16)	78.8% (52)
	d) Slaves as soldiers	69.6% (23)	67.9% (84)	33.3% (30)	68.0% (25)	58.0% (50)
	e) Confiscation	46.7% (30)	63.3% (90)	36.7% (30)	90.0% (10)	84.0% (50)

Table 3.9 (continued)

State dimension	Policy decision	Union Manufacturing activity			Confederacy Manufacturing activity	
		High	Medium	Low	Medium	Low
Client groups	a) Legal tender notes	62.1% (29)	62.2% (98)	56.0% (25)	42.1% (19)	44.4% (45)
	b) Treasury debt	78.9% (19)	76.6% (77)	40.9% (22)	52.6% (19)	54.9% (51)
Extraction	a) Internal revenue	93.3% (30)	90.7% (86)	82.6% (23)	76.5% (17)	58.7% (63)
	b) Direct taxes/internal duties	72.0% (25)	60.9% (87)	24.0% (25)	50.0% (14)	42.0% (50)
World system	a) Tariff	81.8% (22)	80.3% (61)	58.3% (24)	30.4% (23)	15.0% (60)
	b) Negotiated peace	81.0% (21)	71.6% (81)	41.7% (24)	84.2% (19)	71.9% (64)
Average state-building support (all 18 policy decisions)		71.7%	69.8%	51.5%	63.1%	55.5%

Note: Manufacturing activity in congressional districts is measured and categorized according to per capita value-added in manufacturing (in dollars). Per capita value-added in manufacturing is calculated by subtracting the "Cost of raw materials" from the "Annual value of products" in the county schedules of the *1860 Census of Manufacturing*, aggregating the county figures into congressional districts, and dividing by total district population. The High category includes all congressional districts with per capita value-added greater than $60.00. No district in the Confederate Congress reached this level. All districts below $10.00 per capita fell in the Low category. The Medium category includes those between $10.00 and $59.99 per capita.

Table 3.10. *Symmetrical state-building measures: The relationship of congressional support to the percentage of foreign born in district populations*

State dimension		Policy decision	Congressional support for symmetrical state-building decisions				
			Union			Confederacy	
			Foreign-born population			Foreign-born population	
			High	Medium	Low	High/Medium	Low
Centralization of authority	a)	Secret sessions	61.5% (39)	58.3% (72)	59.1% (22)	50.0% (14)	64.9% (74)
	b)	States appoint officers	74.5% (51)	63.7% (80)	53.6% (28)	65.0% (20)	47.5% (61)
	c)	Expulsion of member	65.9% (41)	66.7% (78)	75.0% (20)	68.7% (16)	66.7% (60)
Administrative capacity	a)	Academy appointments	74.4% (39)	51.5% (68)	50.0% (16)	68.7% (16)	41.7% (60)
	b)	Removal of officers	84.8% (33)	85.0% (60)	87.0% (23)	66.7% (9)	33.3% (21)
Citizenship	a)	Conscription	76.5% (51)	69.9% (83)	60.0% (30)	80.0% (20)	62.7% (59)
	b)	Habeas corpus	78.4% (37)	65.8% (76)	50.0% (22)	57.1% (14)	56.6% (53)
Property	a)	Railroad subsidy	51.2% (41)	50.0% (62)	70.6% (17)	76.5% (17)	60.0% (50)
	b)	Control railroads	88.1% (42)	77.9% (77)	72.7% (22)	66.7% (15)	50.9% (57)
	c)	Securities trading	59.2% (49)	54.9% (71)	44.4% (18)	66.7% (15)	79.2% (53)
	d)	Slaves as soldiers	69.2% (39)	63.0% (73)	40.0% (25)	61.1% (18)	61.4% (57)
	e)	Confiscation	57.4% (47)	59.2% (76)	37.0% (27)	85.7% (14)	84.8% (46)

Table 3.10 (continued)

		Congressional support for symmetrical state-building decisions				
		Union			Confederacy	
		Foreign-born population			Foreign-born population	
State dimension	Policy decision	High	Medium	Low	High/Medium	Low
Client group formation	a) Legal tender notes	64.4% (45)	61.0% (82)	46.0% (25)	38.5% (13)	45.1% (51)
	b) Treasury debt	72.4% (29)	73.9% (69)	55.0% (20)	69.2% (13)	50.9% (57)
Extraction	a) Internal revenue	95.5% (44)	86.7% (75)	90.0% (20)	60.0% (15)	63.1% (65)
	b) Direct taxes/internal duties	55.8% (43)	58.9% (73)	47.6% (21)	38.5% (13)	45.1% (51)
World system	a) Tariff	76.3% (38)	78.2% (55)	64.3% (14)	27.3% (22)	16.4% (61)
	b) Negotiated peace	75.8% (33)	70.4% (71)	45.5% (22)	84.6% (13)	72.9% (70)
Average state-building support (all 18 policy decisions)		71.2%	66.4%	58.2%	62.8%	55.7%

Note: "Foreign-born" population taken from the 1860 Census (calculations are for the white population only). The category High includes all congressional districts in which the foreign-born percentage equaled or exceeded 20 percent of the total population. Districts categorized as Medium fell between 5 and 19.9 percent. Low districts contained foreign-born populations under 5 percent. Because only six districts in the Confederate Congress exceeded 20 percent, the High and Medium categories were combined.

than did members from plantation constituencies. In the three most important policy areas of Confederate state building (conscription, suspension of the writ of habeas corpus, and impressment), both plantation and nonplantation districts supported expanded state authority. Here again, however, districts with few slaves had a small but consistent edge. The most remarkable finding to emerge from the voting analysis is that the southern plantation economy was not the most important force driving the Confederate war effort and state development. Plantation economy congressmen were by no means dragging the remainder of the South into a slave leviathan.

Northern state formation presents a striking contrast with this southern experience. In the Union, the handful of slave-holding districts not only provided less support for state expansion than members from free-labor constituencies, but the usual pattern was for slave-state congressmen actually to oppose initiatives sponsored by free-state members (see Tables 3.7 and 3.11). In the decision to use slaves as soldiers, for example, no Union slave-state congressman supported state expansion, while nearly three of every four free-state members backed this enhancement of state authority. In contrast, no relationship between the level of slave holding and use of slaves as soldiers was evident in the Confederate House. Since both Union and Confederate slaveholders had the same material reasons to resist the arming of slaves, the different positions their respective political representatives assumed is a revealing illustration of the differing social bases of the Union and Confederate states. In the South, broader commitments to the Confederate state ultimately overcame more narrow property interests.

Differences between free-state and slave-state Union congressmen are striking in policy areas involving the centralization of authority, citizenship, control of property, client-group creation, extraction, and world-system dimensions (see Tables 3.7 and 3.11). Only on issues involving central state administrative capacity do differences between slave-state and free-state members narrow. Here the requirements of the new Republican party-state directly clashed with the institutional preconditions for bureaucratic autonomy. In this clash, the party generally supported presidential prerogatives when the latter conflicted with more statist proposals to insulate bureaucratic decision making from executive influence. Opposed to the creation of this new Republican party-state, many slave-state congressmen supported expanded administrative capacity because bureaucratic autonomy hedged in Lincoln's executive authority, not because they were more statist than their Republican colleagues. Aside from measures involving administrative capacity, free-state members provided more support for Union state development than members representing slave constituencies on a large majority of both symmetrical and non-symmetrical state-building measures. The evidence indicates that slave-state members were dragooned into Union state formation and, if left to their own devices (assuming they would have fought at all), would have preferred to construct a northern state apparatus much more likely to lose the American Civil War.

Confederate congressmen from "contested" districts gave much more support to southern state expansion than did members from politically secure regions (see Tables 3.8 and 3.12). Differences between contested and secure districts were consistent and in the same direction in every dimension of central state authority except those involving the creation of client groups. In fact, we can conclude that congressmen from contested areas were the strongest advocates of a dominant central state role in the new southern nation. Their more or less consistent support for the expansion of central state authority arose, in part, out of the realization that only a convincing, clear-cut southern victory would lead to the permanent incorporation of their constituencies into the Confederacy.[203] In addition, northern occupation of their homes cut these members off from almost all private sources of income and thus produced a dependence upon congressional salaries and other support from the Confederate government. This dependence led them to resist adjournment resolutions (which reduced per diem income), to support substitution of an annual salary for per diem reimbursement of expenses, and to favor generally an active professionalization of the role of Confederate congressmen.

Members from occupied districts also had several electoral reasons to disproportionately support the growth of central state power. Since their constituents were behind Union lines, these members heard few, if any, complaints concerning the substance of Confederate measures or the way in which they were implemented. In fact, the electorate that sustained these congressmen was largely drawn from the ranks of the Confederate military (soldiers who formerly resided in the occupied states) and a usually smaller number of civilian refugees. Although the electoral record is incomplete, what is known suggests that the soldier vote strongly favored more extreme war measures and, consequently, a stronger central state.[204] As a result of all these factors, the state-expanding tendencies

203. See, for example, Yearns, *Confederate Congress*, pp. 39, 225.
204. On the reasons that explain why congressmen from occupied areas gave disproportionate support for a stronger central state, see Alexander and Beringer, *Anatomy of the Confederate Congress*, pp. 320–8, 336–7. On North Carolina troops (the soldiers' vote) favoring an expanded war effort and stronger central state, see Georgia Lee Tatum, *Disloyalty in the Confederacy* (Chapel Hill: University of North Carolina Press, 1934), p. 132. For an example of the arrangements made to accommodate

of members from contested districts were so pronounced that the decision to allow these congressmen to sit in House of Representatives significantly reinforced the statist orientation of the Confederate Congress. (Even so, we should note that members from contested districts did not provide the margin of victory on any of the state-building decisions analyzed here. All would have passed or failed without their votes.)

The situation was very different in the Union. There members from contested districts were routinely more opposed to central state expansion than members from politically secure constituencies (see Tables 3.8 and 3.11). When the overall relationship between political status (contested or secure) and support for state expansion in the Union and Confederate Congress is compared on the eighteen symmetrical state-building decisions, the direction of the relationship in the Union House of Representatives turns out to be the reverse of that in the Confederate chamber in almost three-quarters of the comparisons (see Table 3.8). In all of these reversals, Confederate members from contested districts were more favorable to statist measures than their more politically secure colleagues; the experience in the Union Congress was just the opposite. Arising as they do out of almost identical state-building decisions confronting both the Union and Confederate chambers, the contrasting direction of these comparative patterns is very surprising. As we noted previously, military occupation of contested regions allowed the Union to impose loyalty oaths and otherwise discourage southern sympathizers and political opponents of the war from participating in elections. By all accounts, these measures significantly increased Union sympathy and statist tendencies among elected representatives from these areas, but they apparently did little to narrow the differences over state expansion between these members and those from secure regions to the North. Thus, in sharp contrast to the southern experience, the decision to allow the representation of contested districts in the northern House of Representatives significantly weakened the statist orientation of the Union Congress.[205]

Though the pattern was weaker than that for exterior members, Confederate congressmen from districts with significant levels of manufacturing activity also provided disproportionate support for state-enhancing

voting by soldiers, see General Order No. 38 (April 7, 1863), which relays "an act of the legislature of Virginia, passed March 26, 1863," in R. H. P. Robinson, *General Orders of the Confederate States Army, 1863* (Richmond, Va.: A. Morris, 1864), pp. 39–40.

205. Exclusion of the votes of members from contested districts would not have reversed any decision except the one to construct a railroad in East Tennessee. In that case, the exclusion of members from contested districts could have meant defeat because border-state congressmen strongly supported the proposed line as a project aiding economic development of the region, not because it was a necessary war measure.

measures (see Tables 3.9 and 12). When broken down into the seven dimensions, the voting patterns of members from manufacturing districts were comparatively less statist in only the creation of client groups. In all those decisions which might have expanded or created client groups, Confederate congressmen from nonmanufacturing regions were more favorable to state enhancement than their more urbanized, industrial colleagues. This exception is striking and we will return to it.

The pattern is in the same direction but more robust in the Union House of Representatives (see Tables 3.9 and 3.11). There, congressmen from heavily industrialized districts (those with a per capita value-added in manufacturing of over $60.00 — there were none in the Confederacy) provided more support for state expansion than their less industrialized colleagues on approximately two-thirds of all symmetrical and nonsymmetrical state-building decisions.[206] The instances in which central state expansion was marginally less favored by industrial members fell, for the most part, under the two structural dimensions (centralization and administrative capacity). Several of these exceptions to the modal pattern related to potential constraints on legislative or executive discretion and thus suggest partisan motives that often led otherwise statist Republicans from industrial districts to restrict bureaucratic autonomy. Aside from these structural dimensions, the pattern of industrial support for central state expansion was uniformly strong and particularly apparent when the policy area involved broad developmental issues (political reconstruction of the South, the place of the United States in the world system, the insinuation of the Treasury into the financial system, and the creation of associated client groups). Although the Civil War agenda of the Union differed in many respects from that of the antebellum period, congressmen representing industrial capitalism remained influential and self-interested charter members of the state-building coalition. From the perspective of these members, the Union state was to be a highly partisan structure for the promotion of internal development and for the emergence of a national market.

When industrial support for state expansion in the Union and Confederate congresses is compared on symmetrical decisions, the two patterns bear a remarkable resemblance. In two-thirds of these symmetrical decisions, both Union and Confederate congressmen disproportionately favored state expansion. In one instance, involving expulsion of members from Congress, both northern and southern representatives from industrial areas opposed state expansion. In several additional policy areas

206. Union members representing the least industrialized districts were comparatively favorable to state expansion in only two policy areas (the expulsion of a member and the administrative capacity of the court of claims).

(secret sessions and legal tender notes), no pattern involving manufacturing activity developed in either Congress and, in several more (presidential removal of officers, conscription, and confiscation), the differences are relatively minor. In only two instances (securities trading and the issuance of Treasury debt) are the patterns in the Union and Confederate Congresses diametrically opposed. These coinciding patterns suggest that the relationship between industrialization and central state expansion would have been similar in both an independent Confederacy and a Union political system without the South, as well as in the reunified and northern-dominated postwar United States.

In the middle of the nineteenth century, politicians often linked rapid industrial development to the presence of relatively high percentages of foreign born in resident populations. One reason for this linkage was that immigrants tended to concentrate in rapidly growing regions, whether they were urban manufacturing centers or the western frontier, because these areas presented economic opportunities and employment not as readily available in more settled, slower growing regions of the nation. In the antebellum years, the flow of immigrants into the United States opened deep cleavages in the political system between nativists and foreign-born citizens. To cite just one example, such a cleavage made the emergence of the Republican party in local politics a much more complex and difficult process than the steady growth that a clear-cut conflict over slavery would have otherwise allowed.[207] Thus, the social and political implications of a relatively high percentage of foreign-born residents in a congressional district included social complexity in a context of rapid economic development. Traditionally, such characteristics have been cited as an impetus for central state expansion. In the Confederate House of Representatives, however, no relationship between immigrant districts and congressional support for state expansion ever emerged. What appears to be a consistent and expected pattern for symmetrical policy decisions (where members from high foreign-born constituencies disproportionately supported state expansion in most cases) is completely reversed when nonsymmetrical issues are examined (see Tables 3.10 and 3.12).

Union congressmen from districts with relatively large foreign-born populations turned in a much more statist record (see Tables 3.10 and 3.11). Of the three categories into which northern members have been classified, congressmen in the highest category (20 percent and over) provided the greatest degree of support for central state expansion in

207. William E. Gienapp, *The Origins of the Republican Party, 1852–1856* (New York: Oxford University Press, 1987), p. 446.

Table 3.11A. Union nonsymmetrical state-building measures: Centralization of authority and administrative capacity dimensions

	Roll call support for nonsymmetrical state-building measures					
	Centralization of authority				Administrative capacity	
Categorization of congressmen	Militia outside state	Freedmen's Bureau	Nationalization of currency	Reconstruction	Court of claims	Board of Admiralty
Contested	0.0% (18)	33.3% (18)	33.3% (15)	25.0% (16)	70.6% (17)	38.5% (13)
Secure	49.2% (132)	53.4% (118)	53.3% (120)	59.1% (115)	67.0% (106)	47.0% (117)
Slave	0.0% (23)	30.0% (20)	41.2% (17)	38.1% (21)	75.0% (20)	43.7% (16)
Free	51.2% (127)	54.3% (116)	52.5% (118)	58.2% (110)	66.0% (103)	46.5% (114)
Value-added in manufacturing (per capita)						
Over $60	38.7% (31)	81.0% (21)	69.2% (26)	67.9% (28)	66.7% (24)	19.2% (26)
$10–59.99	50.0% (90)	44.6% (83)	51.3% (78)	57.7% (71)	65.3% (75)	57.5% (73)
Under $10	27.6% (29)	46.9% (32)	35.5% (31)	37.5% (32)	75.0% (24)	41.9% (31)
Foreign-born population						
20% and more	42.2% (45)	57.4% (47)	54.9% (51)	61.2% (49)	67.6% (37)	40.0% (45)
5–19.9%	48.1% (81)	50.0% (70)	53.1% (64)	53.8% (65)	68.7% (64)	50.7% (69)
Under 5%	29.2% (24)	36.8% (19)	35.0% (20)	41.2% (17)	63.6% (22)	43.7% (16)
Sectional stress	49.2	64.2	54.5	66.1	15.0	45.0

Table 3.11B. *Union nonsymmetrical state-building measures: Citizenship, property, client group, world system, and extraction dimensions*

| | Roll call support for nonsymmetrical state-building measures | | | | | | |
| | Citizenship | Property | Client groups | World system | | Extraction | |
Categorization of congressmen	Emancipation Amendment	Bankruptcy	Homesteads in Confederacy	Pacific railroad	Colonization/ confiscation	National banks	Average support (All 12 decisions)
Contested	66.7% (21)	33.3% (15)	25.0% (16)	63.2% (19)	25.0% (12)	36.8% (19)	37.6%
Secure	68.8% (154)	60.7% (117)	57.7% (123)	61.5% (109)	67.7% (99)	57.7% (123)	58.6%
Slave	70.4% (27)	42.1% (19)	33.3% (21)	60.0% (25)	22.2% (18)	41.7% (24)	42.3%
Free	68.2% (148)	60.2% (113)	57.6% (118)	62.1% (103)	71.0% (93)	57.6% (118)	58.8%
Value-added in manufacturing (per capita)							
Over $60	71.4% (35)	79.3% (29)	71.4% (28)	80.0% (25)	75.0% (20)	50.0% (26)	64.2%
$10–$59.99	71.1% (97)	56.2% (73)	54.8% (73)	57.3% (75)	65.3% (72)	58.6% (87)	57.5%
Under $10	60.5% (43)	40.0% (30)	39.5% (38)	57.1% (28)	42.1% (19)	48.3% (29)	46.0%
Foreign-born population							
20% and more	70.3% (64)	78.8% (52)	61.2% (49)	80.0% (40)	64.1% (39)	63.4% (41)	61.8%
5–19.9%	68.2% (88)	50.0% (66)	55.9% (68)	55.4% (65)	66.7% (51)	50.0% (76)	56.7%
Under 5%	65.2% (23)	14.3% (14)	31.8% (22)	47.8% (23)	52.4% (21)	56.0% (25)	43.1%
Sectional stress	30.9	67.9	64.1	28.6	63.4	45.3	49.5

Table 3.12A. Confederate nonsymmetrical state-building measures: Centralization, administrative capacity, and world system dimensions

	Roll call support for nonsymmetrical state-building measures					
	Centralization of authority	Administrative capacity				World system
Categorization of congressmen	Supreme court jurisdiction	General staff	Exemptions	Civil service test	Establish a supreme court	Blockade cargo
Contested	None voting	85.7% (7)	57.1% (14)	27.3% (11)	46.2% (13)	100.0% (8)
Secure	47.6% (42)	59.6% (52)	45.0% (60)	36.2% (58)	41.8% (55)	82.8% (64)
Slave population						
0–24%	75.0% (4)	69.2% (13)	45.8% (24)	30.0% (20)	33.3% (24)	90.9% (22)
25–49%	47.1% (17)	75.0% (28)	46.7% (30)	33.3% (30)	55.6% (27)	83.3% (30)
Over 50%	42.9% (21)	38.9% (18)	50.0% (20)	42.1% (19)	41.2% (17)	80.0% (20)
Value-added in manufacturing (per capita)						
Over $10	50.0% (4)	61.5% (13)	45.0% (20)	52.9% (17)	54.5% (11)	71.4% (21)
Under $10	47.4% (38)	63.0% (46)	48.1% (54)	28.8% (52)	40.4% (57)	90.2% (51)
Foreign-born population						
5% and more	18.2% (11)	54.5% (11)	53.8% (13)	38.5% (13)	35.7% (14)	71.4% (14)
Under 5%	58.1% (31)	64.6% (48)	45.9% (61)	33.9% (56)	44.4% (54)	87.9% (58)
Sectional stress	70.0	22.7	54.3	16.7	40.0	0.0

214

Table 3.12B. *Confederate nonsymmetrical state-building measures: Property and client-group dimensions*

| | Roll call support for nonsymmetrical state-building measures | | | | | | |
| | Property | | Client groups | | | | |
Categorization of congressmen	Impressment	Destruction of property	Military pensions	Redistribution	Price controls	Veterans' home	Average support (All 12 decisions)
Contested	100.0% (10)	64.3% (14)	0.0% (1)	20.0% (5)	87.5% (8)	28.6% (14)	*56.1%
Secure	85.7% (49)	51.4% (70)	28.6% (35)	35.6% (59)	59.3% (59)	42.0% (50)	*51.6%
Slave population							
0–24%	94.1% (17)	51.9% (27)	0.0% (4)	40.0% (15)	68.2% (22)	40.9% (22)	53.3%
25–49%	85.7% (21)	59.4% (32)	43.7% (16)	25.9% (27)	59.3% (27)	41.7% (24)	54.7%
Over 50%	85.7% (21)	48.0% (25)	18.7% (16)	40.9% (22)	61.1% (18)	33.3% (18)	48.6%
Value-added in manufacturing (per capita)							
Over $10	85.7% (14)	52.4% (21)	None voting	28.6% (14)	55.6% (18)	18.7% (16)	*52.4%
Under $10	88.9% (45)	54.0% (63)	27.8% (36)	36.0% (50)	65.3% (49)	45.8% (48)	*55.3%
Foreign-born population							
5% and more	73.3% (15)	53.3% (15)	57.1% (7)	35.7% (14)	53.8% (13)	18.2% (11)	47.0%
Under 5%	93.2% (44)	53.6% (69)	20.7% (29)	34.0% (50)	64.8% (54)	43.4% (53)	53.7%
Sectional stress	0.0	46.2	20.0	31.8	40.0	28.0	30.8

Note: The summary averages for the "contested/secure" dichotomy do not include the roll call on the supreme court's jurisdiction. Similarly, the summary averages for the "value-added in manufacturing" categories do not include the military pensions vote.

215

almost two-thirds of all policy areas. Congressmen with the smallest proportions of foreign born among their constituents, on the other hand, were comparatively statist in only three instances (the expulsion of a member, presidential removal of officers, and the railroad construction subsidy). As was also the case for members from industrialized districts, statist tendencies among Union congressmen from foreign-born constituencies were comparatively strong across all dimensions of central state authority except those decisions involving administrative capacity. The voting patterns on symmetrical policy issues also display an apparent positive relationship between immigrant populations and support for state expansion for both the Union and Confederacy, since in both states districts with large foreign-born populations were more statist on most decisions. However, this overall pattern is in some ways deceptive. When the record for the two congresses is separately compared on each of the individual issues, for example, the individual patterns coincide in only a third of the symmetrical decisions (see Table 3.10). On the rest, the Union and Confederate results are diametrically opposed. This finding suggests caution in drawing conclusions about the statist inclinations of districts with large foreign-born populations.

Sectional stress also took on very different forms in the northern and southern states. In the Union internal regional divisions on both symmetrical and nonsymmetrical state-building issues were comparatively deep (see Tables 3.11 and 3.13). The average score in the Union House of Representatives, for example, was 43.3 on symmetrical issues and 49.5 for the nonsymmetrical decisions, while the Confederacy averaged 34.0 and 30.8, respectively.[208] On two-thirds of the symmetrical decisions the Union exhibited sectional cleavages more polarized than did the Confederacy. While sectional stress scores ranged widely in the South, the varying intensity of regional divisions in the Confederate Congress seems largely unrelated to the various dimensions of central state authority.

---

208. These sectional stress scores measure the relative depth of sectional cleavages in legislative voting. The higher the score, the more legislative coalitions are sectionally arrayed against each other. For very high scores (60 or more), very few congressmen oppose the positions assumed by the majority of their sectional delegations. These scores were calculated for districts within trade area boundaries drawn from information in *Colton's General Atlas* (New York: J. H. Colton, 1863) and *Asher and Adam's Atlas and Gazetteer* (New York: Asher and Adams, 1873). In brief, the procedure by which these trade areas were determined began with the identification of all cities with populations greater than 8,000 in 1860 that were also more than 75 miles by rail or steamboat route from a larger urban center. Using such cities as the central points of each trade area, the boundaries of their respective hinterlands were then extended to points equidistant by rail or water from other cities. See Bensel, *Sectionalism and American Political Development*, pp. 415–50 for an extended discussion of the similar construction of 1880 and 1890 trade area boundaries and the procedure by which congressional districts are incorporated.

Table 3.13. *Symmetrical state-building measures: Sectional stress in the Union and Confederate congresses*

State dimension	Policy decision		Sectional stress in roll call voting	
			Union Congress	Confederate Congress
Centralization of authority	a)	Secret sessions	38.9	21.2
	b)	States appoint officers	50.9	48.7
	c)	Expulsion of member	35.6	28.0
Administrative capacity	a)	Academy appointments	31.4	38.9
	b)	Removal of officers	17.6	61.5
Citizenship	a)	Conscription	55.1	34.6
	b)	Habeas corpus	51.1	31.0
Property	a)	Railroad subsidy	39.3	50.0
	b)	Control railroads	28.6	45.5
	c)	Securities trading	54.8	25.0
	d)	Slaves as soldiers	59.3	34.5
	e)	Confiscation	52.9	0.0
Client groups	a)	Legal tender notes	22.0	50.0
	b)	Treasury debt	55.9	46.9
Extraction	a)	Internal revenue	14.3	23.3
	b)	Direct taxes/internal duties	51.7	42.9
World system	a)	Tariff	61.5	6.3
	b)	Negotiated peace	58.5	23.8
Average sectional stress score (All 18 policy decisions)			43.3	34.0

In the Union, however, a clear programmatic link emerged between the intensity of sectional stress and northern proposals to reconstruct the southern political economy (Freedmen's Bureau, the Wade–Davis Reconstruction bill, the colonization of freedmen abroad, and southern homesteads for Union veterans). These issues generally divided the slaveholding border regions, immediately adjacent districts in the lower portions of the free states, and New York City against the remainder of the Union. Major questions involving the development of national financial and commercial markets produced only slightly less intense regional cleavages within the Union House (national banks and nationalization of the currency, bankruptcy, the tariff, and securities trading). Both of these broad policy areas were fundamental parts of the Republican program for the national political economy and drove a deep wedge between expanding, free-labor sectors of the North and the slave-dependent communities in the loyal border states and their allies in neighboring districts of the North or New York City. Once again, policy decisions involving administrative capacity constitute the major exceptions to the rule – all produced relatively low sectional stress scores.

A more comprehensive analysis of sectional polarization in the Civil War buttresses this Union and Confederate comparison (see Table 3.14). Here all closely competitive roll calls (those with pluralities less than 55 percent of those voting) recorded in either the Union or Confederate Congress between 1859 and 1869 were analyzed. In all, sectional stress scores were calculated on 648 votes in the North and 306 in the South. The Thirty-sixth United States Congress, which began with the contested election for House speaker and ended with secession, produced an average sectional stress score of 63.0 on closely competitive roll calls – an average probably not matched in subsequent American political development.[209] After the secession of the South, stress scores in the Thirty-seventh and Thirty-eighth Union Congresses subsided a bit but remained at historically high levels. With the admission of Union-sponsored congressional delegations during postwar Reconstruction, the opposition of the South to northern policy proposals was internally divided and stress levels dropped once more. Later, sectional cleavages would again intensify as southern loyalist governments were replaced by regimes led by former Confederate nationalists. The most interesting comparison, however, is between the levels of sectional stress in the two Union and three Confederate Civil War congresses. In the Confederacy, the roll call record of members of the Provisional Congress and the House of Representatives produced an average stress score of 45.6 on 306 closely competitive votes

209.   Bensel, *Sectionalism and American Political Development*, p. 53.

Table 3.14. *Sectional stress in the Union and Confederate congresses*
(December 1859 – March 1869)

Union (dates)	Average sectional stress	Confederacy (dates)	Average sectional stress
36th Congress (Dec. 1859 – Mar. 1861)	63.0 (129)		
		Provisional Congress (Feb. 1861 – Feb. 1862)	52.2 (40)
37th Congress (July 1861 – Mar. 1863)	53.8 (115)		
		1st Congress (Feb. 1862 – Feb. 1864)	42.4 (162)
38th Congress (Dec. 1863 – Mar. 1865)	56.4 (176)		
		2nd Congress (May 1864 – Mar. 1865)	47.9 (104)
39th Congress (Dec. 1865 – Mar. 1867)	51.5 (108)		
40th Congress (Mar. 1867 – Mar. 1869)	46.7 (120)		

Note: Data for the Confederate Provisional Congress include votes taken in the Constitutional Convention. All closely contested roll calls (pluralities less than 55 percent of those voting) are included. The number of roll calls is given in parentheses.

(ranging from 52.2 in the Provisional Congress during the first year of independence to 42.4 in the two subsequent years of the First Congress). In the Union, the roll call record produced a significantly higher average score of 55.4 on 291 votes. Clearly, the Union war mobilization created more serious regional divisions in the North than the southern mobilization produced within the Confederacy.

The sharply sectional basis of Union state formation can be seen in a mapping of congressional support for critical state-building decisions during the Thirty-seventh Congress (see Map 3.3). Opposition to central state expansion was concentrated in the slave-holding border states, the regions of the Union immediately to the north, and New York City and its immediate hinterland. The opposition of members from border states and adjacent districts has already been traced to their ambivalence, even hostility to major portions of the northern, Republican program for the national political economy. In this case, the geographical pattern merely confirms that their hostility to this program was translated into opposition to central state expansion and, theoretically at least, carried plausible separatist implications if the North had lost the Civil War.

The opposition of New York City and its hinterland can be traced to deep involvement in the import/export trade and close, antebellum com-

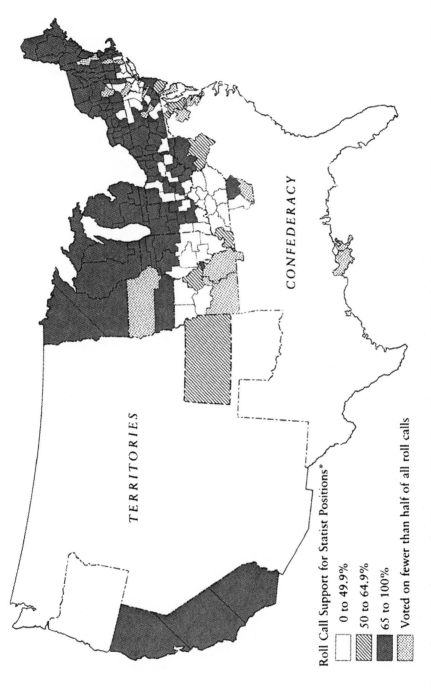

Map 3.3 Congressional support for Union state formation, 1861–3. This analysis includes the twenty state-building measures that were considered in the U.S. House of Representatives in the Thirty-seventh Congress. Several members may have cast the votes that composed the roll call record of individual districts.

Roll Call Support for Statist Positions*

☐	0 to 49.9%
▨	50 to 64.9%
▮	65 to 100%
▦	Voted on fewer than half of all roll calls

TERRITORIES

CONFEDERACY

mercial ties with the southern plantation economy.[210] The subregion was strongly interested in free trade and the early reestablishment of cotton cultivation in the South. The northern war mobilization, instead, brought industrial protectionism, a restructuring of the southern slave labor system, and, in addition, reorganization and intervention in New York money markets by the Treasury. In fact, the opposition of New York City congressmen was so consistent and deep as to substantially reduce the otherwise very strong correlation between industrial manufacturing and support for central state expansion (compare Tables 3.9, 3.11, and 3.15).

The picture in the Confederate Congress was more muddled (see Map 3.4). Two major areas sent comparatively statist congressmen to Richmond: the contested districts of the northern border and the plantation districts of the deep South. A political explanation for the statist orientation of contested regions was offered earlier. With a few minor exceptions, the statist sympathies of the deep South were geographically correlated with regions of intensive cotton production.[211] At first glance, then, Confederate state formation appears to have been the outcome of an alliance between the cotton plantation elite and border-state nationalists. If so, a sharp distinction must be made between cotton production and slavery, because the link between slave holding in secure districts and support for state expansion has previously been shown to be weak.[212] The major centers of opposition to Confederate state formation were located in secure districts outside the cotton belt in Virginia, North Carolina, northeastern South Carolina, northern Georgia and Alabama, and southern Florida. Districts in the first three states composed the resource base for Confederate armies operating in the Virginia theater and probably were exploited more intensively than any other region by southern quartermasters and treasury officials. As Thomas Alexander and Richard Beringer noted in their *Anatomy of the Confederate Congress,* this comparatively high exposure to Confederate resource and manpower mobilization strained civilian morale and, indirectly, may have decreased congressional support for further state expansion. In Georgia and Alabama, congressmen opposed to state enhancement tended to represent upland districts where both slave holding and cotton production were relatively unimportant features of the local political economy. On

210. See Chapter 2. New York City disaffection from the northern, Republican program continued until the end of the nineteenth century. See Bensel, *Sectionalism and American Political Development,* p. 49.
211. Compare, for example, Map 3.4 with the map of cotton production (bales per square mile in 1860) in Sam Bowers Hilliard, *Atlas of Antebellum Southern Agriculture* (Baton Rouge: Louisiana State University Press, 1984), p. 71.
212. Bensel, "Southern Leviathan," p. 131.

Table 3.15. *Support for Union state-building measures by congressmen from manufacturing districts*

State dimension		Policy decision	Support for state-building measures	
			New York City	Other high value-added in manufacturing districts
Centralization	a)	Expulsion of member	60.0% (5)	42.1% (19)
of authority	b)	Secret sessions	33.3% (3)	54.2% (24)
	c)	Militia outside state	50.0% (4)	37.0% (27)
	d)	States appoint officers	50.0% (6)	77.8% (27)
	*e)	Freedmen's Bureau	0.0% (3)	94.4% (18)
	*f)	Nationalization of currency	20.0% (5)	81.0% (21)
	*g)	Reconstruction	0.0% (4)	79.2% (24)
Administrative	a)	Academy appointments	100.0% (3)	85.0% (20)
capacity	b)	Removal of officers	50.0% (2)	80.0% (15)
	c)	Court of claims	50.0% (2)	68.2% (22)
	*d)	Board of admiralty	0.0% (4)	22.7% (22)
Citizenship	a)	Habeas corpus	100.0% (2)	76.2% (21)
	b)	Conscription	33.3% (6)	78.6% (28)
	*c)	Emancipation amendment	16.7% (6)	82.8% (29)
Property	a)	Control railroads	75.0% (4)	92.0% (25)
	b)	Confiscation	40.0% (5)	48.0% (25)
	c)	Slaves as soldiers	100.0% (1)	68.2% (22)
	*d)	Railroad subsidy	0.0% (3)	70.6% (17)
	*e)	Securities trading	0.0% (3)	81.8% (22)
	*f)	Bankruptcy	100.0% (5)	75.0% (24)
Client groups	a)	Treasury debt	33.3% (3)	87.5% (16)
	b)	Legal tender notes	50.0% (4)	64.0% (25)
	*c)	Homesteads in Confederacy	0.0% (4)	83.3% (24)
Extraction	a)	Direct taxes/internal duties	50.0% (4)	76.2% (21)
	b)	National banks	33.3% (3)	52.2% (23)
	c)	Internal revenue	75.0% (4)	96.2% (26)
World system	a)	Negotiated peace	66.7% (3)	83.3% (18)
	b)	Pacific railroad	66.7% (3)	81.8% (22)
	c)	Colonization/confiscation	50.0% (4)	81.2% (16)
	*d)	Tariff	0.0% (1)	85.7% (21)
		Average support	43.4%	73.9%

Note: Asterisks indicate decisions recorded during the Thirty-eighth Congress, when partisan strength generally shifted from Republicans to Unionists and Democrats as a result of the 1862 elections.

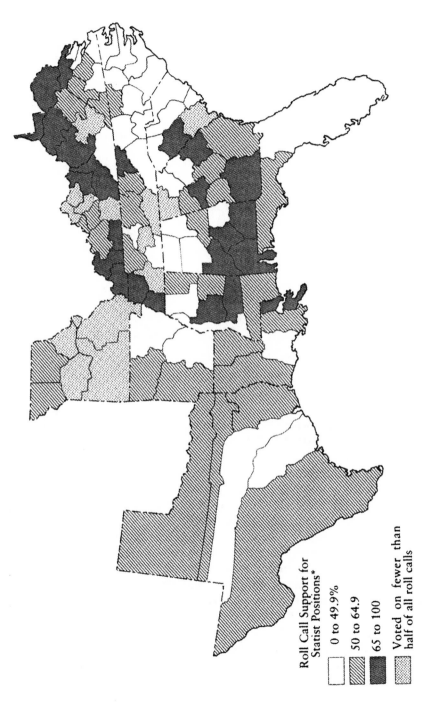

Roll Call Support for
Statist Positions*

☐	0 to 49.9%
▨	50 to 64.9
■	65 to 100
▧	Voted on fewer than half of all roll calls

Map 3.4 **Congressional support for Confederate state formation, 1862–1865.** This analysis includes the twenty-five state-building measures that were considered in the House of Representatives in the First and Second Confederate congresses. Several members may have cast the votes that composed the roll call record of individual districts.

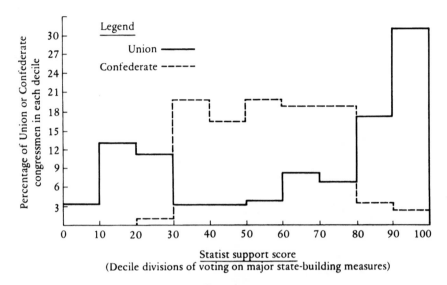

Figure 3.2
Comparison of the distribution of congressional support scores for Union and Confederate state formation.

the other hand, the rapidly expanding cotton districts of the Trans-Mississippi West were also somewhat lukewarm in their support for Confederate state expansion.

Thus, one possible picture of Confederate state formation postulates the existence of a statist alliance between border-state nationalists and cotton producers from the settled regions of the deep South against opponents from upland districts, intensively exploited lowland areas in the East, and rapidly expanding plantation areas in the Trans-Mississippi. There are two very good reasons we should not overstate this interpretation. For one thing, contemporary observers and subsequent historians have not found evidence of a linkage between the cotton belt and the border states (though many have emphasized cleavages between the border states and secure districts and popular discontent in upland regions). Even more important is the fact that Confederate divisions over central state expansion, however described, were shallower than those in the North (see Figure 3.2). In the Union, more than a quarter of all members of the House of Representatives cast under 30 percent of their votes for the state-building decisions (symmetrical and nonsymmetrical) recorded in the Thirty-seventh Congress. Only one member (1.1 percent) fell in this category in the southern House in voting during the First and Second Confederate Congresses. At the high end of the statist spectrum, nearly half of all northern congressmen cast over 80 percent of their votes in support of central state expansion. In the South, only one in twenty members delivered correspondingly high levels of support to Confederate state formation. In the Union, the lopsided, bipolar distribution of statist sentiment reflected deep cleavages within the national political economy over the erection of the Republican party-state and state-sponsored northern development. The southern single-peaked distribution, by contrast, mirrored the more consensual and broadly based political-economic foundation of Confederate nationalism. This characterization of the social bases of the Union and Confederate states is consistent with the Union's emphasis on the repression of southern separatism, a highly divisive project accompanied by a supporting ideology of expansionist nationalism. It is also consistent with the more unifying defensive posture of the Confederacy and the southern state's comparatively centralized direction of the domestic economy. Thus, while we could postulate the existence of a statist coalition in the Confederate Congress, that interpretation could easily obscure a comparatively greater southern consensus on the broad thrust of central state expansion as a reaction to northern invasion. In the South, disagreement over the means to be used by the Confederate state was more serious than disputes over the ends of government policy. In the North, a wide chasm opened between Republican nationalists and the opposition over the ends: the importance of northern victory in the Civil War and the survival of the Union.

In the Union, the central state apparatus thrown up during the American Civil War was the creature of the Republican party (see Table 3.16).[213] On almost every policy decision, the vast majority of Republican members supported central state expansion against the opposition of an equally large majority of the Democratic party.[214] The pattern is slightly different for the railroad construction subsidy, which drew broad support from border-state Unionists. Otherwise, the major exceptions to the over-

213. The thorough identification of the Republican party with a potentially monolithic and all-powerful American state can be seen in Joel Silbey's discussion of Democratic party rhetoric in his *A Respectable Minority*, pp. 72–82.
214. As can be seen in Table 3.16, the number of "unionist" congressmen increased significantly between the Thirty-seventh and Thirty-eighth Congresses. This category includes all members elected by organizations other than the Republican and Democratic parties (Emancipation, Conservative, Union Republican, and Union parties). The Lincoln administration encouraged the creation of "union" parties (including Republicans in their ranks) as a means of broadening the political base for northern war mobilization and some of these were mere facades for otherwise very partisan Republican organizations. In other cases, particularly in the border states where formal Republican organizations were very weak, "unionist" congressmen represented real attempts to find a middle way between the two major parties. See Silbey, *A Respectable Minority*, pp. 41–3, 67–9.

Table 3.16. *Partisan support for Civil War state-building measures in the Union Congress*

State dimension	Policy decision	Partisan support		
		Republicans	Unionists	Democrats
Centralization of authority	a) Expulsion of member	91.2% (91)	81.8% (11)	5.4% (37)
	b) Secret sessions	84.1% (82)	44.4% (18)	6.1% (33)
	c) Militia outside state	71.4% (91)	0.0% (19)	0.0% (40)
	d) States appoint officers	95.7% (94)	48.0% (25)	5.0% (40)
	*e) Freedmen's Bureau	100.0% (36)	66.7% (45)	5.5% (55)
	*f) Nationalization of currency	91.4% (35)	72.3% (47)	5.7% (53)
	*g) Reconstruction	100.0% (36)	75.6% (45)	4.0% (50)
Administrative capacity	a) Academy appointments	80.5% (77)	45.5% (11)	14.3% (35)
	b) Removal of officers	78.3% (69)	94.1% (17)	96.7% (30)
	c) Court of claims	60.8% (79)	66.7% (18)	88.5% (26)
	*d) Board of admiralty	26.3% (38)	48.8% (43)	59.2% (49)
Citizenship	a) Habeas corpus	95.5% (88)	31.2% (16)	3.2% (31)
	b) Conscription	99.0% (98)	57.7% (26)	7.5% (40)
	*c) Emancipation Amendment	100.0% (44)	91.9% (62)	27.5% (69)

Property	a) Control railroads	95.6% (89)	66.7% (18)	47.1% (34)
	b) Confiscation	89.8% (88)	9.1% (22)	2.5% (40)
	c) Slaves as soldiers	94.3% (88)	0.0% (17)	0.0% (32)
	*d) Railroad subsidy	75.9% (29)	83.3% (42)	14.3% (49)
	*e) Securities trading	100.0% (33)	83.3% (48)	5.3% (57)
	*f) Bankruptcy	81.6% (38)	57.4% (47)	38.3% (47)
Client groups	a) Treasury debt	97.4% (77)	42.9% (14)	7.4% (27)
	b) Legal tender notes	80.6% (98)	42.1% (19)	17.1% (35)
	*c) Homesteads in Confederacy	100.0% (36)	76.6% (47)	5.4% (56)
Extraction	a) Direct taxes/internal duties	79.8% (84)	25.0% (16)	16.2% (37)
	b) National banks	77.9% (86)	42.9% (21)	5.7% (35)
	c) Internal revenue	98.8% (86)	94.7% (19)	64.7% (34)
World system	a) Negotiated peace	100.0% (81)	19.0% (21)	0.0% (24)
	b) Pacific railroad	75.7% (74)	47.6% (21)	39.4% (33)
	c) Colonization/confiscation	95.6% (68)	25.0% (16)	3.7% (27)
	*d) Tariff	100.0% (34)	90.2% (41)	31.2% (32)
	Average partisan support	87.2%	54.4%	20.9%

Note: Asterisks indicate decisions recorded during the Thirty-eighth Congress, when partisan strength generally shifted from Republicans to Unionists and Democrats as a result of the 1862 elections.

all pattern appear on policy decisions involving administrative capacity: presidential removal of professional officers, enhancement of the authority of the court of claims, and the establishment of an admiralty board in the Navy Department. In these areas the statist position proposed to constrain the discretionary authority of the executive branch (the Lincoln administration) or the Republican-controlled Congress by insulating the central bureaucracy from the influence of elected officials. While these proposals would have strengthened the structure of the central state by enhancing bureaucratic autonomy, their advocates wished only to weaken the hold of the Republican party on the state in order, paradoxically, to restrain state expansion in more substantive areas. These exceptions only serve to underscore the conflation of party and state during the Civil War and, thus, point out the limitations, from a long-term statist perspective, of party-centered state formation. Put simply, party-led state formation appears to have stifled the development of bureacratic administrative capacity.[215]

In the Confederacy, the relation of political organizations (or the lack of them) to state formation was much more complicated. The most prominent interpretation has emphasized the lack of open competition by organized political parties in the Confederacy. First articulated by David Potter, who suggested that "the Confederacy may have suffered real and direct damage from the fact that its political organization lacked a two-party system," the thesis was fully elaborated by Eric McKitrick in 1967.[216] Among the several arguments McKitrick advances, two best illustrate this general position: first, that formal party organizations and widespread popular identification with them serve as indispensable resources for political leaders, and second, that party organizations in the North mobilized loyalist elements behind the prosecution of the war while

215. This interpretation emphasizes the foundations of mass party competition in the national political economy and the role of the Republican party as the agent of central state expansion during the Civil War. As the Civil War period demonstrates, robust party organizations are not incompatible with rapid central state expansion, although party-led state formation will constrain the emergence of bureaucratic autonomy. For a broad historical overview of the impact of party competition on administrative capacity, see Martin Shefter, "Party, Bureaucracy, and Political Change in the United States," in Louis Maisel and Joseph Cooper, eds., *Political Parties: Development and Decay* (Beverly Hills, Calif.: Sage, 1978), pp. 211–65.

216. David M. Potter, "Jefferson Davis and the Political Factors in Confederate Defeat," in Donald, ed., *Why the North Won the Civil War*, p. 113; Eric L. McKitrick, "Party Politics and the Union and Confederate War Efforts," in William Nisbet Chambers and Walter Dean Burnham, eds., *The American Party Systems: Stages of Political Development* (New York: Oxford University Press, 1967), pp. 117–51. Since McKitrick's elaboration, the argument has become widely accepted in the literature (for example, see Thomas, *The Confederate Nation*, pp. 140, 196; McPherson, *Battle Cry of Freedom*, pp. 689–92).

isolating the disaffected into a separate, easily identifiable, and (as long as it remained a minority) relatively impotent group. The thesis has been most effectively advanced when the ability of the president to lead the nation was connected to the distribution of executive patronage.[217]

Perhaps inadvertently, the theme of lack of political parties challenges one of the most fundamental tenets of conventional political wisdom: that political minorities must organize in order to counter the greater power of their opponent's numbers. McKitrick and others concentrate their attention on the majority side of the state-centered equation: the supporters of the Davis and Lincoln administrations. From this perspective, the Lincoln administration effectively used the Republican party organization to mobilize and, in fact, create loyalist support for the Union. In the South, the Davis administration chose not to organize a supporting political party and, thus, the Confederate war mobilization was impeded. However, from the perspective of the minority side of the same equation, the thesis appears to contend that administration opponents chose not to channel their activity into a formal party and that this choice somehow enhanced their ability to frustrate the Confederate war mobilization. Viewed this way, the thesis contends that opposition to the policies of the Confederate state was more effective than, say, Democratic party opposition in the Union because it was unorganized. By failing to assume a formal organization or to adopt a common platform, opponents of a strong central state were able to blend indistinguishably into the ranks of loyal Confederate nationalists and frustrate the latter's efforts to mobilize the citizenry. Thus, while the nationalists could have reaped large political dividends by assuming a formal organizational identity and should have imposed – it seems to be implied – at least a "negative" identity upon those who could not subscribe to the nationalist program, it is contended that the opponents of centralization would have gained no advantage through organization.

Both the Davis and Lincoln administrations practiced co-optation of opposition members, a classic state-centered strategy not available to opponents. Davis attempted to maintain a broad societal consensus by

217. Van Riper and Scheiber, "The Confederate Civil Service," p. 470. Patronage, as pointed out earlier in the text, is a relatively primitive mode of recruitment and, because of the incompetence that often attends its use, can be employed in wartime only by a relatively resource-rich state. Compared to the well-endowed Union (where administrative corruption and incompetence were rampant), the South could not afford to encourage loyalty through a calculated squandering of limited national resources. For general accounts of Republican patronage policy during the Civil War, see Harry J. Carman and Reinhard H. Luthin, *Lincoln and the Patronage* (New York: Columbia University Press, 1943) and Bogue, *The Congressman's Civil War*, pp. 31–43, 89–92.

frustrating the development of an organized opposition. Lincoln, by contrast, isolated an already existing and relatively extreme opposition in the minority party. Both are optimal strategies for a central state under different initial conditions. A broad southern consensus provided a major justification for Confederate separatism. Because opponents of the Davis administration, by and large, differed over how, not whether, the war should be fought, the Confederate state could tolerate dissent and still mobilize the southern nation. A significant segment of the northern Democratic party, on the other hand, opposed the Union war effort outright. The abundance of materiel and manpower available to the Union allowed the Lincoln administration to forgo a full mobilization of the North and, instead, exploit the political advantage of branding the minority as traitorous.

One perspective from which to evaluate the comparative importance of formal party systems emerges from an examination of the formal policy products of the Confederate and Union political systems. From the perspective of administrative structure and central state authority, the viability of the lack-of-political-parties thesis rests upon the relative strength of the Confederate state. If the formal structure and powers of that state were as fully developed as those in the Union (as we have contended earlier), then the absence-of-political-parties thesis would be hard pressed to explain the failure of the Confederacy by way of state design. In this instance, comparative superiority, not perfection might be the best test of relative state performance.

More immediately, the party thesis questions the leadership ability of Jefferson Davis: whether, on the one hand, the Confederate president recognized the mobilizing potential of centralized state administration of the war effort and, on the other hand, he correctly identified and effectively led a congressional coalition with respect to strengthening central state authority. In examining these questions an additional query emerges concerning the sophistication of the putative executive coalition: whether President Davis and his supporters backed measures that insulated bureaucratic decision making. An executive-led coalition, even while constituting the most effective force in building a strong state, may ultimately limit administrative capacity by maximizing executive prerogatives at the expense of the more statist bureaucracy and judiciary (as did, for example, Lincoln's Republican supporters in the Union). As it turns out, the evidence supports the existence of a relatively sophisticated statist coalition led by Jefferson Davis, thus demonstrating effective presidential leadership in the absence of a formal party system.

In order to pursue this line of investigation, independent identification of presidential supporters is required. Previous work on the Confederate

Congress yields at least two such identifications. Wilfred Buck Yearns published a list of supporters as a part of his appendix ("Biographical Notes on Confederate Congressmen") to *The Confederate Congress* (see the notes to Table 3.17). His identification of presidential supporters is broken down by individual Congress (Provisional, First, and Second) but omits about half of all members, primarily for their failure to vote on a sufficient number of issues. Yearns does not indicate the roll call decisions upon which he relied in identifying supporters and opponents, and as a result, it is not known which, if any, of the decisions analyzed here also entered into his own calculations. The second listing has been taken from Alexander and Beringer's *The Anatomy of the Confederate Congress* and moves closer than Yearns did to a "statist–nonstatist" dimension. They identified members who favored or opposed "the objective of establishing an independent Confederacy with a central government adequate to the tasks imposed upon it in war or peace" and computed an "Average Adjusted Scale Position" for all congressmen regardless of how long or when they served.[218]

By and large, those members identified as supporters of the Davis administration strongly backed legislative expansion of executive discretion. They did so, for example, on all of the measures that proposed major changes in the scope of presidential power (see Table 3.17 and note asterisked measures).[219] In those cases where the expansion of executive power conflicted with other, higher statist principles (decisions involving the establishment of a general staff, a competency test for army engineers, and a home for veterans), Davis supporters consistently favored the administration. Such results probably could not have arisen in the absence of an effective and consistent application of executive influence and leadership. In addition, the data strongly suggest that those members who followed Davis's leadership did not recognize bureaucratic autonomy as a desirable feature of the state when that autonomy conflicted with executive authority. Like Republicans in the Union, southern nationalists concentrated decision-making authority in the more political

218. Chapter 11 and pp. 7, 409–18. Alexander and Beringer do not expand the theoretical basis of their roll call assignments beyond this quote. Their scores, which run from 0 through 9, are based on over two hundred roll calls that include five of the thirty studied here. In each case, the "stronger war effort" alternative is the same as the statist option. For the purpose of analysis here, the scale has been reduced to a dichotomous identification of "supporters" and "opponents" of a stronger war effort.
219. These nine measures are those in which expanded executive discretion constituted a major issue in legislative consideration. Outside the "administrative capacity" and "centralization-of-authority" dimensions, however, the scope of executive discretion was ultimately less important, overall, than the substantive content of central state expansion.

Table 3.17. *Loyalty to the Davis administration, support for a stronger war effort, and voting on state-building measures: 1861–5*

Dimension		Measures	Davis administration loyalty	Support for a stronger war effort
			Relation to	
Centralization	a)	Secret sessions	.36	.47
of authority	*b)	States appoint officers	.57	.82
	c)	Expulsion of member	.71	.92
	d)	Supreme court jurisdiction	−.33	.78
Administrative	*a)	Academy appointments	.88	.86
capacity	b)	Removal of officers	−.71	.17
	*c)	General staff	−.27	−.20
	*d)	Exemptions	.88	.63
	*e)	Civil service test	−.55	−.71
	f)	A supreme court	.66	−.01
Citizenship	a)	Conscription	.86	.95
	*b)	Habeas corpus	.85	.76
Control of	a)	Railroad subsidy	.59	.53
property	b)	Control railroads	−.06	.09
	c)	Securities trading	.44	.08
	*d)	Slaves as soldiers	.82	.60
	e)	Confiscation/sequestration	.02	.33
	f)	Impressment	.11	.13
	g)	Destruction of property	−.36	−.09
Client groups	a)	Legal tender notes	−.55	.21
	b)	Treasury debt	1.00	.47
	c)	Military pensions	−.65	.11
	d)	Redistribution	.49	−.00
	e)	Price controls	.66	.60
	*f)	Veterans' home	−.55	−.80
Extraction	a)	Direct taxes/internal duties	−.16	.25
	b)	Internal revenue	.50	.40
World system	a)	Tariff	.15	.39
	*b)	Negotiated peace	.81	.89
	c)	Blockade cargo	.16	.56

Notes and sources: Figures represent the association between voting in favor of the statist alternative on each of the measures (see text) and (1) "Davis Administration Loyalty" (either support or opposition to the administration; see Wilfred Buck Yearns, *The Confederate Congress*, Appendix, pp. 236–44) and (2) "Support for a Stronger War Effort" (either High, scale positions 5–9, or Low, scale positions 0–4; see Thomas Alexander and Richard Beringer, *The Anatomy of the Confederate Congress*, Average Adjusted Scale Position, pp. 398–405). The association is measured by the statistic Yule's Q. Asterisked measures entailed decisions that significantly affected the scope of executive discretion or, in the case of the veterans' home bill, were vetoed by President Davis.

executive branch of the state, but they, unlike the Republicans, did so in the absence of a party system. In fact, the absence of party competition in the South freed the executive from some of the debilitating constraints of patronage and legislative influence in personnel management that plagued the Lincoln administration.

Aside from decisions involving administrative capacity, Davis administration supporters strongly backed state expansion in almost all policy areas. Yearns's formulation, for example, positively connects administration supporters to backing for the statist alternative on two-thirds of those measures not directly involving executive prerogatives. Alexander and Beringer's listing does the same on almost 90 percent of those decisions. Everything considered, these results indicate a degree of sympathy for central state expansion and direction of the war effort that has not been commonly attributed either to Jefferson Davis or to the Confederate congressmen who backed his administration.[220]

Conclusion

In this comparison of Union and Confederate state formation, most of the surprises are on the southern side of the equation. Apart from the suppression of dissent in the North and plans to reconstruct the southern political economy, the Union relied on an unregulated capitalist market to supply resources and manpower. While some of the financial measures that facilitated this reliance on market procurement had broader, largely unanticipated statist consequences (see the following chapter), most Union policies fell comparatively lightly and transiently on civilian society and economy. The situation could hardly have been more different in the South. In the Confederacy, the central state regulated almost all forms of production and manpower, often assuming direct control of private factories, impressing their production, and even constructing state-owned plants where private capacity was insufficient for the needs of the war effort. In practice, the massive demands of the Confederate war mobilization on southern society steadily consumed the material base of

220. As noted earlier, a statist design for government decision making and central state direction of the economy has been assumed to be the best way to mobilize a society's resources for war. That assumption has allowed the analysis to pose a rough equivalency between "support for statist policies" and "support for the war." By and large this equivalency seems to hold up under scrutiny. However, many scholars might contend that war requires charismatic and politically sensitive leadership in order to maximize resource utilization. Thus effective mobilizations might very well favor strong presidential leadership over more statist designs that promote bureaucratic autonomy. As we have seen, both Republicans in the North and Davis administration supporters in the South behaved in a way that suggests agreement with this exception to the overall relationship between statist organization and war.

the economy, draining the South of the capital plant, infrastructure, and livestock that could have enabled continued war production.

This war mobilization ultimately exposed the entire southern political economy to Confederate confiscation and control. As one Georgia judge wrote:

> It [is] not only the right but the duty of a nation to protect itself, and ... any contract or right flowing out of the operation of law which came in conflict with the preservation of the State [is] an unconstitutional act, not obligatory on the law-making power, and within the constitutional power of the government to repeal.... All rights, all property, all persons who are citizens of a government, may be used by the government in time of war, and it [is] the duty of the courts to sustain the government in the appropriation of the means exercised rightfully by the legislature to protect the whole people from subjugation and ruin.[221]

When understood in the context of a broad social consensus, the southern war mobilization demonstrates the revolutionary nature of the Confederate state. Confronted on the battlefield by an opponent with a much larger and more easily mobilized resource base, the South erected a state that (1) cannibalized the regional political economy by implementing a state-directed system of war-related production and economic development; (2) proposed measures for the adjustment of class conflict that accompanied pressing demands on the plantation economy and manpower mobilization; and (3) increasingly committed the southern state and nation to rapid socioeconomic change as the underpinnings of the antebellum order (for example, the slave system) were eroded by Confederate policy. In contrast, the northern mobilization rested relatively lightly on the robust capitalist markets of the industrializing centers of the East and free-soil agricultural regions of the West. For the most part, the Union drew men and materiel into the war effort through open-market contracts that were quite attractive to producers and potential soldiers at the same time that they severely constrained central state influence over the national economy. While the nature of the northern social base and the political economic goals of the war itself opened deep cleavages within the Union citizenry, this reliance on open-market processes limited the need for northern adjustment of class conflict even while the Union's relatively abundant resource base allowed much more liberal exploitation of clientele-creating possibilities.

---

221. Paraphrased in Moore, ed., *Rebellion Record,* vol. 8, pp. 393–4. This decision upheld the right of the Confederate state to end substitution practices in conscription.

Within the free states of the North, the Union mobilization carried relatively unimportant implications for rapid socioeconomic change. On the other hand, the Union war effort held much more serious implications for the slave states both in and out of the Confederacy. Here the twin goals of the destruction of slavery and the creation of an indigenous social base loyal to the Union led the North to experiment with a number of policies that contemplated massive redistribution of wealth between races and classes, central state determination of access to political power, and direct military rule over the conquered South. While all of these projects were more or less abandoned in the decade following the war, the experiment itself substantially broadened the American state's ability to subject local governmental units to central state policy and brought citizen–state and citizen–citizen relations under the federal umbrella for the first time (through suffrage requirements, labor contracts regulated by the Freedmen's Bureau, and other measures). Viewed as a whole and perhaps oversimplifying a bit, the Confederate state was strong in the South (in its domestic mobilization policies) while the Union state was also strong in the South (in its policies intended to counteract or eliminate southern separatist sentiment). Thus, under both Confederate and Union rule, southerners experienced much more statist regimes than did northerners.

The social groups and economic classes that threw up these northern and southern states exhibited both similarities and contrasts. In the Confederacy, support for state expansion was broadly distributed among the most important groups and classes in the South. Slaveholders, for example, were not (as might have been expected) in the vanguard of most state-expanding coalitions and thus cannot be said to have imposed the war effort upon the rest of southern society. Manufacturing districts gave more support to statist policies, but the most statist group behind Confederate state expansion was composed of representatives from the contested border states. Even this description, however, understates the breadth of the social base of the Confederate state. United by their resistance to northern developmental policies during the antebellum period and by northern invasion during the war, southerners dissolved all party distinctions and subsequently delegated immense power over their property and lives to a bureaucracy largely insulated from political influence. This state-formation process was carried out by a fluid legislative coalition led by the chief executive, Jefferson Davis. In the Union, state expansion was strongly backed by a developmental coalition that brought together industrial capital, farmers, and free laborers across the North. United under the leadership of the Republican party, this developmental coalition thoroughly occupied the state apparatus, directed the war mobilization and developmental policies, and repressed both political dissent and competing political organizations, particularly in the border states.

In many respects, the Confederate state possessed more modern characteristics than this northern regime. Southern leviathan featured more ambitious attempts to adjust class tensions between slaveholders and poor yeoman farmers, more insulated bureaucratic organizations, state-sponsored and subsidized manufacturing activity, a greater use of expropriation and other limitations on the property rights of citizens, as well as a comprehensive allocation of manpower throughout the economy. Overall the Confederate experience generally combined a much stronger boundary between state and society with much more sweeping state authority over the economy. In contrast, the Union state drew great strength from its inhabitation by the Republican party but the emergence of the Republican party-state committed the regime to several premodern practices, such as patronage in the staffing of state bureaus and a reliance on voluntary contractual agreements as the primary means of supplying the war effort. A modern state would have combined a professional, politically neutral bureaucracy with a state-planned and directed war mobilization. On the other hand, many of the policies carried out by the North furthered modernization of American society and economy. Foremost among these were the emancipation of slaves and reorganization of the nation's financial system.

As a consequence of secession and the Civil War, the American state was captured by the Republican party. During the war and the decade immediately following, the American state and the Republican party were more or less synonomous and this near identity was accompanied by an instrumentalist implementation of a broad political agenda, including aggressive tariff protection for industry, western homestead settlement, the promotion of northern and western railroad construction, the creation of supporting clientele groups (for example, through pensions allocated to Union veterans), and the expansion of national markets in capital investment and commerce. With the plantation South out of the political system, the antebellum northern agenda for the political economy was impressed upon the American state with little compromise or mediation.

Among the many results of the emergence of the Republican party-state and the enactment of northern developmental policies was the state-centered reorganization of the nation's financial system. During the Civil War, Treasury policy both insulated the nation's financial markets from foreign influence by abandoning the gold standard and sponsored the creation of integrated capital markets by establishing the national bank system and mandating a national currency. Each of these both modernized the financial system and strengthened the central state's role in capital allocation and development. But, because of the Republican party-state's relatively narrow social base and close alignment with powerful economic classes, including finance capitalists, the postwar period saw a radical change in the trajectory of American state expansion. Where the party-state had sponsored the creation of a new class of finance capitalists during the war – in reality a client group dependent on the successful servicing of Union debt and Treasury policy generally – the postwar decade witnessed a deteriorating Republican coalition in which finance capitalists increasingly advocated a retrenchment of central state intervention in the financial system, massive cuts in federal spending and taxation, and, ultimately, an abandonment of Reconstruction of the South (see Chapters 4 and 5). Though the American state could not have survived secession and the Civil War without becoming the institutional tool of the Republican party, the state expansion that the Republicans carried out had clear limitations. One of these was that continued state expansion depended upon the continued compatibility of the interests of the major wings of the Republican party. The other was that patronage, the life blood of the party-state, was incompatible with administrative competence. Because of its vulnerability to central state policy decisions and the technical requirements associated with successful Treasury intervention in capital markets, the first and most important defection from the Republican state-building project was finance capital.

4

Gold, greenbacks, and the political economy of finance capital after the Civil War

Outside the rebellious South, the Union war mobilization probably fell most heavily upon the financial system, permanently changing both the internal organization of national capital markets and the relationship of the central state to finance capitalists.[1] In part, the policies adopted by the Union were shaped by the North's reliance on uncontrolled markets for supplies and manpower. Voluntary transactions with private manufacturers and civilians required a sound currency and guarantees as to the future credit of the state. At the same time, the huge demands placed upon the domestic economy by the war mobilization forced the financial system off the gold standard – up to this point in American history, the maintenance of that standard had been the foundation upon which the state's credit had rested. As a result of the abandonment of the gold standard and a reliance on unregulated markets for supplies, the Union developed revenue policies that transformed a large part of the financial community into clients of the state. Financiers were both enticed and coerced into becoming the agents of Union fiscal policy and subsequently cooperated with the Treasury in marketing government debt securities and managing the circulation and value of Union currency.

When the Civil War ended, the interests of finance capitalists and the American state were probably more closely linked than at any other point in the nineteenth century. Yet financiers came to oppose central state participation in financial markets and to support a corresponding retrenchment in government activity in most other sectors of the political economy. In this chapter, the origin of this growing opposition to central

1. Because southern banks heavily invested in Confederate bonds that became worthless with the end of the Civil War, the southern financial system was devastated by the collapse of the Confederate state and did not recover in the postwar period. Because the Confederacy did not otherwise influence postwar development, this chapter emphasizes the impact of the northern mobilization on the postwar national financial system.

state power is traced to the stresses that were an inherent feature of the organization of the financial system. Tracing the seasonal rhythms of the nation's money markets and the flow of gold bullion through Treasury vaults and customshouses, we will identify the necessary conditions for financial stability, among them adequate bank reserves, a budgetary surplus in government receipts and expenditure, and a competent accommodation of Treasury transactions to conditions in the nation's financial markets. Administrative incompetence in the management of Treasury intervention in financial markets was the crucial factor in turning finance capitalists away from a potentially neutral or even favorable attitude toward central state expansion. Ultimately, this change in attitude became one of the factors that doomed Republican efforts to remake the southern political economy during Reconstruction.

This chapter begins with a description of how the northern financial system developed during the Civil War, including the impact of abandonment of the gold standard, the strengthening of the dominant position of New York City markets in the financial system, and the rapid growth of a new, national class of finance capitalists. These changes are subsequently related to the organization and operation of capital markets in the postwar period. In this discussion, emphasis is placed on the operating requirements for financial stability and the ways in which government intervention in financial markets could impair or enhance the operation of the financial system. After reviewing the implications of market organization and the government's inability to properly manage the financial system, the chapter concludes with a brief summary of the postwar policy interests of finance capital.

The political economy of finance capital in the antebellum period

In 1861 New York City was the most important financial center in the United States. New York owed its position in finance to its dominant position astride the nation's trade connections with Europe, particularly Britain. During the first half of the nineteenth century, the city had extended its commercial network into the interior of the continent more rapidly than did other important and previously autonomous entrepots, such as Boston, Philadelphia, and Baltimore. In the process, these cities, as well as the remainder of the country, were subordinated to New York markets. This antebellum centralization of the financial system, driven by the international exchange of goods and capital, was expressed in several emerging commercial arrangements and patterns. In one of the most significant developments, state-chartered banks throughout the nation began to keep regular deposit balances in New York institutions.[2]

As these balances concentrated in New York, the capital they represented gave rise to an active "call loan" relationship between the city's banks and the stock exchange. Unused balances were, in effect, lent out to stockbrokers and investors subject to "call" at any time. In most months of the year, this arrangement was not very risky. But during the fall harvest and spring planting seasons, the country banks drew heavily on their New York balances and, in speculative markets, this contraction of credit could produce a financial panic in which the banking system was forced to suspend specie payments on its currency and deposits. The federal government played only a small role in these financial markets and exchanges. In the absence of a central bank or its functional equivalent, the financial system lacked a common reserve and policy coordination. As a result, the New York money market – already by 1850 far and away the dominant center of American finance capitalism – "was an organism without a head."[3] Compared to the postwar period, English capital played a dominant role in New York, with the Liverpool cotton and London securities markets often determining foreign exchange rates and capital investment patterns. This tributary status made the American financial system extremely vulnerable to market conditions in London (as evidenced by the course of the severe business contractions of 1836, 1839, 1845, and 1856).[4]

2. Of the 700 banks chartered in the nation in 1850, almost 600 maintained accounts in New York for the redemption of their currency and bills of exchange. Margaret G. Myers, *The New York Money Market: Origins and Development* (New York: Columbia University Press, 1931; reprinted by AMS Press, 1971), pp. 103–4, 108, 115. For a brief discussion of New York's dominance in the antebellum dissemination of economic information on foreign market conditions and the city's close connections to southern market centers (cotton-exporting ports), see Allan Pred, *Urban Growth and City-Systems in the United States, 1840–1860* (Cambridge, Mass.: Harvard University Press, 1980), pp. 143–5; on the importance of the export/import trade and transportation network to New York's primacy, see Robert Greenhalgh Albion, *The Rise of the New York Port, 1815–1860* (Boston: Northeastern University Press, 1984; reprint of 1939 edition), especially pp. 373–86.

3. On the development of the call loan market, see Myers, *New York Money Market*, pp. 103–25; on the harvest cycle in bank reserves, pp. 141–8, 206–8; and on the absence of central reserves and policy coordination, pp. 204–9. However, Myers notes that founding of the New York Clearing House in 1854 permitted the large banks that comprised its membership to "exercise a genuine regulatory function" and provided "a basis for developing cooperative action in emergency," pp. 96–102.

4. Wallace E. Huffman and James R. Lothian, "The Gold Standard and the Transmission of Business Cycles, 1833–1932," in Michael D. Bordo and Anna J. Schwartz, eds. *A Retrospective on the Classical Gold Standard, 1821–1931* (Chicago: University of Chicago Press, 1984), pp. 464–71. Also see Myers, *New York Money Market*, pp. 52–7, 205–6; on the importance of British capital to the development of New York financial markets, see Vincent P. Carosso, *The Morgans: Private International*

The policies through which the Union financed the war effort changed the antebellum financial system and national political economy in several important ways. First, the material requirements of the northern war effort led the government to develop a much wider array of revenue sources and create a much larger administrative apparatus of collection than had previously existed in the antebellum period. The expansion of revenue capacity enhanced the federal government's ability to consider a broader role in national development and, in addition, created new supporting clientele groups. The most important of these groups emerged in connection with the tariff. Second, the huge national debt floated by the Union altered the composition of capital markets, reshaped the structure and operations of the banking system, and significantly broadened federal involvement in these features of finance capitalism. Both the creation of a large national debt and of a national banking system, in turn, fostered the emergence of a largely new class of financiers dependent on the effectiveness of federal fiscal operations.[5]

Under certain circumstances, the creation of a large national debt can be interpreted as a state-enhancing strategy insofar as it brings into being a broad clientele dependent on the success of central state fiscal policy for interest payments and principal redemption.[6] Such a policy appears

Bankers, 1854–1913 (Cambridge, Mass.: Harvard University Press, 1987), pp. 53–6; Ralph W. Hidy, "The Organization and Function of Anglo-American Merchant Bankers, 1815–1860," *Journal of Economic History* 1 (December 1941): 53–66; for a substantially more positive view of antebellum money market stability and the efficacy of Treasury operations, see Richard H. Timberlake, Jr., *The Origins of Central Banking in the United States* (Cambridge, Mass.: Harvard University Press, 1978).

5. This result was both anticipated and appreciated by well-placed individuals at the time. For example, see the correspondence between Salmon P. Chase (secretary of the Treasury) and Jay Cooke, who later was appointed the chief subscription agent for Treasury loan operations. Ellis Paxson Oberholtzer, *Jay Cooke: Financier of the Civil War*, vol. 1 (New York: Burt Franklin, 1970; a reprint of an unidentified 1907 edition), p. 136. Also see, Amasa Walker, "The National Finances," *Hunt's Merchants' Magazine and Commercial Review*, January 1865, p. 33. *Springfield Republican*, June 19, 1865, quoted in Oberholtzer, *Jay Cooke*, vol. 1, p. 639, more generally, 634–55. Also see, Herbert Ronald Ferleger, *David A. Wells and the American Revenue System, 1865–1870* (New York: Private printing, 1942; reprinted by Porcupine Press, 1977), p. 7. The development of clientele connections that characterized Union finance policy can also be seen as the most direct and unambiguous expression of a general process by which the Civil War accelerated "the emergence of an American industrial bourgeoisie" and "tied the fortunes of this class to the Republican party and the national state." Eric Foner, *Reconstruction: America's Unfinished Revolution, 1863–1877* (New York: Harper & Row, 1988) pp. 21–3.

6. With reference to the new American republic in the late eighteenth century, Thomas Paine argued that "No nation ought to be without a debt. A national debt is a national bond." Noting in a letter to Robert Morris in 1781 that "A national debt, if not excessive, will be to us a national blessing. It will be a powerful cement of our Union," Alexander Hamilton developed this principle into a matter of high state policy. Fritz

to be most effective when (1) the regime possesses otherwise weak claims on sovereignty; and (2) the preexisting revenue demands and obligations of the state are comparatively slight. In such cases, the issuance of debt creates an interest (in the lender) that supports a particular state structure in its efforts both to survive and to exploit the resources of a given society.[7] The two Civil War regimes, Union and Confederate, satisfied these conditions, at least initially.[8] In this chapter we will analyze the ways in which the debt and other Union war mobilization measures focused the attention of finance capitalists, as a class, on central state fiscal operations and decision making.[9]

During the Civil War, the interconnected processes of debt expansion, revenue enhancement, and fiscal centralization continued to accelerate. With the end of the conflict, these processes first stalled and subsequently reversed direction as the U.S. Treasury moved first, to stabilize, stan-

Redlich, *Essays in American Economic History* (New York: G. E. Stechert, 1944), pp. 176–82.

7. If the associated revenue needs are so large that no amount of exploitation can make the debt viable or if these demands themselves threaten the sovereignty of the regime, such policies are clearly counterproductive from the standpoint of state development. There are, of course, many contemporary regimes debilitated by an unmanageable, foreign-held debt. One of the most striking nineteenth-century examples was the Ottoman Empire. Roger Owen, *The Middle East in the World Economy, 1800–1914* (New York: Methuen, 1981), pp. 100–52.

8. Because of the South's economic weakness and the progressive deterioration in its military situation, the Confederacy did not satisfy the second condition for very long. As Bray Hammond put it, "Since the bonds and currency of the confederate government became worthless in the end, the Confederacy's part in the war was financed in reality by a gradual, indirect confiscation of the property of the Southern people and of the foreign investors who bought its bonds." *Sovereignty and an Empty Purse: Banks and Politics in the Civil War* (Princeton, N.J.: Princeton University Press, 1970), p. 259 and, generally, pp. 254–60. The increasing likelihood of southern defeat dried up investor demand for Confederate bonds except at ruinous discounts that impossibly mortgaged the nation's future. Thus the Confederate debt was increasingly discredited both as the obligation of a sovereign nation and as a workable financial policy. Under these conditions, only speculators, very patriotic citizens, and those individuals forced to take bonds in full or partial payment of Confederate obligations would accept new debt issues. The first group usually held only small amounts taken at steep discount from par and were of little aid to the regime. The second group was already strongly committed to the cause and were unlikely to become even more committed as a result of their investments. And members of the third group, while compelled to accept these issues, were more likely to avoid transactions with the regime, if possible, than to become committed to its future. Thus, at some point probably indicated by a steep discount of new issues (against gold) and the relative frequency of involuntary transactions, the Confederacy could no longer utilize a national debt as a regime-strengthening strategy.

9. As the term is used here, the class identified as "finance capitalists" is composed of those individuals who transform or exchange one kind of financial asset into another as their primary vocation. This class thus includes money, commodity, stock, and bond brokers; state, national, and private bankers; insurance companies; import/export houses; and commission merchants.

dardize, and reduce the war debt; then, to reduce the previously wide array of revenue sources and overall level of taxation; next, to cut back war-related government expenditures as part of a general policy of retrenchment; and, finally, to implement, over the sporadic opposition of Congress, fiscal policies that would result in specie redemption of the currency and a return to the gold standard in domestic transactions.[10]

The impact of the Civil War on the financial system

The Union entered the war with a banking system organized and regulated by the individual state governments. Even with the South out of the system, these banks ranged "from the strong solvent institutions of the major commercial centers, to firms, particularly in the newer areas of the West...that were little more than legal counterfeiting shops."[11] The solvency and stability of these institutions, essential to the early mobilization of men and materiel, were undermined after secession by the breaking of commercial ties with southern merchants, the suspension of specie payments in December 1861, and a dependence by the northern financial system on southern state debt as backing for bank currency.[12]

---

10. The common definition of "specie" is money in coin, particularly minted in precious metals. In conformance with nineteenth-century practice, the term specifically referred to gold coin or bullion of precise value. In this chapter "gold" and "specie" will be used interchangeably.

11. Irwin Unger, *The Greenback Era: A Social and Political History of American Finance, 1865–1879* (Princeton, N.J.: Princeton University Press, 1964), pp. 17–19. With the exception of those located in New Orleans, the southern institutions upon which the Confederacy was forced to depend "were the worst of the [antebellum] note-issuing banks." A. Barton Hepburn, *A History of Currency in the United States* (New York: Macmillan, 1915), p. 311; the New Orleans banks were the last southern institutions to suspend specie payments. *Hunt's* January 1861, pp. 76–7; for a general review of antebellum banking conditions, see Bray Hammond, *Banks and Politics in America from the Revolution to the Civil War* (Princeton, N.J.: Princeton University Press, 1957), particularly pp. 671–717; and George Rogers Taylor, *The Transportation Revolution, 1815–1860* (New York: Harper & Row, 1951), pp. 311–51.

12. See, for example, a report issued by the State Bank Controller of Wisconsin, dated October 1, 1860, which itemizes state bonds held as reserves for currency issued by banks in that state. Over 65 percent of the total value of these bonds (valued at par) had been issued by Georgia, Kentucky, Louisiana, Missouri, North Carolina, Tennessee, and Virginia. With the onset of secession, the bonds of all these states began to sell at a deep discount and thus threatened to bankrupt the banking structure. *Hunt's*, January 1861, pp. 76, 94–5; Charles Warren cites estimates that "the indebtedness of the South to the North in 1861 was...$300,000,000, of which $159,000,000 was due to New York, $24,100,000 to Philadelphia, $19,000,000 to Baltimore, and $7,600,000 to Boston....In 1861, 913 mercantile houses in New York at the beginning of the war only 16 were solvent at the end of the first year." (*Bankruptcy in United States History* [Cambridge, Mass.: Harvard University Press, 1935], p. 97). See *New York Times*, April 1, 8, May 23–24, June 6, 1861; for a brief review of the crisis, see William Gerald Shade, *Banks or No Banks: The Money Issue*

As a source of ready capital or as a network for the marketing of war bonds, the financial system on which the Union was forced to depend was still the product of commercial exchange in an agrarian economy tributary to foreign markets. Aggravating an already bad situation, the subtreasury system established in 1846 sharply limited the range of revenue alternatives open to the Treasury and made government transactions awkward and cumbersome (if not destabilizing to the financial system itself).[13]

Excluding outright confiscation or expropriation, the Union could consider only three methods of funding transactions between the government and the economy: taxation, increasing the debt, and inflating the currency. Because the expansion of revenue through taxation required an administrative apparatus that did not yet exist and because the government was reluctant to abandon specie redemption of its currency, the Union relied on new issues of debt at the beginning of the war.[14] From the very beginning, New York banks and financial agents played the major role in distributing Treasury bonds.[15] The earliest of the massive operations that characterized the war years came in the fall of 1861 when the Treasury negotiated a $150 million loan with a syndicate comprising New York, Boston, and Philadelphia banks (see Table 4.1). This offering was apportioned between these three cities according to their capacity to absorb the issue without endangering the stability of financial markets

in Western Politics, 1832–1865 (Detroit: Wayne State University Press, 1972), pp. 224–5.

13. Myers, *New York Money Market*, pp. 182–93; Hammond, *Sovereignty and an Empty Purse*, pp. 18–24; Hepburn, *History of Currency*, p. 203. Viewed from the perspective of finance capital, the imposition of the subtreasury system was only one event in a long chain of incidents arising out of interior mistrust of capital concentration. As the *Commercial and Financial Chronicle* put it: "Very soon after the first organization of banking institutions in this country, a jealousy sprung up against centralization, which effectually prevented the growth of very large institutions, while it stimulated the creation of small banks all over the country. These two opposing forces – the tendency to concentrate the money power on the one hand, and on the other the tendency to disperse and diffuse that power – have continued in operation with various results during the last century." December 16, 1876, p. 583.

14. Timberlake, *Origins of Central Banking*, p. 85; Esther Rogoff Taus, *Central Banking Functions of the United States Treasury, 1789–1941* (New York: Columbia University Press, 1943), pp. 57–61.

15. Negotiations with New York bankers sometimes placed the Treasury in a demeaning position. For example, before the banks rescued an otherwise failing loan offering in December 1860, they compelled the government to dedicate part of the proceeds to the payment (in gold) of the January 1861 interest on the entire national debt. Oberholtzer, *Jay Cooke*, vol. 1, pp. 125–6; 1861 *American Annual Cyclopaedia* (New York: D. Appleton, 1873), pp. 60–8. For other examples of the influence of the financial community on Union war policies, see A. Howard Meneely, *The War Department, 1861: A Study in Mobilization and Administration* (New York: Columbia University Press, 1928), pp. 160, 198, 232, 256, 355.

Table 4.1. *Apportionment of U.S. debt securities: Selected issues, 1862–8*

Broker and/or location	7.3% gold bonds Aug.–Dec. 1861	Securities issued[a]			Total for all four issues
		Three-year 7.3% gold bonds Nov. 10, 1862	Five/twenty gold bonds Mar. 3, 1865– Dec. 1, 1868	Ten/forty gold bonds Oct. 1, 1867– Jan. 21, 1868	
Jay Cooke and Co.	N.A.	$1,073,600 (7.9%)	$87,624,850 (26.0%)	$45,000 (.6%)	$88,743,450 (17.6%)
New York City			(6,727,850)		(6,727,850)
Philadelphia			(13,381,750)		(13,381,750)
Washington, D.C.		(1,073,600)	(853,600)	(45,000)	(1,972,200)
Not specified			(66,661,650)		(66,661,650)
Purchasers in major financial centers[b]					
New York City	$102,056,835 (70.0%)	$11,154,150 (81.9%)	$200,327,250 (59.5%)	$6,586,950 (88.5%)	$320,125,185 (63.6%)
Boston	29,159,095 (20.0%)	341,000 (2.5%)	14,431,810 (4.3%)	103,000 (1.4%)	44,034,905 (8.7%)
Philadelphia	14,579,548 (10.0%)	801,350 (5.9%)	15,531,700 (4.6%)	200,000 (2.7%)	31,112,598 (6.2%)
Washington, D.C.	0	198,100 (1.5%)	10,832,750 (3.2%)	270,000 (3.6%)	11,300,850 (2.2%)
Baltimore	0	0	1,652,000 (.5%)	5,000 (.1%)	1,657,000 (.3%)

Table 4.1 (cont.)

Broker and/or location	Securities issued[a]				Total for all four issues
	7.3% gold bonds Aug.–Dec. 1861	Three-year 7.3% gold bonds Nov. 10, 1862	Five/twenty gold bonds Mar. 3, 1865– Dec. 1, 1868	Ten/forty gold bonds Oct. 1, 1867– Jan. 21, 1868	
Purchasers in selected regions[b]					
Eastern seaboard (N.Y., Mass., Pa.)	0	$40,000 (.3%)	$3,342,450 (1.0%)	$27,400 (.4%)	$3,409,850 (.7%)
Remainder of East and Ohio	0	5,250 (.0%)	1,501,750 (.4%)	39,000 (.5%)	1,546,000 (.3%)
Free-state West	0	0	1,052,100 (.3%)	21,500 (.3%)	1,073,600 (.2%)
South and border	0	0	274,900 (.1%)	148,000 (2.0%)	422,900 (.1%)
Purchasers located (as proportion of total sales)	$145,795,478 (100.0%)	$13,613,450 (100.0%)	$336,571,560 (89.2%)	$7,445,850 (91.5%)	$503,426,338 (92.4%)

[a]Compiled from data in *Hunt's Merchants' Magazine and Commercial Review*, September 1861, pp. 330–1, and March 1862, pp. 308–9; "Schedule of Bids . . . ," Exec. Doc. 1: House of Representatives: 37th Cong., 3rd Sess., Ser. Rec. 1149 (Government Printing Office [GPO], 1863); "Purchase of Government Securities," Exec. Doc. 52: House of Representatives: 39th Cong., 2nd Sess., Ser. Rec. 1290 (GPO, 1867); "Bonds," Exec. Doc. 34: House of Representatives: 40th Cong., 2nd Sess., Ser. Rec. 1330 (GPO, 1868); "United States Bonds," Exec. Doc. 26: House of Representatives: 40th Cong., 3rd Sess., Ser. Rec. 1372 (GPO, 1869); "Ten-Forty Bonds," Exec. Doc. 128: House of Representatives: 40th Cong., 2nd Sess., Ser. Rec. 1337 (GPO, 1868).
[b]Not including the above.

or the institutions themselves. New York banks took 70 percent of the issue.[16]

When the Treasury offered similar three-year, 7.3 percent bonds in the fall of 1862, New York again led the way although, by this time, brokers and private bankers had replaced the larger state-chartered institutions as participants from the financial community. Less than 20 percent of the loan went to individuals or firms outside New York and almost half this remainder went to one broker, Jay Cooke and Company. Cooke's personal connections with leading figures in the Republican party, combined with the clear reluctance of the New York financial community to undertake the development of a national distribution network for bonds, allowed his firm to enter into a special relationship with the Treasury.[17] Although not directly attributed to the firm in Table 4.1, much of the marketing activity outside of New York (particularly in Philadelphia and Washington) and a good portion of that otherwise ascribed to the city was, in fact, coordinated by Cooke as a consequence of these political connections and alliances with other bankers.[18] While active throughout the war, the firm's largest roles came at the end.[19]

As the war continued, the Union abandoned specie redemption of the currency, issued the legal tender notes known as greenbacks, and established a vast internal revenue system. These steps, along with the creation

16. Don C. Barrett, *Greenbacks and Resumption of Specie Payments, 1862–1879* (Cambridge, Mass.: Harvard University Press, 1931), pp. 7–12; Hammond, *Sovereignty and an Empty Purse*, pp. 73–105; Oberholtzer, *Jay Cooke*, vol. 1, pp. 149–52; *Chronicle*, November 11, 1876, pp. 461–2.

17. The Cooke firm was formed in Philadelphia in January, 1861 and, beginning with a $3 million offering for the state of Pennsylvania in June, rapidly came to specialize in government securities, particularly new issues. The Cooke firm's close connections to the Treasury originated in Ohio state politics. Jay Cooke's father had served in the U.S. House of Representatives and his brother, Henry D. Cooke, had developed close ties to Secretary Chase and Senator John Sherman while a newspaper editor in Columbus. Henrietta Larson, *Jay Cooke* (Cambridge, Mass.: Harvard University Press, 1936), p. 103.

18. In his role as general subscription agent, Cooke helped found the First National Banks of Philadelphia and Washington (the latter with his brother, Henry) and the Fourth National Bank of New York. In addition to these closely affiliated institutions, Cooke's allies in his marketing operations included Fisk and Hatch, Livermore, Clews and Company, and Vermilye and Company in New York City and Spencer, Vila and Company in Boston. Oberholtzer, *Jay Cooke*, vol. 1, pp. 92–4, 101–2, 234, 340–50, 551–2.

19. Albert S. Bolles, *Financial History of the United States from 1861 to 1885* (New York: D. Appleton, 1894; reprinted by Augustus M. Kelley, 1969), pp. 127–8. The loan offerings shown in Table 4.1 constituted a substantial portion of all loans offered during and after the war but cannot be considered entirely representative of Treasury activity. In addition, the Treasury did not list the residence of many purchasers in its reports on the 5/20 and 10/40 loans and, while every effort was made to locate these purchasers in city directories, financial almanacs, and other commercial publications, approximately 10 percent of the total offerings could not be located.

of the national bank system, greatly strengthened the federal government's participation in the financial system and commercial life generally. This intervention was accompanied by a substantial abandonment of the subtreasury system, which had previously required that all government transactions with the private economy be conducted in cash. By allowing the government to maintain credit balances with private institutions, abandonment of the subtreasury system promoted the coordination and integration of the financial operations of the national government with the banking system and capital markets. In 1861, for example, legislation authorizing a new bond issue allowed the Treasury to leave the proceeds on deposit with purchasing banks. Subsequently, national banks were permitted under an 1864 revision of the National Bank Act to serve as public depositories for all federal funds except customs receipts. These acts established government accounts in private banking institutions and significantly relaxed the constraints under which the Treasury previously entered financial markets. Abandonment of the gold standard and the issue of legal tender notes similarly released the Treasury from an obligation to restrict market transactions to specie and thus eliminated, for the most part, the previously onerous responsibility to transfer gold bullion from place to place in order to make or receive payments. Subsequent authority to issue "gold notes," backed by Treasury reserves, made specie transactions even easier. While many problems remained, these reforms brought the Treasury into a much closer relationship to money and capital markets.[20]

At the same time the Treasury was assuming a larger and more substantial role in the economy, the Civil War was hastening the development of capital markets and a strong financier class. In the first instance, financial insecurity engendered by the crisis detached American investment from European, particularly British, financing. In 1860, for example, the Secretary of the Treasury estimated foreign investment in the United States at some $400 million dollars.[21] Between 1860 and 1863, concern over the Civil War not only dried up European interest in new securities but also brought on the repatriation of about $200 million of the previous total (the rough equivalent of net foreign investment between 1850 and 1860). As David Wells, Special Commissioner of Revenue, reported to the House of Representatives, "The distrust felt by nearly all foreigners in the future of the United States was so great that the larger portion of American securities – national, State, and corporate – held in foreign

20. Myers, *New York Money Market*, pp. 352–3.
21. Ibid., pp. 36–42; on European hostility to Union debt issues during the Civil War, see pp. 288–90. Also see Bolles, *Financial History*, pp. 327–8; Oberholtzer, *Jay Cooke*, vol. 1, p. 169.

countries, were returned for sale at almost any sacrifice; and to such an extent was this the case that the country in 1863 may be said to have exhibited a clean national ledger in respect to foreign indebtedness."[22]

The withdrawal of European investment strongly encouraged domestic capital accumulation and the emergence of a distinctly American class of financiers. Between 1864 and 1870, for example, the number of New York City bankers and brokers increased more than tenfold (from 167 to 1,800), while bank clearings in the New York Clearing House more than trebled between 1860 and the end of the war.[23] The New York Stock Exchange (NYSE) constructed its own building in 1863 and more than tripled membership fees (from $3,000 to $10,000) between 1862 and 1866. For the first time, specialists in individual stocks, trading on their own account, appeared. The exchange itself admitted only a few new members and trading activity spilled over into less organized markets outside the NYSE.[24] All of these developments were the result of the great expansion of domestic trading and the financial insecurity that accompanied Treasury bond issues whose worth fluctuated in tandem with the changing political fortunes of the government.

While the repatriation of American securities and domestic financing of Union bonds strengthened domestic capital markets, the development of the financial system was further enhanced by the abandonment of the gold standard and the insulating effect a paper monetary unit had upon the nation's sensitivity to foreign economic conditions. The suspension of specie redemption was not the result of conscious policy decisions but, rather, inadvertently followed the government's first major entry into the bond market.[25] In the fall and winter of 1861, the nation's largest banks lent money to the government by buying bonds with gold. These payments rapidly depleted bank reserves while government expenditures widely distributed this gold among the public. When much of this gold was hoarded and did not return to the banking system, the banks and

22. Quoted in Carosso, *Morgans*, p. 98. But also see, Harry H. Pierce, "Foreign Investment in American Enterprise," in David T. Gilchrist and W. David Lewis, eds., *Economic Change in the Civil War Era* (Greenville, Del.: Eleutherian Mills–Hagley Foundation, 1965), pp. 51–2.
23. Dolores Greenberg, *Financiers and Railroads, 1869–1889* (East Brunswick, N.J.: Associated University Presses, 1980), p. 27; *History of the New York Stock Exchange* (New York: Financier Company, 1887; reprinted by Arno Press, 1975), p. 120.
24. Ranald C. Michie, "The London and New York Stock Exchanges, 1850–1914," *Journal of Economic History* 46 (March 1986): 171–88; Francis L. Eames, *The New York Stock Exchange* (New York: Thomas G. Hall, 1894), pp. 42–57.
25. For a contemporary account of suspension, see *Hunt's* March 1862, pp. 308–9; for later treatments, see Myers, *New York Money Market*, pp. 193–9; Hammond, *Sovereignty and an Empty Purse*, pp. 150–9; and Timberlake, *Origins of Central Banking*, p. 86.

the government were forced off the gold standard. Considering the huge
demands placed on the antebellum financial system by the Union war
effort and the repatriation of foreign investments, the North did quite
well to stay on the standard as long as it did (until December 1861). A
good portion of the credit, however, must go to a disastrous European
harvest that produced a surge in grain exports from the United States
and a subsequent importation of specie that temporarily countered the
outflow of capital to Europe.[26] After suspension the United States depended on one kind of money, gold, in foreign exchange and on another,
greenbacks, in domestic transactions. Since bank notes and deposits were
the result of domestic transactions, bank reserves were held primarily in
the form of legal tender notes (though specie was eligible also). As an
explanation of how this paper monetary system insulated the American
economy from foreign "shocks," the following description published by
the *Commercial and Financial Chronicle* is difficult to improve:

> our money market...continues to work easily and is exempt from
> spasms, in face of the heavy foreign exports of coin. Formerly when
> we were on a specie basis the banks were always sensitive to a heavy
> exportation of gold; it never failed to throw the money market into
> confusion, because it drained away from the banks the specie reserve
> on which they did business. If we were now on a specie basis we
> could scarcely escape monetary stringency under the present and
> prospective export of coin. Under our present system, however, legal
> tender notes are just as well adapted as specie for bank reserve; and
> as fast as the banks lose their specie they must replace it with an
> equal amount of greenbacks or clearing-house certificates. Hence...
> our existing monetary system affords a greater protection to the
> money market against disturbance from causes arising in the domain
> of our foreign exchanges.[27]

While a currency standard for the redemption of the notes of private
banks substantially reduced the influence of foreign market conditions,

26. *Hunt's* September 1861, p. 333; Hammond, *Sovereignty and an Empty Purse,* pp.
    38–9.
27. The *Chronicle* continued: "When we return to the solid, stable foundation of specie
    payments we may be able to contrive some method for perpetuating this advantage."
    April 22, 1871, p. 486; for an earlier recognition of the impact of suspension, see
    May 26, 1866, p. 642; for more recent discussions, see Wallace E. Huffman and
    James R. Lothian, "The Gold Standard and the Transmission of Business Cycles,
    1833–1932," Bordo and Schwartz, *Retrospective on the Classical Gold Standard,*
    pp. 455–507, especially, pp. 471–3; Lawrence H. Officer, "The Floating Dollar in
    the Greenback Period: A Test of Theories of Exchange Rate Determination," *Journal
    of Economic History* 41 (September 1981): 629–35; Thomas D. Willett, "Interna-
    tional Specie Flows and American Monetary Stability, 1834–1860," *Journal of Eco-
    nomic History* 28 (March 1968): 28–50.

greenbacks did little to reduce the annual threat to domestic financial stability posed by the harvest and spring planting movement of funds into the nation's interior. These annual drains on bank reserves in New York remained the most important defect in the financial system.

In addition to promoting the return of securities from Europe, the Civil War flooded financial markets with Union bonds and notes to such extent that government debt severely discouraged the issuance of new private stocks and bonds. While the Union was expanding the national debt from $65 million in 1860 to $2,678 million in 1866, for example, only $23 million were added to the total capital stock of railroad companies in the United States. In 1865, the federal deficit amounted to roughly 30 percent of the northern gross national product.[28] When the war ended, the federal government ceased to borrow new funds and began to buy back previously issued bonds and notes.

By ending the government's demands on credit markets, the postwar shift in Treasury policy both permitted and encouraged the transfer of accumulated capital from the government to the construction of railroads. During the four years immediately following the end of hostilities, for example, more than $500 million in new railroad and canal securities entered the market; an essential factor in the success of these offerings was the liquidation of state and federal debt.[29] The ensuing railroad boom in the United States became part of a worldwide speculative mania and, along with the return of relative political stability, produced a vast exportation of both government and private securities to Europe.[30] While

28. U.S. Bureau of the Census, *Historical Statistics of the United States, Colonial Times to 1957* (Washington, D.C.: Government Printing Office, 1960), p. 711. The railroad figures are for 1860 and 1867, respectively. Carosso, *Morgans,* pp. 95–7. The deficit estimate is from Jeffrey G. Williamson, "Watersheds and Turning Points: Conjectures on the Long-Term Impact of Civil War Financing," *Journal of Economic History* 34 (September 1974): 643. On September 1, 1865, Union war debt peaked at $2,757,689,571, itemized in Bolles, *Financial History,* p. 306; on a per capita basis, the U.S. debt was ($59: 1870), not large when compared to Great Britain ($133: 1868), Netherlands ($112: no date), France ($74: 1868), Greece ($50: no date), Spain ($50: 1870). *Hunt's* September 1870, p. 232.

29. Approximately half of these were new stock issues; the remainder were bonds. Railroads took over 95 percent of the total value. For a detailed listing of the bonds, see *Hunt's,* December 1869, pp. 431–4; for a more general discussion, see Williamson, "Watersheds," pp. 644–51. It should be noted that the overwhelming presence of rail securities in capital markets reflected the railroads' preeminence as corporate, industrial enterprises and was not due to their overall impact on the economy.

30. Led by British investors, this speculative expansion came to span five continents, ranging from the Balkans, the Ottoman Empire, and Egypt to Turkey, India, Japan, Russia, and South America. Greenberg, *Financiers and Railroads,* pp. 38–40. For data on railroad investment as a percentage of U.S. gross national product, see Paul H. Cootner, "The Role of the Railroads in United States Economic Growth," *Journal of Economic History* 23 (December 1963): 477–521.

estimates vary, European investments in American stocks and bonds probably increased by $500 million or more between 1866 and 1869.[31]

By the end of 1868, the United States had one mile of railroad for every 876 inhabitants, by far the greatest proportion of mileage to population of any nation in the world.[32] In building this system, the return of the European investor was important, but even more significant to the economic development of the United States was the largely new and controlling role of the American financier. The emergence of northeastern bankers as leading financial agents for railroads and for American economic development generally can be traced to their role in Treasury operations during the Civil War. Some houses, such as the firm of Jay Cooke and Company, arose out of the war itself.[33] Others, like Drexel, Morgan (J. Pierpont Morgan's vehicle) were either formed after Appomattox or less involved in the war effort but found their postwar position vastly enhanced by the conflict.[34]

Thus the American Civil War promoted the development of an autonomous capital market by first, encouraging a repatriation of securities from Europe and a subsequent domestic funding of the war effort; second, forcing the nation off of the gold standard and, in that way, insulating the financial system from the influence of foreign markets; and, last, abetting the emergence of a largely new class of financiers who, upon the withdrawal of the Treasury from the capital market in the postbellum period, moved easily into a dominant position in the coordination and financing of industrial expansion.[35] (The capital mobilizing

31. Greenberg reports European investment in American securities as $350 million in 1866 and $1 billion in 1869. *Financiers and Railroads*, p. 33; the *Chronicle* believed foreign investors increased their holdings of 5/20 federal bonds alone by some $200 million in the three years ending October 1867 (October 19, 1867, p. 485); at the end of 1866, Treasury Secretary McCulloch estimated European holdings at $600 million or more in his *Annual Report of the Secretary of the Treasury, 1866*, p. 12; also see, Oberholtzer, *Jay Cooke*, vol. 1, pp. 513–15.
32. *Hunt's*, May 1869, p. 339.
33. Greenberg, *Financiers and Railroads*, pp. 13–14. As a group, for example, the seventeen most important firms in postwar railroad financing had previously marketed over 44 percent of the 5/20 bond offering analyzed in Table 4.1. This percentage is based on Greenberg's list of firms and the raw data on bond participation used in constructing the table.
34. Relying on his father's connections, J. Pierpont Morgan started his own firm in New York City between April and July 1861; formed a new partnership (Dabney, Morgan) in November 1864, which he re-formed, in an alliance with a major Philadelphia house, as Drexel, Morgan in 1871; and, finally, absorbed his father's London firm in 1890. While but a single, albeit prominent instance of a larger phenomenon, the history of the two Morgan houses graphically illustrates the incremental transfer of financial power and influence from Britain to the United States in the late nineteenth century. Carosso, *Morgans*, pp. 90, 107, 276–7 and passim.
35. Richard E. Sylla also suggests that government bonds indirectly helped link industrial suppliers of Union war material to private capital markets. The American Capital

and concentrating impact of the newly created national bank system, discussed below, could be added to this list.) All of these factors accelerated a process that would have unfolded without the war. For example, other, more constant elements in national money market development were the expanding railroad and telegraph networks that allowed emerging corporate structures to exploit broader market opportunities and brought distant regions into close contact with and reliance upon New York markets.[36] If anything, the requirements of the Union war mobilization retarded the expansion of these commercially important networks. The war effort also held up expansion of the United States economy between 1861 and 1865. A more rapidly expanding economy, through sheer size and increasing maturity, would have reduced the influence of British capital even sooner had the war not occurred.

Within the American political economy, the Civil War encouraged New York's increasing preeminence as the financial and commercial center of the nation. The war, for example, appears to have encouraged the transfer of border-state wealth to the city (as a secure haven for funds that otherwise would have been at risk because of military operations).[37] Both the course of Treasury operations (for example, the department's reliance on New York agents in marketing new bond issues) and the city's role as the primary holder of the country's bank reserves certainly served to centralize the national financial system and further reinforced New York's position. These aspects of government intervention, however, followed the antebellum pattern of economic capacity and were not the product of a conscious attempt to accentuate the city's position. To the contrary, the Treasury's reliance on Jay Cooke and Company, as opposed to originally larger New York houses, could be interpreted as an attempt to develop a competitive alternative to New York markets. On the whole, then, New York did not owe its position to war-related government activity, but the conflict certainly reinforced the city's importance within the financial system. Government policy tended to suppress the emergence

Market, 1846–1914, unpublished doctoral dissertation, Harvard University, 1968, pp. 208–9; cited in Glenn Porter and Harold C. Livesay, *Merchants and Manufacturers: Studies in the Changing Structure of Nineteenth-Century Marketing* (Baltimore: Johns Hopkins University Press, 1971), p. 126.

36. The Atlantic cable was first laid in 1858 but broke after only a couple of months. Laid again in 1866, the cable subsequently became an increasingly important link between the New York and London markets. Richard B. DuBoff, "Business Demand and the Development of the Telegraph in the United States, 1844–1860," *Business History Review* 54 (Winter 1980): 459–79; Lawrence H. Officer, "Integration in the American Foreign Exchange Market, 1791–1900," *Journal of Economic History* 45 (September 1985): 559–60.

37. See, for example, Myers, *New York Money Market*, p. 111.

of other financial centers by recognizing New York City's primacy in the organization of the national bank system and restricting Treasury funding operations to New York money markets.

The financial system during Reconstruction

During the years following the Civil War, the financial system was made up of several interconnected processes and institutions associated with capital mobilization and investment, government fiscal operations, and the movement of foreign trade. Certain government policies were crucially important to the smooth functioning of the major markets and institutions of the postwar financial system. The tight organization of the system in which all of these separate parts were embedded made change in any one mechanism affect operations in many other markets and institutions. Thus, policy choices and institutional performance must be evaluated in terms of the entire system, including the possibility that restructuring in one area might preclude change in another. In addition to indicating the defects and possible reorganizations of the postwar financial system, the following analytical description also provides the criteria that establish the administrative incompetence of the postwar Treasury in its open-market operations.[38] Recognition of this incompetence was the primary cause of the financial community's hostility to central state participation in the financial system and strengthened the community's support for resumption of the gold standard. In turn, these changes in attitudes led the financial community to oppose radical reconstruction of the southern political economy.

In the years between the end of the Civil War and resumption of specie payments in 1879, the financial system can best be summarized with reference to four major types of financial exchange:

38. In laying out the operating requirements of the financial system, markets and institutions will be described as an integrated system in which the availability of gold in the marketplace, the flow of greenbacks in the economy, and the size of Treasury reserves were closely monitored factors influencing financial stability. For example, one of the operating requirements of the financial system was the actual presence of greenbacks in New York City bank vaults so that the redemption of bank notes and deposits could proceed normally. This focus will avoid some of the interpretive problems that might arise from approaching the post–Civil War financial system as the material expression of abstract economic philosophy and theories. Using this approach, three aspects of the interests of finance capitalists within this system will be empirically addressed: (1) their understanding of their position within the national political economy; (2) their policy choices as the product of rational assessment of available options with varying time-horizons and risks; and (3) their recognition of the interdependence between operating stability in different portions of the financial system.

1. The gold market (involving the exchange of specie for government bonds, bond coupons, greenbacks, customs duties, and foreign exchange);
2. the bond market (involving, primarily, the exchange of government bonds for either gold or greenbacks);
3. the currency market (involving, primarily, the movement of greenbacks between the Treasury and the private economy, but also including bank reserves); and
4. the structure and movement of bank reserves (involving, primarily, the pyramidal concentration of country bank reserves in New York, the currency movements associated with the harvest cycle, and the "call loan" connection between New York banks and the stock market).

These will be discussed in turn and, in each case, their particular types of exchange and institutions will be related to the remainder of the financial system. Almost all of the transactions that were important to the determination of market conditions and financial stability took place in New York City.

The gold market

Soon after the banks and the government suspended specie payments, paper currency began to trade at a discount against gold. By January 1862, the gold-currency transactions that turned on this discount began to constitute a significant portion of the business of those Wall Street brokers who dealt in foreign exchange. Largely indifferent, if not hostile, to trading in gold, the New York Stock Exchange provided no facilities for gold-currency operations and, in fact, legislated against the activity in its own trading rooms. So the dealers found temporary refuge in a restaurant ("Gilpin's News Room" by one account). They carried on their business there until October 1864, when the New York Gold Exchange, complete with bylaws and trading pit, was organized.[39] Gold certificates issued by the Bank of New York both provided the basis for trading and served, because access to them required the payment of a $1,000 annual fee and a deposit of gold with the bank, as a qualification for membership on the exchange. In late 1865, the Treasury began to issue its own gold certificates and thus broke down the bank's practical monopoly on entry into trading. In 1870 a prominent financial publi-

---

39. Eames, *New York Stock Exchange,* p. 45; Horace White, *Money and Banking* (Boston: Ginn, 1896), pp. 174–86.

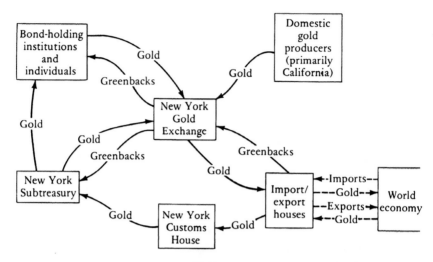

Figure 4.1
The gold exchange and the American financial system, 1862–79. This figure simplifies the
transactions and institutional relationships that related the gold exchange and the remainder
of the financial system. In many of these transactions, for example, national bank notes
were substituted for greenbacks and, on rare occasions, the Treasury bought (as opposed
to sold) gold on the exchange. Imports commonly included capital investment as well as
goods. Gold transferred to bondholders paid interest on the national debt.

cation claimed gold dealers should be well satisfied with their accommodations.[40]

The most important function of the gold exchange in the financial
system was to translate paper dollars into foreign currencies (see Figure
4.1). Because of the dominant position of Britain both in the operation
of the international gold standard and in the foreign trade of the United
States, the gold exchange, for all practical purposes, changed greenbacks
into British sterling. The two most important factors in determining the
value of the greenback were the position of the United States in the world
economy and the financial stability of the U.S. government. For example,
under the international gold standard, American trade deficits were offset

40. Noting that the "Gold Exchange Bank [affiliated with the Gold Exchange] makes
their clearings, to an enormous daily aggregate, with the use of very little *bona fide*
capital" and that "the Treasury, without charge keeps their cumbersome gold coin
in its vaults, giving them paper notes for $1,000 or $5,000 or $10,000, in a convenient
form for rapid, safe and easy transmission from hand to hand," *Hunt's Merchant's
Magazine* went on to assert that "no business in New York is so thoroughly provided
with facilities for economy and efficiency as that of gold speculators." September
1870, p. 185; October 1870, p. 270.

by an export of gold which, in turn, pushed the value of the greenback down relative to the British sterling. Trade surpluses had the opposite effect.[41] Political events that impaired the credit of the United States government, such as military defeats or proposals to inflate the currency, also could drive the greenback down. On the other hand, battlefield victories and Treasury policies that contracted the currency or reduced the national debt tended to raise the gold price of the dollar.

Thus the market price of gold marked, in reality, the greenback's value against British sterling and measured, at least under normal conditions, the present and expected future flows of capital and goods between the United States and the remainder of the world economy. These flows, in turn, were influenced by both economic and political factors that made the gold exchange a highly unpredictable and unstable market. As a consequence, much of the trading in gold can be traced to the hedging operations of import/export houses (in order to protect them from changes in foreign currency rates between the sale or purchase of goods and their delivery).[42]

A distinctly secondary function of the exchange was to provide import houses with the coin necessary to pay tariff duties. The legislation authorizing the issuance of legal tender notes required that all duties be paid in specie and thus established a mechanism by which the Treasury came by the coin necessary for interest payments on the national debt.[43] Gold used to pay customs moved through the New York Customs House to the New York subtreasury (duties, of course, were also paid at other ports in the United States but New York's preeminence must be emphasized).[44] The tariff yielded a supply of gold more than adequate for the

41. Because the United States economy experienced a trade deficit in goods in most years, the export of private and government securities (conversely, the importation of foreign capital) was an important factor in balancing imports and exports and, thus, in maintaining domestic specie holdings. For a general treatment of the role of gold in foreign exchange, see Myers, *New York Money Market*, pp. 338–50; for examples of the potential impact of capital imports on specie flows, see *Hunt's*, January 1870, p. 2, and August 1870, pp. 155–7.

42. Milton Freidman and Anna Jacobson Schwartz, *A Monetary History of the United States, 1867–1960* (Princeton, N.J.: Princeton University Press, 1963), pp. 26, 58, 61; Unger, *Greenback Era*, pp. 152–3. Richard Roll argues that both the gold and bond markets in the postwar era were relatively efficient, even by modern standards, and, by matching up bond prices with major military engagements, demonstrates the markets' sensitivity to political events, "Interest Rates and Price Expectations during the Civil War," *Journal of Economic History* 32 (June 1972): 476–98.

43. *Hunt's*, April 1862, p. 403; for the text of the bill, see May 1862, pp. 477–9; also see, Friedman and Schwartz, *A Monetary History*, p. 27.

44. In the 1866 fiscal year, for example, the New York Customs House collected $133,644,378, 74.4 percent of the national total. "Receipts and Expenditures," Exec.

redemption of bond coupons and, apparently, the Treasury rarely entered the market in order to buy additional coin for this purpose.

The gold distributed throughout the private economy by interest payments on Treasury debt ultimately found its way back to the exchange as it was changed back into greenbacks. The national banks, in particular, held more than one-quarter of all private and public debt by 1866 and, as a routine procedure, bought greenbacks with their gold dividends.[45] Because they traded at par with national bank notes, greenbacks were a much more convenient form in which the banks could hold their required vault reserves for both demand deposits and redemption of bank notes. Thus, gold dividends were exchanged for greenbacks in order to replenish these reserves. Another source of specie arriving on the exchange was the California gold fields. Since greenbacks did not circulate in the Pacific coast states, west coast bullion exports were exchanged directly for imported goods.

With respect to its potential impact upon the remainder of the financial system, the gold exchange presented one major danger. Under a paper monetary standard, the only institutions with a potentially inelastic demand for gold were the import/export houses that required gold to complete their hedging contracts and foreign trade transactions, and to pay customs duties. As a consequence, relatively short-term interruptions in the regular supply of bullion through the exchange could bring foreign trade operations to a halt and seriously undermine the financial foundation of the import/export firms. Over the long term, several weeks or more, gold could be imported from abroad and was, thus, impossible to "corner" but over the short term concerted action by groups of speculators could tie up the supply of specie on the gold exchange and cause a panic as speculators and firms competed with one another for whatever bullion remained available. Because the United States was not on a specie standard in this period (1862–79), a panic on the gold exchange did not directly endanger bank reserves or, as a consequence, overall economic stability. As viewed by *Hunt's Merchants' Magazine*, "So long as our own currency is kept steady in volume, the speculations of cliques in the Gold Room cannot pierce very deeply to injure our sensitive commercial system."[46] However, a corner could indirectly threaten other New York markets by leading gold speculators to liquidate their stock and bond

Doc. 315: House of Representatives: 40th Cong., 2nd Sess., Ser. Rec. 1346 (Washington, D.C.: Government Printing Office, 1868).

45. The estimate on debt holdings is taken from the *Annual Report of the Comptroller of the Currency, 1866*, reprinted in *Hunt's*, December 1866, p. 467.

46. February 1879, p. 98.

holdings in order to satisfy sour trades on the gold exchange. This liquidation of securities, in turn, could spread the panic to the stock market where a rapid fall in security prices would threaten banking reserves (discussed later in this chapter).[47]

One of the operating features of the financial system that made a temporary corner of the gold market possible was the continual flow of specie into the Treasury from the payment of customs. Since this flow was almost always in excess of the requirements of coupon redemption, Treasury vaults over time built up heavy gold balances and, as a consequence, specie was withdrawn from circulation in the rest of the economy. Because of their potentially destabilizing impact on the gold exchange, these gold holdings compelled the government to actively intervene in the New York money markets in order to dispose of surplus bullion. Under normal conditions, the Treasury could select one of three ways to get rid of unneeded gold. First, the government could repurchase bonds in the open market before they matured or, if applicable, call them in for redemption and use surplus gold to pay for these securities. Second, the Treasury could pay upcoming interest in advance of coupon maturity (in effect accelerating future interest payments). Or, third, gold could be sold directly either by the solicitation of bids or, using private brokers as intermediaries, on the exchange itself.[48] Although the Treasury used all three at one time or another, the direct sale of gold was usually relied upon because this method most effectively addressed the problem.

These direct sales withdrew currency from circulation because greenbacks were taken into the Treasury as specie was sold. This withdrawal of currency posed a potential threat to bank reserves, which were held mainly in greenbacks. The Treasury, therefore, was usually compelled to simultaneously pay out greenbacks by purchasing government bonds. The net impact of these two market interventions was to sell gold for bonds (see Figure 4.2). Under some administrations (notably McCulloch's), the Treasury might intervene in the gold exchange in an attempt to stabilize price levels during periods of extraordinary market

47. The most prominent gold "panic" occurred between September 21 and 27, 1869 when Jim Fisk and Jay Gould succeeded in cornering the market. *Hunt's Merchants' Magazine*, October 1869, pp. 312–15; also see November 1869, pp. 342–4, 346–8; for more recent accounts of the crisis and the Treasury intervention that broke the back of the corner, see Barrett, *Greenbacks and Resumption*, pp. 88–94, and Unger, *Greenback Era*, pp. 169–70.
48. Myers, *New York Money Market*, pp. 354–5, 361–2; Barrett, *Greenbacks and Resumption*, p. 87; Unger, *Greenback Era*, p. 164; for contemporary discussion of Treasury activity, see the *Annual Report of the Secretary of the Treasury, 1865* reprinted in *Hunt's*, January 1866, p. 76, and October 1865, p. 313.

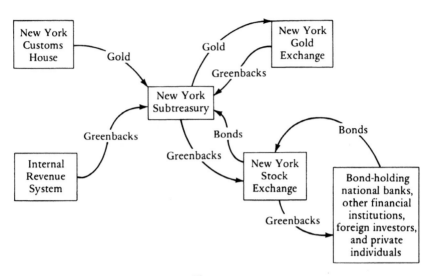

Figure 4.2
Treasury bond purchases and sales of gold and greenbacks, 1862–79. The net result of
these Treasury operations was to sell gold for bonds and gradually to decrease the national
debt. This figure focuses on the bond market's relationship to the U.S. Treasury and does
not include many other transactions, such as those involving Treasury refunding operations
or foreign investment in bonds.

instability but, for the most part, gold disposal was a routine, predictable
feature of the financial system.[49]

While it is important to remember that other ports in the United States
had their own markets, it was the New York Gold Exchange that set
prices throughout the country and linked the American financial system
to the outside world economy. For that and other reasons, this discussion
has focused on the circulation of gold within New York City. As such
it is necessarily incomplete but will provide enough information to support a theoretical description of the broadly conceived arrangements and
policies that were necessary to the stability of the financial system.

The bond market

The market in government bonds was an essential part of the American
financial system for several reasons. In the first place, the federal debt
represented a large portion of all investment in the economy and played

49. On McCulloch's policy, see Taus, *Central Banking Functions*, pp. 65–6; Oberholtzer,
    Jay Cooke, vol. 1, pp. 400–6.

a major role as backing for currency circulated by the national bank system, as well as for savings deposits and potential liabilities on policies issued by insurance companies. In 1875, for example, 63 percent of the value of all investments made by New York City national banks was represented by their holdings in federal bonds.[50] Stability in the bond market tended to secure the foundations upon which these financial institutions rested and rendered an otherwise chaotic economic environment a little more stable.

Even more important, bond transactions were the primary means by which the Treasury could moderate cyclical stringency in the money market caused by the fall and spring movement of funds and by inelasticity in the supply of currency.[51] Because government revenue was chronically larger than expenditure, the Treasury was constantly under pressure to release both gold (from customs) and greenbacks (from internal revenue taxes) back into the economy. The huge war debt and an active bond market combined to make both this disposal of specie and market stabilization possible. The gradual, net effect of Treasury intervention in the bond market was thus the slow retirement of the national debt.[52]

Treasury disposal of excess gold and greenbacks and counterseasonal purchasing of securities were the most important and regular features of the bond market's relationship to the remainder of the financial system. Bonds purchased by the Treasury were drawn from institutional and individual investors in the larger economy (see Figure 4.2) and, while market conditions sometimes determined how large Treasury interven-

---

50. Calculated from data contained in the *Chronicle*, October 21, 1876, p. 392.
51. See, for example, *Hunt's* description of Treasury Secretary Boutwell's countercyclical greenback operations in July 1869, p. 45, and May 1870, p. 376. In order to moderate seasonal cyclicality, the government also moved the date for the payment of annual taxes from September, when money was tight, to July, when money was usually easy. As revenue from the personal and corporate income taxes alone came to $40 million (in 1869), this shift had a major impact on bank reserves and market conditions. *Hunt's*, August 1869, pp. 143–4.
52. For an account of Treasury operations and a discussion of the impact of counterseasonal bond purchases, see Timberlake, *Origins of Central Banking*, pp. 100–1; Taus, *Central Banking Functions*, pp. 67–8; Myers, *New York Money Market*, pp. 355–8; for contemporary comment and approval, see *Hunt's* August 1869, p. 143–4, 153–4, 174–6. *Hunt's* approval was clearly conditional: "Great anxiety prevails in Wall Street to learn what will really be done, as our hopes of an easy money market and of a good fall trade depend largely on the course the Treasury may adopt in this matter; for, however much we may regret the fact, a fact it undoubtedly is, that the money market is under the control of the Treasury, and works easy or tight just as [Secretary] Boutwell locks up currency or pours it out from his vaults" (p. 175). For a discussion of bond purchases between May 12 and October 13 – the easy and tight periods of the year in the money market, respectively – see November 1869, pp. 344–5. For criticism lodged against Secretary McCulloch's administration because he failed to anticipate seasonal market conditions in his operations, see *Chronicle*, September 2, 1871, p. 295; also, October 5, 1867, p. 413; Bolles, *Financial History*, p. 278.

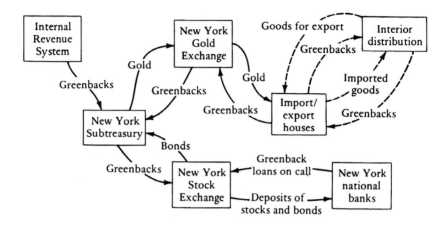

Figure 4.3
The circulation of greenbacks in the American financial system, 1862–79. This figure is
restricted to domestic transactions, does not describe the seasonal movement between New
York City and the interior, and omits the pyramidal structure of bank reserves.

tion would be, government securities were always readily available on
the stock exchange. With respect to the bond market's role in the smooth
functioning of the financial system, the only operating requirement was
that the budget of the U.S. government exhibit a fairly substantial and
consistent surplus. Such a surplus allowed the Treasury to retire bonds
in a gradually improving market because the debt itself was continually
decreasing in size. Only under these conditions could bond purchases
constitute a readily available tool for Treasury intervention in the money
market.

The greenback market

Unlike gold and government bonds, greenbacks did not have their own
central market during the post–Civil War period because no single exchange was the focus of purchases and pricing for paper currency. As a
consequence, any attempt to sketch the circulation of greenbacks through
the financial system must repeat some aspects of the markets already
discussed (see Figure 4.3).

The familiar features of greenback circulation include the continual
collection of legal tender notes into the Treasury through the operation
of the Internal Revenue system and the disposal of specie on the Gold
Exchange, the subsequent purchase of government bonds on the stock
exchange (by which means Treasury greenbacks were returned to cir-

culation), and purchases of foreign exchange through which importers and exporters came by the coin used in foreign trade transactions and customs duties. A close analysis of greenback circulation, however, introduces two new elements into our description of the financial system. In the first instance, greenbacks served a vital role in the movement of goods between the major ports and the nation's interior. This function in the domestic economy paralleled that of gold in international trade and underscored the importance of the markets and institutions that "translated" foreign exchange into greenbacks and vice versa. The movement of greenbacks between the nation's financial centers, particularly New York City, and the interior followed a seasonal rhythm connected to agricultural harvests and planting.

The second new element introduced in Figure 4.3 involves the "call loans" made by national banks to stockbrokers and investors in return for collateral deposits of stocks and bonds. In this relationship of the banks to the stock exchange could be found the only market in which greenbacks could be considered a commodity. When the national bank system was established, the banks were permitted to circulate government-printed notes secured by deposits of government bonds in the Treasury. These national bank notes were redeemable in greenbacks upon demand and were equivalent to legal tender in satisfaction of interbank or government-bank obligations. While greenbacks were a theoretically superior currency (in that they were legal tender in a wider range of transactions), greenbacks and bank notes were normally interchangeable and no distinction was made between them (for example, the term "greenbacks" has been allowed to stand for national bank notes in the figures accompanying this discussion). But in one very important respect they were not equal: greenbacks, because they could redeem bank notes but not vice versa, could satisfy the legal reserve requirements of the national banks.[53] Thus, when greenbacks were used to make deposits in the banks, reserves automatically increased. On the other hand, when bank notes were deposited by customers in otherwise exactly similar transactions, bank reserves were decreased relative to the legal requirement. Most of

53. By law, national banks had to hold reserves in order to secure "1. National bank notes in circulation. 2. State bank notes in circulation. [These were rapidly phased out.] 3. Individual and United States deposits." Reserves could include "1. Specie. 2. All United States legal-tender issues, including the interest bearing legal tender notes. 3. Balances in approved [national banks in New York or other designated cities] ... [4.] Clearing house certificates [issued by the Treasury]. [5.] Balances due from the Treasurer or any Assistant Treasurer of the United States, payable on demand." This description was taken from a circular issued to the national banks by the Comptroller of the Currency, December 15, 1865, reprinted in *Hunt's*, March 1866, p. 236. In practice, most reserves took the form of greenbacks or certificates representing the deposit of greenbacks.

the time this posed no problem to the banks; they just paid out whatever bank notes were deposited and retained greenbacks. But on some occasions, particularly when currency began to move back to New York after harvest or planting, the city's banks were overwhelmed with bank notes and greenbacks became relatively scarce. At those times the national banks traded bank notes for greenbacks at a discount ranging from 1/8 to 1/4 percent or made bank note loans for several days without interest if the borrower agreed to remit greenbacks when settling up.[54]

This sporadic market in greenbacks pointed out the most important operating requirement related to paper currency: in order for the financial system to work smoothly, the national banks had to have access to a ready supply of greenbacks. Even better, this supply should have been so abundant that distinctions would not be made between national bank notes and greenbacks as they passed from hand to hand.

Three situations could create a shortage of greenbacks and, thus, induce a financial panic. First, the government might build up greenback holdings in Treasury vaults through the retention of tax payments or receipts from the sale of surplus gold. Though the major financial publications and other observers found their behavior hard to understand, Treasury secretaries often failed to anticipate shortages or even aggravated them by "hoarding" greenbacks during periods of stress in the money market.[55] A second source of difficulty was the seasonal movement of funds to the interior. The banks could usually adjust to this demand by following a mildly conservative credit policy in the month or so before the movement began. However, factors such as the size and exact timing of the harvest or the emerging recovery of the southern plantation economy, about which little was usually known, introduced substantial uncertainty into bank calculations even under the best of circumstances.

The third situation in which greenbacks could disappear from bank reserves could develop during a downturn in the stock market. Everything else being equal, a steep fall in stock prices would produce a rapid liquidation of call loans. This liquidation would, in turn, feed further selling on the stock exchange and could develop into a vicious downward spiral.

54. See, for example, *Hunt's*, June 1870, p. 467; *Chronicle*, May 6, 1871, p. 550. For a brief description of the importance of greenbacks to national bank reserves, see Myers, *New York Money Market*, pp. 254–6; on the greenback premium, p. 404. In rare, somewhat paradoxical situations, national bank notes could also trade at a premium against greenbacks. See *Internal Revenue Record*, July 11, 1868, p. 12; *Chronicle*, December 28, 1872, p. 854.
55. See, for example, *Hunt's*, July 1869, p. 75. While Treasury operations were often clumsy and, at least to independent observers, indifferent to market requirements, government policy could also be innovative. Unger, *Greenback Era*, pp. 171–2; Taus, *Central Banking Functions*, pp. 67–8.

As stocks fell and loans to brokers turned sour, the financial solvency of the banks could be impaired. This impairment, in turn, could lead creditors to withdraw their deposits and, because greenbacks made up the greater part of ready assets, threaten the ability of the banks to maintain reserves at or above legal requirements. In practice, crashes on the stock exchange were usually induced by the stress that accompanied the harvest/planting cycles and were seriously threatening only during those periods.

National bank reserves and the harvest/planting cycles

Even before the Civil War, a large fraction of all country bank reserves were maintained in New York City. After the establishment of the national bank system, however, country bank deposits became even more concentrated in New York and were an important factor in the emergence of a national money market. The national bank statutes both recognized and reinforced New York's dominant role in the banking system by creating a pyramidal structure in which reserves flowed toward the nation's financial apex. Country banks, for example, were required to maintain reserves equal to 15 percent of all notes in circulation and deposits. Located in small towns and cities throughout the country, these institutions were not required to keep the entire 15 percent on hand, however. Three-fifths of their required reserve (9 percent of circulation and deposits) could, instead, be deposited in approved banks in seventeen designated cities: Albany, Baltimore, Boston, Chicago, Cincinnati, Cleveland, Detroit, Leavenworth (Kansas), Louisville, Milwaukee, New Orleans, New York, Philadelphia, Pittsburgh, San Francisco, St. Louis, and Washington. Their potential liabilities swollen by country bank deposits, institutions in these cities were required to maintain reserves of 25 percent. However, they could place half of their reserve, 12.5 percent of circulation and deposits, in approved New York City national banks.[56]

The country bank reserves deposited in New York were, in turn, lent out in the form of call loans to brokers and investors and, by 1868, the government estimated that "nearly one-half of the available resources of the national banks in the city of New York are used in the operations

---

56. Robert P. Sharkey provides a lucid description of reserve requirements in *Money, Class, and Party: An Economic Study of Civil War and Reconstruction* (Baltimore: Johns Hopkins University Press, 1967), pp. 228–9. Country banks would have maintained balances in New York in any case because they found it profitable to create commercial paper payable in that city. Banks in New York and other reserve cities, however, further encouraged this flow of funds by paying interest on country bank deposits. John A. James, "A Note on Interest Paid on New York Bankers' Balances in the Postbellum Period," *Business History Review* 50 (Summer 1976): 198–202; Myers, *New York Money Market*, pp. 103–8, 118–24, 229–30, 242–9.

of the stock and gold exchange."[57] These loans were secured by the deposit of government bonds or railroad securities and constituted the central reservoir of the national bank system. The potential illiquidity of these loans and their underlying securities was an increasing source of anxiety to finance capitalists during this period. As *Hunt's* described the situation, "the accumulation of capital in all our great monetary centres has been going forward of late with almost unexampled rapidity. It is true that capital is too much concentrated, and is held in few hands. But this very circumstance is favorable to the availability of the capital for the purposes of the loan market, and tends to make money easy. We have, however, to make allowance for the rapidity with which in all parts of the country floating capital is assuming fixed forms." *Hunt's* analysis clearly connects the major advantage and disadvantage of the structure. On the one hand, the concentration of funds in one marketplace was a clear advantage in terms of the mobilization and allocation of the nation's capital. On the other hand, the vulnerability of bank reserves constantly threatened the fundamental stability of the entire financial system.[58]

This movement of currency associated with the harvest cycle represented the most serious challenge to the system's stability (see Figure 4.4). The movement began with the fall harvest of crops in the nation's interior. Agricultural producers would market these crops with merchants in small towns or cities. In completing these transactions, the accounts the merchants kept in country banks would be drawn down and the banks were compelled to replenish their reserves by calling back a portion of the balances they maintained in institutions in New York or other reserve cities. Once this demand for currency began to appear in New York, the national banks in that city started to call in the loans they had made to brokers and investors on the stock exchange. This liquidation of credit, in turn, led the latter to sell their stocks and bonds in the open market. During periods of "easy money," this flow reversed, currency moved toward New York, and the supply of funds on the call loan market

57. *Annual Report of the Comptroller of the Currency, 1868*, reprinted in *Hunt's*, December 1868, p. 461.
58. September 1869, p. 168. The *Chronicle* claimed that, because of the call loan market, "the normal rates of interest fluctuate more in New York than in any other city in the world," January 14, 1871, p. 37. Also see, Myers, *New York Money Market*, pp. 126, 132–5, 265–87. The call loan market was so attractive that *Hunt's* claimed "There are not a few national banks in the country [outside the nation's financial centers] whose officers almost reside permanently in New York, and use the money of the bank in Wall Street to much better purpose, so far as profits are concerned, than if they soberly and quietly sat still at home and lent it to their neighbors in the legitimate way of loans and discounts." August 1869, p. 127. As might be clear from the passage, the journal strongly disapproved of this practice.

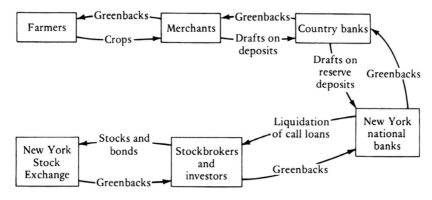

Figure 4.4
The fall harvest and the cyclical drain on New York City bank reserves. National banks
in reserve cities other than New York have been omitted from this figure. In addition, it
should be noted that national bank notes could replace greenbacks in many of these
transactions and, in most cases, funds moved more indirectly than represented here (for
example, a merchant who drew deposits in a country bank might accept a draft on New
York in place of cash). Finally, this diagram emphasizes the harvest cycle associated with
the movement of crops. Currency cycles were also associated with peaks in consumer
purchases in the interior (after harvest and during spring planting).

expanded. A weaker, but similar cycle was associated with peaks in
consumer purchases in the interior during spring planting.[59] With the
harvest cycle in mind, the nation's bankers and other finance capitalists
closely monitored the greenback reserves of the New York City banks
each fall. Every year these reserves would drop (see Table 4.2). However,
the system collapsed only once – in the 1873 panic, which can be clearly
identified in a comparison of the annual reserve patterns.[60]

59. For a conventional critique of the instability-inducing features of the structure of the
national bank system, see Helen Hill Updike, *The National Banks and American
Economic Development, 1870–1900* (New York: Garland Publishing, 1985), pp. 52,
56; also see, Myers, *New York Money Market*, pp. 107, 134, 137, 141–8, 206–9,
258–60; for a discussion of stringency in the money market during the spring months
of 1868, see *Hunt's*, April 1868, pp. 320–1; for a vivid description of the harvest
cycle's potential dangers and official recognition of its impact on the financial system,
see the *Annual Report of the Comptroller of the Currency, 1868*, reprinted in *Hunt's*,
December 1868, p. 463.

60. With respect to its rapid exhaustion of bank reserves, contraction of deposits and
loans, and suspension of bank note redemption (in greenbacks), the 1873 panic almost
perfectly realized the nightmare every financier envisioned. For descriptions, see Timberlake, *Origins of Central Banking*, pp. 104–8; Bolles, *Financial History*, pp.
282–4.

Table 4.2. *Greenback reserves in New York City banks and the onset of the harvest cycle: 1871–5*

Week reporting		Greenback reserves ($ millions)				
		1875	1874	1873	1872	1871
July	29	75.5	65.8	50.0	55.1	73.9
Aug.	5	73.6	66.5	49.0	54.6	72.4
	12	70.7	66.6	47.5	52.5	70.1
	19	70.4	65.9	45.3	59.9	69.5
	26	70.5	67.3	44.7	49.4	68.4
Sept.	2	70.6	65.6	38.7	49.1	66.9
	9	69.2	65.3	36.7	48.1	63.8
	16	67.9	64.8	34.3	44.5	58.4
	23	67.3	65.7	21.2	45.0	55.3
	30	66.5	64.0	12.0	41.9	54.6
Oct.	7	60.4	62.4	10.2	45.8	50.8
	14	56.5	60.7	6.3	52.6	50.0
	21	54.7	58.8	8.8	52.3	50.5
	28	53.5	59.6	14.7	51.7	52.4
Nov.	4	51.3	59.5	21.0	48.3	54.5
	11	49.0	59.5	26.1	46.7	55.2
	18	48.0	57.5	30.9	45.9	53.7

Source: Commercial and Financial Chronicle, October 28, 1876, p. 412.

The national bank system

The most important institution connecting New York markets to the remainder of the American economy was the national bank system. From its establishment in February 1863, the system grew quite rapidly and, by January 1864, 137 banks had been chartered by the Treasury. One year later, the figure was 681. On March 3, 1865, a change in the internal revenue schedule raised the tax on the circulation of notes issued by state-chartered banks from 2 to 10 percent, ten times the rate charged to national banks.[61] The new levy led many

61. While the previous rate had been twice the levy on national bank notes, many state banks, particularly those operating under lax regulatory standards, could still issue notes profitably. The 10 percent levy, however, was prohibitive, and many state banks now hurried to turn in their state for federal charters before the tax took effect on July 1, 1866. By October 1, 1865, 1,566 institutions were organized under the national law with a total capital of some $396 million and the system was already approaching the statutory limit of $300 million that had been placed on national bank note circulation. For that reason the rate of new bank formation now slowed to a crawl. By September 30, 1869, 1,620 were in operation, an increase of only 3.4 percent

state-chartered banks to join the national bank system and, by 1877, the number of operating banks had increased to 2,080 with a total circulation of $318 million.[62]

From the system's very inception, the banks tended to concentrate in the nation's financial centers along the northern Atlantic seaboard and the cities of the northeastern interior. Banks were slow to organize in the South, of course, because of the Civil War. When the 1865 levy on state bank notes was passed, national institutions had formed only in New Orleans, Memphis, Nashville, Knoxville, and Norfolk within the reaches of the dying Confederacy. By 1869, when the system stabilized, circulation had moderately expanded in the South, but the system was still dominated by eastern financial centers and their capital-exporting hinterlands (see Map 4.1). Further progress was made by 1877 but the original pattern established twelve years earlier still characterized the system (see Table 4.3).

Of the nation's five major financial centers, Boston banks issued the greatest number of notes per capita.[63] Per capita circulation was far lower in other major financial centers. The most striking anomaly was New York City's circulation (see Table 4.3). Because New York was the premier financial center in the country, facilities for clearing bank notes and returning them to the issuing institution for redemption in greenbacks were far more efficient there than anywhere else in the nation. As a result, the national banks in New York found it difficult to keep their notes in circulation and thus derived little profit from the note-issuing privilege compared to the remainder of the system.[64] For

over the total in 1865. Subsequent revisions of the law first raised the statutory limit to $354 million (1870) and then removed it altogether (1875). Hepburn, *History of the Currency*, pp. 308–11; Bolles, *Financial History*, pp. 341–2, 353–4; U.S. Treasury, *Annual Report of the Comptroller of the Currency, 1865* (Washington, D.C.: Government Printing Office, 1865), pp. 15, 143.

62. Bolles, *Financial History*, pp. 354–9; U.S. Treasury, *Annual Report of the Comptroller of the Currency, 1877* (Washington, D.C.: Government Printing Office, 1877), p. xv.

63. All city figures reported here are for the counties containing them; for Boston, the figures are for Suffolk county which, in this case, was almost coterminous with the city. In all three years, Boston/Suffolk county's per capita share of bank note circulation led all other counties in the nation. Bristol county, Massachusetts, came in second in 1865 ($36.79). Providence, Rhode Island, was the runner-up in both 1869 and 1877 ($69.17 and $51.18, respectively).

64. *Hunt's*, March 1865, p. 213; Sharkey, *Money, Class, and Party*, p. 249. Since national banks purchased investments (loaned money) by issuing their notes, the amount they could keep in circulation determined the return the banks received on their currency. If the notes did not remain in circulation very long before being redeemed in greenbacks, the banks had to retain larger and more active reserves to secure the currency and bore higher overhead charges associated with their processing. Many New York banks decided that notes were more trouble than they were worth and either did not issue any to begin with or dramatically reduced their original circulation over time.

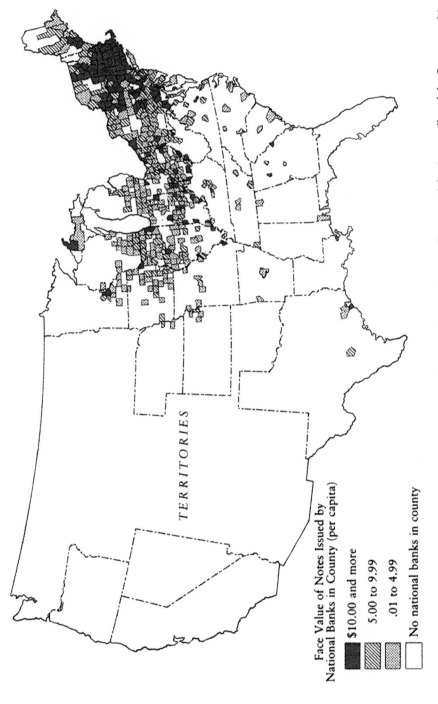

Face Value of Notes Issued by
National Banks in County (per capita)

$10.00 and more

5.00 to 9.99

.01 to 4.99

No national banks in county

Map 4.1 National bank notes issued, by county, 1869. *Source:* Compiled from data in the *Annual Report of the Comptroller of the Currency, 1869* (Washington, D.C.: GPO, 1869) and the *1870 Census of Population.*

Table 4.3. *Currency issued to national banks in selected cities and regions: 1865, 1869, and 1877*

Region or city	Notes issued to national banks (per capita)		
	Mar. 4, 1865	Sept. 30, 1869	Oct. 1, 1877
Major financial center			
New York City	$ 9.28	$36.81	$12.76
Boston	65.33	97.86	65.77
Philadelphia	11.04	16.30	13.14
Washington, D.C.	6.42	6.15	5.33
Baltimore	4.72	21.39	15.98
Selected regions[a]			
Eastern seaboard (N.Y., Mass., Pa.)	$ 6.68	$11.83	$10.18
Remainder of East and Ohio	5.61	13.29	12.25
Free-state West	1.98	3.45	2.91
South and border	.27	1.31	1.42

[a]Not including the above.
Source: Calculated from data contained in the *Annual Report of the Comptroller of the Currency* for the respective years and the 1870 and 1880 censuses. The 1865 data includes only banks chartered through March 4 of that year.

that reason, New York's per capita figures seriously understate the city's actual prominence in the financial system. Outside the five major centers, national banks in the East issued a sufficient amount of currency to bring the per capita average of the region up to levels comparable with Baltimore, New York, and Philadelphia. The free states of the West lagged seriously behind and the southern and border states held banks issuing notes at just over one-tenth the per capita rates of the eastern seaboard and the remainder of the East. For the states of the former Confederacy, indigenous national bank note issues were nine, sixty-eight, and eighty-nine cents per capita in 1865, 1869, and 1877 respectively.[65]

> The results are clearly reflected in the steep per capita decline between 1869 and 1877 and the overall level of New York's circulation.

65. The analysis of national banks has relied upon note circulation as the primary indicator of the extent of regional involvement in the system. Note circulation has an advantage over alternative indicators, such as capital stock or deposits, in that it indicates the extent of constrained investment in government bonds. These bonds, which were held by the Treasury as security for the notes issued by the banks, could not be retrieved unless the banks gathered up their currency and returned it to the comptroller. Since the process by which notes might be gathered was very slow, the investment in government bonds that secured the notes symbolized, for most intents

A number of interrelated factors produced the strongly regional pattern reflected in national bank note circulation. In the first place, the propensity to organize national bank associations appears to have been closely related to the availability of otherwise underemployed liquid capital. For example, the early, strong involvement of the mature, industrial counties of New England in the establishment of the national bank system can be traced to the relative lack of investment alternatives in the region. Unlike the capital-starved reaches of the South and the western frontier, the river valleys and mill towns of the Northeast were comparatively satiated with indigenous capital. For the older, mature regions of the country the national bank system was a comparatively safe method of mobilizing and exporting capital through the New York money market into western development.[66]

A second factor that determined the regional structure of the bank system was the spatial organization of interregional and international trade. In defense of the preponderant position of the Northeast in the distribution of notes, for example, *Hunt's* observed that, "In all modern commercial nations capital shows a strong disposition to concentrate itself on the sea-board, at the confluence where meet the widest currents of interior and foreign traffic. It is consequently natural, necessary, and for the good of the country, that banks and other financial institutions should concentrate there also."[67] The nation's strongest connections within the world economy were with those European nations that bordered the Atlantic Ocean, especially Britain. Their goods entered the country through the major ports of the East Coast, mainly New York, and were subsequently distributed throughout the interior. The commercial links that connected the eastern port cities with the interior can be easily traced in the 1866 postal delivery contracts granted to railroads and steamships (see Map 4.2). As can be seen in the map, the heaviest volumes of mail flowed either between the major commercial and financial centers of the Atlantic seaboard or west from those centers into Ohio.

and purposes, a permanent stake in the fiscal policy of the government. In that respect, note circulation more directly connects the banks to the federal debt than any alternative measure and, thus, most advantageously sums up a general "interest" in the stability of the financial system.

66. A roughly parallel system for mobilizing liquid capital was composed of the life, accident, and casualty insurance companies of the period. New England cities served as the headquarters for firms managing 32.4 percent of all insurance assets, firms in New York State had 43.1 percent of all assets, Pennsylvania and New Jersey held 20.2 percent, and the remainder of the country contained companies holding only 4.3 percent of the total. Assets in all insurance firms added up to $111,440,000 in 1867. Calculated from data in *Hunt's,* September 1867, pp. 198–9.

67. January 1868, p. 28.

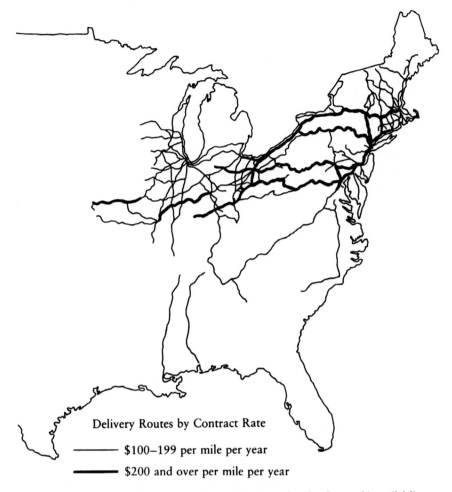

Map 4.2 The United States commercial network: 1866 railroad and steamship mail delivery
contracts. *Source*: Calculated from data contained in the *Annual Report of the Postmaster
General, 1866*, Exec. Doc. 1: House of Representatives: 39th Cong., 2nd Sess., Ser. Rec.
1286, (Washington, D.C.: GPO, 1867) pp. 26–49. A few routes in California and Oregon
have been omitted from this map.

From Ohio, the current divided into smaller, but still substantial streams
that widely distributed mail throughout the more thickly settled regions
of the Midwest. However, only a few middle-level mail routes reached
into the South and these, for the most part, did not connect with each
other in such a way as to compose a network. On the whole, the route

structure almost exactly mimicked the regional pattern of bank circulation.[68]

The last major influence on the regional organization of the bank system was the underdeveloped state of the southern plantation economy and the western frontier. Outside the northeastern corner of the country, many rural, agrarian producers were relatively isolated from the national economy and, while a portion of their production might be marketed with local merchants, the larger share of their harvest either was consumed on the farm or traded for other locally produced goods in quasi-barter transactions. Even where, as in the cotton belt, agricultural production was well integrated into national and world markets, a dearth of capital prevented the development of banking institutions. Thus sectional differences in economic development were reflected in the distribution pattern of national banks. Those regions located at the periphery of the national economy and loosely, if at all, integrated into the national bank system usually exhibited much higher interest rates than the country's money centers. These rate levels can be traced to the greater lending costs associated with an underdeveloped economy: smaller, more administratively expensive loans; higher default rates; and accentuated seasonal demand, which often left capital idle between periods of agricultural activity. Despite these higher, nominal rates, the real return was greater in the nation's financial center. As a result, money flowed through the banking system into New York markets and thus facilitated the capital mobilization necessary for the nation's rapid industrial expansion.[69] As it existed between 1865 and 1877, the national bank system was an integral part of the highly developed markets of the industrial and commercial northeastern core economy, but the social base of periphery regions was only incompletely penetrated and organized by the same system.[70]

68. Businessmen were the leading producers of interregional mail in the antebellum period and, though noncommercial use increased after the war, the strength and consistency of the pattern suggests that commercial communications continued to shape the postal system. On the antebellum period, see Pred, *Urban Growth and City Systems*, pp. 147–9; for similar representations of the postwar commercial network, see David Ward, *Cities and Immigrants: A Geography of Change in Nineteenth-Century America* (New York: Oxford University Press, 1971), pp. 28–46, and John R. Borchert, *America's Northern Heartland: An Economic and Historical Geography of the Upper Northwest* (Minneapolis: University of Minnesota Press, 1987), p. 40.

69. Updike, *National Banks*, pp. 15, 25, 57–77; Richard Sylla, "Federal Policy, Banking Market Structure, and Capital Mobilization in the United States, 1863–1913," *Journal of Economic History* 29 (December 1969): 657–86.

70. Lance E. Davis contended that the narrowing of interest rate differentials between regions in the last quarter of the nineteenth century was due to the growth of more efficient capital markets in the periphery (as part of an overall process of economic development) and that, among other things, the national bank system actually

U.S. Treasury intervention and operations

At the very heart of the post–Civil War financial system was located the combined greenback reserve held in New York institutions for the national banks. Anything that imperiled this reserve put at risk the entire system. Roughly ranked in terms of the gravity of the threat each represented, the most important risks were posed by first, the annual movement of funds through the harvest cycle; second, the possibility of a price collapse on the stock exchange; and, third, clumsy execution or miscalculation of market conditions by the government in its operations. The administrative capacity of the Treasury, in particular, was a continual preoccupation of finance capitalists. As *Hunt's* phrased the concern on one occasion, "it will long constitute one of the perils of the financial situation, that at any moment the government may be selling two or three millions of gold." At another time, the publication observed the "almost despotic control" of the Treasury over the banks "because it could at any time take away their legal tender reserves by sale of gold, by sales of bonds, or by drawing down the balances in the national bank depositories."[71]

While the Secretary of the Treasury normally determined the general policy of the government, his agent in market operations was the assistant treasurer of the New York subtreasury. The person who held this post actually executed the transactions of the government when it intervened in the marketplace. When a vacancy appeared in this position in 1869, *Hunt's* seized the opportunity to sketch the immense responsibilities attached to the assistant treasurer's tasks and the importance of a "sound" appointment:

> The responsibility attached to it exceeds that of any other under the Government. The Assistant Treasurer is custodian of from $70,000,000 to $100,000,000 of money – a larger amount, probably, than is held by any fiscal officer in any country. He is responsible not only for the safe keeping of these funds, but also for the faithful and accurate execution of financial transactions aggregating over $1,000,000,000 per annum . . . the highest business qualifications are required. The officer must have proved himself, through a long experience, to be a man of unquestionable integrity. He ought to be familiar with the banking system of New York and with all the details of practical finance. As the financial representative of the government

retarded southern entry into the national market. "The Investment Market, 1870–1914: The Evolution of a National Market," *Journal of Economic History* 25 (September 1965): 355–99.

71. May 1869, p. 337; April 1868, p. 322.

at the money centre of the country, he is naturally called upon, in monetary exigencies to tender opinions and counsel to the Secretary of the Treasury, who being at a distance from the centre of business often finds it impossible to form an independent opinion of the situation of affairs. At times the Secretary of the Treasury must confide to the Assistant Treasurer an absolute discretion in matters of great magnitude and importance affecting the market for money, gold, and securities.

In contrast to the money market operations of the New York subtreasury, the duties associated with the Treasury Department in Washington were relatively low-level, labor-intensive chores primarily concerned with keeping the nation's accounts.[72] For very good reasons, the administrative competence of postwar Treasury secretaries has been almost universally questioned.

Irwin Unger, for example, called Chase "a rather primitive bullionist Democrat" who narrowmindedly forced the bank system into a suspension of specie payments by compelling the physical transfer of gold to the government during the loan operations of late 1861. In 1863 Secretary Chase again blundered when he moved to check speculation in the New York money market by contracting the supply of greenbacks because, as *Hunt's* described his intervention, "the movement was made suddenly and fell like a thunderbolt from a clear sky. A panic was produced which will be long and sadly remembered in financial circles. A few speculators were made rich by it, but thousands were impoverished."[73]

Following a short term in office by William Fessenden (Chases's immediate successor), Hugh McCulloch was appointed to the position. Upon learning of McCulloch's nomination, Jay Cooke evaluated the new secretary's "calibre" as that of "a bank officer – no higher." Robert Sharkey contends that McCulloch's policy declarations "reflected the processes of a rigid, conservative, and essentially unimaginative mind" and, referring to his program for contraction, observes "The situation called for the delicacy of a scapel, but McCulloch brought only the bluntness of a meat axe."[74] Even after the major financial journals had

72. *Hunt's*, November 1869, pp. 369–71. For a good description of Treasury operations in Washington, see February 1866, pp. 161–3. Also see Leonard D. White, *The Republican Era: A Study in Administrative History, 1869–1901* (New York: Free Press, 1965), pp. 114–5.

73. *Greenback Era*, p. 14; similar interpretations appear in Robert T. Patterson, *Federal Debt-Management Policies, 1865–1879,* (Durham, N.C.: Duke University Press, 1954), pp 25–7; Barrett, *Greenbacks and Resumption*, pp. 12–15; Hammond, *Sovereignty and an Empty Purse*, pp. 349–50; a less severe appraisal is presented in Friedman and Schwartz, *Monetary History*, p. 59, note 64; for the 1863 intervention, see *Hunt's*, October 1866, p. 269.

74. Oberholtzer, *Jay Cooke*, vol. 1, p. 468 (ironically, perhaps, McCulloch joined the

repeatedly warned that a policy of gradual withdrawal restricted to periods between the harvest and planting cycles was the only safe method of reducing the currency, McCulloch still carried his headlong contraction program into the fall harvest and caused near panic conditions in the money market. "He had, it must be believed, no design or intention to produce such disasters," *Hunt's* drily observed.[75]

McCulloch, in turn, was succeeded by George Boutwell, "whose conception of political economy was bounded by one ambition: reduction of the national debt. To this end he would sacrifice not only tariff revision, but tax abatement and currency reform ... [and] spoilsman that he was, Boutwell insisted that the agitation for civil service reform was unfounded."[76] Grant's secretary was faulted for a "needless and mischievous hoarding of greenbacks" throughout his administration and so mismanaged the department's gold sales in the fall of 1872 that a full-blown panic was only narrowly averted.[77] To his credit, however, Boutwell was the first secretary to affirm the Treasury's responsibility for moderating the impact of seasonal cycles in economic activity by retaining currency during slack months and releasing it back into circulation during the fall and spring. In this respect, his performance was measurably superior to that of his predecessors.[78] However, his successor, William Richardson, blundered the nation into, first, a major financial panic and, subsequently, a serious and prolonged economic depression through his reluctance to use the Treasury's powers.[79]

Contemporary explanations of the Treasury's incapacity to manage the financial system attribute the department's failure to the debilitating influence of party politics in a democracy. As Hugh McCulloch, then Comptroller of the Currency, explained in his 1864 annual report,

> Governments should not be bankers. Under popular institutions like ours, no more dangerous, no more corrupting power could be lodged in the hands of the party in possession of the government; none more perilous to official probity and free elections. Give to a party dom-

London office of Cooke's firm after leaving the Treasury in 1869); Sharkey, *Money, Class, and Party*, p. 59 and, generally on McCulloch's administration of the Treasury, pp. 56–120; for a contemporary condemnation of the secretary's plan to reduce the debt, see J. S. Gibbons, *The Public Debt of the United States* (New York: Charles Scribner, 1867).

75. October 1867, p. 288; also see, *Chronicle*, September 2, 1871, p. 295; Bolles, *Financial History*, pp. 277–9; Timberlake, *Origins of Central Banking*, pp. 89–90.
76. Ferleger, *Wells*, pp. 306–7; also, p. 266.
77. *Chronicle*, February 4, 1871, p. 133; July 8, 1871, p. 39; Taus, *Central Banking Functions*, p. 69.
78. Timberlake, *Origins of Central Banking*, p. 100.
79. Timberlake, *Origins of Central Banking*, pp. 105–7; Taus, *Central Banking Functions*, p. 69; Myers, *New York Money Market*, pp. 358–9.

inant in the legislative and executive branches of the government the authority of issuing paper money for the purpose of furnishing the country with its currency, subject as it would be to no restraint but its own pleasure, and what guaranty would there be that this authority would be honestly and judiciously used?[80]

During the 1873 panic, the *Chronicle* received letters urging that the Treasury intervene in order to relieve the crisis in the money market. The financial weekly answered these pleas by contending that government should concern itself with encouraging stability before a crisis sets in and not responding to a panic once it begins.

Maintaining that the Treasury was incapable of effective "administrative government," the *Chronicle* continued "our government is founded on popular principles. It is not fit to control trade or to manage the money market. It is too free and simple in its nature to adapt itself to the complex work attempted by the older governments of Europe, with their bureaucratic habits and centralized power."[81] In short, the federal government could not manage the money market because a robust democracy was too sensitive to the uninformed, ever-changing moods of the people. But there was a more negative side, also. Explaining that "congressmen themselves, as a class, are not venal," Henry Adams offered the observation that "not more than one member in ten of the late Congress ever accepted money" in return for legislative favors to private interests. By liberally supporting individual members and party organizations, the "iron," "whiskey," and "Pacific Railway . . . rings" controlled the course of legislation and frustrated the national interest (as represented in this case by the reform program of Revenue Commissioner Wells). Adams concluded "party organizations have no decency and no shame."[82]

80. From the *Annual Report of the Comptroller of the Currency, 1864*, reprinted in *Hunt's*, February 1865, p. 155. Five years and two comptrollers later, this position had changed little: "The treasury system is so arbitrary in its collections and disbursements, so little in harmony with the business interests of the community, that it frequently absorbs large amounts of currency at most inopportune seasons, and disburses them with just as little regard to the wants of trade. . . . In fact, the current operations of the treasury of the United States are regarded by business men as constituting a powerful, and, at the same time, a very uncertain element, difficult to estimate, but which must necessarily be taken into consideration in all their business transactions." *Annual Report of the Comptroller of the Currency, 1869*, reprinted in *Hunt's*, January 1870, p. 51. Also see, Gibbons, *Public Debt*, p. 100.

81. September 20, 1873, p. 374; three years later, the *Chronicle* repeated this position: "as compared with despotic oligarchies our simple form of government offers fewer guarantees for administrative reform, or for exacting responsibility from those among us who make and execute the laws" (April 1, 1876, p. 314).

82. "The Session," *North American Review*, April 1869, pp. 617–18, partially reprinted in Ferleger, *Wells*, p. 256.

The men who led the Treasury Department during and after the Civil War were products of the intense partisan competition and politicization of policymaking that characterized the period. In the form of potential appointments to office, the Treasury and the Post Office provided well over 80 percent of the "spoils" of party victory. Treasury positions, on the whole, were more lucrative and thus attractive to would-be office holders. Customshouse collectors and internal revenue inspectors, for example, could and did discover many opportunities, primarily involving graft, for raising their standard of living during government service that were largely unavailable to postal officials. Through the Treasury secretary, thousands of such patronage positions were available to the administration, and chief executives were compelled to consider purely political qualifications in naming the head of the department. Above all else, the department head had to possess a political base apart from the department (thus strengthening the administration directly and enabling the secretary to adjudicate intraparty squabbles over particularly choice plums, such as the New York Customs House).[83] The secretary also had to be someone who would place a high priority on administration and party organizational needs in his decisions. Chase, Fessenden, and Boutwell were all party leaders in their own right and sensitive to the major role patronage played in maintaining the party's position in the political system.

An ability to make judicious use of the department's patronage was closely related to the policymaking requirements of the Treasury in that similar brokering skills were a valuable party resource. The major factions within the party disagreed, sometimes violently, over monetary and fiscal policy; so in making his decisions, the Treasury secretary had to be sensitive to the ever-changing political influence each faction commanded. First and foremost, the secretary had to be someone with good contacts within the financial community. McCulloch (as a former president of the State Bank of Indiana), Fessenden (as one of the most influential senators in the formulation of financial policy), and Boutwell (as a Massachusetts congressman with strong links to the commercial interests of his state) all met this condition. Beyond these contacts, however, Treasury heads

---

83. The New York Customs House was only the most corrupt of a revenue system riddled with bribery and fraud. In the *Annual Report of the Commissioner of Customs, 1874,* Commissioner Henry C. Johnson reported that conditions had become so bad that the "mercantile community came to regard the customs-service rather as an agency of personal profit to those who obtained admission into it than as a part of the machinery of a popular government for collecting the revenue necessary to its support, and to look upon the customs officer rather as a parasite, unlawfully living upon themselves, than as a public servant in honorable service." Quoted in White, *Republican Era,* p. 118–19.

were forced to consider the contrary interests of the agrarian and manufacturing sectors of the party. As a result, finance capital did not control or even dominate department policy. Although the leading journals coaxed, cajoled, and flattered secretaries in an effort to influence decisions, the financial community remained deeply disappointed with department performance.[84]

In short, the U.S. Treasury did not possess the administrative capacity to manage the money market in the postwar years. It did not have that capacity because Treasury secretaries either lacked detailed knowledge of how the market operated or were forced to respond to political demands that put financial stability at risk, and sometimes both. (Hugh McCulloch, who perhaps was the best qualified secretary during the period, compiled the worst record by attempting to resume specie payments before the balance of influence in the political system shifted toward inflation.) Examined from a different perspective, the political system was debilitating in another way. In most respects, the Republicans made up the state during the Civil War and Reconstruction and competed with a political party (the Democrats) that offered radical decentralization of central state authority as an alternative organization of the nation's political economy.[85] Because this situation discouraged most statist-oriented elites from entertaining a serious alliance with the Democrats, finance capital and the central state bureaucracy (such as it was) was left little room for political maneuvering between the parties. In the following passage, for example, *Hunt's* expressed a hope that the Democratic resurgence in the 1870 congressional elections would release the executive branch from the debilitating influence of intraparty Republican politics and lead to thorough, "scientific" reform:

> In times of great national danger or effort, it may be desirable to have an overwhelming majority of the legislature in perfect harmony with the Executive ... it remains true [however] that an organized party in undisputed possession of the whole power of Congress, constantly tends to weaken the Executive; while the management of the Government in such a way as to keep the majority compact and earnest in its support, tends constantly to corrupt it. In these respects, there is something gratifying in the simple fact that in the next House

84. On the importance of financial expertise and party prominence as qualifications for Treasury secretary appointees, see White, *Republican Era*, pp. 110–12; Allan G. Bogue, *The Congressman's Civil War* (Cambridge: Cambridge University Press, 1989), p. 32.
85. On the greenback issue and resumption of the gold standard, the Democratic party drifted toward a more statist position than the Republicans ultimately assumed, but differences between the two parties on these issues remained relatively minor until the Bryan campaign in 1896.

... there will be a nearer approach to a balance between parties than for several years before ... new issues, growing up into public notice everywhere, are entirely different in their nature from those which have of late divided parties. They are no longer questions of feeling and prejudice, questions of sections, classes or race, but are questions of opinion or scientific judgment, questions, in short, of financial and economical science. The best reform of the civil service, the method of adjusting the tariff and the tax laws, so as to meet the public dues and wants with the least burden on the people, the regulation of the currency, of banks, of the great national lines or railway, and of State corporations in general ... [requires] a new division of the parties upon economical principles.[86]

Thus one of the major sources of stress in the workings of the financial system was the administrative incompetence of the Treasury. Other problems still facing the system at the end of Reconstruction concerned: the inelasticity of the currency with reference to seasonal movements associated with the harvest/planting cycle; the relationship of a domestic paper money standard with the gold standard prevailing in international transactions; uneven regional development and consequent difficulties in extending the reach of an integrated national market; and, above all else, the vulnerability of greenback reserves held by national banks in New York City. All of these sources of stress have been related to the working of the financial system in individual markets, to the circulation of money within the national and international economies, and to the mobilization and investment of capital. It is to the central interests of finance capitalists in the workings of the system and the political economy in general that we now turn.

Political-economic implications of the organization of financial markets and central state monetary policy

Taken on its own terms, the preceding analysis of market organization and government performance would provide a satisfactory foundation for interpreting the interests of finance capital in the postwar political economy. However, this interpretation will be stronger if we connect this

---

86. *Hunt's*, December 1870, pp. 438–9. In a letter to John Gorham Palfrey (dated August 23, 1866), Henry Adams had previously expressed similar sentiments: "The tyranny of majorities in our country must be tempered by resistance, and I believe it would be good policy to support the most profligate political opposition rather than to allow one party to rule unchecked." Also see his letters to his brother (dated November 10, 1866, May 8, 1867, and April 21, 1868), J. C. Levenson, Ernest Samuels, Charles Vandersee, and Viola Hopkins Winner, eds., *The Letters of Henry Adams, 1858–1868* (Cambridge, Mass.: Harvard University Press, 1982), pp. 509, 512, 533, 570.

analysis to the policy preferences and proposals of the postwar financial community.[87] The class previously identified as finance capitalists included brokers, bankers, insurance companies, import/export houses, and commission merchants. With the partial exception of bankers, individual members of these sectors of finance capitalism were not given to public expression of their views on major public policy questions during the Reconstruction era. When they did give voice to their preferences, their views tended to fix narrowly on the short-term interests of their sector within the system or flesh out a highly abstract, often moralistic position on questions involving abstract economic theory (such as an alleged connection between "public virtue" and the gold standard). For example, Amasa Walker, a prominent Boston merchant, declared that "taking all things into consideration, [in] every way the best money is the gold and silver which God has evidently designed for that purpose." Other academics and business leaders supported their various positions on the "money question" with references to Calvinist principles of self-denial or highly abstract mercantilist notions of the impact of currency inflation on the stock of wealth in society.[88] A summary interpretation of the views expressed by the vast majority of finance capitalists would, therefore, not serve the purposes of this analysis.

The two groups within finance capitalism that did consistently articulate the interests of the system as a whole and, for the most part, kept their attention focused on the policy questions immediately at hand, were the major financial publications serving the banking and mercantile communities in New York City and the long-established New England textile manufacturers. The first group includes *Hunt's Merchants' Magazine and*

87. As we have argued here, finance capitalists did not maintain that this was the only conceivable financial system for its time and place, or that these were the only *set* of structural and policy arrangements that might have made the system work effectively. However, they did contend that the range of possible alternatives was more or less tightly constrained by strong interdependencies among individual elements and the complexity of the system itself. These constraints combined to produce the strong functional advantages of existing financial "practice," inertial resistance to change, and, where restructuring of the system was nonetheless indicated, a preference for incremental reform. As the *Chronicle* expressed this conservatism (for which financiers have long been notorious), "Stability is of more importance in the monetary organism than conformity to any theoretic system, and the practical statesman will bring better results out of an imperfect financial scheme than can be achieved by more symmetrical machinery, if the former have stability, while the latter is inconstant, unsettled, and liable to sudden jerks and unforeseen changes" (January 4, 1873, p. 7). Most adaptive elements of the financial system should not, therefore, be viewed as essential in and of themselves. They should, instead, be seen as facilitating features of the system (some anchor the system through guarantees, others create incentives that encourage functionally supportive and adaptive behavior or provide ways of rescuing the system during crisis).

88. For a review of this literature, see Unger, *Greenback Era*, pp. 120–7.

Commercial Chronicle, Bankers' Magazine and Statistical Register (both monthlies), and the *Commercial and Financial Chronicle* (a weekly – *Hunt's* was folded into the *Chronicle* in January 1871). Together, these publications represented and served the broad banking, merchant, and commercial classes of the nation's financial centers, particularly New York City. (The *Chronicle*, for example, billed itself as "Representing the Industrial and Commercial Interests of the United States.") The advertising carried in these organs gives some idea of their broader role as representatives and servants of the financial community. Among the leading advertisers in *Hunt's* and the *Chronicle*, for example, were insurance companies, brokers and securities dealers, banks, commission merchants, and general manufacturers. Together their advertisements comprised over 80 percent of all advertising space in these journals. Most advertisers were located in New York City with Philadelphia, Boston, and other leading commercial centers trailing far behind.[89]

This wide representation of the financial community among their advertisers supported the broadly conceived role the publications played in commercial and political life. The journals rarely, for example, supported the narrow interests of one sector of finance against another, frequently reprimanded "irresponsibility" by members of the community (failure by the banks to maintain adequate reserves or attempts by brokers to form speculative corners on the exchanges, for example), and generally articulated a systemic approach to questions concerning the course of the political economy. Almost exclusively concerned with both long-term and short-term threats to financial stability, the editorial recommendations of these journals repeatedly urged the adoption of government policies that would have accommodated Treasury operations to changing conditions in the nation's money markets. Though the readership of these publications resided throughout the country, the perspective they offered was from the financial center and articles on important regional events (the Chicago fire, size of the cotton crop, and the like) were always linked to prospective change in market conditions in New York.

Another major and articulate group with a major stake in the general, long-term health of the financial system was composed of the long-established cotton manufacturers and commercial magnates of New England. Concentrated in and around Boston, this subgroup within finance

89. Calculated from advertisements in the January 1867 issue of *Hunt's* and the January 7, 1871 issue of the *Chronicle*. The sectors of finance capital represented on the advertising pages of these journals closely coincides with those cited by Unger as the most important influence on the shaping of "mercantile opinion" on the "postwar currency question": the "importers and exporters, commission merchants, brokers, and private bankers of New York, Boston, and Phildelphia who handled the country's foreign trade." *Greenback Era*, p. 148.

capital was rapidly developing into a rentier class that primarily lived off income from widely diversified investments. The industrial firms and commercial houses that they owned had reached relative maturity and had begun to throw off capital that could not be readily reinvested in these enterprises. The first consequence of this economic maturity was the deep roots the national banks put down throughout New England and, particularly, Boston as this rentier class poured wealth into the new system. Secondary results included substantial New England involvement in the national stock and bond markets and indirect investment in western real estate mortgages. As the new, rentier class emerged, their deep involvement in the banking system and capital markets produced a strong reform movement within the Republican party that strenuously supported both a removal of economic policy from the political arena and a cleansing of the administrative apparatus of government. Using free-trade proposals, civil service reform, and reestablishment of the gold standard as their primary themes, this class viewed the requirements of the financial system and the political economy from much the same perspective as the major New York journals.[90] Of all the spokesmen for this class, the two most articulate were Edward Atkinson (textile manufacturer, investor in Boston fire insurance companies, and economist) and David Wells, a leading political economist of the late nineteenth century. Wells was appointed chairman of the three-person Revenue Commission by Treasury Secretary McCulloch in 1865 and subsequently

90. Though he generally holds to a more cultural interpretation of the attitudes and positions of this class, Irwin Unger's characterization and identification of the group is largely compatible with the one proposed here. After noting the "puritan background the merchants and manufacturers of New England shared with the reformers," for example, Unger goes on to say "Fortunately, the financial environment of New England and the special advantages of the textile industry permitted the Yankee manufacturer to indulge his sense of duty in a way that was seldom open to other business-men. It must be remembered that unlike iron and steel, cotton textiles – and still more, woolens – had achieved relative maturity by 1870, with its period of most rapid growth and change behind them. The need for new capital was not, therefore, as great in Massachusetts as in Pennsylvania and the West; yet at the same time, New England was better supplied with commercial banks, insurance and trust companies, and savings institutions than was any other part of the country. Accordingly, both long- and short-term interest rates in the Boston money market were among the lowest in the nation, and the section exported capital in large amounts." *Greenback Era*, pp. 144–6; also see, 131–43; Foner, *Reconstruction*, pp. 489,498; Sharkey, *Money, Class, and Party*, p. 60; Michael E. McGerr, "The Meaning of Liberal Republicanism: The Case of Ohio," *Civil War History* 28 (December 1982): 307–323. For a contemporary discussion of the export of New England capital to the West, see the letter from Henry Adams to his brother, Charles Francis Adams, Jr. (dated July 30, 1867) in Levenson et al., eds., *Letters of Henry Adams*, pp. 542–3. The correspondence between the Adams brothers relates in detail the investment decisions of the family and, indirectly, the political and financial concerns that influenced New England rentier capitalists (see pp. 503–74).

served as Special Commissioner of Revenue between 1866 and 1870. Given responsibility in both roles to advise the administration and Congress on revenue and fiscal policy, Wells used his position to articulate in detail the policy recommendations of the reform movement.

Though some minor programmatic differences existed between these two subgroups of the financial community (particularly over the pace with which restructuring of the political economy might proceed), both the journals and the emerging New England rentier class shared a broad, informed perspective on the necessary requirements for the stability and smooth functioning of the financial system. These requirements can be divided into three general policy areas:

1. The financial system itself includes currency, banking structure and credit, treasury debt and operations, and capital markets.
2. Federal revenue includes internal duties, the income tax, and the tariff. These are less central to the financial system, but policy decisions here have important implications for the functioning of the system as a whole.
3. Expenditures and operations of the federal government includes the creation of a civil service, corporate subsidies, and public works projects. Policy decisions here are even less central to the financial system except insofar as they affect the quality of federal operations and revenue requirements.

Operating requirements of the financial system

Though the national banking system rapidly became the most important part of the post–Civil War financial structure, many finance capitalists opposed the system's very creation.[91] In the two years before the end of the war, the senior, money-center banks in New York continued to view

91. In an open letter to members of the New York Clearing-house Association (dated September 23, 1863), the president of one of the banks contended that the new national bank system will create "a thousand banks spread over the whole Continent, initiated and managed, in the majority of cases, by inexperienced men, without saying anything of unprincipled adventurers [accompanied by] frantic speculation and elevation of prices, until some political convulsion, or the mere hint of a return to specie payments, pricking the bubble, the 'system' will collapse, spreading desolation and ruin broad-cast over the land, producing such a scene of financial calamity as shall make all our previous convulsions compare with it as a child's rattle to a whirlwind." Printed in *Hunt's*, October 1863, pp. 290–6; for subsequent clearinghouse policy toward the new national banks, see April 1864, pp. 307–8. On the almost unanimous opposition of the New York banks to the formation of the national bank system, see Myers, *New York Money Market*, pp. 220–1; John Jay Knox, *A History of Banking in the United States* (New York: Bradford Rhodes, 1903; reprinted by Augustus M. Kelley, 1969), pp. 100–1.

their junior national bank brethren with suspicion. This critical evaluation of the system's promise was shared by *Hunt's*, which contended that the new institutions did not appear to conduct "much business beyond the receipt and distribution of the public money" and, in fact, argued that "some of them are mere loan offices, and agents of the government, and will not survive the present borrowing exigencies" of the Treasury.[92]

Several factors account for the early hostility of New York banks to the new national bank system. In the first place, before the war the money-center institutions had largely regulated themselves under New York state law. Banks belonging to the New York Clearing House had imposed even stiffer, additional reserve requirements than the already strict statute required and thus viewed their self-policing autonomy as strengthening the financial system as a whole. Furthermore, while many other states might and, in fact, did enact comparatively lax standards for their banks, New York money-center institutions were free to "throw out" the currency of poorly organized banks and otherwise refuse to associate with them. Under the new national bank system, the financial community feared: (1) a loss of the autonomy that allowed the money-center institutions to police themselves; (2) the imposition of relatively low regulatory standards that would significantly increase instability in the financial system; and (3) the compulsory integration of undercapitalized, weak institutions into the banking system on the same terms as stronger ones. When newly organized or rechartered banks began to join the federal system, the financial community could not help but see the division within their ranks as leading to the worst of all possible worlds, a situation in which the new system would be strong enough to survive but too weak to reform or replace previous arrangements. Financial policy, already almost anarchic, would become even more uncoordinated and chaotic.

Once the prohibitive tax on the currency of state-chartered banks was enacted, however, even the money-center institutions in New York joined the new system and the financial community began to take a proprietary interest in the system's maintenance.[93] Once the recalcitrant state-

92. May 1864, p. 368; June 1864, p. 463; for additional critical commentary, also see, November 1863, p. 389; March 1864, pp. 219–21; July 1864, p. 87; and Simon Newcomb, *A Critical Examination of Our Financial Policy during the Southern Rebellion* (New York: D. Appleton, 1865), p. 222.

93. For examples of the protective attitude *Hunt's* assumed toward the national bank system after 1865, see October 1866, p. 317; November 1867, p. 403. For a succinct account of the changing attitudes of the New York banking community, see David M. Gische, "The New York City Banks and the Development of the National Banking System, 1860–1870," *American Journal of Legal History* 23 (January 1979): 21–67.

chartered banks were effectively prohibited from issuing currency, almost all of them converted to the new system. By this time the original 1863 organizing statute had been strengthened by an 1864 revision and regulatory standards were as high as or higher than the requirements imposed by any state. In regulations intended to keep their assets highly liquid, federal institutions were prohibited from investing in or holding mortgages on real estate aside from property necessary for them to conduct their business.[94] Furthermore, federal regulations governed their organization and capital structure and Treasury examiners required regular reports on financial condition and inspected bank records on the premises. These features of the new system combined with the lucrative return on government bonds, national bank notes, and Treasury deposits to make banking in the federal system both profitable and, compared to the previous state-chartered organization, very secure.[95] As *Hunt's* described the situation in 1867, "our National Banks, if founded on a sound basis and conducted with ordinary ability, could scarcely fail to prove extremely remunerative, and we have yet to hear of the first instance in which any National Bank, organized on real capital, has got into difficulties, except by the misconduct of its servants."[96]

Even after the financial community adopted the national bank system as its own, the structure still possessed serious flaws. The major deficiency was the inelasticity of the currency with respect to the harvest cycle. Ideally, a nation in which agricultural production constituted a large portion of all economic activity should have had a money supply that expanded to meet increased seasonal demand and contracted when demand was slack. Under the gold standard and the state-chartered organization of the banks, currency elasticity was introduced by redemption of bank currency either across the counter or at the window of money-center correspondent banks. Even the currency of the strongest banks had some risk and, rather than hold reserves in the form of the notes of other banks, institutions would trade paper currency for gold. As a result, currency would flow back into the vaults of their issuing banks and, once returned, state banks, particularly those in the country, found it more

94. White, *Money and Banking*, p. 409.
95. Harold G. Moulton, *Financial Organizations and the Economic System* (New York: McGraw-Hill, 1938), pp. 328–34; White, *Money and Banking*, p. 410; for a detailed, comprehensive guide to banking practices, see Albert S. Bolles, *Practical Banking* (New York: Homans, 1885).
96. May 1867, pp. 375–6. *Hunt's*, in fact, felt that "the benefits of the National banks may be purchased at too high a price" and entertained the idea that the banks be compelled to accept, as a partial corrective, a lower yield on government bonds deposited with the Treasury, November 1869, p. 366; also see, January 1870, pp. 10–11; April 1870, pp. 246–9.

difficult to reissue their notes during periods of comparatively low commercial activity in early summer or winter. Thus the currency automatically contracted to meet seasonal fluctuations in demand.

Under the national bank system, greenbacks replaced gold as the form
of money into which notes would be redeemed and the notes themselves
were secured by government bonds. As a result, the solvency of the banks
was no longer a factor in the acceptance of their notes (since the Treasury
deposits guaranteed that the notes would be redeemed if the bank failed).
Furthermore, both the greenbacks and the bank notes were almost equivalent in the sense that both ultimately represented government obligations, the greenbacks directly and the notes indirectly through the bonds
deposited with the Treasury.[97] Greenbacks still had some advantage in
that they could satisfy government reserve requirements, but this marginal
difference was not enough to drive bank notes home during slack
demand.[98]

For these reasons, a redemption mechanism for notes did not emerge
naturally out of the restructuring of the bank system. Both the Treasury
and the financial community recognized the need for such a mechanism
(for one thing, it would discourage the overextension of call loans to the
stock exchange during slack seasons and thus alleviate the danger of
contraction during the spring and fall months), but neither the government nor private bankers desired a government solution.[99] A workable

97. Note that, if the United States had been on a gold standard, greenbacks would have
been redeemable in specie. If, under those conditions, there had been any doubt
concerning the government's ability to honor legal tender notes, bank notes might
have been driven back to their respective issuing institutions in exchange for greenbacks that, in turn, would have been presented to the Treasury for gold. By excluding
this possible distinction, the suspension of specie payments would thus seem to have
reinforced the rough equivalency that existed between greenbacks and bank notes.
98. For a discussion of the interrelated problems of inelasticity, the harvest cycle, and
redemption of bank notes, see Unger, *Greenback Era*, pp. 115–16; Bolles, *Financial
History*, pp. 342–7; Myers, *New York Money Market*, pp. 225–6; Friedman and
Schwartz, *Monetary History*, pp. 20–3; for contemporary discussion of the need for
a redemption center, see *Hunt's*, October 1865, pp. 311–12; November 1865,
pp. 392–3; June 1866, pp. 470–2; October 1866, pp. 316–18; October 1867, p. 289;
December 1868, p. 419; July 1869, p. 38; August 1869, pp. 97–9; June 1870,
pp. 401–4. Myers notes that one of the reasons the money-center institutions did not
actively attempt to redeem currency was a fear that redemption would lead country
banks to withdraw their deposits (p. 404).
99. See, for example, Treasury Secretary McCulloch's letter to a national bank officer in
Philadelphia (dated September 26, 1865), reprinted in *Hunt's*, November 1865,
p. 393; for strong endorsements of the principle of redemption, see the *Annual Report
of the Comptroller of the Currency, 1866*, reprinted in *Hunt's*, December 1866,
pp. 464–6; the *Annual Report of the Comptroller of the Currency, 1867* in *Hunt's*,
December 1867, pp. 466–7; the *Annual Report of the Comptroller of the Currency,
1868* in *Hunt's*, December 1868, p. 460; the *Annual Report of the Comptroller of*

solution to the problem, however, never emerged from proposals to privately organize a redemption center, and the federal government finally established a mechanism in 1874.

An equally serious problem involved the quantity of bank circulation and the regional distribution of note-issuing authority. A stable ceiling on the quantity of currency in circulation was a minimum condition for resumption of the gold standard, a high priority in the financial community for many reasons (see below). At the same time, the devastation wrought by the Civil War left the South almost totally unrepresented in the national banking system, a situation that needed rectification for both financial and political reasons. A politically directed redistribution of banking capacity, however, threatened to upset the "natural" distribution of financial resources. A potential solution to the problem was to allow national bank formation and note issuance to proceed whenever and wherever applicants satisfied regulatory requirements. Because that solution would inflate the supply of bank notes, it was often coupled with proposals to contract greenback circulation. Such proposals, however, faced another hurdle. Because bank notes had to be redeemed in greenbacks (and reserves maintained in that form of money), greenback contraction had obvious limits. As greenbacks became scarce relative to bank notes, the supply of greenbacks would become too small to serve as reserves for bank deposits and circulating notes. Thus, a combination of national bank note expansion with greenback contraction would tend to destabilize the financial system by increasing the likelihood of stringency in the nation's money markets. Because the problems posed by the poor regional distribution of note-issuing authority, resumption of the gold standard, and the relative proportions of greenback and bank note circulation were intricately interwoven, the financial community was extremely wary of a politically imposed reform.

If a ceiling on bank note circulation was maintained, the broader issue of greenback contraction and specie resumption was easier to deal with but still presented serious difficulties. Both the government and the financial community favored a policy of contraction in order to prepare the financial system for resumption. Greenback contraction both reduced the outstanding obligations of the government that would have to be redeemed in specie and, indirectly, encouraged a necessary deflation of the American price structure to levels in line with European states.[100] In

the Currency, 1869 in Hunt's, January 1870, p. 48. As late as 1870, Hunt's was still opposed to a state-centered solution (February 1870, p. 114).

100. Unger, Greenback Era, p. 130; Friedman and Schwartz, Monetary History, pp. 29–44; Hepburn, History of Currency, pp. 207–13.

his *Annual Report* for 1865, Secretary McCulloch noted that "the conservative bankers of the country are quite unanimously in favor of a curtailment of the currency, with a view to an early return to specie payments," and he announced that contraction would proceed with that goal in mind. In one of his reports in 1866, Revenue Commissioner David Wells similarly called for "contraction, pure and simple, without artifice or indirection." The secretary single-mindedly pursued his program and, as a consequence, clumsily aggravated seasonal stringency in the money market for several years running. Fearing recession or worse, Congress ended the secretary's program with a flat suspension on further contraction. Trying to put the best interpretation on this legislative setback, *Hunt's* argued that "Congress intended . . . to forbid the abuses of contraction rather than to stop contraction itself or to condemn the country forever to the miseries of a redundant, depreciated, irredeemable circulation."[101]

Throughout the postwar period the financial community sought a solution to the greenback problem. Possible answers had to satisfy several requirements. On the one hand, the Treasury could not be depended upon if the government was assigned a major discretionary role in contraction. The experience with McCulloch's heavy-handed withdrawal was enough to convince most objective observers that such a path to resumption held more risk than reward. Without positive action by the Treasury, however, a workable contraction policy was almost impossible to devise. Although greenbacks would automatically collect in government vaults as a result of the chronic budgetary surplus, the Treasury had to release most of them back into circulation to prevent financial collapse. Furthermore, this release had to be synchronized with the harvest cycle in such a way as to deeply involve the Treasury in the currency supply even in the absence of a long-term contraction policy. Thus a workable contraction policy appeared to combine preservation of the government's ability to moderate seasonal stringency through temporary intervention with a slow, predictable reduction of the currency over the long term.

With these considerations in mind, *Hunt's* had welcomed the limit of $4 million per month placed on the rate of contraction by Congress in

101. The passage taken from the 1866 *Annual Report of the Secretary of the Treasury* was reprinted in *Hunt's*, January 1866, pp. 64–5; also see Ferleger, *Wells*, p. 38; *Hunt's*, December 1868, p. 421; for a summary of congressional debate and Treasury operations from 1865 to 1869, see Bolles, *Financial History*, pp. 263–82; for the text of the "Act to Suspend Further Reduction of the Currency: February 4, 1868," see Charles F. Dunbar, *Laws of the United States Relating to Currency, Finance and Banking from 1789 to 1896* (Boston: Ginn, 1897; reprinted by Augustus M. Kelley, 1969), p. 201.

1866: "Contraction of the currency is necessary. But to contract violently is impossible. To make the leap at once would engulf the whole country in bankruptcy.... The right way is to diminish the volume of our circulating money by slow degrees."[102] Several years later, the journal recommended that further contraction be postponed for a year and suggested a long-term program of permanently retiring mutilated or worn out greenbacks (rather than replacing them in circulation). Such a policy "would produce an imperceptible contraction, which would frighten nobody, and yet would have a great effect on the value of the currency within two or three years."[103]

Another possibility was to allow economic activity to "grow up" to the currency. By retaining a ceiling on greenbacks and national bank notes, economic expansion would gradually deflate the domestic price structure to a point where resumption of specie payments would be possible.[104] The rapid pace of northern industrial development and western settlement made this alternative attractive. In addition, as the South reentered the economic system, the region absorbed vast quantities of bank notes and greenbacks.[105] Much of the currency sent into the states of the former Confederacy failed to return North until utterly worn out from use. Several factors explain the South's heavy reliance on cash. First, in the absence of banking facilities, much of the population hoarded currency as a means of savings and transacted business in cash that in the North might have been done by check. As the southern economy began its slow recovery from the war, cash flowed into the region and was captured either in these hoards or in indigenous circulation. Perhaps even more important was the change wrought by the war in the way the economy was organized. As *Hunt's* observed, the former slave population "being no longer fed and clothed by the planter with goods obtained on credit and paid for in cotton, but hired on wages which they individually

102. October 1866, p. 269; also see, Unger, *Greenback Era*, pp. 159–61; Sharkey, *Money, Class, and Party*, pp. 244–5.
103. May 1870, p. 373.
104. Currency is only one component in the national money supply and, although a ceiling on currency circulation had an indirect impact on other components such as bank deposits and reserves, a ceiling in and of itself would not necessarily combine with economic expansion to produce deflation in the price structure. See, for example, Timberlake, *Origins of Central Banking*, p. 118; for the reasons why a ceiling on circulation tended to have a deflationary effect in the post–Civil War years, see Friedman and Schwartz, *Monetary History*, pp. 50–8.
105. Pacification of the South promoted the resumption of specie payments by increasing cotton harvests (and thus foreign exchange earnings) and by expanding economic activity in the former states of the Confederacy (and thus expanding the volume of transactions in which greenbacks were used). George L. Anderson, "The South and Problems of Post–Civil War Finance," *Journal of Southern History* 9 (May 1943): 186–7.

expend, now handle a large amount of currency in the aggregate. In fact, nearly the whole business of the South has been changed from a system of credit and barter into one of exchanges of commodities effected through a circulating medium."[106] Though a much slower process than other paths to resumption, this passive reliance on economic expansion and growing southern involvement in cash markets would reach that goal without additional Treasury activity. Given the hazards associated with overt governmental intervention and the political opposition to any retirement of greenbacks then in circulation, many members of the financial community viewed the natural deflation associated with economic growth as an effective substitute. This process more or less describes how resumption was in fact achieved.[107]

Aside from the contraction question, the greenback currency posed several additional issues. Greenbacks owed their initial acceptance by the public to the fact that they were made a legal tender for almost all public and private obligations. In 1870, the Supreme Court ruled that the currency was not legal tender for obligations and contracts made before the Civil War broke out.[108] Noting that the decision would probably place at least $350 million in state, municipal, and railroad bonds on a specie-paying basis as well as potentially requiring prewar deposits and insurance policies to be paid in gold, the major financial journals welcomed the development as a major step toward resumption and as a sensible constraint on federal authority over private contracts.[109] A year later, the Supreme Court reversed its previous decision in what the *Chronicle* termed "beyond question one of the most deplorable events in American history." The journal noted that the appointment of two new justices by President Grant had made reversal possible and asserted that the new members of the court were "well known as members and counsel of great railway corporations ... [and] were known to have formed and expressed an opinion adverse to the recent decision of the Court" before they were elevated to the bench. Since the railroads that had previously employed these justices owed large sums of prewar debt that could, under the legal

---

106. March 1870, p. 173; also see, May 1869, p. 388; July 1869, pp. 39–40, 46; August 1869, p. 153; September 1869, pp. 167, 178.
107. Friedman and Schwartz, *Monetary History,* p. 81; Timberlake, *Origins of Central Banking,* p. 89; for a contemporary endorsement of this strategy, see *Chronicle,* July 8, 1871, p. 38.
108. As Secretary of the Treasury, Samuel Chase had recommended passage of the Legal Tender Act in 1862. As Chief Justice of the Supreme Court, Chase wrote the opinion in *Hepburn v. Griswold* that ruled his earlier proposal, at least in part, unconstitutional.
109. See, for example, *Hunt's* March 1870, pp. 161–5; May 1870, pp. 327–8; also, Bolles, *Financial History,* pp. 251–62.

tender act, be repaid in depreciated greenbacks, the *Chronicle* argued that corporate interests had tainted the court's second decision.[110]

In addition to constraining governmental power generally, the financial community wanted to use the Supreme Court's original legal tender decision to enable the enforcement of specie-based contracts. While such contracts, specifying payment in gold, were already being made, they were not enforceable in federal courts as long as the legal tender act was in effect. In keeping with its rather jaundiced view of the impact of government policies on economic stability, finance capital consistently favored the removal of private contracts from a dependence on the ever-fluctuating value of the Union greenback.

Besides greenback contraction and resumption, the other major fiscal problem facing the financial community was the large bonded indebtedness of the government. On this issue, David Wells represented the views of finance capital when he urged that budgetary surpluses be dedicated first to the simplification and reduction of the revenue structure, then to a contraction of the paper currency preparatory to resumption, and only last to a reduction of the bonded debt.[111] After the war ended, Treasury policy went through two phases. In the first, the government undertook the consolidation of a large variety of short-term notes, bonds, and certificates of indebtedness into bonds with medium-term maturities. This phase was largely finished by 1868 and the Treasury subsequently moved to refund the outstanding debt in long-term bonds with substantially lower rates of interest. Since these bonds would be attractive to potential purchasers only if the United States were to resume the gold standard before the bonds matured, the success of the refunding program was linked to progress toward resumption (not achieved until 1879). As a result, refunding went very slowly and was not finished until after Reconstruction had ended.[112] The financial community consistently criticized the government for retiring too many bonds (and not enough greenbacks), for purchasing bonds at the wrong time of the year, and for prematurely attempting a major restructuring of the debt. On all of these issues, financiers generally viewed fiscal policy from a much longer time perspective than did government agents.

Resumption of the gold standard

The most serious deficiency in the workings of the postwar financial system was the paper money standard upon which the domestic economy

110. May 6, 1871, pp. 551–3.
111. Ferleger, *Wells*, pp. 39–40.
112. Patterson, *Federal Debt-Management Policies*, p. 5.

operated. While some advantages could be traced to the use of green-backs, the liabilities far outweighed the assets. For one thing, the green-back system compelled the Treasury to conduct open-market operations for which the department had neither the talent nor, it appeared at times, the inclination. After appraising the destabilizing potential of Treasury operations and focusing on the systemic requirements of the money market, finance capitalists thus endorsed the gold standard as a means of insulating the financial system from the good intentions of Treasury secretaries who were little more than party hacks.[113]

Resumption of the gold standard was an antistatist development for several reasons. In the first place, the monetary regime imposed by specie payments placed control over the supply of currency beyond the reach of the central state. The amount of money in circulation changed as the nation's trade position in the world economy was altered through the import and export of goods and capital investment. As compensation for trade deficits and surpluses, gold flowed out of or into the domestic economy and thus altered the supply of money without government action. In contrast, a paper standard in domestic transactions within an international economy based on gold was equivalent to a system of floating exchange rates in which the currency supply was under the direct control of the central government.[114]

Resumption of the gold standard was not a statist development in another, related respect. Resumption of specie payments would expose the domestic economy to the exogenous impact of specie flows in the

113. For a general exploration of the debilitating effect of patronage and party politics on state development, see Stephen Skowronek, *Building a New American State: The Expansion of National Administrative Capacities, 1877–1920* (New York: Cambridge University Press, 1982).

114. Friedman and Schwartz, *Monetary History*, pp. 51–2. The international gold standard that prevailed in the world economy between 1821 and 1931 was not the unilateral creation of any one nation. Instead, the system depended on conditions beyond the control of any state as well as the facilitating action of individual governments. Anna Schwartz, for example, suggests factors that made the international gold standard possible: "1. the essentially fixed price of gold over the century [1821–1931]; 2. a link between domestic money supply and the gold reserve; 3. relative stability in conditions of gold production; 4. equilibrium in mint pars among gold standard countries; 5. coordination of economic policies among countries adhering to the standard; 6. limited role of government in economic and social affairs; 7. relative absence of political upheavals exemplified by war and revolution and the role of London as the hub of the international monetary system... England – the world's largest trading nation, the center of the world's commodities markets and of the world's gold market, and the world's leading creditor nation – played a central role differing from that of other countries." "Introduction" to Bordo and Schwartz, *Retrospective*, p. 1, 16. In short, governments could choose to adhere to an international gold standard if one existed but no nation or group of nations could create the system if world conditions were unfavorable. As an alternative, a paper system was always available to any nation through unilateral action.

larger, world system and, indirectly, to the potential influence of the leading economic power (in this case, Britain). Adherence to a gold standard might be state-enhancing for the leading economic power in that a marginal increase in that state's ability to influence economic conditions in other nations might compensate for a major loss of direct control over the domestic economy.[115] In such cases, adherence could plausibly be a statist feature of the treasury operations of a major power. For all nations other than the market center, however, specie payments significantly circumscribed economic autonomy within the world system. For the United States, this meant allowing Britain to play a role in determining American economic conditions.

Finance capitalists were not reluctant to expose the American economy to a gold-based international order for several reasons. For one, the British political system was widely admired as a more sophisticated and mature state than the younger and more democratic U.S. government. To the extent that resumption would transfer power from the United States to the United Kingdom, financiers expected better results from the systemic orientation of the Bank of England than the haphazard and poorly executed policies of the U.S. Treasury. Closer to home, that large fraction of the financial community engaged in the management of the nation's export/import trade strongly preferred a gold standard for more practical reasons. An autonomous paper system made trade operations far more complicated and entailed greater risk than an integrated gold standard because merchants were continually forced to translate greenbacks into British sterling and back again in order to complete foreign transactions. In order to hedge their operating margin against changes in the exchange rate, they also became heavily involved in the sometimes volatile futures market of the gold exchange. If the United States resumed specie payments, such operations would become unnecessary.[116]

Finance capitalists possessed several other plausible, self-interested reasons for supporting resumption. Many of them held large creditor positions in the economy and would benefit from a program of deflation. Investors with large holdings of long-term bonds were well situated in this respect. Stockholders in the national banks, with their illiquid deposits of government bonds in the Treasury vaults, were even more committed to deflation than other creditors. These interests were strongly represented in the financial community and may have been a decisive

115. For a good discussion of British monetary policy under the international gold standard, see John Dutton, "The Bank of England and the Rules of the Game under the International Gold Standard: New Evidence," in Bordo and Schwartz, *Retrospective,* pp. 173–95.
116. Unger, *Greenback Era,* pp. 149–53; also see, *Hunt's,* November 1869, pp. 371–4.

factor in preventing a simple devaluation of the currency (as a short-cut to specie payments that would have eliminated the need for radical deflation).[117] Even so, most members of the financial community did not depend on passive, long-term investments for their livelihood, and resumption thus carried little promise of material gain in the form of capital appreciation. Instead, their income came from the rapid exchange of one kind of financial asset for another in which their return arose out of commissions or speculative profits. Within the frenetic, high-risk markets in which these finance capitalists operated, systemic stability was a much more important consideration in their support for resumption than capital appreciation.

An equally plausible motive, at least on its face, might have been that the financial community sought power and influence through resumption. Two major caveats to this interpretation immediately surface from this analysis. First, the discretionary authority assigned to the Treasury under the greenback system disappeared, upon resumption, into market processes that individual financiers participated in but did not control. Furthermore, resumption entailed some transfer of influence from the United States to the Bank of England, an institution even more remote from the American financial community than was the Treasury. In sum, while the Treasury lost influence over the money market under resumption, that influence did not flow into the hands of finance capital. Finance capitalists opposed Treasury influence over the money market not because they wanted that power for themselves but because the government was not up to the task.

While finance capital favored a return to the gold standard, resumption had to be the end result of a gradual process of incremental institutional adjustments.[118] A path to resumption that would not threaten the stability of the financial system would, under ideal conditions, follow four distinct policies. First off, the gold-denominated debt with relatively long-term maturities should be left alone. Aside from the consolidation of short-term and greenback-denominated securities into longer term gold bonds,

117. As Richard Timberlake points out, the mint value of the American dollar could have been reduced from the prewar value (against British sterling) to the level prevailing at the end of the war (after suspension and subsequent inflation). *Origins of Central Banking,* p. 89. Friedman and Schwartz similarly contend that a partial devaluation would have been preferable to the policy actually followed. *Monetary History,* p. 82, n. 95. Such a reduction would have allowed the immediate resumption of specie payments but would have also drastically reduced the gold value of the principal and interest on all outstanding dollar-denominated securities. For this reason, it appears that devaluation was never actively considered as a resumption strategy.
118. See, for example, President Grant's message to Congress in December 1869, reprinted in part in Hepburn, *History of Currency,* pp. 215–16, and *Hunt's* approving commentary, January 1870, pp. 12–13.

the debt should not be reduced or refunded. In addition, contracts specifying payment in gold should become legally binding in the courts. This reform would stabilize many transactions by giving them a specie basis even before resumption.

As a third supporting policy, the national banks should be compelled to redeem their notes in one or more of the country's financial centers. One proposal was to compel New York banks holding country bank deposits to redeem bank notes paid to the government as taxes. Other suggestions included private or government organization of a redemption agency. The last programmatic requirement was for an automatic and gradual contraction of greenback circulation. The most widely cited proposal was for the partial replacement of existing greenbacks with a new issue bearing a low rate of interest. As these issues matured, they would be gradually hoarded and taken out of circulation because they would become worth more than their face value. A wide consensus considered both a rapid reduction of greenbacks and active government direction of contraction dangerous alternatives to the status quo.[119] Even momentary reflection on these policy recommendations reveals how far the financial community was from preferring immediate resumption and how much more complex their position was than a simple interpretation of resumption as a policy intended to deflate the currency and thus favor the interests of creditors.[120]

Federal tax structure and revenue collection

Though the financial community put forward detailed and theoretically developed proposals for reform of the national tax structure and modes of revenue collection, these issues were only tangentially related to the primary political-economic requirements of the financial system. Though a massive force in the economy, the revenue machinery moved slowly and rarely threatened financial stability. On the other hand, a poorly designed tax structure could hinder economic expansion and even throw the government budget into deficit. As most finance capitalists viewed the postwar situation, the tax structure needed reform but could be tolerated as it was.

The general operating requirements of the financial system placed sev-

119. For a good summary of the four points of this program, see an article by George S. Coe, president of the American Exchange National Bank of New York, in *Hunt's*, December 1868, pp. 418–20.
120. Both Unger in the *Greenback Era* and Sharkey in *Money, Class, and Party* describe the politics of resumption as primarily a struggle between debtors and creditors in which financial stability was almost never an issue.

eral broad demands on the tax structure. Most important, the tax system had to extract enough revenue to produce regular surpluses in the federal budget. As we have seen, these surpluses facilitated the Treasury's countercyclical purchases in the bond market by allowing the Treasury to pump greenbacks into financial markets during the annual harvest and spring contractions. Surpluses also tended to support the government's credit in both domestic and foreign markets by giving evidence of the American state's ability to service the national debt. Finally, budgetary surpluses enabled progress toward resumption by permitting the Treasury to retire (and thus contract) the pool of greenbacks that would otherwise have to be redeemed in gold once the gold standard was resumed. Extraordinarily large surpluses, however, were potentially destabilizing because they imposed a serious drag on economic growth and required extensive Treasury intervention in the money market in order to dispose of vault cash and specie. Since the postwar revenue system was producing huge surpluses over government expenditures, one of the primary priorities of finance capital was to cut taxes.

Reductions were proposed in each of the three components of the revenue structure: the internal revenue system, the income tax (technically a part of internal revenue but sufficiently distinct to be treated separately), and the tariff. The hundreds of licensing fees, revenue stamps, and excise charges that were established under the internal revenue acts of 1862 and 1864 survived the war.[121] Most of these levies cost more to enforce than they brought into the Treasury and one of the first reforms proposed was to drastically simplify the system by consolidating the structure around "luxury" taxes on distilled spirits, fermented liquor, and tobacco.[122]

Alcohol taxes, however, were already very high and the revenue collectors were so easily corrupted that "in districts having honest officials, whiskey distillation almost ceased, while in the large cities, where it was easy to conduct the business in a dishonest manner, the number of distillers 'wonderfully increased.' " As a result, fraud and evasion greatly reduced actual revenue from potential collections and spokesmen for the financial community, David Wells most prominent among them, called

121. For a good summary of the internal revenue schedule, see *National Almanac, 1864* (Philadelphia: George Childs, 1864), pp. 90–107.

122. Ferleger, *Wells*, pp. 35, 38–9, 52–72; *Hunt's*, February 1868, p. 113; September 1869, p. 177; *Chronicle*, August 26, 1871, p. 263; for a general review of the period, see Bolles, *Financial History*, pp. 398–444. While the elimination of most taxes was strongly favored by the financial community, the permanent renunciation of the right to tax was not. See, for example, *Hunt's* condemnation of a proposal to renounce federal taxing authority over income from Treasury bonds as the product of "a very dangerous principle" (January 1868, p. 24–5).

for a "scientific" reduction of levies (to encourage compliance), civil service reform of appointments of revenue officers, and a reduction in the "army of officials" then enforcing the large number of unnecessary, "mischievous" taxes. When alcohol taxes were reduced in 1868, revenue from this source in fact increased.[123]

The tariff provided the gold with which the Treasury paid interest on the national debt and also, when reduced to a greenback basis, produced more than half (51 percent) of all federal revenue between 1865 and 1871.[124] While customs collections had to be maintained, the greater part of the tariff schedule produced little or no net revenue to the government. David Wells, for example, estimated that two-thirds of the items subject to duty could be placed on the free list without substantially impairing revenue. As was the case with internal revenue, financial community spokesmen recommended a consolidation of collections around the relatively few goods (such as coffee and sugar) that produced the bulk of the revenue. This orientation made many finance capitalists indifferent or hostile to protectionism, which they viewed as unjustified by industrial conditions and as an obstruction to the natural flow of trade.[125] In taking this position, the financial community again opposed the expansion of central state capacity by constraining the government's ability to reshape the domestic economy.[126] The free-trade policy they supported exposed national development to the trade patterns and commercial pressures of the world economy.

Federal operations and expenditures

For reasons that can be traced to both the Treasury's blunders in money market operations and inefficient, often fraudulent revenue collection,

123. Bolles, *Financial History*, p. 419, 421; *Chronicle*, August 26, 1871, p. 263; Ferleger, *Wells*, pp. 113–14.
124. Calculated from quarterly data on collections in Paul B. Trescott, "Federal Government Receipts and Expenditures, 1861–1875," *Journal of Economic History* 26 (June 1966): 212–13.
125. Ferleger, *Wells*, pp. 270–3; *Hunt's*, February 1866, p. 94; also see, June 1870, p. 425.
126. As was the case with resumption, the antistatist orientation of finance capital reflected a general lack of confidence in the government (though, because tariff schedules were written in Congress, the legislature – not the Treasury – drew criticism). See, for example, this passage from *Hunt's*: "To read some of the [congressional] debates on the pending tariff bill no man would suspect that either the people at large or the Treasury had any concern in taxation. The pig-iron furnaces, the sheep-raisers, the cotton and woolen mills, the shipping trade, the salt, coal, lead, and copper miners, and the theorists upon free trade and protection, all have their representatives ..." (May 1870, p. 373); for a similar interpretation of postwar tariff politics, see Ferleger, *Wells*, pp. 129–82.

finance capital almost unanimously supported civil service reform of government appointments. As the *Commercial and Financial Chronicle* explained:

> A place in the Custom House or in the Internal Revenue is too often given as a reward to some useful political tool who wants an office because he will not or cannot get his living by ordinary business ... we give to these officers so selected by this faulty method, as much discretion, as much power over the purse of the citizen and the revenue of the Government, as if they were the most honest of men. Indeed we give them so much discretion, we confide in them so large a measure of power, that if they were honest at the start they would be very likely to get corrupted by the greed and insolence, the opportunities and immunity of office.[127]

This strong opposition to patronage appointment put financiers in open conflict with one of the paramount needs of the Republican party as a political organization.

Another source of conflict with the party was the financial community's insistence on "the most rigid economy in every department of governmental administration." A general retrenchment of expenditures promised to both further secure the budgetary surpluses of the postwar years and allow, at the same time, a reduction and simplification of the tax structure. With those goals in mind, finance journals and other spokesmen proposed that Congress and the administration turn a "deaf ear" to projects involving land "grants to railroads under any conditions whatever," subsidization of steamship companies, "bounties" to Civil War veterans, purchases of foreign territory (such as Alaska), expansion of civil employment (reductions were indicated here), military spending (reductions indicated here, too), and rivers and harbors improvement.[128]

Though difficult to attribute directly to the operating requirements of the financial system, this blanket condemnation of central state activity can be traced to the negative fiscal implications of growing federal expenditures, the constraining effect of taxation on economic expansion, and the lack of integrity and competence of many civil employees. In general, the political-economic requirements of the financial system added up to something close to a classically liberal economic philosophy of free trade, open markets, and a central state of distinctly limited powers.[129] The most significant exceptions to this regimen involved facilitating state

127.   August 23, 1873, p. 239; also see, Ferleger, *Wells*, p. 41.
128.   *Hunt's*, August 1869, p. 128; December 1869, pp. 440–1; *Chronicle*, November 25, 1871, p. 685; July 29, 1876, pp. 99–100; Ferleger, *Wells*, pp. 40, 75–7, 108.
129.   For a parallel, more cultural interpretation, see Unger, *Greenback Era*, p. 138.

intervention in the workings of the financial system itself: the regulatory direction of the national bank system, prospective resumption of the gold standard, and the distinctly mixed blessing of countercyclical operations in the money market.

During Reconstruction, finance capital was forced to contemplate a relatively primitive central state that was little more than an extension of the political party that had enabled it to survive the Civil War. The federal government did not possess the administrative capacity to manage the interests of finance capital or maintain the financial system. Such tasks, later to be seen by some scholars as the functional characteristics of a mature "capitalist state," were not associated with the federal government in the postwar years. In the latter part of the nineteenth century, individuals who could conceive of tax revenue as the extraction of surplus from the production process or as an income stream dependent on the state-managed health of the capitalist economy almost universally considered the federal government incapable of actively promoting economic development. Given the reality they faced, this conclusion underpinned an entirely rational and well-considered interpretation of the operating requirements of the financial system.

Thus radical reconstruction of the South can be interpreted as antithetical to the contemporary interests of finance capital for a number of reasons. First, radical proposals promised the postponement of a pacification of the plantation economy which was essential to the reestablishment of cotton production (which, in turn, was essential to specie importation through foreign exchange operations). Second, a moderate to high level of government expenditures was a necessary requirement for cohesion within the Republican coalition. Since the party was the political agent of Reconstruction, survival of the Republican coalition was essential to reorganization of the southern political economy. Thus, an active Reconstruction policy expanded the fiscal requirements of the state in two ways: directly by requiring spending for military administration and subsidization of loyal elements in the South and indirectly by requiring spending for benefits to important elements of the national Republican coalition, such as federally financed projects for internal development, political patronage created by federal employment, and direct subsidization of railroad expansion.

These fiscal requirements, in turn, both retarded the dismantling of the internal revenue system created during the Civil War and postponed resumption of the gold standard. Although the Republican party sought to reconcile these goals with Reconstruction policy, the party's success in maintaining its coalition was accompanied by policy failure; radical

efforts to reconstruct the South had largely collapsed by 1871 and the
gold standard was not resumed until 1879. But in order to connect the
politics of Reconstruction and resumption of the gold standard, we now
turn to examination of the ways in which finance policy and Reconstruction were linked in congressional decision making.

5

Legislation, the Republican party, and finance capital during Reconstruction

Reconstruction failed for several broadly related reasons. Perhaps most important, internal contradictions within the Republican coalition emerged as the various wings of the party both achieved their prewar goals and pressed for additional policy concessions in the postwar period. As the interests of the different factions diverged, the party lost the revolutionary zeal that had attended its role as the agent of Union survival and increasingly became a broker organization within which political allies narrowly construed their interests. Factional infighting in the Reconstruction period also made the loyalty of each group to the Republican party more contingent upon the realization of their programmatic goals. In this new political environment, none of the major factions had a direct interest in radical Reconstruction save southern Republicans. Even the latter backed radical policies only as long as there existed some possibility that the national government might back up their tenuous hold on the South. As northern support for Reconstruction waned, however, even these southern Republicans sought their own separate accommodation with former Confederate nationalists.

The establishment of an indigenous loyalist group within the bounds of the Confederacy presented a dilemma for the Republicans from which they never escaped. On the one hand, the freedman could successfully resist resurgent Confederate nationalists only if a thorough redistribution of southern wealth made blacks economically independent of white plantation owners and merchants. On the other hand, state-sponsored confiscation of land owned by Confederate nationalists threatened to create new, even wider class challenges to property rights. These challenges might spread to southern white yeomen and northern workers as the latter groups realized that the state might also redistribute wealth into their hands as well as those of freedmen. To avoid both abandoning freedmen and aggravating wider class cleavages, the Republican party ultimately relied on military occupation as the major prop for southern loyalists, a solution that would have been workable only if the state had permanently committed much larger forces to its attainment (see Chapter 6).

Both the fragmentation of the Republican party and the failure to establish the economic and political independence of freedmen eventually provoked widespread opposition to radical Reconstruction policies. Because of their interests in financial stability, the resumption of the gold standard, the reestablishment of cotton cultivation, and the administrative capacity of the Treasury, finance capitalists became the Republican faction most hostile to continued federal intervention in the southern political system.[1] Against their opposition, southern Republicans and a dwindling number of radical Northerners were just no match. In the dismantling of Reconstruction, military administration of the South rapidly became little more than another arena in which factional interests were adjusted and compromised. In the process, the problem of per-

---

1. The historical literature on the postwar path to resumption of the gold standard tends to see the period as defined by financial and monetary policy questions, particularly those concerning legal tender notes (greenbacks). The literature on Reconstruction, on the other hand, interprets the postwar period as one dominated by questions of sectional reconciliation and the political impact of southern white resurgence in the South. The argument of this chapter attempts to integrate these two "eras," coterminous in time yet separately interpreted in history, within a state-centered political-economic framework. The most recent, comprehensive treatment of Reconstruction is Eric Foner's *Reconstruction: America's Unfinished Revolution, 1863–1877* (New York: Harper & Row, 1988). Foner recognizes the importance of financial policy as an oblique and divisive influence on Republican party cohesion and, thus, on the trajectory of Reconstruction. However, in his interpretation, financial issues are largely confined to currency questions, which are not integrated into his description of Reconstruction as a political process. See Foner, pp. 311, 478, 487, 489, 521–3, and 557. Earlier, Robert P. Sharkey proposed that "high protectionist"/"soft money" attitudes were closely correlated with "radical" Republicanism but did not clearly explain why this would be the case or present much evidence that the relationship held in congressional decision making. *Money, Class, and Party: An Economic Study of Civil War and Reconstruction* (Baltimore: Johns Hopkins University Press, 1967). Though critical of Sharkey's conclusions, Michael Les Benedict briefly suggests a similar connection but does not elaborate. *A Compromise of Principle: Congressional Republicans and Reconstruction, 1863–1869* (New York: W. W. Norton, 1974), pp. 48–56, 262–5, and 275–6. The most influential work from the currency perspective, Irwin Unger's *The Greenback Era: A Social and Political History of American Finance, 1865–1879* (Princeton, N.J.: Princeton University Press, 1964), almost entirely ignores the swirling politics of Reconstruction in an otherwise comprehensive interpretation of the period. While presenting superficially differing interpretive approachs, both the Unger and Sharkey works on Reconstruction monetary policy articulate positions generally consistent with those put forward here. When Unger accused Sharkey of "economic determinism," the latter replied, accurately, that their two interpretations were much closer than Unger allowed: "While admitting the importance and even fascination of ideas and ethics, I would argue that Professor Unger has shown few if any cases where these have diverged from actual economic interests." See Unger, *Greenback Era*, pp. 3–9, and Sharkey, *Money, Class, and Party*, pp. 11–12, 290–311.

manently establishing an indigenous loyalist group within the South – a broad statist goal connected to the conflation of party and state during the war – was transformed into mere tactics by which the resurgence of former Confederate nationalists in regional and national politics was to be postponed.

The characterization of the political landscape presented in this chapter is based on a few simple assumptions concerning congressional behavior. These assumptions concern the way in which congressmen representing different types of districts were sensitive to the pressure of local elites or subject to mass-based electoral influence, both arising out of their districts' relative position in the larger political economy. The accuracy with which these assumptions actually describe congressional behavior is subsequently examined with reference to a representative selection of legislative decisions on major financial issues (including separate analyses of revenue and expenditure policy). From this evidence, a general interpretation of the role of finance capital in shaping Republican party politics is suggested and related to the failure of Reconstruction. Because serious efforts to remake the southern political economy largely ceased by 1871 (some would say even earlier), this investigation is limited to the Thirty-ninth, Fortieth, and Forty-first Congresses (1865–71).[2]

Major sectors in the Reconstruction political economy

During the six years following the end of the Civil War, the American political system continued to be rent by massive cleavages that threatened the very foundations of national unity. The deepest division remained that separating the former slave states, both Confederate and border, from the North. The southern regions of the nation occupied a unique position in the political economy in at least three respects: (1) the presence of a large separatist population that remained unreconciled to federal sovereignty and operated to some extent outside the confines of routine electoral practice; (2) the plantation regime that, through the cultivation of cotton, produced most of American exports in international trade; and (3) a war-devastated economy that, despite some recovery, remained a stagnant, peripheral region in the American system. Although military occupation and dependence on federal protection significantly softened the opposition of southern and border Republicans, the region rapidly

---

2. In his thorough treatment of the impact of southern Reconstruction on national politics, Terry L. Seip observes, "The fate of southern Republicans was probably sealed with the [Reconstruction] plan adopted in 1867." *The South Returns to Congress: Men, Economic Measures, and Intersectional Relationships, 1868–1879* (Baton Rouge: Louisiana State University Press, 1983), p. 275.

reassumed a national position as the major antagonist of the northern Republican party.[3]

Northern Republicans were themselves seriously divided by rifts that paralleled major fractures in the nation's political economy. When Treasury Secretary McCulloch appointed a three-person commission to study federal revenue policy, for example, he insisted that the "different sections be represented as far as practicable." The first person he recruited, David Wells, represented the rentier capitalists and textile manufacturers of Massachusetts. The second was Stephen Colwell, a Pennsylvania iron manufacturer and ardent protectionist. The last appointment, chosen in opposition to Wells's preference for an exclusively eastern panel, was a western agrarian Democrat from Illinois, Samuel Hayes.[4] McCulloch's attempt to balance the commission reflected political reality, the division of the northern political economy into major sectors composed of finance capital, tariff-sensitive industrial manufacturers, and rapidly expanding agrarian settlements in the West. These were the interests that contested most consistently and powerfully for control over the financial policy of the central government. While the three sectors overlapped to some extent and some regions possessed a mixed economic base not closely associated with any of the three, most congressional districts can easily be placed into a theoretical framework based on these distinctions.

The central concern of the financial community was the stability and smooth workings of the New York money market. That market involved the nexus between the mobilization of capital (as exemplified by the national bank system) and the transformation of liquid capital into fixed investment (as exemplified by the stock exchange). A second nexus connected foreign trade and capital flow in the world economy to domestic commerce, including the conversion of transactions based on the American paper system into the international gold standard. Within the financial community, the most broad-based, organized group was composed of the officers and shareholders of the national bank system. Estimated at over 200,000 in number by the comptroller of the currency, these financiers controlled over one-quarter of the entire public and private debt of the United States in 1866. In 1869, these banking institutions formed a national association in order to facilitate the development of a common program and a coordinated response to increasing inflationary

3. For an extensive discussion of the conflicting partisan and economic interests that made congressional policy choices so difficult for southern Republicans during Reconstruction, see Seip, *South Returns to Congress*, pp. 136–294.
4. Herbert Ronald Ferleger, *David A. Wells and the American Revenue System, 1865–1870* (New York: Private printing, 1942; reprinted Philadelphia: Porcupine Press, 1977), pp. 22–8; for a more recent tripartite interpretation of the Reconstruction era political economy, see John G. Sprout, *The Best Men: Liberal Reformers in the Gilded Age* (New York: Oxford University Press, 1968), p. 171.

sentiment in the larger political system. In recognition of their central role within the financial community and the Republican party, the presence of national banks has been used in this analysis as the defining characteristic in the designation of individual congressional districts as potentially susceptible to the influence of finance capital. More exactly, districts have been distinguished by their respective per capita shares of the note circulation issued to national banks in 1869.[5]

Tariff-sensitive industrial manufacturers were of comparable importance in the making of postwar financial policy. While some agricultural producers (notably wool growers) and a wide variety of manufacturing interests benefited from the tariff, the most important group was composed of iron and steel manufacturers. These producers, particularly those from Pennsylvania, played a crucial role in the emergence of the Republican party as a national organization. The congressional representatives of Pennsylvania "iron-men" were, for example, a decisive force in the election of the Republican candidate in the 1859–60 speakership fight in the House of Representatives (see Chapter 2). After winning a protectionist plank in the platform, Pennsylvania sided with the Republicans in the election of Lincoln to the presidency. Subsequently, when the party enacted the Morrill tariff in 1861, Pennsylvania iron producers were the measure's most active proponents and visible beneficiaries.[6] In postwar tariff controversies Pennsylvania iron producers and their representatives played such a pivotal role that the state's very name became synonomous with protectionism.[7]

The impact of this tariff protection conferred upon domestic iron and

5. The 1869 data reflect the stable distribution of notes following the rapid conversion of state banks to the national system in 1865 and subsequent, lagging issuance of notes by the Treasury. Circulation, rather than capital, was used because notes were secured by government bonds deposited in the Treasury. These bonds were thus illiquid investments and tied the banks directly to the success of federal fiscal policy. While national bank circulation has the strong advantages of comparability and accuracy (Treasury records of bond deposits were among the best kept accounts in the nation), the characteristic does not directly represent other groups within the financial community (such as import/export houses).
6. The 1860 platform plank read, in part, "while providing revenue for the support of the general government by duties upon imports, sound policy requires such an adjustment of these imports to encourage the development of the industrial interest of the whole country." Albert S. Bolles, *Financial History of the United States from 1861 to 1885* (New York: D. Appleton, 1894; reprinted by Augustus M. Kelley, 1969), pp. 562–3; Malcolm Rogers Eiselen called the Morrill tariff the "triumph of Pennsylvania protectionism" and gave a good description of the prominent role played by the state's iron producers in antebellum tariff politics. *The Rise of Pennsylvania Protectionism* (Philadelphia: Private printing, 1932; reprinted by Porcupine Press, 1974), p. 266.
7. For evidence and commentary on the prominence of Pennsylvania iron producers and their representatives in Reconstruction tariff politics, see Ferleger, *Wells*, pp. 143–8, 151–2, 154, 157–8, 175, 180, 206, 208, 224, 240–3, 250, 254, 280–5, and 297–8.

steel producers was felt throughout the economy because those metals were used in the fabrication of the vast majority of all manufactured goods. No sector of the economy, however, was more sensitive to the increased cost of iron and steel than the railroads. In the frenzied route expansion of the late 1860s and 1870s, over one-third of all iron produced in the United States was fabricated into rails.[8] Congressmen from western settlement districts, as well as railroad investors and allied interests, generally supported decreases in the iron schedule. Western congressmen from areas in the path of proposed rail lines cited the hindering effect of the tariff on rail expansion as the reason for their opposition, but the tariff generally lowered the prices of agricultural goods relative to those prevailing for protected manufacturing production.[9] For both reasons, tariff protection was detrimental to the interests of western farmers. As many contemporary observers noted, the differential impact of tariff protection within the northern Republican coalition carried the potential for open intraparty warfare.[10]

Because iron and steel producers were the major beneficiaries of protectionism – even to the extent that their political representatives organized other interests into the tariff coalition – iron and steel production was the simplest and most accurate evidence of tariff-sensitive interests in the national political economy. For that reason, iron and steel employment (as recorded in the 1870 census) was aggregated by congressional districts in this analysis and used to designate those representatives who, it is deduced, would support protection as part of a broader, industrial program in Congress. While this selection understates protariff interests in New England and in other smaller regions of the country, the salience of iron producers in both tariff politics and financial policy during Reconstruction outweighed the advantages of alternative choices.[11]

8. Rails comprised 475,000 of 1,324,000 total iron tonnage in 1869. Peter Temin, "The Composition of Iron and Steel Products, 1869–1909," *Journal of Economic History* 23 (December 1963): 451; before the war, total railroad demand for pig-iron production ranged between 15 and 21 percent. Paul F. Paskoff, *Industrial Evolution: Organization, Structure, and Growth of the Pennsylvania Iron Industry, 1750–1860* (Baltimore: Johns Hopkins University Press, 1983), p. 120.
9. For examples of western opposition, see comments by James F. Wilson and John A. Kasson, both Iowa Republicans, in the *Congressional Globe*, 39:1:3515, June 30, 1866, and 39:1:3689, July 9, 1866. Michael Les Benedict suggests that iron producers supported government aid to railroads because they "were among their best customers." *A Compromise of Principle*, p. 54. Such a policy would also have alleviated both railroad and western settlement opposition to protection. On the redistributive impact of the tariff from the agricultural to manufacturing sectors, see Jeffrey G. Williamson, "Watersheds and Turning Points: Conjectures on the Long-Term Impact of Civil War Financing," *Journal of Economic History* 34 (September 1974): 536–661.
10. See, for example, *Commercial and Financial Chronicle*, July 7, 1866, p. 3.
11. On the prominent role of the iron interests in finance legislation, see Unger, *Greenback Era*, pp. 44–119.

The rapidly settling stretches of the western and, in a few instances, southern periphery composed a third faction within the Republican coalition. Distressed by the prospect of both protectionism and the resumption of specie payments, these capital-starved regions constantly threatened to bolt the party.[12] The constituencies classified as settlement districts were those in which the number of rural residents (outside cities of 10,000 or more people) made up more than two-thirds of the total population and, in addition, expanded by more than 25 percent between 1860 and 1870. This classification designates quite well those areas of rapid rural settlement linked with capital importation and railroad development but excludes some districts, most notably those in California, that have traditionally been associated with the western frontier in this period.[13] The regulatory requirements of the national bank system discriminated against these areas of rapid settlement in a number of ways. The relatively high capital requirements ($50,000 for banks in cities of 6,000 or fewer people, for example), prohibitions on mortgages, the exclusive note-issuing privileges (which discouraged the formation of alternative state-chartered institutions), and the ceiling on the total circulation of notes (effective between 1866 and 1870) all combined to make credit less available to rural sections of the country.[14] As a debtor region, settlement districts also would suffer under the deflationary regime imposed by a return to the gold standard. Both hostility to the national bank system and a comparative interest in inflating the currency gave this faction strong reasons to oppose the program of finance capital.[15]

---

12. The Pacific coast states (California, Nevada, and Oregon) remained on a domestic gold standard throughout the Civil War and, though aligned with the remaining settlement states on issues such as the tariff and internal development, strongly supported resumption of specie payments. In the Pacific rim, however, resumption sentiment was for a rather simple "bullion" system and included opposition to the national banking system and other finance policies. For a full, if somewhat diffuse, exploration of the general attitude of residents in the Far West, see John A. Ferris, *The Financial Economy of the United States Illustrated and Some of the Causes which Retard the Progress of California Demonstrated* (San Francisco: A. Roman and Company, 1867; reprinted by Augustus M. Kelley, 1969).

13. In California, San Francisco bulked too large in the first district and the second and third "gold field" districts grew too slowly to qualify as settlement constituencies.

14. See, for example, Richard Sylla, "Federal Policy, Banking Market Structure, and Capital Mobilization in the United States, 1863–1913," *Journal of Economic History* 29 (December 1969): 657–86. Sylla also maintains that these conditions raised rural interest rates by creating local "monopolistic" environments and, at the same time, allowing country banks to export funds to New York City as a ready alternative to local investment. Also see, H. Peers Brewer, "Eastern Money and Western Mortgages in the 1870s," *Business History Review* 50 (Autumn 1976): 356–80.

15. Robert Sharkey, however, notes that farmers and agrarian organizations were silent on monetary issues and most financial questions during the early years of Reconstruction. *Money, Class, and Party*, pp. 135–40.

Thus, the national political economy can be roughly divided into four major sectors. After the South was readmitted into the Union, the largest congressional delegation (85 congressmen) was sent to the House of Representatives by the former Confederate and border states. A smaller number, districts with more than $17.00 per capita in notes issued to their national banks, were particularly sensitive to the interests of finance capital. The 31 districts that met this criterion were all located in the Northeast and two congressmen, both from Baltimore, also represented a border state. All constituencies with more than 1 percent of their total population employed in iron and steel production were classified as potentially interested in tariff protection. Of the 27 districts 14 were in Pennsylvania and 5 each were located in New York and Ohio. Four of these iron and steel districts also fell within the finance category. One more was located in the West Virginia panhandle between Pennsylvania and Ohio and thus overlapped both the iron and former slave-state categories. The settlement category claimed a large number of congressmen, 46 in the Thirty-ninth and Fortieth Congresses, 45 in the Forty-first Congress (after Indiana redistricted). Ten of these districts were located in the South and border regions (one each in Georgia and Florida, 5 in Missouri, and 3 in Texas). The remainder were almost all found in an unbroken block of midwestern territory beyond Ohio. The Northeast contained no settlement constituencies and, as might be expected, no finance or iron district overlapped the settlement category. In all, 172 of the 243 districts in the Reconstruction era House of Representatives fell in one or more of these categories.

Several different concepts of representation undergird the way the major divisions of the political economy have been empirically defined. The settlement category, for example, rests on such a broad population base that the mode of influence can be viewed as mass electoral politics. To a lesser extent, the employment data for the iron and steel designations also suggests electoral influence, but the base is so small that elite influence was probably the primary route for the transmission of constituency interest. The employees of the national banks and the finance community generally never comprised a large cross-section of any congressional constituency (except perhaps in lower Manhattan). Direct elite contact must have been the primary vehicle of political influence here. In the South and, to a lesser extent, border states, both elite influence and mass-based electoral politics shaped congressional behavior, but the region was also subject to extraordinary political forces, including direct military rule by occupying federal armies; violent intimidation of pro-Union segments of the population and other forms of extralegal political activity by elements unreconciled to federal sovereignty; and selective admission of "victorious" candidates to Congress and the readmission of southern states generally. Exogenous political power and bureaucratic authority thus joined electoral competition and elite influence in shaping the tumultuous political reality in which southern congressmen were forced to operate.[16]

With respect to finance policy, the major parties presented confusing and indistinct profiles to the nation. In 1868, for example, Horatio Seymour, the Democratic candidate for the presidency, was nominated on an openly inflationary platform. But Seymour, a former governor of New York, was a "hard money man" and campaigned in support of a fiscal program much of the financial community must have liked: opposition to any change in greenback circulation, resumption of specie payments, retrenchment of government expenditures, and an end to military occupation of the South (presented as a cut in federal spending).[17] Republicans gave lip service to economy in government but, in practice, utilized federal spending for public works projects, military pensions, and railway subsidies to hold their coalition together. From the point of view of finance capital, the party was profligate in managing Reconstruction and setting employment levels in federal agencies. Like the Democrats, the Republicans ended up with a gradualist approach to resumption as a "default" compromise between violently conflicting preferences within the party. In fact, until the Democrats adopted the inflation plank in 1868, it was they, not the Republicans, who had the stronger claim to the "sound finance" title.[18] Basically, however, the major parties were so internally divided over financial questions that there was little basis on which to choose between them as organizations.

Because the Republicans controlled the government, finance capital was compelled to seek influence within the party. In fact, the Republican party can be viewed as a hegemonic coalition in the northern section of the country. It was a coalition in which each of the major sectors of the political economy presented their respective programs and settled their differences before facing the opposition party. The iron interests were most solidly placed within the party, closely followed by the settlement districts with their plans for government-sponsored internal development.

16. For a good review of southern congressional elections in this period, see Seip, *South Returns to Congress*, pp. 69–111. Nineteenth-century congressmen were generally much more deeply involved in finance and industry than is the case in the modern Congress. Bankers, iron producers, and merchants were often found in the ranks of Reconstruction Republicans and, to a lesser extent, Democrats and their presence blurred distinctions between electoral, elite, and personal interests. For present purposes we need only observe the various ways by which the spatial organization of the national political economy found expression in the federal legislature, not the precise mechanism by which influence was funneled in each case.

17. Ferleger, *Wells*, pp. 210–11.

18. Foner, *Reconstruction*, p. 487; Sharkey, *Money, Class, and Party*, p. 281.

Finance capital was less committed to the Republicans, and the party's southern members were considered to be no more than clients by their northern patrons. This hegemonic, quasistatist organization provided an arena in which the major political economic interests worked out a common "program" of side payments and compromise policy agreements. On some things, such as the tariff and some Reconstruction proposals, these agreements were more or less binding on party officials. In other areas, most notably finance policy, defections by congressional Republicans were numerous. Confronting this broad but internally divided alliance, the Democrats attempted to pick up strength from defecting fragments of the major party coalition, from areas not represented by any of the major Republican factions (such as the slow-growing, agrarian, and relatively impoverished regions along the northern bank of the Ohio River), and, most important, from the return of the plantation elite to political dominance in the South.[19]

Turning now to an examination of postwar finance, revenue, and expenditure policies, we find that, in terms of impressing its program upon the national political economy, finance capital was probably the most successful of the four major factions of the Republican party. With reference to central state finance policy, finance capitalists attained most of the policy goals they had set in the postwar period, although the interests and opposition of other factions and the ever-present Democrats delayed their achievement. At the end, we finally take up Reconstruction policies specifically and connect finance capital and Republican factionalism to the central state's abandonment of the freedman.

Congress, finance policy, and the Reconstruction political economy

Scores of roll call votes were recorded in the House of Representatives on major finance questions between 1865 and 1871. From this large number of votes, ten decisions have been selected according to the following criteria: (1) that all major finance policies be included in the analysis; (2) that the votes represent, as far as possible, the clearest test of a finance capital position in their respective policy areas; (3) that the votes selected be evenly spaced over the three congresses in which they were recorded; and (4) that the minority position on each vote attract the support of a sizable fraction of all voting members. Each decision related in some way to the operating requirements of the financial system

---

19. David Montgomery, *Beyond Equality: Labor and the Radical Republicans, 1862–1872* (New York: Alfred A. Knopf, 1967), p. 76.

though none was in and of itself essential to the stability and smooth operation of the system. Finance capital, in fact, lost several of these decisions either in the votes analyzed here or in subsequent political contests. The votes are described briefly here in the chronological order in which they were recorded and their relationship to the program of the financial community is also considered. Analysis of voting alignments and a summary discussion of legislative consideration of finance policy follow.

The first of the ten finance policy votes was recorded upon passage of what became the Bankruptcy Act of 1867, which nationalized the terms and enforcement of debt collection throughout the American economy.[20] In establishing a process of bankruptcy adjudication in the federal courts, the law swept away western and southern statutes that inhibited the collection of interstate debt. In this respect, the legislation was important, for example, to eastern insurance companies that had invested heavily in organized pools of western farm mortgages and to merchants engaged in the distribution of imported goods to the nation's interior. The immediate impact of the bankruptcy act fell heavily on the former Confederate states. In fact, at least some northern lenders "hoped to use the bankruptcy law to reclaim at least a pittance from ruined debtors in the South" and saw the federal statute as a way to prevent peripheral states from enacting laws or procedures that would hinder debt collection.[21] Bankruptcy petitions were most common in the Arkansas eastern district (one petition for every 121 persons), Mississippi northern district (149 persons), Virginia (264 persons), Alabama middle district (280), and Mississippi southern district (287). When allowance is made for the much less well-developed commercial network in the southern periphery, the

20. This vote occurred upon passage of the bankruptcy bill in the House on May 22, 1866 (*Congressional Globe* 39:1:2743). Sixty-eight members favored passage (the finance capital position), 59 opposed, and 56 members abstained. Representative Thomas A. Jenckes of Rhode Island was the primary sponsor and author of the statute (see, for example, his summary and refutation of objections to the bill, 39:1:2742–3, May 22, 1866). For a legislative history, see William H. Barnes, *History of the Thirty-ninth Congress of the United States* (New York: Harper & Brothers, 1868; reprinted by Negro Universities Press, 1969), p. 554, and Charles Warren, *Bankruptcy in United States History* (Cambridge, Mass.: Harvard University Press, 1935), pp. 95–109. This was the third national law on bankruptcy (after 1800 and 1841 statutes which lasted only a couple of years in each case).

21. Lawrence M. Friedman, *A History of American Law* (New York: Simon and Schuster, 1974), pp. 480–1; Warren, *Bankruptcy*, p. 104. Harold D. Woodman estimates the outstanding indebtedness of Southerners to northern merchants to be $150 million at the end of the Civil War. The greater part of this total can be traced to antebellum obligations. *King Cotton and His Retainers: Financing and Marketing the Cotton Crop of the South, 1800–1925* (Lexington: University of Kentucky Press, 1968), p. 203.

disproportion in regional rates is even greater than calculations on a per capita basis suggest.[22]

The second decision analyzed here arose out of efforts by the government to suppress counterfeiting. As we have seen, one of the most important changes wrought by the Civil War was the vast expansion of the central government's role in monetary policy and private financial markets. One consequence of this expanding involvement was an explosion in the sheer number and variety of government securities negotiated in the private economy. Under these new conditions, the old counterfeiting statutes proved inadequate and the legal branch of the Treasury Department drafted legislation that would tighten up laws on the fabrication of counterfeit securities, ban the possession of government dies and engraving plates, and prohibit the passing of fraudulent instruments posing as government obligations in public or private transactions. Reflecting the new, postwar order, the scope of the proposed legislation included "bond, bill, certificate of indebtedness, certificate of deposit, coupon, draft, check, bill of exchange, money order, indorsement, United States note, Treasury note, circulating note, postage stamp, [revenue stamp], postage stamp note, fractional note, or other obligation or security of the United States, or circulating note of any banking association." Passed by a large majority on July 24, 1866, the bill promised to reduce the risk of loss from the acceptance of forged or fraudulent securities.[23]

Throughout the postwar period many suggestions for the abolition of the national bank system and a concomitant replacement of circulating national bank notes with greenbacks were considered in the House of Representatives. The clearest proposal surfaced in the form of a resolution directed to the Committee on Banking and Currency. Rising to address the chamber on December 10, 1866, the author of this resolution, Representative Lewis W. Ross of Illinois, suggested that the committee "in-

22. "Expenses of Proceedings in Bankruptcy," Ex. Doc. No. 19: Senate: 43rd Congress, 1st Session (Washington, D.C.: Government Printing Office, 1874), Ser. Rec. 1580. The data on petitions in some of the districts was estimated by the Department of Justice. Repealed in 1878, the practical impact of the bankruptcy act on the nationalization of commercial transactions was ultimately not as important as the parallel thrust of judicial reinterpretation of creditor rights by the federal courts. On the importance of the federal judicial system to the nationalization of commerce, attempts by the individual states of the West and South to prevent interstate collection of debts, and general accounts of the sectional hostility and conflict in Congress thereby engendered, see Tony A. Freyer, "The Federal Courts, Localism, and the National Economy, 1865–1900," *Business History Review* 53 (Autumn 1979): 343–63; Charles W. McCurdy, "American Law and the Marketing Structure of the Large Corporation, 1875–1890," *Journal of Economic History* 38 (September 1978): 631–49; Morton Keller, *Affairs of State: Public Life in Late Nineteenth Century America* (Cambridge, Mass.: Harvard University Press, 1977), pp. 172, 184, 421–2.

23. *Congressional Globe* 39:1:4095–6. The vote was 89 yea, 25 nay, 67 abstaining.

quire into the expediency of withdrawing the national currency and winding up the national banks and furnishing the country in lieu of said national currency with greenbacks or other currency of similar character." This measure, as did others before and after, neatly combined western agrarian hostility to the bank system with a general predilection for an inflationary expansion of greenbacks.[24] After this resolution was voted down, Representative Samuel J. Randall, a Philadelphia Democrat, introduced legislation pursuing the same goals. Randall's bill presented *Hunt's* with an opportunity to express the financial community's feelings on the subject:

> The opinion...is evidently gaining ground in the country and in Congress, that the National Bank currency could be assumed by the Government without a danger to any business interests of importance, and with manifest relief to the burdens of the people.... As our appreciation is well known of the important part the national banks play in the financial affairs of the country, we need scarcely say that we disapprove of the plan set forth in the foregoing bill, and think it likely, if adopted, to cause serious commotion in monetary and industrial affairs... in the present financial situation we do strongly object to so sweeping, dangerous and revolutionary a change as that contemplated by Mr. Randall and his friends.[25]

This and all other attempts to abolish the national bank system were defeated.

While finance capital strongly endorsed continued government sponsorship of the national bank system, the financial community also wanted to restrict Treasury activity in the money market to those public, predictable operations absolutely required to minimize instability in the financial system. Along this line, one of the most persistent demands was that the Treasury cease its secret sales of specie on the gold exchange. *Hunt's* contended, for example, that these sales encouraged

> vague rumors of collusion between the Department and those speculators and money lenders who wished for stringency [in the supply of greenbacks for bank reserves because gold sales locked up greenbacks in government vaults]. In the atmosphere of mystery and secrecy which have been allowed to gather round and obscure the Treasury movements the most foolish stories get credence, if they be

24. *Congressional Globe* 39:2:48–9. The resolution was tabled by a vote of 87 yea to 58 nay, 46 abstaining. For a discussion of agrarian opposition to the bank system, see Unger, *Greenback Era*, pp. 195–212.
25. *Hunt's Merchants' Magazine and Commercial Review*, January 1867, pp. 78–80; also see "The National Bank Currency," by A. W. Stetson in April 1868, pp. 256–60.

only plausibly and confidently repeated to persons agitated by the terror and dread of a monetary panic.

Two years later the journal again warned its readers:

> few of us... will deny that now, as heretofore, the Treasury has far too much power over the gold market, that that power has too often been used neither wisely nor well, and that it should be sheltered from abuse by being disconnected from so much discretionary authority.

A number of reforms were suggested. Some pushed for daily statements of Treasury transactions. Others sought publication of the size of future Treasury operations but not announcement of the precise timing.[26]

A bill providing for the public sale of Treasury gold through competitive bidding reached the floor of the House of Representatives on January 21, 1867, and passed by a wide majority. The legislation designated New York City as the site for the receipt of bids and ordered public announcement of the sales in both that city and Washington, D.C. (provoking some jealousy among Philadelphia congressmen). In passing, the bill's manager, Representative Justin Morrill of Maine, indirectly acknowledged the growth of a relatively efficient national market by contending that use of the telegraph system made four days adequate notice for a national competition.[27] Though strongly supported by finance capital and, in fact, a majority of every major group in the national political economy, this proposal died in the Senate. While the proximate reason for the bill's failure is not known, the Treasury was understood to be opposed to the measure.

During consideration of a bill to revise the internal revenue schedule on June 26, 1868, the House voted on a section intended to substantially raise federal taxes on national bank deposits, capital, and note circulation. The banks already carried a wide and confusing variety of levies at both the federal and state level. At the time this proposal was debated, for example, the national government levied an annual license fee of $2.00 on every $1,000 of capital, a 5 percent tax on dividends and profits, 0.5 percent on deposits and capital, and 1 percent on note circulation. The revision proposed to raise the tax on capital and private deposits to 1

26. April 1868, p. 323; May 1869, 337–8; *Chronicle* February, 16, 1867, pp. 198–9; Sharkey, *Money, Class, and Party*, p. 90; Bolles, *Financial History*, pp. 312–13; for a discussion of secret Treasury operations in the securities markets, see Ellis Paxson Oberholtzer, *Jay Cooke: Financier of the Civil War*, vol. 1 (New York: Burt Franklin, 1970; a reprint of an unidentified 1907 edition), pp. 194–6, 500–6, 565–6.
27. *Congressional Globe* 39:2:617–18. The vote was 115 yea, 38 nay, 38 abstaining.

percent (doubling the levy), to 3 percent on deposits of federal funds (a sixfold increase), and to 2 percent on note circulation (a doubling of the existing rate). During debate, Representative Ebon Ingersoll of Illinois described the national bank system as "an aristocratic monopoly," and the comments of other supporters made it fairly clear that the revision was a thinly veiled attack on the system itself. The opposition contended that such increases in bank levies would operate in such a way as to discriminate against the country banks, leading those institutions to wind up their business and give up their charters. As a result, deposits would tend to be even more concentrated in the money center banks than they were under the existing tax structure. Congressmen who spoke for the banks also argued that tax increases of this magnitude on note circulation and public deposits would lead institutions in all parts of the country (but particularly New York) to recharter under state laws. The House approved the revision over these objections, but the Senate struck the section out and bank taxes remained unchanged.[28]

Given the size of these rate increases and the fact that levies on alternative investments and occupations would have remained unchanged, at least some of the marginally profitable national banks would have voluntarily folded if the revision had been enacted. In addition, the banks that remained in the system would have been encouraged to reduce their capitalization and thus, to some extent, increase the potential instability of the money market (by reducing assets backing deposits in banks). Even taken together, these developments would not have been fatal to the national banking system in the short run. Existing rates were borne rather easily by the institutions and the banks had relatively secure sources of income from their note circulation and bond deposits with the Treasury.[29] In the longer term, however, the departure of banks from the system (especially in the capital-starved western and southern periphery) and increasing instability from undercapitalization would have significantly impaired the working of the financial system.

On the last day of the Fortieth Congress, the House of Representatives passed legislation embodying several principles of primary importance to the financial community. Later popularly known as the Public Credit Act, the bill provided that, "in order to remove any doubt as to the purpose of the Government to discharge all just obligations to the public creditors, and to settle conflicting questions and interpretations of the

28. Seventy-one members backed the rate increases, 57 opposed them, and 66 abstained. *Congressional Globe* 40:2:3528–3538.
29. Harry Edwin Smith, *The United States Federal Internal Tax History from 1861 to 1871* (New York: Houghton Mifflin, 1914), pp. 139–41.

laws," all Treasury obligations not specifically payable in currency would be redeemed in gold.[30] This pledge explicitly committed the government to a policy of resumption and, in intention at least, settled the controversy that had arisen over whether the principal of some categories of bonds should be paid in greenbacks or specie. A second section provided that all future private contracts specifying payment in gold would be enforced in the courts, a measure that would further stabilize contractual expectations by disconnecting them from the politically sensitive, fluctuating value of greenbacks. This version of the legislation was, however, pocket vetoed by Andrew Johnson. When finally enacted as the first statute signed by the incoming President Grant, the Public Credit Act did not have this second, gold-contract clause.[31]

While the financial community was internally divided over the rate at which circulating greenbacks could be reduced and even whether the Treasury could safely contract the supply at all, finance capital was monolithically opposed to any increase in greenback issues.[32] Despite the endorsement that resumption policy received with passage of the Public Credit Act, legislative attempts to increase the supply of legal tender notes and thereby sabotage resumption continued. On December 11, 1869, for example, Ebon Ingersoll introduced a bill directing the Treasury secretary to issue $44 million in greenbacks in addition to those already outstanding. The greenbacks were to enter circulation through Treasury purchases of gold-bearing securities in the bond market. Though the bill did not become law, a motion to kill the measure failed when it was offered immediately following Ingersoll's introduction. Sixty-five members voted

30. The vote on this bill was 118 yea, 57 nay, and 48 abstaining. *Congressional Globe* 40:3:1883, March 3, 1869.
31. For a legislative history and background, see Unger, *Greenback Era*, pp. 93–4; Seip, *South Returns to Congress*, pp. 149–53; Bolles, *Financial History*, pp. 319–20; Sharkey, *Money, Class, and Party*, pp. 124–9; A. Barton Hepburn, *A History of Currency in the United States* (New York: Macmillan, 1915), pp. 213–14; *Hunt's* called the act "a very satisfactory measure, and indeed it is beyond question the most important financial bill which for some years has been placed on the statute-book" (March 1869, p. 227); the journal later attributed a rapid increase in capital importation from Europe to the positive impact the act had on creditor expectations of financial stability in the United States (July 1869, p. 42).
32. Sharkey maintains that western bankers were generally less interested in contraction, even opposed, for several reasons: Currency was relatively much more important to them than demand deposits (compared to eastern institutions); a return to specie payments would hamper a relatively profitable market for the gold dividends on their bonds deposited with the Treasury; and "the fortunes of these banks were largely bound up with the fortunes of their customers.... Contraction which was another name for deflation could by no stretch of the imagination benefit the credit starved economy of the West." *Money, Class, and Party*, pp. 267–8. For a general discussion of agrarian opposition to resumption, see Hepburn, *History of Currency*, p. 224.

to sustain the finance capital position, 88 members supported the inflationary proposal, and 58 abstained.[33]

Another frontal assault on the Public Credit Act arose out of proposals to pay the principal on the 5/20 government bonds in greenbacks instead of gold. On January 31, 1870, Representative Thompson McNeely of Illinois offered a resolution ordering that the administration adopt this inflationary policy and the House of Representatives summarily tabled (killed) the suggestion.[34] The statutes authorizing the 5/20's did not explicitly state that the principal was to be paid in gold. This oversight (as it must have been as almost all advertisements offering the loan tied redemption to specie) provided a potential loophole from which the above resolution emerged. Greenback redemption of 5/20's were also the basis for the "Ohio Plan," which became the inflation plank of the 1868 Democratic platform.[35]

In July 1870 Congress enacted the National Bank Currency Act, the first broad, postwar revision of currency policy and the national bank system.[36] The heart of the act was an expansion of $54 million in national bank notes. Eighty percent of these notes were to go to the South and West upon application by existing or new banking associations. If this new supply of notes was exhausted, an additional $25 million then allocated to northeastern institutions was to be withdrawn and reallocated to the South and West as acceptable applications were received. At the same time and at the same rate as the new notes were issued, $45 million in 3 percent certificates (negotiable as legal tender and thus held primarily as bank reserves) were to be recalled and permanently retired by the Treasury. Relatively minor provisions authorized the establishment of "national gold banks" that would redeem their notes in specie and a ceiling of $500,000 on the circulation issued to any new national bank or future increase given to an already existing institution.[37]

33. *Congressional Globe* 41:2:75–6. This vote represents a weak version of the operating requirement of the financial system in that the finance policy position only opposed additional legal tender issues and, thus, did not actively support contraction. For analysis of a similar vote (recorded on December 7, 1867), see Sharkey, *Money, Class, and Party*, pp. 110–13.

34. Supporting the resolution were 41 members, 121 opposed the measure, and 52 abstained. *Congressional Globe* 41:2:913.

35. Unger, *Greenback Era*, pp. 82–3; Sharkey, *Money, Class, Party*, pp. 97–101; *Hunt's* strongly condemned the inflationary implications of all such propositions (July 1868, pp. 60–3).

36. The recorded vote on passage of the conference report in the House was 100 yea, 77 nay, and 53 abstaining. *Congressional Globe* 41:2:5303, July 7, 1870.

37. Richard H. Timberlake, Jr., *The Origins of Central Banking in the United States* (Cambridge, Mass.: Harvard University Press, 1978), pp. 94–100; Hepburn, *History of Currency*, p. 315.

Though President Grant and Treasury Secretary Boutwell did not lobby for passage, the redistribution of bank notes contemplated by the act had long been advocated by the Treasury. In 1866, for example, the comptroller of the currency urged that the national bank system be expanded in order to allow participation by the former Confederate states:

> the South should be supplied with all the facilities necessary for the production of the great staples of that section, because the export of these staples would reduce the exportation of gold.... Besides, a community or identity of financial and pecuniary interests would bring into exercise an element of great power for the assimilation of the aims, purposes and hopes of all the people of all the States. The extension of the National banking system throughout the entire Union would bring about such an identity of interest in the credit of the Government, and of the entire system of banks, as would secure the active and zealous co-operation of all sections toward the preservation of such credit unimpaired.

The comptroller's message was based on two arguments that drew wide support in the financial community: (1) that the extension of banking capacity to the South would help organize and promote the expansion of cotton production, the export of which was far and away the most important source of foreign exchange for the American economy; and (2) that participation in the system would associate southern capital more closely with the success of the fiscal policies of the U.S. Treasury and thereby broaden public support for resumption of specie payments. These and the broader goal of promoting loyalty to the national government had also been briefly suggested in a public letter by Secretary McCulloch in April of the same year.[38]

Notwithstanding the beneficial results that a regional redistribution of notes promised, the inflationary potential of the proposal led most of the financial community to oppose the act. *Hunt's Merchants' Magazine and Commercial Review,* for example, objected to the measure because it would inflate the currency (as a sum total of greenbacks and national bank notes). The journal also complained that the legislation would require an adjustment of bank reserves that might produce "a serious temporary disturbance in the money market" because, as 3 percent certificates were retired, greenbacks would flow into bank vaults in order to maintain reserve levels; the demand for greenbacks would also increase because, as national bank notes expanded, the required level of greenbacks in bank reserves would also increase (this effect would be independent of the retirement of 3 percent certificates). As a consequence of

38. *Annual Report of the Comptroller of the Currency, 1866,* reprinted in *Hunt's,* December 1866, p. 468; McCulloch's letter appears in *Hunt's,* May 1866, p. 369.

this adverse change in the ratio of bank notes to greenbacks, a suspension of bank note redemption during periods of stringency was significantly more likely. In addition, the journal was convinced that the low returns on banking in the South and West and the absence of indigenous capital in those regions would prevent the redistributive provisions of the act from having more than "a very trifling effect" on note allocation. Though the final version of the bill was viewed as less objectionable because it appeared to be less inflationary, *Hunt's* still considered passage

> none the less a mistake . . . [because it] is an assertion by Congress of the dangerous power to increase, diminish and regulate the money of the country, according to its own views from time to time, and of the purpose to exercise the power. It is a resolve not to let the currency alone, and leave it to be regulated by the laws of trade, but to interfere with it by artificial measures for the express purpose . . . of affecting the prices of commodities, the value of money and the relations between debtors and creditors. . . . What the people want above all things is stability.[39]

The national bank currency act eventually added some $50 million in national bank notes to the money supply and withdrew $45 million in 3 percent certificates. This apparent net gain in currency of $5 million must be reduced to $4 million once the impact of the 20 percent greenback reserve on notes is considered. The act thus inflated the total volume of currency by well under 1 percent.

One of the most important goals of finance capital in the postwar political economy was the stabilization and refunding of the national debt into long-term securities bearing rates of interest comparable to those prevailing for British consols or French rentes (both of them rep-

---

39. July 1870, pp. 36–40; August 1870, pp. 102–3, for the text of the law, pp. 132–3; September 1870, pp. 176–8; December 1870, pp. 435–7; on the execution of the law, see *Chronicle*, April 8, 1871, pp. 421–2. Also see, Unger, *Greenback Era*, p. 67, 178; Bolles, *Financial History*, pp. 354–9; Sharkey, *Money, Class, and Party*, p. 170; Seip, *South Returns to Congress*, pp. 173–84. Many members of the financial community opposed recall of the 3 percent certificates because they believed that these interest-bearing notes encouraged the banks to hold larger reserves than they would otherwise retain. See, for example, the *Internal Revenue Record*, June 18, 1870, p. 195. As the United States reduced the premium paid for gold by making progress toward resumption, gold-bearing government bonds significantly appreciated in value to the extent that their relatively high market price discouraged the rate of new bank formation. This effect, in addition to the relative low profitability of country institutions, so reduced the incentive to form new national banks in the periphery that the 1870 act had very little real impact on the maldistribution of notes. For a report on the slow progress toward redistribution under the act, see "National Bank Circulation," Exec. Doc. 250: House of Representatives: 43rd Cong., 1st Sess., Ser. Rec. 1614 (Washington, D.C.: Government Printing Office, 1874). For the financial community's consistent commitment to maintaining the $300 million ceiling on national bank note circulation, see *Hunt's*, January 1866, p. 86; January 1868, p. 30.

resenting the epitome of "sound," conservative public finance). This goal was largely achieved in the Refunding Act of 1870, which authorized $200 million in 5 percent, ten-year bonds, $300 million in 4.5 percent, fifteen-year bonds, and $1 billion in 4 percent, thirty-year bonds. Under the act, the Secretary was authorized to accept the outstanding 5/20 bonds (now callable) in exchange for the new securities and to use money from the refunding operations to call in and redeem existing higher interest, short-term debt. The House passed the legislation by a large margin (139 to 54, with 37 members abstaining). For finance capital, the refunding of the 5/20's not only promised long-term economic stability but also removed a major political focus of inflationary agitation. Once the 5/20's were redeemed, the Ohio Plan and other schemes to redeem those bonds in greenbacks would become a dead issue. However, some financiers felt that refunding efforts were premature when considered on strictly financial terms and objected to the timing of the legislation. These predictions that the Treasury might be jumping the gun were, in fact, subsequently borne out by the slow progress of Treasury refunding operations.[40]

Considered together, the ten legislative decisions just reviewed represent a wide sampling of finance policy in the six years following the American Civil War. Four of the decisions directly addressed the size of greenback circulation: the dissolution of the national bank system, the resolution to expand greenback issues by $44 million, the payment of 5/20 bond principal in greenbacks, and the National Bank Currency Act. Often acknowledged as the most important financial question during this period, the role of greenbacks in the domestic economy is thus heavily represented in this review of legislative action. The fate of the national bank system is directly implicated in three of the ten decisions: dissolution of the national bank system, increases in internal revenue taxation of the banks, and the National Bank Currency Act. Given the close connection between greenbacks and bank notes in the political economy of the na-

---

40. *Congressional Globe* 41:2:5523, July 13, 1870; Robert T. Patterson, *Federal Debt-Management Policies, 1865–1879* (Durham, N.C.: Duke University Press, 1954), pp. 81–99; Seip, *South Returns to Congress*, pp. 153–8; Bolles, *Financial History*, pp. 321–3; *Hunt's* repeatedly urged Congress to delay refunding legislation because "The hazard of disturbing the five-twenties resides not only in the probability that any effort at refunding would be unsuccessful at present, but also in the fact that the Government securities lie at the foundation of the financial machinery of the country, and that any attempt to disturb those foundations would not fail to cause perturbation and wide-spread mischief throughout the movements of monetary and industrial enterprise." January 1870, pp. 5–7. Also see *Hunt's*, February 1870, pp. 109–12; April 1870, pp. 315–19; May 1870, pp. 333–4, 374; July 1870, pp. 1–5; the text of the law appears in the August 1870 issue, pp. 130–2.

tion, it is not surprising that two of these three overlap with greenback decisions.

Prospects for resumption of specie payments were implicated indirectly in at least seven of these legislative choices but were most directly involved in passage of the Public Credit Act. That measure and the bill ordering the public sale of Treasury gold also concern the regulation of specie in contractual relationships and on the gold exchange. The federal debt was directly involved in the Public Credit Act, the payment of 5/20 principal in greenbacks, and the Refunding Act of 1870. Finally, Treasury operations and the development of a stable national capital market can be connected to decisions on passage of the Bankruptcy Act of 1867, revision of counterfeiting statutes, and public sale of Treasury gold. In sum, these ten legislative choices represent a broad, balanced survey of the major operating requirements of the financial system, the policy preferences of the financial community, and the range of political controversy during the period.

On these ten questions involving major issues of finance policy, members from districts with relatively high allocations of national bank notes ("capital-rich" districts) delivered much more support for the finance capital position than did members from districts with smaller shares of circulation (relatively "capital-poor" districts – see Table 5.1). The differences are most striking on roll calls involving bankruptcy, dissolving the national bank system, bank taxes, greenback expansion, and the bank currency act. The bank system itself was directly implicated in three of these decisions, and the other two had equally clear ramifications for creditor positions in the national political economy. The voting alignment on the Refunding Act provides the only exception to the pattern. On that issue, members from capital-rich districts, perhaps sharing the financial community's doubts as to the timing of the refunding effort, were marginally less likely to support passage than members from other, relatively capital-poor, constituencies. Though the voting data present few surprises, the pattern strongly suggests that members both responded to the interests of finance capitalists when the latter were prominently represented in congressional constituencies and that the financial community presented a fairly consistent and united front to the remainder of the political system on these questions.

The overall pattern persists when the heart of the Republican coalition is analyzed (see Table 5.2). These are the districts that were represented by a Republican congressman or a member of a closely affiliated party throughout the six-year period. Members from such districts, whether or not they stood for reelection, were supported by strong, local Repub-

Table 5.1. *Currency, banking structure, and Treasury operations: Finance policy and national banks in House voting, 1865–71*

Policy decision	Support for the position of finance capital (percent voting from districts with various levels of per capita note circulation)			
	High districts	Medium districts	Low districts	All districts
National bankruptcy law	88.0 (25)	53.4 (73)	24.1 (29)	53.5 (127)
Ban counterfeiting public securities	90.0 (20)	78.3 (69)	69.2 (26)	78.3 (115)
Dissolve national bank system	88.5 (26)	65.0 (80)	30.8 (39)	60.0 (145)
Public sale of treasury gold	76.0 (25)	83.7 (86)	57.1 (42)	75.2 (153)
Tax on bank capital and circulation	85.0 (20)	50.0 (70)	13.2 (38)	44.5 (128)
Public Credit Act	92.0 (25)	63.6 (88)	62.9 (62)	67.4 (175)
Greenback expansion	77.3 (22)	47.4 (78)	19.2 (52)	42.1 (152)
Pay 5/20's in greenbacks	95.2 (21)	74.4 (86)	67.3 (55)	74.7 (162)
National Bank Currency Act	75.0 (24)	40.7 (91)	37.1 (62)	43.5 (177)
Debt Refunding Act	70.4 (27)	75.0 (100)	68.2 (66)	72.0 (193)

Note: For a description of these issues and the position of finance capital, see the accompanying text. "High districts" are those in which 1869 national bank notes issued to institutions within the district equaled or exceeded $17.00 per capita. "Low districts" are those in which circulation was less than or equal to $2.50 per capita. "Medium districts" range between these two extremes. Per capita circulation was calculated from the *1870 Census* and the *Annual Report of the Comptroller of the Currency, 1869.*

lican party organizations and projected vested political economic interests into intraparty negotiations within the national Republican organization. Congressmen from districts that interrupted Republican representation with opposition party victories, from districts where Democrats or their close allies always held the seat, or districts located within the former Confederacy were, comparatively speaking, either not admitted at all to party caucuses or viewed as clients of the delegations located within the heart of the national coalition.[41] The members excluded from the "Republican district" classification are clearly a heterogeneous group and conclusions drawn from their behavior should be drawn with caution.

Within the heart of the Republican coalition, roll calls on bankruptcy and currency issues provoked strong alignments along the capital spectrum. Divisions on these finance policy issues were at least as divisive within the core of the majority party as they were within the full House membership. On the other hand, differences along the capital spectrum

41. On the exclusion of southern Republicans from "the power structure" of the national party in Congress, see Seip, *South Returns to Congress*, pp. 114–25, 276–8.

Table 5.2. *Currency, banking structure, and Treasury operations:*
Finance policy and national banks in party voting, 1865–71

Policy decisions	Support for the position of finance capital (percent voting from districts with various levels of per capita note circulation)				
	High districts	Medium districts	Low districts	All Republican districts	All mixed/ Democratic districts
National bankruptcy law	94.1 (17)	54.5 (44)	20.0 (15)	56.6 (76)	49.0 (51)
Ban counterfeiting public securities	93.3 (15)	97.4 (38)	93.8 (16)	95.7 (69)	52.2 (46)
Dissolve national bank system	100.0 (18)	70.8 (48)	33.3 (18)	69.0 (84)	47.5 (61)
Public sale of Treasury gold	86.7 (15)	96.2 (52)	85.0 (20)	92.0 (87)	53.0 (66)
Tax on bank capital and circulation	87.5 (16)	48.7 (39)	23.5 (17)	51.4 (72)	35.7 (56)
Public Credit Act	100.0 (16)	79.6 (49)	75.0 (16)	82.7 (81)	54.3 (94)
Greenback expansion	82.4 (17)	58.1 (43)	28.6 (21)	55.6 (81)	26.8 (71)
Pay 5/20's in greenbacks	100.0 (17)	95.8 (48)	100.0 (20)	97.6 (85)	49.4 (77)
National Bank Currency Act	60.0 (15)	26.5 (49)	13.6 (22)	29.1 (86)	57.1 (91)
Debt Refunding Act	100.0 (18)	96.2 (52)	95.7 (23)	96.8 (93)	49.0 (100)

Note: "Republican districts" are those that were represented at all times by a Republican or a member of an affiliated party (such as the Union party in New York). "Mixed/ Democratic districts" include all districts not represented in Congress for the entire period (the former Confederate districts of the South), districts that at one time or another were represented by members from both the Democratic and the Republican parties, and districts that, without exception, were represented by Democrats or members from closely affiliated parties (such as the Conservative party in Kentucky).

almost disappear with respect to the counterfeiting, gold sales, 5/20's in greenbacks, and refunding decisions. The latter were issues upon which the Republican administration had assumed a public stance and the Republican consensus in the House owed something to purely partisan considerations. The administration, however, also backed the National Bank Currency Act, which produced a fairly deep cleavage within the central precincts of the party. This was both the only issue upon which the Grant administration promoted a policy opposed by the financial community and the only instance in which members in the core coalition

of the party were less friendly to finance capital than members representing "mixed" or Democratic districts.

When divided by their districts' position with respect to the four major
sectors of the political economy, the full House membership continued
to cleave most clearly over the bankruptcy, national bank, and greenback
expansion issues (see Table 5.3). Not surprisingly, given the sharp regional differences in the national political economy, these were the five
issues that produced the highest levels of sectional polarization (averaging
53.4 on the index as opposed to 31.4 for the other five). Congressmen
from both settlement districts and former slave-state districts gave much
less support to finance capital than members from bank or iron constituencies. In fact, former slave-state members delivered the lowest level of
support in six cases and settlement congressmen in four. On two issues,
bankruptcy and the National Bank Currency Act, congressmen from bank
and iron constituencies diverged strongly in their support for finance
capital, but on the other eight decisions their behavior was virtually
indistinguishable.

When members belonging to the central coalition of the Republican
party are analyzed separately, the behavior of congressmen from settlement and border-state districts becomes even more closely linked
(compare Tables 5.3 and 5.4 – but remember that the settlement and
border-state categories overlap to some extent). On finance policy at
least, these Republicans from capital-starved regions obviously saw issues
the same way. The linkage between bank and iron districts also tightens
up when central coalition Republicans are considered separately. Though
congressmen from districts producing iron and steel were more likely
than bank members to oppose finance capital on bankruptcy and greenback issues, they otherwise matched capital-rich congressmen in their
devotion to the interests of the financial community. Much has been
made of the relative favor with which iron district members viewed
greenback inflation and some differences in support are evident.[42] However, on one vote (5/20's in greenbacks), iron members unanimously

42. See, for example, Unger's contention that economic difficulties in the 1865–78 period
    "may well have made the iron men receptive to economic panaceas, but they do not
    explain why they became noisy crusaders for soft money." *Greenback Era*, p. 49.
    Unger goes on to identify the "iron men" and their interpretation of their interests
    with the writings and views of Henry C. Carey (pp. 50–9). Sharkey emphasizes the
    reinforcing impact of a high gold premium on tariff protection as one reason iron
    manufacturers supported greenback inflation, *Money, Class, and Party*, pp. 76–7,
    141–71, 285–6. Sharkey also maintains that a "careful evaluation of the evidence
    leads to the conclusion that the opposition to contraction on the part of the iron and
    steel manufacturers of Pennsylvania, New York, and the western states, and their
    allies was the most important single factor leading to the abandonment of [contrac-
    tion] in 1868" (p. 286).

Table 5.3. *Currency, banking structure, and Treasury operations:*
Finance policy and sectors of the political economy in House voting,
1865–71

Policy decision	Support for the position of finance capital (percent of members voting)				
	National bank districts	Iron and steel districts	Settlement districts	Border-state/ Confederate districts	Sectional stress index
National bankruptcy law	88.0 (25)	46.7 (15)	37.0 (27)	47.4 (19)	59.3
Ban counterfeiting public securities	90.0 (20)	76.5 (17)	87.5 (24)	50.0 (14)	24.0
Dissolve national bank system	88.5 (26)	81.0 (21)	39.4 (33)	28.0 (25)	46.6
Public sale of Treasury gold	76.0 (25)	78.3 (23)	83.9 (31)	56.0 (25)	23.7
Tax on bank capital and circulation	85.0 (20)	80.0 (20)	27.6 (29)	12.0 (25)	59.6
Public Credit Act	92.0 (25)	72.7 (22)	57.6 (33)	58.1 (43)	35.1
Greenback expansion	77.3 (22)	70.0 (20)	21.2 (33)	26.3 (38)	52.3
Pay 5/20's in greenbacks	95.2 (21)	81.8 (22)	82.4 (34)	60.5 (38)	31.7
National Bank Currency Act	75.0 (24)	40.0 (25)	26.3 (38)	34.1 (44)	49.4
Debt Refunding Act	70.4 (27)	80.0 (25)	84.6 (39)	65.5 (55)	42.6

Note: "National bank districts" are those in which 1869 national bank notes issued to institutions within the district equaled or exceeded $17.00 per capita. "Iron and steel districts" are those in which employment in those industries equaled or exceeded 1 percent of the entire population. "Settlement districts" are those in which the rural population comprised two-thirds or more of the district total and that rural component grew by 25 percent or more between 1860 and 1870. "Border-state/Confederate districts" are all those located in the former slave states. The "Sectional stress index" is a statistic that roughly indicates the relative level of sectional polarization in roll call voting.

opposed inflation and on two others, dissolving the national bank system and greenback expansion, their differences with members representing finance capital districts were fairly narrow. Only on passage of the National Bank Currency Act, a Republican administration proposal, did differences between the two great wings of industrial capitalism widen to the point of disruption. While members from these two sectors of the political economy moderately diverged on the greenback question, their

Table 5.4. *Currency, banking structure, and Treasury operations: Finance policy and sectors of the political economy in Republican voting, 1865–71*

Policy decision	National bank districts	Iron and steel districts	Settlement districts	Border-state districts
	Support for the position of finance capital (percent of Republicans voting)			
National bankruptcy law	94.1 (17)	66.7 (9)	33.3 (21)	16.7 (6)
Ban counterfeiting public securities	93.3 (15)	100.0 (11)	100.0 (19)	85.7 (7)
Dissolve national bank system	100.0 (18)	86.7 (15)	42.3 (26)	42.9 (7)
Public sale of Treasury gold	86.7 (15)	100.0 (14)	92.3 (26)	75.0 (8)
Tax on bank capital and circulation	87.5 (16)	90.9 (11)	29.2 (24)	20.0 (5)
Public Credit Act	100.0 (16)	91.7 (12)	66.7 (24)	100.0 (2)
Greenback expansion	82.4 (17)	72.7 (11)	26.9 (26)	66.7 (9)
Pay 5/20's in greenbacks	100.0 (17)	100.0 (13)	100.0 (27)	100.0 (6)
National Bank Currency Act	60.0 (15)	14.3 (14)	13.3 (30)	0.0 (9)
Debt Refunding Act	100.0 (18)	100.0 (15)	96.7 (30)	100.0 (9)

Note: "Republican districts" are those that were represented at all times by a Republican or a member of an affiliated party (such as the Union party in New York).

differences were much less wide than those between the capital-rich districts of the East and western settlement and border-state congressmen.

Several factors probably contributed to the closing of ranks among the capital sectors of the Republican coalition. In the first place, greenback expansion was a less central issue to the iron and steel industry than the tariff. Therefore, we should expect a less straightforward representation of iron interests on finance policy than on questions involving protection. Finance policy issues, on the other hand, were of primary importance to the political economy of capital-rich constituencies and many industrial districts, though not in the first rank, were still comparatively well endowed with capital (see the national bank Map 4.1, in Chapter 4). In sum, the combination of only a mild interest in contraction among iron and steel producers and the presence within constituencies of counterbalancing finance capital influence appears to have tilted iron congressmen heavily toward finance capital on issues involving inflation.

Looking at the period as a whole, support for finance capital positions on issues involving the currency, banking structure, and Treasury operations was largely concentrated in New England and New York (see

Map 5.1). Some portions of Pennsylvania, Ohio, and Michigan were also strongly supportive, while the capital-starved sections of the upper Mississippi valley, Pacific coast, and border states were far less sympathetic.[43] While this broad sampling of legislative decisions is representative of the full range of finance policy and financial community views, these ten votes constitute a small proportion of all recorded votes on these issues. With that cautionary note in mind, this sectional polarization of legislative voting remains a striking testament to the party-realigning potential of finance policy in the Reconstruction years and the efficiency with which district political-economic interests were translated into congressional voting records.

Federal revenue and tax structure

For our present purposes, a broad sampling of legislative action on federal revenue policy is not necessary. While the tax structure carried important long-term implications for the development of the American political economy, its immediate impact on the stability and operation of the financial system was more tangential than any of the decisions studied in the previous section. For this reason, both fewer examples of legislative action are analyzed here and the decisions selected for study highlight the political economic position of other major groups in the political economy (as well as those of finance capital).

The first of the five legislative decisions examined under this heading involved a proposed reduction of the tariff on railroad iron. Considered in the House July 10, 1866, the amendment to the tariff schedule would have reduced the duty on rails from one dollar to fifty cents per hundred pounds.[44] Though Pennsylvania iron producers composed the very heart of the protectionist coalition and railroad iron embodied, in turn, their chief interest in the entire tariff, this schedule produced very little revenue.[45] Finance capital, at least that fragment not associated with iron

43. The map displays the voting record of individual *districts* (not individual congressmen though it was, of course, congressmen who did the actual voting).
44. More exactly, the vote was on an amendment to reduce another amendment from seventy to fifty cents per hundred pounds. If adopted, the fifty cent revision then would have come up against the one dollar duty already in the bill under consideration. The proposed fifty cent reduction lost (57 members voting yea, 90 nay, and 35 abstaining). *Congressional Globe* 39:1:3723. The seventy cent amendment returned the duty to the prevailing rate (thus preventing any increase under this bill). Edward Young, *Special Report on the Customs-tariff Legislation* (Washington, D.C.: Government Printing Office, 1877), p. 63. For a general summary of House debate and the politics of this tariff measure, see Ferleger, *Wells*, pp. 144–50.
45. During the 1869 fiscal year, for example, the tariff on railroad iron yielded $3,513,658 – approximately 2 percent of all customs receipts for the year ($180,048,000). Cal-

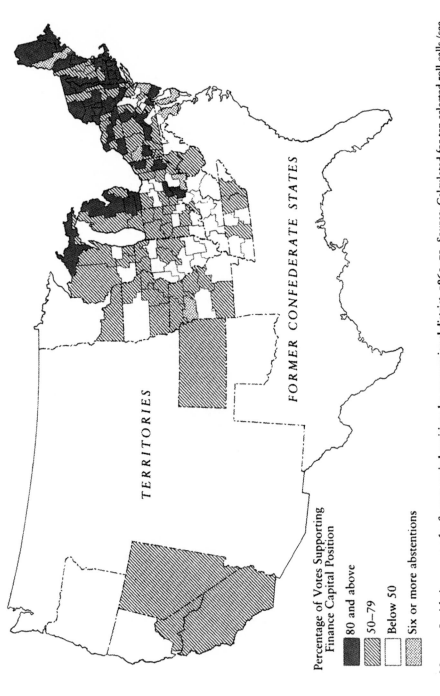

Percentage of Votes Supporting
Finance Capital Position

■ 80 and above

▨ 50–79

□ Below 50

▨ Six or more abstentions

Map 5.1 Legislative support for finance capital positions by congressional district, 1865–71. *Source:* Calculated for ten selected roll calls (see text) on which major questions of national finance policy were decided. The percentages are calculated for all votes cast by the member or members representing each district throughout the entire period.

production, tended to indifference or opposition to protectionism even at this early date.[46] Western agrarians were also opposed because of the negative impact on railroad expansion.[47] Representative John A. Griswold, a "prominent iron manufacturer" from Troy, New York, lumped all opponents of the iron schedule into one group that "have made up their minds deliberately... to obey the behests and dictation of British manufacturers and British capitalists." He then inserted a letter written to the U.S. Consulate in Liverpool, England, in which it was alleged that British manufacturers were campaigning in the western states to repeal the tariff by encouraging the formation of free trade associations.[48]

The financial community was much more interested in repeal of the internal revenue tax on raw cotton. When first enacted the tax stood at two cents per pound; it was raised to three cents in 1866. (This was the only "war tax" to be increased after the war ended.) Both rates were initially but a small fraction of the high price of the fiber during and immediately after the war. By the spring of 1867, however, the levy had become a heavy burden on the commodity in foreign markets.[49] While the excise applied to all domestic sales of cotton, the tax operated in many respects as an export duty because two-thirds or more of the American crop usually moved in international trade. For this reason, as the tax came to comprise a larger percentage of the world price, domestic

culated from data in *Hunt's*, February 1870, p. 131, and U.S. Bureau of the Census, *Historical Statistics of the United States* (Washington, D.C.: 1960), p. 712.

46. Ferleger, *Wells*, p. 147, 162; Sprout, *Best Men*, pp. 46–56; on July 5, 1866, the New York Chamber of Commerce unanimously adopted a resolution condemning proposed increases in the tariff, including those in the iron schedule, Sharkey, *Money, Class, and Party*, p. 272; in a letter (dated February 16, 1867) to his brother, Charles, Henry Adams said "the new tariff is alone enough to ruin the country. It has made me feel more bitter against the Congress than all its other mad or imbecile acts together." J. C. Levenson, Ernest Samuels, Charles Vandersee, and Viola Hopkins Winner, eds., *The Letters of Henry Adams, 1858–1868* (Cambridge, Mass.: Harvard University Press, 1982), p. 519; also see a second letter (dated May 8, 1867), p. 533; for a later statement of the financial community's position, see *Hunt's*, June 1870, p. 413.

47. Well over two-thirds of all railroad construction between 1866 and 1870 occurred in Missouri, the Midwest, and the Pacific coast states. By way of comparison, only 12 percent of all new track was laid in the eleven states of the former Confederacy. Calculated from data in "Report on the Condition of Affairs in the Late Insurrectionary States," Rept. 41, Pt. 1: Senate: 42nd Cong., 2nd Sess., Ser. Rec. 1484 (Washington, D.C.: Government Printing Office, 1872), pp. 222–3.

48. *Congressional Globe* 39:1:3516, June 30, 1866; 39:1:3689, July 9, 1866; also see, Ferleger, *Wells*, pp. 300–3; for western agrarian opposition to the railroad iron schedule during debate on the 1864 tariff act, see Young, *Customs-tariff Legislation*, pp. cxxxv–vi.

49. The market price of cotton reached a peak of $1.65 a pound during the month of August 1864 and had fallen to 28 cents by February, 1867. *Merchants and Bankers Almanac, 1868* (New York: Bankers' Magazine and Statistical Register, 1867), p. 167.

production was increasingly discouraged and competing producers in Egypt, India, and Brazil were encouraged to expand production. The broad effect of the tax, then, was to impair the major comparative advantage enjoyed by the United States in the late nineteenth century and thereby reduce the supply of specie in the country (because exports of specie partially compensated for the reduction of cotton exports in foreign exchange transactions). Over the long term, the impact of the cotton excise would have been to increase the gold premium (against greenbacks) and to delay a return to the gold standard.[50] Radical Republicans, however, viewed this levy as an alternative means of exacting retribution on the southern plantation elite and were not inclined to give it up. They managed to defeat a proposal for outright repeal on February 25, 1867 (the decision included here), but the tax was subsequently eliminated in 1868.[51]

While the cotton excise fell entirely upon the impoverished rural South, the income tax reaped revenue from wealthy northern commercial centers. Probably no two levies in the internal revenue system applied to more distinctly separate classes in the population. When created during the war, the income tax exempted the first $600 of income, levied 3 percent on income from $600 to $10,000, and took 5 percent more on all income beyond $10,000. In 1864 a revision of the internal revenue schedule raised the rates to 5 and 10 percent, respectively, but left the exemption unchanged. In conjunction with a general reduction of revenue rates in 1867, the exemption was raised to $1,000 and all income in excess of the exemption was subjected to a single, flat rate of 5 percent. The income tax came up for review again in 1870 and the decision included here was an amendment to reduce the flat rate to 3 percent. Offered by Representative Samuel Cox of New York City on June 3, 1870, the motion drew 114 yea votes, 77 nay, and 39 members ab-

50. Bolles, *Financial History*, pp. 409–10; Ferleger, *Wells*, pp. 59–61, 84–6, 109–10; *Hunt's*, January 1870, pp. 3–5, also p. 9; for a good discussion of the economic impact of the cotton tax and an early endorsement of repeal, see December 1866, pp. 409–11; also, October 1867, pp. 302–4; January 1868, pp. 31–5. Exports of raw cotton made up 44.2 percent of all exports and 47.6 percent of all merchandise exports between 1866 and 1871, calculated from data in *Historical Statistics of the United States*, pp. 551, 563.
51. Sixty-three members supported repeal, 94 opposed, and 33 abstained, *Congressional Globe* 39:2:1548; on the tax as punitive retribution, see Ferleger, *Wells*, p. 86; also see a broad plea for leniency toward the South on revenue collection generally in the *Annual Report of the Secretary of the Treasury, 1865*, reprinted in *Hunt's*, January 1866, pp. 71–2. When the tax was finally lifted, *Hunt's* claimed the action "emancipated the country from the withering blight of one of the worst of its many bad taxes" (February 1868, p. 114); also see, Frederic C. Howe, *Taxation and Taxes in the U.S. under the Internal Revenue System, 1791–1895* (New York: Thomas Y. Crowell, 1896), pp. 76–8.

stained.[52] Subsequent congressional action further reduced the rate to 2.5 percent, raised the exemption to $2,000, and provided that the tax would expire altogether at the end of 1871.[53]

A second vote on the tariff has been included in this selection of revenue decisions in order to reflect the increasing opposition of the financial community to Pennsylvania "protectionism."[54] This roll call occurred on an amendment to reduce the duty on steel rails from 1.5 to 1.25 cent per pound.[55] First adopted in the Senate, the House accepted the change on July 9, 1870, by a vote of 99 to 72, with 59 members abstaining. As was also the case with the iron schedule, the Treasury received little revenue from the steel tariff.[56]

The steel schedule was part of a composite bill that substantially revised both the tariff and internal revenue structures. From the point of view of the financial community, the legislation was a mixed blessing. In the judgment of David Wells and the finance journals, the rampant protectionism of some portions of the tariff section was a step backward. On the other hand, the changes in the internal revenue system agreeably lowered the income tax rate, abolished dozens of nuisance taxes (such

52. *Congressional Globe* 41:2:4063. For background, see Bolles, *Financial History*, pp. 411–12; Smith, *Internal Tax History*, pp. 52–98; Seip, *South Returns to Congress*, pp. 158–60.
53. Financial journals repeatedly endorsed the principle of an income tax because the levy: (1) required very little administrative expense compared with the revenue it produced; (2) bore some relation to the ability of the citizen to pay and to the interest the citizen had "in the protection afforded by the government; the two considerations which ought to control the distribution of the burden"; (3) constituted an indispensable source of revenue for the Treasury; and (4) did not, compared to commodity taxes and the tariff, perversely distort the normal channels of commerce. One of the complaints lodged against the tax charged that it was associated with much "fraud and perjury" in operation because it depended on voluntary disclosure of easily hidden personal property and income – Treasury officials were said to have estimated that at least one-half of all personal income went unreported and untaxed. With appropriate reforms, the journals opposed repeal of the income tax but recommended, as the 1870 reduction was being debated in the House, a lowering of the tax rate to 3 percent. *Hunt's*, May 1870, pp. 321–6; June 1870, p. 425. On retention of the income tax, see February 1868, pp. 114–15; December 1869, p. 441; January 1870, p. 9; *Chronicle*, February 19, 1870, p. 230; April 16, 1870, p. 487; the *Chronicle* later supported outright repeal (January 7, 1871, p. 7).
54. See, for example, David Wells's increasing advocacy of free trade positions between 1867 and 1871. Ferleger, *Wells*, pp. 222–315.
55. Even after this reduction was adopted, the new rate was higher than that prevailing before revision. Ferleger, *Wells*, p. 298.
56. *Congressional Globe* 41:2:5419. Customs receipts from "Steel in ingots, bars, sheets, or wire not less than one-quarter of an inch in diameter" were $1,069,927 in the 1869 fiscal year, approximately 0.6 percent of all customs revenue. *Hunt's*, February 1870, p. 131. At this time, steel was used in only 5 percent of all rails produced in the United States. William Greenleaf, ed., *American Economic Development since 1860* (Columbia: University of South Carolina Press, 1968), p. 95. By 1880, steel would compose almost two-thirds of all domestic production.

Table 5.5. *Internal revenue, tariff, and the income tax: Revenue policy and sectors of the political economy in House voting, 1865–71*

	Support for the position of finance capital (percent of members voting)				
Policy decision	National bank districts	Iron and steel districts	Settlement districts	Border-state/ Confederate districts	Sectional stress index
Reduce tariff on railroad iron	4.3 (23)	4.3 (23)	65.7 (35)	52.2 (23)	59.6
Repeal cotton tax	24.1 (29)	45.8 (24)	18.5 (27)	86.2 (29)	44.4
Reduce income tax	92.0 (25)	80.8 (26)	23.1 (39)	50.0 (58)	49.4
Reduce tariff on railroad steel	52.4 (21)	29.2 (24)	79.4 (34)	65.9 (44)	58.3
Internal revenue/ tariff bill	76.9 (26)	76.9 (26)	82.5 (40)	69.2 (52)	32.7

Note: For a description of these issues and the position of finance capital, see the accompanying text.

as those on carriages and billiard tables, professional licenses, and small levies on the gross receipts of railroads, theaters, and lotteries), and primarily consolidated revenue around distilled and fermented alcohol, tobacco, banking operations, and a few other goods (such as patent medicines and playing cards). The internal revenue revisions were almost categorically in line with those recommended by the financial community and the relatively obnoxious tariff section was the price that had to be paid to get them. The lopsided vote on final adoption of the combined measure reflected the political success of this shotgun marriage.[57]

In terms of consistency in voting on revenue policy, finance capitalists must have been most satisfied with the behavior of congressmen from the former slave states (see Table 5.5). Though these members split evenly on the reduction of the income tax and supported lowering of the tariff on railroad iron by only a slim margin, the overall record on the five policy decisions was generally in line with the views expressed by the financial community. Not so for the other delegations from the major sectors of the national political economy. Members from settlement constituencies were on the whole more supportive of positions taken by the financial community than were congressmen representing areas more

57. Ferleger, *Wells*, pp. 116, 298; *Hunt's*, December 1869, pp. 441–2; June 1870, pp. 412–15, 420–5. The vote was 144 yea, 49 nay, and 37 abstaining. *Congressional Globe* 41:2:5522, July 13, 1870.

directly linked to the interests of industrial capitalism. Settlement members were particularly sound on the railroad schedules of the tariff and the general revenue bill. Iron members compiled the least desirable record, from the perspective of finance capital, while bank congressmen were only marginally more supportive. On the whole, these voting patterns provide little evidence of finance capitalist influence on legislative behavior with respect to revenue policy. When congressmen from the heart of the Republican coalition are considered alone, support for finance capitalist positions generally declines across the board, but the rough rank ordering of the sectors remains the same (for example border-state districts are most supportive – see Table 5.6). Congressmen from "mixed" or Democratic districts were significantly more favorable to finance capitalist perspectives than members belonging to the core precincts of the Republican party. This surprising pattern originated in the common opposition of Democrats and the financial community to central state expenditures. The former opposed spending because it furthered the interests of the Republicans by servicing their party's coalition. The latter opposed spending because of its negative implications for maintaining a budgetary surplus.

Several factors explain these results. In the first place, the finance capitalist position on all of these decisions favored a reduction in taxation. With the exception of the omnibus revenue bill, which was the result of complex intraparty negotiations and maneuvering, the Republican coalition tended to favor the retention of revenue capacity. The party needed a secure and substantial flow of revenue to make side payments within the core coalition, (railroad subsidies in return for protectionist tariff schedules, for example), to pursue policies that would culminate in the resumption of specie payments, and to maintain a substantial military presence in the southern states. The omnibus revenue bill, when seen in this context, was an attempt to balance those goals against tax relief for commercial sectors. Members not included in the central coalition of the party, particularly Democrats, could support tax reduction measures without the moderating influence of the pacts and informal agreements made within the heart of the Republican party.

As a proximate explanation of voting on these issues, however, direct representation of the political economic interests of the respective districts works very well. On the tariff decisions, for example, the deep divisions that opened up between the iron and settlement delegations can be traced directly to their competing interests in maintaining barriers against the importation of rails. On the whole, members from capital-rich constituencies backed the iron and steel schedules, but the industrial capitalist alliance began to fray a bit as Reconstruction wore on.

Table 5.6. *Internal revenue, tariff, and the income tax: Revenue policy and sectors of the political economy in Republican voting (1865–71)*

Policy decision	Support for the position of finance capital (percent of members voting)					
	National bank districts	Iron and steel districts	Settlement districts	Border-state districts	All Republican districts	All mixed/ Democratic districts
Reduce tariff on railroad iron	0.0 (17)	0.0 (15)	57.7 (26)	33.3 (9)	29.5 (105)	61.9 (42)
Repeal cotton tax	0.0 (18)	14.3 (14)	0.0 (20)	50.0 (6)	9.6 (94)	85.7 (63)
Reduce income tax	88.2 (17)	75.0 (16)	13.8 (29)	33.3 (9)	51.4 (111)	71.3 (80)
Reduce tariff on railroad steel	30.8 (13)	12.5 (16)	77.8 (27)	60.0 (5)	43.9 (98)	76.7 (73)
Internal revenue/tariff bill	100.0 (17)	100.0 (16)	96.8 (31)	87.5 (8)	97.3 (111)	43.9 (82)

Note: "Republican districts" are those that were represented at all times by a Republican or a member of an affiliated party (such as the Union party in New York). "Mixed/Democratic districts" include all districts not represented in Congress for the entire period (the former Confederate districts of the South), districts that at one time or another were represented by members from both the Democratic and the Republican parties, and districts that, without exception, were represented by Democrats or members from closely affiliated parties (such as the Conservative party in Kentucky).

Roll call alignments on the income tax similarly followed district positions in the political economy. On a per capita basis, internal revenue receipts from levies on personal income ranged from over ten dollars in the Boston and New York City revenue districts to a penny or less in western Arkansas (the third revenue district), the coastal plains and hill country of North Carolina (the first, fifth, and seventh districts), piedmont South Carolina (the third revenue district), and central Tennessee (the third, fourth, and sixth districts – see Map 5.2).[58] Receipts were very heavy in almost every major northern city (Philadelphia, Syracuse, Pittsburgh, Cleveland, Columbus, Cincinnati, and Chicago) and in the gold- and silver-bearing regions of the West. Outside of Knoxville, Tennessee, and New Orleans, the South yielded almost nothing from this tax. When broken down by per capita receipts, congressional voting on income tax reduction followed the pattern of revenue flow (Table 5.7). Thus, the strong backing for the finance capital position by capital-rich districts on this issue was probably due to the interests of constituents and not to the comparatively remote systemic considerations suggested by the financial community.[59] As *Hunt's* lamented (a modern lament indeed):

> We have no officer of the Government in Congress whose business it is to consider the interest of the people as a whole, and to devise legislation for them.... Each member of [the congressional] committees has generally local interests to represent, in behalf of his constituents; and the committees sit by months together to hear the statements and arguments of such persons as can bring their own needs to Washington, and command the services of a lobby. If bills thus prepared seem to have been the result of a series of compromises between class interests and local demands rather than an application of the general principle [of the national interest], it is to be accounted for by our system of Government.... To take a single instance of this, there has been in Congress and in the press an earnest demand for the abolition of the Income Tax. [Opposition to the tax has] been reinforced by the intense feeling which is aroused by the personal interest of those who feel this tax heavily, and who feel scarcely any other. Because a large part of the talking and writing men of the country are influenced by these feelings, it has been hastily assumed that the nation, as a whole, is bitterly against it. Yet... if it were

58. The Civil War era tax on personal income was a comprehensive levy with major exclusions limited to corporate income on which taxes had already been paid and, for several years, rent on personal living quarters. See *Hunt's*, May 1863, pp. 397–8; August 1863, pp. 139–41.

59. Between 1867 and 1869, an average of 260,000 individuals paid at least some tax on their income, though more than a third of these taxpayers owed twenty dollars or less. The levy yielded almost $26 million a year during this period. *Chronicle*, January 28, 1871, p. 102.

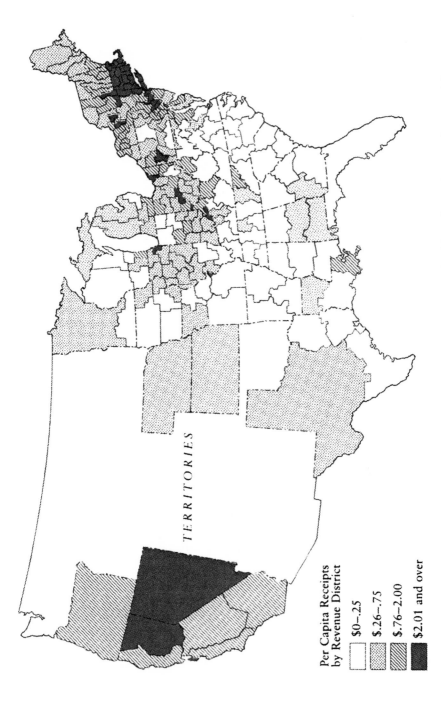

Map 5.2 Per capita receipts from the income tax: July 1, 1866, to June 30, 1867. *Source:* Calculated from data in the *Annual Report of the Commissioner of Internal Revenue*, 1867, the *1870 Census of Population*, and Internal Revenue District boundaries published in the *Internal Revenue Record*, July 24, 1869, pp. 26–30.

Per Capita Receipts
by Revenue District

$0–.25

$.26–.75

$.76–2.00

$2.01 and over

TERRITORIES

Table 5.7. *Voting in the House of Representatives on reduction of the national income tax*

Revenue district receipts (per capita)	Percentage of votes cast in favor of income tax reduction
$ 0 to .25	36.5 (52)
.26 to .75	50.0 (62)
.76 to 2.00	67.7 (31)
2.01 and over	93.5 (46)

Source: Calculations by the author from roll call data and compilations of internal revenue receipts by congressional district (see note to Map 5.2).

abandoned, the whole amount of it would have to be levied from the mass of the people in some way far less equitable and far more oppressive; and it only needs to be reduced to a moderate rate and adjusted upon the principles which we pointed out some time ago.[60]

If a roll call on simple repeal had been analyzed instead of this reduction, congressmen from bank and, to a lesser extent, iron constituencies would, with equal ease, have been thrown into opposition to finance capital (which opposed repeal until, roughly, 1871).

The cotton tax fell most severely upon the plantation districts of the South and pushed overall receipts there to levels comparable to, if not a little above, those in the average northern district (see Map 5.3). Revenues from the cotton excise comprised more than 95 percent of all internal revenue receipts in northeastern Arkansas (97.1, the first district) and the northern two-thirds of Mississippi (97.6 and 98.7, the second and third revenue districts, respectively). In much of the remainder of the deep South, the cotton levy comprised more than 85 percent of all revenue. While the South's dependence on cotton production is unmistakable in these figures, the near absence of any receipts from the other internal revenue schedules also says a lot about the impoverished and underdeveloped state of the region's postwar economy. Not surprisingly, 86 percent of all former slave-state congressmen supported repeal of the cotton tax, as did the same percentage of members from districts outside the heart of the Republican coalition. Finance capital apparently influenced few congressmen from capital-rich districts in the North on this policy even though the financial community as a whole strongly supported repeal. Iron and steel members were more responsive (but not much if they belonged to the central coalition of the Republican party). The cotton

60. June 1870, p. 411.

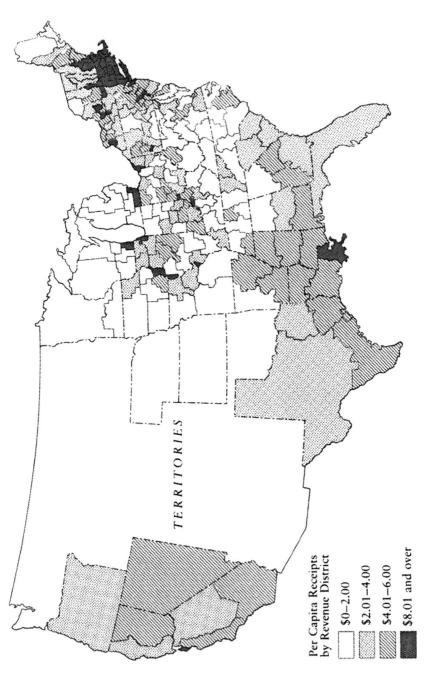

Per Capita Receipts
by Revenue District

☐ $0–2.00

▨ $2.01–4.00

▨ $4.01–6.00

■ $8.01 and over

TERRITORIES

Map 5.3 Per capita receipts from all internal revenue schedules: July 1, 1866, to June 30, 1867. *Source:* Calculated from data in the *Annual Report of the Commissioner of Internal Revenue,* 1867, the *1870 Census of Population,* and Internal Revenue District boundaries published in the *Internal Revenue Record,* July 24, 1869, pp. 26–30.

tax also drove a wedge between cotton-producing and settlement delegations; the latter were the least burdened by internal revenue taxes of any of the major sectors of the political economy.

In each instance, interests more directly implicated by the decision at hand than finance capital appear to have guided congressional decision making. Some relatively slight evidence indicates partisan bargaining within the central core of the Republican party, but, on the whole, voting on revenue policy issues was highly polarized by the weight of revenue demands imposed by the several schedules. Only the omnibus revenue bill indicates that the Republican party as an organization could serve as an effective broker for the major sectors that provided it with a mandate for political rule.

Federal operations and expenditures

Compared to revenue questions, issues involving government expenditures were more tangentially related to the operating requirements of the financial system in that they less strongly redirected the otherwise free workings of the marketplace. While the negative incentives of the tax structure entered into the economic calculations of almost everyone in the nation, federal spending, even in the form of corporate subsidies and military occupation of the South, was less pervasive or effective in shaping private economic activity. Much of government spending, all observers conceded, was either wasted through incompetence or fraudulently diverted from public goals. While waste and corruption were deplored, the financial community viewed government spending as less debilitating, everything considered, than the systemic impact of taxation on economic life. Government corruption and incompetence did, however, lead finance capital to strongly support reform in the criteria and procedures under which appointments to public office were made.[61]

On all of the questions analyzed in this section, the interests of the Republican party as a political organization and the position of the financial community were uncompromisingly opposed. On civil service reform, for example, *Hunt's* backed the operating requirements of the executive branch against the purely partisan interests of majority-party congressmen:

61. See, for example, Unger's observation that civil "service reform attracted many [businessmen] who feared the blackmail often extorted by corrupt politicians from legitimate merchants and manufacturers." *Greenback Era*, p. 144; Stephen Skowronek, *Building a New American State: The Expansion of National Administrative Capacities, 1877–1920* (New York: Cambridge University Press, 1982), pp. 51–5; Ferleger, *Wells*, p. 41.

The one condition of purity and efficiency in a Democratic Government is that the Executive shall be a unit both in power and in responsibility. The custom of Congress is now to regard the Executive as its instrument, expecially in the matter of appointments to office; so that the whole civil service of the country is divided up into lots, for distribution among Congressmen of the fortunate party.... [The Executive's] highest acts of sovereignty are not its own; as a fountain of honor and source of authority, it is a mere mouthpiece of a partisan majority in Congress, each man wholly irresponsible for the excessive influence he wields, often secretly, upon the most solemn and momentous acts of the Executive.... Before any general reform in the administration of public affairs can begin, the Executive authority in its integrity, with the full responsibility for all its appointments, must be restored to the... President.[62]

Because no public policy, no matter how well designed in law, would fail if executed by an incompetent or corrupt bureaucracy, civil service reform was a fundamental requirement for almost all government intervention in the political economy (including active management of the nation's money market). The first serious attempt to reform appointments to government office came in the form of a bill drafted by the House Committee on Retrenchment and sponsored in floor debate by Representative Thomas Jenckes of Providence, Rhode Island (who also managed the bankruptcy legislation). On February 6, 1867, the House tabled and thus killed civil service reform by a narrow, six-vote margin.[63]

The remaining four decisions studied under this heading represent a broad selection of expenditure issues that were important to maintaining the internal cohesion of the Republican party coalition. In each and every case, spokesmen for the financial community indicated unequivocal opposition to the principle that underlay government spending in the respective policy areas (see Chapter 4). The first of these four decisions involved adoption of an amendment offered by Representative Thaddeus Stevens of Pennsylvania, an ardent protectionist and one of the leading members of the Republican party. Stevens proposed that a 20 percent bonus be paid to civil employees of the government who worked in Washington, D.C., and whose salaries were below $2,000 a year. "Seeing the very delightful, wholesome mania for reform which has taken possession of our souls and which pervades this whole country now," Stevens

62. June 1870, p. 408.
63. *Congressional Globe* 39:2:1033–6. The tally was 72 yea, 66 nay, and 52 members abstained. For background to civil service reform, including this vote, see Leonard D. White, *The Republican Era: A Study in Administrative History* (New York: Macmillan, 1958), pp. 279–81; Ari Hoogenboom, "Thomas A. Jenckes and Civil Service Reform," *Journal of American History* 47 (March 1961): 636–58.

claimed he had exercised restraint by instituting the $2,000 cap on the bonus (the previous year's bonus lacked a ceiling). Offered on December 16, 1867, the salary bonus was added to the appropriations bill by a razor thin margin of three votes.[64]

Later in the same session, the House considered a bill to establish a monopoly on the transportation of American mail between the United States and Europe for the steamships of the (to be created) Commercial Navigation Company. The bill provided substantial annual subsidies above and beyond the actual costs for ocean carriage of the mails. These subsidies were to be used by the Post Office to retire the company's bonds, which would be deposited with (but not guaranteed by) that department. If enacted, the legislation promised to do for oceanic shipping what the Pacific railroad acts had done for land transportation. And, in fact, the bill found favor in the House; an early attempt to table the measure failed by a large margin on June 10, 1868.[65]

On January 18, 1869, William Holman of Indiana, who was given the informal title "watchdog of the Treasury" by his colleagues, offered a nonbinding resolution urging: "That in the present condition of the national finances no further subsidies ought to be granted by Congress, either in bonds or money, to railroad or other corporations, or to promote local enterprises, but the whole resources of the country ought to be applied to the pressing necessities of the public service in such manner as will relieve the people from the burdens of taxation." Though Holman was not necessarily a friend of finance capital on other issues (particularly those involving monetary policy), this resolution almost exactly stated the position of the financial community on corporate subsidies. A sizable majority backed the resolution, but the motion was of little or no practical effect.[66]

The last of the five decisions in this section arose in connection with consideration of a sundry civil appropriation bill on February 28, 1871. In previous House deliberations, the membership had "with wonderful unanimity" overridden the objections of the Appropriations Committee and its chairman, Henry Dawes of Massachusetts, and added numerous new public works projects to the measure. After the bill had been loaded up with new projects, the House, in Dawes's words, "shrunk from its own work and strangled its own offspring." In an effort to bring the bill

---

64. *Congressional Globe* 40:2:215. Seventy-three members supported the bonus, 70 opposed, and 44 abstained. The bonus was later taken out of the final bill.
65. *Congressional Globe* 40:2:3031–3. Only 36 members voted to table (the finance capital position), 97 opposed the motion, and 56 abstained. The bill, however, never became law.
66. *Congressional Globe* 40:3:424. The vote was 90 to 67, with 65 abstentions.

back from the grave, the Appropriations Committee offered an amendment to strike all but one of the new projects. The resulting roll call gave the committee a narrow victory.[67] The vote also recorded congressional sentiment on one of the most important sources – along with patronage appointments and railroad subsidies – of political spoils for the Republican party.

The rebellion on the House floor against the leadership of the Appropriations Committee can, in part, be traced to the panel's and the Republican party's discrimination against certain regions of the country in the distribution of projects. This discrimination heavily weighted public works expenditures in favor of the Northeast and left little for the former slave states or settlement districts. For example, the War Department's revised estimates for rivers and harbors improvements for fiscal year 1869 suggested that no projects be awarded to the states of the former Confederacy. Authorized expenditures for rivers and harbors in fiscal year 1870 granted the South just over 5 percent of the national total, but most of the spending was dedicated to improving navigation at the mouth of the Mississippi River, a project just as, if not more, important to the North as it was to the South. Overall, Reconstruction spending heavily favored the already well-developed ports and river courses of the East over the developing and, in the South, war-devastated periphery (see Table 5.8).[68] Given the long southern coastline, the disrepair into which port facilities had fallen, and the importance of cotton exports to the national economy, the discrimination against projects in the states of the former Confederacy was even more marked than these per capita figures suggest.

Congressmen from bank and iron districts were much more favorable to the institution of civil service protection for federal employees than

67. *Congressional Globe* 41:3:1752–7. The tally was 110 votes for the committee substitute (striking out the projects added on the floor), 102 votes for the amended bill (with the projects retained in it), and 28 abstentions.
68. "Appropriations for Harbor and River Improvements," Exec. Doc. 224: House of Representatives: 40th Cong., 2nd Sess., Ser. Rec. 1341 (Washington, D.C.: Government Printing Office [GPO], 1868); "Improvement of Rivers and Harbors," Exec. Doc. 22: Senate: 41st Cong., 2nd Sess., Ser., Rec. 1405 (GPO, 1870); "Public Works in States and Territories," Exec. Doc. 12: Senate: 43rd Cong., 1st Sess., Ser. Rec. 1580 (GPO, 1874), p. 18. The latter included spending on the construction of public buildings, fortifications, and arsenals and armories, in addition to rivers and harbors improvements. Such building construction pushed expenditures in the District of Columbia, for example, over $112 per capita (not included in the table). For slightly different figures on regional expenditures, see C. Vann Woodward, *Reunion and Reaction: The Compromise of 1877 and the End of Reconstruction* (Boston: Little, Brown, 1966), pp. 58–9. Seip points out that southern Republicans were excluded from service on the House Appropriations Committee. *South Returns to Congress*, p. 116.

Table 5.8. *Sectional distribution of rivers and harbors spending,*
1865–73

Region	Total rivers and harbors expenditures, 1865–73	1870 Population	Per capita expenditures
New England	$12,174,852.42	3,487,924	$ 3.49
New York, New Jersey, and Pennsylvania	19,649,132.27	8,810,806	2.23
Midwest	19,540,209.58	11,245,635	1.74
Pacific	7,161,618.97	693,661	10.32
Border	2,167,141.34	4,389,429	.49
Confederate	9,444,945.22	9,487,386	1.00
Territories	251,272.13	311,030	.81

Source: Calculated from data provided by the sources cited in note 68 to the text.

members from settlement or former slave constituencies (see Tables 5.9 and 5.10). Polarization on this issue was even more marked within the heart of the Republican coalition than in the House membership as a whole: Only 14 percent of central coalition Republicans from settlement districts backed the civil service bill, while 92 percent of iron and steel members did so. Heavy backing by congressmen from industrial capital districts (both iron and bank) lifted the overall percentage of central coalition Republicans to 51, nine points higher than the proportion of members representing mixed and Democratic constituencies supporting reform. On this issue, the financial community was apparently influential even though the reform effort failed.

Not so on the other four decisions. In each instance, the financial community's position was opposed to federal expenditures. The one case, opposition to appropriations for new projects, in which members from capital-rich districts supported spending restraint involved conflict over political spoils in which the influence of the financial community probably played little role. The very high sectional stress score and heavy opposition to new, floor-sponsored projects by central coalition Republicans indicate that decision was interpreted as a defense of party prerogatives (as opposed to general considerations of fiscal responsibility). Central coalition Republicans in each of the four political economic sectors, for example, gave a higher proportion of their votes to the committee than their respective cohorts in the full House membership. Although the pattern within the heart of the Republican coalition still reflected the discriminatory inclinations of the committee, the pattern also suggests effective cooptation of majority-party members from settlement and

Table 5.9. *Federal expenditures and operations: Sectors of the political economy in House voting, 1865–71*

Policy decision	Support for the position of finance capital (percent of members voting)				
	National bank districts	Iron and steel districts	Settlement districts	Border-state/ Confederate districts	Sectional stress index
Create civil service	85.7 (21)	75.0 (20)	20.7 (29)	31.8 (22)	40.9
Bonus to federal employees	36.8 (19)	20.0 (20)	58.8 (34)	66.7 (24)	38.6
Establish steamship line	20.0 (20)	20.0 (20)	32.4 (34)	41.7 (24)	27.8
Corporation and railroad aid	69.2 (13)	60.0 (15)	53.1 (32)	33.3 (51)	51.5
Appropriations for new projects	62.1 (29)	45.8 (24)	60.0 (40)	27.1 (70)	56.9

Note: For a description of these issues and the position of finance capital, see the accompanying text.

border-state constituencies that were otherwise allocated small shares of the national pie.

Bank and iron members were also marginally more favorable to spending restraints on corporate aid when the issue was framed in general terms. But when the decision concerned subsidization of a steamship line which would operate out of New York City (the rough equivalent of a Union Pacific railroad to Europe), these members caved in. They also acceded to the bonus for federal employees in Washington, D.C. The central bureaucracy was largely staffed by patronage appointees from Republican districts in the Northeast, rather than party loyalists from the interior, agrarian sections of the country.[69] That connection to local

69. Of the 188 full-time employees of the Office of Internal Revenue in September 1877, for example, 36 were drawn from the immediate vicinity of Washington (the District of Columbia, Maryland, and Virginia – one employee for every 59,382 persons in the total population), 37 hailed from New England (one employee for every 94,268 persons), 53 came from the middle Atlantic states (New York, New Jersey, and Pennsylvania – one employee for every 166,242 persons), 42 were appointed from the Midwest (also the home of the commissioner of internal revenue – one employee for every 267,753 persons), three came from the West (one for every 334,897 persons), six were employed from border states other than Maryland (one for every 601,422 persons), and eleven hailed from southern states other than Virginia (one for every 751,111 persons in the region's population). Calculated from data in Secretary of the Interior, *United States Official Register, 1877* (Washington, D.C.: Government Printing Office, 1878), pp. 62–4 and the *1870 Census of Population.*

Table 5.10. *Federal expenditures and operations: Sectors of the political economy in Republican voting, 1865–71*

Policy decision	Support for the position of finance capital (percent of Republicans voting)						
	National bank districts	Iron and steel districts	Settlement districts	Border-state districts	All Republican districts	All mixed/Democratic districts
Create civil service	84.6 (13)	91.7 (12)	13.6 (22)	28.6 (7)	51.2 (86)	43.2 (52)
Bonus to federal employees	27.3 (11)	27.3 (11)	67.9 (28)	62.5 (8)	52.6 (97)	41.3 (46)
Establish steamship line	83 (12)	8.3 (12)	29.6 (27)	12.5 (8)	18.0 (89)	45.5 (44)
Corporation and railroad aid	50.0 (8)	60.0 (10)	53.8 (26)	28.6 (7)	58.1 (86)	54.9 (71)
Appropriations for new projects	88.9 (18)	71.4 (14)	65.5 (29)	50.0 (8)	76.1 (109)	26.2 (103)

party organizations in their home districts overrode the financial community's preference for fiscal restraint.

On the whole, the voting patterns on these five decisions suggest that finance capital influenced congressional decisions on spending or government operations only when the sector's interests were directly implicated (as in commercial relations with the Customs Bureau and civil service reform). Otherwise, the voting alignments indicate a wide-ranging struggle over political spoils in which the regional distribution of federal largesse and defense of the legislative integrity of the Republican party as a decision-making organization largely determined the pattern of congressional behavior.

Finance capital, the Republican party, and Reconstruction

As a class, finance capitalists had many reasons to view radical Republican plans for Reconstruction of the South with distrust and few reasons to place faith in the process or the outcome. For one thing, a serious effort to remake the plantation political economy could not avoid interfering with the recovery of cotton production and exports (see below). Any delay in the resumption of production would impede efforts to stabilize the national debt through refunding operations, to continue interest payments and ultimately redeem bond principal in specie, to maintain economic expansion in the remainder of the nation by enabling importation of goods and, finally, to resume the gold standard in domestic transactions. In 1865 Treasury Secretary McCulloch spoke for a wide spectrum of the financial community when he allowed that the federal debt was "undeniably large," but went on to say "with the labor question at the South settled on terms just to the employer and to the laborer, and with entire harmony between the different sections, it will be rapidly diminished, in burden and amount."[70] Though McCulloch was far too optimistic about debt reduction, his position clearly reflected the Johnson administration's accommodation to the interests of the southern plantation elite and early readmission of the former states of the Confederacy to full political rights within the federal union. Even when all other major groups in the North had abandoned Johnson, the financial community, particularly in New York City, remained loyal.[71]

70. *Annual Report of the Secretary of the Treasury, 1865*, reprinted in *Hunt's*, January 1866, pp. 69–70. Maintenance of an army of occupation in the South and the establishment of the Freedmen's Bureau were similarly viewed by David Wells and others as obstacles to financial stability. Ferleger, *Wells*, p. 75.
71. During his visit to New York in August, 1866, Johnson delivered a well-received

Radical Reconstruction also presented problems to finance capital in at least two other respects. In order to succeed, a remaking of the southern political economy would have to redistribute landed wealth from separatist elements to those portions of the population that were loyal to the Union (see Chapter 6).[72] Only in this way could the latter, black freedmen and a fraction of hill-country whites, free themselves from an otherwise debilitating dependence on the economic wealth and power of the plantation elite. Some of that transfer had already occurred because, as *Hunt's* observed, "the late great civil war broke down certain sections and classes in this country, and transferred wealth and power to new hands, and . . . such revolutions always unsettle customs, habits of thought and moral judgments."[73] War, however, was a chaotic process of change for which peace and social stability were a strong antidote. The difficulty with a truly radical reshaping of the southern class order was the postwar, bureaucratic involvement of the national government in the determination of property relations.

Radicals urged confiscatory taxation and open expropriation of the property of former Confederates and connected these measures to a redistribution of land to propertyless former slaves. Even if this transfer of wealth had fallen within the administrative capabilities of the federal government (which is to be seriously doubted given the graft and corruption rampant throughout the central state bureaucracy), such intervention in southern property relations was likely to erupt into an uncontrollable, ever-widening threat to the entire capitalist order.[74] It was likely, for example, that a redistribution of southern land to freedmen would make race the defining cleavage in the region's politics by pro-

speech to the financial community in which he observed "You have about three thousand millions of dollars in bonds. How are you going to preserve the credit of them? Will you tell me how the security, how the value, how the ultimate payment of the interest and principal of those bonds is to be secured? Is it by continuing this Government, disrupted as it is, by crippling our energies, and dividing us up into half a dozen petty States? Let me tell you, and mark what I tell you, that there is no way by which those bonds can be ultimately paid, interest and principal than by the consolidation of our nationality, the perpetuity and completeness of the Union of the States." Quoted in Sharkey, *Money, Class, and Party*, pp. 274–5.

72. Seip, *South Returns to Congress*, pp. 269–72; Eric Foner, *Politics and Ideology in the Age of the Civil War* (New York: Oxford University Press, 1980), pp. 119–23, 131–49.

73. June 1870, p. 405.

74. On the administrative incapacity of the national government to reshape the southern political economy, see William Gillette, *Retreat from Reconstruction, 1869–1879* (Baton Rouge: Louisiana State University Press, 1979), pp. 31–3. In carrying out even limited tasks associated with Reconstruction, Gillette observes, "The administrative apparatus of the Department of Justice, the court system, and the military establishment were comparable to a dinosaur – slow, cumbersome, and monumental in inefficiency."

moting blacks as the clients of the federal government while treating whites with comparative indifference or, in the case of those who were expropriated, hostility. In the absence of direct military rule, federal sponsorship of black economic independence could not be the sole pillar of Reconstruction. Some land would have to be distributed to poor whites. But this adjustment in policy would have both expanded the scope of federal intervention and changed the political economic basis. Only a minute fraction of the southern plantation elite had remained loyal to the Union during the war, and most whites who had denied the Confederacy their support came from impoverished hill country regions. In fact, in order to make poor whites in any significant numbers eligible for a redistribution program, the tests for loyalty to the Union during the war would have had to have been set fairly low. The involvement of whites in property redistribution would thus transform a racial cleavage into a class division.

The problem with a class-centered policy of wealth redistribution was that it was difficult to see how it could be limited to the South. Once wealth redistribution under central state auspices was begun, northern labor would almost certainly start to ask that eligibility in the southern transfer of wealth be extended to lower classes in the North that had not only been loyal to but had fought for the Union. Furthermore, once the central state had developed the administrative capacity to redistribute property between classes and legitimated the principle of redistribution, the financial and industrial wealth of the North would have been compelled to develop and defend a logic that distinguished their position in the political economy from that occupied by the southern aristocracy. In the short run, such a defense based on wartime loyalty to the Union would have successfully distinguished northern and southern elites and open challenges to northern capital would have failed. In the long run, however, the necessary logical and ideological distinctions would have weakened (both as the southern aristocracy disappeared and the justifying arguments citing "treason" became shopworn).[75] In fact, in one sense northern capitalists needed the southern plantation elite in order to position themselves as the defenders of "free labor" in the national political economy. Thus, under a program of massive land redistribution, the southern aristocracy not only would have vanished as a useful symbol but, simultaneously, the foundations of capitalist property relations in the North would have been undermined.[76]

75. Foner, *Reconstruction*, pp. 309–10, and *Politics and Ideology*, p. 144.
76. A separate difficulty with a land redistribution in the South was the apparent inclination of land-owning freedmen to adopt subsistence agriculture and thus withdraw from cotton cultivation. From the perspective of finance capital, the most important

The plausibility of this possible trajectory under a regimen of radical Reconstruction depends on several contingencies. One, permanent military occupation of the South, has already been mentioned. In order to see massive land redistribution as politically untenable, permanent occupation (for twenty or more years by as many as 100,000 troops) must be viewed as outside the range of political possibility (in terms, for example, of the maintenance of supporting political coalitions).[77] Other possibilities that might have diverted the energy otherwise feeding this hypothetical, ever-widening spiral of class conflict might include the potential massive use of federal patronage in the South to establish a dependent, white office-holding class to complement the black yeomanry created by land redistribution. What this office-holding class would have done is a salient question here, because the largest (and, in many communities, the only) federal presence in the South, after the military, was the post office (see Chapter 6). Though thousands of postmasters were employed throughout the interior, most were paid trifling salaries and the system could not have served as a durable clientele base if significantly challenged by other parts of the southern political economy.

Though pensions and other government benefits were also theoretically available as alternatives to civil employment, all alternatives under this heading seem both to require a major expansion in central state activity (in order to create the offices to be filled by loyal southern whites) and to invite a parallel spiral of demands, focusing, in this case, on the spoils of federal office (northern workers might very well ask why the comparative security of government employment was limited to southern

reason for establishing a loyalist group in the South was to permanently pacify the region so that cotton exports could resume. Though land redistribution would have strengthened the political economic foundations of the American state, the program would have been a mixed blessing in that the loss of cotton exports would have endangered the health of the financial system. Foner, *Reconstruction*, pp. 54, 108–10, 133–4, 167, 220, 234.

77. On the finance community's attitude toward military occupation, note this passage from *Hunt's:* "We cannot safely permit a colonial system to grow up among us, tending as it does to concentrate power in the hands of the Executive, and to enlarge it even to the dimensions of imperialism.... Till our Southern States are permitted to have their Senators and representatives in Congress, they are but colonies of their sister commonwealths, and can have no joint interest in our great national system." March 1866, p. 170. Also see *Hunt's*, May 1866, pp. 329–31; February 1868, p. 121; March 1868, pp. 188–202; Unger, *Greenback Era*, p. 138; and this passage from a letter (dated August 7, 1867) from Edward Atkinson to Secretary McCulloch: "I am endeavoring in connection with some others who are known as extreme radicals to give such direction to the reorganization of the south as shall prevent the creation of an exclusive black men's party and also to kill the scheme of confiscation." Sharkey, *Money, Class, and Party*, p. 119; for a strong argument that the New York financial community backed Johnson's moderate Reconstruction policies for economic reasons, see pp. 253, 272–5.

loyalists). The purpose of this discussion, however, is not to demonstrate that radical Reconstruction was doomed to failure before it started because the various logics through which it might have operated all ran afoul of the interests of northern capital. Instead, this exposition is intended to suggest that an effective Reconstruction of the southern political economy would almost certainly have implicated northern class relations in some way, depending on the strategy pursued. Furthermore, although these scenarios perhaps seem more likely with the aid of hindsight than they would have appeared at the time, the vested interest of finance capitalists in economic and political stability would have led the financial community to oppose most radical plans for the South in any case.

All radical schemes to reconstruct the South entailed some more or less permanent expansion of central state activity and expenditures. Yet the financial community placed a high priority on retrenchment both as a strategy that would ensure budgetary surpluses and as a necessary precondition for tax reduction.[78] During the 1868 presidential campaign, the Democratic nominee, Horatio Seymour, charged that military occupation of the South was costing the nation some $150 million a year and that, everything included, government expenditures associated with Reconstruction consumed upward of $300 million. In a published reply to the Democratic nominee's claims, Wells countered that direct spending associated with Reconstruction could total no more that $63 million annually. Even the Special Revenue Commissioner's estimate, which appears too low, amounted to over a quarter of all federal spending aside from interest payments on the national debt.[79] In comparison, federal spending on internal improvements and corporate subsidies totaled only about $8.3 million in fiscal 1868. Reconstruction-related expenditures represented a large percentage of all controllable federal spending during the period, and a more effective reshaping of the southern political economy would have been even more costly than the actual level of expenditures.

Finance capital thus had strong reasons to view the designs of radical Republicans with suspicion. The financial community's concern with the stability of the money market, support for the resumption of specie payments, cautious attitude toward governmental regulation of property and

78. For example, Commissioner Wells regularly included the military and the Freedmen's Bureau among his recommended reductions in spending. Ferleger, *Wells*, p. 40, 75, 108.
79. Exceeding by some $70 million all federal spending other than interest in fiscal year 1868, Seymour's top estimate is certainly too high, but the lower figure may be closer to actual Reconstruction costs than Wells's calculation. Ferleger, *Wells*, pp. 210–12; Paul B. Trescott, "Federal Government Receipts and Expenditures, 1861–1875," *Journal of Economic History* 26 (June 1966): 207.

class relations, and desire for a retrenchment in expenditures all weighed heavily and negatively against radical schemes. Henry Adams stated the case well in a letter (dated February 16, 1867) to his brother, Charles. As a consequence of radical Republican activities, Henry wrote, "I look for a struggle for gold combined with a panic, a crash in banks, a Congressional attempt to expand the currency, and a howl of agony from the whole country, as the natural effect of what is passing and has passed. As for politics I care not a damn whether the South rules us or not. In the worst of times they never ruled us so badly as Congress rules us now."[80] On the other side of the balance, the financial community's continued participation in the Republican party necessitated some moderation of this strongly conservative position.

From 1865 to 1871, hundreds of votes on various aspects of Reconstruction policy were recorded in the House of Representatives. In order to summarize the otherwise confusing and vast volume of congressional debate over Reconstruction, nine decisions have been selected from these hundreds of roll calls. Since federal policy toward the South tended to vary from Congress to Congress, these nine decisions have been further divided into three thematic categories. In the Thirty-ninth Congress, the theme is the reorganization of the southern political economy. Under this heading the most serious proposals for federal intervention in southern property relations and the regional class order are considered. The failure of these proposals led radical Republicans to retreat to a program that relied upon suffrage regulation and federal political controls (the theme of the Fortieth Congress). In spite of some striking legislative victories, political intervention also failed to secure the local dominance of southern loyalists. As troops were withdrawn from the region, one state after another fell under the control of resurgent white "redeemers." The last line of defense for radical Republicans became the attachment of special conditions to the readmission of southern states (the theme of the Forty-first Congress). These conditions were intended to make the former Confederate states subordinate members of the Union, always vulnerable to reoccupation by the military forces of the central government if "republican" principles were violated. This last ditch effort foundered in Congress. While the federal government pursued many other more narrowly conceived policies, and although these thematic divisions overlapped in time in ways that defy precise chronological delineation, this categorization neatly captures both the focus of the individual congresses and the sequential ordering of radical Republican efforts to "reconstruct" the South.

80. Levenson et al., eds., *Letters of Henry Adams*, p. 519.

During the Thirty-ninth Congress (1865–7), the most important single decision on Reconstruction policy recorded in the House of Representatives was the rejection of Thaddeus Stevens's substitute for the bill renewing the authority of the Freedmen's Bureau. That measure proposed to open up three million acres of public land in the South to settlement by freedmen and white loyalists, gave temporary title to lands already taken up by freedmen in General Sherman's military district, and ordered federal purchase of land for resale to blacks. Stevens's substitute included land "from forfeited estates of the enemy" among the lands eligible for "homestead or preemption" by southern loyalists. In addition, his proposal reduced the rental on all such lands to a nominal sum "not to exceed ten cents per acre per annum." Stevens also fixed a ceiling of two dollars per acre on the purchase price of land taken up under the act.[81] In general, the substitute envisioned the wholesale confiscation of the landed property of former rebels and its redistribution on easy terms to a new black and poor white yeomanry. As Eric Foner has described it, Stevens "had two related goals. One was to destroy the power of the planter class; the other, to create a new class of black and white yeomen as the basis of future southern political and social power, and as allies of the Republican middle class of the North."[82] On February 6, 1866, the House overwhelmingly rejected this plan for a radical redistribution of southern wealth (126 to 37, with 19 members abstaining).[83]

When finally enacted in another form, public lands in the South were opened up for settlement and southern loyalists were given preferential consideration until 1867. On February 28, 1867, Representative George Julian of Indiana called up a bill to both strengthen this preferential

81. *Congressional Globe* 39:1:655, February 5, 1866; Foner, *Politics and Ideology*, pp. 138–9; more generally, see Kenneth M. Stampp, *The Era of Reconstruction, 1865–1877* (New York: Vintage, 1965), pp. 122–30.
82. *Politics and Ideology*, p. 134. In a speech delivered in his congressional district in Lancaster County, Pennsylvania, on September 6, 1865, Stevens argued, "Heretofore ... Southern society has had more the features of aristocracy than of democracy; the Southern States have been despotisms. Is it possible that any practical equality of rights can exist where a few thousand men monopolize the whole landed property. ... How can republican institutions, free churches, free social intercourse exist in a mingled community of nabobs and serfs, of owners of twenty-thousand-acre manors, with lordly palaces, and the occupants of narrow huts inhabited by low white trash? If the South is ever to be made a safe republic let her land be cultivated by the toil of its owners, or the free labor of intelligent citizens. This must be done even though it drive the nobility into exile. If they go, all the better. It is easier and more beneficial to exile seventy thousand proud, bloated and defiant rebels than to expatriate four million laborers, native to the soil and loyal to the government." Quoted in W. R. Brock, *An American Crisis: Congress and Reconstruction, 1865–1867* (New York: Harper & Row, 1963), p. 101. On the opposition of liberal reformers to Stevens's confiscation plan, see Sprout, *The Best Men*, pp. 27–8.
83. *Congressional Globe* 39:1:688, February 6, 1866.

treatment and make discrimination in southern homesteading permanent by requiring that "any person applying for the benefit of said act shall be required to make oath that he has not borne arms against the United States or given aid and comfort to its enemies." After perfunctory debate and one minor amendment, Julian's bill passed the House by a large margin (97 to 30, with 63 abstentions). Even though the principle embodied in this oath could have been important in other contexts, in this case the practical significance was small. Southern "waste lands" (as one congressman referred to them) were simply too poor to attract or support more than a few thousand of the almost five million freedmen.[84]

The last decision from the Thirty-ninth Congress analyzed here is the vote by which the Senate version of the 1866 civil rights bill was recommitted to the House Judiciary Committee on March 9, 1866. The measure declared all blacks born in the United States to be citizens within the meaning of the Constitution and guaranteed that all residents were entitled to equal rights under the laws, particularly those that enabled individuals "to make and enforce contracts, to sue, be parties, and give evidence, to inherit, purchase, lease, sell, hold, and convey real and personal property, and to full and equal benefit of all laws and proceedings for the security of person and property." The entire machinery of the federal government, including district attorneys, marshalls, commissioners appointed by the district courts, agents of the Freedmen's Bureau, and the military, was to be involved in the protection of individual rights from violations by other persons or state and local governments. As long as state or local governments discriminated in the enforcement or administration of their laws, the operations of their courts would be supplanted by the federal judiciary. Although it fell far short of radical proposals to redistribute wealth, this measure promised a federal administration of civil and property rights throughout not only the South but the entire nation.[85] A slightly amended version of this bill later became law.

During the Fortieth Congress, the regulation of suffrage rights and

---

84. *Congressional Globe* 39:2:1660–1, February 28, 1867; Foner, *Politics and Ideology,* pp. 139–40; Paul Gates, "Federal Land Policy in the South, 1866–1888," *Journal of Southern History* 6 (August 1940):304–13.
85. The House recommitted the measure by a vote of 82 to 70 with 31 abstentions. *Congressional Globe* 39:1:1296, March 9, 1866. When the bill reemerged from the House Judiciary Committee, the rights to be secured were limited to those specifically mentioned in the bill and a section was added that invited an early test of the proposal's constitutionality before the Supreme Court. Passed by Congress, the bill was later enacted over Andrew Johnson's veto. Benedict, *A Compromise of Principle,* pp. 148, 162, 165; Brock, *An American Crisis,* p. 112. For a good summary of this bill and other civil rights measures enacted during Reconstruction, see Robert J. Kaczorowski, "To Begin the Nation Anew: Congress, Citizenship, and Civil Rights," *American Historical Review* 92 (February 1987): 45–68.

direct federal control of state administrative machinery came to dominate legislative deliberations. On July 15, 1867, for example, the House over-whelmingly adopted a resolution requesting the Judiciary Committee "to inquire and report to this House whether the States of Kentucky, Mary-land, and Delaware now have State governments republican in form, and that the committee have leave to report by bill or otherwise at any time." The resolution plainly contemplated the possible erection of Reconstruc-tion regimes in these border states that had never left the Union. Both removal from office of local governmental officials and expulsion of members of Congress could have possibly followed legislative action on this issue. Since congressmen from these states were notoriously conser-vative, expulsion would have strengthened radical Republican influence in both chambers of Congress. Although the House later added subpoena authority to the committee's investigative powers, no bill was ever re-ported.[86]

As congressional Republicans guided southern state conventions in the drafting of new, radical constitutions, the timing and method of the replacement of the incumbent civil governments that had been established by Andrew Johnson presented a rapidly mounting difficulty. Moderates sought to give the military commanders of southern districts discretionary authority over civil officials (thus transferring that power away from the president). Radical Republicans, led by Ben Butler of Massachusetts and Stevens, offered a substitute which declared that in the former states of the Confederacy (Tennessee excepted) "there are no civil State govern-ments republican in form, and that the so-called civil governments in said States ... shall not be recognized as valid or legal State governments either by the executive or judicial power or authority of the United States." The substitute then proposed an arrangement under which the new con-ventions could seize control of the state machinery even before the con-stitutions they crafted had been ratified. As Butler put it, "the majority of every convention in the South is composed of men who have been tried as with fire, and I am quite ready to trust them; and I am certain they will not do wrong with the power." The House rejected the substitute by a substantial margin on January 21, 1868, before adopting the more moderate measure.[87]

The most significant regulation of suffrage rights ever enacted by the national government was the adoption of the Fifteenth Amendment to

86. *Congressional Globe*, 40:1:656–7, July 15, 1867; 40:1:757, July 20, 1867. Maryland was also the subject of a separate investigation. See 40:1:193, March 18, 1867; authority to continue the investigation was granted on December 17, 1867 (40:2:231).
87. *Congressional Globe* 40:2:510–13, January 14, 1868; 40:2:551, January 15, 1868; 40:2:663–4, January 21, 1868. The vote was 53 to 112, with 23 abstentions.

the Constitution. That amendment prohibited the states from discriminating among citizens on the basis of race, color, or previous condition of servitude in granting the franchise. While the measure itself was an important restriction on state authority and a potential expansion of federal power, an even more powerful alternative was rejected by the House of Representatives. Offered by Samuel Shellabarger of Ohio, that alternative would have guaranteed suffrage rights to all males over the age of twenty-one except those who had been convicted of a crime or who "have engaged or may hereafter engage in insurrection or rebellion against the United States." The blanket guarantee would have prevented states from imposing surrogates for race in suffrage laws (as the South later discovered in the "grandfather clause" and literacy tests). The exception created for former rebels would have allowed Reconstruction governments to exclude from voting the vast majority of all whites. In defense of his substitute Shellabarger prophetically argued, "Let it remain possible, under our amendment, to still disfranchise the body of the colored race in the late rebel States and I tell you it will be done. . . . The overwhelming and ocean-like volume of facts which comes to us every single day of our lives in undissenting voice proves that [southern whites] will submit to negro enfranchisement not an hour longer than compelled to by Federal coercion, or as a necessity to reacquire admission to national power." After extensive debate, however, the House rejected Shellabarger's proposal (126 to 61, 35 members abstaining).[88]

After providing suffrage guarantees and new constitutions to the reconstructed states of the South, Congress turned to the question of their readmission into the Union. Three decisions were recorded during the Forty-first Congress (1869–71) which bore directly on the terms that should be placed on readmission. The first arose when Virginia's case was considered by the House on January 14, 1870. Against a bill setting certain conditions on the state's admission (described by one member as the "last gasping effort of the men who feel the offices of Virginia slipping out of their grasp"), John Bingham of Ohio proposed a substitute that simply read, "the said State of Virginia is entitled to representation in the Congress of the United States." Although this motion carried narrowly (98 to 95, with 17 abstentions), the Senate later reimposed "test oaths" as partial qualifications for office holding in the state (the oaths

88. *Congressional Globe* 40:3:722–4, January 29, 1869; 40:3:743–4, January 30, 1869; *Appendix* 40:3:97–100, January 29, 1869. The "grandfather clause" exempted otherwise qualified voters from the operation of literacy tests if they or their forefathers had been qualified to vote in 1867 (the date was chosen because blacks could not vote in the South until after that year). J. Morgan Kousser, *The Shaping of Southern Politics: Suffrage Restriction and the Establishment of the One-Party South, 1880–1910* (New Haven, Conn.: Yale University Press, 1974), p. 58.

vouched for the past loyalty of potential officeholders) and further provided that certain rights guaranteed under the state constitution (relating
to black suffrage, office holding, and education) could not be amended.
The House consented to the Senate conditions and Virginia came into
the Union.[89] When Mississippi came up on February 3, 1870, the Committee on Reconstruction recommended adoption of the same conditions
as had been required of Virginia. A substitute providing for simple readmission was offered by James Beck of Kentucky but rejected by the House
(83 to 100, with 35 abstentions).[90] These two votes thus posed very
similar questions to the House membership.

A slightly different issue was decided by the House on March 8, 1870.
Georgia had previously been readmitted in July 1868 but at the beginning
of the Forty-first Congress was again declared out of the Union. A bill
for readmission containing the same conditions as had been applied to
Virginia and Mississippi was subsequently brought forward but, because
political appointments had already been made under the Reconstruction
process and because of peculiarities in the Georgia constitution, the bill
appeared to prolong the service of radical state officers by congressional
fiat. To quiet conservative fears that the measure would delay "redemption" in the state, Bingham offered an amendment ordering that nothing
in the act could be construed in such a way as to vacate offices properly
filled through election or appointment and that the tenure of officeholders
could not extend beyond the time specified in the state constitution. This
limiting amendment carried (115 to 71, with 36 abstentions) and the
House subsequently voted to readmit Georgia to congressional representation.[91]

On all of these nine Reconstruction decisions the positions of the
financial community and those assumed by radical Republicans were
diametrically opposed. For that reason, the voting percentages reported
in Tables 5.11 and 5.12 can be read as either support for the policy
preferences of the financial community or opposition to a radical Reconstruction of the South. In analyzing these patterns, those for the
members representing the former slave states should be interpreted apart
from the three other sectors of the national political economy. The former
slave states were the object of federal policy and members from the border
and southern states had to reflect upon the way federal legislation would
directly enhance or undermine their political position at home in ways

---

89. *Congressional Globe* 41:2:502, January 14, 1870; W. H. T. Squires, *Unleashed at
    Long Last: Reconstruction in Virginia* (Virginia: Printcraft Press, 1939; reprinted
    Westport, Conn.: Negro Universities Press, 1970), pp. 418–27.
90. *Congressional Globe* 41:2:1013–14, February 3, 1870.
91. *Congressional Globe* 41:2:1765–71.

Table 5.11. *Reconstruction of the South: Sectors of the political economy in House voting, 1865–71*

Policy decision	Support for the position of finance capital (percent of members voting)				Sectional stress index
	National bank districts	Iron and steel districts	Settlement districts	Border-state/ Confederate districts	
Reorganization of the southern political economy					
Stevens's substitute	72.4 (29)	69.6 (23)	71.4 (35)	95.8 (24)	29.7
Homesteads in southern states	15.0 (20)	21.4 (14)	13.0 (23)	48.0 (25)	30.0
Recommit civil rights bill	53.6 (28)	66.7 (18)	28.6 (35)	73.9 (23)	62.9
Suffrage regulation and federal political control					
Republican governments in Kentucky, Maryland, and Delaware	58.8 (17)	40.0 (15)	29.0 (31)	28.6 (14)	17.9
Butler amendment to Reconstruction bill	89.3 (28)	75.0 (24)	51.4 (37)	53.8 (26)	13.2
Shellabarger amendment/voting rights	75.0 (24)	75.0 (24)	63.2 (38)	64.3 (56)	32.8
Conditions on southern state readmission					
Bingham amendment/Virginia readmission	66.7 (27)	40.7 (27)	41.7 (36)	52.0 (50)	43.2
Beck substitute/Mississippi readmission	47.8 (23)	36.0 (25)	34.3 (35)	53.7 (54)	41.0
Bingham amendment/Georgia readmission	68.2 (22)	60.0 (25)	60.5 (38)	49.1 (55)	45.1

Note: For a description of these issues and the position of finance capital, see the accompanying text. In all cases, support for the position of finance capital coincides with opposition to radical Reconstruction of the South.

Table 5.12. Reconstruction of the South: Sectors of the political economy in Republican voting, 1865-71

Policy decision	Support for the position of finance capital (percent of Republicans voting)					
	National bank districts	Iron and steel districts	Settlement districts	Border-state districts	All Republican districts	All mixed/Democratic districts
Reorganization of the southern political economy						
Stevens's substitute	61.1 (18)	56.3 (16)	71.4 (28)	87.5 (8)	67.3 (113)	100.0 (50)
Homesteads in southern states	0.0 (12)	0.0 (9)	0.0 (18)	16.7 (6)	1.2 (81)	63.0 (46)
Recommit civil rights bill	23.5 (17)	50.0 (12)	18.5 (27)	66.7 (9)	37.3 (102)	88.0 (50)
Suffrage regulation and federal political control						
Republican governments in Kentucky, Maryland, and Delaware	53.3 (15)	20.0 (10)	24.0 (25)	11.1 (9)	23.1 (91)	72.0 (25)
Butler amendment to Reconstruction bill	87.5 (16)	64.3 (14)	50.0 (30)	33.3 (9)	60.9 (110)	81.8 (55)
Shellabarger amendment/voting rights	60.0 (15)	69.2 (13)	58.6 (29)	37.5 (8)	56.3 (103)	81.0 (84)
Conditions on southern state readmission						
Bingham amendment/Virginia readmission	43.7 (16)	18.7 (16)	31.0 (29)	20.0 (10)	28.3 (113)	82.5 (80)
Beck substitute/Mississippi readmission	20.0 (15)	13.3 (15)	21.4 (28)	20.0 (10)	18.4 (103)	80.0 (80)
Bingham amendment/Georgia readmission	53.3 (15)	46.7 (15)	56.2 (32)	37.5 (8)	54.8 (104)	70.7 (82)

Note: In all cases, support for the position of finance capital coincides with opposition to a radical Reconstruction of the South.

that northern congressmen did not have to consider. To the Southerners, for example, suffrage eligibility was not only an abstract principle but a potential factor in future electoral victory or defeat. In fact, southern congressmen exhibited very different attitudes toward property redistribution and suffrage eligibility. On the one hand, border-state members within the central coalition of the Republican party were relatively opposed to the property redistribution and civil rights enforcement policies offered during the Thirty-ninth Congress, but subsequently strongly favored, again in comparative terms, proposals for federal suffrage regulation and conditions on the readmission of southern states (see Table 5.12). When the behavior of all congressmen from the border and South are analyzed, however, the former slave-state delegations compiled one of the most conservative records on Reconstruction policy (see Table 5.11). The juxtaposition of the two patterns suggests that a broad bipartisan consensus in the South was lodged against plans for the redistribution of wealth to blacks, but support for purely political Reconstruction measures sharply divided southern party organizations and their respective constituent elements in the political economy.[92]

Of the three other sectors of the political economy, the members from capital-rich, national bank districts were far and away the most opposed to radical Reconstruction of the South and, thus, most supportive of the conservative positions advocated by the financial community. On six of the nine decisions, congressmen from capital-rich constituencies cast a greater percentage of their votes against radical policies than did delegations from both iron-producing or settlement regions (see Table 5.11). In addition, bank and iron delegations both cast 75 percent of their ballots against the Shellabarger amendment. Only on southern homesteads and recommittal of the 1866 civil rights bill were national bank members more radically oriented than, in those instances, members representing iron and steel districts. In every case, congressmen from settlement areas were more favorable to radical Republican proposals than members from eastern, capital-rich districts.

When the heart of the Republican coalition is considered apart from the remainder of the House membership, the picture is more muddled. Iron district Republicans appear, compared to their bank and settlement district colleagues, significantly more radical. Omitting the southern homestead vote upon which northern, central coalition Republicans were

92. Seip sees southern Republican backing for radical Reconstruction measures as ultimately self-defeating: "Locked into a policy based on force which only stimulated the rabidity of their conservative opposition, most southern Republicans supported enforcement legislation because their survival depended on it." *South Returns to Congress*, p. 130.

unanimous, iron district Republicans were the most radical division of the political economy on five of the eight other decisions. Republican members from settlement districts delivered a much more balanced performance, scoring more radical than other northern sectors on three decisions, more conservative on three more, and between the other two on the remainder. Though bank congressmen recorded support percentages for conservative Reconstruction that always placed them as a group first or second, the overall performance was not particularly strong compared to that of the same sector when "mixed" and Democratic districts were included (compare with Table 5.11). The most consistent result reported in Table 5.12 is that central coalition Republicans were significantly more radical than their Democratic and mixed district colleagues – which is no surprise.[93]

In sum, we can say that congressmen from capital-rich districts were more conservative on Reconstruction issues than members drawn from the leading districts within other sectors of the northern political economy.[94] This tendency was very pronounced after the Thirty-ninth Congress and is in general agreement with Les Benedict's observation that as "contractionists and free-traders became more conservative, radicalism tended more and more to be limited to those who advocated expansion of the currency. This became more apparent with each session of the Fortieth Congress."[95] The strong opposition of finance capital to radical Reconstruction can be explained, in the first instance, with reference to the operating requirements of the financial system, and the plausibility of some connection to congressional behavior can be supported by

93. That result was already well known, for example, to Henry Adams, who, in a letter to Charles, called radical Republicans "little better than a mob of political gamblers and timid time-servers" and, on another occasion, denounced bills introduced by Thomas Eliot of Massachusetts and Thaddeus Stevens as likely to produce in the South "a society dissolved and brigandage universal." Levenson et al., eds., *Letters of Henry Adams,* April 3, 1867, p. 528 and March 1, 1867, p. 524.

94. These results coincide with the rankings of congressmen along a "radical–conservative" spectrum that have been reported by other scholars. If Republican congressmen from capital-rich districts are cross tabulated with David Donald's rankings, for example, we find that 16 of 59 (27.1 percent) of members he classifies as "Independents, Moderates, and Conservatives" represented capital-rich districts while the ratio was only 6 of 59 (10.2 percent) for congressmen classified as "Ultra- or Stevens Radicals." *The Politics of Reconstruction, 1863–1867* (Baton Rouge: Louisiana State University Press, 1965), pp. 100–5. Michael Les Benedict reports rankings for all congressmen for several Reconstruction congresses. In the first session of the Fortieth Congress (1867), congressmen from finance capital districts comprised 11 of the 47 (23.4 percent) northern members he classified as "Conservatives," 4 of the 53 (7.5 percent) of those classified as "Centrists," and only 1 of the 26 (3.8 percent) he unequivocally classified as "Radicals."

95. *Compromise of Principle,* p. 276. Butler and Stevens were the most visible proponents of both greenback expansion and radical Reconstruction policies. See, for example, Unger, *Greenback Era,* p. 86; Sharkey, *Money, Class, and Party,* p. 95.

roughly consistent voting decisions on the part of bank congressmen. Most congressmen, however, did not participate in congressional debate or, if they did, failed to mention considerations of financial stability as an explanation for their conservative stands on Reconstruction.[96]

Even though the finance capital sector of the northern political economy spawned the greatest proportional number of conservative congressmen, their overall impact on Reconstruction must be carefully interpreted. If, for example, the failure of radical Reconstruction is traced to the collapse of plans to redistribute southern wealth, then the effort failed before the end of the Thirty-ninth Congress. Yet that period was the one in which bank district congressmen delivered their most radical performance, comparatively speaking. An interpretation of the fate of Reconstruction that places the blame on a general lack of northern determination fares better with the evidence but relies on less persuasive explanations of Reconstruction's failure. Radical efforts failed because no sector of the political economy had a motive to pursue Reconstruction that could override the pursuit of other interests. For example, the iron districts were more interested in the tariff, capital-rich districts in the operation of the financial system, and settlement districts in internal improvements. Each won concessions in these areas from the other groups in the Republican coalition. Southern Republicans, of course, had strong political reasons to favor radical policies but shied away from a major reorganization of southern property and social relations. That left the resurgent southern Democrats who, as they reentered congressional chambers, provided the deciding margin by which Reconstruction died. At that stage and somewhat earlier, the conservatism of the financial community was an important contributing factor.

Conclusion

During the American Civil War, the northern Union reorganized the financial system and established links to the nation's money markets. As one outcome of these policies, a new class of finance capitalists was

96. An exception was William Dodge, "metal importer, iron manufacturer, land speculator, railroad investor, and president of the New York [City] Chamber of Commerce," who on one occasion argued, "The commercial, the manufacturing, and the agricultural interests as they look at [a radical proposal to divide the South into military districts], will see in it a continuance of taxation necessary to support this military array sent to these ten States . . . the men who control the money are waiting to see what shall be the result upon the interests of the country of the measures about to be acted upon in this House [before investing in new ventures and enterprises]." *Congressional Globe* 39:2:629, January 21, 1867; Stanley Coben described Dodge's business interests in "Northeastern Business and Radical Reconstruction: A Reexamination," in Ralph Andreano, ed., *The Economic Impact of the American Civil War* (Cambridge, Mass.: Schenkman Publishing, 1967), p. 157.

created. Compared to their antebellum predecessors, these finance capitalists were both largely autonomous of British influence and dependent on the policies of the U.S. Treasury. This dependence, as well as the positive role of the American state in clearing local barriers to national market expansion, could have transformed finance capital into the national government's strongest ally in the postwar period. Analytical support for this possibility can be found not only in the material interests of the financial community in the structure and processes of the political economy but also in finance capital's clear, sympathetic recognition of the organizational characteristics we now associate with the administrative capacity of the state.[97]

This potential alliance between the Republican party-state and finance capital was a casualty of Treasury incompetence and intraparty factionalism. As the Treasury became recognized as one of the most important sources of instability and risk in the nation's money markets, finance capitalist support for a radical Reconstruction of the South waned both in the major journals of the financial community and within the congressional delegations capital-rich districts sent to Washington. Finance capital, of course, had other reasons for hesitating to embrace radical proposals for reorganizing the southern political economy (protection of property rights from class challenges, reestablishment of cotton cultivation in the South, reduction in government expenditures, among them). Even so, finance capital emerged from the war as the most statist sector of the national political economy and possessed, because of its position, the most well-developed vision of the interdependencies between state capacity, national development, and political integration.

Because radical Reconstruction involved the establishment of an indigenous loyalist group within a militantly separatist society, it was the most important statist project facing the nation in the postwar period.

97. Alternative modes of financing the war effort might have alleviated financial community opposition to Reconstruction. For example, if the Union had more heavily relied on taxation during the war years, correspondingly reduced dependence on legal tender currency issues, and created a nationalized central bank to replace the fragmented, politically exposed operations of the Treasury and the New York Clearing House, the economy might have been able to remain on the gold standard throughout the war (a remote possibility even under these circumstances). Even if the Treasury had been forced off the gold standard by the fiscal demands of the conflict, the nation might have resumed specie payments at the antebellum standard one or two years after the war ended or have adjusted the monetary system to reflect the moderate inflation of the war years expected under this scenario and thus resumed specie payments immediately. All of these possible outcomes would probably have moderated the otherwise strong opposition of the financial community to a radical reorganization of the southern political economy by accommodating the primary interests of finance capital. In the long run, the result might have been a much stronger central state.

But this project was completely in the hands of the Republican party, an organization deeply penetrated by loosely allied economic interests whose separate agendas were often at odds with each other and the developmental implications of Reconstruction. Only those factions of the Republican party that directly connected the fate of southern loyalists to their own positions in the political economy were likely to support radical Reconstruction as a continuing policy interest. As it turned out, radical Republicans were but a minority in every northern sector of the political economy and Reconstruction was a war orphan that no faction wanted to abandon yet none could afford, in the rough and tumble of intraparty combat, to keep. In statist terms, radical Republicans put the survival of the party-state on a par with the narrower interests of their respective constituencies. Conservative Republicans, an increasing proportion hailing from capital-rich regions, placed the interests of their districts above those of party-state survival and, in the process, turned Reconstruction away from the statist goal of a permanent restructuring of the southern political economy and toward a negotiated return to power by former Confederate nationalists.

The Civil War and Reconstruction periods thus describe one of the ways in which particular patterns of state development can be self-limiting. In the case of the Civil War, the Union financed the war effort by floating an enormous national debt and created a dependent financial class to manage the debt's servicing. Because the Treasury lacked the administrative capacity to manage financial markets and radical Reconstruction delayed resumption of the gold standard in the domestic economy, this dependent financial community turned upon the state that created it – thus contributing to an end to radical efforts to reconstruct the southern political economy and preventing a continuation of the process of central state expansion that had been unleashed during the war.

6

State structure and Reconstruction: The political legacy of the Civil War

Union victory left the South occupied by the U.S. Army and the challenge facing the Republican party was to find some way of reintegrating the South into the national political system on terms compatible with the northern social base and the Republican economic agenda. For several reasons, the range of options the Republicans could consider was broader and less constrained by societal structure than those connected with any other major policy choice in the nation's history. The southern political economy was thoroughly devastated and disorganized by the war, leaving secessionists preoccupied with survival and evading prosecution for treason. Moreover, class relations had been completely disrupted by the abolition of slavery and population migration. The Republican opportunity to remake the political economy was further brightened by the absence of southern representation in national political institutions; at least formally, the northern state could work its will upon the South without taking into consideration the sectarian interests of any indigenous group or class. Finally, Republican leaders understood the viable alternatives in the Reconstruction of the South: massive redistribution of wealth between social classes or permanent military occupation. The reasons why neither of these options was chosen were discussed in the preceding chapter. Here the consequences of that choice on subsequent American political development will be taken up.

Reconstruction and American state formation were closely intertwined in a number of ways. Some were directly connected to central state control of the southern political system, which implied either direct state intervention in plantation property relations or military rule. Either alternative (or both) would have required a much larger central state apparatus than actually emerged from the wreckage of Reconstruction, and almost certainly would have committed the state to much wider intervention in the civil and political relations of citizens to each other and to local governments. In addition, the dynamic set in motion by successful state intervention would probably have encouraged a more rapid expansion of social welfare programs such as those suggested by Freedmen's Bureau activity in the early postwar years and radical Republican proposals for federal education subsidies. Such programs were both apparent and logical auxiliaries to the Reconstruction project.[1] The abandonment of Reconstruction also brought to an end the hegemonic supremacy of the Republican party and the thoroughgoing identification of state and party during the Civil War era. As the return of former Confederate nationalists to regional power and national influence accentuated already serious stress within the Republican party coalition, the American state lost its major agent guiding administrative expansion and the most important force propelling centralization. Under these conditions, state expansion ground to a halt – not to resume until the turn of the century.[2]

We begin this chapter with a brief discussion of the Compromise of 1877, which ended Reconstruction and illustrates the alignment of party coalitions when the U.S. Army ceased active intervention in southern politics. Attention is then shifted to the impact of the military on loyalist participation in southern elections between 1865 and 1877. This analysis demonstrates both that loyalist political power in the South was dependent on an active military presence and that the American state failed to commit enough troops to sustain freedmen and loyalist whites in their struggle with resurgent Confederate nationalists. While a major factor in the failure of Reconstruction was the absence of property redistribution, this analysis of electoral support for the loyalist Republican party also yields evidence of the thorough commitment of central state administration to northern economic development, a commitment that left the national government almost unrepresented by civil officials in large regions of the postwar South. As a result, Republican control of federal patronage, which built and sustained powerful party machines in many northern states, was unable to build similar organizations in the former states of the Confederacy. The chapter closes on a brief discussion of the post-Reconstruction path of American political development, focusing on the inheritance of the Civil War as it influenced the composition of party memberships in Congress and the officer corps of the U.S. Army.

1. Examples of bureau activity can be found in Howard Ashley White, *The Freedman's Bureau in Louisiana* (Baton Rouge: Louisiana State University Press, 1970); Roberta Sue Alexander, *North Carolina Faces the Freedmen: Race Relations during Presidential Reconstruction, 1865–67* (Durham, N.C.: Duke University Press, 1985), pp. 99–160. On radical Republican support for a federal role in education, see Eric Foner, *Reconstruction: America's Unfinished Revolution, 1863–1877* (New York: Harper & Row, 1988), p. 452.
2. Leonard D. White, *The Republican Era: A Study in Administrative History, 1869–1901* (New York: Free Press, 1958), p. 2.

The Compromise of 1877 and the end of Reconstruction

In most accounts of late-nineteenth-century American political development, the negotiated settlement of the 1876 presidential election is the event that brought the Reconstruction era to a close. A brief review of the settlement and the characteristics of the legislative coalition that finally closed the door on the Reconstruction era will illustrate the political vulnerability of attempts (in the absence of massive land redistribution) to protect the rights of freedmen in the separatist South and rather striking differences between the partisan allegiance of northern and southern developmental interests. On November 7, 1876, a plurality of some 250,000 voters voted for Samuel Tilden of New York, the Democratic nominee, over his Republican opponent, Rutherford Hayes of Ohio. By manipulating the returns reported by three southern states, however, the Republicans were able to engineer a bare electoral college majority (185 to 184) and continue to control the presidency despite apparent defeat in the election. In the words of C. Vann Woodward, the negotiations that attended the acceptance of this Republican coup renewed the nation's antebellum search for sectional detente:

> in the expanse of territory and the variety of interests embraced, the Compromise of 1877 is readily comparable with the classical compromises that preceded it. These interests ranged from the Eastern seaboard to the Pacific coast. The negotiators concerned themselves not merely with the political problems of two Southern states but with the economic, social, and political problems of the whole South. They sought the fulfillment of Southern hopes and aspirations that were older than the Civil War, as well as relief from grievances arising out of Reconstruction. They enlisted in their efforts the aid of the most powerful capitalists in the country and bestirred the civic ambitions of points as remote as San Diego and Philadelphia, New Orleans and Chicago. They planned a reorientation of Southern politics along the old Democratic–Whig lines and a breaking up of the incipient white solidarity of the region by converting conservative whites to Republicanism.[3]

While accurately conveying the ambitions of the negotiators, particularly on the Republican side, this description overstates the consequences of the settlement. The settlement contained both short-term bargains and long-term possibilities. The short-term bargains were consumated and themselves carried enduring consequences. The long-term possibilities, such as the development of a Whiglike Republican party alliance with

3. C. Vann Woodward, *Reunion and Reaction: The Compromise of 1877 and the End of Reconstruction* (Boston: Little, Brown, 1966), pp. 11–12.

southern whites, were always somewhat unrealistic and, with respect to bargaining over such an alliance, the sincerity of the participants, particularly southern Democrats, should be doubted.

In brief, the proximate issue involved in the settlement was the acceptance of the officially reported electoral votes of three contested southern states (Florida, Louisiana, and South Carolina) and one elector in Oregon.[4] The Constitution provides that the president of the Senate, under normal conditions the vice-president of the United States, was to receive the electoral votes cast by the individual states and announce them to a joint session of Congress. Since Henry Wilson, the vice-president elected with Grant in 1872, had died, the president pro tempore of the Senate was to perform this constitutional duty. Since the Senate itself selected the president pro tem and was solidly controlled by the Republicans, this implied that the party would have a free hand in receiving and announcing the votes sent in by the disputed states. Even though performance of this constitutional duty involved an essentially political decision to accept or reject electoral votes from states that had experienced substantial procedural irregularities (if not outright fraud), Republicans maintained that the president pro tem's decisions would determine the issue.[5] The Democrats, on the other hand, held a substantial majority in the House of Representatives and, when added to their numbers in the upper chamber, could outvote the combined total of Republican senators and representatives. Tilden's supporters therefore adopted the position that, once the president pro tem read the electoral vote of a state, the members of the joint session must vote on whether or not to receive that result as a valid representation of the state's action.

4. The description and analysis of the settlement presented here is broadly based on Woodward's *Reunion and Reaction*; Keith Ian Polakoff, *The Politics of Inertia: The Election of 1876 and the End of Reconstruction* (Baton Rouge: Louisiana State University Press, 1973); Michael Les Benedict, "Southern Democrats in the Crisis of 1876–1877: A Reconsideration of *Reunion and Reaction*," *Journal of Southern History* 46 (November 1980): 489–524; Allan Peskin, "Was There a Compromise of 1877?," *Journal of American History* 60 (June 1973): 63–75; and Paul Leland Haworth, *The Hayes–Tilden Disputed Presidential Election of 1876* (Cleveland: Burrows Brothers, 1906; reprinted, AMS Press, 1979).

5. Whether or not the Republicans would have carried these disputed states in a fair election remains a somewhat open question. Florida, at least, almost certainly should have been awarded to Tilden and, thus, would have given the Democrats the presidency. See, for example, Woodward, *Reunion and Reaction*, p. 19. Also damaging to the Republican case was the fact that Louisiana's electoral votes were put up for sale by its Republican returning board. Although unofficial representatives of the Tilden camp began negotiations in which the board put a price of between $200,000 and $1 million on the state's votes, these talks had not been completed before the board turned around and reported Louisiana for the Republicans. See Polakoff, *Politics of Inertia*, pp. 213–14, and Joe Gray Taylor, *Louisiana Reconstructed 1863–1877* (Baton Rouge: Louisiana State University Press, 1974), pp. 492–3.

Since the Constitution did not indicate which of these equally plausible courses of action was correct, the resulting stalemate threatened the nation's political stability. Prodded by the constitutional crisis, leaders of the two parties hammered out an agreement under which an electoral commission was to be appointed to determine the legitimacy of disputed electoral votes. Under the agreement, the commission was to be composed of fifteen members, five from each congressional chamber and five from the Supreme Court. The ten congressional members were expected to be drawn equally from the ranks of the two parties. In addition, four members of the Supreme Court delegation, two from each party, were designated in the legislation and the fifth and deciding judge (if the remainder of the commission divided along party lines) was to be chosen by these four.

As all the participants realized at the time, only one judge then serving on the Supreme Court could reasonably be considered unaffiliated with either of the major parties. As it turned out and for reasons that remain unclear to this day, Illinois Democrats in the state legislature elected that justice, David Davis, to the U.S. Senate just before the Congress enacted the legislation creating the electoral commission. Since all the remaining judges were Republicans, the electoral commission ended up with an eight to seven Republican majority and subsequently decided every contested electoral vote along party lines. Under the agreement, however, each chamber could separately consider and propose to overturn the commission's decisions. In order to overturn a decision, both chambers had to support reversal. Since reversal was highly unlikely, given Republican control of the Senate, review of commission decisions by the Democratic House of Representatives was a seemingly empty privilege. In fact, however, House Democrats turned that privilege into a powerful bargaining tool by repeatedly postponing their deliberations and thus preventing the completion of the electoral count. These repeated postponements threatened once more to stalemate the process and leave the executive office vacant after Grant's term ended on March 4, 1877.

The Compromise of 1877 thus involved Democratic members of the House of Representatives, on the one hand, and unofficial representatives of the Republican presidential candidate, on the other. The Democrats controlled the pace of the electoral count, including completion, but were not in a position to impose their party's nominee on the Republicans. The Republicans could not complete the count without Democratic cooperation but controlled the electoral commission and, through Grant, the machinery of the federal government, including the military. The broad contours of the compromise thus involved bargains between the incoming Republican administration and Democratic defectors from the ranks of those then supporting postponement of House deliberations.

The Compromise of 1877 involved at least six separate agreements that varied widely in terms of their specificity, participating members, and time horizons. Perhaps the most specific, short-term bargain involved the abandonment of federal military support for the Republican administrations then formally in possession of the state houses in South Carolina and Louisiana. Within two months of Hayes's inauguration on March 5, federal troops in both states had been ordered back to their barracks and new Democratic administrations replaced the Republicans previously supported by federal troops.[6] A second, equally specific bargain entailed the appointment of a Democratic postmaster general by the incoming Republican administration. Hayes subsequently appointed Democrat David Keys of Tennessee, a former officer in the Confederate Army, to that patronage-rich position. Both of these decisions were highly visible and, although they could be described as conciliatory offerings to the South, would be hard to explain without reference to the negotiations that accompanied completion of the electoral count.

The other four agreements were far more ambiguous in both content and performance. Without a doubt, for example, negotiators from both parties attempted to reach some agreement over the continuation of subsidies and land grants associated with the construction of the Texas and Pacific Railroad. Once inaugurated, however, Hayes just as clearly opposed the legislation required to finish the road and thus scuttled whatever understanding existed between the parties on this issue. An even more ambiguous arrangement was conceived in which Republicans would back internal development projects located in the South, particularly Mississippi levees and port dredging, in return for southern Democratic support for completion of the electoral count.[7] Plans were also made for the election of a Republican speaker in the newly elected House of Representatives. Since the Democrats held a narrow majority of the seats in the new House, these expectations entailed a change in party

6. The actual authority of both Republican administrations was, by this point, almost entirely restricted to control of the immediate premises of the respective state capitol buildings and military support for the regimes was lukewarm at best. See Joseph G. Dawson III, *Army Generals and Reconstruction: Louisiana, 1862–1877* (Baton Rouge: Louisiana State University Press, 1982), pp. 243–60; Taylor, *Louisiana Reconstructed*, pp. 496–8; William Gillette, *Retreat from Reconstruction, 1869–1879* (Baton Rouge: Louisiana State University Press, 1979), p. 736; and Francis Butler Simkins and Robert Hilliard Woody, *South Carolina during Reconstruction* (Chapel Hill: University of North Carolina Press, 1932; reprinted by Peter Smith, 1966), pp. 514–41.
7. On the dilapidated condition of the Mississippi River levees, largely caused by neglect during the war, see Taylor, *Louisiana Reconstructed*, p. 319.

allegiance by a handful of southern congressmen. Finally, all of these separate agreements were to be bound up with the emergence of a new party coalition in the South. Representing an alliance between the Republican electorate composed of upland whites and freedmen and antebellum Whigs then affiliated with the Democratic party, the proposed coalition would have competed with the resurging white Democratic party led by planters and former Confederate nationalists.

The large ambitions of these last four agreements possessed a nebulous quality that, in part, can be traced to the fact that they were unlikely to be realized. Despite their infeasibility, however, these tentative agreements did reflect southern interests unaddressed by the policy positions of the two major parties and, thus, potential rearrangements of the political economic bases of party competition. The national Democratic party was dedicated to fiscal restraint and opposed internal development projects on principle. On the other hand, the Republican party was comparatively generous in opening federal coffers to both railroad construction schemes and rivers and harbors improvements. The difficulty with Republican policy, from the southern perspective, was that this generosity was extended almost exclusively to northern and western projects.[8] This unsatisfied demand for federal subsidization of southern transportation projects thus presented an apparent opportunity of uncertain dimensions.

One way to evaluate the political chances of the proposed southern alliance of Republican loyalists and former Whigs is to examine the political economic characteristics of the House coalition that brought the electoral count to completion (see Table 6.1). At the beginning of the contest, before any bargains had been struck, Hayes could only count on fifteen Republicans from the former Confederate states. Tilden, on the other hand, enjoyed a much larger party base of fifty-eight southern Democrats at the start of congressional deliberations. When the political economic characteristics of these two party delegations are compared, the Democrats can be seen to represent constituencies with a per capita value-added in manufacturing almost 40 percent higher, on the average, than southern Republicans. As the much lower median figures suggest, southern manufacturing activity was concentrated in only a few cities, such as Savannah and Augusta, Georgia, New Orleans, Charleston, Nashville, Memphis, and Richmond. Almost all of these cities were represented

8. In fact, northern reluctance to fund projects sponsored by southern Republicans probably undermined the latter's political viability and Reconstruction policy in general. See, for example, Terry L. Seip, *The South Returns to Congress: Men, Economic Measures, and Intersectional Relationships, 1868–1879* (Baton Rouge: Louisiana State University Press, 1983), pp. 269–94; Richard H. Abbott, *The Republican Party and the South, 1855–1877: The First Southern Strategy* (Chapel Hill: University of North Carolina Press, 1986), pp. 178–81, 223–7.

Table 6.1. *Characteristics of the coalitions supporting Hayes's and Tilden's election in the House of Representatives (former Confederate states only)*

Coalition		Characteristics of constituencies			
	Percentage nonwhite	Population growth	Per capita national bank currency	Per capita value-added (manufacturing)	N
Party membership					
Republican (Hayes)	56.4 (59.8)	33.2 (33.2)	$ .81 ($.27)	$5.58 ($4.64)	15
Democrat (Tilden)	38.2 (37.8)	38.9 (31.3)	.90 (.37)	7.49 (4.63)	58
After Texas and Pacific Compromise					
Hayes supporters	50.3 (56.8)	45.3 (32.8)	.76 (.42)	5.06 (4.56)	20
Tilden supporters	39.1 (39.9)	36.9 (33.5)	.93 (.30)	7.61 (4.63)	41
After political compromise					
Hayes supporters	46.9 (54.9)	48.7 (37.5)	.72 (.44)	5.27 (4.56)	24
Tilden supporters	36.2 (35.0)	32.2 (26.8)	1.01 (.35)	7.75 (4.63)	29

Note: The data in this table represents the averages for all members in the respective coalitions (medians in parentheses). The number of members in each group is given at the right end of the table.

Source: Characteristics of congressional districts were calculated from data in the *1880 Census* and *1877 Report of the Comptroller of the Currency.*

by Democrats in Congress (the sole exception being Charleston, South Carolina). Their constituencies also contained national banks that issued marginally greater sums of currency per capita and, finally, their districts were growing substantially more rapidly than did Republican constituencies. Again, as the median figures suggest, much of this difference in population growth was concentrated in a few rapidly expanding areas (primarily in Texas and Arkansas) represented by Democrats.[9] Republican dependence on freedmen voters and consequent heavy concentration in the relatively slowly developing plantation areas of the South was underscored by the much higher average proportion of nonwhites in their constituencies. Though banking and manufacturing activity was still very low in comparison to national levels, southern Democrats represented constituencies that, theoretically speaking, should have been more sympathetic to Whiggish internal development and industrialization policies than the districts of southern Republicans.[10]

After the Texas and Pacific and internal development accommodations had been reached between Hayes spokesmen and a small number of southern Democrats, the two regional coalitions began to take on slightly different characteristics. These accommodations were more or less arranged by January 24, 1877, and, thus, were in place even before Congress began to deliberate on the electoral commission's findings. With respect to these parts of the final compromise, the Hayes and Tilden coalitions have been analyzed as they appeared on a vote recorded February 27, 1877 (see Table 6.1). This vote occurred on a motion to recess

9. Because of continuing economic instability and war-induced dislocation, the 1870 census seriously undercounted the resident population of much of the South. By comparison, then, the 1880 census appears to represent some areas as "rapidly growing" when, in fact, the later count simply corrected the earlier underreporting in 1870. This undercounting was probably more serious in the plantation black belt largely contained in Republican districts (thus describing them as more expansionary than they actually were). The Democratic districts, by contrast, tended to be in western, nonplantation regions where comparison of the two censuses conveys a more accurate picture of actual population growth. On the accuracy of the 1870 Census, see Roger L. Ransom and Richard Sutch, *One Kind of Freedom: The Economic Consequences of Emancipation* (Cambridge: Cambridge University Press, 1977), pp. 53–4 and their "The Impact of the Civil War and of Emancipation on Southern Agriculture," *Explorations in Economic History* 12 (January 1975): 8–10.

10. For the nation as a whole, the 109 Republicans then serving in the House represented constituencies averaging $41.70 in value-added in manufacturing (per capita), $7.61 in national bank currency (per capita), 36.4 percent population growth between 1870 and 1880, and a nonwhite percentage of 9.1. The corresponding figures for the 184 Democrats were $40.60, $5.35, 29.1 percent, and 15.5 percent, respectively. By comparing these national figures with those for the South alone, it will be seen that the Republican party represented a much more developmentally inclined electoral base in the North than it did in the South. Northern Democratic constituencies, on the other hand, scored lower on all developmental characteristics than their Republican opponents – the exact opposite of the situation in the former Confederate states.

the House until ten o'clock the following morning and, because the proposed recess passed by a slim majority (121 to 120), postponed deliberations on the electoral count. This postponement thus occurred well after accommodations had been reached over internal improvements but before agreement concerning the withdrawal of federal troops from active participation in southern political affairs. In fact, the latter issue was the subject of intense negotiations between Louisiana Democrats and Hayes spokesmen at precisely the time at which this roll call was recorded and the former were striving to hold up deliberations just long enough to persuade the Republicans to conclude the bargain.[11]

Party shifts and abstentions produced relatively little change in the earlier pattern of manufacturing capacity or finance capital endowments in the two coalitions. These same shifts, however, significantly reduced the disparity between the two coalitions with respect to the plantation economy (for which the nonwhite percentage is a proxy) and even reversed differences with respect to comparative population growth. Simply put, after the internal improvements bargains, the Hayes coalition came to represent more rapidly settling, but not industrializing portions of the South even as it retained its original base within plantation regions. Much of the change can be directly attributed to the defection of one Arkansas and two Texas congressmen who represented districts within the projected service territory of the Texas and Pacific Railroad.

Following the announcement of an agreement on political aspects of the compromise, the constituency characteristics of the Hayes and Tilden coalitions drew even farther apart with respect to population growth. However, their means remained largely unchanged with respect to characteristics associated with the plantation economy, finance capital, and manufacturing capacity (see Table 6.1). The test of strength upon which these figures are based occurred on the very last motion to recess House proceedings before the completion of the electoral count.[12] Even at this point, only about a quarter of voting southern Democrats (11 of 40) were supporting Hayes. In fact, the proportion of southern Democrats supporting Hayes was smaller than the one-third of voting northern

11. Woodward, *Reunion and Reaction*, pp. 191–9. The roll call can be found in the *Congressional Record*, 44:2:1987–8. On this test of strength, fourteen southern Republicans and six southern Democrats cast their votes against a recess and, thus, for Hayes election to the presidency. One Florida Republican joined forty southern Democrats in support of postponement.
12. This motion was defeated in a recorded vote (147 to 99) on March 1, 1877. *Congressional Record* 44:2:2056. No southern Republican left the Hayes camp on this roll call, while eleven southern Democrats defected to the Republicans. The Democratic defectors included two congressmen from Arkansas, three from Texas, and one from Louisiana.

Democrats (35 of 105) that also bolted their party. What makes the comparative loyalty of the southern wing surprising was the fact that all the bargaining and concessions involved Southerners while Tilden, the former governor of New York, and his closest advisors came from the North. While an analysis of the Compromise of 1877 explains why a handful of southern Democrats, largely drawn from rapidly settling western districts and the lower Mississippi Valley, broke with their party in return for immediate, short-term Republican concessions, it neither accounts for the apparently gratuitous defection of numerous northern Democrats nor provides support for the plausibility of a Whiggish developmental coalition in the South under Republican auspices.[13]

The negotiations surrounding Hayes's ascension to the presidency starkly revealed several features of the late-nineteenth-century American state. For one thing, the changing coalitional patterns highlighted the importance of the central state's role in aiding (or hindering) regional economic development. They also suggest the strongly contrasting class bases of the Republican and Democratic parties. In the North, the Republicans represented relatively prosperous industrial manufacturers, merchants, and yeoman farmers. The Democrats depended on working-class immigrants and marginal agrarians. In the South, however, the Democrats were the party of the plantation elite and development-minded merchants, while the Republican party contained impoverished freedmen and marginal, upland whites. These incongruent class constituencies implied that, while the Republicans were the political agent of modernization in the North and, by extension, the nation, the Democratic party played that role within the formerly Confederate South.[14]

Although the possibility of a combination of northern and southern developmental elites occurred to the negotiators, such a hegemonic class

13. By a slightly different route, Seip also reaches this conclusion in *The South Returns to Congress*, pp. 257–63. Michael Perman similarly contends that southern Whigs were already committed to the Democratic party much earlier than 1876 and had, in fact, moved the Democrats into a much friendlier attitude toward government-sponsored economic development, at least as far as the South was concerned. He argues that whatever opportunity may have existed for converting former southern Whigs to the Republican party was lost by 1868. *The Road to Redemption: Southern Politics, 1869–1879* (Chapel Hill: University of North Carolina Press, 1984), pp. 264–7. Also see James Tice Moore, "Redeemers Reconsidered: Change and Continuity in the Democratic South, 1870–1900," *Journal of Southern History* 44 (August 1978): 357–78. On the comparative support of the southern wing of the Democratic party for the House filibuster, see Benedict, "Southern Democrats in the Crisis of 1876–1877," pp. 514–16.

14. For the commitment of postwar southern Democrats to regional development, see C. Vann Woodward, *Origins of the New South, 1877–1913* (Baton Rouge: Louisiana State University Press, 1951), pp. 1–22.

alliance would have defied two realities of the American political economy. The first was that northern economic development was heavily subsidized by the South. The affiliation of southern economic elites with the Republican party would have reduced, if not eliminated, this interregional subsidization (for example, by lowering customs duties) and cut the South in for a share of federal developmental aid. With these changes, the redistributive implications of state-sponsored economic development could not have constituted an important basis for major party competition. Put crudely, central state-led economic development was a zero-sum political program of winners (the North and West) and losers (the South). Once the loser joined the winners in a new party coalition, there probably would have been a reduction in the redistribution of wealth from the South to the North and West and a concomitant reduction in central state revenue. This reduction in revenue would have come at the very moment developmental subsidies ceased to be a major political issue. Thus, the outcome of such an alliance might in fact have been a paradoxical, net reduction in developmental aid. The failure of negotiations to produce more than a mere suggestion of a bisectional developmental alliance confirmed these programmatic realities of party structure and political economy that placed a premium on regionally exclusive developmental coalitions.

The Compromise also confirmed the political priorities of nineteenth-century American state formation. While central state subsidies to railroads and waterway improvements were worth bargaining over, these aids to economic development clearly rated second compared to the primary challenge presented by southern separatism. When northern Republicans and southern Democrats began to bargain in earnest, asking for written commitments and honor-bound promises, the subject of negotiations was not the Texas and Pacific Railroad but withdrawal of federal troops from the Louisiana and South Carolina state houses. The care with which these negotiations were conducted underscored their important implications for subsequent state development. One of these was that the Republican party could no longer advocate central state intervention in the southern political process and also win elections. By weakening the party's commitment to a larger central state role in the national political economy, internal stress within the Republican coalition thus permitted a resurgence of hostile southern separatism. Both developments corroded the link between the Republican party and the American state. The Compromise of 1877 accelerated this corrosion by bringing military involvement in the South to an abrupt end, a withdrawal that virtually guaranteed Democratic control over the former states of the Confederacy by formally committing the Hayes administration to nonintervention for at least four years and by making subsequent military intervention a breach of the status quo in sectional relations.

The central state, Reconstruction, and the Republican party

By 1877, many observers had already concluded that Reconstruction had failed and that the Compromise merely recognized political fact.[15] The continued viability of Reconstruction can be evaluated, however, only if we have a fairly clear statement of the program's goals and if alternative means of achieving those goals are explored. From the perspective of American state formation, Reconstruction of the South was intended to create a self-sustaining, competitive (if not dominant) loyalist political base within the states of the defeated Confederacy. Because of the identification of the Republican party with the national state, this problem involved, in practice, the creation of a self-sustaining Republican party in the South.

In the establishment of a southern Republican party the primary administrative agent was to be the U.S. Army, which at the close of the war stood astride the South as a victorious power occupying an enemy nation.[16] As a result of the war, most Southerners had been both citizens of the Confederacy *and* traitors to the American regime. Only two indigenous groups appeared likely to voluntarily swear allegiance to the federal government: black freedmen and a comparatively small number of mountain whites. These groups subsequently composed the foundation of the southern Republican party. Because freedmen composed the vast majority of the new party and because mountain whites defected from the coalition in the early stages of Reconstruction, the electoral base of southern Republicanism rapidly became identified with former slaves. Thus, the welfare of the southern freedman, the success of the national Republican party, and the continued expansion of the American state were all intimately connected within the Reconstruction project.[17]

The successful installation of a freestanding loyalist party required a

15. On the relative insignificance of the electoral crisis to an already failed Reconstruction, see Gillette, *Retreat from Reconstruction*, pp. 333–4.
16. William L. Richter, *The Army in Texas during Reconstruction, 1865–1870* (College Station: Texas A&M University Press, 1987), pp. 194–5. The previous experience of the U.S. Army in administering occupied enemy territory was limited to nine months in Mexico in 1848 and approximately four years in territory annexed as part of the Mexican War settlement. See Dawson, *Army Generals and Reconstruction*, pp. 2–3.
17. Gillette, *Retreat from Reconstruction*, pp. xiii, 6; Perman, *Road to Redemption*, p. 41.

massive redistribution of property from Confederate plantation owners to Republican former slaves. Since land comprised the vast bulk of southern wealth and was held by former Confederates, redistribution of land between plantation owners and freedmen would have strengthened black autonomy while impoverishing disloyal whites. The dilemma facing the national Republican party was that land redistribution from disloyal whites to former slaves might have instigated a sequence of class claims ultimately involving the entire political economy (see Chapter 5). A radical assault on Confederate property by Republican-controlled southern legislators would have thus carried important implications for the class basis of the northern wing of the party. Perhaps for this reason, property redistribution was never a serious issue in the South and, in fact, never occurred.[18] Without redistribution, freedmen were left economically dependent on their former masters and Reconstruction became a rear guard action carried out by the retreating forces of federal sovereignty against the political resurgence of former Confederate nationalists.[19] Although a self-sustaining Republican party could not be established in the South without land redistribution, the political position of a loyalist class could be propped up by direct central state intervention in southern political and economic institutions.[20]

18.   As Michael Perman noted, southern Republicans "expressed little interest" in a re-distribution of land to freedmen even though it "was obviously essential to guarantee emancipation." *Road to Redemption,* p. 31; also see Foner, *Reconstruction,* p. 375.
19.   Roger Ransom and Richard Sutch emphasized the necessity of land redistribution in their *One Kind of Freedom.* "The reason, of course, that emancipation and the demise of the plantation did not destroy the planter class was that they retained firm control over the primary form of productive capital in the southern economy. Indeed, the only way the dominance of the planter class might have been ended would have been through a sweeping redistribution of land to the freedmen at the time of their emancipation. . . . in light of subsequent events, the failure to carry forward plans for land redistribution appears as a great tragedy of this era." P. 80. From their discussion of "The Trap of Debt Peonage" in ch. 8, it seems likely that the impact of land-ownership on political power would have been felt after an initial redistribution of land to freedmen when merchants and landowners would have been unable to create "lien" law "rights" to the cotton crop. Without "crop lien" legislation, freedmen would have been able to resist most of the grinding economic exploitation of the postwar era, including the loss of land. Also see, Roger L. Ransom, *Conflict and Compromise: The Political Economy of Slavery, Emancipation, and the American Civil War* (New York: Cambridge University Press, 1989), pp. 223–9, 247–9. Though the possibility is a prominent theme in his work, Foner is a little more skeptical that land redistribution might have established black political autonomy. *Reconstruction,* p. 109.
20.   Citing the comparatively successful experience of immigrant groups in American history, William Gillette and David M. Potter have both suggested that land redistribution was not essential to black political autonomy. They have also contended that redistribution would have failed in any case because the collapse of the cotton economy in subsequent decades would have caused freedmen to lose their land, as actually happened to thousands of "economically independent" poor whites. Thus

Direct federal intervention assumed a variety of forms. The Freedmen's Bureau and southern homestead policy have already been discussed (see Chapter 5). These along with direct military administration of the South were all applied with decreasing vigor between 1865 and 1877. Aside, perhaps, from the immediate postwar years, none of these programs were ever given enough material support to do more than delay the return of Confederate nationalists to power.[21] In fact, the rapid demobilization of the Union army after Appomattox may have doomed Reconstruction even before the project began. On May 1, 1865, the military force available to the Union stood at just over one million men. By November 15, 1865, over 800,000 of these troops had been mustered out.[22] Aside from those troops assigned to Indian suppression on the Texas frontier, the army occupying the South numbered little more than 10,000 men by January 1866 and, with little variation in trend, steadily decreased to about 3,000 at the time of the 1876 presidential election.[23] These small numbers were surprisingly effective but still only retarded and could not prevent the collapse of the southern Republican party.

In fact, Reconstruction generally combined almost absolute political

forced into sharecropping and tenantry, freedmen would have ended up in a subordinate relationship to the plantation elite similar to that which emerged without land redistribution. *Retreat from Reconstruction*, pp. xiii–xiv, and *Division and the Stresses of Reunion, 1845–1876* (Glenview, Ill.: Scott, Foresman, 1973), p. 187. These parallels between the experiences of freedmen, immigrant groups, and southern yeoman whites are misconstrued in several respects. Immigrants in the North, for example, were never as strongly perceived to be the client group of an alien power (as much as nativists wanted to believe immigrant Catholics took their marching orders from the Pope). Compared to the experience of immigrants in the North, southern freedmen and scalawag whites faced a much more implacable hostility to political participation, a hostility reinforced by a belief that these groups were "delegitimized" by their cooperation with the federal authorities. Furthermore, any effective land redistribution would have involved a massive confiscation of wealth held by white former Confederates. Such a massive transfer of wealth would have meant that the consolidation of land holdings in subsequent decades (assuming that such a consolidation would still have occurred) would have delivered wealth into a very different and much more "loyalist" set of hands because Republican freedmen, not Confederate nationalists, would have dominated the plantation economy.

21. For data on criminal prosecutions and enforcement of voting rights in the South by the federal government, see Gillette, *Retreat from Reconstruction*, pp. 31–3, 42–5, and n. 39; Stephen Cresswell, "Enforcing the Enforcement Acts: The Department of Justice in Northern Mississippi, 1870–1890," *Journal of Southern History* 53 (August 1987): 421–40.

22. The *1865 American Annual Cyclopaedia* (New York: D. Appleton, 1866) provides the dates, units, and branches demobilized during this period as well as an account of the assignment of remaining units to military districts (pp. 78–80).

23. See the "Letter of the Secretary of War," Exec. Doc. 12: Senate: 39th Cong., 1st Sess., Ser. Rec. 1237 (Washington, D.C.: Government Printing Office, 1866), pp. 36–63, and various annual reports of the Secretary of War between 1867 and 1876. For an example of the impact these reductions had on Reconstruction as a political project, see Richter, *The Army in Texas*, p. 180.

authority with grossly inadequate material force. In Texas, for example, the military commander could censor the press, selectively suspend the writ of habeas corpus, remove at will the governor and hundreds of other civil officers, and determine the outcome of elections by ruling on the legitimacy of county returns.[24] In one form or another, most commanders exercised similar powers throughout the South even as they were increasingly powerless to deter intimidation of black voters or enforce their edicts much beyond the immediate vicinity of federal garrisons.[25] The discrepancy between authority and force can be attributed to the rapidly emerging contradictions within the national Republican coalition. Industrialists, western agrarians, and finance capitalists were all committed to repression of southern separatism. However, their respective programmatic priorities either demanded that the nation's resources be turned to internal development or postulated, as in the case of finance capital, an absolute retrenchment of government expenditure. Formal grants of repressive authority to military commanders were cheap. Enforcement was expensive. The end result was a slow starvation of the Reconstruction project.[26]

Direct military rule alone could not create a new political economy in which a self-sustaining loyalist party could emerge. For one thing, in no southern state did loyalists make up a majority of the white population. In most, white Union sympathizers composed only a small fraction of the potential electorate. Freedmen were, however, a majority in several states but were clearly vulnerable to economic retaliation and physical

24. Richter, *The Army in Texas*, pp. 178–9 and passim.
25. James E. Sefton, *The United States Army and Reconstruction, 1865–1877* (Baton Rouge: Louisiana State University Press, 1967), pp. 113, 118–27, 137–43, 209; Edward McPherson, *The Political History of Reconstruction* (New York: Solomons and Chapman, 1875; reprinted by Negro Universities Press, 1969), pp. 428–30; Gillette, *Retreat from Reconstruction*, pp. 34–5; Jerrell H. Shofner, *Nor Is It over Yet: Florida in the Era of Reconstruction, 1863–1877* (Gainesville: University Presses of Florida, 1974), p. 226.
26. Some scholars have assumed that the lack of material support for Reconstruction and the failure to include southern Republicans in internal development allotments signified a basic lack of faith and interest in building the party in the South. See, for example, Abbott, *The Republican Party and the South*, pp. x, 242–3; and Michael Perman, *Reunion without Compromise: The South and Reconstruction, 1865–1868* (New York: Cambridge University Press, 1973), Preface (no pagination). As these authors note, the creation of a freestanding Republican party in the South took second place to competing policies that promised direct material benefits to their northern constituents. And, as Reconstruction proceeded, the southern wing of the party became an increasing liability in national politics as the struggle to survive increasingly involved southern Republicans in corruption and electoral fraud. Still, the national party never entirely lost interest in Reconstruction (at least until 1877), because it relied on the southern wing to retard the reemergence of Democratic supremacy in the former states of the Confederacy.

intimidation.[27] Military rule could temporarily counter economic retaliation through political patronage and reduce violence by extending physical protection to loyalists, but these political structures and arrangements would vanish as troops were withdrawn from the South. What remained was the implacable hostility of southern separatists to the central state and the Republican program for the national political economy.[28]

However, even inadequately funded military rule was surprisingly effective. In order to demonstrate that effectiveness and, subsequently, to discuss how a more statist program might have aided the establishment of a loyalist party, we will now turn to a comparison of Republican party strength in the South at the beginning and at the end of Reconstruction. When the first postwar presidential election was held in 1868, the Republican party drew just under 49 percent of all ballots cast in the former Confederate states (see Table 6.2).[29] At that point, the Republicans were at the apex of their power in the region. The party had controlled the constitutional conventions in which suffrage eligibility requirements, including barriers to former Confederates, had been enacted and administered the election machinery through which the ballots were cast and counted. In both instances, southern Republicans enjoyed the active assistance and protection of the federal military.[30] In addition, the 1868 presidential election posed a choice between Ulysses S. Grant, the general who accepted Lee's surrender at Appomattox, now leader of the Republican party, and Horatio Seymour, the Civil War governor of New York who had opposed the abolition of slavery, now the candidate of a party that unequivocally condemned Reconstruction of the South. In no other presidential contest in American history were the contrasts with respect to central state power more starkly drawn between the two major parties.[31] Thus the 1868 election returns reflected fundamental attitudes

27. In 1870 the Bureau of the Census counted 3,939,032 blacks among the 9,488,206 residents of the eleven former states of the Confederacy. Blacks constituted a majority of the resident population in the states of Louisiana, Mississippi, and South Carolina. *American Almanac for 1878*, p. 258. These figures were not adjusted for under-enumeration.

28. Richter, *The Army in Texas*, pp. 191–2; Perman, *Reunion without Compromise*, pp. 11–12.

29. Seven southern states participated directly in the 1868 presidential election. In one other state, Florida, the Republican-controlled state legislature determined which way the state would cast its electoral votes. In that state, as well as Mississippi (1868), Virginia (1869), and Texas (1869), where presidential elections were not held, election figures for gubernatorial elections were used to represent Republican strength.

30. Perman, *Road to Redemption*, pp. 22–3.

31. As Gillette reports, former Confederate soldiers and political leaders "were on conspicuous display at the Democratic convention in New York City" at which Seymour was nominated. *Retreat from Reconstruction*, p. 13. For stump speeches in which Democrats condemned Reconstruction, see Perman, *Road to Redemption*, p. 4; Ed-

Table 6.2. *The impact of federal troops on southern support for the Republican party in the 1868 and 1876 presidential elections*

Presence of federal troops (by county)	Total number of votes cast in 1868	1868 Republican percentage	Total number of votes cast in 1876	1876 Republican percentage	Change in Republican percentage
Federal troops present in both 1868 and 1876	229,917	43.6	310,504	44.9	+ 1.3
Federal troops present in 1876 but not 1868	91,849	47.6	145,066	40.6	− 7.0
Federal troops present in 1868 but not 1876	352,467	54.1	542,604	41.8	− 12.3
No troops present in either 1868 or 1876	599,851	48.0	837,765	37.7	− 10.3
All categories	1,274,084	48.8	1,835,939	40.3	− 8.5

Note: Each category includes the votes of counties in which troops were stationed and immediately adjacent counties. Newly created counties in 1876 were included in 1868 totals only if the parent county either contained federal troops or was adjacent to a county in which troops were stationed in 1868. All votes were cast in the 1868 or 1876 presidential elections, respectively, except for Florida, Mississippi, Texas, and Virginia. In these four states, gubernatorial elections in 1868 or 1869 were substituted for presidential returns because these states did not hold presidential elections in 1868.
Source: Calculated from data in W. Dean Burnham, *Presidential Ballots, 1836–1892* (Baltimore: Johns Hopkins University Press, 1955) and the *1871 Tribune Almanac*. Troop dispositions can be found in *1868 Report of the Secretary of War*, Exec. Doc. 1: House of Representatives: 40th Cong., 3rd Sess., Ser. Rec. 1367 (Washington, D.C.: Government Printing Office [GPO], 1869), pp. 732–69; *1869 Report of the Secretary of War*, Exec. Doc. 1: House of Representatives: 41st Cong., 2nd Sess., Ser. Rec. 1412 (GPO, 1870), pp. 164–5, 170–1; and *1876 Report of the Secretary of War*, Exec. Doc. 1, Pt. 2: House of Representatives: 44th Cong., 2nd Sess., Ser. Rec. 1742 (Washington, D.C.: GPO, 1877), pp. 42–57. Dispositions were reported as of October 28, 1868, October 30, 1869, and October 14, 1876, respectively.

in the electorate toward the legitimacy of central state authority in the South.

In the 1868 election, the Republican party was particularly strong in the Virginia and North Carolina piedmont, the Georgia and South Car-

---

ward L. Gambill, *Conservative Ordeal: Northern Democrats and Reconstruction, 1865–1869* (Ames: Iowa State University Press, 1981), pp. 137–46; and McPherson, *Political History*, p. 368.

olina coast, north-central Florida, almost the entire state of Tennessee, the Alabama black belt (the dark-soil region of intensive cotton cultivation), central Mississippi, most of Arkansas, the Louisiana portion of the Mississippi River Valley, and the Brazos River basin of Texas (see Map 6.1a). Even though the Republicans were the dominant force in the region, the vulnerability of the party was already evident in the absence of Republican support in the Georgia black belt, the river counties of Mississippi and Tennessee, and upland regions of North Carolina and Virginia. The former cases demonstrated that freedmen could be intimidated into abstention or even led to vote for Democrats. The latter suggested that the mountain whites' flirtation with Republicanism would be brief. In fact, the erosion of white Republican support had begun somewhat earlier than the fall elections. The returns from the adoption of the new state constitutions in the spring of 1868 had already indicated serious white disaffection among putative loyalists in Alabama, Arkansas, Georgia, Louisiana, and South Carolina. Only in North Carolina did the Republicans draw as much as a quarter of the white vote that spring.[32]

By 1876, almost every area of loyalist strength had experienced significant erosion in Republican support (see Map 6.1b).[33] Erosion was particularly severe in the Appalachian regions of east Tennessee and northern Georgia, as well as central Texas and Florida.[34] Previous centers of loyalist sentiment in central Mississippi and the Arkansas Ozarks vanished altogether. The one area of expanding Republican support was the Mississippi and Red River counties of Louisiana. In the South as a whole, the Republican party lost almost one-sixth of its electoral strength between 1868 and 1876, along with control of nine of eleven state houses

32. In Louisiana, upland whites opposed Republican Reconstruction from the very beginning, Taylor, *Louisiana Reconstructed*, p. 159; Michael W. Fitzgerald argues that southern support among mountain whites was always low in absolute terms and rapidly collapsed after 1867 in his "Radical Republicanism and the White Yeomanry during Alabama Reconstruction, 1865–1868," *Journal of Southern History* 54 (November 1988): 565–96; for a discussion of upland, white support for ratification of the North Carolina constitution and data and crude estimates of white voting on state constitutional conventions throughout the South, see Perman, *Reunion without Compromise*, p. 341, 348; on upcountry unionism generally, see Foner, *Reconstruction*, pp. 300–4; Abbott, *The Republican Party*, pp. 159–60.
33. Presidential elections returns for 1876 were used for all states in this map. Where the returns were disputed in the electoral crisis (the states of Florida, Louisiana, and Mississippi), the returns of the Republican reporting boards were used except where the boards threw out the results of individual counties. In those cases, the voided results were included as an indication of local Democratic strength even though the returns themselves were not accepted by the state boards.
34. On the collapse of the Republican party in the Appalachians between 1868 and 1876, see Gordon B. McKinney, *Southern Mountain Republicans, 1865–1900: Politics and the Appalachian Community* (Chapel Hill: University of North Carolina Press, 1978), pp. 32–3.

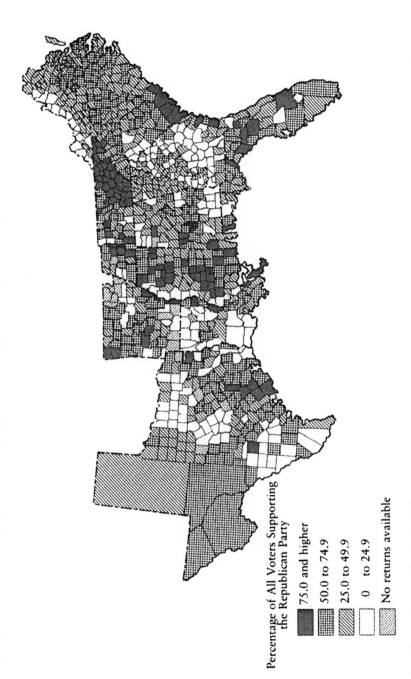

Percentage of All Voters Supporting
the Republican Party

◼ 75.0 and higher

▦ 50.0 to 74.9

▨ 25.0 to 49.9

☐ 0 to 24.9

▒ No returns available

Map 6.1a Electoral support for the Republican party in the states of the former Confederacy, 1868. *Source:* Calculated from data in W. Dean Burnham, *Presidential Ballots, 1836–1892* (Baltimore: Johns Hopkins University Press, 1955) and the *1871 Tribune Almanac*. In order to facilitate comparison, counties created between 1868 and 1876 were consolidated with their parent counties so that the geographical units represented in these maps were consistent over both elections.

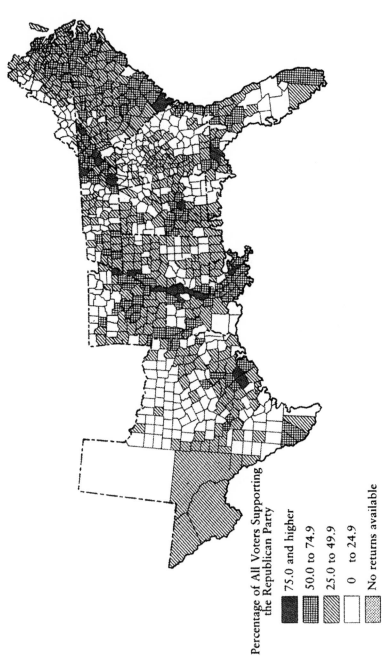

Percentage of All Voters Supporting
the Republican Party

■ 75.0 and higher

▨ 50.0 to 74.9

▧ 25.0 to 49.9

☐ 0 to 24.9

▦ No returns available

Map 6.1b **Electoral support for the Republican party in the states of the former Confederacy, 1876.** *Source:* Calculated from data in W. Dean Burnham, *Presidential Ballots, 1836–1892* (Baltimore: Johns Hopkins University Press, 1955) and the *1871 Tribune Almanac.* In order to facilitate comparison, counties created between 1868 and 1876 were consolidated with their parent counties so that the geographical units represented in these maps were consistent over both elections.

and over three-quarters of the region's congressional seats. This striking collapse of Republican strength during the Grant administration suggests that only early and massive intervention would have successfully planted a loyalist party in the South.[35]

Even as Republican strength steadily waned through the eight years of Grant's presidency, there is some evidence that sustained military intervention might have produced at least a stalemate between loyalist freedmen and former Confederate nationalists (see Table 6.2). The disposition of federal troops in the South during the 1868 election varied widely between individual states and military districts but tended to concentrate soldiers in plantation areas and urban centers. White, upland rural countries, on the other hand, were only weakly garrisoned. Counties occupied by the army in both 1868 and 1876, in the aggregate, gave the Republican party 43.6 percent of the vote in 1868. This level of loyalist support was lower than any of the other three categories in Table 6.2 and reflected the separatist leanings of the Confederacy's state capitals and plantation-dependent port districts. Occupied more or less continuously, these cities contained the military headquarters from which Reconstruction was directed. They were Mobile (Alabama); Little Rock (Arkansas); Atlanta and Savannah (Georgia); Shreveport, Baton Rouge, and New Orleans (Louisiana); Jackson (Mississippi); and Charleston and Columbia (South Carolina).

In analyzing the election returns for 1868 and 1876, the presence of the army has been assumed to influence both the expression of loyalist, Republican sentiment in the counties to which the troops were formally assigned and, also, the political environment on election day in countries immediately adjacent to those stations. The assumption is that troops were more likely to be deployed into adjacent countries on election day than to be dispatched to comparatively remote areas. In addition, the military was more likely to have developed a network of informants through which political intelligence could be gathered in these neighboring areas than could be established in other, comparatively distant regions of the district. Thus, the influence of the military's presence on the expression of loyalist sentiment was likely to have been restricted to the immediate vicinity of the individual garrisons. This assumption, at least in so far as it refers to deployment, appears well founded.[36] By all

---

35. For a differing interpretation, see Gillette, *Retreat from Reconstruction*, p. xii.
36. For example, when the military took up temporary positions in Mississippi during the 1868 referendum on adoption of the state's constitution, thirty-four of those forty-five positions (75.6 percent) were either in or immediately adjacent to a county containing a permanent garrison. (One of the temporary positions could not be located. There were actually forty-six postings in all.) Calculated from locations given in "Condition of Affairs in Mississippi," Misc. Doc. 53: House of Representatives:

reports, both troops and commanders varied widely in both competence and their personal political sympathies. However, we do not have enough information on individual officers to distinguish among them with reference to performance of their duties. Simply put, the presence of federal troops is thought to have reduced the level of intimidation and violence directed at loyalists by southern separatists and, in addition, made the recording of Republican ballots more likely.[37] Violence between separatists and federal troops performing election duty was exceedingly rare even though the number of men posted in most counties was very small.[38] On the other hand, the limited capacity of these small garrisons to impose order made accurate political intelligence as to separatist intentions vitally necessary to the successful suppression of terror and intimidation.[39]

40th Cong., 3rd Sess., Ser. Rec. 1385 (Washington, D.C.: Government Printing Office, 1869), pp. 134–5. To convey some idea of the duties troops were expected to perform, the general orders under which they operated are worth quoting: "During the election to be held in the State of Mississippi, commencing on the 22d instant, commanding officers of posts, stations or detachments in this sub-district will be held responsible for the preservation of peace and good order at their respective posts or stations, and in the vicinity thereof, taking such measures as may be considered necessary to that end. Assistance will be rendered to registrars, sheriffs, and other civil officers, when called for; the commanding officer being the judge of the necessity for such assistance. Commanding officers are authorized to send detachments or parties to such places in the vicinity of these posts or stations as may be considered necessary to preserve the public peace, bring offenders to justice, and protect all classes of the community in the right of voting free of intimidation." On the difficulty of overland transportation (which made rapid and distant troop deployment almost impossible), see Taylor, *Louisiana Reconstructed*, p. 338.

37. See, for example, William C. Harris, *The Day of the Carpetbagger: Republican Reconstruction in Mississippi* (Baton Rouge: Louisiana State University Press, 1979), p. 195; Shofner, *Nor Is It over Yet*, pp. 310–11; Richter, *The Army in Texas*, pp. 182–90; George C. Rable, *But There Was No Peace: The Role of Violence in the Politics of Reconstruction* (Athens: University of Georgia Press, 1984), pp. 108–10. In Texas, the army went far beyond simple policing of the polls and actively participated in administration of the election. In addition, General Reynolds ruled on the acceptability of all returns in his capacity as both civil governor and military commander. For analytical simplicity, the text emphasizes the security role of the army in the enforcement of voting rights. However, federal troops also protected local Republican returning boards as the latter carried out more or less partisan audits of county tabulations. Since these audits required at least some support in the form of firsthand reports of vote fraud by Democrats, the military often served Republican boards in two capacities: as witnesses to voting practices across the state, and as armed protectors. For examples of such activity from the 1876 elections in Louisiana and Florida, see Dawson, *Army Generals and Reconstruction*, pp. 224–35, 240–1; Shofner, *Nor Is It over Yet*, pp. 311–25; Gillette, *Retreat from Reconstruction*, p. 315.

38. As James Sefton put it, "Even a very small detachment, just to 'show the flag', was often sufficient to keep a community quiet. . . . Sometimes it sufficed for the Army merely to pretend it was sending a force to a particular area." *The United States Army and Reconstruction*, p. 209.

39. As is widely recognized in the historical literature, attacks on loyalist whites and freedmen were an almost ubiquitous feature of the Reconstruction landscape. See, for

In the counties in which troops were posted in 1868 but not in 1876, the Republicans polled an impressive 54.1 percent of the vote in the first election. Unlike the urban centers continuously garrisoned over the period, these counties tended to be much more rural and contained a comparatively large proportion of freedmen. The plantation regions of Alabama, Arkansas, North Carolina, Tennessee, Texas, and Virginia were the most important areas abandoned by the military over the eight-year period. However, other plantation counties, particularly in Louisiana and South Carolina, also constituted the major area in which federal troops took up new stations between the two elections. The aggregate Republican vote in these latter areas was 47.6 percent in 1868, slightly below the loyalist performance in the South as a whole. Finally, almost half of all southern ballots in the first postwar election were cast in areas not garrisoned by the military during either the 1868 or the 1876 election. These usually rural, sparsely populated, upland areas contained a particularly large portion of the electorate in Georgia, North Carolina, and Virginia – states captured fairly easily and early by the Democrats.

While the presence of federal troops undoubtedly bolstered loyalist turnout and their absence gave some license to separatist schemes of intimidation and violence, these effects were comparatively unimportant in the 1868 election because of federal inexperience in administering the election process and the relative uninvolvement of separatists in most of these contests.[40] The Republican percentage of the vote was, in addition, somewhat inflated by varying levels of discrimination against participation by former Confederates.[41] Although these factors undoubtedly

example, Foner, *Reconstruction*, pp. 119–23, 425–44, and Rable, *But There Was No Peace.*

40. Perman, *Road to Redemption*, p. 23; for an account of the 1869 Virginia gubernatorial campaign, see Jack P. Maddex, Jr., *The Virginia Conservatives, 1867–1879* (Chapel Hill: University of North Carolina Press, 1970), pp. 73–83; on the Mississippi gubernatorial election (rendered null by defeat of the constitution), see Harris, *Day of the Carpetbagger*, pp. 194–6, and James W. Garner, *Reconstruction in Mississippi* (Baton Rouge: Louisiana State University Press, 1968), pp. 208–13.

41. In some of the southern states that participated in the 1868 presidential election or held 1869 gubernatorial elections in connection with readmission to the Union, former Confederates suffered minor barriers to voting or outright disfranchisement. Tennessee and Arkansas appear to have imposed the most discriminatory conditions on suffrage with Louisiana close behind. Suffrage requirements in the rest of the region, however, appear to have been fairly open. Perman, *Road to Redemption*, pp. 12, 25–6; McPherson, *Political History*, pp. 327–33; Foner, *Reconstruction*, p. 324; William A. Russ, Jr., "Registration and Disfranchisement under Radical Reconstruction," *Mississippi Valley Historical Review* 21 (September 1934): 163–80; the constitution defeated in Mississippi in 1868 probably would have disqualified a majority of all white voters but was never enacted, Garner, *Reconstruction in Mississippi*, p. 211; on the local impact of Confederate disfranchisement, see Stephen V. Ash, *Middle Tennessee Society Transformed, 1860–1870: War and Peace in the Upper South*

had some impact, we can probably assume that the 1868 returns roughly approximated the actual distribution of loyalist sentiment in the South.⁴²

The impact of military occupation can be clearly seen by comparing the 1868 election returns with the 1876 count. In those areas in which the military maintained permanent installations, we should expect to find the least erosion of Republican strength. In those areas, political intelligence networks would be most well developed. In addition, the commissary requirements of the military would have deepened the central state's ties to at least some elements of the local economy and expectations of future occupation would have substantially reduced, if not eliminated, loyalist fear of separatist retaliation. If military occupation had any influence on loyalist prospects, that influence should have shown up here. In fact, these political centers and port districts actually gave a greater proportion of their aggregate vote to the Republicans in 1876, an increase of 1.3 percent as the South as a whole was experiencing a decline of 8.5 percent.

In the two categories where military occupation was intermittent, we should have very different expectations. In both, Republican performance should be inferior to areas in which the military presence was continuous. In addition, we should expect a better performance in areas where troops were newly positioned in 1876 than in areas abandoned by the military over the period. Newly positioned troops would inhibit separatist activity, but their effectiveness would be limited by the brevity of their experience with the local political terrain. The withdrawal of troops over the period would, on the other hand, allow white Democrats a comparatively free field for violence and economic retaliation against loyalist voters. As it turned out, these expectations were borne out by the relatively moderate decline of 7 percent in the aggregate vote of newly occupied counties, while the decline was a much steeper 12.3 percent in areas abandoned by the military.

In regions where the army did not take up stations in either of the two contests, the Republican portion of the aggregate vote should be expected to decline over the period as white separatists captured the political machinery of local governments and more effectively translated their dominant position in the local economy into political influence. The decline should be steeper than that in areas into which troops were moved in 1876 because the military would not have inhibited separatist activity

(Baton Rouge: Louisiana State University Press, 1988), p. 218. By 1876, discriminatory barriers had been removed in every state of the South.
42. The outstanding exception was Louisiana where the Republican governor advised blacks to abstain from the 1868 presidential election because they could not be protected at the polls. Taylor, *Louisiana Reconstructed*, pp. 161–72.

in the ungarrisoned counties. The decline should, on the other hand, be less steep than that in areas from which troops were withdrawn, because the process of "redemption" had already begun by 1868 (and, thus, loyalist strength had less far to fall over the period of Democratic resurgence). In fact, Republican strength declined by a little over 10 percent in areas never occupied by the army. This decline, as expected, was less than that of abandoned areas but greater than that of newly occupied regions. Compared to areas in which the military was continually stationed, the decline in loyalist support was quite dramatic. In 1868 regions never occupied by the military cast a Republican vote 4.4 percent greater than that cast in counties continuously occupied by the military; however, in 1876 these same areas returned 7.2 percent less than continuously occupied counties (37.7 and 44.9 percent, respectively) – a movement of almost 12 percent in relative Republican support in the two regions.

Before we conclude that the military could have successfully sustained a loyalist party in the South, one aspect of the central assumption should be subjected to at least rudimentary investigation. The assumption that needs at least cursory scrutiny connects the depth of federal involvement in the local political economy with the extensiveness and effectiveness of auxiliary political networks. Here we must remember that military occupation was not the only form in which the central state imposed its authority throughout southern society. While certainly a less dramatic and important force in the region, the civil administration of the federal government also positioned officials in most counties of the South. Tied to the national Republican party through appointment and to the federal government through official duty, these officers constituted a political network naturally allied with the occupying forces of the army. In some ways, they were even better equipped to gather information on election-related separatist activity than the military because the routine exercise of their duties brought them into more intimate day-to-day contact with a larger and more heterogeneous cross-section of the community. In addition, where the administrative apparatus was comparatively strong, Republican-controlled federal patronage could strengthen the loyalist leadership and electoral base by ensuring at least partial autonomy from the separatist-dominated local economy.[43]

The relative density of the civil administrative apparatus had, in fact,

43. Foner, *Reconstruction*, pp. 349–50, 362. As an illustration of the importance of federal office to loyalist political activity, it should be noted that almost 10 percent of delegates to the postwar Reconstruction conventions were U.S. Army veterans or former Freedmen's Bureau agents. Richard L. Hume, "Carpetbaggers in the Reconstruction South: A Group Portrait of Outside Whites in the 'Black and Tan' Constitutional Conventions," *Journal of American History* 64 (September 1977): 315, 319.

Table 6.3. *Troops, federal civil employment, and support for the Republican party in the 1868 and 1876 presidential elections*

Presence of federal troops/employees (by county)	Total number of votes cast in 1868	1868 Republican percentage	Total number of votes cast in 1876	1876 Republican percentage	Change in Republican percentage
Troops present in 1876					
Administrative center	117,820	40.9	146,498	45.8	+ 4.9
At least one employee	187,456	49.0	287,650	43.1	- 5.9
No civil employees	16,490	24.4	21,422	34.8	+ 10.4
No troops present in 1876					
Administrative center	228,939	54.2	304,346	45.0	- 9.2
At least one employee	650,605	50.1	960,573	38.5	- 11.6
No civil employees	72,774	39.4	115,450	30.6	- 8.8

Note: Each "troops present" category includes the votes of counties in which troops were stationed and immediately adjacent counties. A county was classified as an "administrative center" if it contained at least one employee from three of the following four branches of the civil government: internal revenue, customs, the federal judiciary, and the post office. In addition, the density of civil federal employees must have been at least one for every 3,500 people. The votes of all counties that did not meet the criteria for classification as an "administrative center" were aggregated in the two other catgories. All votes were cast in the 1868 or 1876 presidential elections, respectively, except for Florida, Mississippi, Texas, and Virginia. In these four states, gubernatorial elections in 1868 or 1869 were substituted for presidential returns because these states did not hold presidential elections in 1868.

Source: Calculated from data in W. Dean Burnham, *Presidential Ballots, 1836–1892* (Baltimore: Johns Hopkins University Press, 1955) and the *1871 Tribune Almanac.* Troop dispositions can be found in *1868 Report of the Secretary of War,* Exec. Doc. 1: House of Representatives, 40th Cong., 3rd Sess., Ser. Rec. 1367 (Washington, D.C.: Government Printing Office [GPO], 1869), pp. 732–69; *1869 Report of the Secretary of War,* Exec. Doc. 1: House of Representatives: 41st Cong., 2nd Sess., Ser. Rec. 1412 (GPO, 1870), pp. 164–5, 170–1; and *1876 Report of the Secretary of War,* Exec. Doc. 1, Pt. 2: House of Representatives: 44th Cong., 2nd Sess., Ser. Rec. 1742 (GPO, 1877), pp. 42–57. Dispositions were reported as of October 28, 1868, October 30, 1869, and October 14, 1876, respectively. The location of federal civil officials was obtained from the *1877 Official Register of the United States* (GPO, 1878).

a clear influence on the effectiveness of military occupation (see Table 6.3). When southern counties are divided into categories roughly corresponding to their respective density of federal officers and cross tabulated with the presence and absence of troops in 1876, this impact can be seen in the superior Republican electoral performance of administrative centers and comparatively poor loyalist showing in areas in which no civil officers were located.[44] The pattern holds for both the 1868 and 1876 elections and, separately, for areas in which troops were present in 1876 and regions that were not occupied during the contest. The Republican advantage ranges from 16.5 percent in the 1868 returns of counties occupied in 1876 to 11 percent in the 1876 returns of those same counties. In all but one of these comparisons, areas with at least one civil officer turned in a Republican performance superior to counties without any officials, but inferior to those areas in which the administrative apparatus was more developed.

Overlaying the influence of federal patronage and civil administrative activity was the independently positive impact of military occupation. Where federal troops occupied administrative centers in 1876, for example, the Republican share of the aggregate vote actually increased 4.9 percent over the eight-year period. Where administrative centers were not occupied, on the other hand, the Republican proportion declined by over 9 percent. Compared to occupied centers, the relative trend was a decline of 14.1 percent. For counties in which at least one civil officer was located, the Republican vote declined 5.9 percent when troops were present and 11.6 percent when soldiers were not posted. For counties with no civil officials, Republican support actually increased by 10.4 percent when troops were posted but declined by 8.8 where they were absent.[45] In fact, the impact of federal occupation in 1876 turned the prior 1868 pattern of Republican support on its head. In 1868 the Republican vote was lower in areas in which troops were posted in the subsequent 1876 election in all three categories of civil employment (compare 40.9, 49.0, and 24.4 percents with 54.2, 50.1, and 39.4, respectively). In 1876 the pattern is diametrically reversed (compare 45.8, 43.1, and 34.8 with 45.0, 38.5, and 30.6, respectively). In these patterns, we can see both the influence of military supervision of elections and the supporting role of civil officials.

44. Although the primary influence of federal officials on the expression of loyalist sentiment was probably their role as an extension of military administration, the posting of civil officials also had a small, positive impact on local economies in terms of salaries and federal expenditures on construction and services. This impact probably encouraged, at least to some extent, loyalist leanings in the local white population but, because of the relatively small amounts of money involved, the impact was probably small.

45. Though generally consistent with the expected connection between the presence of troops and Republican voting, this increase of 10.4 percent in loyalist electoral support is anomalously large. In part, this significant addition to Republican ranks can be attributed to the extraordinary effort of the federal military to protect black voters in rural Louisiana counties in the 1876 election and the somewhat creative attempt by the Republican election board to adjust the returns from these counties in order to compensate for fraud and intimidation. All of the increase in Republican support in this category can be attributed to these Louisiana returns.

On the whole we know little about how military occupation and civil administration may have strengthened southern loyalists and the viability of the local Republican party. What we do know suggests that federal patronage available in the form of appointments to civil administration was generally used to bolster radical elements in local Republican parties closely allied with freedmen. In contrast, offices controlled by governors of the individual states tended to be given to moderates who generally preferred to accommodate the interests of white former Confederates.[46] Not only were federal officers more likely to be linked to radical factions of the Republican party, their connections with the occupying forces also were apparently much deeper than the ties maintained by officials of local governments or private citizens.[47] Coordination between revenue agents, U.S. marshals, and the army, for example, seems to have been closer than that between most other branches of civil administration.[48]

46. Perman, *Road to Redemption*, pp. 42–3, 49–53, 115, 143, 163. For a list of the major officeholders in the federal bureaucracy in Louisiana in 1867, 1871, and 1875, see Ted Tunnel, *Crucible of Reconstruction: War, Radicalism and Race in Louisiana, 1862–1877* (Baton Rouge: Louisiana State University Press, 1984), pp. 148–50, 162, 239–41. Almost half of all carpetbaggers who served in Congress had previously held federal patronage positions, but the national Republican party never gave these or other southern Republicans full control of local patronage. Seip, *South Returns to Congress*, pp. 73, 119–25; Foner, *Reconstruction*, pp. 348–57.

47. Between October 1873 and October 1874, for example, the Adjutant General's Office in the War Department reported thirty-one requests for federal troops in the former Confederate states. Only two came from private citizens (one of these was forwarded to the War Department by U.S. congressmen). Five more came from southern governors and local government officials. The remaining twenty-four, representing roughly three of every four requests, were made by federal officials requesting military assistance in the performance of their administrative duties. Most of these were sent by internal revenue collectors and U.S. marshalls. *1874 Report of the Secretary of War*, Exec. Doc. 1, Pt. 2, Vol. 1: House of Representatives 43rd Cong., 2nd Sess., Ser. Rec. 1635 (Washington, D.C.: Government Printing Office, 1875), pp. 87–9.

48. Administrative cooperation between these branches often appears in accounts of the use of troops in the apprehension of moonshiners and the execution of court orders. See Wilbur R. Miller, "The Revenue: Federal Law Enforcement in the Mountain South, 1870–1900," *Journal of Southern History* 55 (May 1989): 206–8; *Internal Revenue Record* 13 (February 18, 1871): 50–1; 14 (July 8, 1871): front page; 15 (March 9, 1872): 69. The Ku Klux Klan violently harrassed revenue officials in Mississippi, *Internal Revenue Record* 13 (March 25, 1871): 90–1; Sefton, *The United States Army and Reconstruction*, pp. 214–15, 219–27. A congressional investigation reported that the internal revenue collector in Greensboro, North Carolina, "advocates the appointment of those who have served in the Union army as collectors of internal revenue throughout the South, upon the ground of its securing a more cooperative system between collectors, and of contributing materially to the suppression of fraud and increase of revenue." "Civil Service of the United States," House Report 47: House of Representatives: 40th Cong., 2nd Sess., Ser. Rec. 1358 (Washington, D.C.: Government Printing Office, 1868), p. 69. The collection of the excise tax on tobacco created, in fact, an extensive network of internal revenue offices that played a major role in the life of the North Carolina Republican party. Miller, "The Revenue," p. 201; McKinney, *Southern Mountain Republicans*, pp. 48–9, 96–8.

Everything considered, then, military occupation of the South was a rather effective means of supporting a southern loyalist party; William Gillette was probably too negative when he concluded:

> At the end of Grant's administration a string of federal forts still existed throughout the South, but as no more than isolated and beleaguered islands. The American flag still flew over the forts, but they were besieged on all sides, not by a rival army but by something more effective – an entrenched, armed, determined political opposition, civilian in appearance yet paramilitary in nature. The federal forts served both as a beacon of hope to local Republicans and as a rallying cry for the counterrevolutionaries who put pressure on the government to withdraw the remaining army units. But formidable as the fortresses might appear from the outside, they were in fact hollow shells. The complement of soldiers had decreased to a mere handful of men pulling garrison duty and rarely venturing outside. The edifices were jerry-built and rested on the frailest of foundations. They were but fortresses of failure.... Overwhelming federal force was necessary to enforce law and to command obedience.[49]

While the number of troops occupying the South was never large enough to prevent the gradual collapse of the Republican party, the garrisons did influence the expression of loyalist sentiment throughout Reconstruction. Furthermore, they were hardly as isolated as Gillette reports. Instead, they were the central element in a widely distributed administrative apparatus that included the federal court system, U.S. commissioners, internal revenue collectors, postmasters, and customs officials. Even while the project as a whole was withering away for lack of material support, Reconstruction still remained, in 1876, a moderate success in administrative centers garrisoned by the army – at least in the sense that the Republican party was both a competitive and expanding political force in these occupied counties.[50]

State structure and the American political economy in 1877

As the preceding analysis demonstrates, civil administration could not substitute for military occupation but, instead, was a necessary supplement to Reconstruction. The analysis also suggests why one of the pri-

49. *Retreat from Reconstruction*, pp. 170–1.
50. Nowhere in the South was the army more active or the federal administrative apparatus more extensive than Louisiana. Although the state was the last one to fall to the Democrats, the federal presence was even there not enough to sustain loyalist forces.

mary goals of southern Democrats in the bargaining over the 1876 election was the appointment of a friendly postmaster general. The postmaster general made 1,748 administrative appointments in the South that carried salaries sufficiently large to potentially ally their recipients with the central state (see Table 6.4).[51] These appointments covered over three-quarters of the counties in the South and comprised roughly 40 percent of all civil administrative officials in the region. In fact, once these patronage positions were conceded by the Republicans, most southerners probably resided in counties in which no federal official was sympathetic to the central government. When they fought for postal patronage in the 1877 negotiations, southern Democrats were not bargaining for the spoils of political competition but for a strengthening of sectional political autonomy.

The collection of internal revenue spawned the second largest civil administrative apparatus in the South. Most of these officials were more concerned with suppressing illegal distilling operations ("bootlegging") than with the collection of tax revenue. Concentrated in rural districts of North Carolina, Tennessee, and Virginia where excise taxes on alcohol and tobacco were difficult to enforce, internal revenue employees played a comparatively unimportant role in the political life of the rest of the South.[52] In these other states, the federal courts were a more significant force, because both judges and U.S. commissioners were directly involved in administrative oversight of elections and were widely distributed throughout the region. Less numerous and, in some respects, less useful to Reconstruction were the employees who collected the tariff. Confined almost entirely to Atlantic seaboard and Gulf coast districts, most customs officials resided in the region's major ports. New Orleans alone

51. Only federal officials whose total compensation equaled or exceeded $220 a year were included in Table 6.4, and the discussion in the text. This threshhold roughly equaled one-fifth of the annual salary of the average full-time federal employee and, after adjustment for a 10 percent increase in the price index, was also equivalent to the figure used in the 1859 analysis of federal employment (see Chapter 3). Whether or not this figure in fact separated "state-oriented" employees from those who saw their federal employment as honorific or as of secondary importance to their private occupations can be no more than a reasonable assumption. However, the thousands of federal employees who drew smaller salaries as country store postmasters, lighthouse keepers, and part-time customs officials were very unlikely to have been able to play an important role in Reconstruction politics. Such a role often required more economic autonomy than that conferred by their small stipends.

52. Illegal distilling, for example, was primarily centered in three mountainous regions of the southern and border states: the Blue Ridge, Smoky Mountain territory between eastern Tennessee, western North Carolina, and northern Georgia; the Cumberland Mountains between eastern Kentucky, Virginia, and West Virginia; and the Ozark Mountains of southwestern Missouri and northwestern Arkansas. Miller, "The Revenue," p. 198.

Table 6.4. *Federal officials in the South, 1877*

State	Internal revenue	Customs	Federal courts	Post office	Light-houses	Army	Other	Total
			Branch of the federal service[a]					
Texas	39	93	59	256	22	3,355	4	3,828
Tennessee	144	4	80	181		38	19	466
Georgia	46	42	53	207	14	79	9	450
Virginia	140	38	70	243	59	277	212	1,039
North Carolina	210	25	74	120	36	18	9	492
Alabama	22	20	40	161	14	5	11	273
Mississippi	15	8	126	131	14		3	297
South Carolina	24	32	35	105	36	175	7	414
Louisiana	34	176	60	182	37	144	47	680
Arkansas	27		53	115		13	12	220
Florida	9	53	26	47	69	194	12	410
Total	710	491	676	1,748	301	4,298	345	8,569

[a]Officials included in the post office category include mail messengers. The army includes paymasters, quartermasters, and surgeons assigned to locations outside military installations. The "other" category includes steamboat inspectors, architects, and employees of the lifesaving service, mint (New Orleans), assay office, marine hospitals, subtreasury (New Orleans), arsenal, federal cemeteries, general land offices, pension bureau, and navy yards. Over half of all officials in the last category were employed in the navy yard at Norfolk, Virginia. States are ranked by population, largest to smallest (1880 census), in order to give some idea of relative density. This tabulation includes all officials who drew an annual salary of over $220, drew a daily wage in excess of $1.00, or were paid in fees (some internal revenue and court employees).
Sources: 1877 Official Register of the United States and *1877 Report of the Secretary of War.*

employed over one-third of the total for the entire South. The large majority of the remainder were posted in Norfolk (Virginia), Wilmington (North Carolina), Mobile (Alabama), and Galveston and Brownsville (Texas). In these urban centers they formed a significant patronage base for local Republican organizations but, because of their redundant concentration along the coast and absence in the interior, were almost useless as an auxiliary information network for occupying forces.

Even less useful to Republican Reconstruction were the lighthouse keepers located on relatively isolated islands, sand bars, or rocky promontories along the coast or at entry channels to southern ports and river systems. Their location and working routines apparently limited their contact with the remainder of southern society. In any case, their silence in the Reconstruction record is complete. Most employees in other minor

Table 6.5. *Federal officials, 1877*

Section	Internal revenue	Customs	Federal courts	Post office	Light-houses	Army	Other	Total
			Branch of the federal service					
South	710	491	676	1,748	301	4,298	345	8,569
Border	603	267	260	1,136	99	389	81	2,835
Northeast	682	2,314	414	6,405	444	2,161	1,644	14,064
Midwest	748	261	631	4,671	198	2,367	565	9,441
West	97	239	139	553	90	845	819	2,782
Territories	44	37	135	221	18	11,734	557	12,746
Nation	2,884	3,609	2,255	14,734	1,150	21,794	4,011	50,437
District of Columbia								7,918
Grand total								58,355

Note: See explanatory note to Table 6.4.
Sources: 1877 Official Register of the United States and *1877 Report of the Secretary of War.*

branches of state administration were, like customs officials, confined to the region's urban centers. There, particularly in New Orleans and Norfolk, steamboat inspectors, architects supervising federal construction projects, workers minting the nation's coinage, superintendents of marine hospitals, navy yard employees, and others further expanded the party's patronage base without strengthening the intelligence network of the army.

Aside from the far-flung frontier garrisons in west Texas, fewer than a thousand troops still remained in the South in 1877. Almost half of those were stationed in just two posts: Hampton Roads in Virginia and Charleston harbor in South Carolina. The small size of these garrisons reflected the abandonment of Reconstruction by Hayes and the national Republican party. By comparison, almost 12,000 troops were posted in the western territories (see Table 6.5). When frontier posts in Texas, the Pacific coast states, and the Midwest are included, over 80 percent of the army was assigned to Indian suppression and western settlement duty. Many of these soldiers were serving in Montana where, a little more than a year earlier, Custer and his men had been wiped out on the Little Big Horn. Another 1,700 troops were also still positioned in Pennsylvania following summer strikes by miners in the anthracite region.[53] In 1877

53. For a brief account of these strikes and the federal response, see Robert V. Bruce, *1877: Year of Violence* (Chicago: Quadrangle, 1970), pp. 294–9. Also see the

no part of the army was committed to national defense other than scattered garrisons along the Rio Grande that primarily protected settlers from Indian raiding parties and in major port cities where they did little more than show the flag.

As for civil servants, the South was allocated more than a quarter of all the federal government's lighthouses, largely because of the region's long coastline. These marked hazards along the principal coastal routes and the entry channels to major harbors; the density of these installations was directly related to the traffic generated by local ports. A large number were located along the southern littoral of the Great Lakes (particularly Michigan) and on the Mississippi and Hudson rivers. Even more closely linked to commercial activity on the high seas were the relative sizes of the nation's customshouses. Largely because of the New York port, over two-thirds of all customs officials were located in the Northeast.

In the nation as a whole internal revenue employees were concentrated both in the largest northern urban centers and in rural areas of the South and border states where tobacco and alcohol production were locally important. Because the Department of Justice played important roles in the enforcement of federal revenue and election laws, U.S. commissioners (falling under the heading "federal courts") were a prominent feature of the federal administrative apparatus in the South. No other region of the nation had as many federal officials in this category. However, the southern extension of the national postal system was much less developed than that in the North. Since the largest portion of postal volume originated in commercial activity and personal letters written by private citizens, the poverty and high illiteracy rates of the South made the region a relatively weak generator of postal revenue. The Northeast, for example, had over three times as many postal officials on a per capita basis. With most of the nation's navy yards and other specialized services, the Northeast also led in "other" federal employment. In the western states and territories, employees on Indian reservations also pushed up totals in the "other" category.

In 1877 the central state distributed federal officials in ways that systematically reduced the government's profile in the very areas where loyalist sentiment was weakest. In the nation as a whole, the central state employed one person for every 860 citizens. (Though a precise figure cannot be calculated from available data, the current ratio of population to federal officials would almost certainly be below 60.) As always had

commanding general's report in 1877 *Report of the Secretary of War* (Washington, D.C.: Government Printing Office, 1877), pp. 86–98. During the summer the army was stretched so thin that troops throughout the South and as far away as Wyoming were mobilized to suppress labor unrest in the East.

been the case in the past, the density of federal officials was greatest on the frontier. In Wyoming, the central state posted one agent for every 12 citizens counted in the 1880 census. In Montana, the figure was 16. All of the other western states were also thickly posted with troops and agents. Frontier duty also raised the density of officials to population along the band of settlement activity in the northern portions of Minnesota, Wisconsin, and Michigan as well as Kansas, Nebraska, and Texas. Excluding the states in which settling the frontier was continuing, the greatest density of federal officials was found in the Northeast.[54] Massachusetts, Maine, Rhode Island, New York, and Pennsylvania all had population to official ratios of 1,000 or less. Maryland, a neighboring border state, also fell within this range. On the other hand, five of the six states with ratios above 3,000 were within the former boundaries of the Confederacy: Alabama (4,625), Mississippi (3,810), Arkansas (3,648), Georgia (3,427), and Tennessee (3,310). The one nonsouthern exception was West Virginia (4,386). In fact, New York State alone held more civil officials than did the eleven states of the former Confederacy.

Viewed from the broadest perspective, troops and officials were concentrated in the western frontier, in a continuous band along the nation's coastline (including the Great Lakes littoral), throughout the thickly settled and commercialized regions of the Northeast, and most of the nation's major urban centers. The central state's limited role in the settled, rural areas of the southern interior was highlighted by an almost complete absence of agents in portions of the lower Appalachians, the Ozarks, and pine districts of Texas, Louisiana, and Alabama. This striking spatial pattern resulted from the interplay of three general central state commitments within the national political economy: the provision of marketplace infrastructure and facilitating services; the extraction of revenue from the national economy; and internal development policies associated with the pacification of indigenous native populations and territorial administration.

The central state's commitment to the expansion and facilitation of a national market materialized in the form of an extensive postal system (second only to the army in size) that penetrated all but the most sparsely populated parts of the nation, the coastal distribution of lighthouses along the primary waterways and ports of entry for foreign commerce, and the strategic location of steamboat inspectors for the inspection of boilers. Though patronage and political favor were also of some importance, the driving influence in the spatial design of the postal system was the network

---

54. The one exception was Florida where military installations, lighthouses, and tariff collection all contributed to a relatively large federal presence.

of economic exchange between the nation's urban centers and between those centers and more rural populations. The postal system, through contracts for mail carriage, was also an important force in the development of the nation's railroad network (as were contracts for the carriage of troops and military supplies). Lighthouses served somewhat dual purposes. While these beacons were primarily intended to mark water hazards that endangered access to the nation's ports, no federal lighthouse marked the way to a harbor that lacked a customs official. In that sense, at least, they could be considered an auxiliary to revenue collection. Requiring but few federal employees, public works expenditures on rivers and harbors similarly facilitated waterborne commerce while tending to concentrate activity in a way susceptible to revenue extraction and aiding internal development. The location of public works projects was more vulnerable than many other state activities to political influence, and an inordinate number of northern ports and rivers benefited from central state subsidies during the late nineteenth century (see Chapter 5).

The rate and point at which the state appropriated economic surplus dictated the administrative structure necessary to collect revenue in a number of ways. Because almost all federal revenue came from taxes on alcohol, tobacco, and imports, these levies produced a strong federal presence in the major commercial centers of the Northeast, where foreign imports entered the nation and much of the country's liquor production was concentrated. Northeastern branches of the internal revenue and customs network, as a consequence, collected the bulk of the state's revenue. Taxation, however, could potentially reshape the distribution of economic activity. New York, for example, was normally the port of entry for the importation of railroad iron. Steep tariffs made evasion through unmonitored harbors potentially profitable and, if the state did not police the entire coastline, these tariffs could direct commerce to alternative ports. An efficient revenue system policed almost all areas where evasion might erupt into abnormal networks of commercial exchange. As a consequence, the networks and marketplace relations that were subjected to taxation were left more or less unchanged by revenue collection. Even so, the administrative apparatus of any tax system was disproportionately oriented toward collection in areas where revenue is greatest and turned to enforcement in all other regions of the country. For that reason, the major supporting auxiliaries for collection (such as lighthouses and subtreasury offices in which government revenue was deposited) were concentrated in revenue-rich urban centers while those used in suppressing evasion were concentrated in relatively revenue-poor rural areas (revenue agents, U.S. commissioners, and marshalls). Thus, although the extraction system had some links to marketplace facilitation and infrastructure support, the overall design responded to distinctly different imperatives.[55]

An entirely different set of priorities brought together the army, Indian agents, and the administrators of federal land offices. In the field operations of these branches of the central state, both the facilitation of national markets and the extraction of revenue in the nation's urban centers were but distant, almost irrelevant concerns. Instead, these federal officials brought an immense (in proportion to the resident citizenry) developmental apparatus to bear on the twin projects of Indian removal and frontier settlement. In a very real sense, the federal government incubated new political and social communities on the frontier. Once these achieved some degree of maturity, recognized by admission into the Union, the central state rapidly dismantled this apparatus only to erect it again closer to the line of current settlement. For most of the nineteenth century, the major task assigned to the military was this work of internal development and territorial expansion. In the antebellum period, this work not only confronted hostile Indian populations but also, at times, ran into active competition from other national states. At the end of Reconstruction, however, no major power threatened American control of the West.

These, then, were the three major material commitments of the American state at the end of Reconstruction: national market facilitation, revenue extraction, and western development. To these must be added two more inextricably linked but distinct commitments: the protection of American industry from foreign competition and the servicing of the national debt, which brought treasury operations into close, continuous contact with national capital markets. Overlaying all of these was the reliance of the state on the recruitment of civil administrative officials through the operation of political patronage, an arrangement that reinforced the Republican party's identification with the interests of central state survival and expansion during the Civil War era. Given the material commitments of the government and the spatial concentration of state officials in the Northeast and much of the Midwest, the rise of powerful Republican machines in the North was inevitable.[56]

55. Governments generally have a strong interest in maintaining and strengthening robust, visible marketplaces in which the extraction of revenue through excise taxes and tariffs is relatively efficient. See, for example, the discussion of Civil War revenue systems in Chapter 3.
56. On the importance of the Boston customshouse to Massachusetts politics, see Margaret Susan Thompson, *The "Spider Web": Congress and Lobbying in the Age of Grant* (Ithaca, N.Y.: Cornell University Press, 1985), pp. 239–40. For a colorful account of many of these Republican machines, see Matthew Josephson, *The Politicos, 1865–1896* (New York: Harcourt, Brace, and World, 1966).

As this review of state commitments perhaps suggests, civil employment in the former Confederate states could only have been expanded if the state had heavily subsidized the creation of a specifically southern officialdom. Even as things stood in 1877, for example, 45 percent of all tariff revenue gathered in southern ports was used to pay the administrative costs of collection. The percentage, by way of comparison, was only 2.5 in New York City and under 10 for all of the Northeast.[57] The administrative burden was not the result of a bloated federal bureaucracy in the South; only one in every seven customs officials was stationed in the region. The burden, instead, grew out of the proportional emphasis of southern customshouses on policing potential evasion (smuggling) rather than on collecting revenue. For similar reasons, southern branches of the internal revenue system also consumed large portions of all the taxes they collected. In the third district of Louisiana administrative costs in the 1876 fiscal year ate up over 80 percent of everything brought in. In Alabama's third district, administration consumed 71 percent of total revenues. In the state of Mississippi, the figure was 57 percent. Outside the tobacco districts of Virginia and North Carolina, administrative costs stood at 20 percent or more of total revenue in most southern revenue districts. In New York State, on the other hand, administrative costs ate up less than 5 percent of all revenue. The proportion for the entire North was probably a third that of the South.

Once Reconstruction was abandoned, there was, literally, little for the American state to do in the former states of the Confederacy. The region was too poor to tax, too thickly settled for frontier administration, too capital-starved to participate in the national bank system or financial markets, and too underdeveloped to benefit from tariff protection. The late-nineteenth-century American state was a state committed to northern industrial, financial, and territorial expansion. The one and only asset the South brought to that project was cotton, and capitalist markets worked quite efficiently to turn the foreign exchange earned by the crop into lines of foreign credit and debt servicing bullion without government assistance. In order for Republicans to plant a loyalist client group in the South they would have needed to create new federal activities that would have necessitated a doubling or trebling of the bureaucracy of civil administration in the region. When combined with substantially larger

---

57. Calculated from revenue and expenditure figures in the *1876 Report of the Secretary of the Treasury,* Exec. Doc. 2: House of Representatives: 44th Cong., 2nd Sess., Ser. Rec. 1752 (Washington, D.C.: Government Printing Office, 1877), pp. 550–1, 604–6. Because they do not include costs associated with auxiliary officials such as U.S. commissioners and the federal courts, these calculations considerably understate the proportion of all revenue consumed in administration.

military garrisons, such an expansion of civil administration would have held former Confederate nationalists at bay without massive land redistribution. However, given existing commitments to northern development and the refusal to restructure the economic basis of southern class relations, the required expansion of the administrative apparatus and military presence in the South promised a heavy drain on the Treasury that would have postponed, if not permanently sidetracked, efforts to resume the gold standard in the domestic economy. Heavy subsidization of southern loyalists was at best a long-term commitment that seriously compromised the interests of major factions of the Republican alliance.

For all these reasons, Reconstruction slowly wasted away. The process suggests why Reconstruction governments in the South so often turned to corruption and deficit spending in their efforts to conserve political resources and distribute them to potentially supportive clients. Systematic corruption displaced resources onto favored social groups despite formal arrangements that otherwise would prevent such transfers. By informally increasing their personal incomes, corruption also strengthened the autonomy of government officials from private holders of wealth. Both corruption and deficit spending were closely linked to schemes of southern railroad expansion.[58] The fiscal starvation of Reconstruction also partially explains why most patronage positions were denied to blacks, since, under the circumstances, southern Republicans had to assume the loyalty of the freedman and concentrate patronage on marginal whites.[59] Even so, not enough loyalist whites could be found to fill up the patronage positions that existed and tests of loyalty, such as the "iron-clad" oath, had to be weakened or abandoned in the search for a broader Republican coalition.[60] Under these conditions, proposals for civil service reform must have seemed, to southern Republicans fighting Reconstruction's last rear guard battles, an absurd luxury. Merit exams without loyalty oaths would have delivered control of civil administration into the hands of

58. Without central state backing, however, these southern railroads collapsed in the depression that followed the 1873 panic. The most complete account is in Mark W. Summers, *Railroads, Reconstruction, and the Gospel of Prosperity: Aid under the Radical Republicans, 1865–1877* (Princeton, N.J.: Princeton University Press, 1984).
59. For an account of black demands for federal patronage in Georgia – demands that went largely unsatisfied – see Edmund L. Drago, *Black Politicians and Reconstruction in Georgia: A Splendid Failure* (Baton Rouge: Louisiana State University Press, 1982), pp. 60–2, 157.
60. On the lack of loyal, qualified applicants for patronage positions, see Maddex, *Virginia Conservatives*, p. 73; Garner, *Reconstruction in Mississippi*, pp. 231–3; Russ, "Registration and Disfranchisement under Radical Reconstruction," pp. 167–9; and the comments of a Little Rock, Arkansas, internal revenue collector in "Civil Service of the United States," p. 54.

former Confederate nationalists and sabotaged what little remained of the effort to plant loyalists in the South.

While other powerful explanations for failure could also be put forward – among them irreducible white racism, northern Republican indifference to the fate of their southern wing, and fatal mistakes in political tactics – Reconstruction of the South depended ultimately on a choice between massive land redistribution and an equally massive, permanent occupation of the region accompanied by a much expanded civil administration. As the chief architect and guiding force behind central state development in the Civil War era, the Republican party chose neither alternative and thus doomed the project.

Confederate congressmen and Yankee generals: The post-Reconstruction state

The end of Reconstruction brought on a rapid resurgence of separatist political power that remained the major influence in southern politics until just before the end of the century (see Figure 6.1).[61] In the first three postwar congresses, Union veterans actually outnumbered Confederate veterans in the congressional delegations representing the former Confederate states.[62] By 1871, six years before Hayes assumed the presidency, the South was electing roughly twice as many Confederate as Union veterans to the U.S. House of Representatives. Though a few former rebels crossed over to the Republican party during Reconstruction, almost all Confederate veterans were Democrats, and Union veterans were Republicans.[63] By 1875, well over half of all southern congressmen had fought for the Confederacy and the proportion remained over 50 percent until the Populist era. At the peak, 79.5 percent of all southern representatives were former rebel officers or enlisted men. If political officials who did not join the army are included (such as Alexander Stephens, the Confederacy's vice-president), former Confederates occupied 83.6 per-

61. On the persistence of southern separatism as a cultural form, see Charles Reagan Wilson, *Baptized in Blood: The Religion of the Lost Cause, 1865–1920* (Athens: University of Georgia Press, 1980).

62. In the Thirty-ninth Congress, only Tennessee had been readmitted into the Union, so the percentages in Figure 6.1 are based on only eight members. In the Fortieth Congress, the southern delegation was also incomplete because Mississippi, Texas, and Virginia were still out of the Union.

63. At the beginning of the Forty-fourth Congress (1875–7), 98 percent of all Confederate veterans serving in southern delegations were Democrats. Eighty-nine percent of all Union veterans were Republicans. Outside the South, all five Confederate veterans were border-state Democrats, but only 59 percent of Union veterans were Republicans.

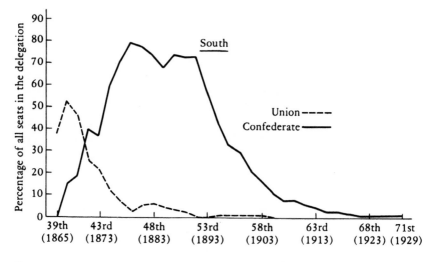

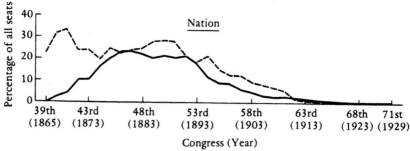

Figure 6.1
Confederate and Union veterans serving in the United States House of Representatives:
The South and the nation, 1865–1929. *Source*: Calculated from biographical entries in
Biographical Directory of the American Congress, 1774–1971 (Washington, D.C.: Government Printing Office, 1971). Only the first members sworn in from each district in each
Congress were included.

cent of all southern seats. This was in the Forty-sixth Congress which
met following the 1878 elections. By then Union veterans had almost
disappeared and a southern Democratic caucus in the House of Representatives was both a sectional and a separatist conclave. A decline in
Confederate dominance did not come until 1893. By this point, even
enlisted men who had fought for the South in their teens were approaching fifty years of age. Most former officers were in their seventies or
eighties. This aging generation was rapidly displaced by younger political
leaders in the century's last decade in a transition undoubtedly accelerated

by Populist-led agrarian insurgency.[64] The last Confederate congressman was Charles Stedman of North Carolina, who served as a major under Lee in Virginia and died in office in 1930 at the age of eighty-nine.

The border states of Maryland, Delaware, West Virginia, Kentucky, and Missouri also sent significant numbers of Confederate veterans to Congress (see Map 6.2). Though former Union officers and enlisted men dominated these delegations until the Forty-fourth Congress (not one Confederate was even elected until 1871), for the next four decades former rebels almost invariably outnumbered Union veterans among border-state congressmen. Confederate strength peaked in 1881 when former rebels controlled a third of border-state seats and dropped precipitously after the 1893 election. Generally speaking, the pattern of Confederate political resurgence in the border states matches that of the South with a lag of several years and much lower overall proportions. Though Union veterans were more competitive in the border states than they were in the South, Confederate dominance in these ostensibly loyalist former slave states underscores the ambivalent unionism of their residents and the crucial role early military occupation played in preventing their secession.

After the end of Reconstruction, almost all Union veterans were elected from the North and West but, unlike southern Confederates, were drawn from the ranks of both major parties. In the nation as a whole, Union veterans usually outnumbered former rebels in the postwar years. In the Forty-sixth Congress (1879–81), however, the House of Representatives held sixty-seven members who had fought in blue and sixty-eight who had served in Confederate gray. The Fifty-second Congress, in which the number of Union and Confederate veterans both stood at seventy-one, was also an exception. Added together, veterans on both sides of the Civil War occupied from 40 to 50 percent of all House seats between 1877 and 1891. Only in the Fiftieth Congress (1887–89), however, were Civil War veterans a majority of the House. As was true of southern

---

64. Near the end of *Reunion and Reaction*, C. Vann Woodward wrote, "In less than a year after the Compromise of 1877 an irresistible tide of agrarian radicalism was sweeping the South out of control of conservative leaders and into alliance with the agrarian West" (p. 237). A lot depends on how "agrarian radicalism" and "conservative leaders" are defined, but Woodward does seem to suggest that the failure of a developmental coalition between former Confederate Whigs and Republicans was thwarted by insurgent agrarians. Such a conclusion would have been much more appropriate for the early 1890s than in 1878 if only because the coalition thesis was so weak in the earlier period and the evidence for agrarian insurgency is so much stronger later in the century. In addition, there were very sound reasons for an alliance between even "conservative" southern leaders and western "radicals" in that they confronted a common foe in rampaging eastern industrial and commercial expansionism.

Confederates, the proportion of Union veterans dropped sharply during the Populist era as agrarian insurgency and old age took their toll. Even at the turn of the century, however, one in every five members of the House of Representatives had done military service during the Civil War.

With few exceptions, former Confederate veterans and officials were sent to Congress from all parts of the South (see Map 6.2). The exceptions were the loyalist mountains of east Tennessee and the recently settled lowland marsh country of southwest Louisiana.[65] Confederate congressmen were also a prominent feature of the political terrain in the plantation districts of Kentucky and Missouri, the remote mountain regions of West Virginia, and the industrializing areas near and in Baltimore. Outside of the South, Confederates served in Kansas (a Populist congressman elected at large) and New York City. After the turn of the century – too late for inclusion in this map, Confederate veterans were also elected from Idaho (a Populist) and Colorado (a Democrat). Although in smaller proportions than Confederates in the South, Union veterans were sent to the House from almost every region of the nation between 1865 and 1900 (see Map 6.3). Largely because they were admitted to the Union comparatively late in the period, the western states usually did not send many (aging) Union veterans to the House. California, Nevada, and Oregon, however, were entitled to representation throughout the postwar period and were notably reluctant to elect Union veterans. Outside east Tennessee, the spotty strength of Union veterans in the South was almost entirely a product of the early Reconstruction period. Even during military rule, however, portions of most southern states were never represented by former Union military men. Lower New England, New Jersey, and central New York State were all areas of substantial or at least competitive Republican electoral strength, yet were also unlikely to select Union veterans as their congressmen. On the whole, the proportion of Union veterans in the Northeast delegation ranged from 10 to 20 percent lower than that in the Midwest. At no point in the entire period did Union veterans ever comprise as much as half of all northern congressmen.

All of these patterns suggest that Civil War veterans played different roles in the two major parties and sections of the nation. Though the

65. Because congressional district boundaries changed frequently, constituencies were first broken down into their counties before recording the military service, if any, of their congressman. Since congressional districts, not counties, elected representatives, it is possible that a county could regularly vote against Confederate or Union veterans and still be represented by them. A good example would be Winston county, Alabama, whose Republican ballots were overwhelmed in congressional races by surrounding Democratic communities. Thus, only broad patterns permit an inference of separatist sentiment from Confederate representation. Unlike Figure 6.1, the small number of Confederate officials who did not serve in the military are included in this map.

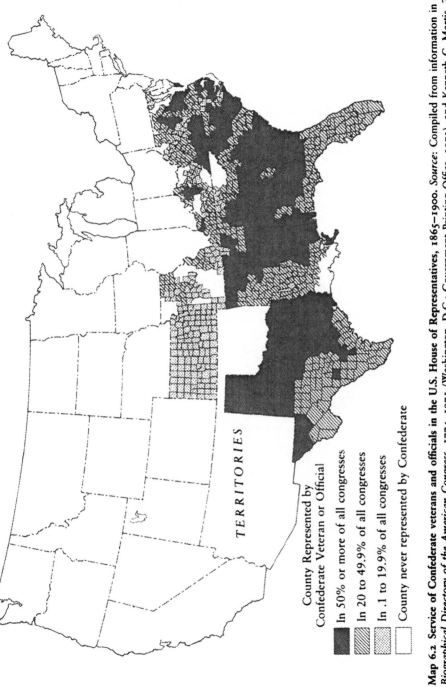

County Represented by
Confederate Veteran or Official

■ In 50% or more of all congresses

▨ In 20 to 49.9% of all congresses

▦ In .1 to 19.9% of all congresses

□ County never represented by Confederate

Map 6.2 Service of Confederate veterans and officials in the U.S. House of Representatives, 1865–1900. *Source:* Compiled from information in the *Biographical Directory of the American Congress, 1774–1971* (Washington, D.C.: Government Printing Office, 1971), and Kenneth C. Martis, *The Historical Atlas of United States Congressional Districts, 1789–1983* (New York: Macmillan, 1982).

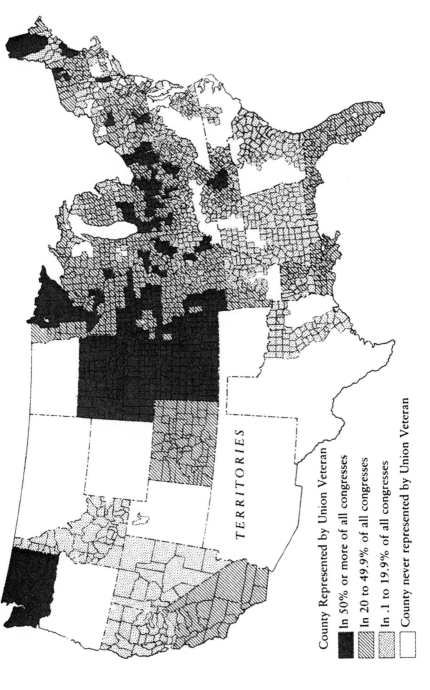

County Represented by Union Veteran

■ In 50% or more of all congresses

▨ In 20 to 49.9% of all congresses

░ In .1 to 19.9% of all congresses

□ County never represented by Union Veteran

TERRITORIES

Map 6.3 Service of Union veterans in the U.S. House of Representatives, 1865–1900. *Source:* Compiled from information in the *Biographical Directory of the American Congress, 1774–1971* (Washington, D.C.: Government Printing Office, 1971), and Kenneth C. Martis, *The Historical Atlas of the United States Congressional Districts, 1789–1983* (New York: Macmillan, 1982).

connection must remain unexplored here, Union veterans and pension politics probably played a more important role within the Republican party organizations of the Midwest than in the Northeast. Eastern constituencies more concerned with financial policy and the tariff may have been less preoccupied with the war service of their congressmen than western communities with generally higher proportions of Union veterans in their populations.[66] In the North as a whole, veteran status carried an implication of sympathy for the cause of pensioners but held a comparatively weak symbolic connection to either sectional or party identity. In the South, on the other hand, Confederate service became almost synonymous with both party and section despite the complete absence of a direct clientele connection (Confederate veterans were not eligible for federal pensions). Unlike the North, where loyalty to the Union was more or less taken for granted and was only loosely connected to war service, the South elected Confederate veterans to Congress precisely because they had demonstrated a commitment to disunion. The war had been lost and the South would not attempt secession again, but the continuing strength of separatist sentiment could not have been more dramatically demonstrated than by the serried ranks of former rebels who occupied the Democratic side of the House chamber.

The prominence of former Confederates in the Democratic party and national political institutions made Republican "bloody-shirt" remonstrations more than campaign platitudes. In the Forty-seventh Congress (1881–3), for example, Confederate veterans actually held a majority of all Democratic seats in the House of Representatives. In several other periods, former rebels approached 50 percent of the party. In this era of legislative dominance, the probable indifference, if not open hostility, of these Confederate veterans to American military security posed a substantial challenge to both the leadership of the Democratic party and the central state itself.[67]

One solution was to pack sensitive congressional committees with Union veterans. Almost every Republican who served on the House Military Affairs Committee between 1865 and 1893, for example, had seen

---

66. For more discussion of some of these issues, see Richard Franklin Bensel, *Sectionalism and American Political Development, 1880–1980* (Madison: University of Wisconsin Press, 1984), pp. 60–70.

67. The national leadership of the Democratic party rarely included Confederate veterans and the party, both North and South, was often reluctant to put former rebels on prominent display. See Woodward, *Reunion and Reaction*, pp. 142–3; Gambill, *Conservative Ordeal*, p. 138; Maddex, *Virginia Conservatives*, p. 289. On southern opposition to modernization of the American military establishment between 1877 and 1898, see Stephen Skowronek, *Building a New American State: The Expansion of National Administrative Capacities, 1877–1920* (New York: Cambridge University Press, 1982), pp. 98–105.

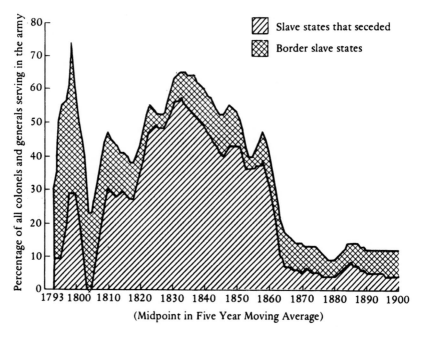

Figure 6.2
Slave-state representation in the officer corps of the regular army of the United States,
1791–1902. Percentage of colonels and generals who resided in slave states at the time of
their initial appointment. Percentages calculated on a five-year moving average. *Source*:
Calculated from information in Francis B. Heitman, *Historical Register and Dictionary of
the United States Army, 1789–1903*, (Washington, D.C.: Government Printing Office,
1903).

military service with the Union during the Civil War. More significantly,
the Democratic party discriminated against Confederates in determining
the membership of this important panel.[68] For most of this period, the
proportion of Confederates on Military Affairs was smaller than that
within the Democratic party or the entire House (calculated for Democrats alone and the entire House membership, respectively). The other
solution was the denationalization of the officer corps of the U.S. Army
(see Figure 6.2). Before the Civil War, Southerners had comprised the
major sectional component of the officer corps, but the command was
genuinely integrated in regional terms. The secession of the South, the
resignation of the vast majority of southern officers, and the coincident

68. These generalizations are based on data collected from the *Congressional Directories*
    for the respective congresses.

rapid expansion of the officer corps to meet the requirements of the Civil War all combined to reduce southern share of the command to well under 10 percent of all officers. There it remained even after the Spanish-American War almost forty years later. Undoubtedly, separatist hostility to federal occupation of the South during the Civil War and Reconstruction must have discouraged many erstwhile southern soldiers from entering upon a military career, and the hostility of Northerners within the army must have meant slower rates of advancement and promotion. The most powerful influence was, however, a federal statute that systematically discriminated against Southerners for command appointments.[69] The result was that the U.S. Army, the largest and most professional arm of the central state, remained a *northern* army until after the turn of the century. As such, control of the military was safely placed well beyond the influence of southern separatists as they regained an otherwise substantial share of influence over central state policy.[70]

Conclusion

By formally abandoning Reconstruction of the southern political economy, the Compromise of 1877 merely ratified the results of a massive process of central state consolidation and adjustment to debilitating stress within the Republican party coalition. The most important result of this process was the return of local control of the region to former Confederate nationalists. With a much larger, permanent military occupation and a massive expansion of civil administration in the region, a loyalist party could have been sustained. Under those circumstances, a much more powerful central state would have been necessary to support the required level of political and social intervention. One possible outcome of a successful Reconstruction effort might have been the continuation of central state expansion in other areas of the national political economy. One certain outcome would have been a weaker resurgence of southern separatism as a major factor in American political development. All of the evidence here connects the failure of Reconstruction to the stalemated American state of the late nineteenth century.

69. In 1866 Congress barred all Confederate veterans from regular commissions in the Union army and allocated vacancies in the officer corps among the various states in proportion to the number of volunteers from each that served in the northern army during the Civil War. The formula, of course, virtually prohibited Southerners from rising to command in the postwar period. Edward M. Coffman, *The Old Army: A Portrait of the American Army in Peacetime, 1784–1898* (New York: Oxford University Press, 1986), p. 219.

70. For a review of late-nineteenth-century central state policy that emphasizes the influence of sectional competition, see Bensel, *Sectionalism and American Political Development*, pp. 60–103.

Another result of the failure of Reconstruction was the retardation of southern political and economic development. The American Civil War would have retarded southern modernization in any case if only because the Union state apparatus was thoroughly imprinted with northern developmental policies. As the description of the Reconstruction state indicates, these policies were either indifferent or openly antithetical to southern developmental interests. In fact, both the American Civil War and Reconstruction reinforced the sectional division of labor that had existed in the antebellum period by widening the disparity between the subsequently stagnant southern and accelerating northern economies. The failure of Reconstruction further undercut southern modernization by knocking the props out from under its one positive development: the abolition of slavery and the potential emergence of a free labor market. As Reconstruction governments fell one by one across the South, resurgent separatists placed controls on black labor throughout the southern plantation economy by enacting legislation and enforcement authority for crop liens and labor contracts.[71] In combination with other forms of discrimination (such as underfunding of education), these measures immobilized and reduced the productivity of the southern labor force in such a way and on such a scale as to retard what little industrialization might have occurred under the American state in the late nineteenth century. This legislative assault on free black labor may have been in the direct interests of plantation owners and country merchants, but a major reason for enactment was the erection of economic controls on the political behavior of a class allied, from the separatist perspective, with an alien power.

As the foregoing analysis suggests, responsibility for the weak American state in the late decades of the nineteenth century should not be placed on widespread political participation and a robust party system. Indeed, as the Civil War and Reconstruction demonstrate, the American state could be very strong and could even attempt Reconstruction, a project on a scale and an ambition that would have astounded contemporary European regimes. In fact, that strong state was synonymous with a robust political party (the Republicans) and rested on wide electoral participation (by southern freedmen and poor whites). These were

71. Perman, *Road to Redemption*, pp. 237–63; William Cohen, "Negro Involuntary Servitude in the South, 1865–1940: A Preliminary Analysis," *Journal of Southern History* 42 (February 1976): 31–60; Harold D. Woodman, "Post-Civil War Southern Agriculture and the Law," *Agricultural History* 53 (January 1979): 319–37; for an argument that planters needed governmental action, in the form of crop lien legislation, in order to hold and exploit rural labor, see Ralph Shlomowitz, " 'Bound' or 'Free'?: Black Labor in Cotton and Sugarcane Farming, 1865–1880," *Journal of Southern History* 50 (November 1984): 569–96.

strengths, not weaknesses. If the substance and rhetoric of the party system seem irrelevant to the building of an administrative state after 1877, it is because the fundamental issue facing the nation during the latter half of the nineteenth century was southern separatism, not the economic and social dislocations of northern industrial expansion. In that context, the "bloody shirt" tactics of the Republican party were not empty slogans addressed to the low-order prejudices of aging soldiers but, instead, underscored a fundamental and continuing clash of interests within the national political economy.

One of the ironies of American political development is the way in which important parts of national modernization and state expansion finally became associated with the underdeveloped South. The irony does not appear during the initial, repressive response of the North to southern secession. Nor is it yet evident during the Reconstruction era or the coincidental state-sponsored nationalization of the market economy. Only in the post-Reconstruction period does the modernization of the American state become associated with southern demands in the national political economy, as the defensive reaction of the agrarian South to economic nationalism leads the region's politicians to support expansion of central state administrative and regulatory authority over the industrial and financial system of the North. The irony is that the southern separatists who provided the raw political power behind the expansion of central state regulatory authority were still in the American political system only because they were not allowed a separate nation of their own.[72]

72. The best account of the importance of southern congressmen to the development of the regulatory powers of the modern American state will be published by Elizabeth Sanders, *Farmers, Workers, and the State* (Chicago: University of Chicago Press, forthcoming).

7

Southern separatism and the class basis of American politics

Emerging from the Civil War and Reconstruction as both agent and product of northern economic development, the American state's close identification with the interests of northern industry and finance created a political economy in which the South was systematically impoverished. Estimates of war devastation within the bounds of the vanquished Confederacy range as high as 40 percent of antebellum wealth, and the postwar American state contributed little or no assistance to the rebuilding of the region.[1] The temporary imposition of cotton excise taxes even further depressed what little recovery occurred in the years immediately after the war. Over the longer term, the operation of the tariff, military pension disbursements, Treasury debt and money policies, transportation subsidies, and the concentration of federal services and employees in the North all contributed to a massive redistribution of wealth out of the South into northern industrial and westward expansion. The systemic impact of these policies reinforced the already significant advantages the North possessed in the national marketplace. The South's weak position in the national political economy was most evident in the structure and operation of the financial system.[2] Charter restrictions on entry into the

1. James L. Sellers estimated that the war destroyed 43 percent of all southern wealth (excluding the prewar value of slaves), including 32 percent of all horses, 30 percent of the region's mules, 35 percent of the cattle, 20 percent of all sheep, and 42 percent of the swine between 1860 and 1866. Restocking the agricultural economy was a "slow process" in which eight of eleven southern states still could not match prewar (1860) levels of livestock valuation in 1900. "The Economic Incidence of the Civil War in the South," *Mississippi Valley Historical Review* 14 (September 1927): 179–91. Also see Claudia G. Goldin and Frank D. Lewis, "The Economic Cost of the American Civil War: Estimates and Implications," *Journal of Economic History* 35 (June 1975): 299–326; Albert W. Niemi, Jr., *U.S. Economic History: A Survey of the Major Issues* (Chicago: Rand McNally, 1975), pp. 166–70; Willard Range, *A Century of Georgia Agriculture, 1850–1950* (Athens: University of Georgia Press, 1954), pp. 61–74.
2. For example, Mark Aldrich has argued that greenback/gold transactions in foreign exchange, heavy importations of capital from abroad (primarily for railroad invest-

national bank system, for example, retarded bank formation in peripheral agricultural regions, while reserve requirements promoted the consolidation of capital in national financial centers, where it accelerated industrial expansion. Destruction of the southern banking system with the fall of the Confederate government also contributed to the underdevelopment of the southern economy and the rise of debt peonage as the major form of labor organization in cash crop agriculture. The lagging convergence between interest rates in the South and the remainder of the nation suggests that the destruction of southern banks severely retarded the region's integration into national finance markets and that the war's impact could be felt as late as 1914.[3]

The forced integration of the plantation system into the American political economy meant that the higher level functions of capital formation and technologically advanced production would be performed outside the South in the core regions of the Northeast and Midwest.[4] During the Civil War, the Confederate mobilization stimulated industrial and commercial expansion in southern cities such as Richmond, Augusta, Columbus, and Nashville. Under southern independence, these cities would have continued to develop core characteristics as the coordinators of the southern economy and primary mediating agents between cotton production on the plantation and marketing in the world economy. With

ment), and a Treasury policy to resume specie payments combined in the marketplace to significantly reduce the value of cotton exports (relative to other sectors of the domestic economy), thus retarding the South's recovery from the war. "Flexible Exchange Rates, Northern Expansion, and the Market for Southern Cotton: 1866–1879," *Journal of Economic History* 33 (June 1973): 399–416.

3. Richard Sylla, "Federal Policy, Banking Market Structure, and Capital Mobilization in the United States, 1863–1913," *Journal of Economic History* 29 (December 1969): 657–86; Roger L. Ransom and Richard Sutch, "Debt Peonage in the Cotton South after the Civil War," *Journal of Economic History* 32 (September 1972): 641–69 and *One Kind of Freedom: The Economic Consequences of Emancipation* (Cambridge: Cambridge University Press, 1977), ch. 6; Lance E. Davis, "The Investment Market, 1870–1914: The Evolution of a National Market," *Journal of Economic History* 25 (September 1965): 355–99; B. Michael Pritchett, "Northern Institutions in Southern Financial History: A Note on Insurance Investments," *Journal of Southern History* 41 (August 1975): 391–96.

4. For a discussion of the resumption of the cotton trade through New York City and the reintegration of the South into the national and world economies as a quasicolonial, dependent region, see Harold D. Woodman, *King Cotton and His Retainers: Financing and Marketing the Cotton Crop of the South, 1800–1925* (Lexington: University of Kentucky Press, 1968), pp. 246–53, 345–59; also see, George Ruble Woolfolk, *The Cotton Regency: The Northern Merchants and Reconstruction, 1865–1880* (New York: Octagon Books, 1979; reprint of a 1958 edition). For evidence that the resumption of political ties and the "very process by which the post–Civil War North and West developed...hampered the South's recovery from the war," see Aldrich, "Flexible Exchange Rates, Northern Expansion, and the Market for Southern Cotton"; also, George L. Anderson, "The South and Problems of Post–Civil War Finance," *Journal of Southern History* 9 (May 1943): 185.

postwar reunification, southern cities were again relegated to secondary roles as marketplace crossroads and gathering places for bulk commodity exports. With reference to the South, then, the net impact of the American Civil War was a severe retardation of economic development, which was, in turn, a major contributing factor in the relative demodernization of the region in the last decades of the century.[5]

Though mobilization diverted resources from expansion, the northern economy still grew during the American Civil War and, unlike the South, emerged almost unscathed.[6] The real acceleration in northern economic growth, however, came after the conflict ended and the war had transformed the American state into the coordinating agent of northern development. State agencies such as the national bank system and government subsidies to railroad construction and waterway improvements promoted the formation of national markets in almost every economic field. The concentration of capital in the Northeast meant that only the North would be able to exploit the opportunities thus created; national market formation meant northeastern penetration of southern and western periphery economies. The American state, in fact, served as a major barrier to periphery attempts to regulate the giant industrial and financial combinations that flourished in the late nineteenth century. In addition, the North benefited from the massive redistribution of wealth that inhered in tariff protection and federal programs generally.

Underlying all of these factors was the forced integration of the plantation system into the American political economy. Because the South was in the Union, the core regions and sectors of the North were larger than they would have otherwise been and the interregional division of labor was more pronounced. Reunion meant that higher functions such

5.   On the persistence of southern economic underdevelopment until and beyond 1900, see Morton Rothstein, "The New South and the International Economy," *Agricultural History* 57 (October 1983): 385–402; C. Vann Woodward, *Origins of the New South, 1877–1913* (Baton Rouge: Louisiana State University Press, 1951), pp. 291–321. The South's colonial relationship to the North in the postwar economy was, for example, so pronounced that northeastern and midwestern commercial interests were able to purchase some 85 percent of the more than 2.5 million acres of public land sold in lots of 5,000 or larger in Louisiana and Mississippi between 1880 and 1888. Purchases by outside interests were smaller in other southern states but still amounted to a quarter or more of sales. Paul Gates, "Federal Land Policy in the South, 1866–1888," *Journal of Southern History* 6 (August 1940): 303–30.
6.   The major exception was the northern merchant marine. Confederate raiders on the high seas caused higher insurance premiums to be placed on Union vessels and thus put them at a competitive disadvantage with foreign flag carriers. As a result, the merchant marine was largely transferred to foreign ownership during the war and, for other reasons, never recovered afterward. George W. Dalzell, *The Flight from the Flag: The Continuing Effect of the Civil War upon the American Carrying Trade* (Chapel Hill: University of North Carolina Press, 1940), pp. 237–62.

as the mediation of cotton production in the world economy would be performed in New York City as opposed to Savannah, Galveston, and New Orleans. Reunion also meant that southern markets would subsidize industrial expansion in Pittsburgh as opposed to Richmond. Because the South was compelled to foot a major share of the bill associated with northern industrialization, western agrarians tolerated the increasing consolidation of eastern economic power for a much longer time than probably would have been the case had the South won independence. Without the redistribution of wealth out of the South and without the foreign exchange earned from cotton exports, the burdens associated with northeastern capital accumulation and industrialization would have fallen much more heavily on the agrarian West. Assuming that the West would not have borne these heavier costs without protest, southern secession would have split the developmental alliance of western agrarians and northeastern capital. With the South in the Union, western resistance to the rise of giant corporate institutions and national market facilitation was muted and the American state not only did not constrain but, indeed, promoted capital consolidation. For all these reasons, then, the American Civil War significantly accelerated the modernization of the northern political economy.[7]

The conflict's starkly contrasting impact upon northern and southern development must be viewed in comparison with what might have resulted had the Confederacy won the war. A victorious South, for example, would have developed and modernized at a faster pace than actually occurred within the Union, and northern development would have been retarded. The conclusions drawn from this comparison are different, however, from those that might be reached by contrasting sectional trajectories if the war had never been fought at all. Given the huge expenditures associated with both the Confederate and Union war mobilizations, the loss of life and labor productivity resulting from the vast number of casualties, and widespread property destruction in south-

---

7. For colorful but theoretically unsatisfying accounts of the impact of the American Civil War on northern economic development and the rise of the giant industrial corporation, see Charles A. Beard and Mary R. Beard, *The Rise of American Civilization* (New York: Macmillan, 1930), vol. 2, chs. 18 and 20, and Louis M. Hacker, *The Triumph of American Capitalism* (New York: Columbia University Press, 1940), chs. 25 and 26. Opponents of this school have sometimes described a Beardian theory much more elaborate and, ironically, internally coherent than the original texts can support. See, for example, Irwin Unger, *The Greenback Era: A Social and Political History of American Finance, 1865–1879* (Princeton, N.J.: Princeton University Press, 1966), pp. 3–9. For a more balanced evaluation of the impact of the Civil War that still calls the conflict a limited "triumph of industrial capital interests," see Roger L. Ransom, *Conflict and Compromise: The Political Economy of Slavery, Emancipation, and the American Civil War* (New York: Cambridge University Press, 1989), pp. 253–84.

ern military theaters, both the North and South probably would have developed more rapidly if the war had not been fought, regardless of whether or not the South had separated from the Union.[8] This conclusion is clearly easier to reach for the South, because most of the destruction took place in that section.[9] For the North, the comparison is complicated by the redistribution of wealth from the South in the postwar period, which to some extent compensated for the cost of the Union mobilization, and by the economies of scale that a larger national market conferred on northern industrial and financial corporations.[10] The latter consideration emerges as a major factor if southern secession is seen as but the first stage of a general breakup of the northern Union (see Chapter 2). From that perspective, a failure to suppress the South might have produced a fragmentation of the American political economy that would have retarded overall economic development to such a serious extent that prosecution of the war made sense for the North as a long-term, balance-sheet calculation. Given the southern orientation to world commodity markets and lack of industrial and financial capacity, on the other hand, the South might actually have benefited from a division of the antebellum Union into three or more new nations. Because the South, for the most

8. Goldin and Lewis, "The Economic Cost of the American Civil War," p. 322.
9. Ransom and Sutch have contended that, as was the case with German and Japanese recovery after the Second World War, southern recovery from the Civil War's immense devastation was surprisingly rapid and that other factors must account for the region's underdevelopment in the decades following 1880. *One Kind of Freedom*, pp. 41, 324n. Their argument must, however, be amended in several respects. In the first place, postwar Germany and Japan were the recipients of massive American aid which, in part, assisted their rapid recoveries. In sharp contrast, the post–Civil War South received no recovery aid and was even further devastated through the operation of the Union political economy. In the second place, sovereign nations, regardless of their relative weakness, are better able to establish and direct their own financial systems than integrated, dependent regions. Sovereignty, for example, appears to be a major contributing factor in the rapid Japanese recovery in that central direction of investment played an important role. See, for example, Chalmers Johnson, *MITI and the Japanese Miracle: The Growth of Industrial Policy, 1925–1975* (Stanford, Calif.: Stanford University Press, 1982). Finally, investment in rebuilding the South was one of the major factors in the capital impoverishment of the region in that, particularly in the huge agricultural sector, the reestablishment of production and the repair of supporting infrastructure absorbed what little capital survived the war itself. And Ransom and Sutch cite capital impoverishment as the major cause of the development of debt peonage as the dominant form of labor organization in the postwar economy which, in turn, they blame for subsequent underdevelopment. Thus it would seem that the war's devastation, through its impact on the southern financial system and the rise of debt peonage, made an important contribution to the region's long century of underdevelopment.
10. See, for example, Edward Chase Kirkland, *Industry Comes of Age: Business, Labor and Public Policy, 1860–1897* (Chicago: Quadrangle Books, 1961), pp. 262–77, and Alfred D. Chandler, Jr., *The Visible Hand: The Managerial Revolution in American Business* (Cambridge, Mass.: Harvard University Press, 1977), pp. 207–39.

part, relied upon world (not national) markets for cotton, breaking up the Union would not have damaged the position of the region in the world economy but, instead, would have allowed the South to erect political barriers to predatory northeastern economic penetration.

For the nation as a whole, Union victory in the American Civil War probably accelerated economic expansion over what would have taken place if the South had won independence. The subsequent retardation of southern development was more than offset by the acceleration of northern growth and the exploitation of scale economies permitted in a consolidated American market. In addition, the presence of the South in the national political economy almost certainly facilitated the continuing dominance of the Republican party as the agent of northern and, by implication, American modernization. The exploitation of the southern economy, for example, permitted the party to expand military pensions as a partial compensation to western agrarians for tariff protection of eastern industry. Pensions, homestead land settlement, and federal subsidies to railroad construction all worked to delay the revolt of western agrarians against the tariff, the gold standard, and unrestrained industrial consolidation.

Even more important, the cross-sectional inversion of class alignments of the two major parties made the emergence of coherent lower class claims difficult, if not impossible, in the national political arena. Class alignments were inverted because, in the North, the Republican party represented industrial and financial elites, while the Democrats drew support from immigrant workers and subsistence farmers but, in the South the Republicans were aligned with freedmen and poor mountain whites and the Democratic party was heavily influenced by the plantation elite.[11] This cross-sectional inversion of class alignments made the articulation of coherent class claims (consistent across the entire nation) impractical in national politics, because an attack on economic privilege could only be made by sacrificing the elite interests of one of the two major parties.[12]

With respect to the impact of the Civil War on modernization, one of

11. For a description of the American party system following the Civil War that emphasizes differences in class alignments within the North and South, see Richard Franklin Bensel, *Sectionalism and American Political Development, 1880–1980* (Madison: University of Wisconsin Press, 1984), pp. 368–402.

12. Note that these party coalitions were "incoherent" only within a developmental interpretation that emphasizes national class conflict between capital and labor as the primary driving force behind political change. If the party system is viewed, instead, as fundamentally oriented toward the process of American state formation and derivative southern separatist claims, the regional class structures of the two parties can be easily interpreted in terms of the political economic commitments of the central state and the existence or absence of associated client groups.

the most important outcomes was to propel the Republican party into its subsequent role as the major political agent of economic development, a role already evident in the legislative struggles of the last antebellum congresses. The Republicans and the American state so thoroughly inhabited by their party organization carried out the fundamental task of American political development: the successful repression of southern separatism. The party then effectively pursued the important but secondary goals of the formation of national markets for commercial transactions and investment, the facilitation of links between American finance capital and European credit markets (for example, through a gradual return to the gold standard), and successful opposition to proposals for central state regulation of economic activity (particularly rail movement of agricultural commodities) and corporate consolidation.[13] All of these positions contributed to the development of national markets, massive corporate mobilization of resources and investment reserves, and a strengthening of the position of nationalist elements in the political economy. On the other hand, the two most significant failings of the Republican party from a developmental perspective were its continuing reliance on patronage and on corruption.

Of the two, patronage was the less objectionable since the practice of political appointment to federal office was a state-enhancing asset during the Civil War and Reconstruction periods. During the war, loyalty to the Union could not be assumed within large sections of the North and the appointment of Republican partisans to office ensured Union loyalty.

13. Given the fact that most of the political support for economic regulation originated in southern and western hostility to corporate consolidation, Republican opposition to government activity in this area should be seen as "modernizing" because, if successful, periphery resistance to consolidation and integration into national markets would have promoted parochial fragmentation. Under different circumstances (particularly under the auspices of a core intelligentsia more concerned with the coordination of corporate capacity than with its dismantlement), most scholars might view central state regulation differently. See, for example, Stephen Skowronek, *Building a New American State: The Expansion of National Administrative Capacities, 1877–1920* (Cambridge: Cambridge University Press, 1982), pp. 248–9. Among the many definitions that might be adopted in this discussion, the following one seems most appropriate: "Modernization may refer to such varied but related innovations as the impersonalization of relationships, the erosion of traditional local or parochial loyalties and the rise of more cosmopolitan identities, the specialization and synchronization of economic activities, and the growth of a national social structure that embodies a transfer of social, political, and economic authority from local to central levels which can coordinate massive activities in a presumably rational manner." Michael J. Cassity, "Modernization and Social Crisis: The Knights of Labor and a Midwest Community, 1885–1886," *Journal of American History* 66 (June 1979): 41. Also see, Morton Keller, *Affairs of State: Public Life in Late Nineteenth Century America* (Cambridge, Mass.: Harvard University Press, 1977). Here, of course, we are drawing a sharp distinction between economic and political modernization (also see the discussion of the Civil War and modernization in Chapter 1).

During Reconstruction, any merit-based system would have handed over southern branches of the state apparatus to disaffected former Confederates, because there were not enough qualified southern Republicans to fill federal posts. After Reconstruction was abandoned, however, patronage appointments no longer strengthened the foundations of state authority beyond the superficial reinforcement of Republican organizational strength. With the rebirth of a competitive Democratic party, in fact, continued reliance upon patronage appointments increasingly impaired administrative capacity by preventing the emergence of an independent state bureaucracy that might have been able to play the two major parties off each other. For example, a Democratic victory in a presidential election could wipe out the institutional memory of career Republican appointees, replacing them with inexperienced Democrats.[14] By 1877, the increasing inability of the Republican party to win every election and the declining threat of renewed civil war should have shifted statist strategy from patronage to civil service recruitment of federal employees. Republican corruption can be traced to the long dominance of the party organization in national politics during the Civil War and Reconstruction periods and the close association of railroads and government contractors with the interests of the American party-state. The informal redistribution of government largess between allied groups within the Republican coalition appears to have contributed little, if anything, to overall political development.

The Democratic party was the agent of resistance to American political development. Cloaked in a states' rights ideology, southern separatism became the dominant element in the party, but the Democrats also represented a wide range of northern groups opposed to central state direction and subsidization of economic expansion. However, the existence of a competitive Democratic party – as long as it lost most elections – benefited political development in several ways. First, as a critic of Republican patronage appointment practices, the Democratic party became a participant in a political dynamic by which civil service standards were steadily expanded and the central state bureaucracy became professionalized.[15] Both public exposure of patronage abuse and the enrollment of party appointees into the civil service just before a defeated administration left office contributed to a process by which partisan motives ultimately

14. In a seriously divided political system with a single dominant party almost always controlling the state, patronage appointments may be almost as effective as a merit-based civil service in strengthening central state authority and administrative capacity. In such a system, national unity (not bureaucratic autonomy) should have higher priority among state-building agents.

15. Elizabeth Sanders, "The Social and Geographic Roots of American Bureaucracy," *Center for Studies of Social Change Working Paper* no. 28 (July 1986): 2–9.

underpinned the emergence of (limited) bureaucratic autonomy.[16] Similarly, Democratic exposure and criticism tended to limit the extent of Republican involvement in corrupt transactions with allied, private interests.

Separatism, party alignments, and social democracy

Southern separatism, the inverted class alignment in cross-sectional party competition, and the role of the Republican party as the agent of northern economic development all had profound implications for the course of subsequent American state development, particularly the comparative failure of social-democratic party organizations in the United States and the anemic expansion of national social welfare policies.[17] In this area, the two questions that have preoccupied both social scientists and historians are why a socialist vision never emerged as a realistic alternative in American politics and why American labor has had so little political influence. Most answers to these questions have emphasized either internal divisions within the American working class or the hegemonic influence of an ideological worldview hostile to the exercise of governmental authority and friendly to capitalist marketplace relations. As a consequence, these approaches have either focused on the social development of northern working-class communities or relied on a conception of American society that stressed national homogeneity and unity.[18] Both perspectives pay little attention to regional differentiation within the United States. In the first case, the answer was assumed to lie exclusively within the peculiar formation of the American working class, and other features of the political economy were believed to be of, at most, secondary importance. In the second, the inhibition of political conflict

16. Ari Hoogenboom, *Outlawing the Spoils: A History of the Civil Service Reform Movement, 1865–1883* (Urbana: University of Illinois Press, 1968), p. 261; Skowronek, *Building a New American State*, pp. 70–1, 73.

17. On the comparative weakness of American socialists in the late nineteenth century, see R. Laurence Moore, *European Socialists and the American Promised Land* (New York: Oxford University Press, 1970), p. 104. Also see Aristide Zolberg's careful comparison of working-class formation and the emergence of working-class political parties in the United States, Germany, the United Kingdom, and France. "How Many Exceptionalisms?," and Ira Katznelson, "Working-Class Formation: Constructing Cases and Comparisons," both in Katznelson and Zolberg, eds., *Working-Class Formation: Nineteenth-Century Patterns in Western Europe and the United States* (Princeton, N.J.: Princeton University Press, 1986), pp. 28–41, 397–455.

18. For example, Richard Ostreicher virtually ignores sectional differences in the United States in his "Urban Working-Class Political Behavior and Theories of American Electoral Politics, 1870–1940," *Journal of American History* 75 (March 1988): 1257–86. Also see Alan Dawley, *Class and Community: The Industrial Revolution in Lynn* (Cambridge, Mass.: Harvard University Press, 1982), pp. 238–41.

between labor and capital has often been attributed to an ideological or cultural hegemony in which socialist visions of societal organization could not emerge because most Americans just could not conceive of alternative developmental paths.[19] The latter interpretation appears most powerful when all internal variation, not just differences within industrial communities, is downplayed.

The major problem with both explanations is that they fail to recognize that the United States in the late nineteenth century was really two nations joined together by force of arms. The upper classes of the United States were deeply divided into two branches with almost entirely conflicting interests within the national political economy. On the one hand, the northern industrial and financial elite was committed to the exploitation of its dominant position in the nation and to the suppression of southern separatism. The primary vehicle for its interests was, of course, the Republican party. On the other hand, the plantation elite, even in defeat, was committed to maintaining its dominant position in the southern political economy, to resisting northern economic exploitation and integration into national markets generally, and to promoting the development of formal political structures that could underpin sectional autonomy.

This deep division within the American elite produced the previously described inverted class basis of the great national parties as each organization attempted to exploit class divisions within the other party's regional base. Thus, the Republican party joined northern economic elites to southern freedmen and native-born northern labor, and the Democrats combined plantation owners and immigrant workers. This schism within the American upper class was the primary problem facing American state-builders in the late nineteenth century and carried serious implications for political stability and social integration. The Civil War was only the clearest expression of the potential impact of upper class schism on American political development. Seen from this perspective, the social dislocation that accompanied industrialization – often emphasized as a potential contributing factor in the emergence of a social democratic party – was of secondary importance.[20] This interpretation is not intended

19. On these two general explanations, see Eric Foner, "Why Is There No Socialism in the United States?," *History Workshop* 17 (Spring 1984): 63–7. For other plausible causes of social democratic weakness, see Seymour Martin Lipset, "Why No Socialism in the United States?," in Seweryn Bailer and Sophia Sluzar, eds., *Sources of Contemporary Radicalism* (Boulder, Colo.: Westview, 1977), p. 88.

20. David Shannon, for example, traces the origins of the American Socialist party to "the social and economic conditions created by the mushrooming industrialism of America after the Civil War." *The Socialist Party of America: A History* (New York: Macmillan, 1955), p. 2.

to denigrate the harsh impact of industrialization throughout the northern manufacturing belt, but it does recognize that this source of social and political stress was not the primary factor behind the alignment of party competition or the trajectory of American state development.

A social-democratic party can be defined as a political organization dedicated to the regulation or socialization of capitalist enterprise with an intention to redistribute wealth to the lower classes of society and to insulate those classes from some of the debilitating features of open market competition. Such a social-democratic party could have emerged as a major force in American politics in one of two ways: through capture of one of the two national parties or by replacing either the Democrats or Republicans as one of the two major party organizations. Capture of the Republican party by an insurgent, social-democratic coalition was never plausible even as hypothetical speculation. The party in the late nineteenth century was solidly entrenched in the national political economy as a vehicle of elite interests in tariff protection, the operation of financial markets, and the subsidization of railroad expansion. For allies, the party was able to attract marginal, middle- and lower strata support throughout the North through the distribution of patronage appointments, military pensions, and the establishment of land grant colleges. In the South, the party enjoyed the near universal backing of the black community. As the tariff and other Civil War era features of the American political economy became increasingly less important in the early decades of the twentieth century, the Republicans broadened their appeal by giving at least superficial support to "progressive" reform.[21] But even Theodore Roosevelt cannot be considered a social democrat and Robert LaFollette, who could be, was never a serious contender for party leadership.

Capture was much more plausible in the Democratic party. For one thing, the southern plantation elite was much weaker vis-à-vis the party's northern, lower class wing than the Republican industrialists and financiers were in relation to southern freedmen. For another, agrarian resis-

---

21. One of the causes of the deterioration of the Civil War political economy was the increasing competitiveness of American industry and manufacturing in world markets. Exports of American manufactured goods to Europe took off in the last years of the nineteenth century, rising from 7.4 (1895) to 15.5 (1910) as a percentage of all United States exports to Europe. Matthew Simon and David E. Novack, "Some Dimensions of the American Commercial Invasion of Europe, 1871–1914: An Introductory Essay," *Journal of Economic History* 24 (December 1964): 591–605. Also see R. A. Church, "The Effect of the American Export Invasion on the British Boot and Shoe Industry, 1885–1914," *Journal of Economic History* 28 (June 1968): 223–54. As American industry became more competitive in world markets, fewer sectors of the economy were dependent on tariff protection and one of the most important developmental policies of the Republican party lost much of its popular appeal.

tance to industrialization created a much wider community of interests between western and southern farmers (including plantation owners) than the Republican developmental program ever produced between southern freedmen and northern industrial labor. Within the Democratic party, agrarian insurgency could attract western farmers in areas that were marginally productive or vulnerable to transportation monopolies; southern sharecroppers and tenant farmers producing for world markets; and the plantation elite, which was also highly vulnerable to the Republican developmental program. These groups came together behind the Bryan presidential campaigns of 1896 and 1900 but, even though Bryan's coalition inherited much of the Populist party's strength, the Democratic platforms of those years tended to stress monetary reform and gave only a passing nod to other proposals for central state intervention in national markets.[22]

The Populist party organization of the 1890s fell within the penumbra of our definition of a social-democratic party because of the redistributive potential of the substitution of silver for gold as the nation's monetary standard, proposed socialization of the marketing and transport of agricultural commodities, and the favorable attitude of the party toward the regulation of working conditions and organizational rights for industrial labor.[23] The Socialist party of the early twentieth century advocated an even more explicit and comprehensive program of redistribution and socialization. As formal party organizations, the Populists were a stronger but less permanent force in national politics. James Weaver, the party's candidate in 1892, drew 8.7 percent of the popular vote and carried four states with twenty electoral votes. (Two more electoral votes were cast for Weaver by electors who won election on fusion tickets in North Dakota and Oregon.) In addition, eight Populists were elected to the United States House of Representatives and more than 1,500 Populists won local offices across the nation.[24] Four years later, however, the organization was almost entirely absorbed by the Democratic party. The Socialist party had a more lasting presence in American politics but peaked in 1912 with only 6 percent of the popular

22. By the beginning of the Progressive Era, however, both agrarians and labor had joined forces within the Democratic party behind a much more assertive program of central state regulation and controls. For a description, see Elizabeth Sanders, "Farmers, Workers and State Expansion in the Progressive Era," *Center for Studies of Social Change Working Paper* no. 72 (July 1988).

23. Lipset has called the Populist movement "the most sustained and successful effort to build a left third party which appealed to farmers and workers." "Why No Socialism," p. 61.

24. John D. Hicks, *The Populist Revolt: A History of the Farmers' Alliance and the People's Party* (Lincoln: University of Nebraska Press, 1961; reprint of a 1931 edition), p. 267.

vote and never carried a state. Though other third-party efforts, such as Robert LaFollette's Progressive campaign in 1924, might also be mentioned, the Populist and Socialist parties represent the two most important and plausible attempts to establish a social-democratic organization as a major force in national politics.

The failure of these independent organizations and insurgent efforts to capture one of the two major parties was, from a political-economy perspective, a result of the patterning of wealth redistribution and capital accumulation in the United States. In order to understand why this was the case, a distinction must be made between interregional and intraregional redistribution. In the late nineteenth century, interregional redistribution drained wealth from the southern and, to a lesser extent, western periphery into the northeastern and midwestern core. The larger part of this redistribution took place through the normal, automatic operation of a market economy in which higher level financial and technologically advanced sectors held a strong strategic advantage over commodity production in agriculture or industrial raw materials. Within the national political economy, it was the struggle over interregional wealth redistribution – the direction and flow enhanced by a wide range of central state policies – that attracted industrial workers to the Republican party (as in the 1896 campaign) and southern yeomen to the Democratic party (as in the Reconstruction period).[25] Simply put, political conflict over in-

25. Leon Fink has described the "pivotal presidential campaign of 1896" as pitting "the forces of producer republicanism against a Supreme Court mindful of the security of corporate and finance capital. Indeed, perhaps more radical than any economic changes that William Jennings Bryan's Populist-Democratic forces proposed were the Democrats' platform commitments promising an end to 'government by injunction,' proposing jury trials in all contempt cases, opposing life tenure for federal officials, and even suggesting 'reconstituting' (adding new members to) the Supreme Court." "Labor, Liberty, and the Law: Trade Unionism and and the Problem of the American Constitutional Order," *Journal of American History* 74 (December 1987): 913. While Fink downplays the importance of monetary issues in the campaign, his emphasis on the open appeal of "producer republicans" for labor support in a crusade against their common enemy (eastern capital) makes all the more paradoxical the widespread labor support enjoyed by the Republican party in 1896. James L. Huston has recently argued that the "Republicans ... realized that industrialization had upset the lower working class. In the establishment of the high tariff policy during the Civil War and the maintenance of the policy in the years thereafter, the Republicans became the first political party to wield consciously the power of the federal government in order to smooth over some of the social dislocations generated by the industrial revolution." "A Political Response to Industrialism: The Republican Embrace of Protectionist Labor Doctrines," *Journal of American History* 70 (June 1983): 35–57. What Huston does not say is that the ameliorating impact of the tariff was achieved by displacing some of the cost of industrialization onto the agrarian periphery, particularly the cotton-exporting South. For iron workers' support for a high protective tariff, see John Jarrett, "The Story of the Iron Workers," in George E. McNeill, ed., *The Labor*

terregional wealth redistribution tended to efface class divisions within both the core and periphery regions of the United States.[26] Within both the northern core and southern periphery, however, intraregional conflict over income shares tended to aggravate class-based political divisions. While northern capitalists and workers agreed on the broad outlines of interregional redistribution (from the agrarian South and West to industrial Northeast and Midwest), the sharing of that appropriated wealth between capital and labor produced intense intraregional class divisions, with the Republicans tending to represent capital and the Democrats, labor. However, because interregional redistribution was the dominant force shaping the political system, most of the energy generated by contests over intraregional income shares could not find an outlet in party competition and spun off into largely nonpartisan, apolitical, strike activity.[27] Intraregional conflict over income shares in the South was most intense between black sharecroppers and tenant farmers, on one side, and plantation owners and merchants, on the other. Historical racial divisions

Movement: The Problem of Today (Boston: A. M. Bridgman, 1887), pp. 287–9, 310–11.

26. Gary Marks has recently argued that a broad-based working-class party did not emerge in the United States because the structure of the two-party system strongly discouraged third-party insurgencies and thus prevented the development of an independent political base for a national labor party. *Unions in Politics: Britain, Germany, and the United States in the Nineteenth and Early Twentieth Centuries* (Princeton, N.J.: Princeton University Press, 1989), pp. 217–25, 232–4. While his argument correctly notes the inhibiting impact of the electoral system on the emergence of new national parties, his case is weakened by the fact that the Republican party, under the same electoral system, did replace the Whig organization as a major contender for national power. As the Republican experience demonstrated, even under a "winner-take-all" electoral system, insurgent movements can develop into major parties if they represent massive social forces in the political economy. The problem for labor parties in the late nineteenth and early twentieth centuries was that their response to the process of industrialization was ultimately a less salient force in American political development than the interregional conflicts engendered by northern economic expansion and southern separatism, around which the two-party system continued to be organized.

27. As Foner puts it, "what needs to be explained is the coexistence in American history of workplace militancy and a politics organized around non-ideological parties appealing to broad coalitions." "Why Is There No Socialism?" p. 59. Also see, Leon Fink, *Workingmen's Democracy: The Knights of Labor and American Politics* (Urbana: University of Illinois Press, 1983), p. xi; John Laslett, "Reflections on the Failure of Socialism in the American Federation of Labor," *Journal of American History* 50 (March 1964): 651. In a few states along the border dividing the manufacturing belt and the agrarian periphery, insurgent alliances between labor and farmers did develop in the early twentieth century. See Richard M. Valelly, *Radicalism in the States: The Minnesota Farmer-Labor Party and the American Political Economy* (Chicago: University of Chicago Press, 1989).

and slavery were important factors in determining the intensity of this competition, but this race alignment in the plantation economy also overlay the cleavage between Union loyalists and Confederate separatists. Although blacks were tied to the Republicans because of the party's role as a guarantor of civil and political rights (albeit an inadequate one), the inevitable result of their alliance with northern Republicans was that southern blacks were seen as the pliable allies of those who directed northern economic and political exploitation of the South.[28] Another difficulty was the fact that white subsistence farmers and small land-owning producers had interests less antagonistic to those of the plantation elite. While black sharecroppers and plantation owners struggled over their respective shares of the land's harvest, the plantation elite and small white landowners shared a common antipathy toward the interregional redistributive policies of Republican nationalists.[29] Yet another barrier to cooperation between blacks and poor whites grew out of the economic dependence of blacks on white landowners and merchants; blacks were often intimidated by threats of economic retaliation into supporting candidates backed by the bourbon elite. Thus, left alone, blacks overwhelmingly supported the Republican party and, where intimidation was successful, provided votes for upper class whites.

Both the alignment of blacks with the Republican party and their vulnerability to intimidation tended to delegitimate black political participation in the eyes of poor whites. In fact, many poor whites acquiesced in the disfranchisement of a large part of their own ranks in the constitutional conventions of the late nineteenth century in order to push blacks out of the electorate. Thus, the complex politics of disfranchisement, in which many poor whites were often indifferent toward or even supported suffrage restrictions, recognized a perverse reality – a reality in which deep divisions within the American upper class and cross-sectional class inversion in major party competition retarded social-democratic campaigns.[30]

28. On widespread southern white interpretation of Republican regimes as alien governments imposed by an outside power and their supporting black constituencies as illegitimate participants in the political process, see Eric Foner, *Reconstruction: America's Unfinished Revolution, 1863–1877* (New York: Harper & Row, 1988), pp. 346–7; George C. Rable, *But There Was No Peace: The Role of Violence in the Politics of Reconstruction* (Athens: University of Georgia Press, 1984), pp. xi, 11, 15, 58, 63, 81, 188, 191.
29. Ransom and Sutch document that poor whites in every wealth strata were much more likely to own land than were poor blacks. *One Kind of Freedom*, pp. 85–6.
30. For similar reasons, the "white primary" also allowed open political discussion of intraregional wealth distribution in connection with Democratic party nominations without threatening either local race relations or cohesive sectional opposition to national, Republican policies. Because blacks were barred from participating, the

In the Populist and Bryan campaigns, even mild social-democratic appeals failed to reformulate the basis of major party competition, because industrial workers preferred the hard-money, high-tariff interregional program of the Republican party to central state regulation of capitalist markets under the auspices of periphery agrarians. Even though the Socialists were weaker both locally and nationally than the Populist party at their respective peak strengths, the Socialists established a deeper organizational base throughout the nation and maintained a grass roots organization in local politics over a longer period than did the Populists. In addition, the Socialists attracted at least some support from most sectors of industrial labor, whereas the Populist alliance with the Knights of Labor proved barren throughout the manufacturing belt and the Bryan campaigns drew only perfunctory loyalty from foreign-born workers. Furthermore, the Socialists maintained a deafening silence on most of the major issues involved in interregional wealth redistribution, such as the tariff and the monetary standard, issues that provided the very foundation of the Populist movement.[31] This silence focused the Socialist party's attention on the potential common interests of core and periphery

Democratic primary in effect settled questions of intraregional shares of southern wealth within the white community before confronting Republican candidates in the general election. During the 1890s, for example, the Populists in Alabama and Louisiana proposed that a white primary be held with the Democrats in order to nominate the "white" candidate in the general election. Morgan Kousser attributes their overture to a belief that plantation Democrats controlled a significant share of the black vote and thus exploited an economically dependent group in elections. The white primary, it was hoped, would even the odds in a contest between lower class and upper class whites by denying the plantation elite the votes of dependent blacks. At the same time, a restricted primary would have brought agreement on a common candidate and thus eliminated divisions within the white community that potentially allowed black Republicans to play a balance-of-power role in the general election. *The Shaping of Southern Politics: Suffrage Restriction and the Establishment of the One-Party South, 1880–1910* (New Haven, Conn.: Yale University Press, 1974), p. 75. Kousser takes pains to recognize widespread Populist opposition to disfranchisement. However, many elements in his account suggest that the complex politics of disfranchisement involved poor white recognition of the fact that black identification with the Republican party and vulnerability to economic intimidation tended to weaken political insurgency in the South. For example, the escape clauses, such as the grandfather clause, provided to poor whites helped to target suffrage restrictions exclusively on blacks. In addition, the contradictory electoral strategies of poor white political leaders (for example, whether to embrace blacks in a class coalition or exclude them from voting altogether) illustrates the ambivalence with which white insurgents viewed their potential allies. Finally, the fact that any definition of a national lower class would necessarily include the vast majority of all southern whites meant that no suffrage restriction could have been enacted in the South without substantial white lower class support.

31. See, for example, the Socialist party platforms of 1904, 1908, and 1912 in Kirk H. Porter, ed., *National Party Platforms* (New York: Macmillan, 1924), pp. 265–70, 311–18, 361–8.

lower classes in pressing redistributive claims in national politics. Finally, the Socialist party possessed a modern, professional preoccupation with electoral success that insured, within the limits of socialist doctrine, a pragmatic optimalization of the organization's electoral appeal, whereas the Populists were a much more loosely coordinated and less cohesive organization.[32] All these contrasts suggest that the two parties represented different potential routes to social democracy.

   In local politics, the Socialist party was strongest in the Northeast and Midwest, where intraregional redistribution was an appealing issue.[33] In the core economy, the party pressed working-class claims on corporate income in a number of ways (such as redistributive policies enacted by municipal governments and regulation of working conditions), and elected members to state legislatures and to the mayoralties of industrial cities. The party, however, was much less successful in national elections in these regions. In presidential elections during the early twentieth century, Socialists were a much more powerful force in the southern and western periphery, where the party's program could combine both interregional redistribution (through the socialization of transportation and regulation of industry) and intraregional redistribution (through state-sponsored agricultural collectives in warehousing and marketing as well as unionization of workers in extractive industries).[34] The leading So-

32.   As Shannon put it, "In being all-inclusive, in being a fairly loose alliance of regional political groups, the Socialists unconsciously were following the pattern of the major political parties. As the party of Lincoln had within it Western agrarians and Pennsylvania manufacturers, so the party of Debs had within it Oklahoma share-croppers and New York garment workers; . . . the Socialist Party was firmly committed to the ballot box, to attempting to attain its objective, the cooperative commonwealth, through political and parliamentary action." In later years, Shannon argues, the party's electoral strength faded away because it attempted "to cast all its members in the same mold, [violating] one of the basic principles of American political parties." *The Socialist Party*, pp. 6, 260. Not all scholars would agree either with this characterization of the party or the impact of ecumenical electoral strategies on leftist party strength. For a review of the literature, see Lipset, "Why No Socialism," pp. 131–3.

33.   Of the nineteen Socialists in state legislatures in 1913, for example, fourteen were elected in the Midwest, one in the East, four in the West, and none in the South. Ethelwyn Mills, *Legislative Program of the Socialist Party* (Chicago: Socialist Party, 1914), pp. 10–11. For a description of Socialist party strength in local elections, see Ira Kipnis, *The American Socialist Movement, 1897–1912* (New York: Monthly Review Press, 1952), pp. 345–63; Nathan Fine, *Labor and Farmer Parties in the United States, 1828–1928* (New York: Rand School of Social Science, 1928), pp. 224–9.

34.   The subsequent persistence of Socialist party support in eastern industrial centers has misled some scholars into describing the party's strength at its peak in 1912 in terms more appropriate to later periods. See, for example, Zolberg, "How Many Exceptionalisms?" p. 427. In fact, however, it is quite possible that the votes cast by small landowning farmers, tenants, and sharecroppers, as well as rural laborers, exceeded in 1912 the number of Socialist ballots cast by manufacturing workers and miners.

cialist states in the 1912 presidential election were Oklahoma (16.6 percent), Nevada (16.5), Montana (13.6), Arizona (13.5), Washington (12.5), California (11.7), Idaho (11.3), Oregon (9.7), and Florida (9.3). Among the worst states for the Socialists were Indiana (5.6 percent), Connecticut (5.3), Michigan (4.2), New York (4.0), New Jersey (3.7), Massachusetts (2.6), Rhode Island (2.6), New Hampshire (2.3), and Maine (2.0).[35]

The Socialist failure to break into the Civil War party system reflected the enduring American state-building problem of inadequate political and economic integration. This problem persisted until the New Deal restructuring of the political economy partially nationalized the class structure of national party competition by bringing blacks and labor into the Democratic party. Even so, the equivocation of New Deal reformers on race segregation, southern disfranchisement, and the confinement of social welfare programs to northern constituencies all represented concessions to the plantation elite. What united New Dealers between 1932 and 1965 was not a social-democratic vision but a common assault on the privileges of northern capital.[36]

From this perspective, Barrington Moore may have erred in arguing that Union victory promoted the development of social democracy in the United States. If the North had lost the Civil War, both the northern Union and the new Confederacy would have had internally coherent class coalitions as the basis of their respective major parties. Without the southern insistence on devolution of authority (states' rights), the post–

Though they constituted a much smaller proportion of the total electorate of the nation, the states of the South, West, and Plains contributed over 37 percent of the Socialist presidential vote. Subtracting from this total the ballots cast by miners and manufacturing workers (important but small fractions of all periphery support) and adding rural votes cast in states such as Minnesota, Iowa, Missouri, Wisconsin, and Kentucky, the agrarian wing of the Socialist party probably reached rough parity with what was, under most definitions of "working class," the support given by American labor. For a description of Socialist voters in the Southwest, see James R. Green, *Grass-Roots Socialism: Radical Movements in the Southwest, 1895–1943* (Baton Rouge: Louisiana State University Press, 1978), pp. 228–69.

35. Calculated from vote totals reported in Edgar Eugene Robinson, *The Presidential Vote: 1896–1932* (Stanford, Calif.: Stanford University Press, 1947), *1914 World Almanac*, and manuscript returns in individual state archives. The breadth of Socialist strength within some of these states was truly remarkable. Of Oklahoma's 77 counties, for example, all but one reported Socialist percentages that exceeded the 5.2 percent cast for the party in New York County (Manhattan), New York. For a discussion of the 1911 campaign and Socialist strength in the periphery generally, see Elizabeth Sanders, *Farmers, Workers, and the State* (Chicago: University of Chicago Press, forthcoming). Formal party membership figures, adjusted for population, convey a very similar picture of Socialist party strength across the nation. See *The Party Builder*, numbers 12 and 15, December 18, 1912, and January 11, 1913, respectively.

36. Bensel, *Sectionalism and American Political Development*, pp. 147–74.

Civil War Democratic party could have embraced a state-centered program of social-welfare expansion and marketplace regulation that might have competed successfully with Republican developmental policies. At the very least, the resulting major party debate over such proposals would have borne a much closer resemblance to that in contemporary European movements. Even more, such a class-coherent alignment might have radically changed the trajectory of American state development (in the North) in a more centralizing, interventionist direction.

The evolution of the South as an independent nation could have followed several possible paths. Each depended on the timing of the abolition of slavery, which in turn appears to have depended on the point at which independence was achieved. If independence had been established very early in the war, the institution might have survived intact and endured beyond the elimination of serfdom in Czarist Russia (1861) and slavery in Brazil (1888).[37] However, war rapidly corroded the foundations of the institution and, under most probable scenarios, slavery was already one casualty as early as the autumn of 1862, when Lincoln issued the Emancipation Proclamation.[38] Even the Confederate government itself began to contemplate emancipation as a war measure by late 1864 and, in the spring of 1865, the South enacted "slaves-as-soldiers" legislation promising freedom in return for military service (see Chapter 3).

Emancipation, of course, did not necessarily imply full political and civil rights for blacks and, with southern independence, the possibility of a Reconstruction-like period of black political participation and power sharing would have been foreclosed. On the other hand, the freedman would not have been aligned with the alien Republicans of the North and subsequent political integration may not have been either as painful

37. Both the Brazilian and Russian experiences provide indirect support for the argument that an independent South would have found a peaceful road to abolition. In Brazil, for example, the plantation provinces peacefully acquiesced in slavery's abolition as the national government (in which advanced industrial or financial interests had little or no influence) gradually withdrew institutional supports for the system and slaves simply walked away from their masters. See Robert Conrad, *The Destruction of Brazilian Slavery, 1850–1888* (Berkeley: University of California Press, 1972), ch. 17. On the abolition of Russian serfdom, see Jerome Blum, *Lord and Peasant in Russia: From the Ninth to the Nineteenth Century* (Princeton, N.J.: Princeton University Press, 1972), pp. 577–600. For a somewhat narrow comparison that reaches a different conclusion, see Peter Kolchin, *Unfree Labor: American Slavery and Russian Serfdom* (Cambridge, Mass.: Harvard University Press, 1987), pp. 50–1, 373–5.

38. For an excellent introductory narrative that concisely chronicles the impact of the Civil War on slavery as an institution, see Ira Berlin, Barbara J. Fields, Thavolia Glymph, Joseph P. Reidy, and Leslie S. Rowland, eds., *Freedom: A Documentary History of Emancipation, 1861–1867* (New York: Cambridge University Press, 1985), pp. 1–56.

or such a long time in coming. One of the most important barriers to poor white–black political cooperation would have been removed under this scenario by the elimination of potential interregional wealth redistribution. Even handicapped by black identification with northern Republicans, southern Populism was much more radical and, in regional terms, more politically successful than the western wing of the movement. A similar insurgency within an independent Confederacy might have been even more powerful. In any event, it is difficult to imagine how populist insurgency could have ended in disfranchisement of poor, whites if the South had been a separate nation.

Furthermore, an independent South would almost certainly have been a more prosperous region, especially if the war had been won early. Under reunion, some of the bitterness and violence associated with postwar, intraregional redistribution can be attributed to the fact that there was so little wealth to redistribute in the South.[39] If an independent South had been more prosperous, the adjustment of black and lower class white claims on production probably would have been less violent. Finally, in evaluating the social-democratic possibilities of each of these scenarios, it must be remembered that what actually occurred in the South – the long century of violence, segregation, and disfranchisement that drew to a close only during the 1960s – was a tragic and traumatizing period in American history.[40] If Lee and the Army of Northern Virginia had prevailed at Gettysburg in July 1863, before the immense destruction that accompanied subsequent Union invasions of the South but after military action had fatally undermined the institution of slavery, southern independence might, as was the case in the North, have enhanced the prospects of social democracy within a new southern nation as well.

The political legacy of the American Civil War and Reconstruction can therefore be briefly summarized under three headings. Under economic development, the events of these periods accelerated northern expansion, retarded southern growth, and probably contributed to net national economic development in a global perspective (that is, in developing a major industrial economy). In terms of the modernization of private economic organizations, by which is meant their expansion, consolidation, and nationalization, the impact of the Civil War was a positive factor from all perspectives, North, South, and nation. For the South, modernization

39. Rable, *But There Was No Peace*, p. xi; on the extreme poverty of the late-nineteenth-century South, see Ransom and Sutch, *One Kind of Freedom*, ch. 9.
40. Southern society and economy between 1865 and 1965 is, in fact, often compared to South African apartheid. See, for example, Stanley B. Greenberg, *Race and State in Capitalist Development: Comparative Perspectives* (New Haven, Conn.: Yale University Press, 1980).

came in the form of integration into a national market dominated by northeastern corporations. In terms of social democracy, by which is meant the emergence of formal political organizations dedicated to a redistribution of wealth from upper to lower classes and the insulation of the latter from some of the hardships imposed by open market competition, the long-term impact of this period was almost certainly negative for the North and possibly also for the South. What little social-democratic potential the Civil War possessed was embodied in emancipation and largely abandoned during and after Reconstruction. From a social-democratic perspective, subsequent American development was debilitated by the legacy of southern separatism that imposed incoherent class coalitions upon the national political system. Thus, the weak, decentralized social-welfare commitment of the American state was very much the product of the Civil War and Reconstruction political economy, and Union victory meant that the continuing dilemma of southern separatism, not social dislocation associated with industrialization, would be the major problem facing late-nineteenth-century state-builders.

Index

Adams, Green, 80
Adams, Henry: condemns radical Republicans, 353, 362n; condemns tariff, 331n; on political parties and government policy, 278, 281n
Administration Democrats: oppose antebellum development policies, 76, 77; oppose federal prohibition of polygamy, 91n; policy positions in Thirty-sixth Congress, 49–50; refuse to compromise on tariff, 51, 54–7; support Breckinridge, 64
administrative capacity: comparison of Union and Confederate policies, 125–35; creation of Republican party-state and, 207–8, 227–8; dimension of state authority, 107–11; in Confederate state, 230–3; Treasury operations in financial markets and, 239, 275–81
Alabama, 37; administrative costs of revenue collection in, 403; antebellum federal officials in, 105; assistance to soldiers' families, 165n; bankruptcy petitions in, 313; enlists Creoles in army, 153; congressman expelled from Confederate Congress, 121; distribution of federal officials in, 400; postwar occupation of, 389; postwar Republican strength in, 384; support for Confederate state expansion, 221; white primary in, 431n
Albany, New York, 265
Alexander, Thomas B., 177, 221; on supporters of Confederate war effort, 231, 233
Alleghany Arsenal, 86, 87
American party, 24; policy positions in Thirty-sixth Congress, 49–50; resistance to secession and, 80–5; supports antebellum development policies, 76, 77; supports federal prohibition of polygamy, 91n; supports high tariff, 44–5; tactics during speaker's contest, 54–6
Anti-Lecompton Democrats, 24; back Douglas, 64; policy positions in Thirty-sixth Congress, 49–50; support antebel-

lum development policies, 76; support federal prohibition of polygamy, 91n
Arizona, 433
Arkansas, 123; antebellum federal officials in, 105; bankruptcy petitions in, 313; Confederate election in, 196n; construction of Pacific railroad and, 76; cotton tax receipts in, 339; distribution of federal officials in, 400; illegal distilling in, 396n; income tax receipts in, 337; postwar occupation of, 389; postwar Republican strength in, 384; rapid population growth in, 374; rivers and harbors projects in, 74; secession of, 59; suffrage in, 389n; suspension of writ of habeas corpus in, 143
Arlington, Virginia, 195n
army: see United States Army
Atkinson, Edward: opposed to Reconstruction, 351n; spokesman for financial community, 284
Atlanta, Georgia, 189, 195n, 387; suspension of writ of habeas corpus in, 143
Atlantic cable, 253n
Augusta, Georgia, 195n, 372, 417

Baltimore, 408; banks and fiscal policy, 244–7; commercial relations with South, 243n; impact of secession on, 37–8; martial law in, 142; national bank system and, 265, 271, 310; position of in antebellum financial system, 239; Union troops attacked in, 140
Bank of England: American resumption of gold standard and, 295, 296
Bank of New York, 255
bankruptcy, 323; impact on national political economy, 313–14; passage of national law, 158–9, 313–14
Barney, William, 27
Bateman, Fred, 31
Baton Rouge, Louisiana, 387
Beard, Charles A., 419n
Beck, James, 358
Bell, John: nominated for president, 64
Benedict, Michael Les, 308n; on connec-

437

416–24, 435–6; origins of state authority in, ix, 1–2
claims, court of, 128
Clark, John G., 121n
Cleveland, 265; income tax receipts in, 337
client-groups: comparison of Union and Confederate policies, 161–7; dimension of state authority, 111–12; government debt created by, 163, 241–2
Cobb, Howell, 86
colonization: of freedmen, 178–9
Colorado, 90, 408
Columbia, South Carolina, 189, 387
Columbus, Georgia, 195n, 417
Columbus, Ohio, 337
Colwell, Stephen, 306
Commercial and Financial Chronicle: as organ for financial community, 282–3; condemns legal tender decision, 292–3; on capacity of democratic governments to manage financial system, 278; on civil service reform, 299–300; on interest rates in New York, 266n; on interior distrust of capital concentration, 244n; on paper currency and insulation from foreign panics, 250; on stability in financial system, 282n
Commercial Navigation Company, 343
Committee of Thirteen, 56n, 59
Committee of Thirty-three, 56n, 59
Committee on Appropriations, House, 343–4
Committee on Banking and Currency, House, 314
Committee on Elections, House, 47n
Committee on Military Affairs, House, 87, 411–12
Committee on Reconstruction, House, 358
Committee on the Confiscation of Rebels, House, 157
Committee on the Judiciary, House, 23, 355, 356
Compromise of 1877, 3, 413; and post office patronage, 371, 395–6; description and analysis of, 368–78
Confederate Bureau of Conscription, 137–8
Confederate Congress, 79; information concerning, 115; members from contested areas and, 195–7, 207–9; patronage and, 126–7; presidential coalition in, 230–3; prior service of members in

U.S. Congress, 100n; secret sessions in, 117–18, 198n; structural weakness in Confederate state, 183; *see also* roll call analysis
Confederate Nitre and Mining Bureau, 146, 186
Confederate Post Office department, 101–2
Confederate States of America: absence of Supreme Court in, 132–4; border state congressmen and, 207–9; conscription and war mobilization in, 135–9; early development of, 99–105; expansion of and immigrant populations, 211, 216; expansion of and lack of party system, 228–33; expansion of and manufacturing areas, 209–11; expansion of and slave holding, 198, 207–8; impact of financial policy, 238n, 242n; nationalism in, 11; redistribution of wealth in, 165–6, 167, 183–4; sectional stress in, 216–19; slavery and, 153–6; social base of, 192–3, 225, 235; southern economy and, 146–7, 169–72, 183–8, 233–4; state authority in compared to Union, x, 12–13, 94–9, 191–2, 233–6; stimulated southern economic development, 417–18
Confederate Supreme Court: organization of, 132–4; proposed jurisdiction, 124–5
confiscation: colonization of freedmen and, 178–9; comparison of Union and Confederate policies, 156–8; redistribution of wealth to southern loyalists and, 191, 303, 349–50, 354, 379–80
Congress: expulsion of members, 120–1; patronage and, 126–7; secret sessions in, 117–18; state authority and, 108–9
Connecticut, 433
Conrad, Charles, 119, 154
conscription: comparison of Union and Confederate, 135–9; Confederate economic controls and, 183–6; exemptions to Confederate, 130–1
Constitutional Union party, 59; nominates John Bell, 64; platform, 65
Cooke, Jay, 241n; as alternative to New York banks, 253; markets Union debt, 247; on McCulloch's qualifications as Treasury secretary, 276; postwar railroad boom and, 252
Cooper, Samuel, 119
cotton: export duty on, 176; internal revenue tax on, 331–2, 339, 416; northern economic development and, 403; production and Confederate state

cotton (*cont.*)
    expansion, 221–2, 224; regional con-
    centration of banking capacity and,
    274; resumption of gold standard and
    export of, 301, 348, 416n; southern
    economic ties with the North and, 41–2
Cottran, Wade S., 175
Coulter, E. Merton, 139n
counterfeiting: federal legislation to pre-
    vent, 314
courts, *see* judiciary
Cox, Samuel, 162
Crawford, George, 119
Crittenden compromise, 60
Crockett, John, 196
Cuba: and the extension of southern slav-
    ery, 36, 65, 67
currency: autonomy of financial system
    and paper, 250–1; devaluation and re-
    sumption of gold standard, 296; ex-
    change controls on, 151–3; gold notes,
    248; legal tender, 111, 162; legal tender
    cases, 292–3; market exchange of, 255;
    nationalization of, 124; *see also* green-
    backs, national bank notes
Custer, George A., 398
customs: *see* tariff

Dabney, Morgan, 252n
Danville, Virginia, 148
Davis, David, 370
Davis, H. Winter: backs coercion of the
    South, 80; casts decisive vote for Re-
    publican speaker, 54; on secession, 37–
    8; proposes board of admiralty, 128–9;
    Wade–Davis bill and, 123–4
Davis, Jefferson, 60, 79, 119; appoint-
    ments to naval academy and, 126; con-
    trols on export/import trade and, 180;
    leadership of statist coalition and, 229–
    33, 235; on arming slaves, 154–5; op-
    poses legal tender legislation, 162n; or-
    ganization of army and, 130; peace
    negotiations with Union and, 177; sup-
    ports railroad subsidy, 148; suspends
    writ of habeas corpus, 142–4; vetoes
    soldiers' home, 166
Davis, Reuben, 33n, 59n
Dawes, Henry, 79–80, 343
Delaware: free blacks in, 29; proposal to
    reconstruct, 356; sends Confederate vet-
    erans to Congress, 407
Democratic party: absorbs Populist party,
    427; American political development
    and, 423; as southern developmental
    coalition, 374, 376–7; composed of ele-
    ments outside Republican coalition,

312; Compromise of 1877 and, 368–
    78; Confederate veterans in Congress
    and, 405–6, 411–12; during Recon-
    struction, 3–4; 1868 platform supports
    currency inflation, 311, 319; expansion
    of slavery and, 27n; hostility to central
    state authority, 11, 280; in border
    states during Civil War, 197; New Deal
    realignment and, 433; opposed to nativ-
    ism, 46; opposed to Reconstruction,
    382; opposed to tariff protection, 44–5;
    opposition to Union war mobilization,
    225–7, 229–30; patronage and, 423;
    social democracy and, 426–7, 433–4;
    splits in 1860, 64–6; *see also* Adminis-
    tration Democrats, Anti-Lecompton
    Democrats
Detroit, 265
direct taxes: comparison of Union and
    Confederate policies, 168; *see also*
    extraction
District of Columbia: loyalty oath for mi-
    litia in, 78–9; quartering of troops in,
    79; slavery in, 24, 60
Dodge, William, 363n
Donald, David, 362n
Douglas, Stephen: candidate for president,
    64; platform, 65–6, 75; support for
    popular sovereignty and state forma-
    tion, 89–91
Dred Scott decision, 24, 40, 65, 91
Drexel, Morgan, 252

East: American state formation and, 10;
    capital formation in, 417–18; distribu-
    tion of federal officials in, 399–403;
    growth of Republican party in, 22;
    postwar share of rivers and harbors
    spending, 344–5; rivers and harbors
    projects in, 74; Socialist party in, 432;
    source of federal employees in capital,
    346; Union veterans in Congress and,
    408, 411
Edgerton, Sidney, 168
Egypt, 332
Eiselen, Malcom Rogers, 307n
Eliot, Thomas, 362n
emancipation: amendment to constitution,
    144–5
English, William, 80
Erie Canal, 38
Etheridge, Emerson, 90n
Europe: export of manufactured goods to,
    426n; harvest in and suspension of gold
    standard, 250; hostility to Union debt,
    248–9; postwar railroad boom and,
    251–2

civil service reform, 341–2; on congressmen and the income tax, 337, 339; on currency circulation and abolition of slavery, 291–2; on federal taxing authority, 298n; on greenback contraction, 290–1; on impact of Civil War on southern class relations, 349; on military occupation of the South, 351n; on National Bank Currency Act, 320–1; on national bank system, 286, 287, 315; on organization and operations of the gold exchange, 256n, 258; on Public Credit Act, 318n; on qualifications of Assistant Treasurer for New York, 275–6; on Refunding Act of 1870, 322n; on repeal of cotton tax, 332n; on regional concentration of banking capacity, 272; on tariff politics, 299n; on Treasury operations and financial stability, 275, 276, 277, 278n; on Treasury operations in the bond market, 261n; urges public sale of Treasury gold, 315–16; on virtues of two-party competition, 280–1
Huston, James L., 428n

Idaho, 408, 433
Illinois, 22; resistance to secession and, 80
Illinois and Michigan Canal, 38
immigrant populations: support for Civil War state expansion and, 211, 216
import/export houses: tariff and hedging operations on gold exchange, 257, 258, 295
impressment: in Confederacy, 135, 159–60, 170n, 183–6
income tax: finance capitalists and reform of, 298–9, 332–3; receipts from, 337–9; *see also* extraction
India, x, 332
Indiana, 46n, 433
Indiana, State Bank of, 279
Ingersoll, Ebon, 317, 318
internal revenue: administrative costs of collection of, 403; comparison of Union and Confederate policies, 168–72; finance capitalists and reform of, 298–9; regional distribution of employment in bureau, 346n, 396, 399, 401; tax on cotton, 331–2; tax on state-chartered bank notes, 124, 268, 286–7; taxation of national banks, 316–17; total receipts from, 339–40; Treasury holdings of greenbacks and, 262; *see also* extraction, income tax
Interstate Commerce Commission, 16
Iowa, 75, 433n; support for Blake resolu-

tion, 23–4
Iverson, Alfred, 26n

Jackson, Mississippi, 189, 387
Jarnett, Daniel de, 78–9
Jenckes, Thomas A.: sponsors bankruptcy legislation, 313n; sponsors civil service bill, 342
Johnson, Andrew: pardon policy of, 122–3, 157; Reconstruction policy of, 348, 356; vetoes Public Credit Act, 318
Johnson, Henry C., 279n
Johnston, Joseph E., 119
Joint Committee on Conduct of the War, 178n
judiciary: Confederate organization of, 101, 103; nationalization of commerce and, 314n; state authority and, 107–9, 124–5, 128, 132–4; writ of habeas corpus and, 139–40
Julian, George: sponsors southern homestead bill, 354–5

Kansas, 80; antebellum army in, 105; as issue in 1860 election, 65; distribution of federal officials in, 400; Lecompton constitution and, 40; proposed admission as slave state, 40–1; sends Confederate veteran to Congress, 408
Kentucky: American party in, 77; contested by Union and Confederacy, 195–7; illegal distilling in, 396n; proposal to reconstruct, 356; resistance to secession and, 80; sends Confederate veterans to Congress, 407–8; service of militia, 122; suspension of the writ of habeas corpus in, 141
Keys, David: appointed postmaster general, 371
Knights of Labor, 431
Know-Nothings: *see* American party
Knoxville, Tennessee, 144, 269; income tax receipts in, 337
Kousser, J. Morgan, 431n
Ku Klux Klan, 394n

La Follette, Robert, 426, 428
Lancaster county, Pennsylvania, 354n
land-grant colleges, 69, 73; support for and resistance to secession, 82–5
Larrabee, Charles, 43
Latham, Milton, 61
Leach, James T., 177
Leavenworth, Kansas, 265
Lecompton constitution, 40, 49; *see also* Kansas
Lee, Robert E., 154

Republican party (*cont.*)
South between 1868 and 1876, 382–94;
as agent for northern economic expansion, 69, 76–8, 421, 426; as agent of
state formation, 2–4, 10, 89–93, 225–
30; as alliance between industrial East
and agrarian Midwest, 43; as loyalist
group in postwar South, 378–9, 391–5;
as nationalist force, 11–12, 18–19, 63–
4; as northern developmental coalition,
374n, 376–7; as threat to slavery, 20–
6; backs tariff protection, 73–4, 307,
426, 428; changing strategy toward Reconstruction, 353–8; coalition and Reconstruction, 301–2, 303, 311–12, 365,
381; Compromise of 1877 and, 368–
78; discriminates against southern wing,
372n, 381n; 1860 platform and northern economic development, 66–8; expansion of slavery and, 27–9; leads
resistance to secession, 78–85, 86–8;
legislative support for finance capitalist
program and, 323–9, 335; legislative
support for Reconstruction, 358,
361–3; nativism and, 45–6, 66, 211;
patronage and, 300, 367, 402, 422–3;
patronage and appointment of Treasury
secretaries, 279–80; policy positions in
Thirty-sixth Congress, 49–50; postwar
divisions in, 306, 308; reduction in federal spending and, 300, 311, 335, 341–
8; social democracy and, 426–7; Union
veterans in Congress and, 405, 411–12;
see also party-state, party system
revenue, *see* direct taxes, extraction, internal revenue
Rhode Island, 400, 433
Richardson, William: performance as
Treasury secretary, 277
Richmond, Virginia: Civil War expansion
of, 417, 419; Confederate employment
in, 103; manufacturing in, 195n, 372;
martial law in, 143
Richmond and Danville Railroad, 148
Richmond *Dispatch*, 162n
Richmond *Examiner*, 121n, 187n
river and harbor improvements, 401:
Compromise of 1877 and, 371–2; defeated in House, 74–5; postwar spending on, 343–5; support for and
resistance to secession, 80–5
Robinson, William, 100
roll call analysis: of amendment to Interstate Commerce Act, 16n; of Blake antislavery resolution, 25–6; of decisions
on federal expenditures and operations,
346, 347; of New York City support

for Union state expansion, 222; of partisan support for Union state expansion,
226–7; of postwar financial policy decisions, 324, 325, 327, 328, 330; of postwar revenue policy decisions, 334, 336;
of presidential coalition support for
Confederate state expansion, 232; of
Reconstruction legislation, 359–60; of
reduction in income tax, 339; of resistance to secession, 81–2, 84; of sectional stress in Union and Confederacy,
217, 219; of southern support for the
Compromise of 1877, 373; of Union
and Confederate state expansion, 199–
207, 212–15, 220, 223–4
Roosevelt, Theodore, 426
Ross, Lewis W., 314–5
Russel, Robert, 75
Russia, 434

St. Joseph, Missouri, 77
St. Louis, Missouri, 156, 195n, 265; suspension of the writ of habeas corpus in,
141
Salisbury, North Carolina, 143
San Francisco, 75, 265
Santo Domingo, 12n
Savannah, Georgia, 195n, 372, 387, 418–
19
Schaefer, Donald, 28n
Schmitz, Mark, 28n
Schwartz, Anna: on factors underlying international gold standard, 294n
Scott, Winfield: response to secession, 85,
86
secession: compromise efforts to avoid,
56–7, 59; election of a Republican president and, 48; explanation for, 18, 35–
9, 57–60, 69, 92–3; future of slavery
and, 19–20, 32; impact on national political economy, 12; nonslaveholding
whites and, 34–5; northern decision to
resist, 18, 60–4, 78–85; of regions
other than the South, 43, 61–3; response of American state to, 85–91;
states' rights and, 13; urged by southern
congressmen, 59–60
sectional stress, 77n; analysis of in Union
and Confederacy, 216–19
Sefton, James, 388n
Seip, Terry L.: on fact of southern Republicans, 305n, 361n
Sellers, James L., 416n
separatism, southern: advantages of a
southern nation, 35–9; American state
formation and, ix–x, 10, 414–15, 425,
436; central state authority and, 60–1;

CPSIA information can be obtained
at www.ICGtesting.com
Printed in the USA
LVOW12s2007150416

483838LV00002B/220/P